T0396336

Influencing Organizational Effectiveness

In this book, Linda Holbeche offers a historical narrative on the changing landscape of work since the 1980s and considers how definitions of organizational effectiveness have changed over time. She discusses the characteristics and effects of the neo-liberal work culture of new capitalism, and how HRM practices have contributed to shaping this work culture.

Influencing Organizational Effectiveness challenges mainstream thinking around business strategy, change and organizational effectiveness, and about the roles of HRM and management. While the overall tone of the book is critical, Holbeche argues that HRM can play an active and constructive role in giving voice to employees and advancing organizational effectiveness.

Grounded in research, this book includes reflective questions, case studies and helpful guidelines to support HRM and OD professionals and master's-level students. It illustrates what 'better' might look like and how HRM can contribute to a new definition of effectiveness which is aligned to the needs of modern organizations and their key stakeholders.

Linda Holbeche is the former Director of Research and Policy for the CIPD, Director of Leadership and Consultancy at the Work Foundation and Director of Research and Strategy at Roffey Park, UK. She is now Visiting Professor in HRM and Organization Development at Cass Business School and four other UK universities, and Fellow of the Institute for Employment Studies and Roffey Park.

Influencing Organizational Effectiveness
A Critical Take on the HR Contribution

Linda Holbeche

LONDON AND NEW YORK

First published 2017
by Routledge
2 Park Square, Milton Park, Abingdon, Oxon OX14 4RN

and by Routledge
711 Third Avenue, New York, NY 10017

Routledge is an imprint of the Taylor & Francis Group, an informa business

© 2017 Linda Holbeche

The right of Linda Holbeche to be identified as author of this work has been asserted by her in accordance with sections 77 and 78 of the Copyright, Designs and Patents Act 1988.

All rights reserved. No part of this book may be reprinted or reproduced or utilised in any form or by any electronic, mechanical, or other means, now known or hereafter invented, including photocopying and recording, or in any information storage or retrieval system, without permission in writing from the publishers.

Every effort has been made to contact copyright holders for their permission to reprint material in this book. The publishers would be grateful to hear from any copyright holder who is not here acknowledged and will undertake to rectify any errors or omissions in future editions of this book.

Trademark notice: Product or corporate names may be trademarks or registered trademarks, and are used only for identification and explanation without intent to infringe.

British Library Cataloguing in Publication Data
A catalogue record for this book is available from the British Library

Library of Congress Cataloguing in Publication Data
Names: Holbeche, Linda, author.
Title: Influencing organizational effectiveness : a critical take on the HR contribution / Linda Holbeche.
Description: Abingdon, Oxon ; New York, NY : Routledge, 2017. |
Includes bibliographical references.
Identifiers: LCCN 2016028689| ISBN 9780415740081 (hbk) |
ISBN 9780415740098 (pbk) | ISBN 9781315815862 (ebk)
Subjects: LCSH: Manpower planning. | Strategic planning. |
Personnel management. | Organizational effectiveness.
Classification: LCC HF5549.5.M3 H653 2017 | DDC 658.3–dc23
LC record available at https://lccn.loc.gov/2016028689

ISBN: 978-0-415-74008-1 (hbk)
ISBN: 978-0-415-74009-8 (pbk)
ISBN: 978-1-315-81586-2 (ebk)

Typeset in Bembo
by Out of House Publishing

To the late Dr Geoff Esland, who inspired me to write this book. To my dear husband Barney, my late mother and father, Elsie and Bill, thank you for everything.

Contents

List of figures	ix
List of tables	x
Preface	xi
Acknowledgements	xx

SECTION I
Context 1

1	Introduction	3
2	Key concepts and theories	19
3	A neo-liberal landscape	35
4	The new work culture	54

SECTION II
Managerialism and HRM 75

5	The HRM 'project'	77
6	The shaping of subjectivities	99
7	The conflicted HR practitioner?	119

SECTION III
The impact of the new work culture on employees 137

8	The emerging psychological contract	139
9	The search for meaning	160

viii *Contents*

SECTION IV
Phoenix out of the ashes?   183

10 The 'crisis' of capitalism   185

11 New organizational effectiveness   201

SECTION V
HR influencing organizational effectiveness   223

12 HRM, stewardship and organizational effectiveness   225

13 A high-performance workplace   245

14 Building a healthy, ethical and changeable organization   266

15 Conclusion   287

References   306
Index   332

Figures

4.1	The law of self-defeating consequences	67
8.1	The effect of insecurity on loyalty (2000–3)	142
8.2	The effect of insecurity on motivation (2000–3)	143
8.3	How does your organization make excessive demands of you?	144
8.4	Percentage who experience stress as a result of work	145
8.5	What impact has change had on your role?	150
8.6	Why are you considering leaving your organization?	152
8.7	I have made sacrifices for my career	155
8.8	Have you sacrificed your career for your personal life?	155
9.1	Correlations of meaning	175
9.2	An emerging model of meaning	176
12.1	Models of national and international regulation: a frames of reference approach	232
13.1	Values and behaviours framework	259

Tables

5.1	Evolution of Personnel	81
8.1	Work–life balance-related questions	147
8.2	How important is work–life balance?	147
11.1	Quadruple bottom line	209
11.2	The Clarkson Principles of Stakeholder Management	217

Preface

A not-so-funny thing happened on the way to the twenty-first century: people stopped caring about their jobs…Now after years of downsizing, outsourcing and a cavalier corporate attitude that treats employees as costs rather than assets, most of today's workers have concluded that the company no longer values them. So they, in turn, no longer feel engaged in their work or committed to the company. The reality of mutual co-dependence between employees and organizations, and the advantages gained from long-term mutual commitment and engagement, have been lost.

(Bardwick, 2007:13)

This book offers a historical narrative on the changing landscape of work since the 1980s and considers how definitions of organizational effectiveness have changed over this period. It takes a long-term view of the way that changes in the white-collar employment relationship, mainly in the UK, have fed into people's perceptions of their working lives. Key themes include the characteristics and effects of the neo-liberal 'work culture of new capitalism' (Sennett, 2006) as reported by white-collar employees between 1997 and 2016; and how human resource management (HRM)[1] practices have contributed to shaping this work culture. This review of how we got to where we are leads us to consider some of the options open to human resource (HR) teams in future about how they might contribute to a new definition of organization effectiveness more appropriate to meeting the emerging needs of organizations of the twenty-first century.

My own experience is that of a researcher-practitioner in a variety of organizational contexts (Hodgkinson and Rousseau, 2009). The book's empirical component involves a re-examination of research conducted by colleagues and myself during this period. This research focuses on the individual actor and attempts to explicate how white-collar workers responded to pressures put upon them within the new work culture and to which they were required to adapt. A key thread running through my arguments relates to inherent tensions between the exercise of agency (individual autonomy) and structures (social, political, cultural and economic forces) shaping the new work culture.

My interest in how the 'new work culture' and HRM practices impact on the employment relationship of employees in white-collar careers stems from my own values and work experience. I believe passionately in the right of individuals to exercise a degree of autonomy over their work and to have enriching and satisfying work lives. Yet a number of trends which I chart in the book appear to erode this possibility. In my own working life, I have experienced or witnessed at first hand the transformation of the UK secondary education system in the 1980s, and also the impact of major organizational restructurings on employees in the

xii *Preface*

late 1980s and 1990s during my time working as a management developer for a major international corporation.

I have also had the opportunity to research the experience of the changing work world from the perspective of employees, mainly between 1994 and 2005 when I was Research and Strategy Director at Roffey Park, a UK management institute. There I was able to work with many "white-collar" workers, i.e. executives, managers, professionals and HR practitioners from all sectors of the UK economy, as a management developer and consultant. I became aware of how widely managerialist ideas appeared to be gaining currency across all sectors from the mid–late 1990s onwards.

Through my work as a consultant, I was witness to the types of culture change intended to inject market disciplines into previously non-commercial workplaces, such as education, public service and not-for-profit organizations, or that typically accompanied the privatization of previously public sector bodies. Characteristics of this 'new work culture' included managerialism, ongoing change, performativity, work intensification through technology, the flexibilization of work, such as through outsourcing, and the proliferation of human resource management. It became apparent that, within the emerging new work culture, value systems based on vocationalism and professionalism were on a collision course with those based on flexibility and expediency. I saw the damaging effects on the morale of many workers as their working conditions altered.

To explore the changing workplace from an employee perspective, I devised an annual survey, the Roffey Park Management Agenda, that was, and still is, completed by white-collar (managerial, professional, administrative, technical) employees from many sectors of the UK economy and elsewhere. Thanks to this, it was possible to learn about what was happening in contemporary workplaces, and also to 'drill down' into emerging issues in more depth. My focus was on the individual actors, whether as agents involved in shaping the work culture or as white-collar employees experiencing and reacting to the effects of such changes on their social and psychological contracts.

I wanted to gain a better understanding of where this new work culture was coming from. This led me to the first research question in this book: what were the macro political, economic and technological changes which led to the emergence of a 'new work culture'? I began to read literature from a variety of sources and fields, including economics and politics, that could shed light on the new work culture and the human consequences of neo-liberalism. I read Braverman's *Labor and Monopoly Capital: The Degradation of Work in the Twentieth Century* (1974) and found interesting parallels between Braverman's description of the degradation of clerical work in American office-based workplaces in the 1960s and what appeared to be happening in UK workplaces at the turn of the twenty-first century.

Similarly, Richard Sennett's books *The Corrosion of Character* (1998) and *The Culture of the New Capitalism* (2006), and other literature relating to the psychological contract and trust, were a spur to my thinking. From this literature, together with Management Agenda findings and other survey data, such as from the UK government's Workplace Employment Relations Study, it became evident that many of the workplace changes underway were the consequence of neo-liberal economic policies, of managerialism and the use of technology to commodify white-collar work.

Essentially the Management Agenda acted as a tracking mechanism with respect to workplace change and its effects on employees. For instance, I was interested in understanding how the new work culture might be affecting the career psychological contract of white-collar workers. I carried out several research projects looking at managers' careers in 'flatter' structures and published a book in 1997, *Motivating People in Lean Organisations*. However, as

I explored people's accounts through the Management Agenda survey, my interest broadened beyond the theme of careers to understanding how the new work culture was being experienced by people, in particular with respect to their satisfaction.

Another of the key themes arising from the Management Agenda, most noticeably between 2000 and 2004, was about a perceived loss of existential meaning at work reported by many white-collar employees. With a colleague, Nigel Springett, I explored this theme in more depth, using focus groups and interviews, during 2003–4. There were many willing volunteer participants in this study, suggesting that the topic was potentially of relevance to white-collar workers from many organization types and sectors. The findings from this study are discussed in Chapter 9.

From such research themes I was struck by the seeming mismatch between business aspirations to achieve financial success through innovation and finding more flexible and cost-effective ways of operating, and the needs and aspirations of employees, on whose productive output such business results largely depend. This made me increasingly question the view that organizational effectiveness must always be defined in terms of the results expected of organizations. After all, how were organizations to achieve their strategic aspirations if the surviving workforce was potentially demotivated as a result of restructurings and downsizings? Surely effective organizations were those that engaged those affected in their transformation? Accordingly, I wrote two books in 2005 in which I attempted to marry up these different needs and prescribe 'better' management and HR practice that could lead to greater employee engagement in a collective effort. These were: *Understanding Change: Theory, Implementation and Success* and *The High Performance Organization: Creating Dynamic Stability and Sustainable Success*.

My interest in understanding the broader macro-political context of the contemporary workplace was sharpened when I became Leadership and Consultancy Director at the Work Foundation, a left-leaning think tank, whose core mission was to promote 'good work' (Coats and Lehki, 2008), a concept that suggests that for work to be 'good' it must not only achieve desired business results, but must also involve ethical and fair treatment of employees.

Good work is defined as 'whatever advances development by supporting the fulfilment of individual potentialities while simultaneously contributing to the harmonious growth of other individuals and groups' (Csíkszentmihályi et al., 2001: 244). Under this rubric, employees should have 'voice', i.e. not only be kept informed of developments by management but also have the chance to participate actively in issues relating to business and the workplace. Employees are assumed to want to exercise agency, and to be motivated to achieve mutual benefits for themselves and their employers. While this may sound idealistic, I feel very attuned to this agenda and it is the standard by which I am evaluating changes in work patterns that have occurred.

Alongside this, I was curious about the role played by human resource management theory and HR practice in the development of the 'new work culture'. I wrote many practitioner-oriented articles and a book, *Aligning HR and Business Strategy* (1999), specifically aimed at HR practitioners, that describes ways that HR could best help their organizations to become effective, in my view. However, I became increasingly sceptical about the contribution to organizational effectiveness of some HR practices, such as performance management. As a developer of HR professionals throughout the period in question, I became very aware that many HR staff who had started their careers in 'Personnel' departments and who had been attracted to this function because they were interested in working with people, were becoming disillusioned with their roles and feeling obliged to conform to a new stereotype of business partner for whom the needs of employees should come second to those of business.

xiv *Preface*

I was also interested to discover how senior HR practitioners, especially those who might be considered leading HR professionals, viewed the role of HR with respect to the new work culture. Did they see HR as shaping, responding to or challenging aspects of the new work culture? To what extent did they appear to recognize the impact of change on the employment expectations of white-collar workers? How much did they give priority to business interests? So I carried out a series of interviews with HR leaders over a number of years to find out about the sense-making process used by participants in the formulation of their role. Watson (2007b) criticizes Boxall et al. (2007) for failing to acknowledge that different social actors may pursue different goals in HRM. As Watson observed, my interviews with these HR leaders revealed many different perspectives, motivations and goals pursued by people in HR leadership roles, as we shall discuss in Chapter 7.

Over time I have gradually adopted a more critical stance towards HRM which was reflected in my rewriting of *Aligning HR and Business Strategy* (2009). The issue that appears to fundamentally divide Critical scholarship from the HRM mainstream revolves around managerialism. I have increasingly become an 'internal critic' of managerialism, adopting an 'inside-outside' perspective (Goodman, 2010) and attempting to work with the tensions implicit in a more balanced dialectic. I am generally sympathetic to the mainstream HRM argument that performance is critical to organizational success, without which the employment relationship becomes largely irrelevant. I am also critical of the lack of emphasis within much critical theory on improving practice. On the other hand, I am wary of the potential uses of managerialism, including HRM, and technology to degrade jobs in order to increase shareholder value.

Consequently, I am aware of my own cognitive dissonance with respect to management and managerialism. As Berger (1974) argued in his psychosocial analysis of modernity, the pluralization of social life worlds and modernity's effects on the subjective consciousness (i.e. self-concepts) of individuals mean that: 'Modern man (postmodern?) is afflicted with a permanent identity crisis' (Berger, 1974: 77–9).

However, as Watson (2010) makes clear, antipathy towards managerialism is not the same as antipathy towards managers. The concerns, goals and objectives of managers and HR practitioners are of interest to me. They are often dealing with multiple complex challenges within tight constraints. Indeed, based on my experience, I agree with Legge (1995) that managers (and HR) often feel 'powerless' (or portray themselves as powerless) to act within the managerial system in which they find themselves, and find themselves coping with divided identities and motivations.

Business school academics may find themselves with similar divided identities. As Grey et al. (1996) point out, the influence driving the development of mainstream management knowledge and education is functionalist and does not problematize itself. It fits within a 'given' context of a neo-liberal system, therefore management knowledge is compromised and becomes a 'marketized epistemology', i.e. the market favours the non-problematized in which there is no reflexivity about whether the effects of such approaches are good or bad, especially in human terms.

A similar cognitive dissonance is reflected in stereotypical manager attitudes towards HR policies. Are managers themselves passive subjects of HR policies? While HR policies are in theory aligned to business strategies, in my observation HR policies often seem to be considered by managers to be irritants or constraints on what the managers themselves are trying to achieve, rather than enablers. In many cases I have come across, including my own, managers deal with HR policies by ignoring them, challenging or subverting them, especially if these are perceived to have a strong controlling intent over managerial freedom to act.

A pragmatist–realist approach

In writing this book, I have embraced the pragmatic-realist approach described by Watson (2010: 917). This 'pragmatic style of thinking' is aimed at developing knowledge which might more realistically inform action than what has come before. I have mainly, but not exclusively, drawn on a partial secondary analysis of existing data derived from the Management Agenda annual survey of UK employees working in all sectors of the UK economy (1997–2016). The survey incorporated both quantitative and 'open-ended' elements to explore how UK white-collar employees described structural and other changes taking place at work, such as delayering and restructuring, as well as the effects on them of work intensification, long working hours, performativity and other pressures.

Essentially I used the Management Agenda in two main ways; both for trend analysis and as a sensitizing exercise to identify themes and issues which were worth pursuing in more depth. I followed up on intriguing signals within the data through other strands of research in order to obtain a more nuanced understanding of the issues. These included themes such as the perceived loss of meaning at work, as reported by Management Agenda participants; and the accounts of HR practitioners about their role in developing the new work culture.

These themes were explored mainly using qualitative methods, including focus groups, interviews and discourse analysis. As Van der Ven (2007) notes, a complex reality demands the use of multiple perspectives. Watson argues for a wide variety of conceptual-theoretic and methodological resources, such as in-depth qualitative analyses and, in particular, various forms of discourse analysis which have been influential in the deconstruction of HRM. Watson (2007b: 9) advocates setting up 'participative' research projects which draw on the 'perspectives' of the range of 'stakeholders' who are involved in the area being researched. Such parties include the researchers themselves, together with 'users, clients, sponsors, and practitioners'. The research method used in the project entitled 'The Search for Meaning' is an example of such an approach.

The core questions I have sought to address in this book are as follows:

1   What are the macro-political, economic and technological changes which have led to the emergence since the 1980s of a 'work culture of new capitalism' (for brevity I shall refer to this as the 'new work culture')?
    - How do neo-liberal economic theory, technological advances and managerialism impact on the development of the 'new work culture'?
    - How is 'new work culture' defined in the literature?
2   How is HR's contribution to organizational effectiveness defined under neo-liberal forms of capitalism?
    - How is HRM represented in the mainstream and critical HRM literature?
    - How do HRM practices contribute to the development and perpetuation of the new work culture, e.g. in destabilizing the 'old' white-collar psychological contract?
    - How does HRM practice and discourse aid the 'normalization' of the new work culture?
3   What were the characteristics of the new work culture as experienced by employees in the first decade of the twenty-first century?
    - To what extent was work being intensified, flexibilized and commodified?
    - To what extent were employees able to exercise agency in the face of these changes?
    - How were employees reacting to increasing workloads and long working hours?
    - What was the reported effect on employee trust in their employers?

xvi *Preface*

4   How is the 'old' white-collar psychological contract changing?
  •   What evidence exists of employees experiencing increasing job insecurity?
  •   What evidence exists that employees are willing to continue to make personal sacrifices in order to progress their careers?
  •   To what extent is the 'employability thesis' working?
  •   What support do employees expect/hope for from their employers?
  •   To what extent are people adjusting by adopting attitudes described by Sennett (2006: 5) as the 'cultural ideal' of new capitalism, i.e. 'a self, oriented to the short term, focused on potential ability, willing to abandon past experience'?
  •   To what extent are employees experiencing existential loss of meaning in the new work culture?
5   How do HRM professionals view their roles with respect to the new work culture?
  •   To what extent are practitioners aiming to balance the needs of business and of employees?
  •   How conflicted are practitioners by their 'business partner' roles?
  In the latter part of the book I shift focus to consider developments in the macro context of work, and potential shifts in HRM's role, since 2009. In particular:
6   To what extent has the contemporary 'crisis' of capitalism brought to the fore the need for a different form of capitalism, and related changes to behaviours and working practices? How have demographic shifts and 'connected' practices fed into this?
7   What might this mean for HRM's future contribution to organizational effectiveness, in particular with respect to:
  •   the employment relationship,
  •   employee wellbeing,
  •   employee careers, and
  •   ethics?

So in this book I am attempting to develop a well-constructed line of argument for a particular way of understanding the origins, practices and effects of the new work culture, from which choices for potential action might subsequently be derived. Of course I recognize many limitations in methodology, nature of samples and so on, which I discuss later in the book. I recognize that my narrative may be biased and that I may have omitted many other possible interpretations.

The account I give is a personal one and, as Van der Ven (2007) points out, our understanding of the 'real world' is limited. All facts, observations and data are theory laden and consequently a reliance upon linear, statistical modelling fails to capture this dynamic, and is often perceived to be unhelpful to practitioners because of a lack of attention to the 'real world' of practice.

Watson (2010) argues that a coherent CHRM (critical human resources manager) theorization requires a clear acknowledgement of the sociological, socio-psychological, economic, political and ethical aspects of working, managing and organizing. This is what I seek to do throughout the book. As Watson suggests, pragmatism is not about pursuing absolute or final truths about reality. It is about attempting to make theoretical generalizations which might inform human practices and help us better appreciate the relationships between individuals' predicaments and institutional and historical patterns better than others. In addressing the core research questions above in this book, I hope to open up new areas of dialogue about some of the pressing social and technical issues facing organizations, employees and communities today. I believe that, potentially, this approach offers a grounded, intellectually coherent and explanatory framework for understanding the changing employment relationship which can both make a contribution to the body of knowledge and be useful to employees and to organizations.

How the book is organized

Section I: Context

In the first chapter I set the scene by considering the work of two authors – Harry Braverman and Richard Sennett – who will be my leitmotivs throughout the book. Braverman argued that there was a systematic process of degradation of work underway that would ultimately affect even highly skilled workers, while Sennett proposed that the work culture of what he calls 'new capitalism' has damaging effects on workers. These are some of the assumptions I consider throughout the book, drawing on research carried out by Roffey Park that provides an employee perspective on these matters.

With respect to organizational effectiveness, many early definitions focused almost exclusively on shareholders as key beneficiaries of organizational efforts. These replaced the earlier, less defined view that the purpose of organizations is to provide returns for a range of stakeholders. In later chapters we shall look at how changing definitions of business success may again redefine organizational effectiveness, broadening the outcome focus beyond simply delivering financial returns for the benefit of shareholders to results that benefit a wider group of stakeholders.

In Chapter 2 we consider some of the main theories I have used to develop my argument. In Chapter 3 we consider key drivers for change in the workplace over the last few decades, looking in particular at the effects of neo-liberalism and technology. We shall consider whether degradation of work is a feature of, and is made easier by, the 'new work culture'; indeed, whether this culture is an active force in the degradation of work. It could be argued, for instance, that the neo-liberal new work culture and technological advances have simply extended the range of instruments available for managers to increase control. We then look at changes to work and workplaces as reported by employees in Roffey Park Management Agenda surveys (1998–2016) in Chapter 4.

Section II: Managerialism and HRM

In Chapters 5, 6 and 7 we consider whether HR itself may have been captured by an exclusively shareholder value-focused business agenda. From such a perspective, HR's contribution to organizational effectiveness involves managing the human resource cost base and increasing performance. We contrast themes from the mainstream literature about HR's role with respect to performance with critical perspectives on HR's role with respect to the degradation of work. We consider how the use of HR discourse and performative HR practices helps secure worker compliance to the demands of the work culture of new capitalism and question the ethics and sustainability of such approaches.

Section III: The impact of the new work culture on employees

In Chapters 8 and 9 we look in more detail at the impact on the psychological contracts of white-collar workers of the changes taking place in the workplace in the early years of this century, as reported in Chapter 4.

xviii *Preface*

Section IV: Phoenix out of the ashes?

In Chapter 10 we consider whether contemporary capitalism itself is in crisis and if neo-liberalism has run its course. A possible indication of this is that, since writing this book, in its referendum in June 2016 over continued membership of the European Union, the UK voted marginally in favour of exiting the EU, or 'Brexit'. The range of arguments given by politicians leading the 'Leave the EU' campaign, and by voters voting to leave, appeared to be based on a mixture of xenophobia and a range of fears and grievances relating to the risks of poor jobs and unemployment as a consequence of the EU's requirement for freedom of movement of workers. Ironically, as I point out in earlier sections of this book, many of the long-standing systemic issues relating to poor jobs can be traced back to the 1980s and the rapid advance of Anglo-Saxon forms of neo-liberalism with its pursuit of global competitive advantage, labour flexibility and extraordinary rewards for so-called wealth creators. The development of poor jobs was aided by the UK's own form of industrial relations with the decline of the collective voice, the possibility of using technology to replace low-skill work and the overall 'buyer's market' with respect to lower-skilled jobs, which has allowed employers to neglect workforce issues and enabled practices such as 'zero hours' contracts to flourish.

Arguably such practices have little, if anything, to do with the EU since EU member countries take different tacks with respect to employment law and how executives are rewarded relative to the rest of the workforce, and for what they are rewarded. For instance, unlike their German counterparts, UK and US executives are often handsomely rewarded for acquisitions and restructurings that lead to significant job losses – and with no consultation with local communities. The UK's de-industrialized towns bear witness to the chronic and ongoing after-effects of abandoning failing industries to the whim of the market. This is in contrast to many EU countries which have retained state ownership or involvement in their own traditional industries and infrastructure firms. Indeed, the EU has arguably done more to protect the rights of UK employees than any UK government of its own accord, with the possible exception of the introduction of the national living wage in recent times. The many notorious cases of unethical business practice, enabled by a largely unregulated financial market, particularly evident since the economic crisis that began in 2008, have led to widespread public cynicism about institutions and people in positions of authority in general. Brexit could perhaps be an indicator of a more widespread malaise in the UK with the kinds of capitalism which permit social polarization, with the EU used as a convenient negative *cause célèbre* by various politicians for their own ends. These include a desire to reject a European institution which has largely acted to curb the worst excesses of Anglo-Saxon forms of capitalism.

Will a more sustainable form of stakeholder capitalism emerge to replace it? In Chapter 11 we consider what a stakeholder-oriented form of capitalism might look like and how organizational effectiveness might be defined from this perspective. How this might be operationalized by HR is what we shall explore in the final section of this book.

Section V: HR influencing organizational effectiveness

The remaining chapters of this book address what HR's contribution might be to realizing this alternative scenario. In Chapter 12 we consider what an 'employee-centric' approach to the employment relationship might involve, in particular the implications of a more mutual and plural perspective for current labour management practices. We shall look at how people might have more genuine voice, decent work and reasonable career opportunities. In Chapter 13 we revisit the contested topic of performance management through this lens. In

Chapter 14 we consider how organizational change can be implemented with, rather than on, people. Here we consider the role of HRM in developing more ethical business culture and practices and what kinds of 'leadership' are fit for purpose in the twenty-first-century workplace. In Chapter 15 we conclude with alternative visions for HRM and for organizational effectiveness – one for continuity of the status quo, the other a more utopian aspiration for the kinds of contribution HR could make to redefining what business 'success' and 'organizational effectiveness' might mean in today's world.

My aim, as recommended by Watson (2010), is to have selected theoretical resources on the criterion of 'their power to illuminate aspects of the realities of social life'. The outcomes should be to challenge practices that have become counter-productive to healthy work and working lives and to suggest how HR might play a pivotal role in producing better, more ethical and sustainable organizational practice in future.

Note

1 In using the term 'Human Resource Management' (HRM) I am conscious that I risk conflating under the terms 'HRM' and 'HR practice' the work of specialist functional areas such as Human Resource Development (HRD) and even related disciplines such as Organization Design and Development (OD&D). While these different disciplines contribute to organizational effectiveness in different ways, the common factor with HRM is the unitarist assumption on which they are built i.e. that what is good for the business is good for its employees and vice versa. So except when otherwise stated, I have used the terms 'HRM' and 'HR practice' generically to apply to elements from a wide spectrum of functional practice.

Acknowledgements

I am extremely grateful to all the people, too numerous to mention, who have contributed to this book. These include sources of inspiration, such as the Center for Effective Organizations at the University of Southern California, and all those who have kindly helped me to develop the case studies on their organization's practices.

Throughout the book I refer to various research projects carried out during my time as Director of Research and Strategy at my former employer Roffey Park, as well as to more recent work. For their support and encouragement, I would like to express my gratitude to Roffey Park's CEO Michael Jenkins and to Andy Smith, Director of Research, Practice and Qualifications and his team. Similarly, I am delighted to refer to some of the recent thinking emerging from the CIPD, the professional body for HR in the UK and Ireland. In particular, I would like to thank CIPD's People and Strategy Director, Laura Harrison; Head of Public Policy, Ben Willmott; and Research Associate, Ksenia Zheltoukhova, for their help and insights.

I should also like to thank Isobel Fitzharris and the production team at Routledge for their patience and encouragement.

Finally, I should like to thank my husband and my family for their ongoing support and understanding.

Whilst every effort has been made to contact copyright holders, the author and publisher would like to hear from anyone whose copyright may have been unwittingly infringed.

Section I

Context

1   Introduction

> The essential difference today…is the changing character of industrial societies … the change in the rate of change.
>
> (Ling, 1954: 15)

We live in an age of rapid transition as economic, political and social changes converge to create a tumultuous pace of change that is shaking the global business world to its core. Today's 'febrile' form of 'flexible' capitalism, which Sennett (1998) calls the 'New Economy', is characterized by political and economic uncertainties, increasing competition, rapid technological change and the changing demographic. To address these complex performance drivers, organizations are attempting to pursue strategies of innovation, and to become sufficiently agile that they can rapidly adapt to changing circumstances and shape new opportunities.

Indeed, some might argue that we have reached an inflection point in business – driven by technology and globalization. According to 'Moore's Law' – based on Gordon Moore's famous 1965 prediction – the number of transistors on a chip would double every two months. This pace of change in technological advances has been significantly outstripped in reality and is accelerating. It is hard to imagine how things might look in this rapidly changing landscape in 15, 30 and 45 years from now. And yet arguably, business success requires a future focus, to anticipate and adapt to the changing context.

With a backdrop of such rapid change, how will companies build a robustly adaptable advantage when conventional strategies no longer produce differentiation? For instance, competing simply on product excellence is undermined by the fact that competitors can replicate technical breakthroughs made by one company in a matter of weeks, driving down the cost of their product to consumers, as anyone who has bought a camera recently would attest. Nor is cost leadership a sustainable strategy for success. Not only does cost saving ultimately wear away at a firm's capability, but all competitors are attempting to keep their costs low anyway. So in conventional business strategy terms, the main strategy for enduring success would seem to revolve around the customer – the deep relationship forged with present and future customers which relies on deeply human, rather than android, foundations.

What does the future hold for work and workers?

Given that, in today's complex environment, the world of work is volatile and uncertain and the status quo is being pressured from all sides, change is the new normal. The nature of work itself, the workplace and the workforce are all being transformed.

4   *Context*

Technology in particular is proving a major driver of social and business change, with new technologies applied immediately, virally and globally, disrupting business practice and creating new ways of communicating, making social connections and spreading knowledge. The advent of digital personal technologies, such as smartphones, tablets and smart watches has led to a boom in 'on-demand' access to data and in discussing and collaborating in real-time through the written word, via instant messaging and social media. Perhaps as a result, the future of work is increasingly being associated with bridge building, collaboration, co-creation and innovation among partners.

What is happening relates to world patterns in trade and employment that produce winners and losers in the share of benefits that economic development can provide. For instance, in the wake of the financial crisis and debates about the ethics of business, there is debate about whether the shareholder value model will remain dominant in the twenty-first century. On the one hand, despite the crisis of contemporary capitalism which was signalled by the global financial downturn that began in 2008, there appears to be a high degree of continuity of this thinking and related practice. On the other hand, today's business environment is increasingly described as the 'collaborative economy', which recognizes the need to create 'shared value' for a wider range of stakeholders, not least customers and employees.

Who will be the 'winners' and the 'losers' in the brave new world of work?

These world patterns will continue to have an impact on the way people live and consume, on the shape and nature of organizations, on work, and on the state of the employment relationship. Post economic crisis, it is still consumption which drives economies and people need good jobs in order to be able to spend. People's access to good jobs depends on their relative power in the labour market. Perceptions about 'talent' are changing since the skills required to thrive in the knowledge economy may be higher than those previously thought sufficient.

In the knowledge economy, talented employees with scarce skills can look forward to a bright future since skilled labour is becoming a scarce resource. The global workforce gained around 70 million workers in 2005. By 2039, that figure is forecast to fall to 30 million a year. In Europe the demand for abstract skills has risen by 20 per cent in recent years. On the other hand, in Europe the demand for low-skilled workers has decreased by 20 per cent in the last decade. Fifty-five per cent of the working population lack the basic problem-solving skills required when working in technology-intensive environments.

Those with less clout in the labour market may be at risk of serial unemployment. Automation is increasingly being applied to many types of work. Are robots going to take over jobs or will the next wave of automation open up the possibilities of more meaningful work for most workers? Will the knowledge possessed by the few remaining workers be ever more important and highly valued? The IMF fears that this skills premium, and persistent global technological divide, will compound inequality, making the skilled members of Generation Z richer, and the less skilled poorer, highlighting the need to potentially upskill a whole generation of the workforce. So can we drive consumption and jobs based on fair pay, good jobs, inclusion of women and people with caring responsibilities while reducing the skills gap?

Organizational effectiveness

In this changing context, how will 'organizational effectiveness' be defined, and what will HR's contribution be to achieving this? These are the core questions we explore in this book.

Organizational effectiveness is a floating, ill-defined concept that changes over time and has multiple dimensions. In broad terms, organizational effectiveness is the concept of how effective an organization is in achieving the outcomes the organization intends to produce. Thus it encapsulates both the results an organization sets out to achieve and its means of achieving those results, hence organizational effectiveness.

Organizational effectiveness is itself something of an emerging trend, and interest in it has grown during the economic downturn, moving on from an earlier focus on organizational development (OD) and managing change. While specialist organizational effectiveness roles exist in some organizations, these are often focused on measurement – of culture and climate, employee engagement levels and so on. Increasingly, organizational effectiveness is becoming perceived as a broader discipline, practised by a wide range of functions including HR, OD, internal communications and some line managers.

One of the main debates is about how 'performance' and success are defined. Organizational performance is one of the most important constructs in management research and how performance is defined reflects the organization's nature and context. In private-sector organizations, outcomes are conventionally expressed in terms of economic valuation, including productivity, net profit and so on, while in non-profit organizations, organizational effectiveness is often defined as 'outcome accountability', or the extent to which an organization achieves specified levels of progress toward its own goals (Richard et al., 2009).

Thus definitions vary according to the lens applied and the results expected by the business' primary beneficiaries. Intended results are reflected in organizational priorities and have consequences for other beneficiaries. In a shareholder value model, what produces high dividends for shareholders may result in job losses for employees. In a stakeholder value model, 'success' and 'results' might be judged very differently.

Therefore, if there is a shift underway from a purely investor-driven agenda, definitions of 'performance' and 'organizational effectiveness' must adapt too. Yet ironically the typical binary thinking and the traditional, often adversarial discourse between representatives of business, the state and workers reduces the possibility of finding common ground in addressing these issues. There is need for genuine dialogue and potentially new ways of thinking about how to lead in the emerging world of work. Throughout this book we shall be looking at how these definitions shift and change over time as we track the journey from a purely investor/shareholder/owner-driven perspective to a more diffuse 'stakeholder' perspective, increasingly measured through a 'quadruple bottom line'.

What contributes to organizational effectiveness?

Similarly, there are many debates about what contributes to organizational effectiveness. In the late 1950s and 1960s it became recognized that a variety of factors – internal and external – can play a part in organizational effectiveness. Accordingly, systems models became more prominent. For instance, Hirsch (1975) used an open systems model to consider the alignment between the organization's (internal) task environment and the institutional environment that conditioned and set the context for industry profitability; and second, the way that the external environment influenced senior management decisions over strategy.

Sparrow and Cooper (2014) point out that today's focus on organizational agility was evident then. In his review of 17 models of the time, Steers (1975) found that 10 out of 17 models used adaptability and flexibility as the main criteria, followed in order of importance by productivity, satisfaction, profitability, resource acquisition, an absence of strain, control over the environment, development, efficiency, employee retention, growth, integration, open communications

6   *Context*

and survival. However, Steers' (1975) review of the operationalization of performance highlighted the limited effectiveness of commonly accepted measurement practices in tapping this multidimensionality. Measures were generally inconsistent and used in isolation, with the most popular being productivity, profit or rate of return, employee satisfaction and employee withdrawal or turnover (the latter two seen as being value-laden and less objective).

A myriad of frameworks has since been applied in the hope of isolating the key things that might make a difference to output – for instance by improving the functioning of service-value chains. Typically, in non-profit organizations, whose output is social, logic models are used that specify how programme inputs, such as money and staff time, produce activities and outputs, such as services delivered, which in turn lead to impacts, such as improved beneficiary health.

As Richard et al. (2009) have found, reviewing past studies reveals a multidimensional conceptualization of organizational performance related predominately to stakeholders, heterogeneous product market circumstances and time. Katz and Kahn (1966) argued that, although senior managers could attend to activities associated with internal issues of efficiency from an economic perspective, it was evident that effectiveness was a political judgement made about organizations best viewed externally (Sparrow and Cooper, 2014).

How people contribute to business success

In particular, the focus of ongoing debate is how people contribute to business success, a focus that dates back to the origins of organizational effectiveness in the human relations theories of the 1930s. This followed the widespread adoption of scientific management practice in manufacturing sectors during the early decades of the twentieth century in which the primary focus was on improving efficiency, dissecting work processes into discrete activities that only managers had oversight of. The Human Relations School and the Hawthorne studies appeared to identify links between employee satisfaction and organizational performance. In 1955 Brayfield and Crockett reviewed existing literature at the time to establish whether such a link existed, and broadly concluded that the link was, at best, weak. Nevertheless, scholarly attempts to establish links between employee attitudes, organizationally relevant behaviours and performance continued. For instance, the concept of commitment (Steers, 1975 and Stevens et al., 1978) was thought to link attitude and behaviour, though commitment itself has been studied from so many perspectives that Hall (1977) suggested abandoning the concept altogether.

With respect to organizational practice, human relations theories put the 'people' back into the frame. From the 1950s onwards, management and leadership theories were developed that emphasized taking account of employee needs. For instance, situational leadership theory suggested that if managers wished to get the best performance out of people, they would need to vary their own styles to match the specific situations in which people were working and people's readiness, skill or 'development level' for the task in hand. Refinements of such theories, largely psychological, continue to this day, with newer variations coming from neuroscience, for example, and reflected in 'employee engagement' initiatives. The assumption is if managers understand employees' motivations, and attempt to meet their needs, so performance will improve. Thus employees are a means to an end.

Today, theory that seeks to explain linkages between HR practices and organizational performance sits within HRM theory, as we shall discuss in Chapter 5. Currently much of the thinking is tactical – for instance, how to use integrated business and HR analytics to pinpoint specific organizational variables which appear to make a difference to performance output in order to improve them.

Today, as the nature of work and the workplace are being rapidly transformed in the knowledge and service-based economies, there is growing recognition in the business community of the importance of people, and organizational culture to business success. This book focuses in particular on HRM's place within this, which is probably timely since there is also growing potential regulatory and competitive pressure on leaders to be able to account for exactly how people contribute to business success. As Dr Anthony Hesketh (2014), author of the report *Valuing Your Talent*, comments: 'HR leaders, CFOs and other members of the finance community interviewed for this research, place people – or human capital – at the heart of such an integrated understanding of the capacity of businesses to deliver sustained value-creation through their people.' UK analysts are increasingly paying attention to the 'human capital' factor when they assess the value of companies, and some of the UK's leading financial institutions are considering how to implement common assessment metrics that would require leaders to be able to articulate the performance of their people. The *Valuing Your Talent* framework is designed to dovetail with the increasingly influential and global Integrated Reporting Initiative, which provides a format for organizations to report on how their strategy, governance, performance and prospects lead to the creation of value in the short, medium and long term. If implemented, these new measures would require greater collaboration between HR, finance and strategy communities to understand how and where value is created and the related investments and initiatives which most drive sustainable business performance.

What is HRM's role with respect to improving organizational effectiveness?

Given the assumed linkages between employee attitudes, behaviours and skills with organizational performance, it might be expected that HRM will make a major contribution to organizational effectiveness. The HR function is a changing, evolving phenomenon. In its earlier historical incarnation, as Personnel, it too was heavily influenced by human relations theories that took account of the emotional, behavioural and motivational needs of employees. As we shall consider in Chapter 5, the development of HRM in the 1980s arose in response to the dominance of neo-liberal economic theories, that emphasize market freedoms and the promotion of managerialism. This has meant that priority has overwhelmingly been given to HR practices aimed at producing shareholder value, often at the expense of the needs of other stakeholders, such as customers, employees, unions, suppliers, communities, the environment and society as a whole. Yet productivity in the UK is consistently lower than in other countries, and generally weak levels of employee engagement are reported in many surveys.

Today, there is an argument, which I shall pursue throughout this book, that HR is pivotal to redressing this imbalance by shifting the dial to focus on culture, ethics and, above all, people. After all, there are many examples where business has not done well in behavioural and ethical terms – Enron, FIFA and Volkswagen are just some of the more obvious cases. The financial crisis and the unethical business practices that contributed to triggering it suggest that the motivational systems at work that are impacting on work today, including reward and leadership behaviour, need to change. However, related debates – about how to increase productivity, innovation, improve business culture – are largely not being led by HR.

Using HR influence

Looking ahead, human resource professionals will find themselves increasingly on the front line of these issues, and many more besides, dealing with a host of unprecedented 'known-unknowns' (to quote Donald Rumsfeld) which will have a major impact on work and the

8 *Context*

global workforce by the middle of the century. Business leaders will look to respected HR professionals for a steer on what might be anticipated with respect to the people businesses need, and how to build organizational cultures conducive to learning, innovation and sustainable high performance. We need real principles on which to base decisions and a more balanced view of priorities to ensure that stakeholders, including employees, and society as a whole, benefit from improved productivity.

Looking back to look forward

So how will the needs of employers and workers change in coming years? How will organizational effectiveness be defined and what is HRM's contribution to this?

Since the future can only be subject to conjecture, it is useful to look back over the past to determine how we reached where we are now and consider some of the choices we may have for the future. That is why this book takes a historical perspective that is grounded within both sociological and managerial theoretical contexts on the changing world of work, on the development of HRM and changing definitions of organizational effectiveness.

Shedding light on possible futures could be approached in a number of ways. For instance, we could look at what is already happening within organizations in order to create an 'evidence base' from which to deduce possible trends that might have an impact on the future world of work. We could consider some of the high-performance and organizational effectiveness models and attempt to 'stress test' them against today's fast-moving context. We could consider contemporary debates about strategic and business model change, organization design, talent management, agile and resilient organization, balanced scorecard, employee engagement, ethics and reputation, the nature and purpose of HR. Equally, we could attempt to focus on some of the intermediate outcomes that can lead on to strategic business outcomes, such as how HRM can help build broad dynamic cultural capabilities such as innovation, customer centricity, operational excellence, globalization, knowledge exchange, resilience and agility.

However, if we focus only on contemporary management fashions we run the risk of missing the bigger picture – the whole system effects which influence what happens in every walk of life. There are increasing calls for discussion about the workplace to break out of functional disciplinary siloes and be multidisciplinary. As Sparrow and Cooper (2014:3) point out:

> There is a need…to understand the implications that these problems of organizational effectiveness have for both the people and organizational processes, and to seek to challenge these through research lenses that synthesize and integrate important logics of action, theories and models. To the extent that they address issues of people and performance, we need to tap disciplines beyond those typically associated with organization effectiveness and HR, such as consumer behaviour, operations, risk and crisis management, political economy, population ecology, industrial sociology, amongst others.

Moreover, I believe that any study relating to the world of work must take into account the political, economic and other features of the changing context. Therefore, in this book I attempt to 'look outside' and broaden analysis beyond contemporary debates about human capital by locating my argument in a historical political economy context. As Sparrow and Cooper (2014:3) also argue,

> in an age of constrained growth we have returned to an era when HR functions also have a responsibility to start 'looking out' again – to understand the changing nature of work

and its place in society, and the issues that cut across organizations but will strongly impact the internal world of any of them.

HR practitioners will need to be able to articulate how the management of people can serve to create value for the organization, capture that value, leverage it, whilst also protecting and preserving what is of value. They will need to collaborate with colleagues in disciplines such as employee communications, operations, risk and crisis management and political economy, amongst others, and be able to convert their insights into action. Whether HR itself is up to the challenge is a question that will be explored throughout this book.

Looking through a critical lens

In exploring these themes, I shall mainly use a critical lens and will seek to question the assumptions made within mainstream HRM as a philosophy and practice, and how the norms inherent within this approach have implications for the ways that employees are conceptualized, managed and treated within organizations. First, let me distinguish between the orientations of mainstream and critical management and HRM theory.

Mainstream theory

Managerial discourses such as HRM are now central to the modern political, social and cultural body. There are different schools of thought in the field of management studies, of which HRM is an offshoot. Grey and Mitev (1995) distinguish between the dominant mainstream, i.e. 'managerialist', and 'critical' management studies (CMS). The purpose of much mainstream HR and OD research, to which I have contributed, is to identify links between HRM practice and organizational performance, in order to develop the 'holy grail' – an evidence-based and robust theory of HRM. In Chapter 5 we shall consider some of the many ways in which mainstream scholars have attempted to define HRM's contributions to organizational performance.

Mainstream management theory gained a high public profile across developed economies from the 1980s onwards through the well-publicized management theories of a variety of 'management gurus' (mainly American management consultants). For example, Peters and Waterman's influential book *In Search of Excellence* (1982) popularized the notion of organizational culture and strategy as being key to competitive success. The quest for the management 'formula' for lasting corporate success continues unabated to this day (see, for example, Collins and Porras, 1994; Kotter and Heskett, 1992; Katzenbach, 2000; Joyce et al., 2003; Ulrich and Ulrich, 2010; Goleman, 2011).

'Managerialist' researchers consider that research should be unitarist, i.e. operating for the benefit of management and aiming to contribute to organizational and managerial effectiveness. One of the arguments given to support unitarist practices is that, since the interests of all lie in the success of the business, management is merely exercising its mandate to manage in that common interest (Legge, 1995). The dominant theoretical framework for mainstream scholars is functionalism, focusing upon possible modifications to the design of organizational structures or processes, or changes to external factors in order to improve the situation of an organization. Much practitioner-focused research, including my own, is aimed at being of practical use to those who are struggling to meet the challenges of the status quo.

10   *Context*

Contemporary mainstream human resource theories mostly conceive of employees as resources (rather than people), both costs to be managed and assets to be optimized. Yet most HRM theory lacks a real focus on employees, who, importantly, are active agents and 'subjects' who can and do shape the world around them (Grant and Shields, 2002; Dundon and Ryan, 2010). It is, therefore, necessary to explore beyond firm-level reported data to tease out the role of employees in shaping HRM (Heffernan and Dundon, 2016).

Critical management theory

In contrast, the field of CMS is more diverse in its range and intent. Its overall purpose is not to improve the current system but to critique and problematize management practice with reference to its social, moral and political contexts (Grey and Mitev, 1995). Various scholars have attempted to summarize the intellectual character and analytic agenda of CMS (see, for example, Alvesson and Willmott, 2003; Spicer et al., 2010). For Watson the common core of what CMS offers to mainstream management theory is deep scepticism regarding the moral defensibility and the social and ecological sustainability of prevailing forms of management and organization. Fournier and Grey (2000: 18) argue that boundaries should be drawn around what CMS is on the basis of anti-performativity, denaturalization and reflexivity.

While critical management scholars are probably agreed upon their antipathy towards managerialism, this does not necessarily reflect a rejection of management *per se*. For Watson (2010), CMS's motivating concern is the social injustice and environmental destructiveness of the broader social and economic systems that these managers and organizations serve and reproduce, rather than focusing simply on the practices of managers themselves.

Grey et al. (1996) note that mainstream functionalism is underpinned by the basic assumptions of positivism, a legacy of the influence of scientific and engineering disciplines upon management. This assumes a direct correspondence between the forms of representation used and the 'objective' world. Critical scholars have comprehensively critiqued positivism – the view that the application of science to the problems of management is able to generate true, value-free knowledge since such a view assumes political neutrality, and does not acknowledge the influence of the interpretative framework of the author or the context within which the representations of reality are constructed.

Critical scholars are generally united in their attack on the dominance of one-sided accounts of change, written largely from a managerial perspective (Pettigrew and Whipp, 1991; Quinn, 1980; Mintzberg, 1988, 1994) since much of this literature trivializes the socio-political dimensions of change. This has led to demands for more robust theoretical models which can also be accessible to practitioners.

CMS is itself often accused by mainstream scholars of being critical without making a positive contribution to the development of new theory. Some CMS researchers have rejected the notion that they should seek to encourage 'better management'. Moreover, there remains a significant gap between academic and practitioner worlds (Cascio, 2007), and debate has intensified about the nature and reasons for this gap, together with calls for research to be more 'evidence-based' (Briner, 2007).

Theoretical approach

In writing this book I recognize that I fall between these two broad 'camps' – seeking to problematize management practice while also wishing to help improve it. Therefore, I propose to take a stance advocated by analytical pragmatists such as Watson (2010). Critical pragmatism

Introduction 11

derives from critical theory and is a methodological orientation that believes that social science research should illuminate ideological domination, hegemonic practices and social injustice and advocates an eclectic methodological experimentalism in the pursuit of this illumination. This is with a view to radically transforming management practice.

The book problematizes the ethics of HRM from a position of essentially modern ethical frameworks: notions of justice and the social contract. For instance, it could be argued that HR has been instrumental in installing what Sennett calls 'the work culture of new capitalism' in the early years of the twenty-first century. Keenoy (2009) argues that HRM is a discourse of control, that embodies a discipline of 'individualized performativity'. We shall consider some of the main HR mechanisms of performativity in Chapters 2, 5 and 6.

Both Herbert Marcuse (1964) and Antonio Gramsci (1971), from whose work critical pragmatism derives, urge the need for research into the ways in which societies reproduce themselves and the ways in which people are persuaded to embrace ideas, beliefs and practices that may not be in their best interests. According to Watson (2010), this approach involves treating sceptically all taken-for-granted, received or conventional assumptions about labour management practices and their links with both their societal/global and organizational contexts.

Representing the employer, HR is responsible for managing the employment relationship with employees. The employment relationship can be defined according to a general perspective, for instance on the labour market, and also from an individualized/employee perspective which concerns an individual's relationship with her/his employer, the term 'psychological contract' (see Chapter 2). Consequently, this term is often used in the same breath as 'new employment relations' and refers to the perceptions of employer and employee about what their mutual obligations are towards each other – the unwritten rules and expectations that govern day-to-day behaviour, the 'way things are done round here'. These implicit signals can prove much more important in the management of the employment relationship than any formal contract of employment since in essence this represents the moral bargain of work that revolves around understandings of obligations, expectations and promises. We shall explore how from the late 1990s onwards, white-collar employees in UK organizations experienced a significant shift in their psychological contracts as employers one-sidedly rewrote the employment relationship in favour of the employer.

Taking a pragmatist critical-analytical study of HRM should allow me to adopt both a critical approach to exploring what I believe to be some of the key contributory factors that have created current norms, and also to maintain an optimistic view about the possibilities for 'better' with respect to HRM's contribution to organizational effectiveness. Therefore, I intend to link the analysis across time and contextualize today's concerns in the structures of the past, and to examine these performance issues across several levels of analysis such as the individual, team, function, organization and societal (policy) level.

Watson argues that a critical-analytic HRM study 'would give us a good idea of how things work in the employment sphere and, thus, be as useful a guide to action to the employer or the employed, just as a "good" map of a country would be as valuable to invaders of that country as it would to its defenders'. What should be produced will be knowledge that people involved with HRM, whether they be workers, managers, policy-makers, trade union officers or HRM academics, can use to inform their understandings and hence their actions with regard to those HRM phenomena, whether the aim is to work to perpetuate the patterns that have been identified or to attempt to destroy them.

Debate about the nature and impact of the 'knowledge practice gap' in HRM has attracted growing interest in academic and management circles (Rousseau, 2006; Starkey et al., 2009). It is within the context of these debates that 'relevance' and 'usefulness' are discussed as creating

12   *Context*

value for practitioners (e.g. Lepak et al., 2007), or developing actionable knowledge that has maximum impact (Antonacopoulou, 2009). From a critical pragmatist stance, I am interested in theory and methodological orientation that illuminates ideological domination, hegemonic practices and social injustice. And, while I am seeking to be critical in tone, I am also interested in theory that can promote improved management practice and that can be practically useful.

Braverman and Sennett as points of departure

As a means of narrowing the focus of a potentially very wide sphere of discussion relating to the changing workplace, I have used as a leitmotiv throughout the book the predictions and observations made about the workplace by two very different authors, writing in different periods, and have examined more recent evidence for their claims drawn from a variety of sources. The first of my points of reference is Harry Braverman, whose book *Labor and Monopoly Capital: The Degradation of Work in the Twentieth Century* was published in 1974.

Braverman was an American Marxist political economist who had become radicalized during his early working life in the steel industry during the Great Depression. Braverman's (1974) book provides an interesting perspective on the social psychology of work under capitalism and when it appeared gave a significant spur to the emerging field of labour process studies. Marx (and thus Braverman) asserts that work is central for the human animal. It is through work that men and women realize their humanity. However, under a capitalist system, work is degraded to serve the interests of capital.

Braverman considered the capitalist 'mode of production', or the manner in which labour processes are organized and carried out, as the 'product' of capitalist social relations. Braverman wrote about the use of technology and 'scientific management' practices by managements to commodify clerical white-collar work in the 1960s. The deskilling of workers, he argued, was an inevitable tendency under Anglo-American monopoly forms of capitalism since this process enriched 'owners' of capital. This process of degradation, he continued, was often carried out at the expense of labour's wellbeing and enjoyment of work. Braverman predicted that the capitalist labour process would involve further worker deskilling, and the degradation of work more generally, and that this would extend beyond blue-collar to most forms of white-collar work during later periods.

Braverman had little time for the Personnel function, seeing this as a handmaid of management which in turn was in service of owners. Of course it could also be argued that the capitalist mode of production is the determining factor since it includes certain types of social relationship and constitutes the foundation on which all other relations within the society tend to get constructed, rather than the other way round.

With the publication of *Labor and Monopoly Capital*, Braverman set in motion a debate which has not yet run its course. For a time, his book stimulated considerable discussion and political/socialist commentary by Marxist writers. In the UK, labour process theory was highly influential, with industrial sociologists in the 1970s and early 1980s (Nichols and Benyon, 1977; Thompson, 2009) finding theoretical coherence in Braverman's work. Then the debate started by Braverman was followed by accusations of the exhaustion (Storey, 1985) and irrelevance (Lash and Urry, 1994) of labour process analysis, whilst repeated doubts have been expressed about its theoretical coherence and purchase (Littler and Salaman, 1982).

Braverman died in 1976 before the coming to power in the UK of Margaret Thatcher and the New Right project in the late 1970s or the collapse of the Soviet bloc from the end of the 1980s. Braverman's attempt to fill the gap in the theory of monopoly capitalism stimulated great debate when *Labor and Monopoly Capital: The Degradation of Work in the*

Twentieth Century (1974) first appeared. His labour process theory did much to stimulate renewed research into changing trends in work processes and labour relations in the late twentieth century. Eventually, after Thatcher's policies led to a tightening of control over the UK's higher education establishment, much of the academic debate which Braverman's book had prompted died down and was later subsumed into a general critique of Thatcherism or else suppressed beneath largely neo-liberal mainstream economic theories.

Richard Sennett and the 'work culture' of 'new capitalism'

My second point of reference is Richard Sennett, a contemporary sociologist, whose book *The Culture of the New Capitalism* (2006) provides an overview of the rapid and radical changes to the work world of modern capitalism since the mid-1990s. Like Braverman, Sennett begins by examining the nature of work under earlier forms of industrial capitalism but he also surveys the major differences between this earlier version of capitalism and the more global, more febrile version that is taking its place. When global capitalism came into being, Sennett argues, the focus in many businesses shifted from producing goods to be sold, to share price and to trading in companies rather than goods. As a result, companies tend to operate to very short-term agendas and this affects the way they deal with workers.

In *The Corrosion of Character: Personal Consequences of Work in the New Capitalism* (1998), Sennett argues that there is a 'new work culture' of capitalism that has deleterious effects on the social and psychological contracts of white-collar workers (see below for a more detailed explanation of psychological contracts). The emphasis on short-term gains for shareholders, usually at the expense of employees' wellbeing and job security raises questions about what 'organizational effectiveness' means in such contexts. While Sennett (2006: 10) draws his conclusions from his observations of knowledge workers in elite high-tech, finance and media industries which are only 'a small part of the whole economy', Sennett argues they 'exert a profound moral and normative force as a cutting-edge standard for how the larger economy should evolve'. My book focuses on the white-collar populations Sennett refers to and his depiction of the new work culture resonates strongly with me.

In *The Culture of the New Capitalism* (2006), Sennett provides an overview of the changes which have taken place in recent decades with respect to work and labour. Sennett first looks at bureaucracy in early capitalism. Most businesses were short-lived and unstable. However, in the latter half of the nineteenth century, business was modelled on predictable military lines where all roles were defined and career progression could be mapped out. Within the bureaucratic model, described by Max Weber, pyramid-like corporate structures aimed at social inclusion. Individuals knew their place and planned their futures – most would work at the base of the pyramid, hopefully progressing to the tip.

Sennett explores how new forms of work are changing people's communal and personal experience. In modern management practices there is an emphasis on flexibility – of working and also of contract. Sennett (2006) provides an ethnographic account of how middle-level workers make sense of the 'new economy'. He argues that the new ideal of the lean, flexible firm, which appears to liberate society from oppressive and inefficient bureaucracies, has destructive practical consequences for workers.

In *The Corrosion of Character*, Sennett contends (1998: 16) that, instead of Weber's 'iron cage' of bureaucracy, which rationalized use of time, modern capitalism requires that people constantly adapt and prove themselves to be assets. Today's corporations provide no long-term stability, benefits, social capital or interpersonal trust. In the work culture of new capitalism, work is reshaped to stress short-term goals, chop-and-change professional paths, decentralized

14   *Context*

structures, incessant risk and teamwork as against the hierarchies of yesteryear. Due to mecha-nization and the need for 'upskilling', managers as well as their subordinates face the possibility of obsolescence. The notion of career in such circumstances is no longer a meaningful concept.

Therefore, in large modern businesses, the effects of the new work culture are largely nega-tive for the majority of workers who face uncertainty and find it difficult to conceive of a life narrative. As a result, Sennett argues, personal character as expressed by loyalty and mu-tual commitment, or through the pursuit of long-term goals, is corroded. In such a context, he asks,

> How do we decide what is of lasting value in ourselves in a society which is impatient, which focuses on the immediate moment? How can long-term goals be pursued in an economy devoted to the short-term? How can mutual loyalties and commitments be sustained in institutions which are constantly breaking apart or continually being redesigned?
>
> (Sennett, 1998: 10)

In *The Craftsman* (2008), Sennett contends that, in today's organizations, concepts such as craftsmanship and getting the job right are seen as wasteful and somewhat obsessive. In the modern world, skills – interpersonal and managerial – substitute for craft and are often acquired in order to compete with others, rather than for their own sake. Moreover, the development of skills is often treated as a mechanical exercise, with the learner relieved of having to think through unsolved problems to find solutions since s/he relies instead on the use of technical and other tools to cut corners in the development and application of a skill. As a result, 'skill' is reduced to mere procedure rather than a disciplined struggle to master a complex technique. With echoes of Braverman's depiction of Taylorism, for Sennett the separation of hand and head does not lead to a state of real knowing.

Yet, Sennett argues, every human being can become a craftsman in ways which play to their intrinsic motivations, i.e. they can learn a skill and adjacent skills deeply, gain pride in achieve-ment and self-respect. However, to truly acquire a craft takes time and requires the craftsman to think about, experiment and learn deeply, understanding the relationship between problem solving and problem finding. It is only by reaching a more balanced state, developing an out-ward focus and rediscovering the discipline of practice that the craftsman can really build up his/her own capacity for learning.

Psychological contract

In various chapters of this book we shall consider self-reported evidence for how employees experience the changing work landscape and the new work culture. To make sense of people's accounts of their working lives, the concept of psychological contract provides a useful integrative concept around which to converge the concerns of the contemporary workplace. In an environment of rapid organizational change, where ideas of employee satisfaction and motivation could be seen as potentially meaningless, it is useful as an analytical device in social and organizational research to describe, understand and predict the consequences of changes occurring in the employment relationship (Shore and Tetrick, 1994).

Psychological contract theory is part of a widely accepted paradigm in organization the-ory, that of (reciprocal) social exchange between parties. March and Simon (1958) argued that employees and employers are in an exchange relationship in which each party makes demands of the other while providing something in return: employees provide production and participation in return for organizational 'inducements'. Chris Argyris was an early pioneer of the psychological contract theory in 1960 though the theory came to greater prominence in the 1990s at a time of considerable organizational change.

Over the past two decades in particular, a number of researchers have used the term to describe what is implicit within the employment relationship in terms of reciprocity and exchange. Because psychological contracts involve employee beliefs about the reciprocal obligations between themselves and their employers, they can be viewed as the foundation of employment relationships (Rousseau, 1995; Shore and Tetrick, 1994). Various scholars suggest that it is the psychological contract that mediates the relationship between organizational factors and work outcomes such as commitment and job satisfaction (e.g. Marks and Scholarios, 2004; Guest and Conway, 1997).

Central to the working of a healthy psychological contract is the notion of trust. As long as both parties maintain their contribution, the employment relationship is likely to function constructively. When one or other party is perceived to have reneged on their obligations towards the other, trust starts to break down and the psychological contract is considered 'breached', or in the case of severe breaches, 'violated'. In such cases, the psychological contract will be rebalanced by the 'damaged' party by for instance withdrawing goodwill, reducing effort and commitment, exiting or even sabotage.

The assumptions on each side of the 'psychological contract' between employees and employers, about what can/should be expected from each side, and what cannot reasonably be expected, have changed over time. In the 1980s, the 'old' white-collar psychological contract described by Herriot and Pemberton (1995a), represented a form of social exchange – of job security and potential career progression for the employee in return for performance and loyalty for the employer. I argue that this psychological contract type, at the heart of the white-collar employment relationship, was deliberately dismantled by employers, since it was considered a costly obstacle to labour flexibility. In its place was supposed to be a 'new deal' by which employees would offer hard work, flexibility and commitment to the employer in return for which 'good' employers would offer the employee scope to develop 'employability' – skills and experiences which might secure them work in the firm or elsewhere. We shall look for evidence throughout the book of how psychological contracts were impacted by the changing circumstances people experienced, and will look in more detail at psychological contract theory in Chapter 2.

Increasing confluence of theory

There is a small but detectable confluence of thinking from within the mainstream and to a lesser extent among critical theorists to close the 'knowledge–practice' gap (Pfeffer and Sutton, 1999). Boxall et al. (2007: 7), for instance, developed the notion of 'analytical HRM' to emphasize that 'the fundamental mission of the academic management discipline of HRM is not to propagate perceptions of "best practice" in "excellent companies" but, first of all, to identify and explain what happens in practice'. Analytical HRM is concerned with why management does what it does; with how contextualized processes of HRM work in practice; and is interested in questions of 'for whom and how well, with assessing the outcomes of HRM, taking account of both employee and managerial interests, and laying a basis for theories of wider social consequence'.

Boxall et al. (2007) also acknowledge that HR practices are not universally applicable, that much HRM research has failed to recognize adequately the cultural and organizational context, or that different social actors may pursue different goals in HRM. There

16 *Context*

is also acknowledgement that the employee experience of HRM needs 'to be more closely examined for moral and ethical reasons' (Paauwe, 2004; Boxall and Purcell, 2008). Critical pragmatist theorists Spicer et al. (2010) advocate the 'denaturalizing' of taken-for-granted assumptions underpinning the plethora of 'how to' guides on HRM which tend to encourage an unreflective adoption by practitioners of dominant vocabularies at play within organizational settings and beyond. However, other critical HRM scholars such as Delbridge and Keenoy (2010) still consider the managerial intent of analytical HRM to be the key divisive issue between the mainstream (performance) and critical scholars.

It is within these debates that I am attempting to ground my book, both from the practitioner perspective and from the academic, in which relevance is seen as a necessary condition for rigour (Starkey et al., 2009). In this book I examine if, and how, managerial and professional work is currently undergoing a transformation similar to that described by Braverman, looking at some of the available evidence of the effects of these changing employment patterns since the late 1990s on white-collar workers mainly based in the UK. A key source of data I will draw upon is the Roffey Park Management Agenda, an annual survey of white-collar workers from a variety of sectors which has been conducted since 1997 to this day.

I shall draw on a summary meta-analysis of annual Roffey Park Management Agenda surveys over ten years (1997–2006),[1] when I was Director of Research and Strategy at Roffey Park, and compare findings from more recent Agenda surveys (2015–16). This annual survey material was completed by white-collar workers – including professionals, specialists and managers – mainly based in the UK. Many respondents of the Agenda 2000–3 were managers, but were asked to respond as employees unless there were specific questions probing particular aspects of people management where it was appropriate to answer from a management perspective. The Management Agenda survey continues to be carried out each year and in later chapters I draw on this latest data to bring some of the issues discussed here up to date.

My interest was in how respondents in this study reported the nature of changes within the work culture at the time and how they responded to pressures put upon them within the new work culture, to which they were required to adapt. In particular, I examine ways in which employees appear to have experienced the dismantling of the conventional assumptions of the 'old' psychological contract, i.e. job security and career progression.

In seeking to understand how HRM contributes to shaping the new work culture, my aim is to challenge the overtly unitarist and managerialist framing of HRM that has progressively edged out pluralist perspectives on employment management including what are described as traditional personnel management or old-style industrial relations (Francis and Sinclair, 2003; Wright and Snell, 2005). I shall be arguing that HR practices, aided by technology, have contributed to the ongoing degradation of white-collar work, in particular by substituting a one-sided white-collar employment relationship in favour of employers in place of one which represented mutual obligations between the parties.

In this book, I shall be arguing in favour of including the voice of employees, and for employee-centric HR. Watson (2010: 920) identifies the need for CHRM 'to ensure that the voices of those who tend to be excluded from mainstream analyses are better represented in HRM theory and practice'. Increasingly, scholars such as Paauwe (2009: 134) call for mainstream HRM research which 'attends to the concerns and well-being of employees, recognizes the potential differential interests of the various "stakeholders" and takes a more multidimensional perspective on performance'. I am therefore interested in the extent to which HR practitioners, given their transformation into 'business partners', have maintained a focus on employee wellbeing and employee interests and shall explore this in Chapter 7. To date, employee-focused studies have been strongly influenced by the field of organizational psychology, largely located within the literature on the psychological contract, and used to examine the direction and strength of employee reactions to HRM, with the focus usually placed on how employees 'respond to' HRM (Grant and Shields, 2002). There remains a tendency to treat employees in instrumental terms, viewing them as largely 'consumers' of HRM practices (Paauwe, 2007), or of employer brands (Martin and Dyke, 2010), rather than 'producers' of HRM/brands, thereby failing to sufficiently acknowledge the 'agency role' of employees in shaping HR practice, nor accommodating competing conceptions of HRM (Janssens and Steyaert, 2009; Grant and Shields, 2002; Francis, 2006).

Within this context there are increasing calls from analysts to move beyond the either/or orientation about HRM, to new ways of thinking that create a more 'balanced agenda' (Francis and Keegan, 2006; Boselie et al., 2009). For instance, Boselie and colleagues acknowledge that the conceptualization of performance used in the performance stream is highly managerialist and unitarist in outlook, often represented as what is good for the employee is good for the organization, and the other way round (Boselie et al., 2009; Guest, 2002). This idealistic view of the workplace places managers in the 'driving seat' of change and adopts an optimistic (if not naïve) view of the HR function's role in generating employee commitment in order to enhance organizational performance.

With such debates as a backdrop, there is some evidence of competing perspectives coming closer together, reflected in more 'intellectual space' being given to CHRM in mainstream journals (Delbridge and Keenoy, 2010). Current developments within this body of literature have been described as a promising way forward in terms of developing more nuanced and employee-centred approaches to the study of HRM–Performance (HRM-P) (e.g. Grant and Shields, 2002), and in combining different levels of analysis. Within the HRM-P stream, this is reflected in the following quotation by Paauwe (2009: 134): 'Bringing employees back into the equation between HRM and various kinds of both individual and organisational level outcomes, including financial performance, is a "*conditio sine qua non*" for advancing the field as a respected discipline.'

Conclusion

Both Braverman and Sennett argue that the capitalist labour process is potentially damaging to workers. In this book I will consider if their commentary is borne out in the various forms of evidence I have gathered. In particular, is deskilling being extended into most types of white-collar work, including many professional jobs, with special skills, knowledge and control reserved for those at the top of the hierarchy, as Braverman predicted? I shall attempt to link this with the debate about managerialism, and reconnect it to employment practice of the current time.

Alongside examining the cultural, political and economic significance of the new work culture in UK organizations within the recent history of the UK, my second focus is on how the conventional notions about exchange in the employment relationship and reciprocation in the 'old' psychological contract have been undermined in the new work culture from the mid-1990s onwards. I examine how these shifts in the employment relationship have impacted on employees' perception of their working lives. In this book I am attempting to reveal the reality of the daily lived experience of HR policy and practice, within which the

18   *Context*

psychological contract acts as the weather gauge of the employment relationship. I believe that, potentially, this offers a grounded, intellectually coherent and explanatory framework for understanding the changing employment relationship in a way that can be useful to employees and to organizations.

Note

1 The annual surveys were written in January of each year and featured data gathered between July and November of the previous year. Therefore, the data gathered in 1997 features in the 1998 survey.

2 Key concepts and theories

> The principle that human nature, in its psychological aspects, is nothing more than a product of history and given social relations removes all barriers to coercion and manipulation by the powerful.
>
> (Noam Chomsky, 1975)

This book attempts to explore the changes happening to work, the workplace and workers over the last few decades. As discussed in the last chapter, Sennett suggests that work in today's dominant form of capitalism has largely negative consequences for workers. For Sennett, the work culture of new capitalism prevents people from developing a life narrative.

For Braverman, workers become commodities who are essentially dispensable. A large part of Braverman's argument centred on the systematic effort in a capitalist economy to 'deskill' jobs in order for capital and its representatives to be able to more efficiently control and coordinate the labour force, pay lower wages and thus maximize profit. It is this drive that is behind the ever more detailed division of labour, the adoption of computers and other technologies to commodify work and replace workers, leading to the 'degradation' of work and workers, and growing polarization within societies. So, by deskilling workers, capitalist managements could find cheaper, alternative means of production.

But are employees merely hapless pawns to be moved around at will by a chess grand master, or can they exercise free will in the form of agency?

We shall examine this question throughout the book using various sociological and psychological theoretical lenses, together with key concepts such as performativity, which I introduce in this chapter. We shall cover:

- structuration theory;
- scientific management;
- the degradation of work
- work as a commodity;
- performativity;
- alienation;
- psychological contract;
- new capitalism as discourse driven.

Structuration theory

Structuration theory (Giddens, 1986) is one structural theoretical resource drawn upon within this book. This draws together the two principal strands of social thinking – structure and agency. In the structuralist tradition, the emphasis is on social structure (which is

20   *Context*

primarily seen as a form of constraint over human behaviour). Structure consists of the rules (or behavioural norms) and resources (accumulated knowledge and expertise) that guide behaviour in a social system. In the phenomenological and hermeneutic traditions, which this book embraces, the human agent is the primary focus. For Albert Bandura (2001), a prominent social learning and social cognitive theorist, agency is the 'essence of humanness' which is contained in a 'capacity to exercise control over the nature and quality of one's life'. Bandura's definition of human agency incorporates his theory of self-efficacy:'To be an agent is to intentionally make things happen by one's actions…the core features of agency enable people to play a part in their self-development, adaptation, and self-renewal with changing times' (2001: 2). People exhibit agency through developing intentions and thought before events; self-regulation through self-reaction; and self-reflectiveness about their capabilities, performance and the meaning and purpose of what they do in life. Bandura developed the concept of reciprocal interaction, in which humans are regarded as highly active processors of information who are continually interacting with the social environment.

Structuration theory attempts to recast structure and agency as a mutually dependent duality. Behaviour and structure are intertwined; people go through a socialization process and become dependent on the existing social structures, but at the same time social structures are being altered by their activities. In other words, human actors display agency, but in a structural context, and this mutually dependent relationship (structure influences action, action influences structure) evolves over time and space. Structure both limits and constrains organizational behaviour because organizational members tend to adhere to existing rules for interaction.

Moreover, individual behaviours are constrained by the knowledge resources available to them; organizational members tend to behave in ways which conform to existing mental models for how the organization should operate (Senge et al., 1999).The phrase the 'way we do things around here' is often used to describe organizational culture, which is both shaping and being shaped by human agents. However, when individuals or groups begin to draw on new resources or apply new rules for carrying out their work together, the structure of the social system becomes amenable to change. In this way, many micro actions come to constitute the social interaction.The theory helps illuminate both how participation is embedded in its social context and how it evolves over time. Technology is in this context socially transformative, as well as socially transformed, and hence any process study needs to consider the interdependence of human action and social structure.

This theory allows for the Marxian idea that capitalism stabilizes itself through structures which then become naturalized and taken for granted. Pre-existing frameworks of interpretation, as shaped by various contextual, cultural and normative assumptions, necessarily affect processes of knowledge construction (Kuhn, 1970). In capitalist societies, positivist assumptions become rationalized in institutions, denying the reality of underlying structures and thus reinforcing the status quo.

Scientific management

Amongst the structural forces with a direct bearing on employee agency in the labour process is scientific management, or 'Taylorism'. Braverman's book began with a historical analysis of work and employment, starting with pre-capitalist production, moving to the outworking system, to the factory, to the detailed division of labour, to mechanization, Taylorization, and to personnel management. In the past, the labour process (how the work is planned and done) was the responsibility of the craftsperson; now it is the responsibility of the capitalist and his handmaiden or surrogate agent, the manager.

Above all, Braverman argued, the history of the labour process from the early twentieth century was dominated by the acceptance – and promotion – of the battery of techniques associated with scientific management and the scientific technical/revolution as an instrument of control. These are also known as Fordist or 'Taylorist' practices since they were devised by Frederick Winslow Taylor and famously adopted by the Ford Motor Company in the US in the 1920s. Since Taylor did not generally trust or respect labour, scientific management's application was contingent upon a high level of managerial control over employee work practices which necessitated a higher ratio of managerial workers to labourers than under previous management methods.

After careful study of individuals at work, including via time and motion studies, Taylor advocated replacing traditional working practices and decisions based upon rules of thumb by precise procedures. This involved the codification and re-engineering of craft workers' knowledge in the shape of the moving production line (Brown et al., 2010a). Thus mechanical Taylorism fragmented workers' skills, separating mental from manual tasks (or conception from execution), and resulted in the deskilling of much of the labour force – the 'artisan' or 'craft worker' of the working world – and a decline in workers' intellectual input into their individual work product. The monopoly over knowledge was held by management to control each step of the labour process. Taylorism's manifestations included work intensification. Workers were increasingly seen as machines which could be adapted to the requirements of any job. Thus deskilled, workers became dispensable and replaceable.

Taylor's methods and performance-measurement processes were widely adopted in manufacturing firms as a means of improving productivity. In the decades following the Great Depression of the 1930s, some of the worker dissatisfaction and resistance to such methods was manifested in low productivity, an increase in absenteeism, wildcat strikes and a reluctance of workers to commit themselves to their work tasks (Braverman, 1974: 31).

The 'degradation' of work

In his explicitly anti-Taylorist critique of the practices of leading US corporations during the 1960s, Braverman (1974: 320–4) found evidence of classical Taylorist approaches to monitoring and measuring the output of the growing ranks of workers employed in large offices through the early applications of computerized data processing which turned office routine into: 'A factory-like process in accordance with the precepts of modern management and available technology...the modern office becomes a machine' (p. 348). This 'degradation' of work through the divisions of labour achieved using Taylorist methods (Braverman, 1974: 347–8), he argued, ended any residual pretence of mutuality of interest between labour and owner. Owners and workers fell into their separate camps. Moreover, Braverman portrays management as having no concern for the workforce as people. Management was the 'new working class' that included engineers, technical specialists, scientists, lower supervisors and lower management (including personnel management), and other specialists or professionals including marketing, finance, administrators and workers in the hospital, school and government businesses (pp. 403–4). Braverman considers these as agents of the capitalist because they have a position of control over the labour force (pp. 404–6). Similarly, Mandel (1968: 5) argued that, since capital's appetite for profit is unlimited, and since this involves exploiting human surplus labour, capitalists 'haggle ever more furiously over seconds and fractions of seconds, as in time and motion studies'. Braverman predicted that capital would eventually increase its control over professionals and higher-skilled workers by continuously deskilling and proletarianizing them through the use of technology.

For the capitalist class, Braverman argued, this view of man as a machine has become more than mere analogy, it is also how it has come to view humanity. Such views of man as machine

22 *Context*

or commodity, Braverman argued, typically generate friction between workers and managers, and social tensions between the blue-collar and white-collar classes.

Work as commodity

Commodification refers to the way that market values can replace other social values, or the way a market can replace a communal system. The process of proletarianizing workers described by Braverman is consistent with the conceptualization of work as commodity from mainstream (neo-classical) economic theory. According to labour relations scholar John Budd (2010), when work is commodified in this way (conceptually), it is analysed as an economic quantity independent of non-economic concerns and ignores issues of human agency and dignity. Work and workers are thus treated like any other factor of production, as 'resources'. When work is viewed as a commodity, its allocation is seen as governed by the impersonal 'laws' of supply and demand in a free market. On the supply side, work is something that individuals choose to sell in varying quantities in order to earn income and maximize their individual or household utility.

Budd (2010) and others argue that commodity production has become the predominant mode of relation between worker and work, extending across ever-wider reaches of society, touching every sphere of human existence and causing other conceptualizations of work to be overshadowed. For instance, employment relations scholars see work as occupational citizenship – an activity undertaken by citizens with inherent equal worth who are entitled to certain rights and standards of dignity and self-determination, irrespective of what the market provides (Crouch, 1998). The overshadowing of organizational citizenship by commodity conceptualizations of work is evident in much mainstream contemporary HRM theory that also embraces the notion that employees are 'resources' and costs to be managed and reflected in HR practices which install and reinforce performativity.

The concept of work as commodity is embedded within the new individualized HRM industrial relations. In Ulrich's influential model of HR roles (1997), the roles of 'employee champion' and 'administrator' were considered to be tactical and therefore of lesser value than the strategic business partner and change agent roles (see Chapter 5). In essence, HR practices are intended to ensure that organizations have the people they need, and the means of achieving performance from their workforces, in the most productive and cost-effective way possible. The basis of shared purpose – the 'common goal' referred to by Scott (1994) – is about survival in the marketplace. Market survival applies not only to organizations but to individuals too: 'Employees are simultaneously required, individually and collectively, to recognise and take responsibility for the relationship between the security of their employment and their contribution to the competitiveness of the goods and services they produce' (Willmott, 1993: 522). Unless employees possess specific forms of labour power, they are essentially resources which can be deployed or dispensed with at the will of the employer. Contemporary HRM practice may therefore be at odds with stereotypical organizational rhetoric such as 'our people are our greatest asset'.

Performativity

The employment relationship is put under particular strain by the structural demands of performativity. This policy imperative, manifest in performance-related organizational processes such as targets, performance monitoring, appraisals, performance-related pay and so on, can be examined under the lens of labour process theory. From this perspective, performativity is a contributing factor to the degradation of white-collar work.

As we shall discuss in the next chapter, much of the academic literature on performativity focuses on changes within the UK's education sectors which were implemented by the 'New Labour' governments (1997–2010). The political goal of performativity involves installing work cultures supportive of neo-liberal managerialism, and undermining cultures which could potentially compete with, or be a source of critique of such practices. Ball (2003) argues that in the case of education, performativity, the market and managerialism are three interrelated policy technologies used to 'reform' the education sector to the ends of business. Within the broad strategy to produce stronger links between education outputs and the requirements of a capitalist economy, 'the manner in which education is delivered is increasingly subject to market scrutiny and commercial management practices and values' (Hatcher, 2001: 48).

Ball makes the connection between policy decisions taken by New Labour and their 'rendering of education itself into the commodity form' (1999: 198). Commodification (first appeared in the Oxford English Dictionary in 1975, origins Marxist political theory) is used to describe the process by which something that would not normally be seen as 'goods' such as ideas, becomes a commodity and is assigned a value. Hence it describes how market values can replace other social values including a modification of relationships, formerly untainted by commerce, into commercial relationships in everyday use.

For Ball (2003: 217) what helps create these new work cultures is the constant flow of changing demands and related structure of surveillance: 'a flow of performativities...expectations and indicators that makes us continually accountable and constantly recoded'. New roles and relationships are reflected in new terms. In professional settings such as schools, some teachers become 'managers' who have the right to assess the work of other teachers. Within the public sector, resources and responsibilities are split out so that work is carried out by 'suppliers' and assigned and measured by 'commissioners'. Ball (1999: 190) argues that the re-forming of relationships creates new power bases and subjectivities. Language reflects seemingly self-renewing 'regimes of truth' in Foucauldian terms, forming and legitimizing market, management and individual-rights discourses, as well as the movement of consumerism (described by Bauman, 2002) into society. There is increasing polarization of the workforce with respect to career opportunities, based on whether people are judged to be 'on-side' with managerial priorities and language. With the loosening of job security, employees take fewer risks in speaking their minds. Recruitment activities gradually bring into organizations people who conform to the new work culture.

Ball (2003: 216) argues that what have been lost with the erosion of professional cultures are values, integrity and an ethical basis for work. The new ethical systems are based upon institutional self-interest. This can be empowering for some but for others may require 'intensive work on the self' to set aside personal beliefs and commitments and live an existence of calculation. Thus it would seem that performativity is a key plank in realizing Braverman's prediction that all forms of work would eventually be commodified and workers deskilled.

Alienation

For critical theorist Herbert Marcuse (1964), alienation and dehumanization were the inescapable hallmarks of capitalism. This process of turning workers into commodities, Braverman claims, becomes a permanent and ever-expanding feature of a capitalist economy. Each succeeding generation has to be acclimatized to the new mode of work, socialized to overcome the initial revulsion to the ever more detailed division of labour and the consequent rending of human beings.

Braverman hints at the moral, social and human impacts of the capitalist labour process and the degradation of work. Misery for labour accumulates in direct proportion to the

24   *Context*

accumulation of capital in the pockets of CEOs (1974: 396): 'The pyramids were built with the surplus labor of an enslaved population' (p. 64). Coercive methods were required to turn 'free' craftspeople into 'habituated cogs in the machine'. Thus for the worker, work would be transformed from being a source of meaningful activity into a mindless, machine-based and powerless activity. Workers who remain employed must work even harder for lower wages to produce surplus value. In time, fewer skilled workers would be needed and they would suffer the personal consequences of deskilling, rationalization and hierarchy (1974: 415).

Sennett (2006) has charted the disorienting effects and personal consequences for workers of this form of capitalism with its short-termist regimes. He argues that alienation, that was once considered the preserve of the old proletariat, is now being experienced by workers in the 'knowledge economy' and public sector. As the work ethic changes, new beliefs about merit and talent displace old values of craftsmanship and achievement and 'careers' are no longer a meaningful concept.

Mandel too argued that the three characteristics of modern labour under capitalism as defined by Marx – i.e. its key role in the productive process, its basic alienation, its economic exploitation – were extended in the neo-capitalist society of the twentieth century to include a wider range of skilled workers, since the productive process, especially automation, tends to universalize industry, and to integrate a constantly growing part of the mass of wage and salary earners into an increasingly homogeneous proletariat. Given the dictates of capital accumulation, capitalists and their managements are constantly driven to renovate the productive process. Therefore, under a neo-capitalist economy (see the next chapter), labour is more than ever alienated:

> forced labor, labor under command of a hierarchy which dictates to the worker what he has to produce and how he has to produce it. And this same hierarchy imposes upon him what to consume and when to consume it, what to think and when to think it, what to dream and when to dream it, giving alienation new and dreadful dimensions. It tries to alienate the worker even from his consciousness of being alienated, of being exploited.
>
> (Mandel, 1968: 9)

In *The Corrosion of Character*, Sennett (1998) argues that, with the degradation of work, pride among workers has dissipated and people don't look 'long-term'. In today's workplace one must be very flexible, therefore loyalty and commitment are not part of a fast-paced, 'short-term' society. Workers know that they are simply a tool that can be replaced with the twist of a wrench. Consequently, Sennett argues, people's interests are with themselves. People don't look at what they can offer, but instead at what they want to receive. In such a context, Sennett argues, people struggle to sustain a life narrative that comes out of their work. As a result, Sennett (1998) argues, personal character is corroded.

Psychological contract

In various chapters of this book we shall consider self-reported evidence for how employees experience the changing work landscape and the new work culture. Psychological contract theory is part of a widely accepted paradigm in organization theory, that of (reciprocal) social exchange between parties. Social exchange theory has arguably become one of the most influential frameworks for understanding exchange behaviour within organizations and, while there are various definitions, there is a general consensus that it involves a series of social and economic interactions that generate obligations to reciprocate, engendering 'feelings of personal obligations, gratitude and trust' (Blau, 1964: 20). It has been used to explain a number of different interactions, including psychological contract theory and perceived organizational support (Shore et al., 2004), and more recently, employee engagement (Saks, 2006).

Chris Argyris was an early pioneer of the psychological contract theory in 1960, though the theory came to greater prominence in the 1990s at a time of considerable organizational change. Social exchange theory argues that, when one party gives something to another, it expects the other party to reciprocate by providing some contributions in return (Blau, 1964). March and Simon (1958) argued that employees provide production and participation in return for organizational 'inducements' from the employer. Whereas the traditional employment relationship model of industrial relations consists of 'regulated exchange' and collective representations between management and employees (Sparrow, 1996: 76), today's exchanges with the employer are more individualized and run the risk of becoming unbalanced as well as unregulated.

Over the past two decades in particular, a number of researchers have used the term to describe what is implicit within the employment relationship in terms of reciprocity and exchange. As well as explicit social exchanges, there are also more implicit and psychological or social exchange processes occurring within the workplace. Because psychological contracts involve employee beliefs about the reciprocal obligations between themselves and their employers, they can be viewed as the foundation of employment relationships (Rousseau, 1990, 1995; Shore and Tetrick, 1994; Guest, 1997; Coyle-Shapiro and Kessler, 1998). Aspects of employment relationships such as job security, performance management, human capital development, opportunities for growth and the firm's core philosophies of HRM may have a profound impact on the development of perceived mutual obligations (Rousseau, 2001; Francis and D'Annunzio-Green, 2007; Sparrow and Cooper, 2003).

Various scholars suggest that it is the psychological contract that mediates the relationship between organizational factors and work outcomes such as commitment and job satisfaction (e.g. Marks and Scholarios, 2004; Guest and Conway, 1997). The employment relationship is therefore increasingly conceptualized as involving a 'psychological contract' which reflects the individual and subjective nature of the employment relationship.

There are two main definitions of the psychological contract. The first, which is described by Herriot and Pemberton (1995a) as the 'classic' definition, derives from the work of Argyris (1960) and Schein (1978). This refers to the perceptions of mutual obligation, held by the two parties in the employment relationship, the employer and the employee (Herriot et al., 1997). According to the second definition, which is based on the work of Rousseau (1989: 122), the psychological contract is:

> An individual's belief regarding the terms and conditions of a reciprocal exchange agreement between the focal person and another party. A psychological contract emerges when one party believes that a promise of future returns has been made, a contribution has been given and thus, an obligation has been created to provide future benefits.

In this definition, the psychological contract is formulated only in the mind of the employee and is therefore about 'individual beliefs, shaped by the organization, regarding terms of an exchange between individuals and their organization'. However, in terms of underlying constructs, there remains no overall accepted definition of the psychological contract and this exchange relationship is very complex and dynamic, with a wide range of factors shaping employee perceptions of how they experience the deal.

While there is ongoing debate about whether the psychological contract is based on 'expectations' or 'obligations', there is consensus that psychological contracts extend beyond

26   *Context*

legal contracts to beliefs or expectations an individual and an employer might hold toward the other. In other words, psychological contracts relate to individuals' beliefs regarding reciprocal obligations: what obligations the employee owes the employer and vice versa. When individuals believe they are obligated to behave or perform in a certain way, and also believe that the employer has certain obligations towards them, these individuals are said to hold a psychological contract.

Research has commonly focused on contract content and outcomes, i.e. the nature, scope and impact of exchanges between employer and employees (e.g. Rousseau et al., 2009; Guest et al., 2004). Critics argue that, in its present form, the concept of psychological contract symbolizes an ideologically biased formula designed for a managerialist interpretation of contemporary work and employment (Cullinane and Dundon, 2006). Moreover, in terms of underlying constructs there remains no single accepted definition of the psychological contract and this exchange relationship is very complex and dynamic, with a wide range of factors shaping employee perceptions of how they experience the deal. Any psychological contract is malleable, since it is personal to every employee and will change as an individual's needs and expectations change over time.

Despite these difficulties, as Coyle-Shapiro and Kessler (2000) point out, the psychological contract framework may be of particular value in understanding non-traditional employer–employee linkages since it provides a complementary or alternative framework for examining changes occurring in the employment relationship at the individual level. The extent of the balance/imbalance appears more important to the nature and health of the contract than the specific content of the contract.

Social and psychological contracts

Some authors argue that psychological contracts are strongly conditioned by existing and changing social contracts. Indeed, Edwards and Karau (2007) question whether the changes taking place in the workplace are impacting the social contract or the psychological contract. They define a social contract as the set of norms, assumptions and beliefs that society conceives as fair and appropriate for parties involved in employment relationships. This includes the general beliefs and norms pertaining to reciprocity, job security, loyalty, good faith and fair dealings that should be maintained by employees and organizations. Most centrally, organizations significantly influence the social contract (Morrison and Robinson, 1997).

Different social contracts can exist that define what is appropriate behaviour in different societal contexts, such as employer–employee, teacher–student, etc. Behaviour that is considered appropriate according to one social contract may be considered inappropriate under another (Clark and Waddell, 1985). Rowan and Cooper (1999) argue that individuals adapt to different social settings and roles as 'plural selves', and can thus operate successfully within different and changing contexts.

The psychological contract differs from the social contract in several ways. Whereas the social contract is developed at societal level and establishes assumptions and norms regarding a wide variety of employment relationships, the psychological contract is developed at an individual level and is the set of assumptions and expectations between a specific employee and a specific employer. Therefore, actions that may violate a specific individual psychological contract may be within the norms of the social contract. Thus, breach of a psychological contract between an employee and employer will be perceived at an individual level (Robinson and Morrison, 1995; Robinson et al., 1994), whereas violation of the social contract will, most likely, be perceived at an organizational or societal level.

With respect to career expectations, for instance, various writers (Hakim, 1994; Ellig, 1998; Maxwell et al., 2000) suggest that the new employment relationship consists of a social contract requiring that employees be responsible for acquiring their own skills and employability. These changing social contract assumptions may or may not influence how individual employees view their psychological contract with their employer at any point in time. The interplay between the social contract and the psychological contract has been little explored (Edwards and Karau, 2007).

Who speaks for the organization?

The question about who speaks for 'the organization' in psychological contracting is undertheorized within employment relationship research and analysts warn against the anthropomorphizing of the organization in this regard, giving it its own human-like set of intentions (Herriot and Pemberton, 1997; Coyle-Shapiro and Shaw, 2007; Guest and Conway, 2001). While we naturally talk about organizations much of the time as if they had a more concrete existence, Watson (2002: 96) warns us of the risk of falling into a unitary language that oversimplifies the actual reality of organizational life, glossing over differing perceptions and values held by organizational members.

Nevertheless the personification of the organization usefully allows people to find a way of relating to it (Lievens et al., 2007). In general, however, it is assumed that the HR function plays a key role in the psychological contracting process since it is responsible for employer branding, recruitment and induction processes through which employee expectations are shaped before, or at the start of their employment.

Psychological contract fulfilment or breach

Social exchange theory and the norm of reciprocity have been used as theoretical frameworks to explain how psychological contract fulfilment produces beneficial outcomes. For instance, in what Tsui et al. (1997) describe as the 'mutual investment model', there is a mutually beneficial transaction between an employer willing to ensure the wellbeing of the employee (e.g. health and wellbeing, career opportunities, training and appraisal), and an employee who knows what is expected and offers up the appropriate behaviours to meet those expectations. High mutual obligations are significantly more likely to lead to better outcomes for the organization, such as higher employee commitment and the associated benefits of discretionary effort, pro-social organizational behaviours and so on.

Central to the working of a healthy psychological contract is the notion of trust. As long as both parties maintain their contribution, the employment relationship is likely to function constructively. Guest (1997) argues that, from an employee standpoint, the value of the new psychological contract will be assessed according to:

*   The extent to which the organization has kept its promises/commitments about job security, careers and the demands of the job and workloads (delivery of the 'Deal').
*   Trust in management to keep its promises and look after employees' best interests.
*   Fairness of treatment in general and specifically with regard to reward allocation.

This ideal balance of interests is, however, unlikely to be achieved in a context of downsizing and ever-increasing tight control of resources by employers, in which employees who survive redundancy are expected to take on increasing workloads. When one or other party is

28　*Context*

perceived to have reneged on its obligations towards the other, trust starts to break down. Breach of the psychological contract occurs when an employee feels that the organization has failed to deliver satisfactorily on its promises (Morrison and Robinson, 1997; Rousseau, 1995). For example, if an employee's psychological contract is founded on the expectation that the organization will provide training and development opportunities, failure to do so results in a contract breach. In the case of severe breaches, the psychological contract will be considered 'violated' and the exchange relationship is likely to break down.

There is ongoing debate amongst academic writers about the nature, extent and consequences for both parties of breach and violation. However, since the psychological contract is perceptual, unwritten and hence not necessarily shared by the other party to the exchange (Rousseau, 1989; Lucero and Allen, 1994), employees and employers may hold different views on the content of the psychological contract and the degree to which each party has fulfilled the mutual obligations of the exchange.

Rousseau (1995) argues that, because psychological contract breach is a subjective experience which emanates from a sense-making process, its effects on employee behaviours may be influenced not only by situational variables (e.g. perceptions of (in)justice – Kickul et al., 2001) but also by individual difference characteristics (e.g. Ho et al., 2004; Raja et al., 2004). Some theorists argue that organizationally imposed change continues to threaten evolving forms of psychological contract (Hiltrop, 1996; Holbeche, 1997), while Guest and Conway (2001) argue that the extent of the impact of change on employees has been exaggerated. They suggest that, despite the downsizings and restructurings of recent years, many elements of the so-called 'old' psychological contract have remained in place.

Amongst the possible causes of breach, HR policies and practices can and do represent implied promises or obligations on the part of the employer in the employee's understanding of the contract (Guest and Conway, 1997). If employees perceive that the employer has changed the terms of their psychological contract without explicit negotiation, for instance when employers impose more flexible employment contracts, there is significant likelihood of ongoing psychological contract breach and violation, with potentially negative consequences for employees and employers. Circumstances like organizational timing (e.g. mergers) or market factors (e.g. redundancies, cutbacks) can lead to feelings that the contract has been broken (Turnley and Feldman, 2000).

Social exchange theory and the norm of reciprocity are also used to explain how perceived psychological contract breach results in negative consequences. In such circumstances, employees tend to redress the balance in the relationship through reducing their commitment and their willingness to engage in organizational citizenship behaviours. If balance cannot be achieved longer term, one or both of the parties will seek to terminate the relationship or the 'damaged party' will seek to rebalance the deal by, for instance, withdrawing goodwill, reducing effort and commitment, exiting or even sabotage.

Fisk (2002) points out that not all employees feel the same about the new working environment and the psychological contract is constantly being redefined, while Rousseau argues that some impacts will generically affect most employees.

The psychological **career** *contract*

The assumptions on each side of the 'psychological contract' between employees and employers, about what can/should be expected from each side, and what cannot reasonably be expected, have changed over time. A major focus of psychological contract theory during the 1990s concerns careers, especially the shifting locus of responsibility for career management, which was widely acknowledged to have moved from the employer to the employee. The reason for the prominence given to this issue was the destabilization of the employment relationship described as the 'old' (paternalistic) psychological contract. For white-collar workers this is typically described as based on mutual expectations that in return for job security, and the possibility of vertical promotion/career progression, the employee will work hard for and be loyal to the employer. Essentially, such psychological contracts are based on an assumed 'relationship' between employer and employee; a belief that a good employer will 'look after' its employees.

While it might be argued that many of these assumptions were based on myths, nevertheless such beliefs were common and there was a social contract around white-collar careers which was reflected in the career practices of medium to large organizations from the 1950s onwards when white-collar workers would tend to work for one employer throughout their working life (or 'career'). However, the restructurings, downsizings and delayerings (or flattening of management hierarchies) of the 1990s challenged the assumptions underpinning the 'old deal' and the notion of a 'job for life' became anachronistic.

I argue that this psychological contract type, at the heart of the white-collar employment relationship, was deliberately dismantled by employers, since it was considered a costly obstacle to labour flexibility.

The 'new deal'

The core elements of this old deal were to be replaced by a less clear-cut 'new deal' (Herriot and Pemberton, 1995a). These authors present a contextual and processual model of the new psychological contract. They describe elements of the modern career as follows:

- In place of promotion and job security, employees should focus on developing their employability and job portability.
- In place of loyalty, employers should focus on enabling high performance and developing high-commitment work practices.

Employers are demanding more flexible hours and ways of working from employees (Herriot et al., 1997; Johns, 2001). People remain employed on the basis of their current value to the organization, as opposed to long service and seniority. However, as Cappelli notes: 'Managers who believe that they can draw up a new employment contract that will deliver high performance based on lowered expectations and heightened individual responsibility for "employability" have some nasty shocks in store' (in Sparrow and Cooper, 2003: 60). There are two popular theses on how this 'new deal' is operationalized. The first, labelled the 'employability thesis' (Rajan, 1997), suggests that since 'enlightened' employers can no longer offer job security they have instead been offering a new deal to employees by providing assistance to enable and encourage employees to develop, mainly as a way to add value to the organization, but also as a backstop should they need to look for other employment. The assumption is that the modern employee will be 'flexible' and self-manage his or her career, making themselves more employable through skills and abilities which they accumulate through training, willingness to learn, performing a variety of tasks, and adapting their portfolio of activities. By so doing, employees become more efficient for the organization and better equipped to handle the pressures of the new marketplace (Herriot and Pemberton, 1995a; Sparrow and Marchington, 1998). Thus, organizations are expected to become 'learning' organizations in which 'empowered' employees take on greater responsibility for their work, training and careers (Hendry and Jenkins, 1997).

30   *Context*

Byrne (2001) argues that the enlightened 'new deal' environment represents a risk to the employer since it will encourage employees to hoard their specialist knowledge to retain their employability value. He argues that the 'new deal' is a contradiction to the 'knowledge company' and that companies should choose one approach or another. However, in practice it is questionable how much the 'learning' organization concept has come to fruition in organizations.

The other main thesis is that the new deal will drive an increase in demand for training which will be less employer driven and more employee driven. As Herriot et al. (1997) have suggested, it is employees who are looking for more training because they perceive the old psychological contract to be broken (i.e. security for loyalty) and have low trust in the rhetoric around 'employability' in place of job security. The new contract has a self-reliance orientation that is significantly removed from the concept of 'devotion' to a specific employer, with the role of the organization open to debate as individuals move with much greater frequency between different employers to attain the rewards that they believe are due to them (Maguire, 2002).

Beard and Edwards (1995) suggest that, as employees adjust to the new climate of job insecurity by taking on board the rhetoric of employability, they may have developed a heightened set of expectations about what they are 'owed' by employers in training and development, and often feel let down by what is actually delivered by their organizations.

Hall and Moss (1998) describe these self-propelled careers as the new 'protean' career contract which is directed by the needs and values of the individual, with success being described as internal (psychological). To pursue a 'boundaryless' career (Arthur and Rousseau, 1996) individuals will experience more frequent changes between jobs and periods of inactivity. This will require constant readjustment, lifelong learning and an entrepreneurial mindset on the part of employees. Given this 'new deal' career definition, is it appropriate for employees to develop a set of expectations concerning mutual obligations between themselves and the organization?

Maguire (2002) examined the extent to which this increased emphasis on self-serving personal and organizational strategies made the concept of psychological contract irrelevant. It was expected that, with increased mobility as a consequence of organizations becoming more competitive, the psychological contract in such an environment would tie the individual more to a profession rather than an organization. Maguire (2002) found that the psychological contract still continued to provide a means of establishing effective relationships between organizations and their employees. Assertions that the workforce was more likely to change employment rather than remain with an employer if there was a perception that a better deal could be struck elsewhere were not empirically supported by Maguire's study. However, this study also suggested that employers would need to adjust the terms of the psychological contract to meet the needs of a potentially increasingly mobile and less predictable workforce (Maguire, 2002).

With a workforce increasingly self-focused, it has been suggested (for example, Rousseau and Fried, 2001; Shore et al., 2004) that the uniqueness and peculiarities of each work context could allow for the negotiation between employer and employee of specific work arrangements. Such agreements have been referred to as idiosyncratic deals (i-deals), and it could be argued that the existence of such understandings may negate the need to change employer (Rousseau, 2005).

Although responsibility for career development lies primarily with individuals, it is argued that the new psychological contract still represents a form of partnership of mutual interests between individuals and organizations, with different requirements of both 'partners' (Herriot and Pemberton, 1995a) consisting of 'an individual commitment to career self-management' and 'organisational support for career self-management' (Lankhuijzen et al., 2006: 94). HR practitioners are key to the organizational partnership since many of these areas are traditionally the focus of HRM policy (Guest, 1997).

Of course, the expectations and practices of the two parties to the new psychological contract may not converge. For instance, the level of self-management with regard to career development is the significant dimension along which expectations about careers may vary (Lankhuijzen et al., 2006). People who do not self-manage their careers are viewed as traditional careerists, and are most likely to suffer through the loss of the old psychological contract. With the removal of the default retirement age and the general reduction in pension values, it is likely that many people will have to work into their mid-sixties and beyond. As employees age, it is possible that their ability to continue to work at the pace required in today's workplace will reduce, leaving them facing the 'specter of uselessness' described by Sennett (2006).

Under-researched areas include the extent to which employees think of their careers according to these concepts; the extent to which organizations are willing to give employees the freedom and support required for career self-management; and the extent to which people in mid-career have adjusted their expectations of career to embrace the flexible career model is also a relatively under-researched area. Other underdeveloped areas of research include the potentially different career expectations of younger employees, stereotypically referred to as Generation Y or Millennials; and, given the likelihood of longer working lives, the implications for careers in a multigenerational workforce.

Herriot and Pemberton (1997) contend that, in addition to the mitigating factors identified by Guest (1997a), the 'new deal' is also mitigated by perceptions of fairness such as workloads, equal opportunities, bullying in the workplace, pay and performance and working conditions. They argue that, from an employee perspective, the 'new deal' is violated mainly in these areas rather than by changes in career practice. For instance, in the current economic and employment climate for the public sector, with pay freezes, public-sector pension issues and redundancies, perhaps the most obvious perceived collective psychological contract violation of all must be the one between the state and its staff. The implicit deal for public-sector employees in the past was that, though paid less than workers in the private sector they would, in return, have more secure jobs and decent pensions. Even if employees do not blame the employer, what will such broken promises do to trust, commitment and the desire to perform well?

We shall look for evidence throughout the book of how psychological contracts were impacted by the changing circumstances people experienced in the early years of the twenty-first century.

In the context of ongoing change and a more diverse and 'boundaryless' employment landscape, the psychological contract is viewed in much of the literature as dynamic and evolving (Hall, 1996; Cappelli, 1999, McInnes et al., 2009). New kinds of employment contracts are emerging, in particular 'organization-centred' contracts that tend to be imposed and short-term, giving the organization greater control. The flexible firm theory, shortened planning horizons and internationalization of market forces have led to management practices that stress labour force flexibility and reinforce market forces within the firm. There is a growing literature (Korten, 1999) which suggests that corporations themselves are the biggest cause of such turbulence, so much so that the main threat in the environment comes from other organizations. In contrast, Cappelli (1999: 243) argues that, in a fast-moving context, any single organization's discretion is extremely limited and, in their quest for flexibility, employers will offer mainly short-term and unstable jobs.

32   *Context*

Moreover, McInnes et al.'s research (2009) suggests that, whereas organization-centred contracts were previously restricted to contract workers, they are now applied to employees in general. Herriot and Pemberton (1997) argue that the new employment relationships are no longer relational but strictly transactional, in which contributions and benefits are actively negotiated, with the risk in the employment relationship resting with the individual. Employees with transactional contracts tend to show less normative and affective commitment. Guest's research suggests that employees working for large organizations are likely to experience a poorer psychological contract than those working in small and medium-size organizations.

New capitalism as 'discourse driven'

Fairclough (2003) argues that the common idea of new capitalism as a 'knowledge-based' or 'knowledge-driven' socio-economic order implies that it is also 'discourse driven', suggesting that language may play a more significant role in contemporary socio-economic changes than it has in the past. If so, discourse analysis has an important contribution to make to research on the transformations of capitalism.

Discourse can be seen as a set of 'rules' that shape the way people construct their world (Watson, 2002; Fairclough, 2001). Foucault used the concept of discourse as a 'framework and logic of reasoning that, through its penetration of social practice, systematically forms its objects' (Alvesson and Sköldberg, 2000: 250) and 'in the practice of doing so conceal their own invention' (Foucault, 1977: 49). That is because, although discourses are concerned with language, they extend beyond it to shape consciousness and action. Discourses work in three ways: they enable, they constrain and they constitute (Storey, 2001: 129).

Foucault (1977) traced the role of discourses in wider social processes of legitimating and power, emphasizing the construction of current truths, how they are maintained and what power relations they carry with them. Coining the phrase 'power-knowledge', Foucault (1980) stated that different forms of knowledge are in the service of power and they function in a disciplinary way, amongst other things by establishing normality and deviation. Discourse is related to power, according to Foucault (1977, 1980, 2004), since it operates by rules of exclusion. Discourses not only order the possibilities for thought and speech, but also who is authorized to do so. Power produces reality: through discourses it produces the truths we live by, as well as constrains the truth.

Foucault's concepts of 'regimes of truth' and 'technologies of power' provide useful additions to neo-Marxian understandings of power and knowledge and may also be considered as complementary to social constructionist analyses of knowledge. Discourse therefore is controlled by objects, what can be spoken of; ritual, where and how one may speak; and the privileged, who may speak (2004: 29). If ideas are believed, they establish and legitimate particular 'regimes of truth'. Modern societies create regimes of truth that are enforced by power structures or the truth-generating apparatuses of society (schools, disciplines, professions, laws).

Established conceptions in science and other societal institutions thus contribute to regulating the self-consciousness and the actions of individuals. Indeed, governmentality is contingent upon the structuring of knowledge for the purposes of regulating, supervising and governing specific groups of individuals: knowledge is necessary to the operation of disciplinary power. This is exercised by governments at state level by establishing specific ends, means to these ends, and particular practices that should lead to these ends (Foucault, 1997 [1978]). Of course, attempting to control outcomes in such ways may have unintended consequences. In the state sector, relentless targeting may well have made public services, such as teaching, narrower and more instrumental (Marquand, 2008b).

Neo-liberalism characteristically develops indirect techniques for leading and controlling individuals without being responsible for them. Within organizations, governmentality is achieved through 'technologies of power' – the technologies of the market, and of self, through which individuals transform themselves in order to attain a certain state. For instance, one technology of self – responsibilization – entails subjects transforming social risks such as unemployment into a problem of 'self-care' (Lemke, 2001: 201), all of which, critical scholars would argue, are manifest in HRM.

Conclusion

Following its publication, Braverman's book was criticized by many academics for its broad-ranging theoretical sweep. However, Braverman's orthodox (i.e. Marxist) labour process analysis has been criticized for its neglect of agency, subjectivity and resistance which are central to the structuralist and economistic features of Marx (e.g. Burawoy, 1979; Knights, 1990, 1997; Knights and Willmott, 1989; O' Doherty, 1993; Willmott, 1994, 1997; Thompson, 2009). For the critics of this orthodoxy, the marginalization of worker subjectivity is problematical because, not infrequently, 'employees' feelings of identification with...the enterprise' are supportive and stabilizing of a 'modus vivendi' between managers and workers (Littler and Salaman, 1982: 260).

Some critics wanted to take a more nuanced view, finding Braverman too deterministic, and argued for a greater recognition of agency and organizational context. Smith (2011) points out that labour process analysis carries through inequality from market relations into capital–labour relations in the workplace and suggests that the dynamic of this unequal social relationship both limit, condition and drive the structuring of work. However, Smith also points out that, in some countries, labour process analysis lost its way when it became imbued with discourse analysis, which according to Smith (2011: 3) produced: 'highly abstract and rarefied commentaries far removed from Braverman's desire to link the practical experience of those working for capitalism with a grounded political theory of the dynamics of the system'.

The general form of Marxian critique today is that core labour process theory is alienated from its Marxian roots and that it is managerialist, meaning that it treats managers as having too much discretion, independent of any systemic profit or surplus–value extraction imperatives, to determine the nature of work (Tinker, 2002; Hassard and Rowlinson, 2001). This critique is rooted in a belief that core labour process theory is fundamentally flawed because it derives from Braverman's (1974) analytical concepts which were applicable to understanding monopoly capitalism, though are perhaps not helpful in understanding contemporary global-competitive capitalism. Smith also points out that Braverman's book undervalued the way the labour process is embedded within socio-cultural contexts which lay out different ways of putting together the employment relationship. Therefore, Braverman's message about work degradation fits some societies better than others.

Nevertheless, Braverman's criticism of the labour process of monopoly capitalism has had a lasting impact on the sociology of work and labour relations. His labour process theory has come to sit within CMS. Critical management theorists such as Alvesson, Willmott and O'Doherty have continued the debate. Post-modernist writers O'Doherty and Willmott

34   *Context*

(2001) develop a third, 'hybrid position', one that is informed by post-structuralist insights but does not neglect or reject established traditions of 'modern' sociology and labour process research. This may offer a means of understanding how people are rendered subjects and become complicit in the accomplishment and reproduction of capitalist employment relations and is the approach I embrace in this book.

3   A neo-liberal landscape

> Any discourse about people management lacks context without consideration of the changing
> nature of the organisational environment, employment models and the employment relationship.
> (Wong et al., 2009b)

Introduction

CMS assumes that the practice of management can only be understood in the context of the wider socio-economic, political and cultural factors which shape – if not determine – those practices (Wong et al., 2009a, 2009b). Therefore, in this chapter, we shall take a historical perspective on how the neo-liberal agenda underpinning Anglo-American forms of global capitalism since the 1980s has led to the installation of a 'new work culture' of capitalism. By stepping back, we can consider how organizational practices that today have become the norm, were the result of a gradual implanting of a modus operandi which placed achieving competitive advantage within a free market to the benefit of shareholders as the highest value.

Since Braverman's time, capitalism has undergone a transformation which has, if anything, accelerated the process of the degradation of work he described. The widespread adoption of neo-liberal economic policies has provided the rationale, or legitimization, for the unbridled pursuit of market freedoms by corporations since the 1980s until the financial crisis began in 2008. Allied to this, we shall also consider the emergence in the UK during the 1980s of a political agenda reflecting the belief in effective management as a route to economic regeneration.

Definitions of organizational effectiveness changed over this period to reflect the dominant neo-liberal ideology and the pursuit of shareholder value. Within UK organizations of every sector, a corresponding cultural shift was presided over, with an emphasis upon the enterprise economy, self-improvement and competitive individualism. The practices of this 'new work culture' have long been accepted as inevitable and therefore seemingly unchallengeable. 'Management', and human resource management in particular, constitute an important area of practice where a number of these issues become manifest.

We shall look at:

- The impact of neo-liberal forms of globalization on the white-collar employment relationship and on the commodification of white-collar work.
- The role of technology in transforming work.
- Changing definitions of organizational effectiveness.

36 *Context*

Monopoly capitalism

Work has the potential to play a constructive role in our lives and to contribute to the creation of a healthy society. Marx considered work a positive thing since it should be integral to our wellbeing, our growth and our sense of purpose. Today however, the trends relating to work are not all pointing in this direction.

Marx considered capitalism a progressive development, since, in overthrowing feudalism, it prepares the way for the revolution that will bring about communism. Marx was writing during the emergence of industrial capitalism. He observed the damaging effects of industrial intensification on workers and identified the essentially different interests of employees and employers. Unlike the classical economists, Marx recognized that such an economy was inherently unstable and impermanent and was essentially a battle of competition fought by cheapening commodities.

Among Marxian economists 'monopoly capitalism' is the term widely used to denote the stage of capitalism which dates from approximately the last quarter of the nineteenth century and reached full maturity in the period after the Second World War. The early post-war decades were a period of rapid capitalist expansion during which the US established its global hegemony.

It was then that the concentration and centralization of capital, in the form of the early trusts, cartels and other forms of combinations, began to assert itself; it was then consequently that the modern structure of capitalist industry and finance began to take shape. Marx's theory remains basically unchanged, and even more so the role of what Marx called the credit system, now grown to enormous proportions compared to the small beginnings of his day.

The 1940s and 1950s witnessed the emergence of new trends of thought within the general framework of Marxian economics, though these had their roots in Marx's theory of concentration and centralization. Keynesianism, as it came to be called, was the dominant theoretical framework in economics and economic policy-making in the US and UK in the period between 1945 and 1970. Its strategy was to build a mass market for consumer goods which would sustain demand for industrial production. It was thought that a high rate of economic growth, falls in unemployment and the expansion of welfare provisions would curb working-class disenchantment with capitalism and would incorporate labour into a lasting political consensus.

Corporate capitalism

The particular form of monopoly capitalism that Braverman wrote about was corporate capitalism (i.e. a marketplace characterized by the dominance of hierarchical, bureaucratic corporations, which are legally required to pursue profit). This dominated the latter part of the twentieth century. This transition of capitalism from its competitive to its monopoly phase was accompanied by an equally important transition in the labour process. Braverman contended that capitalist ideology becomes a material force in the machines and procedures of work and that so-called progress in advanced technological societies has been achieved through the ongoing commodification and intensification of work and worker alienation within the 'free' labour force.

Braverman extended Marx's writings on the impact of capitalist industrial growth on the labour process, paying specific attention to the growth of giant corporations and oligopolistic industries. For Braverman, monopoly capitalism:

> embraces the increase of monopolistic organizations within each capitalist country, the internationalization of capital, the international division of labor, imperialism, the world market and the world movement of capital, and changes in the structure of state power.
>
> (Braverman, 1974: 252)

The process of expansion of capital by large corporations extending their operations beyond their country of origin was largely achieved with the active and positive support of their governments. Corporations have limited liability and remain less regulated and accountable than sole proprietorships. Many of these large multinational corporations have become powerful enough to develop their own strategies of expansion beyond the control of individual government policies.

A turbulent period

Braverman's book brings to the foreground some of the moral dangers that can befall a capitalist society, especially in the area of employee management and job satisfaction. The dominant culture of pre-sixties America was that of 'science, protestantism and capitalism'. It was characterized by 'modernism'; a belief in science and technology; trust in 'objective truth' and 'objective reality' which people were confident would lead to a better world; individual freedom and care for the planet.

During this time, there was a growing protest culture towards the monolithic modernist US culture. The counter-culture was concerned that the values, attitudes and methods of science were so thoroughly integrated into modern industrial society that they threatened to destroy all humanistic values and would lead inevitably, according to Marcuse (1964), to the domination of man by man. As Braverman himself states, the 'radicalism of the 1960s' was 'animated' by the discontent with capitalism in its success (1974: 14). Braverman argues that the disquiet of workers in the 1960s lends credence to Marx's view that the greater accumulation of capital and wealth by the few is directly proportionate to the increase of misery and unemployment for the many (p. 389).

Braverman's book was published following a decade of what he refers to as 'a period of dissatisfaction with work' (1974: 31). By the late 1960s, Britain's and America's old model of mass industrial production and capital accumulation was beginning to fail. This was a period of chronic industrial unrest in the US and UK. Growing pressure from organized labour for increased wages was undermining profitability. Auto industry manufacturing moved out of the UK. The 1970s was an era of political change and the price of oil became a major driver of industry, as OPEC (Organization of the Petroleum Exporting Countries) recognized the value of the black gold its countries abounded in. The oil price crisis created great discontinuity. There was collapse in the rate of profit and a systemic crisis.

A neo-Keynesian view of price and wage flexibility was adopted, especially strongly by American economists. In effect, this stated that economic rigidities were responsible for unemployment and that these rigidities included such factors as trade unions and minimum wage laws. In a sense, the American neo-Keynesian position was implicitly a forerunner of today's neo-liberal labour market flexibility agenda.

Neo-liberalism

Palley (2004) argues that out of this crisis a 'great reversal' took place by the 1980s. The economic theories of John Maynard Keynes and his followers, and the Keynesian fixed rate system, were abandoned. These were replaced by the more 'monetarist' approach of money-supply targeting inspired by the neo-liberal theories and research of the Chicago School, notably Milton Friedman (1962) and Friedman and Schwartz (1963). While nineteenth-century economic liberalism was predicated upon laissez-faire economics and closely associated with free trade, neo-liberalism advocates that individual freedoms should be actively increased through the deregulation of markets, enabling competitive capitalism to be free from interference from the state and thus maximize the production of wealth, so that, in principle, everyone gains.

A period of capitalist expansion began (Gamble, 2009: 69). The development of this post-industrial form of capitalism was assisted by the development of new information and communication technologies which were beginning to transform traditional manufacturing and distribution systems. Much traditional manufacturing capability migrated away from the developed countries to parts of the developing world. However, this resulted in massive layoffs in industrialized countries that pushed unemployment rates to their highest levels since the Great Depression, a sharp rise in global real interest rates and significant financial market volatility.

The US sought to maintain its dominance by crafting a different kind of order which was less unpredictable and which depended on the expansion of the financial markets as a leading sector (Hutton and Giddens, 2001). In the UK too during the Thatcher years there was a vigorous political commitment to new forms of market, in particular, the growth of the financial services industry. This new and invigorated global capitalism was subsequently advanced as a political project by the 'New Right.'

Capitalist expansion

The adoption of neo-liberalism on both sides of the Atlantic gave spur to markets and reduced governments. Since then, 'neo-liberalism', i.e. monetarism and related theories, has dominated macro-economic policy-making, as indicated by the tendency towards less severe state regulations on the economy, and greater emphasis on stability in economic policy rather than 'Keynesian' goals such as full employment and the alleviation of abject poverty. Power and wealth are, to an ever increasing degree, concentrated within transnational corporations and elite groups (Saad Filho and Johnston, 2005).

Neo-liberalism gives priority to capital, so capitalism came to be treated as a global system of accumulation. The discrediting of the Keynesian and social democratic regimes allowed the new philosophy of deregulation and arm's-length regulation to flourish. The priorities of finance came to predominate in the shaping of economic policy and industry was expected to adjust to the rules that this establishes. The utilization of knowledge and culture as economic resources created new types of post-Fordist firms, products and markets. The West became predominantly a service economy, with the UK in particular seeing the development of high technology, financial services and travel and tourism as major growth areas.

Late capitalist or post-industrialist ideology points to the advantages of capitalism, free enterprise and self-organizing markets. However, Palley (2004) argues that the neo-liberal ideology is also used to oppose all forms of state control and to celebrate private ownership. Similarly, neo-liberalism proposes that labour markets should be made as flexible as possible in order to create the best conditions for markets to flourish. It is the market that 'determines', 'legitimizes' and 'rationalizes' layoffs, downsizing, mergers, acquisitions, plant relocations and temporary employment (Alvesson and Willmott, 1986: 158–9). The market is meant to ensure that people – the factors of production – are paid what they are worth, obviating the need for institutions of social protection and trade unions. Indeed, Krzywdzinski (2014) notes that investors tend to avoid firms with strong unions or labour regulation. Moreover, neo-liberal theorists argue that when institutions of social protection interfere with the market process, they can lower social wellbeing and cause unemployment.

Despite its dominance, neo-liberalism has been applied inconsistently and opportunistically to macro-economic policy and has sometimes departed from its theoretical rhetoric.

In practice, the result has been widening wage and income inequality. 'For neoliberals, this is because the market is now paying people what they are worth; for post-Keynesians, it is because the balance of power in labor markets has tilted in favor of business' (Palley, 2004).

Organizational effectiveness and shareholder value

Early economic theory viewed each business as a type of machine with various inputs and profits being the output. The neo-liberal view was that the ultimate purpose of business is always to maximize profits for investors. This originated with the Industrial Revolution's earliest economists such as Adam Smith and is an idea that has remained with us ever since. Indeed, shareholder theory defines the primary purpose of a firm as value maximization (for shareholders).

Profits are one of the most important goals of any successful business and investors are one of the most important constituencies of the business. The success of business therefore is primarily measured in terms of financial outcomes only, often at the expense of other important outcomes. Mackey (2006) argues that Industrial Age entrepreneurs thought they had discovered a 'perpetual motion machine' – enterprises organized to maximize profits, and through the reinvestment of these profits, the promise of indefinite continued growth so that everyone benefits. Early large investors and entrepreneurs often took substantial risks by investing large sums of their own money in firms and therefore expected to reap substantial rewards.

With respect to organizational effectiveness theories, under neo-liberalism, shareholder value came to be seen as preferable to the earlier stakeholder theories that had been prevalent in the 1950s and 1960s since success can be measured more simply. Stakeholder theory on the other hand can only be defined more broadly, the interests of stakeholders (such as shareholders, employees, customers, suppliers, creditors, local community, state and others) may differ and cannot be expressed using a unique measure. As Jensen (2001) argued: 'it is logically impossible to maximize in more than one dimension; purposeful behaviour requires a single, valued objective function'. Indeed, Jensen claimed (p. 302) that social welfare is maximized when all firms in an economy maximize total firm value. Sadly, various notorious examples of major global firms maximizing profits in the UK in 2016 while using tax loopholes to pay only a tiny percentage of the corporation taxes due, or avoid paying them altogether, suggest that firm success does not automatically lead to social welfare.

Moreover, the world has become much more complex since those simple Industrial Age machine metaphors were first developed. Today's investment community has become large and diverse, with relatively few individual investors taking substantial risks with their own money. Rather, they expect managements to pursue strategies which will increase their dividend payments, such as restructurings, sell-offs and headcount reductions. Carried to excess, such strategies are thought to reduce shareholder value in the long term since they result in loss of intellectual capital and goodwill – of employees and customers. Thus while stakeholders such as employees and customers may not benefit from such actions, even investors may not benefit from strategies which appear to treat them as the sole beneficiary of a firm's efforts in the long term. We shall return to shareholder and stakeholder capitalism in more detail in later chapters.

Globalization

With the restructuring of capitalism in the 1970s and 1980s, there was a resulting intensification of the processes of globalization which accelerated in the 1990s following the fall of the Soviet

40   *Context*

Union (Gray, 1999). With the collapse of the Soviet Union and the widespread adoption of neo-liberal economic policies within the newly independent former Eastern Bloc countries, US-style capitalism was ascendant and neo-liberalism unchallenged by the end of the 1990s.

Globalization is often referred to as the triumph of capitalism on a world scale over national and local identity. Within industrialized countries, the economic agenda has been dominated by policies associated with the 'US model'. According to Amin (1997), globalization is 'not to be stopped if you side with neo-liberalism or to be resisted through trans-national anti-capitalist or social democratic forces if you take an opposite view'.

Globalization is understood as both a set of processes which it is often claimed are gradually creating an integrated global economy, and also as a particular ideological discourse about those processes (Michie, 2003). Separate from this is the discourse promoted by some business schools about hyper-globalization, intertwined with neo-liberalism, which has 'gripped the imagination of many in the political class across the world' (Gamble, 2009: 68) and is about the end of the nation state, the creation of a borderless world in which connections (especially economic ones) between different kinds of societies were multiplying.

Globalization is leading to major changes in the way businesses compete and organizations operate. As discussed, changes in the structure of the global economy have seen a shift from traditional manufacturing to services (Romero and Molina, 2011), where the economic base has seen a transformation of working practices due to shifts in dominance of the working population from blue-collar to white-collar. As a result, the employment relationship between employers and employees is being rewritten.

Box 3.1 Labour as a commodity

Braverman's position is that capitalists treat labour as they do other raw product resources. A monopoly capitalist sees labour as a human resource that can expand his ownership of more and more capital, and therefore as a cost to be controlled (1974: 149). Braverman classifies a large portion of the labour force as proletariat and when he refers to 'old working class' he describes general labourers. Under capitalism, labour itself becomes a commodity to be sold; in fact, labour power is the only commodity that the worker has to exchange for necessary goods and services. In order to expand his capital, the capitalist invests in the purchase of labour for wages, then attempts to get more value out of this labour than he has invested in it. The more surplus the capitalist can expropriate from the workforce, the greater the profitability and accumulation of capital.

The decline of collective employee voice

Until the 1970s, British industrial relations were characterized by a collectivist culture. British industrial relations since the 1980s have been based on bounded Europeanization since, as Maas (2004) points out, the internationalization of markets and capital means that national industrial relations regimes are no longer able to deliver what they once did for trade unions and this forces them to look further afield for solutions: 'Unions may be pushed or forced to seek co-operation across national borders because they no longer find allies, protection or rewards in national arenas' (Visser, 1998: 231, in Maas, 2004: 3). Globalization therefore has a multidimensional impact on employment relations (Lansbury et al., 2003). Distinct changes in the relative power of capital and labour and work regulations within and outside countries and regions have brought new interactions between different stakeholders.

However, the greatest transformation in the climate of industrial relations in Britain took place after Margaret Thatcher came to power in 1979. Thatcher wanted to cure the 'British disease' of industrial unrest by weakening the unions and a conscious political attempt was made to restructure employment to support the market freedoms demanded by employers.

Thatcherism began with a policy of non-intervention in the markets, allowing areas of industry to decline, finding their natural levels. State-owned organizations were sold off or closed down and subsidies were withdrawn from highly unionized industries such as the automotive manufacturing industry. The recession of the early 1980s saw manufacturing, the main area of union strength, shrink by half, while unemployment soared to over 3 million. In effect this was a policy of deindustrialization and, to obtain non-intervention, the power of the unions was reduced; they would have fought to prevent industries going into decline (Wheen, 2004). Following the ending of the miners' strike in 1984, the unions went into steep decline. They lost their power, influence and a large swathe of their rights. Union membership plummeted from a peak of 12 million in the late 1970s to almost half that by the late 1980s. Margaret Thatcher's economic policies emphasized deregulation, particularly of the financial sector (which was largely not-unionized) and flexible labour markets.

UK governments since the 1980s until the present day have consistently promoted the interests of business over those of workers, making the unitarist argument that the economic growth that business can generate when freed from control is in the interests of workers (Marquand, 2008b). Indeed, governments have actively sought to deregulate and release business from obligations and responsibilities to workers. For instance, the New Labour governments resisted, 'opted out', or caused to be significantly modified the Working Time Directive. British employment law on equal opportunities had to be imposed by EU directives. The implementation of the Information and Consultation Directive, again a European policy initiative, operates inconsistently in the UK and appears to be an accommodation between European models and British voluntarism.

In contrast to UK and US forms of capitalism, 'social Europe' has long favoured stakeholder capitalism, where shareholder needs are only one set under consideration (Hyman, 2003; Kelly et al., 1997). Stakeholder capitalism encompasses collective regulation, decommodification and solidarity, and 'social partnership' is institutionalized in many European countries. An embedded workplace voice is not left to the choice of employers but mandated. This institutionalized relationship creates forms of dialogue and constrains parties to negotiate with each other to find solutions. However, the European social model is imprecise and systems vary radically across countries. The impact of European enlargement means that there is increasing fragmentation of bargaining, with a range of systems being brought into Europe which are more similar to the UK voluntarist models than to European kinds.

The emergence of HRM

The emergence of HRM in the UK was aided by the undermining of trade union power and the deliberate transformation of industrial relations by the political establishment following unions' political confrontations with the Thatcher government. HRM formed part of the Thatcherite political project to replace the largely adversarial collective relationships with a new industrial relations based on human resource management practices geared to winning employees' 'hearts and minds' to a shared task (i.e. the managerial agenda). Managers' 'right to manage' was asserted and managerialism was gradually installed across all sectors of the UK economy from the 1980s onwards.

Within UK organizations, collective employee relations involving unions have been largely replaced by individualized HR practices (Beardwell et al., 2004). This individualism has been mirrored by the reduction in collective bargaining. Without collective

42   *Context*

protections, an individual can only show dissatisfaction with the organization by leaving their employment. This does not wield any power; only if there was a mass exit of employees would the organization investigate the cause (Farnham, 2002). Trade union researchers speak of this in terms of 'the transformation of industrial relations' (Kochan et al., 1986), of 'new industrial relations' (Kelly and Kelly, 1991) and of the 'new workplace' (Ackers et al., 1996). The aim of mainstream HRM is to foster a more positive and less adversarial organizational culture, within which greater performance (and lower labour costs) can be achieved from employees (Keenoy, 2009).

Despite the inherently contested nature of HR discourse, it has been evident for some time in mainstream HRM writing, increasingly consensus in orientation (Keegan and Boselie, 2006), that HR work is largely framed as a business issue and the hegemonic project of commerce is now widely naturalized within mainstream HRM theory (Boltanski and Chiapello, 2006). This acceptance of HR's business-facing priorities is manifest in the development of HR business partnership as part of the academic discourse (Paauwe, 2007; Kenton and Yarnell, 2005; Reilly and Williams, 2006, Lepak et al., 2005; Guetal and Stone, 2005).

As Keenoy and Reed (2007) argue, there appears to be little challenge to what they call 'HRMism' with its focus on strategic 'fit' and its concern with identifying 'mechanisms to facilitate "high commitment" and "high performance" organizations'. Watson too points out that 'the field of HRM has become almost co-terminus with the new managerialism of the putative globalised economy' (2007a). Indeed, HRM has emerged as the global discourse and a recognized semiotic for 'modern people management' (Paauwe, 2007: 9). So HRM becomes a tool of management (within capitalism) as a means of controlling the labour process.

The gradual consolidation of HRM (in organizations), into the general repertoire of managerialism is the outcome of a complex and paradoxical cultural process. On the one hand, HRM appears to have become less coherent, less centred, more dispersed and insubstantial when compared with other technical specialities of management such as strategy or marketing. In spite of this appearance, though, HRM has become a very strong cultural programme capable of extending its range to emerge as one of the most significant grounds of managerialism itself (Costea et al., 2007). Delbridge and Keenoy (2010) point out that, since mainstream HRM became the dominant discourse relating to management practice from the mid-1980s on, what Keenoy (1997) terms 'HRMism' has enjoyed 'unparalleled success'.

Managerialism

Management is a key feature of organizations in a neo-liberal economy.

Box 3.2 Controlling labour

According to Marx and Braverman, labour and capital are opposite poles of capitalist society; antagonism is therefore integral to their relationship (Braverman, 1974: 377). Braverman argued that, while early capitalism used outright force and coercion to attain maximum advantage over labour, with a 'free' labour force, management must now exercise more subtle methods of control.

At the core of the labour process of extracting surplus value on behalf of capitalists would be so-called 'unproductive' labour. This is found in those occupations that do not directly engage in production, such as accounting, finance, human resources, marketing, surveillance. People with senior salaries 'rest upon the backs' of productive labour (pp. 206–7). This is why we have a field of study and management specialists in human resources

---

> training, development and management. However, rather than these fields aiming at improving labour's job-quality situation, Braverman argues that they simply reflect management efforts 'to reduce costs and improve profits' (pp. 37–8).

As well as breaking union power in the UK, Thatcher also sought to produce a more proactive and professional cadre of management. Charles Handy's 1987 report entitled *The Making of Managers*, often referred to as the Handy Report, assumed a link between national economic performance and a deficit of good managers. The report recommended that Britain should develop her managers more systematically through business school education. Management was increasingly professionalized and placed at the vanguard of social and economic restructuring throughout the 1980s and 1990s (Pollitt, 1993; Marquand, 2004). With the decline of collective UK industrial relations and the subsequent rise of the 'New Right', efficient management came to be seen as a panacea for a number of economic ills. Since that time, supportive governments have encouraged confidence in the right and power of managers to manage.

Margaret Thatcher also sought to reduce the power of intermediate institutions (Marquand, 2008a) which might represent sources of potential critique of government policies. She 'virulently attacked the progressive social influences of the civic counter-cultures of the 1960s while at the same time marketising them in consumer culture and in the social relations of new industries' (Rutherford, 2008). For instance, the cultural power of the BBC as the public service broadcaster was challenged and undermined, leaving the BBC damaged and seemingly delegitimized. The civil service, the educational establishment and universities in particular, as potential centres of intellectual challenge, were effectively neutralized by a modernization agenda which included the development of business schools. Government and university-funding bodies became directive in overtly managing academics and academic work.

In its application to the private sector, the term 'managerialism' is usually associated with a critique of maximization for a single interest group, i.e. passive shareholders. However, managerialism is more generally held to refer to the adoption by public-sector organizations of the organizational forms, technologies, management practices, ideologies and values more commonly found in the private business sector (Deem, 1998; Pollitt, 1993; Cutler and Waine, 1994).

New public management

During the 1980s a series of reports commissioned by the Thatcher government resulted in the public sector becoming progressively managerialized, with power over decision-making gradually wrested away from professionals. By the 1990s, references to managerialism in the literature had become associated with the introduction of 'new public management', described as follows: 'A new paradigm for public management has emerged, aimed at fostering a performance-oriented culture in a less centralised public sector' (Organisation for Economic Co-operation and Development, 1995: 8). These reports were all part of a political 'reform' agenda, i.e. a 'top-down' system-wide ideological approach to the organization, finance and culture of public-service management based on external processes and sometimes referred to as 'new managerialism' (Deem, 2004). For instance, the Griffiths Report (1988) launched general management into the National Health Service (NHS), replacing so-called consensus management. This led to a managerial cultural revolution and a period of significant change within the NHS which continues to this day.

For Deem (1998), new managerialism is a 'complex ideology which informs ways of managing public institutions by advocating many of the practices and values of the private-for-profit sector in the pursuit of efficiency, excellence and continuous improvement' (Deem, 1998: 48). It is a 'set

44   *Context*

of beliefs and practices, [that] will prove an effective solvent for…economic and social ills' (Pollitt, 1990: 1). In the case of higher education, considerable emphasis was placed on culture change, shifting away from the idea of higher education as a social institution to higher education as an industry.

A key feature of the political attempts to achieve a 'modernizing' of the public sector according to the precepts of new public management was the replacement of 'administration' by 'management'. This wholesale shift in power towards 'managers' (Parker, 2002), reflects the dominance of organizational interests within the employment relationship. Lord (Norman) Fowler, the then social services secretary who implemented the Griffiths Report's recommendations, remarked in 2009 on the political nature of the subsequent 'reforms' this made possible: 'You could not have done the internal market without general management. It was absolutely crucial that you changed the management structures. Once you did that, you could go on to other things' (Davies, 2009). The managerialist work culture installed was characterized by performativity, work intensification and the commodification of workers (Scott, 1994). Pollitt (1993: 2–3) described its features as follows:

- The use of 'ever more sophisticated technologies'.
- A labor force disciplined to productivity.
- Clear implementation of the professional manager role.
- Aimed at continuous increases in efficiency.

Managerialism's ideological language reflects economic concepts such as 'freedom of choice' (Bauman, 2002), 'best value' and 'the customer'. With the strengthening of the power of management came the rhetoric of accountability. Managements (and government) were able to force these changes through, it is argued, because high levels of unemployment during the 1990s allowed managers to control recruitment, introduce more flexible structures and to further embed managerialism in diverse social spheres beyond the private sector. New public management penetrated public organizations such as schools, social services and healthcare from the beginning of the 1990s (Christensen et al., 2002; Dent, 2004) and could now be said to have been adopted in all sectors of the economy, including charities.

New Labour continued the Thatcherite trajectory with regard to controlling and potentially deskilling the professional classes. As Rutherford (2008: 10) points out, 'New Labour achieved power by appealing to this social democratic sensibility while accommodating itself to the neo-liberal ascendancy. To manage this contradiction, it abandoned traditional class-based politics for its own brand of aspirational individualism.' Fairclough (2003) suggests that the transformation taking place towards 'new capitalism' involved both the 're-structuring' of relations between the economic, political and social domains, including the commodification and marketization of fields like education (which becomes subject to the economic logic of the market), and the 're-scaling' of relations between different scales of social life, i.e. the global, the regional (e.g. the European Union), the national and the local. A key aspect of this is performativity. This serves as a key managerial tool in producing the outcomes described above since it is 'a policy technology, a culture and a mode of regulation that employs judgements, comparisons and displays as a means of control, attrition and change' (Ball, 2003: 216). These policy technologies have the 'capacity to reshape in their own image the organisations they monitor' (Shore and Wright, 1999: 570). Centrally imposed public-sector targets, subsequent measurement regimes and tight control of funding streams, for instance in higher education, challenged the 'trust-us-the-professionals' model.

Whether or not such practices have led to improved services, they have had the function of enabling politicians to be seen to hold public servants to account, and also to be able to publicly castigate institutions or individuals who are perceived to be failing. Individual stellar practitioners are brought in to 'turn around' or close down institutions, such as schools which are perceived to be failing. Perhaps not surprisingly, there is currently a national shortage of qualified people wishing to take on some public-sector leadership roles such as head teachers.

Managerial state?

Clarke and Newman (1997: ix) talk about the 'managerial state' and consider managerialism as a cultural formation and a distinctive set of ideologies and practices which form one of the underpinnings of an emergent political settlement. They further argue that such changes 'have installed managerialism as new regimes of power structured through the domination of decision-making, agenda setting and normative power' (1997: 82). Davis (1997: 305) argues that, in its latest mode, managerialism has 'refashioned the world in its image and captured for itself the modern state'. According to Deetz (1992), the increased influence of management may be interpreted in terms of a 'corporate colonisation of the lifeworld' in that all cultural and institutional forms become progressively subsumed within the logic of capitalism.

Critical management scholars argue that managerialism, with its development of pervasive management controls, aided and abetted by technology, consists of an updated version of an older tradition embodied in the work of Frederick Winslow Taylor (Terry, 1998; Pollitt, 1990). They typically argue that this 'new', or 'neo'-managerialism has been pushed as a form of social domination (Clarke and Newman, 1997) and that managerialism involves an abuse of power, either by government or by the professional manager class (Grey, 1996).

The pursuit of flexibility

In the highly competitive Anglo-American form of capitalism of the 1980s, business leaders increasingly came to see flexibility as necessary to the pursuit of competitive advantage. Flexibility ostensibly allows organizations to react quickly and easily to changes in their environment as well as to develop highly cost-efficient ways of producing and selling goods and services. However, to enable business flexibility, management wanted labour flexibility.

For instance, Atkinson and Meager's (1986) flexible firm strategy explains how Western firms consciously subdivided their workforce into core and non-core (peripheral) groups in order to achieve greater flexibility in hiring and firing, in the numbers of hours worked and in worker remuneration. However, in the large organizations of the 1970s and early 1980s – with their bureaucratic structures based on the division of labour with a central unit of control, vertical integration, command and control management styles, and a large pyramid of managers and supervisors, working in remote command chains decentralized their structures and created independent business units with specific remits and targets – labour flexibility was low. Post-Thatcher, and without powerful trade unions to protest, managements were free to actively reshape the employment relationship to achieve ever greater labour flexibility, increase productivity and reduce labour costs (Gamble, 2009; Reed, 2010; Millward et al., 2000). Flexibility has been used by employers as the rationale for widespread organizational restructurings and for sourcing workers via a flexible labour market rather than maintaining the traditional, rigid and more costly white-collar employment relationship with employees.

This move was encouraged as part of a political, economic and cultural transformation project driven by the policies of the Thatcher and successor governments, since 'inflexible' employment arrangements were considered an obstacle to the pursuit of market freedom. In terms of economic policy, the Keynesian concept of full employment was replaced with the neo-liberal notion of a 'natural rate of unemployment'. This natural rate is unobservable and is supposedly determined by the forces of demand and supply in labor markets (Palley, 2004).

46   *Context*

The pursuit of business and labour flexibility has continued apace since then. A quick look at labour flexibility through the last few decades illustrates the shifts taking place.

The 1990s

Corporate capitalism itself underwent further transformation during the 1990s. Although large firms remained influential, many of those that had survived the turbulence of the 1970s and 1980s were radically restructured to make them leaner and more 'flexible' rather than heavily staffed and tightly integrated. The organizational metaphor used by Charles Handy in his 1994 book *The Empty Raincoat* was that of the doughnut in which the small essential core of the organization contains all the necessary jobs and employees, surrounded by an open and flexible space which is filled by contractors, consultants and, these days, outsourcers.

Structural forms increasingly reflected aspirations to move beyond the 'modernist' era of large bureaucratic production to smaller, leaner 'post-modern' organizations with responsive and delayered management structures. These 'flatter' structures were presented to workers as enabling greater initiative, being freer, more flexible and participative, although the primary reason for delayering, as many employees perceived it, was to achieve cost savings (Holbeche, 1996). There was medium labour flexibility at this time. The 1990s saw considerable restructuring of the UK's public sector, with 'purchaser/provider' splits and many public services outsourced to third parties, often to the lowest-cost bidder. For the first time since the Second World War, job security for white-collar workers started to be destabilized.

Many workplaces became subject to 'new' management ideas, such as 'Japanese' management practices, including the redesign of core processes, total quality management, continuous improvement and horizontal integration (Hasegawa and Hook, 1998; Hammer and Champy, 1993; Peters and Waterman, 1982). Similarly, HRM high-performance work practices, such as teamwork, were promoted. Hudson (1989) argues that the use by organizations of technology and methodologies designed to increase productivity gains in effect resulted in employee deskilling and represents just a reworking of modernist production methods.

2000s

The current period, it is argued, is that of so-called nimble or 'agile' production (Francis, 2001), where organizations pursue ever greater flexibility and global reach. In their quest for agility, organizations attempt to incorporate new ways of working – collaborating across organizational boundaries, for instance – as well as pursuing multiple new and often transient prospects for competitive advantage.

Thanks to a determined approach to use technology to replace expensive 'human resources', the nature of work and the workplace continues to be transformed. Technology facilitates the rise of the virtual world and the opening up of new markets and means of production, organizations are increasingly task-oriented organic structures, rather than being a fixed entity, characterized by a small core centre and alliances with suppliers and customers. Many firms operate 24/7 on a global basis with a highly complex and diverse workforce and set of supplier relationships. The flexible and the informal co-exist with formal, integration mechanisms. The interconnectedness, multiplexity and hybridization of social life at spatial and organizational levels attributed to globalization (Amin, 1997: 129) are directly related to the changing nature of the employment relationship where contradictory dynamics emerge.

Various terms describe the 'post-bureaucratic' organization (Heckscher and Donnellon, 1994) which is designed to be able to adapt quickly and easily to changes in the environment.

These include the 'ambidextrous organization' (O'Reilly and Tushman, 2004) 'knowledge-creating' (Nonaka and Takeuchi, 1995), 'high-performance' or 'high-commitment work' systems (Pfeffer, 1998), and 'boundaryless company' (Devanna and Tichy, 1990). Decisions are supposed to be based on dialogue and consensus rather than authority; the organization is a network open at the boundaries rather than a hierarchy (Heckscher and Donnellon, 1994).

Thus neo-liberalism has been the central tenet of UK and US corporations and has spread more widely as a global movement. Hansmann and Kraakman (2000) and Höpner (2001) focused their research on evaluating the Anglo-American corporate governance model. According to their findings, the Anglo-American shareholder-oriented governance model would soon prevail over other models because of globalization and increased competition on the international capital markets. Indeed, prior to the financial crisis which began in 2008, within Europe there increasingly appeared to be bounded convergence with Anglo-American capitalism, with a general consensus in Brussels towards market liberalism and maximizing shareholder value. Firms with shareholder-oriented corporate governance have access to cheaper capital sources, providing them with a competitive advantage over firms with other corporate governance models (Fiss and Zajac, 2004).

In a similar vein, Hansmann and Kraakman (2000) showed that firms with shareholder-oriented governance enjoy competitive advantages on the market, as their corporate governance is more flexible and allows fast adaption to market changes. As these firms are not burdened with the interests of other stakeholders, they can adapt their management structures, enter the market more aggressively and exit from inefficient investments more rapidly.

'Untamed' capitalism

Various names have been given to this stage of capitalism since it made its appearance: finance capitalism, imperialism, new capitalism, late capitalism and entrepreneurial capitalism, defined as:

> The system of markets energized by a shift from industrial and labor capital to intellectual capital that has been forced by a continuously increasing rate of technology-related businesses by individuals who can, in many cases, act without enormous quantities of financial capital, and who bring their innovation to markets eager to embrace new products and services that, in turn, yield more innovation.
>
> (Schramm, 2006: 2)

'Financialization' or the attempt to reconstruct the finances of every organization and of every individual citizen to allow them to borrow and increase their spending became the driving force of the new growth model that was to produce the 1990s boom.

Marquand (2008a) labels the period of New Labour (1997–2010) as 'phase three' or the renaissance of 'untamed capitalism' characterized by 'the strange mix of ferocious centralism in the polity and hyper-individualism in the culture and economy, that it seems to have brought in its train' (2008a: 363). Under New Labour, the Thatcherite ideology was continued and extended (Monbiot, 2000), resulting in an ongoing and sustained attack on bureaucratic structures in the UK's public sector, bringing about their wholesale transformation or 'modernization' in line with neo-liberal political agendas underpinned by notions of value-for-money, competition and marketization (Esland et al., 1999: 175). New Labour enthusiastically adopted the funding of major public infrastructure projects such as the building of roads, schools and hospitals through private finance initiative arrangements with the

48 *Context*

private sector. Marquand (2008a: 376) notes that, far from rejecting neo-liberalism, Blair sought to: 'root Thatcher's legacy in the nation's soul by softening its hard edges and making it less divisive. The most frequently used word in his speeches was "we".' By the mid-1990s the successful growth of the financial services industry and the burgeoning market for new financial products resulted in rapid global movements of capital. Business and investment analysts and bankers, along with governments, to a large extent now appear to set the mandate within which firms operate. Corporations, especially multinationals, were beginning to wield more power than national governments. By changing their investment patterns, they can put local economies at risk. In Anglo-American forms of globalization, driven by capital, the role of business was conceived as being exclusively about making wealth for shareholders and investors.

In such a context, a longer-term perspective is penalized; organizations become vulnerable to takeover by investors or competitive predators if they appear too cash-rich and/or are considered too organic and long-term in their approach to strategic development. As a consequence, Sennett (2006) argues, many organizations have come to see themselves purely as short-term investment vehicles. Within firms, senior management, as representatives of 'owners', set short-termist agendas which derive from these mandates. These are the agendas which shape the new work culture and to which employees are required to respond.

The knowledge economy

As access to capital became more equal across the developed world, intellectual capital has supplanted financial capital in competitive importance. Much of the business and policy literature focuses on knowledge, innovation and creative enterprise and a new alignment of institutional forces which have coalesced to allow a resurgence of entrepreneurial activity. The flexibility that businesses have sought may now work against them if they are unable to attract and retain the 'talent' their business needs.

Schramm (2006) argues that, in the emergent system, the predictability and order of bureaucratic capitalism is being replaced by the unpredictable. As Binnie (2005) points out, new sources of competition are creating an ever more cut-throat backdrop to organizations and their supply chains: 'There is a feeling that short-term cost advantages take priority over long-term relationships. Whoever in the world can pop up now on the Internet and offer to supply at the lowest cost, will get the business – and the long-term welfare or development of the supplier is of no importance.'

The new entrants, the entrepreneurial firms, are 'aggressively non-bureaucratic' (Binnie, 2005: 10) and the idea of starting and scaling firms without the need for capital has significant implications for capital markets. In an increasingly knowledge-driven economy the value of labour, as 'human capital' producing intellectual capital, has provided the rationale for major investment in higher skills in Organisation for Economic Co-operation and Development (OECD) countries.

A high-skill economy?

The first major element in any model of high performance working is the competence of the workforce. Writers in the 1990s, including the political economist Robert Reich (1991) and management writer Peter Drucker (1993), argued that prosperity was based on a global competition for ideas, knowledge and skills. It was assumed at the time that the technological superiority of Western countries would limit this competition to OECD economies. UK government policies at the time echoed this thinking. New Labour's adoption of the politics of individualization is reflected in the 1998 competitiveness white paper, *Our Competitive Future: Building the Knowledge-Driven Economy*, which set out a policy framework in which the market and its values were central. UK government economic and education policies since the late 1990s have been based on the assumption that Britain will successfully compete in the global marketplace on the basis of a high-skill/high-pay economy.

However, as Brown et al. (2010b) point out, technology and the educational policies of developing economies such as India are enabling them to compete globally on the basis of high skills/low cost. Consequently, UK white-collar workers are likely to find themselves competing in a high-skills/low-pay labour market and are left seriously exposed to the full force of the 'global auction' for talent, as Brown et al. (2010b: 141) note:

> People may…be doing everything that is expected of them in terms of acquiring marketable skills, investing in further learning, or going that extra mile to meet unrealistic sales targets, but it may not deliver the expected returns in terms of jobs, salary, or career progression.

As a result, there is growing inequality on a grand scale. French economist Thomas Piketty (2014) argues that, because returns on capital exceed wage growth in the long run, business owners will continue to benefit at the expense of workers. Saad-Filho and Johnston (2005: 1) share the quite common view that power and wealth are, to an ever-increasing degree, concentrated within transnational corporations and elite groups. Robert Reich (1991) argued that in a global economy, there would be increasing polarization of opportunity, with wealth following the elite 'symbolic analysts' who become key to economic wellbeing in the information age. As noted previously, the skills premium and persistent global technological divide are predicted by the IMF to compound inequality by making the skilled members of Generation Z richer, and the less skilled poorer. However, contemporary demographic trends may redress the imbalance since skilled labour is becoming a scarce resource. The global workforce gained around 70 million workers in 2005. By 2039, that figure is forecast to fall to 30 million a year.

In contrast, there are growing concerns that the next raft of knowledge work will be automated. Who will be impacted and will new jobs replace the ones being eliminated? Can today's workers be retrained for this emerging world of work?

Technology as a management tool

By applying Taylorist methods, Braverman argued, managements could organize, measure and control white-collar work. As a result, work could be degraded and workers commodified. With less labour bargaining power, employees would have less employment security and lower wages. Similarly, Graeber (2015) argues that since the 1970s there has been a shift from technologies based on realizing alternative futures to investment technologies that favour labour discipline and social control. He suggests that the internet is one such mechanism, but that 'The control is so ubiquitous that we don't see it'.

By the 1990s the general evolution of office work was as a result of the far-reaching organizational changes taking place in the banking industry linked to the introduction of new generations of information and communication technologies (Bain et al., 2002). Thanks to call centre technology, 'back-office' operations could be centralized and a new form of 'front-line' facility developed in the form of 24/7, customer service call centres. Routine office and

50   *Context*

production work is often outsourced to third-party suppliers in locations where requisite technical and English language skills are available, where labour costs are relatively low compared with the UK and where service is available on a 24/7 basis.

Sennett (2006) argues that new information technologies appear to cut through traditional hierarchies and communication channels. Automation, along with the casualization of labour, has exacerbated the relative flattening of hierarchies by eliminating much of many firms' blue-collar base and white-collar middle strata. But at the same time as they undermine older forms of bureaucratic command, such technologies also support a new kind of centralization, giving upper management a kind of panoptic control over the far reaches of the firm. Bain et al. (2002: 173) argue that the call centre labour process represents new developments in the Taylorization of white-collar work. As a result, 'Companies developed the capability to not only distribute work and measure output, but also had the means to assess – and intervene in – the quality of an employee's performance in "real time"'.

Today, the kinds of data analytics that are applied to customer interactions can be applied to the workforce, enabling a combination of target setting and monitoring in 'real time' which makes management control of the labour process more complete.

Commoditization and 'digital Taylorism'

Braverman predicted that high-skill work would eventually be proletarianized and that technology would be a means whereby capital could apply Taylorism, which involves the separation of conception from execution, to the work of professionals, in order to be able to more efficiently control and coordinate the labour force to maximize profit. Since manufacturing has been declining in the West for so long now that there is little left to offshore, highly skilled white-collar work becomes the next and most obvious target.

Commoditization is the process by which goods that have economic value, and are distinguishable in terms of attributes (uniqueness or brand), end up becoming simple commodities in the eyes of the market or consumers (Rushkoff, 2005). With respect to high-skill work, the trend is towards greater experimentation with 'high-end' work in low-cost locations. Brown et al. (2010b) refer to Blinder's (2007: 16) analysis of the potential impact of offshoring on the jobs of American workers which shows that higher-skilled workers are just as likely to see their jobs offshored as low-skilled workers.

International service centres now offer a wide range of professional or functional services in a diverse range of fields. In publishing, for instance, previously 'core' knowledge-based activities such as editing are increasingly outsourced to vertically integrated production units which can be based in any geographic location and are staffed by multilingual, professionally qualified graduates working for lower wages than their counterparts elsewhere. Consequently, within a couple of decades, the publishing world has become one of the least secure employment prospects for workers in the West.

Moreover, in the current era of knowledge capitalism, commoditization of high-skill work is being achieved through 'digital Taylorism' (Brown et al., 2010b). Digital Taylorism is the technology-assisted process of knowledge-capture whereby companies attempt to increase surplus by reducing the cost of knowledge work.

In their policy review of the implications of the globalization of knowledge for the UK economy, Brown et al. (2010a) describe the shift towards global standardization within companies and efforts to digitalize knowledge that had previously been the preserve of high-skilled workers. They consider this a manifestation of 'digital Taylorism' since it involves the 'extraction, codification and digitalisation of knowledge into software prescripts and packages that can be transmitted and manipulated by others regardless of location' (p. 15). Thus codified, the idiosyncratic knowledge of workers becomes available to the company rather than being the 'property' of an individual worker: 'In short new technologies have increased the potential to translate knowledge work into working knowledge, leading to the standardization of an increasing proportion of technical, managerial and professional jobs that raise fundamental questions about the future of knowledge work and occupational mobility' (Brown et al., 2010b: 8).

As a result, even highly skilled and professional forms of work are potentially exploitable by managements as commodities, leaving workers deskilled and with less control over their 'knowledge capital'.

In the US higher education system, Tinker and Feknous (2003) describe how the widespread take-up of distance learning on the premise of enormous cost savings in educational delivery systems is leading to a 'real subsumption' of educational labour. Educators are reduced to being 'minders' of software and hardware delivery systems that are developed and delivered by other specialists. This loss of control and autonomy frequently results in educators feeling powerless when confronted with changes that seem beyond their control.

In the UK, creative work is being separated from routine analytics and 'permission to think is restricted to a relatively small group of knowledge workers'. Brown et al. (2010a) argue that, while it took decades for manufacturing to 'lift and shift' through standardization, the process when applied to service-sector employment is likely to be much faster, 'because the only hardware you need can fit on the average office desk'.

While the full extent of the application of scientific management techniques in Britain is debated, it could still be argued that the combination of managerialism, performativity and digital Taylorism results in the degradation and commodification of high-skilled work, together with the reduction of labour power over professional work. Today, Sennett (2006) argues, automation, globalization and restructurings cause workers to fear the encroaching 'specter of uselessness'.

The wider consequences of neo-liberalism

The broader social consequences of the adoption of neo-liberalism in the West became increasingly evident in all walks of life during the 1990s. The market dominated all forms of life and social provision. Scase (2006) describes this as the 'Age of Individualism' whose popular ethos was about individual freedom, entrepreneurialism, consumerism, greed and wealth creation. Films like *Wall Street* exemplified the fiercely competitive behaviours and values of extreme forms of capitalism. This was to some extent reflected in Margaret Thatcher's infamous, if misquoted, 1980s dictum 'There is no such thing as society', which in turn echoes the neo-liberal views of Milton Friedman. Friedman described the growing demands in the 1970s for US business to have a social conscience as 'pure and unadulterated socialism'. He argued that 'business has a duty to make profit first; anything else will create confusion'.

Within UK society, the last two decades have witnessed the ever deepening advance of capitalism. Materialist and secular values have become dominant, the media have promoted a cult of celebrity, authority figures are generally discredited and the Westminster MPs' expenses scandal suggests that the culture of greed, rule bending and personal enrichment has spread from the bonus hunters, mortgage hawkers and tax avoiders of the financial sector into the heart of Britain's representative democracy.

52   *Context*

These individualized values are reflected in what Sennett (2006: 178) calls 'the culture of the new capitalism', as follows:

> Consuming passion (i.e. passionate consumerism)…meritocratic concept of talent… idealized self publicly eschewing dependency on others…These are cultural forms which celebrate personal change but not collective progress. The culture of the new capitalism is attuned to singular events, one-off transactions, interventions.

Sennett argues that the cultural ideal of the new capitalism involves people developing their potential, getting rich by thinking short term, and regretting nothing since they no longer hang on to the past. In order to progress, Sennett concludes, a longer-term perspective is needed.

Left-wing economists and commentators, such as Will Hutton and John Kay, urged a redesign of the architecture of British capitalism but this call was ignored. Like Tony Blair, his successor Gordon Brown saw renascent global capitalism, gross inequalities of reward and increasingly powerful financial markets as givens. Even the financial crisis and its causes appear not to have fundamentally changed business practices, although the era of relative austerity that has ensued has perhaps reset the dial on consumerism fuelled by cheap credit.

Conclusion

There were of course alternative economic models to neo-liberal Anglo-American capitalism available to politicians. As Giddens (1999) points out, 'globalization is political, technological and cultural, as well as economic'. However, other forms of capitalism afford more protection for workers, and could therefore reduce business flexibility and profitability.

No doubt some would argue that the neo-liberal political agenda driving the development of the flexible labour market in America and Britain has resulted in economic growth over the past two decades. How successful neo-liberalism has really been in achieving its economic objectives is a moot point. International economic policy has long been dominated by the 'Washington Consensus', which advocates privatization, free trade, export-led growth, financial capital mobility, deregulated labor markets and policies of macro-economic austerity. Business practices have been driven both by profit growth and by cost reduction. However, it has become apparent in the wake of the economic crisis and recession of 2007–9 that the relatively sustained growth of the UK economy (1998–2007) was largely fuelled by consumer spending, thanks to cheap credit and low-cost Chinese imports, while the underlying 'real economy' may have been growing less strongly. And, as Palley points out, compared to the (mostly Keynesian) 1945–80 era, this recent period has seen substantially slower economic growth and widening income inequality, both within and between countries.

Indeed, perhaps the defining characteristic of neo-liberalism these days is widening inequality. Post-Keynesians argue that labour is not automatically paid what it is worth by an anonymous neutral market process, as neo-liberals would suggest. Rather, the pattern of income distribution is impacted by labour market institutions, and institutional interventions are needed because markets tend to favour capital over labour. One of the fastest ways of boosting profits in an era when trade unions are weak and union representation in much of the private sector has collapsed is to downgrade employees' terms of employment and working conditions and reduce wages. Average wage growth in the US between 2002 and 2012 remained stubbornly low; the vast majority of wage earners have already experienced a lost decade, one where real wages were either flat or in decline (Shierholz and Lawrence Mishel, 2013).

This is in contrast to sky-high executive pay, out of all proportion to effort or contribution. Managements' bargaining power has been further increased by the threat – and sometimes the reality – of moving work offshore.

In his strong critique of the neo-liberal values upon which our current economic model is based, Hutton (2010) argues that a lack of basic fairness in our economic system is driving inequality to levels that threaten democracy, capitalism and civil society and has become a challenge to us as moral beings. What Hutton calls the 'cancer of inequality' causes trust to evaporate. Trust evaporates. There is no sense of common purpose. Creative social, economic and political interaction and deliberation become impossible. Capitalism distorts itself and ceases to innovate. Hutton calls for a wholesale reconstruction away from the ideals of 'free market fundamentalism'.

In the next chapter we shall consider some of the changes taking place in British workplaces during the period 1998–2006 and some of their reported effects on employees.

4   The new work culture

> Where rapid change takes place, the whole social structure is dislodged. Change means that individuals no longer play their accustomed roles, with resulting confusion and conflict.
>
> (Ling, 1954: 15)

In the previous chapter we looked at some of the background context factors contributing to the changing world of work. In this chapter we examine evidence for these factors in the workplace. We will look for indications of what Sennett describes as 'the culture of the new capitalism' and its reported impact on UK white-collar workers.

Sennett (2006) argues that the organizational work culture of the new capitalism arises from the increasingly international nature of markets and capital; the intensifying competition between major corporations and a move towards shareholder power in large companies, where empowered investors demand short-term results rather than looking to the long term. This work culture reflects the competitive ambitions of managements and owners of organizations; it is one of enterprise, based on free market principles, individualistic values and employer-centric employment relationships. Sennett proposes that this culture has now permeated organizations of all sizes and sectors, transforming the nature of what organizations do, and how they do it.

What Sennett calls the 'new regime' views stability and routine as a sign of weakness in an economic environment that now prefers the language of change, innovation, new opportunities and enterprise. Within organizations, the work culture is characterized by managerialism, the use of technology to transform products and commodify work, by performativity, a focus on customers, and by the ongoing quest for greater flexibility, efficiency and cost effectiveness. The new work culture offers employers labour flexibility, with reduced employment security for employees and the increasing use of contingent labour.

Was there any evidence of Sennett's 'work culture of new capitalism' or for Braverman's labour process argument in the Management Agenda surveys from the end of the 1990s? In this chapter I intend to interweave findings from a summary meta-analysis of the Roffey Park Management Agenda surveys carried out between 1997 and 2006, together with background trends which were reported in the business and management press, and in the media more generally, during this period. The majority of respondents of the Agenda were middle managers or other professional white-collar staff. Managers were asked to respond as employees unless there were specific questions probing particular aspects of people management where it was appropriate to answer from a management perspective. The majority of Agenda respondents were not members of unions.

From the volume of data available to me, in order to test out the evidence for Braverman's predictions and Sennett's observations about the nature and effects on employees of the 'new work culture', I have restricted my selection to those items which give the clearest demonstration of employer trends and employee responses. The summary meta-analysis of the Management Agenda remains at a level of broad generality rather than examining a specific sector, gender or age group. However, there was sufficient commonality of response across sectors that I will refer to these broad trends that provided my jumping-off point for obtaining a more nuanced view of issues arising, investigated using qualitative research methods and findings from these strands of research which are discussed in the coming chapters. In particular, we shall consider:

- What are the salient features of the emerging new work culture, such as work intensification and the increasing flexibilization of work?
- To what extent does work appear to be degraded and commodified in the new work culture?
- How were employees affected by the new work culture? Was worker alienation apparent? Were there indications of worker attempts to ameliorate their lot?

Developments in the UK employment context (1997–2006)

In this section I combine some of the key features of the UK employment landscape around the turn of the century, with findings from the Management Agenda. When the first Management Agenda was published in January 1998, shortly after the coming into power of 'New Labour', it presented an overall picture of the UK economy, and organizations, 'gradually returning to economic growth' after a period of economic turbulence. There were generally tight labour markets and high levels of employment. Globalization at that stage was reported by most respondents as 'a future trend'.

Changing structures

Throughout the period, the management of change remained the dominant theme. The first Management Agenda survey in 1998 followed a lengthy period of organizational restructurings including 're-engineering', downsizing and 'delayering' (or flattening of organizational structures), in which swathes of middle managers lost their jobs. Organizational restructurings were very much the order of the day, with 86 per cent of respondents reporting that their organization was downsizing, outsourcing or delayering its structures. In 1999 the survey highlighted the ongoing consolidation of mature industries such as construction through merger and acquisition. Many companies were expanding through partnership with other providers or strategic alliances such as joint ventures. By 2005, 92 per cent of Agenda respondents reported that their organization had undergone change over the previous two years, with medium–large organizations reporting the highest levels of change. Managing change and poor communication were reported to be the biggest challenges facing organizations (63 per cent).

It would appear that many organizations entered the twenty-first century with a workforce still struggling to adjust to some of the 'realities' of the new world of work and its work culture. Agenda respondents frequently reported having to continually adjust to new requirements and not understanding the rules of what Archer (1995) calls the 'new game'. For Archer, this is the morphogenesis underway in business and society and is evident in the fast-changing nature of work and employment, the end of 'jobs for life' and the global transfer of skills. In everyday life, people will have to confront more discontinuities and the scope for

56　*Context*

routine action is reduced. To cope with this 'new game', Archer calls for greater reflexivity at all levels. This is the mental capacity of all normal people to consider themselves in relation to their social contexts and vice versa.

Flexibilization

Flexibilization was especially evident in Agenda surveys between 1998 and 2003 as the outsourcing of 'non-core' routine work areas got under way in commercial sectors. Call centres were increasingly described in the popular press as latter-day 'dark, satanic mills' for their heavy use of technical monitoring and controls imposed on employees. Within a short time, jobs in UK call centres were being lost as employers 'offshored' or exported operations overseas. The number of part-time workers reached a record high, reflecting the seemingly inexorable shift away from secure, full-time employment to less secure flexible patterns and casualization.

By 2002 almost half of respondents' organizations were outsourcing business processes and third-party contract management became a new challenge for managers. The increasing casualization of the workforce meant that many managers found themselves managing a flexible workforce, including contractors and temporary staff, who, managers feared, had no loyalty to the organization. Forty per cent of manager respondents indicated that they were increasingly expected to manage people not directly employed by the organization. Over half of the 2002 sample reported being increasingly required to work in a variety of forms of team. More 'flexible' matrix structures, with complex reporting lines, seemed to be especially challenging to work in, as illustrated by this comment by a technical specialist then working in a matrix: 'There are too many senior managers. Consensus cannot be reached, therefore delay in making decisions. Managers are not secure in their own positions.'

Redundancies

At the time of the first Management Agenda survey in 1997–8, the overall impression was of turbulent workplaces and confusion, with redundancies becoming increasingly commonplace. Most comments concerned the generally inept way redundancy processes were handled rather than questioning whether redundancies should be happening at all. Interestingly, respondents on the whole seemed to accept that redundancies were inevitable. This might be explained as a manifestation of what Scott (1990: 72) describes as the 'thin' version of Marx's 'false consciousness' theory: 'The thin theory…maintains only that the dominant ideology achieves compliance by convincing subordinate groups that the social order in which they live is natural and inevitable.' As Scott points out, 'the thin theory settles for resignation.' Typically, respondents instead expressed deep scepticism about the fairness of the process by which people were selected for redundancy:

> There is a naive belief that staying with the business is an end in itself, so we have no compulsory redundancy programme to assuage the vanity of the union and Personnel Director, which means that those who want to stay get pushed out; those who want to go, can't.
>
> (A senior manager who had opted for voluntary
> redundancy but was refused)

Redundancies in particular are a touchstone of employee perceptions about organizational justice. Justice researchers typically distinguish between three types of justice: the perceived fairness of outcomes (distributive justice), the fairness of the processes whereby outcomes are allocated (procedural justice), and the interpersonal treatment received during the implementation of the procedure together with the perceived adequacy and timeliness of information given (interactional justice) (Colquitt et al., 2001; Heffernan and Dundon, 2016). When managers are seen to satisfy employees' need for organizational justice, this is reciprocated where employees respond positively to the organization via positive attitudes (Frenkel et al., 2012).

However, perceived inequity can result in disengagement and increased turnover (Kenny and McIntyre, 2005). In the Agenda surveys, widespread perceived injustice was reported in the way job losses were handled. There were many criticisms of the HR function's role, perceived 'resource' focus and lack of respect for people: 'Treated like a number'; 'The time Personnel has to assist is reduced'. Respondents were asked if their organization had handled redundancies compassionately (yes/no). Ninety-two per cent of respondents chose the 'no' answer. Correlations with other questions suggested that those 'survivor' employees who felt the process was badly handled also then began to focus more on their own needs, rather than those of the organization, suggesting perhaps that trust had been lost.

Since traditional 'relational' psychological contracts depend implicitly on trust, loyalty and a degree of job security as the basis of employees' willingness to expend their discretionary effort for their employer, it could perhaps be argued that these were being replaced by 'transactional' contracts, where the employment relationship becomes a calculated negotiation, with employees providing, for example, long hours and extra work in exchange for high pay.

Growing industrial relations tensions

The government drive to modernize public services continued throughout the period. School, further and higher education sectors were undergoing 'reform'. Across the UK's public sector, targeting and 'partnership working' in cross-sector service delivery in areas like health and social services were leading to rationalization of services, and of staff. Local government employees were experiencing the early thrusts of purchaser/provider splits which were later extended under a 'best value' rubric. Central government services were starting to be amalgamated, such as the merger of the Benefits Agency and the Employment Service. For many employees such arrangements brought into sharp relief issues relating to job security, career progression, cultural differences and complexity.

In 2005 a worsening industrial relations climate was becoming evident in the hardening of attitudes among some union leaders towards the then UK government, and increasing incidences of strikes. The growing assertiveness of trade unions was reflected in industrial action, such as that of the Fire Brigades' Union, on a scale not seen for a number of years. By 2006 the New Labour government admitted that too many targets had been centrally imposed on public bodies and that a culture of managerialism may not be the answer to improving standards of public service.

In the 2006 Agenda, the closure of many final salary pension schemes to new recruits was widely reported, with many employees expressing concern about the prospect of having to work for longer, both to compensate for poorer pensions and the likely later age at which they would be able to access pensions.

The challenges of change

Throughout the period in question, employees were subject to growing workloads, increased demands and uncertainty as organizations pursued growth through flexibility and cost

58   *Context*

containment. There was little evidence of effective change management happening or support being provided to help employees make the necessary transitions. Of course individuals are likely to experience many organizational changes during the course of a working lifetime. Research into mergers and acquisitions carried out by the author and colleagues between 1998 and 2003 found that even in one merger, an individual will typically experience multiple 'waves of change' as different phases of the merger hit home in cognitive, affective and material ways (Hirsh et al., 1999). Managers who have already experienced their own transitions may not be aware of the effects of change on employees who are only later experiencing the impact of change and they may not provide the support individuals need to make the transition successfully. In the Agenda surveys, people reported that there was too much focus on the 'hard technical issues' of change and too little staff involvement.

Do more with less

One of the main management challenges at the time was motivating teams. The concentration on cost cutting and redundancies in both contracting and expanding organizations had an inevitable knock-on effect on the workloads of those who remained employed as they struggled to do more with less. There were higher expectations of employees, including being required to learn new skills and increase both the quality and quantity of output. The main reported sources of demotivation included poor management, bureaucracy, lack of recognition and demands always to do more, as reflected in this comment by a manager in the 2002 Agenda: 'I'm increasingly expected to do more and better with less and for no more reward or recognition.' This meant that other valuable activities were relegated to the 'nice to have' category. The majority of respondents between 2000 and 2003 described their working conditions as stressful, unproductive, time consuming and destructive of enjoyment of work. Employees reported that the things that motivated them as people – such as enjoyment of the job, personal drive and achievement, challenge, helping others and recognition – were difficult to achieve in the new work climate. Financial rewards were mentioned by only a tiny minority. In particular people reported feeling under pressure to deliver, especially bottom-line results.

Confusion

In 2000, 90 per cent of Agenda respondents reported that their workplace was undergoing a variety of changes, including business process re-engineering, restructurings and internationalization, and in many cases all of these change processes were underway at the same time. The impact of change was being keenly felt and contributing to a lowering of performance levels in some cases. A financial services manager talked about the effects of change in his organization: 'Morale in affected areas is very low. There's a high rate of attrition, services delivered from these areas have deteriorated due to lack of knowledge and lack of resources.' For many 'survivors' one of the consequences of the sheer volume of change initiatives was confusion and a lack of clarity. In 1998, half of respondents reported loss of direction as a result of: 'too many changes being introduced at one time', 'directionless leadership', 'authoritarian management' and 'too much politics'. This comment by a manager in 2002 highlights the implications for individuals of lack of clarity: 'Less people have the overall view to fight their corner, whereas before people knew more of what went on and could balance matters off.' As one respondent put it in 2002, the sheer volume of change was producing 'sink or swim' responses: 'Frequent restructuring within the organisation results in either "change fatigue" or an acceptance of constant change as the norm.' The majority of respondents reported a decline in morale of 'survivors' of downsizing, loss of trust, poor communication and lack of role clarity following restructurings. These employee perspectives echo findings from other studies. In the CIPD Employee Outlook survey (2009), 58 per cent of respondents reported feeling anxious about the future, even though very few of them felt their own job to be at risk of redundancy.

Sutton (1990) researched both the short- and long-term effects of workforce reduction in the context of organizational decline processes. He found that employees at all levels experience anxiety and stress; lower-level employees because they fear loss of jobs, higher-level employees (managers) because they make the decisions about layoffs, transfers and demotions. Doherty (1996) argues that downsizing has a significant effect not only on people who lose their jobs but also on the 'survivors' who face a number of unsettling changes such as the loss of peers, extra work, different progression opportunities and so on. In Doherty's studies, people who survived layoffs commonly experienced guilt, lack of commitment and fear since within organizations, decision-making and planning became more short-term, and work climates typically became more politicized.

Technology

Technology appears to have a dual positive/negative aspect, according to how it is used. Many new developments have the potential to help mankind solve some of society's most complex problems and bring great advances for society. For instance, technologies like driverless cars may improve road safety and robotic surgery is likely to save millions of lives. Equally, technology has the potential to be deployed for less benevolent purposes, such as surveillance, for intruding into personal lives and for creating weapons of mass destruction.

Back in the 1970s there was widespread optimistic belief in the power of scientific and technological progress to change people's lives for the better and John Meynard Keynes predicted that technology would lead to more leisure time: 'Man [sic] will be faced with his real, his permanent problem – how to use his freedom from pressing economic cares, how to occupy the leisure, which science and compound interest will have won for him, to live wisely and agreeably and well.' However, critical analysts have drawn attention to the 'tyrannical dimension' of new technology, such as driving employees to engage in intranet discussion forums for fear of being 'unseen and left behind' (Maravelias, 2009: 350), or the perception by workers that they may lose advantage and status through sharing and codifying knowledge (Flood et al., 2001). For his part, Braverman focused on the increasingly dehumanizing effects of technology on work and workers, and the sinister intentions of its deployers. He argued that technology is driven more by the capitalist machinery and not for the wellbeing of mankind: that science and technology have changed from a 'relatively free floating social endeavour' to a tool of capitalism (1974: 156). His form of labour process theory highlights how 'the rationality of technique in the modern industrial enterprise is not neutral in respect of class domination' (Giddens, 1982: 38).

Similarly, Braverman's contemporary, E.F. Schumacher (1974: 80) proposed that there is a form of Parkinson's Law by which the prestige carried by people in modern industrial society varies in inverse proportion to their closeness to actual production. He argued that the potential of technology to ease mankind's burdens had instead been used to enslave him, turning virtually 'all real production into an inhuman chore which does not enrich a man but empties him'. In particular, the type of work which modern technology is most successful in reducing

60   *Context*

or even eliminating is skilful, productive work of human hands, in touch with real materials of one kind or another.

What Schumacher and others observed is arguably even more pronounced today. David Graeber (2015) argues that, rather than freeing mankind, technology has been marshalled

> to figure out ways to make us all work more. Huge swathes of people, in Europe and North America in particular, spend their entire working lives performing tasks they believe to be unnecessary. The moral and spiritual damage that comes from this is profound. It is a scar across our collective soul.

Transformation of work through technology

The period of study saw technology being used as Schumacher and Braverman had predicted, i.e. both to intensify work, since with the advent of email and the internet more work could be carried out at speed and remotely, and to commodify white-collar work in order to increase flexibility and efficiency. Thanks to the development of call centre technology, routine work was being 'parcelled up', outsourced and/or 'offshored' to less expensive centres of production or of customer service.

The speed with which work practices and workloads were being transformed through technology is evident in Agenda surveys. In 1998, the use of electronic means of communication was still in its infancy; less than 50 per cent of Agenda respondents regularly used computers at work and only 73 per cent of respondents reported using or having occasional access to emails. Many managers still employed secretaries to do their typing. By 1999, company use of information and communications technology had grown so significantly that there were real concerns about the risks (which proved unfounded) posed to company systems by the 'Millennium Bug'.

Some respondents lamented the advent of electronic communications. They were already noticing how email was replacing face-to-face communication, and remarked on the increased workloads and speed of response expected. The growing intensification of work is evident in this complaint by one respondent about 'the added pressure when all those who wish to talk to me do so by e-mail, currently 50–100 messages a day at peak; could multiply by 3 or 4'. There were calls for a new form of etiquette around emails, in particular how to avoid causing offence with the inadvertent use of capital letters, and HR teams reported drafting new policies or protocols relating to appropriate use of email. By 2000, information and communication technology was an accepted feature of the workplace, and email in particular was used more extensively. Its main reported drawbacks included the increase in or overload of communication, with people continuing to copy in large numbers of people on messages just to 'cover their backs'.

Digital Taylorism (Brown et al., 2010b) was proceeding apace throughout this period. In 2005, knowledge management was reported as a high business priority (83 per cent, compared with just 32 per cent in 2001). Agenda respondent comments in 2002–3 about the growing use of integrated information systems such as SAP highlight the uneasiness many people felt about the introduction of such systems. These concerned partly the expense and slow progress of implementation, but also people's reluctance to place on the system valuable information which might once have been their own preserve, thus potentially making them expendable. In 2005, 90 per cent of respondents reported having little inclination to make their own knowledge available to others via information systems. People were at that stage reporting various means by which they had managed to side-step the apparent organizational requirement to share e.g. client knowledge via these systems. Low trust in employers and a recognition of career vulnerability were widely reported.

Decline in job quality

Alongside the use of integrated systems to 'absorb' workers' knowledge, the increased pressure people were experiencing meant that many employees had little control over their workloads and were experiencing job strain. Green (2009b) argues that worker autonomy (or 'task discretion') in the UK has been in decline since the 1990s. This is significant because, as Green points out, this development signals a deterioration in job quality for people, not only because it goes hand in hand with lower trust, but even more fundamentally because it lessens the extent to which workers can fulfil themselves through their work.

A common assumption in much occupational health literature is that job strain is the result of an imbalance between the demands made of employees and the resources they have at their disposal. Much research in industrial-organizational psychology and occupational health psychology has concerned the impact of job or organizational features. For instance, Karasek's (1979) study found that the highest levels of depression were in employees who experienced low levels of job control. Similarly, Guest's CIPD research used Health and Safety Executive data to examine the extent to which respondents had reasonable demands to deal with and some personal control over their work. The score should be 85 or over. This mostly was not the case, suggesting that poor-quality jobs are rife.

Other studies also highlight the corrosive effect on employee wellbeing of lack of control over workloads. For instance, the longitudinal 'Whitehall II' studies of a cohort of 10,308 women and men, all of whom were employed in the London offices of the British Civil Service at the time they were recruited to the study in 1985. These studies found that the most stressed workers were those in the middle, with mortality higher among those in the lower grade when compared to the higher grade. High blood pressure among the lowest grade servants at work was associated with greater 'job stress', including 'lack of skill utilization', 'tension' and 'lack of clarity' in tasks assigned.

Various models suggest a linear relationship between job characteristics and employee wellbeing. Karasek's (1979, 1998) job demand-control model argues that the combination of having little scope for decision-making and a heavily demanding job gives rise to stress and job dissatisfaction. High job demands (particularly work overload and time pressure) and low job control by the individual produces job strain. The control that workers have over what they do is often described as 'autonomy'; too little control and they cannot participate fully in the work, which is an important aspect of their needs. High job demands, such as a high work pressure, emotional demands and role ambiguity are primarily related to the exhaustion component of burnout and may lead to sleeping problems, exhaustion and impaired health (e.g. Doi, 2005; Halbesleben and Buckley, 2004).

The effort-reward imbalance (ERI) model of Siegrist (1996) derives from equity theory. This emphasizes the reward, rather than the control, structure of work. The ERI model assumes that job strain is the result of an imbalance between effort (extrinsic job demands and intrinsic motivation to meet these demands) and reward (in terms of salary, esteem reward and security/career opportunities, i.e. promotion prospects, job security and status consistency). The basic assumption is that a lack of reciprocity between effort and reward (i.e. high-effort/ low-reward conditions) will lead to arousal and stress.

62   *Context*

Work-related stress tends to be triggered by pressure or demands on an individual and occurs when there is a mismatch between the demands of the job and the resources and capabilities of the individual worker to meet those demands. It can impact upon the individual's ability to cope, or rather his/her perception of that ability. Self-efficacy theory (Bandura, 2001) concerns a person's perception that he or she is competent in relation to present demands reflects people's view of their competence in the past, in relation to their ability to cope in the future. Scheck and Kinicki (2000) found that employees' positive assessments of their self-efficacy during organizational change were linked to lower perceptions of threat and potential harm. Conversely, an employee's perception that he or she has failed to prevent a controllable negative event might give rise to even more unhappiness.

Relatively few investigations into environmental factors affecting work have also focused on the cognitive and affective processes of workers. Warr (1990) found a non-linear relationship between job demands and decision latitude and employee wellbeing. The strength of Warr's study was its large sample size, as non-linear relationships can only be examined with a large heterogeneous sample. Although most psychological research focuses on affective wellbeing, Warr distinguishes five components of mental health: (1) affective wellbeing; (2) competence; (3) autonomy; (4) aspiration; and (5) integrated functioning. According to Warr's Vitamin Model, certain job characteristics, similar to the effect of vitamins on physical health, initially have a beneficial effect on employee mental health, whereas their absence impairs mental health. Beyond a certain level, a plateau has been reached and the level of mental health remains constant.

The Vitamin Model empirically indicates nine environmental factors that influence work and employment policy in a non-linear way as sources of happiness or unhappiness. These include personal control. In any job or setting, the opportunity for personal control is essential for meeting personal goals, for sustaining a sense of personal agency and for reducing feelings of helplessness. Environmental clarity is generally desirable both to reduce anxiety about the future and to make it possible for people to plan and regulate actions. Other factors include the opportunity for skill use and acquisition, externally generated goals, variety, environmental clarity and contact with others. The features thought to have a constant effect beyond moderate levels are availability of money, physical security, valued social position, supportive supervision, career outlook and equity (Warr, 2007; Warr and Clapperton, 2010).

Some environmental characteristics at very high levels can become punishing, and are likely also to be accompanied by extremely high levels of other features that yield an additional strain. Thus features identified as 'opportunities' (for control and for skill use) become an 'unavoidable requirement' at very high levels, and are likely to yield unhappiness since behaviour is then coerced rather than being encouraged or facilitated. Environments that call for unremitting control through extremely difficult decision-making and sustained personal responsibility, or which demand continuous use of extremely complex skills, can give rise to overload problems as very high demands exceed personal capabilities. If externally generated goals become very difficult and/or numerous, the load may become unmanageable, producing harmful effects. De Jonge and Schaufeli (1998) also found support for a non-linear relationship between job demands and job-related anxiety, job autonomy with emotional exhaustion (depression), and workplace social support with job satisfaction (discontented-contended) and emotional exhaustion.

The long-hours culture

Therefore, work effort is negatively related to employee wellbeing if it becomes too intense and hours are excessive, and if people have little control over the demands made of them, or few resources to call upon, resulting in job strain and stress. Occupational stress is a pattern of emotional, cognitive, behavioural and physiological reactions to adverse aspects of work content, work organization and work environment, including the responsibilities associated with the work itself.

From the late 1990s onward, employees typically had little time at their disposal as British workplaces became known for their long-hours culture. UK workers were reported to have the longest working week of European countries, with official figures suggesting that 3 million people regularly worked longer than 48 hours a week. Government policy effectively endorsed this by exercising its right to 'opt out' of the EU Working Time Directive (June 2000). This directive was intended to protect people's health and safety by restricting work to no more than 48 hours per week on the basis that excessive working time is a major cause of stress, depression and illness. In contrast, France passed stricter legislation, limiting the maximum working week to 35 hours.

Blurring of work/home boundaries

As reported in Agenda surveys, with internet access, every desk gained its PC and workers were progressively equipped with laptops and mobile phones. New forms of flexible working were enabled, including remote and home working. As a result, the boundaries between work and home life started to fragment. One of the companies participating in the Agenda survey sold off its head office and required all workers to work from home, thus transferring the related financial overhead and social costs of work to employees.

Longitudinal comparison of data (1992 and 2001) from a survey designed by the Policy Studies Institute and a team from the London School of Economics suggested that British workers were becoming more dissatisfied with longer working hours and growing work pressures, and that this was having serious repercussions on their motivation at work. The most dissatisfied workers were those who were highly qualified or were among the workforce elite.

These findings were echoed in the Agenda, which started to examine the working hours of managers in 2000. The majority of Agenda respondents then reported that their workload had increased significantly over the previous two years. Between 2000 and 2002, the vast majority of respondents (typically over 87 per cent), regardless of their gender or age or the sector they worked in, reported that they consistently worked longer than their contracted working week. At the same time bureaucracy was seen as adding to the pressure since it slowed down the speed at which work could progress. The size of the organization only appeared to have an impact in 2003 when 72 per cent of people working in smaller organizations of 1–250 people reported consistently working longer hours compared to 84 per cent of those in organizations of 251–5,000 people and 90 per cent of those in organizations of over 5,000 people.

Moreover, since technology enabled faster communication, employees were expected to respond quickly. Agenda respondents increasingly talked about taking their laptops on holiday and 'just keeping on top of their emails' for a couple of hours each day. Bunting (2004) argued that employees were becoming 'willing slaves' of the system at the expense of their health and wellbeing and without guaranteed employment security.

As employees rose to the challenge of increased workloads, what might have been previously thought to be an exceptional effort now became accepted as the norm for performance, with consequences for the individual. During the early 2000s there was evidence that many Agenda respondents were experiencing job strain during this period, that for some people may have had long-lasting effects. As Guest (1995) pointed out, the idea of being out of

64   *Context*

balance is tolerable, as long as the illusion is retained that this is a temporary phenomenon. Similarly, Brown et al. comment (2010b: 141):

> The problem many confront today is that doing one's best may not be good enough. Even extraordinary efforts to improve performance will count for little if everyone else does the same thing. But whatever the outcome, the constant striving for perfection also comes at a personal price.

By 2002 the overriding impression was that employees were overworked, spending long hours both at the office and at home on business issues. Working long hours (or being seen to be) was one way some employees attempted to protect their career interests in demanding work cultures. With greater competition for reduced promotion opportunities inherent in downsizing organizations and flatter structures, some employees appeared to accept long hours as the price to be paid for success and as a means of demonstrating visible commitment to the organization in order to gain an advantage over others (Clark, 1997). A report by insurer Royal and Sun Alliance suggested that one in three men and one in six women were too busy to go on holiday, leaving £4 billion of work going unpaid in Britain each year.

There was growing debate in the management press about the effects of the long-hours culture which was defined progressively as an equal opportunity (gender issue), then a family-friendly issue, then a work–life balance issue, followed by a diversity issue and now falls under the human rights banner. Many companies during the early 2000s developed work–life balance policies, yet flexible working options available were often not taken up, sometimes because they were poorly communicated and therefore little known about. More often though (reflected in verbatim responses to the employee surveys), employees did not take up these options because they feared being perceived as unable to 'cut it' in the increasingly 'dog-eat-dog' work climates.

Discussion

Despite the potential of technology to improve working lives, we seem to be working harder, not smarter. Indeed, it could be argued that new technologies, especially information and communications technology, have been used to provide new means of intensifying work, rather than increasing satisfaction. The use of mobile internet technology has enabled remote working but has also contributed to increased workloads and shorter lead times. Today, thanks to email and the internet, work has no real boundaries of time or space. Work can be, and is, carried out from anywhere, leading to a blurring of boundaries between work and other aspects of life for many people. With 24/7 operations, faster-paced communications and rapid developments in technology, for those who let it, work can take over all waking hours. And no matter how much work is done, it is never enough. The phenomenon of workers who take their laptops on holiday and work each day is not uncommon. Many people find themselves working in stressful working environments and subject to work intensification and uncertain futures. Productivity is slowing, engagement levels are languishing and stress is becoming endemic – fuelled partly by the growing 'always on' work culture that technology supports.

Hartley (1999) has argued that, when the balance of exchange between the individual and organization is altered, in the context of insecurity, the individual may perceive the organization as implicitly demanding more from him or her, while offering either the same or reduced rewards. As reported in the Agenda, employers did expect employees to work long hours and do more with less. The bond of trust between employee and employer, which underpinned the old psychological contract, became strained during this period.

How well people were able to cope with the growing demands made of them appeared to vary considerably. These different responses perhaps reflected individuals' confidence in their own employability in the buoyant labour market of the time. Some people undoubtedly chose to meet these heavy work demands, perhaps through love of the job and/or because they were ambitious and were willing, wittingly or unwittingly, to forego other rewards they wanted – time and balance. Younger workers in particular appeared to respond to the challenges of the new workplace as both a developmental opportunity, and as necessary to fulfil their ambitions. For the struggling majority, the demands of structure appeared to have driven out agency and many were complying with increased demands and reduced control and 'rewards' because they felt they had no option.

Aronowitz and DiFazio (1999) suggest that the scientific-technological revolution of our time, which is not confined to new electronic processes but also affects organizational changes in the structure of corporations, has fundamentally altered the forms of work, skill and occupation. They argue that the redistribution of skilled work due to technological advances has destabilized the employment relationship, polarizing work opportunities between people who are 'work-rich', overloaded and in full-time employment, whose working hours know few boundaries thanks to instant access via laptops and mobile phones; and those who are 'work-poor', whose jobs may have been deskilled or who may have few, if any, prospects of paid employment. Reich (1991) too envisaged growing disparities of opportunity between American 'symbolic' workers who are able to compete in the global skills market and 'routine' workers, who cannot compete. Reich in particular argued that social cohesion and a sense of national community would dissipate as a result.

As with Sennett, for Aronowitz and DiFazio (1999) the whole notion of tradition, and the identification of persons with their work, has been radically altered. They argue that there is increasing proletarianization of work at every level below top management and a few scientific and technical occupations. They suggest that Western societies may have reached a historical watershed in which the link between 'work', as the Western cultural ideal, and 'self' is in crisis, since both qualified and mass labour is increasingly considered redundant. I agree with them that, as a result of these profoundly altered circumstances, expectations of both employers and employees have changed, creating new social contracts within which new psychological contracts emerge.

The new work climate

Throughout the first few years of the Agenda survey in the late 1990s, the increasingly competitive nature of organizational cultures was reflected in the reported increase in political behaviour as people sought to protect themselves or gain personal advantage in these more complex workplaces. Some of the many forms this took included: 'power struggles; attacks on my credibility; blame culture by immediate manager; different powerful players pursuing incompatible agendas and making demands of me that cannot be reconciled'. 'Tribalism' in organization cultures, where information is power and therefore not shared, was considered one of the main barriers to knowledge management in 2000. One manager's comment in 2002, typical of many, highlights one of the reasons for his growing sense of insecurity: 'People manoeuvring for power. Change has created opportunities for new networks to form, creating increased political activity.' While it might be argued that work environments have always been sites of struggle, what we are seeing here are significant changes to the terrain in which these

66   Context

struggles take place and the opening of new fronts, for example those enabled by technologies, on which hostilities can be conducted.

Loss of trust

In an economy increasingly dependent on exploiting knowledge and service-intensive work, information technologies and new structural forms should in theory enable greater human interaction for the purposes of knowledge and value creation. However, Sennett (2006) argues that, if anything, the new work culture is counter-productive to knowledge creation. Trustful relationships may be a casualty of change, undermining the reciprocal knowledge exchange between employers and employees. Similarly, for Whittington and Mayer (2002) the exchange of knowledge works better through the enduring and trustful relationships to be found in more integrated organizations than across diverse centres.

The context more generally in the early 2000s was one of low trust. Public trust in institutions and their leaders was shaken in the wake of the WorldCom and Enron scandals, and the 'fat-cat' director pay debacle in 2001–2. Governance issues were in the spotlight, Sarbanes–Oxley[1] was implemented and a variety of reports such as those by Higgs[2] and Tyson[3] recommended guidelines to improve board performance and accountability. A study on trust in Britain and around the world (Elliot and Quaintance, 2003) showed that the proportion of the population believing that other people 'could generally be trusted' had dropped from 60 per cent in the late 1950s to 29 per cent in 2003. Experts variously blamed the demise of the job-for-life culture, greater social mobility, the rising divorce rate, greater immigration, changes in the way we work, more short-term contracts and a more aggressive dog-eat-dog commercial ethic.

Not surprisingly, the growing public scepticism about leaders and institutions was reflected within organizations and evident in the Agenda data. The effectiveness of traditional sources of managerial control had been in decline for some time. Company after company appeared to be in a perpetual state of flux as managers tried to respond to fast-changing markets and technology. They had flattened hierarchies, reduced the role of headquarters, tried to dismantle central bureaucracies, set up matrix organizations and outsourced activities. A casualty of the changes was the perceived authority and honesty of senior managers. Throughout the period 1998–2006, Agenda surveys reported a continuous drop in reported levels of employee trust in senior leaders from 60 per cent in 1998 to only 24 per cent in 2004, as this comment from 1999 illustrates: 'Senior management are completely unaccountable: they have a chief concern with their organisational status above all else.'

In his book *Fat and Mean: The Corporate Squeeze of Working Americans and the Myth of Managerial 'Downsizing'*, David Gordon (1996), one of Braverman's intellectual heirs in the US, used an array of quantitative evidence of overall employment patterns of the previous decade to argue that US corporations had gone 'mean' rather than 'lean', and that they were employing more managers and supervisors per worker than ever before. These ever-increasing functionaries control company payrolls and pay themselves generous salaries – at the expense of average workers. Instead of sharing profits with their employees, thus encouraging them to work harder, management has more often opted to prod workers by instilling fear of layoffs.

In the 2003 survey, lack of trust was reported as one of the main barriers to empowerment along with organizational politics, cynicism, risk-averse senior management, abdication by managers, individualism and having no parameters within which to be empowered. As one manager in 2002 put it, 'I like to do things well, and in the current context I feel it's quantity and politics over quality'. One middle manager in a building society which had recently

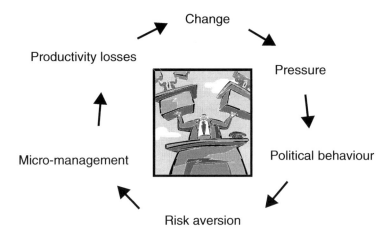

Figure 4.1 The law of self-defeating consequences

become a bank was re-evaluating his commitment to his organization because, 'I'm tired of the politics and seeing poor managers progress because they are good at "playing the game"'. While some people saw conflict as a source of energy, others pragmatically accepted that conflict was now a feature of working life: 'not pleasant but inevitable'. For many Agenda respondents the breakdown of trust and collaboration between colleagues was a major source of job dissatisfaction.

By 2007, the main issues reported to affect trust at work were uncertainty and lack of communication during change. As a result, as one manager put it, there was 'a lot of pressure and responsibility without adequate information or tools to do the job'. The overall picture was one of a growing disenchantment and some resignation towards working conditions within the competitive new work culture. Since trust is considered a cornerstone of a healthy psychological contract, the widespread cynicism amongst employees towards management suggests alienation arising from widespread psychological contract breach or even violation.

So commonly were the negative effects of these changes on employee motivation reported via the Agenda that, to prompt debate among management audiences at conferences, I presented various Agenda correlations in process form under the title of 'The law of self-defeating consequences' (Figure 4.1). By presenting these elements in this form, I am conscious that this could imply causality rather than relationship between behaviours and organizational outcomes, such as productivity losses. However, there was generally strong recognition by audiences of the interplay of factors which gave face validity to the extensiveness of such behaviours and their consequences for many people's working experience. For me this was additional evidence that, for many people, work was being degraded.

'War for talent'/volatile labour market

Highly skilled knowledge-intensive work was becoming a major generator of GDP from the mid-1990s. By the end of the 1990s, major consultancy and other professional service firms wishing to expand were experiencing a shortage of skilled employees. They competed with each other in what McKinsey and Co. (2001) dubbed the 'war for talent' to attract highly skilled recruits on the basis of individualized pay and benefits packages tailored to the individual's lifestyle.

68   *Context*

However, 2001 was a year of economic turbulence and political shock, as events of September 11 reverberated throughout the developed economies. In UK manufacturing alone, 150,000 jobs were lost and even organizations which depended on high-calibre specialist labour, such as the telecoms, investment banking and IT industries, were badly affected by the potential global recession. In the UK, company pension schemes, endowment mortgages and personal share-based savings schemes were badly affected and house prices were predicted to fall.

In practice it seemed that, rather than resorting to layoffs, some employers did recognize the importance of retaining skilled staff. In the 2002 Agenda, a slight majority (56 per cent) of companies were reported to be slowing down the downsizing process, some because they feared 'corporate anorexia', a condition in which a corporation does not have enough employees to meet its goals or needs. Others (29 per cent) were reversing the 'delayering', or flattening of management hierarchies, by 'relayering', because they were concerned about being able to retain talent, given the lack of career opportunities.

In 2004, various economic reports suggested that consumer spending in the UK would continue to rise. This accounted for the strength of the UK economy, with spending fuelled in many cases by the more easily available credit and the remortgaging of properties. Economic growth slowed towards the end of 2004. Factors such as rising interest rates, gloomy and disturbing news from events in Iraq and elsewhere appeared to be leading to a slowdown in consumer confidence and spending.

By the mid-2000s, with a tight labour market, more jobs overall and an ageing workforce in many cases, skills shortages were reported to exist in many sectors. According to the management press in 2005, a new 'war for talent' had broken out. The demand for unskilled and semi-skilled workers was largely being met by migrant workers from the new EU accession states who made up the shortfall of British workers able and willing to service the burgeoning consumer markets. More generally, organizations were reported to be competing for the best talent by offering attractive 'employment value propositions' and targeted 'employer brands'. The emphasis appeared to be mainly on improving reward packages.

Some employers were already attempting to differentiate themselves in the white-collar labour market by focusing on work–life balance, developing a 'high benefits strategy' to strengthen recruitment and retention, incorporating both significant fringe benefits and family-friendly practices. However, several City firms reinforced the importance of being seen to be capable of working long hours by providing a wide range of human resource 'benefits' – such as concierge services, childcare vouchers, Indian head massages at employees' desks – to ensure that workers could work long hours.

With today's renewed focus on talent, companies are again making headlines through the benefits they offer. For instance, in 2016 tech giants Apple and Facebook added a new benefit for women to staff packages. This allows women who work for them to undergo highly invasive medical treatment in order to have their eggs frozen. While this 'offer' might be in response to what their employees have requested, critics have argued that the subtext of this benefit could also be seen as an encouragement to women to defer family life so they can continue to work very hard in a sector where typically they have a less than 10 per cent chance of making it to the top. Indeed, this could be seen as an implicit psychological contract expectation of employers that people should dedicate their lives to work.

New roles and skills

Structural changes were leading to new roles and forcing the need for new skills. For instance, in the 2000 Agenda, 73 per cent of respondents from all sectors reported that they were expected to develop new skills such as performance management, communication, IT and interpersonal skills. These reflected the customer-facing shifts taking place in organizations, where it seemed no longer sufficient for people in non-managerial roles to be technical specialists alone, they needed also to be able to work effectively in teams and to demonstrate a swathe of 'soft' skills that would enable them to work well with other people.

With respect to the emerging 'new deal', in line with Sennett's observations and Rajan's employability thesis, employees generally seemed aware of the need to develop new skills and were keen to actualize their potential. In 2000, 94 per cent of respondents felt confident that they had the new skills required to work in changing organizations. However, many people were less sanguine about their prospects and considered development as a means of hanging onto their jobs.

The concept of leadership in particular had widespread appeal for the practitioner community as idealized management types were promoted by management 'gurus'. One example was the influential book *Good to Great* by Jim Collins (2001), which featured regularly in leadership-development programmes. Thus, managers were exhorted to become 'level five'-type leaders, and to demonstrate 'humility', one of the attributes of such leaders. These attitudes were widely incorporated into organizational competency frameworks for assessment and development purposes. As Sennett (2008) points out, the value placed on such skills has replaced in modern organizations that previously placed on craftsmanship, with its possibilities for deep learning and real achievement.

Fifteen years on, (how) have things changed?

Do these findings still hold true today? Arguably yes, according to the Management Agenda findings for 2015 and 2016. The sample sizes were larger than earlier surveys (1,000+ white-collar/managerial/professional respondents).

Change continues

In 2016, change was as extensive and pervasive as ever. Both HR and line managers considered lack of appropriate leadership and change fatigue key barriers to effective change. Both groups reported a general lack of understanding about the need for, and direction of, change. Perceptions of how well change was being received varied according to hierarchical position. Junior managers in particular typically felt that they were not involved in change, whereas more senior leaders considered that staff at all levels were widely involved. Although some of the reported changes were technology-driven, very few organizations appeared to be using the potential of social media and mobile technologies to support change. After all, these have the potential to support more 'bottom-up change' by acting as vehicles for sourcing ideas and responses quickly and efficiently from a wide group of employees, and increasing the connectedness across the organization (especially in large organizations).

Cost restrictions

More than half of all organizations (57 per cent) were putting in place cost restrictions as a means of responding to the political and economic challenges they faced. Consequently, maintaining staff morale and engagement was proving difficult, as a respondent from the production and manufacturing sector comments: 'We are going through a difficult period financially and we had a voluntary redundancy programme. Another problem is that, as a

70   *Context*

business, we don't measure engagement in a sophisticated way and, as a business, we don't really know what engages people and what doesn't.' This was particularly the case in the public sector, where 75 per cent of managers reported their organization attempting to constrain or reduce costs, partly through redundancies (52 per cent of managers in the public sector report their organization making redundancies) and seeking greater efficiencies through redesigned processes and systems (64 per cent). As the 2016 Agenda report's authors (Lucy et al., 2016) point out, 'The dangers of this approach may be that, in streamlining processes, what makes for good work may get lost and jobs become unfulfilling'.

Lack of resources and control

The trend towards organizations slimming down and wanting more for less was reflected in the finding that the majority of managers at all levels say that they never have enough time to get work done (whilst this is true for all managers, it is increasingly so the more you move down the organizational hierarchy). Managers at all levels reported not having a high level of control over aspects of work, in particular the pace of work, and one in two said they worried a lot about work outside of hours, as this public-sector respondent points out:

> We are under-resourced and overstretched. There is a very, very high level of expect-ation coming from the very top which is divorced from the actual reality on the ground. So people expect things to happen, which they should obviously, the Chief Executive or whatever should expect things to happen. But they seem to be unaware of the fact that people lower down in the chain are not as well-resourced as they were in the past. There's cuts going on all the time, there's restructures going on all the time, people are losing their positions. And there are fewer people to do the work, so there's that challenge.

Lack of clarity

Moreover, many respondents reported that confusion and lack of clarity about priorities made it very difficult to balance operational and strategic pressures, as this not-for-profit-sector respondent points out:

> Vague strategic objectives with no timeframe and what the expected outcomes are. Because they're not clear enough and we don't know what we're supposed to achieve as a result of them, it's that balance of, well, okay, how do I know when I've got there, be-cause I can't measure it?

In combination, such issues have negative implications for people's sense of wellbeing and, perhaps, ability to perform at their best.

Stress is still prevalent

Not surprisingly, stress was still a prevalent feature of many people's working lives. In the 2016 Management Agenda, the majority of managers at all levels reported not having enough time to get work done and lacking control over key features of work, in particular the pace at which work is done. This was especially the case for junior managers who reported having considerably less control over a number of features of work than their more senior colleagues.

It seems then that the sheer volume of work and worries about it may be spilling over into what is meant to be time away from work. For many people with jobs, work has come to define how they view their entire lives.

Nearly one in two (44 per cent) managers, rising to 59 per cent of junior managers, said that their level of stress had increased over the previous six months. Junior managers were less likely to feel that their job was secure (42 per cent of junior managers compared with 52 per cent of senior managers who felt that their job was secure); or that they were fairly rewarded financially for the work they did (49 per cent of junior managers compared with 65 per cent of senior managers felt that they were fairly rewarded financially). Both these factors may, at least in part, explain the increased stress levels reported.

Ability to cope?

Moreover, in today's connected era, mobile technology and social media were reported to be extending the work world beyond the confines of the job, blurring the lines between work and non-work. One fifth of 2016 Management Agenda respondents found the constant connectedness offered by the smartphone in their pocket, and the need to be 'always on', a source of stress. In some cases, this pressure (whether perceived or real) was experienced as 'pervasive' or 'relentless'. One interviewee described the expectation in her organization to respond to out-of-hours emails as a 'hierarchy of who is most committed, in the same way that the hours you put in at the office used to be'.

On the other hand, 31 per cent of managers felt that the abundance of social media and mobile technology was having a positive impact on the balance between their work and home life. And in spite of much discourse on the evils of the abundant technology at our fingertips, the main positives cited in interviews included the ability to work from home, to work whilst travelling and in other locations and to be able to work flexible hours. Some people spoke at length about the need to 'feel connected' and the benefits of this not only for the business, but for them as an individual. Overall, it would appear that UK managers recognize and experience the pitfalls of the 'always-on' culture as enabled by mobile technology and social media, but regard these potential risks as secondary to the benefits offered in terms of speed, agility and connectedness.

A better work–life balance

Despite not having enough time to get work done and worrying about work outside of hours, the vast majority (66 per cent) of managers reported having a satisfactory balance between their work and home lives. This may perhaps be linked to the gradual recognition by employees that they alone must strike the right balance for them between work and non-work activities. Only a few (paternalistic) employers appeared to force the issue by deliberately role modelling new practice, or introducing new customs such as 'no-email Fridays'. This may also reflect the embedding of the 'employability thesis' (Rajan, 1997) and the 'new deal' (Herriot and Pemberton, 1995a).

Throughout this period, there has been a growing popular focus on self-help with regard to coping mechanisms, with publications and reports galore on themes such as 'mindfulness', neuroscience and thinking skills (fast and slow – Kahneman, 2013) selling in large numbers. Roffey Park's research on personal resilience (Lucy et al., 2014) has suggested that maintaining a sense of perspective about work is a key capability for developing personal resilience, including not allowing work to encroach and overshadow other parts of one's life. It would

72   *Context*

seem, then, that some employees have managed to adjust to their demanding work conditions, perhaps by building their capacity for resilience.

Conclusion

We have considered how the 'new work culture', described by Sennett, was becoming a reality for many employees – both blue- and white-collar – from the late 1990s on. Its features included degraded work conditions resulting from work intensification and reduced job security, declining job quality and loss of autonomy, as Braverman had predicted. In terms of how the employment relationship was shifting, Herriot and Pemberton (1995a) contend that the 'new deal' is mitigated by perceptions of unfairness in terms of workloads, equal opportunities, bullying in the workplace, pay and performance and working conditions. They argue that, from an employee perspective, the 'new deal' is violated mainly in these areas rather than by changes in career practice. This would seem to be the case for the majority of Agenda respondents.

The majority of Management Agenda respondents experienced the new work culture as stressful and demanding, and continue to do so. It would therefore seem that, for many employees, the social exchange and effort–reward ratio became, and remains, unbalanced. Much of the recent survey data suggests that in real terms, change is not being managed any more effectively than in the past. Moreover, despite all the promise that technology offers, we seem to be working harder, not smarter. Far from liberating people, technology has indeed 'enslaved' them as Schumacher (1974) claimed. In that sense, the capitalist machine is voracious and unforgiving.

Braverman's (1974) book highlights the unfairness and imbalance inherent in capitalist employee relations and the seemingly inexorable advance in the process of degradation. With little employment protection, white-collar workers become subject to commodification. The Agenda findings suggest that the individualized nature of the employment relationship appears to leave British employees very exposed to the vicissitudes of the market and at the mercy of employers in the new work culture.

Key organizational players within this new work culture are representatives of capital, including managers, leaders and HR professionals who devise and implement policies and working practices supportive of the new culture, as well as employees themselves. Employees whose skills are in significant demand may find negotiating an individualized deal (Rousseau's i-deal, 2005) is not so difficult. However, the extent to which we will see the renegotiation of psychological contracts between organizations and their managerial populations remains debatable (Doherty et al., 1997). It seems unlikely that individual employees who are not elite 'symbolic workers' (Reich, 1991) really have sufficient power in the employment relationship to negotiate a psychological contract truly based on the principle of mutual benefit. More research will be needed to understand the differentiated contracts for 'talented' employees and the relative benefits for employee and employer.

It is possible that future workforce generations will be better equipped to cope with the demands of working in the new work culture and be less prepared than their predecessors to put up indefinitely with a lack of work–life balance or with an unbalanced social contract. Given the significant changes in the composition of today's labour market, more research is also needed to explore whether today's more mobile, diverse, global and increasingly multigenerational workforces are looking for different psychological contracts from their forebears. And given the variety of organizational forms and working arrangements which are emerging, there are likely to be a multitude of psychological contract types.

There are now a number of studies looking at the psychological contracts of contract workers, of workers in call centre environments, of people working in cross-boundary partnership arrangements (Marchington et al., 2005). Within 'boundaried' organizations, more research may be needed to explore whether it is possible for the majority of employees who become 'plateaued' to not only remain productive but also 'psychologically satisfied' and keep their jobs!

In presenting these findings I am aware of a number of limitations, both in the data and in the generalizations I am making from these. I have aimed for breadth and overview, rather than depth and specificity. Therefore, limitations could be placed on the inferences that can be drawn from this study since, in this necessarily selective, re-presentation of the original material, I may have tended to select data that supported my argument and downplayed counter-evidence. I may therefore have overlooked and failed to report some of the positive responses to the new work culture. I have been aware of this risk, and have attempted to achieve some balance in the reporting.

Moreover, I am not relying solely on the Agenda data to explore the nature and impact of the new work culture on the while-collar psychological contract. The Agenda provided the spur to the qualitative research, through which I explore aspects of the nature and impact of the new work culture more in depth. These include the themes of performativity, which we shall examine in Chapter 6, and meaning (Chapter 9). In addition, I explore the perspectives of HR practitioners on the role of HRM in embedding the new work culture in the next chapter. I believe that, taken together, these research strands build up a rich picture of the changing work world during the first decade of the twenty-first century.

Notes

1 The Sarbanes–Oxley Act of 2002, also known as the 'Public Company Accounting Reform and Investor Protection Act' and the 'Corporate and Auditing Accountability and Responsibility Act' is a United States federal law which set new or enhanced standards for all US public company boards, management and public accounting firms.
2 The Higgs Report (2003) reviewed the role and effectiveness of UK non-executive directors.
3 The Tyson Report (2003) reviewed the processes for the recruitment and development of UK non-executive directors.

Section II

Managerialism and HRM

5 The HRM 'project'

> We can now say with increasing confidence that HRM works. But this is a skeletal finding and we need to put a lot of flesh on the bones.
>
> (Guest 1997b:274)

A central argument of this book is that, within the 'work culture of new capitalism', white-collar work and workers have become progressively degraded and commodified by managerialism and that this exemplifies the Marxian contention that capital progressively dominates and deskills labour and subsumes knowledge artefacts for profit. Braverman predicted that deskilling would be achieved through latter-day Taylorism, the essential elements of which, according to Braverman (1974: 119) are the: 'systematic pre-planning and pre-calculation of all elements of the labour process which now no longer exists as a process in the imagination of the worker but only as a process in the imagination of a special management staff'. HRM theory and practice, it could be argued, represent the site *par excellence* where this process occurs.

In this chapter I shall review some of the main conceptual moves which feature at the core logic of HRM and its role in the development of a 'new work culture'. I outline some of the central debates relating to the purpose, nature, role and impact of HRM on organizations, work and workers. In doing so, I will draw on literatures of HRM, organizational behaviour, labour relations and strategic management to explore the managerialist functions and justifications for employment practices under the rubric of human resource management.

Within managerialism, HRM has emerged and become consolidated around a particular framing of work, management and identity which places subjectivity and a particular kind of 'self' at the centre. 'Work' has become the ground upon which the modern 'self' defines its life. In later chapters I shall explore in more detail the ways in which subjectivity and 'work on self' have become central to work and management in contemporary organizations.

More specifically we shall consider:

- The contested nature of HRM.
- HR's functional transformation journey.
- Perspectives on the employment relationship.

Human *resource* management

In recent decades, HRM has come to be the preferred international discourse to frame employment management issues. It has also emerged as a pervasive theme in the literatures of organizational behaviour, strategic management, business policy, international and inter-cultural management. As a field of practice, HRM and its sister disciplines – human resource development (learning and development), organization development (OD), compensation and benefits and so on – differ significantly in a number of ways. Indeed, the depth of research

78 *Managerialism and HRM*

in the HR subfunctions has grown enormously over the years and some areas, such as human resource development and OD, can rightly claim to be fields in their own right. However, I am focusing here on the common strands these subfunctions and organizational disciplines share with respect to the influence of HR over organizational effectiveness.

The nature of HRM is contested and its practice within organizations is often constrained and determined by dimensions of size, structure and culture. However, there is some consensus that HRM is a business concept reflecting a mainly managerial view of the employment relationship, with theory, policies and practices geared to enabling organizations to achieve flexibility, competitive advantage and high performance through people. Thus the field of HRM provides a framework for analysis of a wide range of issues relating to work and work organization, management policy and practice, employee resourcing and development, organizational culture, employee motivation and performance as well as employee relations and employment regulation (Boxall et al., 2007).

As with management studies, there are two broad categories of theory within the growing theoretical field of HRM: mainstream and critical. The dominant managerial mainstream offers many models of HRM theory and encompasses 'hard' and 'soft' approaches (which will be discussed later in this chapter). In American and British models of HRM, the predominant view is unitarist, i.e. it assumes that employees and employers are united in the common endeavour of achieving business success. Such views represent a legitimizing management point of view. The organizational effectiveness task of the HR function is to secure the people the organization needs and to bind employees tightly to the production of the organization's goods and services. One definition of HRM is:

> A philosophy of people management based on the belief that human resources are uniquely important to sustained business success. An organization gains competitive advantage by using its people effectively, drawing on their expertise and ingenuity to meet clearly defined objectives. HRM is aimed at recruiting capable, flexible and committed people, managing and rewarding their performance and developing key competencies.
>
> (Price, 2003: 31)

This overtly unitarist and managerialist framing of HRM has progressively edged out pluralist perspectives on the employment relationship, including what are described as 'traditional' personnel management or old-style industrial relations (Francis and Sinclair, 2003; Wright and Snell, 2005).

The other category of theories derives from critical management scholarship and is known as critical HRM (CHRM). This disparate field encompasses critical versions of postmodernism (Alvesson and Deetz, 2005) and radical humanist approaches (Burrell and Morgan, 1979), among others. Watson (2010) defines human resource management as the

> managerial utilisation of the efforts, knowledge, capabilities and committed behaviours which people contribute to an authoritatively co-ordinated human enterprise as part of an employment exchange (or more temporary contractual arrangement) to carry out work tasks in a way which enables the enterprise to continue into the future.

As Watson points out, the use of the term 'authoritatively co-ordinated enterprise' in this conceptualization is a recognition that human resource management, in the modern world, is utterly and absolutely a bureaucratic phenomenon. In Weber's (1978 [1922]) ideal-typical characterization, bureaucracy involves the control and coordination of work tasks through a

The HRM 'project' 79

hierarchy of appropriately qualified office holders, whose authority derives from their expertise and who rationally devise a system of rules and procedures that are calculated to provide the most appropriate means of achieving specified ends. In this characterization, HRM is primarily a control function.

Critics argue that the mainstream largely ignores the Marxist view that the employment relationship has been characterized by 'three great struggles' – over interests, control and motivation: 'In one respect "HRM" is merely the latest managerial discourse deployed to massage the perennial issue of how to optimize labour costs and ensure employee performativity while simultaneously stimulating and maintaining employee motivation to work' (Keenoy, 2009: 466).

The emergence of HRM

Jacques (1999) argues that the origins of 'HRM' can be found in the ideas which emerged between 1900 and 1920 from the historical conjunction of scientific management, the employment managers' movement and industrial psychology. Others argue that HRM's beginnings can be traced to Walker's (1978) call for a link between strategic planning and human resource planning.

With regard to the HR function itself, both practical mainstream business discourse and academic textbooks transitioned during the 1980s from speaking of 'personnel management' in favour of 'human resource management' (often modified with the related terms 'strategic' or 'strategy'). That's because, as strategy literature moved away in the 1980s from looking at external factors (such as industry position), it looked towards internal firm resources as sources of competitive advantage (Hoskisson et al., 1999). Resource-based theory and the resource-based view of the firm (Barney, 2001) in particular were influential in the development of HRM as a subfield of managerialism.

Beer et al. (1984) were the pioneers of this 'new HRM paradigm' with their concern to make corporate HR functions more 'strategic' (Boxall et al., 2007: 34). They saw HRM as a synthesis between labour relations, personnel and organization behaviour/development. As Boxall et al. put it, this means treating HRM as 'a broad generic term equivalent to "labor management"' (2007: 49). Beer and colleagues' Harvard model (Beer et al., 1985) suggested effective organizations should serve the needs of a range of stakeholders, not simply shareholders. The Harvard style of HRM displays tendencies towards developmental humanism, stresses cooperative labour process and not overtly coercive employment governance. More recent 'employee engagement' initiatives are heir to this tradition.

While the Harvard model was analytically better than the Michigan model, it was complex to use and fell away in practice. The more prescriptive and normative Michigan 'matching model' (Fombrun et al., 1984) focuses on links with strategy and proposes that, for competitive advantage to be gained, a tight fit is needed between human resource strategies and the overall (and predominantly short-term) strategies of the business. Policies for managing people should be integrated with strategic business planning and organizational culture.

More recently, Ulrich's (1997) work, which has been influential with practitioner audiences, emphasizes the primary role of the HR function as creating 'value' for business and its stakeholders, including customers and investors. Across the Western world and beyond, a raft of practices has emerged that attempts to ensure that people management within an organization is successfully aligned with business strategy in the hope of facilitating success. Critical scholar Keenoy (2009: 466) argues that HRM, which began as a local US cultural artefact, has emerged as a global naturalized discourse which informs the social practice of international corporations.

80   *Managerialism and HRM*

David Guest (1987) presents a normative model of HRM that defines functional areas of personnel management and sets an agenda regarding what HRM must achieve – which includes integration of HRM to organizational business strategy, employee commitment, flexibility and quality. He represents HRM as having two focuses within a single framework with specific links that can be tested. Guest argues that HRM's scope extends beyond that of personnel management since it is both a new way of managing people and also focuses on creating a workplace culture that leads to employee commitment to the organization.

Those who view HRM as simply a new, commodified form of managing employment argue that the stimulus for the development and application of new managerial techniques and the demand for cooperation and commitment in labour relations was aided by the socioeconomic, legal and political changes of the 1980s, in particular the intensification of international competition (Foley et al., 1999; Scott, 1994).

As discussed previously, the development and expansion of HRM in the UK since the late 1980s, at the expense of personnel management and industrial relations, reflects the perceived political need to expose all parts of the UK economy to the values of business. HRM's task is to achieve a closer functional relationship between the needs of business and 'human resource' practices.

HR's own change journey

Within the mainstream HRM discourse, the case has long been made for the HR function to provide cost-efficient and effective HR services that are perceived to add value to its 'customer base', including employees, line managers, the senior management team and relevant external stakeholders. The HR transformation agenda is also being shaped by talk of 'reputational drivers' – as employers seek more sophisticated technocratic means to link their people strategy and company brand in order to achieve differentiation in the labour market (Martin, 2008; Leary-Joyce, 2004).

These issues can be understood within the long-running debate about the changing roles of HR professionals (e.g. Legge, 1995; Tyson and Fell, 1986; Ulrich, 1997). As a result of its unitarist and technocratic (Alvesson and Willmott, 1996) framing, the HR function has itself undergone large-scale structural transformations in HR service delivery to reduce costs, increase firm competitiveness and achieve a tighter alignment between HR practices and business strategy. Such transformations are presented as 'self-evident', urgent and inevitable, and the morphing of ordinary HR practitioners into HR business partners is seen as a natural step in the evolution of HR work in a globally competitive environment (Ulrich and Brockbank, 2005). It has also to a large extent obscured questions around HR's role in advocating employee wellbeing, a theme that I will develop throughout this book. The evolution of the HR function is summarized in Table 5.1

A specific contribution to the emerging form of HR structures was the publication of Ulrich's book *Human Resource Champions: The Next Agenda for Adding Value and Delivering Results* (1997). Ulrich promoted a business-oriented philosophy of HRM and proposed an HR Business Partner model by which HRM was urged to align itself with business strategy and so organize itself to be able to 'partner' with the business. In its more developed form this would mean that HRM would be systematized and focused around an organization's strategic-planning functions where decisions about the deployment of staff are seen in relation to the financial and market pressures which impact upon it (Esland et al., 1999: 162). While there is no single model of business partnering, generally it is seen as a way forward for HR staff to build greater links with senior managers and the strategic aims of their organizations,

The HRM 'project' 81

Table 5.1 Evolution of Personnel

Approximate dates	Key business issues	Organizing principles	HR role	Title for role
1920s–30s	Organic growth New technologies	Time and motion Collective employee relations	Hiring, paying, training, caring for employees	Clerk Personnel
1940s–70s	Diversification Competition	Top down Low trust Administrative efficiency Pluralist ER	Productivity Negotiations Succession planning	Personnel Employee relations Labour relations
1980s and 1990s	International competition Survival Shift to services Differentiation	Centralized Formally defined roles Mechanistic Unitarist ER	Downsizing Compliance Leadership and high potential programmes Change programmes Performance management Competencies Rewards	Human resources
2000–10	Globalization Innovation Reinvention	Flattening of structures Decentralized Flexible roles Bottom up Improving performance Cost minimization and efficiency Fragmented unitarism	HR transformation Talent management and development Strategic capabilities Polarized 'deals'	Strategic HR Business partnering
2011–	Growth vs austerity Rapid technological advances Greater scrutiny Agility Knowledge management Organizational reputation Talent shortages Big data Partnering/ collaborating	Networked organization Fragmentation of roles Automation Maximum utilization Cultural transformation Adaptive workforce Optimizing diversity New pluralism?	Organization design, development and improvement Ethics, transparency, governance Leadership cultures Team development Sourcing scarce talent Simplifying HR policies Employee engagement, wellbeing and reciprocal commitment Internal communications	People and strategy

Adapted from a Mercer Delta slide presentation

so requiring them to gain and display greater business awareness and skills, and often internal advisory, coaching and mentoring skills (Caldwell, 2003).

The 'HR Transformation' agenda has spawned a rich stream of research into new HR service delivery models (e.g. Martin et al., 2008), typically exploring the application of

82 *Managerialism and HRM*

the 'Ulrich model' in order to fulfil its business function. In this discourse, HR work is considered too important to be left to HR managers, and is in fact ideally carried out by line managers and senior executives (Beer, 1997). In fact, line and general managers have been instrumental in the adoption of HRM – often pushing changes through despite the resistance of personnel specialists (Storey, 2001: 7). Integrated HR functions are being replaced (wholly or partially) with variations of the 'Ulrich' framework of operational delivery through shared services, 'centres of excellence/expertise' and business partnering, with strategic alignment achieved through a small corporate centre (Reilly et al., 2007; Reilly, 2009). 'Centres of expertise' refer to the concentration of advice on HR specialisms such as recruitment, development and legal services, often as part of a shared services centre (Reilly and Williams, 2003).

The development of shared services models is primarily driven by cost reduction and service-efficiency goals, with provision often outsourced to third-party suppliers. These represent a highly integrationist approach to centralizing HR administrative and operational processes, related to the desire of the HR function to make line managers and employees more responsible and accountable for their own HR data in the form of technology-mediated self-service often referred to as 'e-HR'. With respect to e-HR, the subtext could therefore be seen as largely Taylorist, as being about more centralized control (Pullen and Linstead, 2005), making people do more for less, putting workers under increased surveillance and increasing job instability as the employment relationship and the psychological contract are re-engineered.

As research into the field of HR transformation has grown, new theoretical frameworks have emerged to explore the 'absorptive capacity' of HR functions, and the problems faced in moving from face-to-face HR to a technology-mediated model associated with the segmentation of roles, the distancing of HR from employees and front-line managers and the imbalance between business–focused and people-centred roles (Martin et al., 2009; Hope-Hailey et al., 2005; Keegan and Francis, 2008). A relatively neglected area of research concerns the question of the potentially conflicted identities of HR practitioners with respect to the roles they are required to carry out under the HRM/business partner discourse. We return to this topic in Chapter 7.

These issues can also be understood as part of the debate about the centrality of line managers in the enactment of HRM practice (Purcell and Hutchinson, 2007; Purcell and Kinnie, 2006). This includes a body of literature that draws on the construct of the psychological contract and perceived organizational support to examine this pivotal role of line managers and associated 'black box' of processes that link HRM with organizational performance (e.g. Boselie et al., 2009; Purcell and Hutchison, 2007; Boxall and Purcell, 2008).

Mainstream HRM-P research

Organizational effectiveness is the concept of how effective an organization is in achieving the outcomes the organization intends to produce. This reflects a common belief in both the business and the academic world that the human 'resources' of an organization (more than the technology, products or marketing strategies), if well managed, can be a source of competitive advantage: 'The distinctive feature of HRM is its assumption that improved performance is achieved through people in the organisation' (Guest, 1997a: 269). The enduring assumption in most organizational theory is that there is a link between individuals' attitudes, motivations and behaviours and the performances they produce. For instance, the relationship between job satisfaction and job performance has been extensively researched since the 1970s but studies are often based on different assumptions and have different goals. Frameworks such as Attitude,

Motivation, Opportunity (Purcell et al., 2003) assume links between employee attitudes and performance.

In their meta-analysis of previous studies, Judge et al. (2001) found that, with regard to situational constraints, job complexity and autonomy play a moderating role. When there are fewer situational constraints and demands on behaviour, correlations between individual characteristics and attitudes (e.g. job satisfaction) have a stronger potential to affect behaviours (e.g. job performance), resulting in higher attitude–behaviour correlations (Barrick and Mount, 1993; Herman, 1973). The common theme of two reviews (Locke, 1970; Schwab and Cummings, 1970) was to issue a strong call for theory-driven investigations of the satisfaction–performance relationship.

Thus mainstream HRM research continues to be dominated by a concern with the HRM-P issue (Paauwe, 2004; Keenoy, 2009). This explores the links between HRM (people practices) and business performance; in particular, how the human resource function can deliver and develop 'human capital' by increasing employees' organizational commitment to, and identification with, organizational goals (Alvarez, 1997). The urgent issues within this mainstream HRM discourse are how to make HRM more effective in achieving managerial interests, and how to forge ever tighter links between HR work and firm financial performance. Increasingly the focus of much HRM research is on how HR functions seek to reduce costs or increase impact. However, there is a dearth of longitudinal studies to establish whether, and how, HR practices lead to high performance outcomes.

Variants on high HRM-P theory

Theorists take different positions with respect to if, and how, HR practices actually impact on organizational performance outcomes.

HRM is conceptualized in terms of carefully designed combinations of practice (variously defined and often referred to as the 'black box') that are geared to employee identification with the organization's goals and to enhancing organizational effectiveness and performance. Numerous studies by academics and management consultants have attempted to find causal links between particular 'bundles' of HR practice which simultaneously promote employee 'high commitment' and 'high performance' and produce measurable firm performance (Huselid, 1995; Purcell et al., 2003; Fleetwood and Hesketh, 2006; Guest et al., 2003; Wright and Snell, 2005).

Boxall and Macky (2009) explain that any 'HR system' encompasses two broad types of practices: employment (i.e. concerning the recruitment and deployment of workers in line with the job and organizational requirements) and work practices (i.e. the way work is organized, e.g. self-managing teams). It is argued that together these practices, embedded in an HR system, should affect performance on multiple levels from the collective to the individual (Purcell et al., 2003).

High-performance work systems

Amongst the HRM-P theories, high-performance work systems (HPWS) is the dominant approach and has its roots in the business strategy/resource-based view. The focus is on management techniques for building a productive work climate and high-performance work practices such as team working and so-called 'Japanese-management' methods, such as continuous improvement and 'six sigma'.

The trend towards HPWS was one of the top 'trends your organisation is embracing for the future' in the Roffey Park Management Agenda surveys of the early 2000s. These included

84　*Managerialism and HRM*

HRM-P elements such as self-managed learning; reorganizing; 'winning team' philosophy; European Foundation for Quality Management; flexible working/annualized hours; call centres; internationalization; and top-line growth. However, the practice of HRM reported in the surveys appeared implicit and unsystematized and what HR functions were actually focusing on was mainly transactional and operational in nature.

Recent, mostly American, HRM theory focuses on 'human capital' – its measurement, value and cost. Employees are seen as a means to the end of high performance. As 'human capital management professionals', HR practitioners are expected to play a key role in organizational performance, profitability and growth. They are increasingly required to act as finance professionals, measuring and monitoring workforce and talent initiatives with an understanding of how these impact the bottom line. Analytical links can be made with strategic workforce planning, for example. While evidence does suggest that there is an association between HPWS and financial performance, research typically focuses mainly on large organizations rather than smaller units and little attention is paid to employee wellbeing. The means to an end of this approach raises ethical issues too.

Best practice or best fit?

There has been extensive debate in recent years about whether HRM most effectively improves performance by applying universal 'best practices' in labour management, that advise managers how to manage labour better, or through 'best fit' (contingency) approaches, adapted to context. 'Best-fit' approaches became dominant by the 1990s, though earlier 'best-practice' emphasis has been revived in much of the writing on what is now called 'HRM', most notably in influential works by Pfeffer (1998), and is now evident in a range of studies which look for links between particular employment management practices and business performance (Becker and Gerhart 1996). For example, many contemporary studies in employee engagement, mostly conducted by consultancies, could be seen as seeking to identify universalist 'best-practice' approaches.

While opinion varies as to which HR practices are most closely correlated, if not causally linked with performance, the most extensively adopted performative practices within organizations include performance management and variable (performance-related) pay. Yet in real terms, the jury is out about if and how these links work.

'Hard' and 'soft' HRM

Further distinctions can be drawn between what Storey (1992) described as 'hard' and 'soft' versions of HRM. The 'hard' version focuses on cost reduction and containment, links with business strategy and the role of HRM in furthering competitive advantage. It is widely acknowledged to place little emphasis on workers' concerns and, therefore, within its paradigm, any judgements of the effectiveness of HRM would be based on business performance criteria. In contrast to the rhetorically dominant high-performance/high-commitment or 'soft' models of HRM, the 'hard' version of HRM tends to emphasize the value of data, risk assessments and measurements which attempt to tie HR activity to delivery of business strategy. 'Hard' theorists argue that HR practices will be contingent on context.

High-commitment HRM

The roots of 'soft' high-commitment HRM are in the changing nature of the employment relationship and build on human relations traditions. Early proponents include Walton and the

Harvard Business School (Beer et al., 1984). Some claim that HRM offers a new model of the management of people at work, based around attempts to increase their commitment (Guest, 1999). The task of this 'high-performance', 'high-commitment', 'high-involvement' HRM is to ensure that employees are 'engaged' in their work, 'aligned' to what the organization needs and managed in ways that enable them to perform at their best. This is achieved by inducing employee commitment through identification of the employee with the goals, values and brand of the firm. By so doing, Bunting (2004) argues, companies can both shape employee behaviour and also sell more products.

A key feature of new-style HRM practices is their focus on notions of high trust, high commitment, teamwork and increasing worker autonomy in the workplace, often grounded in the idea that employees can (and are willing to) become self-managing and self-reliant in ways that serve the firm's interests. While 'soft' HRM is therefore primarily concerned with business performance, it is also likely to advocate a parallel concern for workers' outcomes since its function is to identify employment practices directed towards winning the commitment of employees in order to build a common cause of organizational advancement (Guest, 1999; Walton, 1985; Kochan et al., 1986). Therefore, organizational effectiveness measures would focus not only on performance outcomes but also on worker wellbeing and engagement.

Today, typical employee engagement 'outcome' measures include performance variables such as discretionary effort – willingness to 'go the extra mile' – and commitment to achieving the organization's objectives; positive affect for the organization – organizational pride, loyalty and optimism for the future; positive identification with the organization – employee advocacy, willingness to recommend the organization as a good place to work, and overall satisfaction (Francis, 2003).

This notion of the self-reliant worker has led to increasing interest in the development of 'emotional capital', where employees are required to effectively manage their feelings and displays of emotion at work, arguably leading to a more, rather than less instrumental orientation of employees (Fineman, 2000). Employees are still seen as a means to an end. The nature of commitment required is to the organization rather than to the employee's own interests. Moreover, this approach lacks a comprehensive view of HRM.

High-involvement HRM

This approach has its roots in the nature of work and participation and recognizes that organizations have a variety of stakeholders. The central notion is that people should be involved in decisions that affect them. Leading thinkers include Lawler, Boxall and Macky. Lawler's (1986) 'PIRK' model of high-involvement work processes, developed in work conducted primarily in the private sector, recognizes that if employees are to help improve organizational performance, they must have *power* – especially in the areas of budget, personnel and work processes – to make decisions that influence organizational practices, policies and directions. However, power alone is insufficient; employees also need three other organizational resources that should be decentralized in order for employees to have the capacity to create high-performance organizations. These are: *information*, *rewards* and *knowledge*, which are seen as mutually reinforcing (Mohrman et al., 1992):

*   Knowledge that enables employees to understand and contribute to organizational performance. Knowledge includes technical knowledge to do the job or provide the service; business knowledge for managing the organization; and interpersonal, problem-solving and decision skills for working together as a team.

86   *Managerialism and HRM*

- Information about the performance of the organization. Such information includes data related to production (revenues, costs, sales, profits, cost structure); customer satisfaction; and benchmarks with other companies.
- Rewards for high performance, including adjusting the compensation structure to be aligned with the behaviours, outcomes and capabilities required for high performance. Employees may be paid on the basis of the knowledge and skills needed in the work environment to get the job done. There also may be performance-based pay that is allocated on a group or team basis and may include, for instance, profit sharing, gain sharing or group-based salary bonuses.

In summary, Lawler's model posits that knowledge, power, information and rewards create the conditions that enable employees within the organization to restructure for high performance. Yet this model omits many HR practices and take-up in large organizations is often limited.

Within the mainstream there is no overall theory of HRM or of how HRM affects organizational performance. Moreover, there is evidence to suggest, for example, that higher firm performance may be due to work intensification (Ramsay et al., 2000) rather than greater discretion or higher job satisfaction (Wood and de Menezes, 2011). Research into the potential effect of HPWS on employee wellbeing is rare (Harley et al., 2007; Boxall and Macky, 2014).

Indeed, research on the links between HR practices and firm-level performance is often managerially biased, with insufficient attention devoted to those at the 'receiving end' of HR policy (Boxall and Macky, 2014). Critics argue that the underlying premise of such approaches is that employees are passive objects to be moulded into appropriate attitudes and behaviours. The style of HRM discourse reflects how management controls the labour process. The language of mutuality ('people are our greatest asset') implicitly encourages employees to commit to the organization and to further its aims (Heffernan and Dundon, 2016).

These conflicting HRM priorities – of organizational identification and control/cost reduction – are reflected in the annual Management Agenda surveys between 2000 and 2016. The key organizational challenges reported by HR practitioner respondents were the retention of key employees, addressing work–life imbalances and also the need to change culture and drive performance improvements. Progressively the focus switched to improving the quality of line management. For instance, in 2006, HR staff recognized the need to address inappropriate leadership and management styles, to build succession plans and develop team working. However, while these were top priorities recognized by HR functions, in practice most HR teams in the 2006 survey were focusing on training and development, introducing performance management and modifying reward systems. As Guest (1987: 505) notes, 'there is a danger of confusing "management thinkers" with management practitioners and assuming that because human resource management is being discussed, it is also being practised'.

Does HRM really deliver performance?

With respect to theories that link HRM to performance, the field has moved on from rather simplistic models in the 1990s, in which HR practices were assumed to correlate directly to rather remote indicators of (financial) performance, to today's more sophisticated ways of thinking about the relationship between HRM and performance. 'High-commitment' practices in particular are commonly thought to lead to high performance since they are assumed to affect the attitudes and behaviour of employees at an individual level which, in turn, affect key behavioural or HR outcomes which, subsequently, might impact on organizational or firm-level outcomes.

However, the 'evidence' that has been presented about how HRM achieves its objectives is highly contestable, as is the meaning and role of HRM in relation to other business practices.

Notions such as 'empowerment', flexibility and organizational levelling were trumpeted in the 1980s as leading to an 'era of productivity and justice' (Humphries, 1998). As Dyer points out, 'these co-options have long been defrocked' (Grice and Humphries, 1997; Sewell and Wilkinson, 1992). For instance, with respect to 'high-performance' work practices, HRM came to be seen as an influential element in theory about the high-performance manufacturing organization, often referred to as the 'Japanese model'. The dominant discourse in this literature is about the apparent success of certain manufacturers in combining 'high-commitment' HR practices and HPWS 'team-based work systems' with the technical features of 'flexible production' plants such as Just-in-Time and total quality management and the 'lean-production' model of manufacturing management. The 'Japanese model' and lean production have been used to argue that employees no longer need the protection of trade unions from their employer since a new unitarism will characterize contemporary workplace relations.

The debate around 'Japanese practices' centres on whether this combination of tightly controlled technical systems with flexible, high-commitment, team-based social systems that incorporate increased worker skill and involvement is a 'universalistic model' which can and should be transposed, regardless of setting. Theorists question how well these new approaches are working in practice and whether the benefits outweigh the costs (Marks, 2000; Marks and Lockyer, 2004). Delbridge (1998), for example, in his study of two manufacturing plants using Japanese methods, found strong evidence to question the intentions of management at the plants with regard to worker participation and also that the workers themselves were not persuaded to contribute discretionary effort. The research shows that the workers at the two plants had not identified with, nor accepted, managerial goals. They were experiencing a harsh and coercive managerial regime and were complying because they believed that they 'had to'.

Manning (2010: 151) argues that, 'there is a need to question the veracity of the link between Human Resource Management (HRM) and performance'. Boselie et al. (2005: 80–1) analysed 104 studies of HRM and concluded that 'no consistent picture exists of what HRM is or even what it is supposed to do' and because of the 'sheer variety of methods used for measuring HRM, performance and the relationship between the two, it is not possible to compare results from different studies'.

Similarly, in a detailed analysis charting 25 years of HR practice in Great Britain, Guest and Bryson (2008: 142) observe that, although personnel management practice is now more embedded and more professionalized than in the past, overall results 'are almost the opposite of those we expected to find. There is precious little evidence to support the assumption that HR practices have improved performance.' They go on to suggest that where personnel specialists are present, including qualified specialists, performance tends, if anything, to be poorer. Despite this, the quest remains to increase profit and growth, as does the desire to control the behaviour of others in the interest of a very limited notion of efficiency and effectiveness.

Literature on implementation has instead examined the relationship between managers and employees. This raises challenging questions for the personnel profession and has also created residual analytical problems; in particular, a failure to develop a coherent theorization of HRM. This issue has increasingly exercised leading proponents of HRM (see Guest, 2001; Paauwe, 2004; Boselie et al., 2005).

So from a mainstream perspective, how can HR contribute to organizational effectiveness?

A significant movement of practice has grown in the UK with respect to employee engagement, with a variety of studies examining what appears to drive engagement as well as its links to business performance. More recent thinking has included a focus on HRM as a 'decision

88   *Managerialism and HRM*

science' (Boudreau and Ramstad, 2007) in which detailed analytics can play a part in pinpointing aspects of a firm's value chain where HR interventions – for instance to produce different behaviours and capabilities – can help improve a firm's productivity.

As Lawler (2014a) points out, HR's best route to developing effective organizations may be through a focus on talent and its procurement, development, retention and motivation. It's not a matter of just being a provider of good talent; it is important to identify the critical talent that makes a difference between the organization being effective and not so effective. Lawler argues that, if HR can identify key talent areas and provide coherent, well-developed plans for obtaining, developing and managing critical talent, it has opened the door to being a major strategic player with respect to organizational effectiveness.

Critical management and CHRM perspectives

As the debate about the HRM 'black box' has heightened, more intellectual space is being given to critical management studies in HR research (Delbridge and Keenoy, 2010; Spicer et al., 2010). Keenoy (2009) argues that the adoption of the managerialist conception of the discourse of HRM which has come to dominate research over the last 30 years has meant that the analysis of employment management has become increasingly 'myopic and progressively more irrelevant to the daily experience of being employed' (Keenoy, 2009: 456).

According to Watson (2010), CMS's motivating concern is the social injustice and environmental destructiveness of the broader social and economic systems that these managers and organizations serve and reproduce, rather than focusing simply on the practices of managers themselves. In this respect, CMS has an explicitly political agenda which draws its inspiration from an eclectic mix of Marxian, Weberian, post-structuralist and humanist roots. As Watson points out, such a position stands in sharp contrast to mainstream management research, both by reintroducing pluralism and by analytically privileging a concern with the structures of domination and the distribution of power within and between organizations.

The strand of studies called CHRM is wide and diverse. It is beyond the scope of this book to provide a comprehensive review of CHRM literature, so what follows is necessarily a selection of current debates within the field. Key critical research themes include the control of employee subjectivities (Rose, 1999; Alvesson and Willmott, 2002), the management of meaning (Gowler and Legge, 1983) and the cultural construction of employee identities (Keenoy and Anthony, 1992). The most common methodology employed by critical theorists is some form of discourse analysis.

For Keenoy (2009: 466), what unites all CHRM perspectives is a concern with the absence of any meaningful consideration of social power, differential interests, cultural variation and potential value conflict in the HRM literature. Watson (2010) summarizes three broad themes which characterize the CMS/CHRM agenda and have direct relevance to a contemporary understanding of HRM. These are an overriding emphasis on the socio–political context of social action; a wide-ranging critique of management discourse (or 'denaturalization' – see Chapter 6); and a concern to include excluded and alternative voices in any account of management practice.

Emphasis on the socio-political context

In contrast to mainstream HRM theory, with its primary focus (echoing the philosophical concerns of market individualism) centred on the psychology of the employee and on such factors as individual motivation, discretionary effort and commitment, CMS assumes that the practice of management can only be understood in the context of the wider socio–economic, political and cultural factors which shape – if not determine – those practices. Of fundamental significance here are the essentially capitalist economic relations which are seen to regulate the global economy.

Legge (1995) was among the first of the commentators who critically questioned the consequences for HRM of the economic determinism of neo-liberalism. Legge's work (2001) critically evaluates and confronts the rhetoric of organizations with the realities of practitioner existence in a post-modern context (Keenoy, 1999).

Reality versus rhetoric

For critical theorists a recurring theme is the guise of mainstream HRM in purporting to represent a new, more altruistic form of employee management when, in reality, it constitutes a rational response to wider, contextual drivers. In a flexible labour market, the driver is to reduce fixed costs such as labour.

Based on the Roffey Park surveys, I argue that the 'hard' or cost/control function of HRM was dominant throughout the first decade of the twenty-first century. In contrast to Walton's (1985) argument that HRM must move away from control to commitment styles, reported HRM practices in many organizations seemed to be more about control, resource and cost management. HR practitioners commonly reported introducing performance management and performance-related pay, running assessment processes, handling redundancies, dealing with grievances and employment tribunals and transfers of undertakings. Similar findings were evident in CIPD's Employee Outlook surveys from 2010 onwards. In other words, echoing Keenoy (1999), HRM has something of a 'wolf in sheep's clothing' about it.

In their analysis of HRM's contribution to the flexibilization of the UK further education sector in the 1990s, Esland et al. (1999) describe the agenda pursued by HRM as follows:

> Our central contention is that, in spite of its emphasis on employee development and the importance of skill enhancement through training, HRM is often perceived by both managers and those 'managed' as a means of reducing an organisation's human resource costs and of increasing 'flexibility' in staffing.
>
> (Blyton and Morris, 1992 in Esland et al., 1999)

Esland et al. (1999) point out that, in further education, HRM achieves these aims in two ways: first by enabling teaching inputs to the learning process to be redefined as a variable cost, so that greater output can be achieved for less. Second, HRM is capable of being deployed as a disciplinary instrument for the identification of 'underperformance' or inadequate commitment among employees, if necessary as a basis for downsizing, redundancy or casualization (Cunningham, 1997).

Similarly, Ball argues that, in teaching contexts, conflicting aims are achieved through high-commitment HRM: both an increasing individualization, including the destruction of solidarities based on a common professional identity and trade union affiliation, and the construction of new forms of institutional affiliation and 'community' based on corporate culture. HRM is thus both a means of proletarianizing professional skills and judgement and of achieving greater compliance and cost reduction.

How genuine is 'mutuality'?

Within mainstream HRM theory, mutuality of interest between employers and employees is emphasized, implying a social contract through which employees are governed but

90 *Managerialism and HRM*

receive benefits through which they are enriched and renewed. HR functional activity is conventionally aimed at attracting, motivating and retaining people through, for instance, developing an enticing 'employer brand', initiatives geared to 'employee engagement', opportunities for development and reward strategies. This assumes that employees and employers share a common interest in the success of the business and that what is good for the business must be good for employees. Walton (1985) defined HRM as 'mutual goals, mutual influence, mutual respect, mutual rewards, and mutual responsibility' and furthered the notion that HRM must enhance employee commitment and move away from control styles. As Legge (1995: 64) points out:

> The new HRM model is composed of policies that promote mutuality-mutual goals, mutual influence, mutual respect, mutual rewards, mutual responsibility. The theory is that policies of mutuality will elicit commitment, which in turn will yield better economic performance and greater human development.

Similarly, Walton (1985) further added that, although the 'psychological contract' under this high-commitment model is one of mutuality, it is a mutuality strictly bounded by the need to operate within an essentially unitary framework.

'Captured' by business agendas

Critics argue that, under HRM, HR itself has been 'captured' by business agendas. Braverman (1974: 415) considered Personnel/HR as 'unproductive' labour at the heart of the labour process, extracting surplus value on behalf of capitalists by 'riding on the backs of productive labour', who experience the personal consequences of deskilling, rationalization and hierarchy. The legal structures built around the employment relationship concern themselves both with ensuring that labour markets operate smoothly and with the need to protect employees from unfair practices. However, the overshadowing of organizational citizenship by commodity conceptualizations of work is evident in Ulrich's influential model of HR roles (1997), in which the roles of 'employee champion' and 'administrator' were considered to be tactical and therefore of lesser value than the strategic business partner and change agent roles. According to Esland et al. (1999: 178):

> To overcome the supposed burden of inflexibility, superstructural devices such as HRM and HRD are put in the service of change management, and employees, often unaware that they are now regarded as a variable cost, are actively encouraged to procure their place in the new flexibility, and to ignore the paradox that long-term employment is now based on an ability to move from one insecure job to another in a never-ending series, and possibly all the way to retirement.

Since the 1990s, HRM emphasis has moved away from attempting to change culture by altering employee values, to change programmes described as 'results driven' that focus on outputs/behaviours, based on the view that organizations can achieve fundamental change in employee behaviours in the short term through 'hard' structural change strategies that are more 'task driven' (Burnes, 2009; McHugh, 1997). For instance, advanced people analytics are increasingly used by HR practitioners to improve cost management and for better targeting of people practices. Emphasis is typically put on efficiency and effectiveness rather than on employee wellbeing, for instance:

- Effectiveness. Are your people programmes, policies and processes yielding the right outcomes? For example, if we are talking about the hiring process, improving effectiveness would result in hiring better performers over time.
- Efficiency. Can we get to the same outcomes in a shorter time span or by spending less money or with fewer people? In the hiring example, higher efficiency would result in a lower cost per hire.

Consequently, it could be argued that, since its inception, HRM's appeal to management was the claim that it was a route to high performance (Overell, 2005) and that 'soft' human resource management, in practice, was deployed in service of the managerial agenda to the disregard of workers' concerns.

Despite the unitarist rhetoric and implied mutuality statements such as 'our people are our greatest asset', which may be true in the case of a relative minority of exceptional employees, people are commonly viewed as an organization's greatest cost. A win–lose relationship can occur where the application of HPWS can lead to negative employee outcomes for employees such as longer working hours, increased job demands and stress (Cafferkey and Dundon, 2015). Similarly, based on an analysis of large-scale British workplace data, Peccei (2004) questioned whether the set of HR practices that are good for management, from the point of view of enhancing productivity, for example, are necessarily equally good for employees in terms of enhancing their wellbeing. Ramsay et al. (2000) suggest that performance gains are usually made through increased control and work intensification rather than through increased worker job satisfaction. And despite invocations of shared organizational purpose, market-driven differentiated HR practices such as talent management and high rewards favour some, but not others. This may be one reason why so much attention has been paid to deconstructing the ethical pretensions of the discourse of HRM.

Herriot and Pemberton (1997: 46) argue that, with the advent of HR ideology and practice, the implicit assumption in many formulations (that employees are human capital to be deployed in the interests of business) has frequently been expressed in practices which operate upon that human resource without its consent. This clearly raises important questions about potential trade-offs between organizational performance and employee wellbeing in contemporary organizations, and the role that HRM plays in such trade-offs (Peccei, 2004). Paauwe (2007) argues that more research is needed to examine the benefits of a 'value-laden' approach for management as well as for employees and other stakeholders.

The 'new industrial relations'

This suggests that an understanding of how the employment relationship is structured and regulated, and a concern with how managers manage such endemic potential conflicts, ought to be at the heart of HRM. At present, this is not the case: the employment relationship is treated very much as a given, part of the 'background' context; and its complex impact on managerial practice is of marginal concern (Boselie et al., 2009; Keenoy, 2009).

Frames of reference on the employment relationship

This leads us to consider different frames of reference with respect to the employment relationship, i.e. the essential ideologies that underpin them and to some degree define how work, and the relationship between employer and employee, are viewed by most employment relations

92 *Managerialism and HRM*

scholars, policy-makers and practitioners (Budd and Bhave, 2008). The employment relationship is the fundamental socio-economic axis which articulates any and all varieties of HRM policy and practice (Delbridge and Keenoy, 2010). Similarly, the nature of work itself is a key variable influencing the choice of HR policy. This highlights the argument that different technological, labour and market contexts may require different HR management strategies and practices.

Budd (2010) defines four alternative models of the employment relationship – Critical, Pluralist, Egoist and Unitarist – together with their related perspectives on work.

Critical

Marx argued that the interests of owners and their representatives (managers) and those of workers were inherently in conflict. The employment relationship is therefore one of an unequal power relation embedded in complex socio-political inequalities (Budd, 2004), with markets representing one element of these. Managers and workers are locked into a relationship that is both contradictory and antagonistic, what Edwards (1986) calls 'structured antagonism'. This is typically cast within the familiar terrain of management seeking to maintain control and generate worker consent, creativity and commitment (D'Art and Turner, 2008). Work is seen as deeply human, about identity, citizenship and caring for others.

Edwards (2003) posits a radical, Marxian view of the employment relationship as follows: 'The employment relationship is about organizing human resources in the light of the productive aims of the firm but also the aims of employees. It is necessarily open-ended, uncertain, and, as argued below, a blend of inherently contradictory principles concerning control and consent.' The contract is indeterminate because although workers are the only people who produce a surplus in the production process, they do not determine how their labour power is deployed to meet the objective. So even though it may well be in workers' interests that a surplus is generated, this should not disguise the fact that they are exploited. Edwards' ideas have been criticized by Ackers (2014) who argues that, in a market economy, not all workers are treated the same way, nor are they all passive pawns of management, suffering as a result of having their talents exploited, illustrating his argument by highlighting the wide disparities of income generated by a factory worker and by David Beckham.

Marxist scholars such as Mandel (1973) argue that the structural crisis of late capitalism led to the reinvention of a more subtle means of control over labour – through worker participation. Burawoy (1979) suggests that capitalists (owners or employers) are increasingly using such methodology as a means of subtle coercion and to manufacture consent. Thus employer-initiated voice mechanisms are viewed as methods for increasing management's control of the workplace. Such practices may represent Marx's 'invisible power' whereby employees have 'false consciousness' or are unaware that it is not in their interests to be subservient to the organization. Scott (1990: 72) argues that Marx's 'false consciousness' occurs in 'thick' and 'thin' versions:

> The thick version claims that a dominant ideology works its magic by persuading subordinate groups to believe actively in the values that explain and justify their own subordination. The thin theory on the other hand maintains only that the dominant ideology achieves compliance by convincing subordinate groups that the social order in which they live is natural and inevitable. The thick theory claims consent; the thin theory settles for resignation.

In this frame, strong, militant labour unions are seen as important advocates for employees' interests. These can counter their exploitation under capitalism by mobilizing and raising

The HRM 'project' 93

the consciousness of the working class, and by fighting for improved compensation, better working conditions and greater control over workplace decision-making.

Pluralist

In contrast, (non-Marxist) traditional pluralists, such as industrial relations experts, argue that, since markets are imperfect, they need regulation. Conflict in the employment relationship is inevitable as the various parties' interests are different. Therefore, the employment relationship is a wage–effort bargained exchange between employers and employees, who have unequal bargaining power, such that employment outcomes depend on the elements of the environment that determine the other's bargaining power (Budd et al., 2004). In this frame, work is seen as occupational citizenship.

Pluralists propose that, instead of a unitary denial of any rational basis for conflict, managers should recognize the inevitability of disputes and seek means to regulate them, for instance through collective bargaining. From such a perspective, unitarism appears naïve, since as we have discussed in previous chapters, what is good for the organization is not always good for employees, and vice versa.

Scott (1994) puts forward two contrasting possible explanations for this seemingly passive acceptance by employees of the new balance of power within the employment relationship. On the one hand, as the old orthodoxy declined, the lack of employment protection afforded employees was accepted by some workers in return for higher wages, thus re-establishing a new wage–effort bargain. On the other hand, the more collaborative working relations between management and unions in the form of 'partnership working' in recent years may reflect their increasing consensus and 'realism' about the necessity for change given the challenges of the increasingly competitive global marketplace. Most unions now feel that, with the increase of individualism, partnerships are the only way they can be involved in employee negotiations (Blyton and Turnbull, 2004). Similarly, a growing number of organizations within the UK have replaced union presence with 'partnerships', though these do not have the power to change a corporate agenda. Moreover, many new workplaces, especially those in international, more knowledge-intensive and the creative industries, have preferred not to recognize unions at all (Millward et al., 1992). With relatively little employment protection, despite European employment legislation, and low job security, many employees have had to accept an extension of managers' prerogatives.

Equity and voice are therefore very important for human dignity and freedom. Voice is frequently seen as industrial democracy that requires collective voice mechanisms that are legally and functionally independent of management, such as works councils or labour unions to ensure free speech and due process protections.

Egoist

In this frame, employment is a mutually advantageous transaction between self-interested legal and economic equals in a free market. Work is viewed as 'lousy' and commoditized, to be endured in order to earn money (Budd, 2004). Yet for some workers, such a free market experience can be advantageous since they can come and go as they please if they have transportable skills.

Unitarist

In the reframing of Personnel as HRM, the fundamental discursive shift, as Keenoy (2009: 460) points out, is the replacement of the pluralist framing of the employment relationship

94 *Managerialism and HRM*

(in which it is assumed to recognize and institutionalize different interests) with a 'unitary' framing of issues (in which all members of an organization are assumed to have harmonious and mutual interests). Work is seen as a source of personal fulfilment.

In this sense, HRM advances a 'vision of the ideal organisation which amounts to a sophisticated unitarism…its policy prescriptions have advocated practices which have inhibited employees' belief that their interests were separate and distinct from those of management' (Scott, 1992: 12). Within the perspective of a more modern, sophisticated unitarism, managers have been encouraged to refashion employee relations in ways that have encouraged workers to relate to the organization as individuals, rather than primarily as members of a distinctive interest group.

The high-commitment/involvement HRM perspective proposes that employees are partners within the organization, that they can wield the same power as their employers. From this 'high-commitment' perspective, it is rare for texts on HRM to conceive explicitly of the employment relationship in terms of the contested nature of work (Marchington and Wilkinson, 2005). There is no mention of worker interests or trade unions, nor is there any wider concern about social justice and the uneven distribution of rewards. Conflict within the employment relationship is seen as an aberration, to be dealt with on an individual basis. Indeed, Budd argues that in the unitarist employment relationship, the presence of a union is interpreted as a signal of poor managerial methods since managers are expected to align employee and employer interests.

Theoretically employees have voice – they are able to have a say over work activities and decision-making issues within the organization in which they work (Wilkinson and Fay, 2011). In contrast to the critics, mainstream HRM theories view positively cultural approaches that replace conventional industrial relations through direct communication, participation and employee involvement, whether these take the form of meetings for diffusing information or dialogue between managers and employees. Higher voice is reported to lead to higher employee engagement and lower emotional exhaustion (Conway et al., 2015). However, in practice, despite the growing use of social media for internal communications, the extent to which employees have the opportunity for direct involvement in decision making may be limited.

With its long and divergent history in organizational sciences (Morrison, 2014), the construct of employee voice lacks conceptual clarity (Dietz et al., 2010). Moreover, for Sennett, the advent of new information technologies has also changed the style and substance of management communications. With email, for instance, directives can now be communicated from the top of organizations to all staff without the need for mediating and interpretative layers of bureaucracy. Having delivered the orders, bosses expect them to be acted on immediately. Failure of employee communication programmes is commonly attributed to the lack of genuine intent to solicit and incorporate employees' views in business decisions (Dessler, 1994). In today's fast-changing environment, many employers are reported to be in a state of flux about giving greater decision-making to employees in order for them to feel empowered and to use their skills. Indeed, many managers are said to prefer tighter surveillance and control in order to increase a sense of predictability, as Gallie et al. (2001: 1090) point out: 'Organizational pressures may then have combined with technological opportunity to swing the balance from empowerment to control, irrespective of the costs in terms of the commitment of employees to their organisations.' Moreover, even where policies might purport to encourage 'direct involvement', Willmott (2003: 24) argues that, without collective employee relations, employees may be unable to make full representation of their views, leaving them vulnerable to coercion: 'Might it not be that the pressures placed on workers to conform to management plans have been increased?' The extent to which these practices are genuinely employee-centric, except for a few elite employees, is doubtful.

Discussion: power and differential interests

What pluralist and critical frames of reference have in common is their recognition of the relative and changing nature of the power distribution between employers and workers. Unitarism tends not to acknowledge this, so workplace change, for instance, may often be presented as if total unity can be assumed, even though employers and workers find themselves in different positions at different times and may experience different fates (Edwards, 1995).

The underlying premise of the unitarist managerial orientation of mainstream contemporary HRM theory is that employees are 'resources' and costs to be managed. In a market economy there are inevitable tensions between the 'buying in' and use of labour as a commodity and its human element. Moreover, when work is viewed as a commodity, its allocation is seen as governed by the impersonal 'laws' of supply and demand in a free market. On the supply side, work is something that individuals choose to sell in varying quantities in order to earn income.

Yet the extent to which workers can look after their interests depends to a large extent on their labour market value at any given time. The commoditization of labour will be more or less pronounced depending on the particular approach to people management and prevailing economic and political circumstances (D'Art and Turner, 2008). For instance, in a context of rising unemployment in the 1980s, many managers took advantage of their increased bargaining power afforded to them by applying measures to 'increase the degree of effort which the employee is expected to surrender to the firm' (Baldamus, 1961: 105–7). Moreover, as Sparrow and Cooper (2003: 85) suggest: 'The pursuit of downsizing and the intensification of work effort have not created the best conditions for implementing high commitment work practices in a coherent and sensible way.' Given the increasing flexibilization of the workforce, the growing use of contract or temporary workers, the increase in job insecurity, the rise in the measurement of performance and performance-related pay and the decline of collective protections through trade union membership, employers may have the dominant hand and many workers are likely to be treated simply as hired hands. In a purely contractual relationship, employees are unlikely to be consulted in the event of change.

On the other hand, in a more lasting employment relationship, members of an organization have rights which need to be respected; they might expect to engage in its key choices. After all, a truism of organization development theory maintains that giving workers a say in decisions that affect them may improve organizational functioning in some way (and is therefore more efficient), for instance through various direct participation such as team working or problem-solving groups. Despite this, many employers continue to impose change without involving staff.

Similarly, the different lenses on the employment relationship reflect relative balances of power in the labour market and in turn shape the nature of HR provision. In the egoist employment relationship, HRM practices are seen as essentially dictated by the labour market – where HR's challenge is not to pay too much for labour (and therefore raise employer costs) or too little relative to the value of workers at any given time (Befort and Budd, 2009). The pluralist perspective rejects a reliance on employer goodwill and HRM practices for serving employee interests (since by assumption there are some interests that clash) and elements of the internal labour market result from a mixture of pressures, such as economic efficiency, relative bargaining power and customs. From the critical perspective, HRM practices are not seen as

96 *Managerialism and HRM*

methods for aligning the interests of employee and employer, but rather as disguised rhetoric that quietly undermines labour power and perpetuates the dominance of capital (Budd and Bhave, 2008).

In the unitarist model, well-designed HRM practices are seen as the key managerial mechanism for creating profitable organizations because these practices are the way to align the extrinsic and intrinsic interests of employees and employers. These include such practices as 'soft' HRM, with its emphasis on training, career development, 'empowerment' and benefits typical of more traditional paternalist relationships that foster personal growth, security and work–life balance; and open channels of communication to prevent conflict. However, such practices also tend to be shaped by market dynamics and reflect the duality of 'hard' HRM control and coercion. For instance, in recent times, many employers have actively worked to reduce their pensions' and other obligations towards long-term staff.

The commodity conceptualization of work is embedded within the new individualized HRM industrial relations and reflected in HR practices which install and reinforce performativity. In essence, HR practices are intended to ensure that organizations have the people required, and the means of achieving performance from their workforces in the most productive and cost-effective way possible. The basis of shared purpose – the 'common goal' referred to by Scott (1994) – is about survival in the marketplace. Market survival applies not only to organizations but to individuals too: 'Employees are simultaneously required, individually and collectively, to recognise and take responsibility for the relationship between the security of their employment and their contribution to the competitiveness of the goods and services they produce' (Willmott, 1993: 522). Unless employees possess specific forms of labour power, they are essentially resources which can be deployed or dispensed with at the will of the employer. In practice, power in the employment relationship tends to be one sided, with the employer holding the largest share: 'the employment relationship, although it is contractually based and freely entered into, removes all the freedom of action from the individual' (Beardwell et al., 2004). Contemporary HRM practice may therefore be at odds with stereotypical organizational rhetoric such as 'our people are our greatest asset'. Ethics are subsumed within a taken-for-granted market mechanism. As Keenoy suggests (1990: 4), HRM practices may therefore have something of a 'wolf in sheep's clothing' element about them.

Excluded voices

What unifies the critical accounts is a concern about the absence of any meaningful consideration of social power, differential interests, cultural variation and potential value conflict in the HRM literature. As CHRM theorists point out, the fundamental shift in the move to HRM involved the replacement of a 'pluralist' framing of the issues – in which the employment relationship is understood to involve and articulate differential interests – with a 'unitary' and managerialist framing of the issues – in which all members of an organization are assumed to have mutual interests. Scott describes the 'new industrial relations' as comprising techniques which emphasize that employment should theoretically be founded upon extensive mutual obligations and a shared sense of dedication towards a common goal. In reality, mutuality of interest may be largely missing.

This mainstream framing of HRM has resulted in more and more alternative voices being excluded. Such a perspective 'naturally' marginalizes the possible contribution of those 'external' to the organization, such as the state or trade unions, as significant actors in devising HRM policies and practices. It also excludes overtly pluralist perspectives such as those described as traditional personnel management or old-style industrial relations (Francis and Sinclair, 2003), where HR practitioners had a clear role in balancing the interests of workers and employers. Within mainstream HRM literature there is little specific reference to unionized workplaces or to the rise in highly repetitive and highly programmed call centre work arising from the various forms of subcontracting to which HRM itself has been exposed in the pursuit of greater flexibility and cost-effectiveness (Deery and Kinnie, 2004). Other excluded voices in the employment relationship within mainstream HRM are non-Western, small and medium-sized firms, feminists and the potentially rich diversity of cultural influences thanks to globalization. Any employment relations not characterized by HR 'bundles' (MacDuffie, 1995) are marginalized or excluded.

The most obvious voices that are routinely marginalized in the evaluation and analysis of management practices are those of employees themselves (Delbridge and Keenoy, 2010). Scott (1994: 5) points out that, in practice, as the balance of power in the employment relationship has shifted towards managers: 'Driven by awareness of greater market competition, the ascendancy of "realism" may therefore have encouraged managers to believe that their decisions no longer required workers' approval.' Yet employees are, after all, the primary recipients and consumers of HRM. At best employees are assumed to have a passive role, irrespective of which approach is adopted (Grant and Shields, 2002). This includes managers who, more often than not, are subject to the same discourses of control as any other employees. Legge (1978) produced a highly sophisticated and innovative analysis of the personnel function which focused on the relative powerlessness of those entrusted with people management. The power relations implicit in such role relationships will be examined in Chapters 6 and 7.

Paauwe (2009) has argued for a wider and 'more balanced approach' to HRM research which attends to the concerns and wellbeing of employees, recognizes the potential differential interests of the various 'stakeholders' and takes a more multidimensional perspective on performance. I echo his call.

Conclusion

Despite the existence of critical research, the technical mainstream still prevails, thereby reinforcing rather than challenging technicist understandings of management (Grey and Mitev, 1995). The way performance is conceptualized in most studies looking at the impact of HRM on the employee is predominantly unitarist and managerialist (Boselie et al., 2009). The success of this discourse in academic spaces can be attributed, at least in part, to its resonance with broader socio-economic changes, including what Fairclough (2003: 4) describes as 'new capitalism', to refer to the most recent of a historical series of radical restructurings through which capitalism has maintained its fundamental continuity. Yet, even while critical stances are largely marginalized, so too 'the mainstream itself has, in turn, been largely ignored by practitioners' (Delbridge and Keenoy, 2010: 799).

In the next chapter I consider the role played by HRM practices such as performance management, in shaping the performative 'new work culture' and in securing worker compliance. In practice, HR's control function is potentially at odds with the dominant grand discourse of high-commitment HRM. After all, aligning people to short-term business agendas that require flexibility means that HRM's task involves loosening the in-built rigidity represented by an employment relationship within which employers showed real commitment towards employees by offering them longer-term job security. At the same time HRM demands commitment from employees, and focuses on increasing employee productivity through ever-tighter controls and performativity.

98 *Managerialism and HRM*

The contrast and tensions between these two roles give rise to what Legge (1995), refers to as the gap between rhetoric and reality and call into question the accuracy of mainstream research which has argued that HRM may win over workers' 'hearts and minds', provide better employment relations and secure for management the heightened commitment and obligations of workers. I shall argue that HRM practices are the site where the seemingly one-sided balance of power in the employment relationship is at its most obvious.

Points to ponder

- Is any form of participation scheme potentially a new way of bending workers to capital's demands?
- Is mutuality within the employment relationship achievable only when labour has equal or greater power than capital in the employment relationship?
- How might mainstream HRM include more excluded voices? What difference would this make to HR practice?

6 The shaping of subjectivities

> To work in this kind of organization, employees are expected to bring ever more of their subjectivity and put it to work producing economic value.
>
> (Brannan et al., 2011)

As we discussed in the last chapter, mainstream HRM theory emphasizes the importance of HR in creating coherence between organizational strategy and the management of employees, on the assumption that employees can make a major contribution to an organization's efficiency, performance and productivity if organized, developed and trained in line with organizational goals (Esland et al., 1999: 168). What is HRM's role in advancing the performative and flexible 'new work culture'? From an organizational effectiveness perspective, this involves HR creating the conditions within which people willingly do what the organization requires, and indeed demonstrate high levels of 'engagement', thus releasing their 'discretionary effort' on behalf of the organization.

This raises questions about how employees are controlled to meet the ends of neo-liberalism. How does HRM contribute to achieving employee compliance within the new work culture? After all, as discussed in Chapter 4, the increasingly performative new work culture is a harsh regime. CHRM scholars have argued that, while high-commitment HRM practices may provide enhancements in employee discretion, these come at the expense of stress, work intensification and job strain (Legge, 2001). They point to the controlling effects of the language of commitment and engagement, the potentially damaging consequences for human social relationships at work and for employee wellbeing, and the extent to which these pose a threat to employees, materially and emotionally.

Why do employees appear to have acquiesced to these working conditions, becoming 'willing slaves' (Bunting, 2004) to the demands made by employers? This suggests that the key to understanding group practices, such as acceptance of performativity, is through analysis of the reciprocal interaction between structure and agency.

In this chapter we shall consider if, and how, HRM discourse and practices help shape employee subjectivities and contribute to the development and perpetuation of the 'new work culture' of capitalism. First we discuss how HRM 'grand discourse' and related 'technologies of power' (Foucault, 2004) are used to engender employee compliance, causing people to moderate their behaviour in line with organizational expectations, even at cost to their own wellbeing. Then I shall examine how HRM mechanisms of performativity, such as performance management and performance-related pay, render employees as subjects, expose them to scrutiny and contribute to embedding a work culture of competitive individualism.

HRM grand discourse

Managerial discourses such as HRM are now central to the modern political, social and cultural body. These frame how people think about the world around them, their identity and, in the case

100 *Managerialism and HRM*

of HRM, the nature of the employment relationship. As an offshoot of managerialism, HRM's 'distinctive character stems from an attempt to persuade workers to give their best efforts to the enterprise for which they labour' (Scott, 1994: 4). For Keenoy (2009), the projection of a seemingly humanistic 'philosophy' of HRM, along with the deregulation of markets, was part of the strategic shift from state and collective regulation to the 'market' and 'management of meaning' (Peters and Waterman, 1982; Legge, 2005). Here, HRM represents a more insidious form of ideological control and identity appropriation, rather than offering any real substantive change in the employment relationship (Geary and Dobbins, 2001; Legge, 2005).

Critical management scholars contend that HRM discourse and practices aim to redefine how individuals relate to employers, with the aim of encouraging employees to align to a value system that prioritizes business values. For instance, Keenoy and Anthony (1992) argue that from the late 1980s onwards HRM has played a key role in manufacturing, mediating and administering cultural transformation in an environment of work softened up by recession and unemployment. They argue that the ideology of neo-liberalism and discourse of managerialism have been used to legitimate the status quo of power over the production process and play a role in continuing the gap between hierarchical control by capital/management and workers' democratic governance of their work. Underpinning neo-liberal thinking is the discourse of market individualism. 'Work' has become the ground upon which the modern 'self' defines its life.

It is argued that, as HRM has become discourse-driven, it has mobilized cultural resources external to work organizations to develop a variety of vocabularies and practices through which subjectivity has become the central element of the management of people at work. Signalling theory proposes that HR practices send signals to employees about expected workforce behaviours and managerial intentions (Den Hartog et al., 2013). The discursive attempt to leverage maximum advantage from what Legge (1995) calls the twin discourses of the 'market' and the 'community' – which differentiate the so-called 'hard' and 'soft' approaches to HRM – serve to conceal the tensions inherent in the management–employee power relationships and the gaps between rhetoric and the reality of employee or practitioner experience, as described by Legge (Delbridge and Keenoy, 2010).

'Human resources'

I argue that the discursive shift from the 'Personnel' to the human resource function in the 1980s represents more than just a change in jargon, but rather reflects a change in managerial mindset. 'Personnel' are persons and people, and as such, are subjects. 'Human resources', as assets and property for supplying 'some want', are objects. By applying managerial concepts such as 'customers', 'return on investment' and 'markets' to HRM, both the nature of work and labour itself become commodified (Grey and Mitev, 1995a).

Inkson (2008: 272) argues that, while treating people as a resource to be invested in, rather than as a cost to be minimized, is a 'step in the right direction', emphasis on the 'resource' metaphor means that labour continues to be treated as a commodity, to be used as management sees fit. As objects, employees may be treated discursively as one would with other 'material resources', making them subject to discussions of economic optimization, without recourse to analysis of the impact of actions on real human beings. As objects whose cost must be minimized, the discursive construction of employees as 'human resources' has then allowed for other managerialist discourses such as 're-engineering', 'right sizing' and 'outsourcing' to be normalized as the accepted direction of travel.

Critical scholars argue that managerial ideology promotes performance and competitive advantage as the 'natural' routes to follow for 'success'. For instance, Peters and Waterman (1982)

The shaping of subjectivities 101

argued that 'excellence' requires a 'strong culture' and that employees should be persuaded to 'buy in' to a managerially dominated labour process. The extensive business-driven restructuring of organizations of all sizes and sectors in recent years is often presented as an inevitable response to market requirements, rather than as a strategic choice which involves shedding jobs to save labour costs. After all, changes have been made over the years to work system design to accommodate the pursuit of agility. Labour flexibility and productivity are explicit or implicit goals for HR functions. Yet technology has often resulted in work intensification. More fluid organizational structures have been complemented by 'non-employment' options such as 'zero-hours' contracts.

As Dyer (2007) points out,

> The fashion-makers in management discourses of the 1980s, for example, took up notions of 'empowerment', flexibility and organisational levelling as heralding a 'new era of productivity and justice' (Humphries, 1998). These co-options have long been defrocked... Yet, this interesting wrinkle in the management literature seems not to have dented the overall embeddedness of the aspiration to increase profit and growth and the desire to control the behaviour of others in the interest of a very limited notion of efficiency and effectiveness.

Critics argue that such discourses work by:

> masking specific interest (e.g. capital accumulation of labour surplus into senior management/owners hands) through general theories, demonstrating how bourgeois conceptions of justice or democracy (e.g. Total Quality Management, Business Process Reengineering, team management) mystify capitalist hegemony (power manipulations that are too subtle to notice) over the working class.

(Best, 1995: 248)

For instance, Boje (2010) argues that Hammer and Champy's business process re-engineering reinforces Taylorist managerialism by bringing in expert 'science imitators' to divide the labour process into outsourceable chunks and to make designs more controllable by senior management. Boje critiques 'Japanese' management practices, including total quality management, arguing that, contrary to its rhetoric, total quality management does not promote democratic worker control but instead, like Taylorism, shifts worker knowledge to technocratic experts who tweak the system as a whole into higher states of centrally controlled labour process. By creating 'quality', 'customer visions' as in the general interest of workers, the particular interests of senior executives are masked by clever rhetoric. These managerial ideological assumptions and discourse become 'naturalized' and assumed to be the correct order of things. More broadly, from a critical perspective, HRM reflects: 'implicit issues of performativity, surveillance, information and communication technologies, empowerment, self-actualisation, the demise of hierarchies, individualism and instrumentality as well as aspects of consumerism and consumption-based values' (Foley et al., 1999: 170). This unitarist and 'technocratic' (Alvesson and Willmott, 1996) framing of HR transformation as 'natural' and 'self-evident' plays an important role in obscuring questions around HR's role in advocating employee wellbeing, a theme that I develop throughout this book.

The role of HRM in shaping employee subjectivity

A key thread running through my arguments relates to inherent tensions between employee agency (individual autonomy) and structures (social, political, cultural and economic forces)

102 *Managerialism and HRM*

shaping the new work culture. Critical researchers pay attention to the processes through which structured antagonism is realized, and to the discourses which are deployed to legitimize inequalities of power and persuade social actors to accept and endorse managerial objectives. From a critical HRM perspective, mainstream HRM practices and discourse are a managerial tool for controlling and managing the workforce in ways which are designed solely to meet business needs but which appear less directive than the command and control structures of previous decades. Such 'power-knowledge' mechanisms are thought to play a decisive discursive role in constituting employee subjectivities to ensure that employee performance(s) can be 'managed'.

Braverman (1974) contended that, under capitalism, workers became 'habituated' to comply with the mode of production by repeated detailed operations and various petty manipulations, rather than by coercion. But are employees merely passive objects moulded by, and complicit with, performative practices or are they able to exercise agency, if only in the form of overt or subtle resistance?

The manipulation of meaning

Much has been written about the politics, ethics and practicalities of 'meaning making' in the workplace which are reflected in the way the 'levers' of HRM draw on the language of commitment and engagement and are used to shape people's understanding and behaviours (e.g. Keenoy, 1997; Legge, 2005). Critics argue that mainstream HRM academics have provided an almost unique, humanistically inclined voice among the seductive, dominant discourses of 'business as usual' despite the adverse impacts of increasing competitiveness on the quality of life. Keenoy and Anthony (1992), for instance, argue that the language of HRM is riddled with metaphors and rhetorical devices used to hide the harsh realities of the 'Thatcherite' free enterprise effects on many businesses. They argue that managers become missionaries in this context, using the figurative language of HRM as an evangelical discourse to elicit enthusiasm and commitment from staff.

The ever-changing working conditions and concepts of flexibility, teamwork, decentralization, control and delayering are presented as offering new opportunities for self-fulfilment to employees, but in reality these create new forms of oppression, ultimately disorienting individuals and undermining their emotional and psychological wellbeing (Sennett, 1998). According to Sennett (p. 99), teamwork

> is the work ethic which suits a flexible political economy. For all the psychological heavy breathing which modern management does about office and factory teamwork, it is an ethos of work which remains on the surface of experience. Teamwork is the group practice of demeaning superficiality.

Because of the superficiality of content and focus on the immediate moment, because of the avoidance of resistance and deflection of confrontation within teams, the concept of teamwork is only 'useful in the exercise of domination' and has no further value (1998: 115). Similarly, the widespread UK Skills Survey (Felstead et al., 2007) found that 'teams' merely accentuate the stress and pressure experienced by employees by intensifying the control and monitoring of their work.

As we discussed in Chapter 4, the impact of organizational change on employees is often perceived by them to be harsh. Bunting (2004) argues that work has enslaved us, as it has taken over our consciousness, creating psychological hardships such as stress and burnout, with the result that other aspects of our lives suffer, such as family relationships. Bunting (2004) argues that the weakening of the trade union movement, neo–liberalism and New-Ageist ideology have all contributed to a work environment that is more and more intolerable for workers. Arguably these shifts have been enabled by the transformation of the white-collar employment relationship from one based on genuine mutuality to one in which the pretence of mutuality remains. Unitarism is manifest both in the HR pursuit of 'employee engagement' strategies and the separation of individuals on compromise agreements. Why do employees appear to have acquiesced to these working conditions? How does HRM discourse contribute to this?

Foucault theorized that it is through discourse that compliance is achieved. Discourse is a medium through which power relations produce speaking subjects. The individual is an effect of power. Foucault took the view that historically and culturally determined practices precede and form subjects. In other words, subjectivity itself, as a complex, contradictory and shifting view of the self, is transformed or reproduced through social practices, which express power (Knights and Willmott, 1989: 541). As Rowan and Cooper (1999: 2) put it:

> Within a modern world characterized by 'one man, one job' – along with such 'grand narratives' as linear development, progress, and the scientific search for truth – the notion of an autonomous, singular self, moving towards its own most future seems deeply credible, to the point of being transparent. But in a world characterized by multi-fragmented social positioning and the deconstruction of absolute truths, the notion of a unified self begins to stand out like a relic from a bygone era. In its stead, postmodern thinking has heralded the 'death of the subject' swallowed up by the 'blank and pitiless' (Gergen, 1991: 157) forces of language games, discourses and texts. From this perspective, subjectivity is no longer the writer but the written; no longer the signified but a signifier in a two-dimensional world of free-floating, interconnected signifiers.

In their sustained ethical critique of HRM discourse, Winstanley and Woodall (2000) argue that such quasi-normality contrasts starkly with the waves of dishonesty and venality common in the commercial world. With its stereotypical claim that 'people are our most valued assets' HRM is a discourse that encourages employees to 'work on self' often to the detriment of their own wellbeing. Even the language framing of 'soft' commitment-seeking models of HRM 'bespeaks passivity by the employee'. Wood (1999) argues that high-performance approaches or 'high-involvement' and 'high-commitment' practices, such as the development of shared visions, individualized reward and direct employee communications, are just another way for managers to gain control over labour through 'attitudinal restructuring'.

Willmott (1993: 517) goes further, arguing that many of the 'soft' or high-commitment best practice approaches to HRM amount to 'governance of the employees' soul'. From this position, the 'manipulation of meaning' by employers (Townley, 1998; Francis, 2007) and contemporary managerial rhetorical ambition now embraces 'the subject in its totality as an object of governance' (Costea et al., 2008: 670). As Ball (1994: 22) notes: 'We are the subjectivities, the voices, the knowledge, the power relations that a discourse constructs and allows.' But are employees powerless to resist and unable to exercise agency in such contexts? Understanding of agency within the field of HRM is relatively weak and both CHRM and HRM-P streams have been criticized for sharing a common view of the worker as essentially 'objects' that are being exploited for the benefit of the organization, thereby slipping into some kind of structural determinism (Fleetwood and Hesketh, 2010).

As discussed in Chapter 2, Giddens' structuration theory (1986) conflates structures and agents, seeing connections between the most 'micro' aspects of society – individuals' internal sense of self

104 *Managerialism and HRM*

and identity – and the big 'macro' picture of the state, multinational capitalist corporations and globalization. Archer (1995: 14) criticizes the 'elisionism' of Giddens' structuration theory, arguing that structure should be reconceptualized since today's context of rapid change represents 'untrammelled genesis between the cultural and structural domains', producing 'new games'.

Work on self

With respect to power relations Foucault (1980) introduces the concept of 'domination' to refer to the establishment of 'stable and asymmetrical systems of power relations' in which 'the possibility of effective resistance has been removed' (Patton, 1994:64). HRM also employs another technology of power – normalization – which achieves its ends by causing workers to 'work on self' to conform to what they believe is required of them. This works on the basis that those who wish to achieve 'normality' will do so by controlling their impulses in everyday conduct and habits, and inculcating norms of conduct into others, enforcing norms through the calculated administration of shame (Rose, 1999: 73). Graeber (2015) describes the normalization process involved in the structural transformation of universities over the past two decades. Whereas universities were once 'havens for oddballs', now academics must 'work on self' if they wish to fit in. As one academic put it, 'Now, if you can't act a little like a professional executive, you can kiss goodbye to the idea of an academic career'.

HRM practices

The second strand under discussion is how specific HR practices contribute to the degradation and the subsumption of white-collar professional work.

Box 6.1 Scientific management

Braverman (1974) contended that, given the dictates of capital accumulation, managements are constantly driven to renovate the productive process. Moreover, 'Management is habituated to carry on labor processes in a setting of social antagonism and, in fact, has never known otherwise. For corporate management this is a problem of costs and controls, not in "humanization of work"' (1974: 377). Thus, he argued, as long as labour tries to attain higher pay and benefits or improvements in the work environment, while at the same time management tries to reduce production costs, the distance between the goals and desires of two parties will grow.

Braverman considered that the capitalist labour process would seek to retain control of the labour process by subsuming the skills and knowledge of even highly skilled workers within managerial control systems, rules and procedures, reducing them to the status of routine production workers. Braverman also argued that the principal means for achieving this systematic deskilling and dehumanizing of labour in the twentieth century was the battery of techniques associated with scientific management and the scientific/technical revolution.

Within organizations, HRM functions exercise governmentality in a very real way since they organize practices (mentalities, rationalities and techniques) through which subjects (employees) are governed. Barbara Townley (1993, 1994, 2004), a significant exponent of Foucault's post-modernist notions, focuses on how HR practices impact on employee sensibilities and privilege the regulatory effects of such practices. These approaches include 'high-performance work practices', such as team working and performance management.

So is scientific management, or Taylorism, alive and well in the twenty-first century?

As discussed in earlier chapters, it could be argued that the drive for increased productivity and cost control has led to the development of a performative work culture. Performativity is a process rooted in the political economy that is deliberately geared to changing workplace cultures and underpins 'reforms' of the public sector to enable greater organizational flexibility and productivity (Organisation for Economic Co-operation and Development, 1995: 29). These shifts have involved 'giving managers greater freedom in operational decisions and removing unnecessary constraints in financial and human resource management' (p. 29). Critical scholars argue that mainstream HRM approaches construct a highly utilitarian approach to people management that form part of an array of means of securing management domination over work. They argue that the prevailing paradigm is one of performativity and the degrading instrumentality that this assumption engenders.

The nature of control exercised through performative HRM is both explicit and subtle. From an organizational perspective, 'HR practices send strong messages to individuals regarding what the organization expects of them and what they can expect in return' (Rousseau, 1995: 162). HR practices represent communications, 'calculated messages' or 'intended signals' regarding the relationship between the employer and employee. Townley (1993, 1994, 1998), drawing on Foucault, has argued that HRM practices such as appraisal and selection have an important shaping effect on employee subjectivities, discursively reconstituting them in line with local organizational objectives. This analysis of the discursive shaping of the individual project emphasizes the relational and constructed nature of the self, embedded in social (power) relations. As Cullinane (1996: 190) points out, 'Management does not need stand-over tactics to control the labour process because the style of employment governance ensures that workers themselves maximize the transformation of the labour process'. The design of routine low-skill jobs grounded in scientific management's separation of the conceptual from the practical dimensions of work is one example of employer strategies to obtain power and control over the employment relationship through the manipulation of HRM practices. Above-market compensation policies and informal dispute-resolution procedures are viewed as union substitution strategies to prevent employees from gaining more power by unionizing (Budd and Bhave, 2008).

HRM/high-performance rhetoric

The greater managerial control and employee behavioural shifts required by performativity within professional/bureaucratic cultures have profound implications for organizational culture. These include HPWS, the use of which was widely reported in Management Agenda surveys by the end of the 1990s. Almost every organization in the 1999 Management Agenda had 'high-commitment' HRM practices, such as a mission or vision statement and a set of organizational values. Scott (1990: 72) argues that organizational values are a manifestation of the 'thick' version of Marx's 'false consciousness' theory: 'The thick version claims that a dominant ideology works its magic by persuading subordinate groups to believe actively in the values that explain and justify their own subordination. The thick theory claims consent.' However, organizational values were mostly perceived by employees as more of a public relations exercise than a reflection of reality; the lack of congruence between espoused and

106 *Managerialism and HRM*

practised values was a consistent source of low trust and growing cynicism. This would suggest that employees do have some choice in how they respond, even if their response is not explicit.

Many different forms of culture clash were reported between 2000 and 2003, not least caused by the gap between the espoused HRM/high-performance rhetoric of teamwork and empowerment versus the reality of authoritarian management styles, traditional top-down budgeting and planning processes and biased rewards. Aggressive, inconsistent and occasionally threatening and bullying behaviour by managers (and colleagues) was frequently reported. The main mismatch was over stereotypical claims that 'people are our greatest asset', whereas in reality, people believed they were seen as resources. As one middle manager reflected in 2002, there was a gap between what was said and what was done:

> We say that people are our most valuable asset yet we don't invest in them. We say we want people to innovate yet our first instinct is to criticise any new ideas rather than nurture them. We say we want our first line leaders to lead the organisation yet we constantly measure them against top-down compliance.

Far from feeling valued, employees were working excessive hours and were expected to shoulder ever-increasing workloads. As a result, there was widespread loss of trust. The Agenda survey findings suggest that this had direct consequences for employee commitment. Many of the 2003 response themes pointed to the negatives of the 'new work culture' for employees. These included lack of appreciation, poor management and no promotion prospects. Along with pressure, employees generally reported a more aggressively paced work climate. Many comments referred to the 'cold, unfriendly environment' and the 'reducing quality of the work environment'.

The 2006 survey highlighted the differences of perspective between senior managers and those of other employees with respect to values. Amongst board directors, 73 per cent believed that executive/senior manager behaviour was in line with the espoused values, whereas only 26 per cent of middle managers and 20 per cent of junior managers believed this to be the case. Similarly, the 2004 Workplace Employment Relations Survey (Kersley et al., 2005) found that managers considered that employment relations had improved since 1998, whereas employees considered that it had changed little (Brown et al., 2008). In 2007, 85 per cent of Agenda respondents said that managers did not 'walk the talk'. As one person reported, it was senior managers' inability to be honest about bad news and lack of 'emotional intelligence' that 'messed it up'. The 2016 Agenda findings echo similar themes.

For employees, the contrast between HRM rhetoric and reality as perceived by employees can be significant. The greater diffusion of HRM systems can lead to negative employee experiences, including lower perceptions of job security and increased job strain (Green, 2004). Too many high-performance management initiatives can lead to overload for employees. As Macky and Boxall (2007: 558) have previously pointed out, outcomes for employees 'become less optimal as complexity increases: when, for example, performance appraisal is added to teamwork in a flattened hierarchy, along with increased participation in decision-making, enhanced information flows, and so on' (in Heffernan and Dundon, 2016).

The 'tyranny of teamwork'

Similarly, 'soft' HRM concepts, such as teamwork, which Sennett (1998: 28) describes as 'the work ethic of a flexible political economy' since it relies on 'the fiction of harmony' and stresses mutual responsiveness at the expense of original thinking, is a means of shaping employee subjectivities.

By way of example, Organization A, a major financial services organization whose culture was competitive and performative, was facing considerable business challenges in the light of competitive pressures at the end of the 1990s. For the first time in many years, staff redundancies were implemented, producing shock waves among surviving employees and the local community which depended heavily on the company as a source of income. The company recovery strategy entailed strengthening its commercial brand and company culture. HR was to play a key role in cultural transformation as well as 'right sizing' the organization. Alongside ongoing restructurings, various kinds of training and 'soft' HRM culture change and 'values-based' management processes were imposed on regional offices by the US centre. 'Leadership' and 'team working' became mantras and HR tools such as competencies were developed as a template by which organization/person 'fit' at recruitment and performance management could be judged.

While there was some widespread employee scepticism and grumbling about these practices, there was very little overt resistance to the dominant ideology; instead, employees were encouraged to embrace the company brand, feel proud to work for Organization A, to advocate its interests to external parties, and to feel a sense of personal failure or shame if an individual could not, or would not, fit in with the company culture. Employees were encouraged to give feedback to each other, and also about each other to HR. If an employee was branded 'not a team player' that was a signal to the employee to move on since they would be shunned by colleagues and passed over for promotion.

The power play involved was usually akin to that deployed by bullying playground gangs, with groups conspiring against individuals. In essence 'teamwork' required 'group-think' conformity and compliance to group norms and subsumption of individual agency to the dominant rhetoric. Thus both the 'thick' and 'thin' versions of false consciousness (Scott, 1990) were perpetuated by encouraging employees to feel a sense of failure for not being part of what was purported to be not only 'natural and inevitable' but also the 'right thing'. As Ball (2003) argues, 'the policy technologies of market, management and performativity leave no space for an autonomous or collective ethical self'.

Pause to reflect

- Can organizational identification go too far? What are the risks to employers and employees?
- What does 'healthy' teamwork consist of?
- What could HR put in place to guard against 'group-think'?

Performance management

Alongside performativity and efficiency, the new work culture is characterized by the pursuit of flexibility. With the ending of 'jobs for life' for white-collar workers, continuous employment depends on an individual's ability to meet specific standards and changing targets.

Box 6.2 Employment governance

By the 1990s, labour process theory had moved on from Braverman's deskilling thesis. Instead the focus shifted to the variety of ways management use to exercise employment governance and control the workplace. As Cullinane (1996: 189) points out, first capital must control the labour process in order to maximize the transformation of labour

> power into labour (see Braverman and Marx). Second, management is the means capital uses to control the labour process and maximize the transformation of labour power, and third, management divides work into component parts to assist control of the labour process (Thompson and Hartley, 2007).

Performance-management systems and processes in particular appear to have a strong shaping and controlling effect on employee behaviours (Armstrong and Baron, 1998; Beardwell and Holden, 2001). 'Performance management' roughly denotes a varying set of HRM practices that are aimed at managing the job performance of individual employees, tied together by 'a strategic and integrated approach' (Armstrong and Baron, 1998) which stresses both control and 'development' of employees. They include features such as mission, strategy, organizational structure, performance measures, feedback systems and rewards and practices such as appraisal interviews, 360-degree feedback, competence assessments, performance-related pay, peer appraisal and others. These collectively constitute the 'disciplinary practices' regulating social behaviour at work. Their use has grown steadily in the private sector over the last 20 years, particularly in medium-sized and large organizations (Bach, 2000), though within public-sector institutions the emphasis on performance measurement and management is more recent.

When the old control-oriented performance-appraisal systems first started to be rebranded as 'performance management' a few years back, the aim was for a much more positive, strategic, organizational performance-related and employee engagement-oriented agenda. After all, performance management is intended to align organization strategy, personal objectives and action and so maximize individual performance. The process should provide the space (and the impetus) for managers and employers to meet and discuss how things are going and it should formalize development discussions which might otherwise not take place. Performance management should also be a means whereby people receive the recognition, reward and development investment they deserve if they really are a firm's 'greatest asset'.

Moreover, by linking together many of the disparate strands of HR policy – such as goal setting, appraisal, training and development, talent management, reward and diversity – a performance-management system (PMS) should reinforce employee motivation, drive continuous improvement and meet business needs. A PMS should ensure that employees feel fairly treated and that their development needs are met; and from the firm perspective, it should provide concrete evidence on which talent spotting, promotions, or separation decisions can be based.

The problem is that these positive intentions are hard to realize in practice.

Problems also occur when appraisal processes become overly complicated. Tamkin (2016) points out that some HR departments are too ambitious in their expectations of how PMS can be used. They set themselves 'an expanded and formidable agenda of goals to achieve', seeking to use performance-management processes to link together disparate strands of HR practice – performance assessment with talent management, development, reward and diversity.

Performance management is often marketed internally as being employee-focused, stressing the development of innate qualities of individuals, since one of its ostensible aims is to ensure that employees can receive fair feedback and be appropriately rewarded for their performance. Yet appraisal discussions with line managers can often become formulaic and low quality, especially as managers consider performance management a burdensome addition to their real 'day job'. The use of standard competencies that bear little relation to people's real jobs and the often reductionist assessment processes in which these are applied tend to produce fixed views about the nature of real contribution, with inappropriate or little focus on growth and potential. Implementation is often poor, with performance management reduced to a complex, bureaucratic HR process, mechanistic data collection and non-existent follow-up and only a vague connection to

The shaping of subjectivities 109

short-term business strategy. All too often performance-management systems seem designed to catch out the underperformer rather than to identify potential or reward great contribution.

In recent times, numerous studies, including CIPD research, have identified that employees and managers alike are dissatisfied with their performance-management systems. The main focus of the debate about performance management has been characterized as being about ratings – whether or not they are fair, and whether or not they achieve their stated objectives. Moreover, when forced ranking forces line managers to demotivate talented people by assessing them as average performers, performance management loses its overall benefits.

More recent critical commentary has highlighted neuroscience research which suggests that when the appraisal-system ratings are directly linked to pay, conversations can provoke a fight or flight reaction among employees which inhibits any learning response (Nabaum et al., 2014). Forced ranking in particular initiates a fight or flight brain response, which prevents the genuine reflection and considered conversation that are so important in performance reviews. Rock et al.'s (2014) SCARF framework is based on neuroscience findings and helps explain why. This model has been widely discussed in management circles and in the field of learning and development since its introduction. It is concerned with five domains of experience which activate strong 'threats' and 'rewards' in the brain, namely:

1. Status (sense of importance relative to others).
2. Certainty (one's need for clarity).
3. Autonomy (sense of control over events).
4. Relatedness (sense of connectedness and security with another person).
5. Fairness (just and non-biased exchange between people).

For example, an employee who is not recognized for their contribution at work may consider this a 'threat' to Status, whereas appropriate recognition would trigger the 'reward' response, so boosting motivation. In the 2016 Management Agenda findings, of the five SCARF dimensions, the lowest rated by employees is that of 'Certainty', suggesting that managers may need to get better at being clear about what they can and cannot be certain about, and setting clear expectations even in environments characterized by change and uncertainty.

Rock et al. (2014) argue that traditional forms of performance management can be demotivating and potentially damaging to the employment relationship. They conclude that not only does performance management have negative consequences for employees, it also affects managers who may dislike trying to both encourage employees and judge them, for the following reasons:

1. Status: ranking people often creates status differentials, which can cause tension within teams.
2. Certainty: because ranking not only reflects individual performance, but often relative performance to others, individuals can feel a loss of certainty and control.
3. Autonomy: performance management typically reflects past performance, rather than future potential. This fosters a 'fixed' view, and employees may feel they have less influence over their own performance than they actually do.
4. Relatedness: employees may begin to compete with each other, rather than competing to meet external challenges.
5. Fairness: forced ranking can mean making arbitrary decisions because of the need to meet quotas or an ideal distribution. This can lead to significant challenges to the perceived fairness of the system.

110 *Managerialism and HRM*

Consequently, managers may feel undue pressure to raise performance ratings over time. Rock et al. (2014) argue that the only people who benefit from such a system are senior executives overseeing the process, who experience feelings of status, certainty and autonomy as a result.

From a critical perspective, such practices form part of an array of managerial domination over work. Within the new (performative) work cultures, employees are subject to regular appraisal, review and performance comparisons since performance at individual, group and organizational levels is understood as capable of being dissected, measured and assessed. Within call centre environments, for instance, the level of monitoring is overt; in other situations, monitoring might be more subtle. Organizational flexibility and efficiency require that those who do not perform to the right standard are replaced by others who can. Consequently, HRM practices make it ever more difficult for individual workers to exercise agency, despite the appearance of joint interest between the organization and the employee, unless employees themselves exercise considerable power in the employment relationship because of their specific market value.

Such instrumental utility of the HRM banner without adoption of any HRM ideals has led to accusations of HRM being 'amoral' (Miller, 1996) in that HRM becomes 'a covert form of employee manipulation dressed up as mutuality', whose aim, according to Fowler (1987), is to achieve 'the complete identification of employees with the aims and values of business– employee involvement, but on the company's terms'.

Trust?

In bureaucratic or professional cultures, trust is traditionally an assumed feature of the work environment. In performative cultures, the assumption is that employees cannot be trusted to perform to the levels required without management and monitoring. The activities of management drive performativity into practices and relationships (Gallie et al., 2001: 1086): 'The drive to accountability in all corners of organisational life – what Michael Power (2001) calls an "audit explosion" – has meant that too many organisations are leaning too heavily on the rule book to the detriment of professional intuition and ethical behaviour'. The task of the manager is to instil the 'attitude and culture within which the worker feels themselves accountable and at the same time committed or personally invested in the organisation' (Ball, 2003: 220). For those not able to perform at the level required, there are 'managed exits'. As a result, professionals become gradually subsumed and controlled within a set of standards and practices imposed by managers.

Given the instruments of performativity, there should be no requirement for 'command and control' management styles (such as McGregor's 'Theory X' which assumes that workers cannot be trusted to work). After all, through HRM's performative instruments, such as appraisals, reviews and performance-related pay, the individual performances of employees are made visible to others and the managed are 'opened up' to assessment and control. Through HRM rhetoric, managers are overtly encouraged to embrace 'Theory Y' – the participative management styles which encourage employees to trust and share their best ideas with their employer.

There is a paradox in that the apparent move away from 'low trust' (Theory X) methods of managerial control via high-commitment HRM, in which management responsibilities are delegated and initiative valued, has been simultaneously matched by the installation of very immediate surveillance and self-monitoring through appraisals, making employees subject to greater control and potential manipulation, itself implying low trust (Ball, 2003; Inkson, 2008; Overell, 2005). In practice, it could be argued that performativity instruments perform an ever-strengthening 'Theory X function' within HRM practices purporting to Theory Y.

The shaping of subjectivities 111

In the UK's education sector, for example, the performance regime imposed upon teachers, or (in Stephen Ball's phrase, inherited from Lyotard) the new 'terror' of performativity, makes it ever clearer that they are part of a productive process that feeds the global market (Ball, 1999: 2). Workers who lack such power, such as teachers who are situated within the nexus of education production as pedagogical workers, have found their very capacity to work defined exclusively by the conceptual structures of commodity production (Boxley, 2003):

> Thus through a system of staff appraisal, the employee is invited to collude in a process in which he or she accepts the attribution of specific 'deficiencies' in respect of skills and qualities thought to be functional to the organisation's success, and takes responsibility for 'correcting' them. This is particularly challenging for employees when the organisation's culture is perceived as threatening to employee security, and where hidden personnel agendas are seen to be operating amongst its senior management. Then HRM – under its legitimizing guise of 'staff development' – can become a major resource in the operation of organizational power politics.
>
> (Esland et al., 1999: 163)

Such approaches encourage the discursive shaping of the 'individual project', i.e. employees self-regulate their attitudes and behaviours to be consistent with business needs and comply with the demands of the market (Townley, 1998). The employee is seen as an object to be practised on, and in this regard there is little acknowledgement of the agency role of employees (Grant and Shields, 2002; Francis, 2006). So in performance-appraisal discussions, for example, as employees recount and evaluate their work experiences and ambitions, they do so in a situation where they are observed and judged by others in social (power) relations. They create a narrative of their experience using the discursive resources of the local organizational context (Alvesson, 2003), with all the intricacies and implicit values embedded within these resources.

Critical HRM scholars have long argued that such practices in fact reconstitute the subject by means of a set of linguistic concepts, which graft performativity in the self and simultaneously reinforce the notion of a free, autonomous individual (Iles and Salaman, 1995; Fournier and Grey, 2000; Deetz, 2003; Keenoy, 1997, 1999; Du Gay and Salaman, 1992; Keenoy and Anthony, 1992; Legge, 1995).

The new performative worker is an enterprising self, with a 'passion for excellence'. Ball (2003) points out that teachers, for instance, are encouraged to work on themselves, to think of themselves as 'enterprising subjects', or as 'neo-liberal professionals'. The requirement to comply or mould self, according to the prescribed discourse of the 'good' worker, can be an opportunity for some employees to make a success of themselves. For others, while theoretically free to opt out if they choose, embracing such an identity creates cognitive dissonance, inner conflict, inauthenticity and resistance. This, Ball argues, creates within employees 'a basis for ontological insecurity – are we doing enough?', leaving employees with constant doubts and uncertain self-worth (2003: 220). This new subjectivity produces feelings of guilt and uncertainty; we act upon ourselves and one another in order to make us particular kinds of being (Rose, 1999: 161).

Foucault used the imagery of Bentham's Panopticon (1787) to illustrate how these ends are achieved. The panopticon was a design for a prison, at the centre of which is a tower that allows the inspector to observe all the prisoners in the surrounding cells, without the prisoners knowing whether or not they are being observed. According to Foucault (1980: 201):

> The major effect of the Panopticon [is] to induce in the inmate a state of conscious and permanent visibility that assures the automatic functioning of power...surveillance

112   *Managerialism and HRM*

is permanent in its effects, even if it is discontinuous in its action; that the perfection of power should tend to render its actual exercise unnecessary.

In Foucauldian terms, performance management and other HR practices serve to control employees through 'self-esteem'. Self-esteem is a technology of self, similar to other psychological technologies borrowed from technologies of the market, for 'evaluating and acting upon ourselves so that the police, the guards and the doctors do not have to do so' (Cruikshank, 1996: 234). This has more to do with self-assessment than with self-respect, as the self continuously has to be measured, judged and disciplined in order to gear personal 'empowerment' to collective yardsticks determined by performative norms. As Foucault points out:

> He who is subjected to a field of visibility, and who knows it, assumes responsibility for the constraints of power, he makes them spontaneously upon himself; he inscribes in himself the power relation in which he simultaneously plays both roles; he becomes the principle of his own subjection.
>
> (1980: 202–3)

As a result, according to Lemke, 'By taking up the goal of self-esteem, we allow ourselves to be governable from a distance' (2001: 202).

Potentially, this has important effects on the way in which people look upon their working life. The employee's conception of the employment relationship shifts away from former collectivist ideas toward a more individualist version, where the primary responsibility for performance lies with the employee and the primary risk in the employment relationship is theirs. Such practices have exposed as a myth the assumptions of mutuality of interest in the employment relationship that are implicit in high-commitment 'soft' HRM.

Measurement against 'ideal' templates

Measurement and monitoring are key features of performativity and of scientific management. In order to achieve this, Kallinikos (1996: 37) argues that:

> Management implies and reproduces compartmentalization and fragmentation as a means of mastery and control. For, in order to be managed, the totality of physical and social processes, whether within limited instrumental contexts or in society as a whole, needs to be broken down into narrow domains that can be inspected, measured and handled.

One form of compartmentalization involves the use of competencies, which prescribe the desired skills, attitudes and behaviours against which employee performances are assessed, and with which employees are expected to comply. In their study of the labour process in call centre environments Bain et al. (2002) argue that the use of both 'hard' (quantitative) and 'soft' measures represents 'new developments in the Taylorisation of white-collar work'.

In the 2000 Management Agenda, many large company HR functions were organizing assessment centres as a means of 'objectively' assessing potential as well as for graduate-recruitment purposes. In such processes, individuals are observed as they perform tasks and are assessed against competency-based criteria. In many organizations, employees were encouraged to view invitations to participate in such assessment processes as a mark of favour, almost a rite of passage to senior management in which it was important that there was a good 'fit' with the company against an idealized template. Ambitious individuals sought to be selected to participate in such assessment processes as gateways to promotion.

Employee opinion about these processes was polarized in the 2000 survey. While a few respondents considered these an exciting development, many people raised concerns about competencies and the use of assessment centres, about their objectivity, consistency and fairness. The skills and impartiality of assessors and the relevance of the competencies on which assessment was based were called into question. Indeed, employees generally regarded competencies with scepticism and respondents working in international organizations reported cultural resistance to their use.

Similarly, Boxley (2003) reflects on teacher-appraisal processes which require the evidencing of teachers' capability and performance against a list of 16 'professional characteristics' drawn up after extensive analysis by Hay McBer (2000):

> The data required of teachers in this area is of a qualitatively different order. Evidencing capability in this regard rests upon claiming personal qualities compatible with…such immeasurable descriptors as 'respect for others', 'conceptual thinking', 'initiative', 'holding people accountable' and 'understanding others'. In this, the fifth of the five categories, there is clearly a difficulty of accounting for the assessor. This situation has necessitated the construction of a relationship between 'personal characteristics' and performativity.

Performance is thus judged on the 'what' as well as the 'how' and a strong degree of conformity with these normative descriptors is required if an individual's performance is to be judged acceptable. Since such descriptors are also used in recruitment and promotion processes, there is a strong incentive for teachers to behaviourally comply, or at least appear to do so, at the risk of potentially undermining others' and their own view of themselves as professionals. Moreover, the processes of evaluating performance are often perceived by employees as being far from neutral or fair since the question of who gets to set the standards and judge performance is more often the outcome of political processes of domination that present themselves as rational decision-making. As Scott (1994) suggests, where standards of performance and discipline have been set in new and different ways, the scope for workers legitimately to challenge these processes may also have been restricted.

Monitoring and technology

Technology's 'panoptic' potential is assisting in the creation of employee subjectivities. In addition to the potential of technology to 'hollow out' skilled jobs, it also offers the means through which work and workers can be continuously monitored in ways F.W. Taylor could only have dreamed about. While the possibility of controlling the labour process using technology was discussed in the 1980s, it was only with the growing use of personal computers in offices from the 1990s that more attention was focused upon how managers could attain total knowledge in 'real time' of how every employee's time was being deployed using electronic monitoring (Bain et al., 2002).

Increasing use of performance data analytics is enabling managements to differentiate between levels of individual performance and to closely monitor employee activity and reduce worker autonomy. In many call centre environments, workers are continuously measured on their response times and the time it takes to address a client's needs. They are also typically restricted in terms of the time they can take away from the work station to address personal needs. While this monitoring is often dressed up as competition between teams, with small

114   *Managerialism and HRM*

rewards for the most productive workers, at the same time the information is used to sanction less high-performing employees.

In an extreme example, workers at one establishment have cameras and digital sensors fitted to their work stations which enable worker energy levels and performance output to be measured constantly. In another, an entrepreneur had himself surgically fitted with a microchip, and encouraged his employees to do the same, so that they could gain easy access to buildings and equipment without the need for security passes. While such moves could in theory be open to a humanistic interpretation, for instance enabling support to be provided to the worker if needed, it is tempting to view them as intrusive surveillance in order to increase worker productivity, a panoptic equivalent of making workers wear an electronic tag. The advance of 'big data' is lauded in HRM media as assisting employers to locate potential recruits, identify trends and improve customer-satisfaction levels. At the same time, it allows employers to monitor their workers' social media activity out of work, with a view to gauging their personal preferences, reliability and loyalty to the company.

Does performance management achieve its ends?

As previously stated, performance management should be a means whereby organizational objectives can be achieved, and individual performance fairly assessed and rewarded. However, it would seem that in practice, the systematization of performance management has had some perverse consequences. Various surveys conducted by academics and consultants (e.g. Workplace Employment Relations Survey, Department of Trade and Industry 2008; Towers Watson, 2008; EAPM/Boston Consulting Group, Caye et al., 2008) provide evidence that in increasingly performative organizational cultures, there is usually a combination of systematic work intensification, profound employment insecurity and new forms of performance management which, together, produce a strong coercive impetus to drive employees to achieve ever more challenging work targets and higher performance.

Communications technology also assists in the shaping of worker subjectivities since it plays a major part in enabling work intensification. Thanks to emails, laptops and continuous connectivity, work can extend beyond time and spatial boundaries. However, work intensification appears less harmful to worker wellbeing than the lack of autonomy afforded by a high-strain job (high effort, low discretion). The 2006 UK Skills survey (Felstead et al., 2007) found that the design of such a job makes a large difference to the wellbeing of the job holder, with the effect relative to the existing distribution of wellbeing being much larger than the difference in wellbeing that would be associated with a reduction in work hours from 50 to 40 hours a week.

The Tayloristic nature of these processes is reported to be largely harmful to employee wellbeing, since it has resulted in a reduction in worker autonomy and an increase in work pressure. Official skills surveys show a significant decline in the proportion of workers who report that they have much influence over how they do their daily tasks – from 57 per cent in 1992 to 43 per cent in 2006 (Felstead et al., 2007). Gallie et al. (2001) suggest that: 'declining task discretion has played a major role in preventing a substantial rise in organizational commitment…changing forms of control make a further negative contribution' (p. 1095). Similarly, Willmott (2003) refers to how new performance-driven production methods at a car plant placed workers under high levels of continuous stress. Even though workers believed that their jobs were secure and their prospects good, these traditional sources of anxiety were replaced by new ones based upon close monitoring of individual performance.

Performance-related pay is also intended to focus employees' attention and efforts on achieving specific desired organizational outcomes, yet it appears to have a number of unintended consequences, especially when applied to roles in which there is not a clear link between individual/team effort and measurable results, for instance in sales. Employees may focus only on those (few) tasks which deliver the variable pay, whereas the 'core role' may be neglected. The broader contribution of employees towards longer-term goals may be ignored in the allocation of rewards since these typically focus on short-term achievements. Individual rewards may drive individualistic behaviours and undermine teamwork, with the possibility of employees hoarding information or 'leads' which will enhance their own results but not those of others. On the whole, such systems are perceived to be unfair and ineffective at stimulating employee motivation or performance (Rose, 2011).

The economic drivers of performativity include strong cost management, where work is intensified while costs are reduced. Yet the development in recent years of monitoring and evaluation regimes means that at an institutional level there are two cost challenges: both from the intensification of first-order work (e.g. to serve the customer) and also from the costs of second-order activities such as performance monitoring and management. Consequently, in order to serve the customer and monitor performance, costs go up.

Moreover, if performance orientation is dominant in the culture, without a learning orientation, 'There is an increase in strategic behaviour; a focus on looking good rather than learning well' (Watkins, 2010: 5). Watkins argues that, in a school context, while a focus on learning can enhance performance, a focus on performance (alone) can depress performance. The effects of a performance orientation include greater helplessness, reduced help seeking, more maladaptive strategies and a greater focus on grade feedback. This, as Watkins points out, is not a strategy for success.

As Sparrow and Cooper (2003: 85) suggest, 'The risk then is that new technologies continue to create the conditions in which positive gains in the employment relationship are masked by ill-considered HR strategies'.

Employee perspectives on performance management

Though performance management had become relatively common in large private-sector organizations by the end of the twentieth century, it was still relatively rare in professional service firms and in parts of the public sector. In 1999, 55 per cent of private-sector Management Agenda respondents reported the introduction of performance-related pay in the previous two years. In particular, it was felt that only 'hard' results (outputs) were really taken into account in decisions about bonus payments or about who came to be promoted and that inputs (i.e. extra effort, complying with values and behavioural standards) were taken for granted. In 1999 I reported that the performance-management process was becoming more complex, with the annual review of performance (appraisals) now being generally supplemented by integrated objective-setting and development-planning processes. The use of 360-degree feedback was increasing but many respondents expressed distrust of this in assessing performance. Most respondents wanted more regular feedback from their manager and from the 'end user' of their work, such as the customer.

Incentive schemes were reported as being extended to a wider employee population than to those traditionally so rewarded, such as sales people, and as favouring short-term performance only, regardless of other consequences. By implication, those issues which might yield longer-term benefits would not be treated as priorities. Many respondents also reported that incentive

116   *Managerialism and HRM*

schemes tended to set colleagues against one another and favoured individual or departmental performance as opposed to corporate/collective targets. In 2000, only a third of respondents reported that their organization offered flexible benefits packages.

Perceived lack of fairness in the way performance-management schemes worked was increasingly reported between 2001 and 2003. Many employees reported a lack of confidence in their organization's appraisal system and the link with reward. While some felt recognized through the performance-appraisal process, they did not feel equitably rewarded. In many cases, people remarked on the lack of clear goals which meant that their performance could never be fairly judged as in one junior manager's remark: 'the manager is unprepared to provide parameters for performance, therefore you are always wrong'. A public sector (central government) senior manager was blunt about performance management *per se*: 'I do not believe that performance appraisal is necessary – rather it is fundamentally damaging.' As he explained, the appraisal process undermined faith in professional standards and judgement and resulted in loss of trust between colleagues and managers.

The effects of performative climates on employees were evident in Management Agenda surveys in the first decade of the twentieth century. Many respondents between 2000 and 2003 reported that a culture change would be necessary if empowerment was to become a reality in their organizations. A culture conducive to empowerment was characterized as being 'no blame'; with clear accountability levels, an acceptance of risk taking, managers who were willing to let go of power, good systems and deliberate trust building. It was only in such a culture that people believed they were likely to be fully motivated and accountable for their performance.

Commodity relations

In today's new work cultures and uncertain employment markets, genuine social relations are increasingly replaced by information structures and peer pressure: 'The sociality of postmodern community does not require sociability' (Bauman, 1992: 198). It is more likely that people's individual psychological contracts are then re-formed within a broader social contract of competitive performativity. Since performativity effectively silences alternative voices, employee compliance may not be genuine. Ball points out how 'judgement and authenticity within practice are sacrificed for impression and performance' (2003). People have to fabricate accounts of themselves to create the impression of compliance and these accounts become embedded in systems of recording and reporting on practice. As a result, ironically performativity may produce opacity rather than transparency as individuals and organizations take ever-greater care in the construction and maintenance of fabrications. Moreover, without a basis for trust, employees may keep their best work to serve their own interests.

As Sennett suggests, it is arguable that employees experiencing alienation of self, linked to the requirements of performativity, are paying a heavy price in terms of their personal and psychological wellbeing. Brooks (2009) points out that Marx conceptualizes alienation as a contradictory phenomenon. Although commodity relations are alienating, workers are not blind to the realities of capitalist labour process (Lukacs, 1974). They strive to ameliorate their alienation through a mix of informal shop-floor culture, misbehaviour and even overt resistance (Linstead, 1996). Pragmatism and self-interest rather than professional judgement and ethics are the basis for new organizational language games, or as (Bernstein, 1981: 169) puts it, 'value replaces values'.

It is possible that older employees, who may aspire to end their careers with their current employers, have had to adjust to changing demands in order to keep their jobs. Whether younger employees will do so is a different matter. Various studies have examined stereotypical age groupings in today's multigenerational workforces in terms of the experiences which have shaped them, their attitudes, values and expectations. Cannon (1997), for instance, studied the attitudes to work of 'Generation X'. On the one hand they are well equipped to deal with the technological demands of work – they are heavy users of technology, including the internet, and are able to see some of the potential applications of transformational technology. Stereotypically they expect honesty from employers, especially with regard to career opportunities and dislike feeling manipulated. Cannon found that Generation X employees reacted with cynicism to performative work cultures. They did not trust their employers since they did not provide secure employment and employees were wary about commitment to anything long-term since loyalty to an employer was no longer an appropriate concept for them.

While the increasingly performative nature of the 'new workplace' may be challenging for people in mid-career, it is possible that young people entering the workplace now would have less trouble adjusting to workplace demands. We shall consider the reported needs and expectations of Generation Y in later chapters.

Conclusion

In this chapter we have focused principally on critical literature which examines the role of HR professionals as institutionalized employer 'agents' in shaping and embedding the 'work culture of new capitalism' (Sennett, 2006). The new work culture is characterized by flexibility, work intensification, performativity, short-termism, flexibility, managerialism, performativity and the replacement of direct by indirect controls over the workforce.

We have considered how HR practitioners provide significant input into creating the new work culture by designing specific policies and practices, by developing and transmitting the discourse in which these are constituted, and by the level of support around the devolution of HR work to line managers (Wong et al., 2009a, 2009b).

We have explored how HRM appears to exercise governmentality within organizations and in culturally consolidating the primacy of business interests as the dominant rationale for the way people and work are organized and managed, irrespective of the consequences for employee wellbeing. HR policies and practices are not merely managerial tools but first-order factors impacting on the employment relationship. HRM practices represent and produce the establishment of a new form of control, a 'controlled de-control', a 'hands-off, self-regulating regulation' (Du Gay, 1996). We have considered how HRM discourse and mechanisms of performativity, such as performance management, produce worker subjectivity.

HR's role is therefore complex and potentially paradoxical. How might such tensions be resolved to improve HR management practice? For Watson (2010), significant attention should be paid to denaturalizing the taken-for-granted categories and assumptions which typically inform the mainstream analysis of HRM (and management practice more generally). In particular, the morality of the use of performativity to produce a compliant workforce should be questioned. In later chapters we shall consider, for example, if it is possible that HR practices can lead to both improved performance and employee wellbeing.

In the next chapter we shall consider the perspectives of senior HRM practitioners, on their role as agents of managerialism, in delivering a compliant, hard-working, cost-effective and ultimately expendable workforce.

Points to ponder

- What is the relationship between specific HR practices and employee performance in particular contexts?
- Is attempting to align staff to an uplifting organizational purpose simply the co-option of that purpose within existing neo-liberal discourse?
- How might the focus of HRM discourse become more 'balanced'?

7 The conflicted HR practitioner?

> Doing to others an act you'd rather not have done to you reveals a powerful internal conflict.
>
> (Alexandra Katehakis)

The role and purpose of the HR function continues to evolve and different stakeholders, not least HR practitioners themselves, have widely varying expectations of HR. As Francis and Keegan (2006) point out, within this discursive space, the expressed priorities of HR work change over time and are a source of debate and contention. While for some scholars and practitioners, the protection and advocacy of employee interests are integral to HR work where the ethical treatment of workers is emphasized (Winstanley and Woodall, 2000; Legge et al., 1999; Kochan, 2007; Holbeche, 2012), for others the main priority of HR work is to contribute to firm competitive advantage and maximize the returns to shareholders.

Schuler (1992), for example, argued that the HR function had the opportunity to shift from being an 'employee advocate' (associated with personnel management) to a 'member of the management team'. This would require HR professionals to be concerned with the bottom line, profits, organizational effectiveness and business survival. In other words, HR issues should be addressed as business issues. As we have discussed previously, HR itself appears to have been captured by the business agenda but is not generally accepted as a business partner. Line-manager perceptions are often coloured by a widespread view that HR practitioners do not understand their business, so why should managers listen to them?

In this chapter we shall discuss what a number of HR leaders consider to be their roles and priorities. In particular, we shall explore whether they have embraced the role of business partner and how this operates. Many HR practitioners were no doubt attracted to a career in HR management in order to work with people. Does the potential for conflicting needs create cognitive dissonance for these practitioners? Given that HR practitioners and line managers are the organizational agents with whom the process of psychological contracting with employees generally takes place, I consider the extent to which HR practitioners manage the inherent duality of their role, i.e. balancing the interests of both the organization and its employees.

We shall cover:

- a challenging role;
- business partner literature themes; and
- HR leader discourse themes.

A challenging role

The HR function is often in a seemingly 'no-win' situation. As representatives of Weber's 'ideal type' of bureaucracy, with resourcing, cost and control responsibilities, HR functions are

120 *Managerialism and HRM*

often caught at the intersection of conflicting stakeholder expectations. Moreover, as we have discussed, HR functions often send out mixed messages. In contrast to HR discourse, which is often aspirational and values-based, much HR practice under the shareholder-value model is short-termist, cost-driven and instrumental. Despite the rhetoric of mutuality, in most cases, power in the employee relationship tends to be one-sided in favour of employers. Many HR practitioners are themselves conflicted about what they feel required to do, versus what they believe is the right thing to do.

Moreover, HR is often criticized for not being proactive: for continuing to carry out administrative duties that had theoretically passed to line managers with the development of the business partner model. With heavy administrative workloads, HR is usually intensely busy carrying out activities which maintain the status quo operationally speaking – which Ulrich calls the 'doables' – but which lack the broader impact on business performance, or on business culture, practices and dynamic capabilities which might be expected by stakeholders – the 'deliverables'.

Such observations are reflected in Management Agenda surveys between 2006 and 2016 where HR was consistently described as reactive. Not surprisingly, HR respondents themselves tend to report HR's contribution more positively. In 2006, over half of HR respondents stated that HR added value, while only 17 per cent of all other respondents believed this to be the case. In some contexts, respondents considered HR to be too powerful and to be interfering with business decisions in a damaging way. How value is defined therefore depends on the vantage point of each stakeholder in their specific situation.

More generally, it seems that HR's influence and perceived value has waxed and waned over the years. Lawler has observed that HR is at its most powerful during periods of industrial unrest, when the HR function actively negotiates and manages relations with trade unions. Similarly, in his article 'Why we love to hate HR…and what HR can do about it', Peter Cappelli argues that HR's perceived value is linked to what is happening in the broader economy. When there is plenty of available labour, managers perceive HR as a nuisance, imposing 'unnecessary' procedures and bureaucratic requirements. Conversely, when labour is in short supply, HR is considered useful in sourcing necessary labour. Cappelli highlights the positive role played by personnel departments in the 1920s in making supervisors treat employees well. However, during the economic slowdown of the 1970s, with high levels of unemployment, employers unravelled many of the good people-management practices of previous decades since people were considered easily replaceable.

Cappelli points out that the post-war period, which he calls 'the gray flannel suit era', was a high point of Personnel influence. At that time executive jobs were mostly filled from within and about one third of executives died in office – many of them from heart attacks. Personnel became a powerful function as it started to develop succession plans, but also practices such as coaching, developmental assignments, job rotation, 360-degree feedback, assessment centres, high-potential tracks in order to attract and retain talent. However today, most executives are external appointments, and succession planning and related development processes have mostly died down. Moreover, with flatter structures and more fluid staffing arrangements, managers have wide spans of control so staff receive little development. This has been exacerbated by the devolution to managers of many tasks previously carried out by HR such as recruitment and pay decisions.

In their business partner roles, Cappelli argues, HR have to persuade managers to follow procedures without having any direct power over them, which to line managers can feel like unhelpful interference. The lack of influence of HR was evident in a report published near the beginning of the 2008 recession, which found that only a third of HR departments were consulted on company decisions about which people should be laid off, despite this being an area where HR has considerable expertise.

Business partner literature themes

Within the discursive space of HRM (Francis and Keegan, 2006; Francis and Sinclair, 2003; Keenoy, 1999; Legge, 1995), the greater focus is placed on the role HR plays in supporting business goals by 'partnering with the business'. The primacy of the economic model has been evident in forging the roles of HR practitioners since the 1980s. For David Guest, the adoption of the Business Partner model has become so widespread that the focus on employees has become secondary to the supremacy of business needs. Similarly, within the 'practitioner paradigm' genre, Ulrich's (1997) business partner modelling of HR has been promoted as the one to which the profession should aspire (Caldwell, 2003: 988).

Though since revised (2005), the Ulrich (1997) model has formed the basis of extensive restructurings within HR functions which are seen as an essential part of HR transformation. Talk of HR transformation is typically advanced and defended by 'experts' focusing on ends such as 'improved efficiency' and 'greater strategic focus'. Large-scale structural transformations in HR service delivery to reduce costs, increase firm competitiveness and achieve a tighter alignment between HR practices and business strategy are presented as urgent, inevitable and politically neutral. Technology is presented simply as a means to an end – typically the streamlining of HR services in order to free up high-end HR practitioners to engage in strategic HR activities, while line managers and employees are trained to be responsible for an ever-widening array of basically administrative HR activities. The transformation of ordinary HR practitioners into HR business partners is framed as a necessity and presented as a natural step in the evolution of HR work in a globally competitive environment (Ulrich and Brockbank, 2005).

HR professionals are required to identify closely with line management through enactment of a strategy not unlike that of the 'conformist innovator' described by Legge (1978), where dominant business values are treated as a 'given' by HR professionals. Ulrich and Brockbank (2005) remark on the prominence and attractiveness of the 'strategic partner' role amongst HR professionals, noting that it is sometimes used as a synonym for the business partner, consistent with CIPD research which shows that the strategic partner role is proving the most attractive of Ulrich's original four roles for most HR people (Brown et al., 2004).

Unitarist HRM models like HR business partnership work on the assumption that what is good for the business is good for employees. These ignore the inherent duality of HR work raised in more critical accounts of HRM. In particular, the model developed by Ulrich (1997) specifically works to downplay the responsibilities of HR practitioners in securing and protecting the interests of employees (Francis and Keegan, 2006; Hope-Hailey et al., 2005) while also failing to adequately consider the difficulties and tensions faced by HR practitioners as they are urged to adopt strategic roles (Caldwell, 2003). Indeed, I wrote a book for HR practitioners, *Aligning HR and Business Strategy* (1999), which provided pointers as to how such alignment could be achieved. When I wrote the second edition of this book in 2009, I argued that the pursuit of such strong unitarist and inherently short-term alignment was mistaken, since I now believe that pursuing short-termist business agendas derived from a neo-liberal mandate is fundamentally counter-productive. Not only does the development of people require a longer-term perspective but also the mechanisms used to extract performance from employees raise ethical concerns for me and no doubt many practitioners.

122 *Managerialism and HRM*

A key issue for practitioner-focused research is the extent of influence HR can exercise, often described as 'a seat at the (board) table'. However, the position HR occupies in terms of its power and influence within organizations is highly contested both within and without organizations. Even though people issues have now become a key business driver in knowledge and service-intensive firms in particular, HR is still fighting to exert influence at the highest level.

Discursive resources reflect different understandings of the priorities of HR work, and are invoked to influence the way language constructs particular types of HR reality and governs the way HR issues are talked about, understood and experienced (Harley and Hardy, 2004). Given the history of HR practitioners' struggles for acceptance as key organizational players (Guest and King, 2004; Legge, 1978), it is hardly surprising that a way of discursively modelling the concept of HR as 'hard' and relating it to other concepts such as 'business-driven agendas' and 'strategic management' has become so popular. It offers perhaps some hope of escaping the 'perpetual marginality' (Watson, 1996) of HR practitioners by offering a way out of the dualism when they seek to claim a share of strategic decision-making, while at the same time attending to the kinds of employee-centred and administrative aspects of the role.

Indeed, the transformation of HR functions into business partnering appears to be ever advancing. Keegan and Francis (in Delbridge and Keenoy, 2010) interviewed 44 HR professionals, all of whom appeared to have redefined themselves and their responsibilities as business partners. What they demonstrate is that, through the discourse of 'competitive advantage', the activities of HR management have seen an ineluctable transition from a professional and ethical concern with 'people management' to a more instrumental, functional management focus on providing a 'business service' to general management.

HR leader discourse

In this section my interest is in localized senior practitioner discourses, and in whether these reflect broader academic discursive trends towards business partnership (Harley and Hardy, 2004; Watson, 2004). Given the shaping effect of HRM discourse, I wanted to explore where senior HR practitioners themselves placed their priority emphasis, and the extent to which they viewed the mutual employment relationship as 'mutual', as implied in 'soft' HRM, or whether they viewed employees as 'subjects'. To that end, the core of this study is a qualitative theme analysis of interview-based texts, treated here as a form of social practice (Bazely, 2009; Aronson, 1994; Constas, 1992). In addition, I include findings from the Roffey Park Management Agenda survey 2016.

The 24 senior UK-based HRM practitioners I interviewed for my book *HR Leadership* (2009) were considered 'discourse shapers' in their own contexts and more widely within the HR profession, since some were quite well-known within broader management circles. The interviews were carried out between 2004 and 2009, as the recession was becoming entrenched in the UK. During that period, I interviewed several people two or three times as they moved to new jobs. Most of the practitioners were known to me personally or by reputation as people considered to be exemplars of professional HRM.

The organizations for which they worked included a national charity, a central government department, two local government authorities, a large police authority and a professional body. Private-sector respondents worked for companies involved in electronic communications, publishing, retail, fast food, banking, utilities, telecommunications and manufacturing. Two of the respondents were CEOs, having previously been HR directors; ten were group HR directors or equivalent; all had been HR directors. Finally, nine of the respondents were female and 15 were male; five respondents were aged 28–35; four were aged 36–45; 15 were over 46.

My aim was to discover how senior HR practitioners conceived their role, and HR's contribution to organizational effectiveness; also, how they ascribed particular positions to themselves and others within the changing employment relationship. I was curious to explore the extent to which HR professionals themselves appeared willing to embrace their roles as agents of managerialism, pursuing the needs of business which is itself operating according to short-termist, neo-liberal agendas in pursuit of competitive advantage. This was with a view to understanding the dominance of business in HR practitioner discourse; the ways in which HR practitioners exercise power; the extent to which these HR leaders were agents and discourse shapers or were themselves subjects of performativity.

I used a semi-structured life-history interview method which covered areas such as respondents' early career and why they had pursued an HR career. Empirical question areas relating to their roles included:

1. The nature of their role now, current challenges, key priorities and how they measure their success.
2. Their view about how much agency, influence and power they believe they have.
3. Their view about employee relations.
4. How they develop their own teams and their view about how future HR professionals should be developed.

I shall variously refer to these respondents as 'HR leaders' and 'HRDs' (HR directors).

Discourse themes

HR leader careers

The importance of business/market knowledge to HR career success is reflected in the career experiences of most interviewees, many of whom had not started their own careers in HR. Early career routes included other 'people'-related fields such as teaching (4), becoming a qualified solicitor (1), marketing (3), sales (4), priest (2), acting (1), general management (1) and recruitment (2). Two had started out in finance or as economic analysts; one as a research scientist. Two of those who had started their career in HR had moved into HR when they were on a graduate scheme and found that they enjoyed the work. One of the people who had deliberately chosen to work in HR had moved jobs reasonably frequently, working his way across business sectors and organizations of different sizes in order to expand his experience and understanding of both HR and business.

Most interviewees argued that having business understanding is a crucial foundation for HR's credibility and several respondents commented that, unless HR practitioners demonstrate a real understanding of the business, non-HR people tend to be brought into HR leadership roles.

What attracted them to HR?

Two male interviewees admitted that they had been attracted to a career in HR because they believed HR jobs to be well paid and 'out of the firing line'. Another had chosen HR as a career route after a period of indecision about what he wanted to do. This was during a

124   *Managerialism and HRM*

period of industrial strife in the UK. What attracted this HRD was the chance to 'earn his spurs' through industrial relations and to be part of the 'management action'. He certainly achieved that since he found himself in the front line of confrontations with striking workers at various factories. He admitted that this was a very challenging but exciting aspect of his role. He had gone on from industrial relations to an ever more senior range of generalist roles in organizations from different sectors.

Many respondents described their early career choices deriving from the strong, people-oriented personal missions of their youth. The desire to develop people was a common theme, although HRDs mostly saw this as a means to a unitarist end, i.e. developing people in order to improve the business. One person, who was initially attracted to a career in the Church, saw some similarities between that and HR: 'Both are rooted in helping people to achieve their full potential. And both have a welfare aspect – supporting people through difficult times.'

Several wanted work that was of social value; for instance, one person's early career involved working part time as an HR professional, doing social change work as a volunteer in his spare time. His personal politics were about social change:

> You see things in HR which at least demonstrate the impact of what HR does. In the 1990s I saw a site of engineering/manufacturing go from a headcount of 5000 to 2500 in 2 years flat. I saw the social impact – shops in the High St became Charity shops, the level of violence in the town centre went up, you can see the link clearly. If you live in the locality, you can see the impact. It was a defining experience.

So for many respondents their personal value-set was altruistic, about doing something 'worthwhile' to help people, business and for some the community also.

Many of these HR leaders are high-flyers by any standards and most have learned significantly through early exposure to challenging situations. Interestingly, many of these involved making people redundant, and despite their early motivations most appeared to have adopted a 'macho' approach to the task. One person relished the early opportunity to restructure a large business, working as part of a small team setting up a wholly owned subsidiary. Another person left teaching to work for a big pharmaceutical company, in sales and then marketing. As the highest-performing person in the company, she was plucked out of the 'oblivion' of the marketing department and put to work for the MD running a major change programme:

> I remember day two, my boss called me into the room and said, 'Look [X], we've got to shed about five thousand people', and I went, 'mm…okay. When?' It was November, and he said 'December', and I said, 'Oh that's fine – we've got thirteen months.' And he said 'No – *this* December!' So I was thrown into massive reorganization, losing five thousand people in about four or five weeks, and then taking the company through chapter eleven. Huge, huge learning; fantastic learning, because no-one else could tell me what to do. So that was a hideous set of circumstances, having to let people go and refinance the business and stuff, but hugely developmental.

This example illustrates the apparent degree of trust invested in this person and the autonomy she was able to exercise in carrying out major downsizings. She gained considerable credibility and influence as a result. She saw the downsizings as a career -defining moment; as an opportunity to prove herself and conceived her role very much about serving business interests.

HR's core role

In what Legge (1995) calls the twin discourses of the 'market' and the 'community' it is the market and business interests which dominate HR leaders' discourse. Without exception, the HR leaders in this study believed the purpose of their role was to be a business partner, supporting business success by recruiting capable, flexible and committed people, managing and rewarding their performance and developing key competencies. Most were working to very short-term agendas. The common mantra was: 'business first, people second'. One HRD described the mark of a great HR leader as being 'as un-HR like as possible'.

Alignment with business strategy was considered crucial and for one group HR director, the HR functional structure across her complex business needed to reflect this, so she spent a year restructuring the HR function globally to signal alignment: 'So now it certainly is absolutely integrated and is not seen as some odd separated group that does its own thing'. A number of respondents referred to the opportunities to increase HR's influence afforded by the economic crisis:

> If you are emerging from the downturn and you aren't a strategic partner with your CEO, I think you have lost your way. Yes, do the basics and the operational piece brilliantly, but be seen as that go-to person and true strategic partner. There's never a better time to raise the profile of HR in the organization.

HR transformation

Every HR leader appeared to view the transformation of the HR function as urgent and inevitable, ostensibly to enable more cost-effective operational delivery and to free up HR capacity for more strategic roles. However, cost reduction appeared to be the main driver. While the pace of transformation was slow, the seeming inevitability of such transformations was accepted by all the respondents, especially in public-sector organizations as spending cuts started to bite. All appeared to be adopting structures akin to those associated with the 'Ulrich model', i.e. some form of devolution to the line accompanied by e-enabled self-service, centres of expertise/excellence, business partners and a small corporate centre focused on corporate strategies such as executive compensation. HR leaders considered that they should be seen to lead this transformation before they were forced to do so. Many expressed doubt as to whether the new structures would prove successful in practice, but there were no accepted alternatives:

> Many of us have developed, or are developing, service centre-type structures. It is the only model in town and we have to make it work. What I have seen so far impresses me, but the longevity of this approach will be the real test. I don't know another model that is affordable.

For many respondents, without this transformation, the HR function was on the road to obsolescence. As one senior public-sector organization HR director commented:

> Put simply, there are cheaper – and probably more effective – ways of handling personnel matters. It is called clerking and doesn't, in all cases, require qualified HR professionals. That is, unless we refocus. And we need to do so pretty darn quickly. For too long, we have navel-gazed about what HR is, and worried far too much about processing.

126 *Managerialism and HRM*

None of the HR leaders was satisfied that the process of functional transformation was complete or entirely effective in their institutions and in many cases was proving all-consuming, becoming the end in itself rather than the means to greater effectiveness and value creation. While most appeared to consider the task of restructuring HR as bowing to the inevitable, some presented HR transformation in a more dynamic light, as enabling them to better support the business and keep pace with the company's changing needs. The importance of context was evident, especially when HR was transformed to meet the specific needs of the firm in its own business environment. For example, one pharmaceutical company HRD describes his motivation for transforming HR: 'I found the clutter of the day job getting in the way of the real value.' In his company, for instance, HR was positioning itself as an organizational change agent and was perceived to be of value:

> There is now a very concerted effort to better re-align HR to what the business really needs and that coincides with the business itself changing very dramatically in the pharmaceutical industry and [this company] is at the forefront of making that change. We, as an HR function, are definitely integral to not only making that change ourselves, but supporting that change in the organization. We are strategically positioned to help in that.

For all the HRDs interviewed, the 'people as resource' metaphor was dominant. For example, one senior HRD described the devolution of HR responsibilities to the line as entirely appropriate and what HR should be doing anyway, arguing that HR has perhaps inappropriately taken over many aspects of the role of managers in the past:

> A manager must manage and be accountable for their people, just as they are accountable for the goods and services that go out from their businesses or the provision of goods and services from their business. I think we are getting managers now to respond to both of those dimensions in the business.

However, HR leaders were aware their own proposed change of role would be politically contested by other influential players in their own context. Many recognized that the 'Achilles' heel' of HR credibility was being accused of poor-quality service delivery. So crucial was getting operational delivery right that many respondents found themselves spending considerable time on improving the detail of the service quality required to achieve the right outcomes, ironically leaving little time to attend to more strategic agendas, as one person commented:

> At times I probably have to rein back a little bit. I have been very concerned by the quality of our service from our (outsourced) partners so I've kind of got in there and rolled up my sleeves as well, to make sure that the quality of service we are delivering is meeting our KPIs and that people feel the service is at least as good as it was when it was provided internally – and hopefully it is better because that is the whole point of outsourcing it.

The HR team

In this, most HRDs were agreed that the measure of success of a good HR director is their ability to create a diverse team that can bring the right blend of skills to the business, since no HR director will have every single skill required around the HR table. For instance, one HRD spends two working days of every week having one-to-ones with her staff. She genuinely believes that 40 per cent of her time is spent coaching, managing and supporting her team, then 20 per cent of her time coaching and counselling senior managers, letting them blow off steam and helping them sort out organizational issues. She then spends the rest of her time working on the learning and development agenda, looking at how to develop people, how to ensure that they keep learning as an organization, as well as general operational things like salary planning and hiring.

Some HRDs put less emphasis on building the quality of their team and more on building their relationship with the team, considering this crucial to the team's ability to deliver at the right standard. Other HRDs were clear that they did not have the time or inclination to develop people who they did not feel were of the right calibre. Instead they tended to move people out and actively recruit high flyers from outside, or bring in line managers and other specialists on secondments.

The need to improve the calibre of HR professionals

Many of the HRDs were aware of criticism about the HR profession. Only one HRD said that he was impressed by HR practitioners' ability, knowledge and thoughtfulness. He did, however, say that HR people probably lack some of the consulting and project-management skills that you see in the consultancy profession and that there may be too many people in HR who have either come in from outside and not been professionally trained or have overprogressed and been overpromoted.

Apart from this HRD, all the interviewees had a strong opinion about the current population of HR professionals. One said that there were a lot of people going into this sphere of life, at HR conferences and so on, who he thought were an embarrassment. Another said that it was crucial to equip your function with professional, capable people who were credible, have integrity and deliver on time and not when it suits HR.

Yet another said that, at a time of economic crisis, some HR teams were employing mechanistic and bullying tactics which is a sad reflection on HR. He cited one organization's HR team who had sent half of their people to one hotel and the other half to another and sent a text to one half of them saying 'you have been made redundant; don't come back to the office'. The HRD thought that was an appalling HR tactic, and yet the HR department in question is seen to be really slick and effective at dealing with a problem and an HR yardstick.

Another HRD thought that there was hardly anybody who was really good in HR at the time. She thought that historically the function attracted people who probably entered the profession because they got a bit of a power kick out of knowing a lot of basic people data, so she surmised that there were a lot of people in the function who didn't have the integrity they should. Yet another HRD referred to the HR team before she arrived as 'very employee relations based, hand holding, smiley, smiley sort of HR people', that she had subsequently 'supplemented and complemented' with some internal business partners with OD expertise. Thus 'employee champion'-type orientations were not deemed of any value. Another had reduced the HR team from 400 'form fillers' to 40 'deliverers'. All of this was with a view to building a positive reputation for HR within the business. The HRD's reputation was only as good as that of their team.

HR leaders' power and influence

So on the one hand, these are powerful individuals who are perceived as influential players in their organizations and within HR professional circles, yet they recognize their essential

128 *Managerialism and HRM*

subordination to the business interests and vulnerability to the possibly negative perceptions of others. Only five of the 24 HR leaders interviewed for this study were members of their executive board, although all were, or had been, members of their organization's management team. Most argued that the 'seat at the table' question is irrelevant to HR leaders' ability to deliver, with some dismissing this as a '90s issue'. One respondent put the point more forcefully: 'I suppose in terms of the balance of power it's time the profession generally got off its bottom and began to make a difference rather than just talking about how life could be so much better if they had a seat around the table.' One HRD argued that the emerging, more strategic contribution from HR was starting to be valued in his company:

> I also think that the business leaders want, and have recognised the power and the usefulness of having an HR business partner, or the HR leader work alongside them, who really understands their business and can work with them on an equal footing in the context of people issues. I don't mean just be a supporting function, but actually work strategically alongside them in a more consultancy kind of relationship.

But the same HRD points out that the success of this more strategic role depends on the 'HR basics' being delivered effectively:

> They also recognise they want that foundational, day-to-day, operational stuff that HR does carried out more efficiently, whether it be paying people on time, delivering bonuses on time, having good employee relations, environment support, problem-solving and all the other lifetime career management aspects that HR can support.

The extent of HR leaders' power and influence appears to a very large extent determined by their personal credibility and relationship with executives at the highest level. According to Hesketh and Hird (2009), executives use personal strategies which involve them in power struggles over limited resources. They deploy material, symbolic and ideological power to secure distributional advantages for themselves and the functions they represent. The importance of these (power) networks in constructing, shaping and ultimately determining the outcome of material resources is generally underestimated.

Most of the respondents recognized the crucial importance of a close working relationship with the CEO. One HRD, for instance, would not go to work in an organization if she didn't think that she could build a good relationship with the CEO: 'If at interview I've not felt that I could work with this guy, and this guy would be totally open with me and I'd be his confidante and part of his kitchen cabinet, I wouldn't want to work at the company.' The nature of the HR leader's relationship with the CEO was variously reported to be that of 'ally', 'confidante', 'counsellor', 'conscience', but in all cases the HR director appears to act as subject, rather than overt agent – the 'power behind the throne'. As one HRD comments:

> The most important job I do is supporting the most senior person that I work with; no question. And one thing that I've learnt over time is you have to be a very different sort of person to be able to do that. You have to be willing to get a kick out of hearing a CEO using your words, and not tell anyone they're yours. You have to genially think that's really cool, and I do. Of the time I spend with the senior team, I would say the vast majority of it I spend with the CEO and that's where I get my kicks and that's what I love doing. And I would just leave my job if I didn't have that relationship with the CEO – I just wouldn't stay.

So on the one hand, this HR director appears subject in relative power terms, yet also appears in a position to manipulate and control agendas behind the scenes. Another (group) HRD of an international corporation talked of her influence over colleagues:

> I probably am the main confidante of not just the Chief Executive, but also with my colleagues on the executive. That is an extremely important role for an HRD to do well. It's probably the most important part of the role and one which I personally take very seriously. I will often be the conduit between colleagues and between colleagues and the Chief Executive. That's a role that, if you play it well, is extremely valuable for the organisation.

At the same time, this interviewee argued that HR participation on the wide business agenda is absolutely critical and that HR should have much more courage of its own convictions to make sure that it does that role, and is seen to play that role, especially around the executive committee tables of the company.

Indeed, all of the HR leaders interviewed for this study recognized that, for their role to grow in scope and influence, they needed close working relationships at the top, particularly with the CEO and the chief financial officer. This they all felt was when HR's power and influence is at its highest. I term this 'the charmed circle' which can also act as a 'closet cabinet'. One HRD meets with the group executive informally. The focus is on reflection, 'temperature' assessment, counsel, discussing linkages to the corporate centre, business performance 'hot spots', and acting as a mini think tank for the organization on the micro and strategic people issues, including some conflict resolution and development of the senior team itself.

This close relationship has also been termed 'the golden triangle' by Hesketh and Hird (2009) to describe the informal, tacit or intangible network of executive relationships and conversations – typically, but not exclusively operating between the CEO, finance director and their director or vice-president of HR. As Hesketh and Hird point out, the lack of a formal boardroom place makes membership of the golden triangle all the more important for achieving strategic voice for HR. But however valuable this role, it is not without its risks, not least to the HRD's integrity. The HR leader has to be willing to find themselves in the middle of the political power games of executive networks, whether or not these are to their taste. If not, they can be forced out of the charmed circle. As the group HRD quoted earlier points out:

> Play it incorrectly and your trust and ethics just go down the tubes. So you have to be quite clever to play it because you also have to be able to articulate on issues which may have been brought to your attention or require resolution and try and come up with some ideas on how you can problem-solve those to avoid conflict for example, or to ensure that everybody's voice is heard, including your own, around the table.

For those who are able to 'play it correctly', HR's performance tends to be judged less on hard, quantifiable measures and more on qualitative measures of success which reflect their growing influence: 'It's whether the senior team are coming to my room all the time to talk to me, before they do anything organisationally. That's how I know if I'm being successful of not'.

Hesketh and Hird (2009) argue that a number of structural influences determine the potential power of the HR leader. These include size – large, complex organizations with high labour costs – or scientific and technical contexts, where managers have little preparation for managing people. HR then becomes powerful as a source of support on labour relations and development. The presence of powerful trade unions – which tend to make CEOs

130   *Managerialism and HRM*

nervous – and industrial-relations tensions – where HR becomes the ultimate management negotiator – provide a strong power base for HR directors. Ironically, when employee relationships are less adversarial, this can reduce HR's power base.

These conditions are reflected in the comments from respondents in this study whose accounts confirmed that HR's power and influence is highest when HRDs are seen to be protecting the organization against industrial action, acting as a counter-weight to poor line management and reducing labour costs. Some drew power and influence from their growing role in managing risk and reputation, both in terms of preventing large numbers of industrial tribunals and 'doing deals' where necessary to silence 'the awkward squad'. Managing tough change involving restructurings and redundancies is also a time when HR's power appears high.

HR as 'employee champion'

The CIPD's (2016) research into ethics asks the question: who should HR serve? While CIPD respondents believed that workers should be treated as legitimate stakeholders of a business, in actual practice only about half (47 per cent) of practitioners said that they always apply the principle 'Work should be good for people' in their day-to-day decisions, with a further 35 per cent suggesting they may compromise this principle under certain circumstances.

With respect to the HRDs I interviewed, employees were mostly mentioned in the context of change – such as handling exits well or re-engaging 'survivors'. Only a few showed empathy with employees. Talent management was discussed entirely with respect to what business needed from talent, rather than the other way round. There was strong consensus that making the case for greater investment in people for its own sake was likely to diminish HR's credibility.

Another HRD said that, as people are integral to a business, everything you do with respect to your people has to be integrated with what your business strategy and goals are.

One HRD acknowledged the potentially alienating effects of the pace of change within large organizations:

> I think that staff can feel increasingly anonymous and isolated, a cog in the wheel, in these large fast-moving companies where people come and go from jobs much more quickly than they used to. You don't necessarily know your colleagues for very long; then you've got another colleague, another report, another boss. It's far more turbulent, and I think the word is turbulent, rather than changing, than it used to be.

Another HRD argues that the employee-champion role will inevitably become more prominent since the future workforce will make different demands of employers:

> If you think about Generation Y, and certainly Generation Z when it comes along, people's expectations will be enormous in terms of what a working career and job and occupation will provide for them, whereas the Baby Boomer generation was much more content to do what they were told, and be much more loyal naturally. Now I think people are more disloyal naturally and they want to know what your ethical policy is and what you are doing about saving the planet. I think the future of business is much more around people understanding and being comfortable with your ethics behind the scenes than it ever used to be. And that's a good thing but it's also something you have to think about for the future.

Similarly, in the 2016 Management Agenda, HR managers see managing the needs and expectations of different generations as among their key people challenges for the future. Given that working lifespans are extending, organizations will have to find ways to adapt to the changing nature and diversity of the workforce. However, beyond a recognition of the shift, few HR leaders seem to have developed specific employee-value propositions that might be relevant to different groups.

Ethics?

The CIPD's people and strategy director, Laura Harrison, argues that as a profession, HR should be ensuring that there is ethical practice in organizations. As she points out (CIPD, 2016),

> Respected and successful companies are questioning what makes a 'good' business and what their fundamental purpose is, asking whether and how they are serving a range of stakeholders, including business owners, people, economies and communities. They're doing so because they understand that in an uncertain and interconnected world, businesses are unlikely to survive in the long term if short-term profit persists as the sole end goal.

Against this context, Harrison states,

> HR should ask a similar question – what is the end goal for the profession? Is it to implement the people aspects of the business strategy – efficiently and with minimal risk – whatever the human cost? Or, is it to act as a critical adviser, asserting human-centred business practice and nurturing healthy organisational cultures that deliver sustainable value for all stakeholders, including people?

Up to a point, the HRDs I interviewed recognized that they had this dual and potentially conflicting responsibility. Several argued that we must learn lessons from the banking crisis and transform HR leadership by so doing. One person commented, 'never be paid too much you can't afford to leave – the table stakes can be high and provide real tests for personal integrity'. Moreover, there was recognition that HR's role as a tool of the market has proved a contributory factor to the kinds of performative cultures in which irresponsible behaviour is rewarded:

> 'You have to pay what you have to pay' has proved counter-productive, especially when the behaviour that has been encouraged by such payments causes the business to go broke. HR leaders need to ask themselves if there are other things that make working for an organisation more motivating than just money.

Encouraging though such comments are, the extent to which such reward systems are being revised remains in doubt.

The wider debate about the role of business in society is beginning to place a premium not just on the ability of a firm to meet the bottom line in the short term, but also on trust in its capacity to maintain that performance sustainably. The 2016 Management Agenda findings suggest that HR is still failing to address the ethical challenges in their organizations. In times of change and uncertainty, employees' awareness of their own vulnerability is heightened. They are more sensitive to management actions. If they feel they cannot trust their employers, employee morale and commitment are likely to be damaged. Breaches of trust occur not so much over what is done, but how it is done. And, in this, organizations' espoused values become a touchstone. Many organizations' values can appear like wish lists or corporate branding, inspiring but distant from our experience of them as stakeholders of one form or another. Alternatively, they may act as the connective glue that binds the organization together and captures what makes the organization different.

In the 2016 Management Agenda, roughly one third of employees felt that organizational values as practised by management did not reflect those espoused by the organization. Gaps between espoused and experienced values were greater in the public sector (43 per cent of managers in the sector saw a gap compared with 31 per cent and 24 per cent in the private and not-for-profit sectors, respectively); and for junior compared to more senior managers (46 per cent of junior managers saw a gap compared with 31 per cent of senior managers and 12 per cent of board directors). The most common barrier to 'living the values' was a lack of senior management buy-in. More than three quarters (77 per cent) of managers saw this as a barrier. This is interesting given that the perceived congruence between actual and espoused values rises through the management grades. Are those at the very top of organizations deluded? Or, perhaps, it only takes one senior manager behaving out of line with the values to make a significant impact on perceived congruence. The danger for organizations is that values imposed top-down for the sake of brand reputation rather than for their own sake generate employee cynicism and distrust at a time when trust is fragile and ever more important.

Feeling pressured to compromise one's own or the organization's ethical standards is another potential source of broken trust. The 2015–16 Agendas highlighted that the majority of managers did not experience such pressures. Those that felt pressured to compromise their own standards blamed the need to follow orders, meet overly aggressive business targets and schedule pressures their organization survive. In 2016 there was a sharp increase in the percentage of managers from the not-for-profit sector feeling the need to compromise their organization's ethical standards to help the organization survive. The pressure to meet overly aggressive business targets has also increased in the sector. Funding pressures may force decisions that meet short-term financial needs but which may be contrary to long-term sustainability. It seems that more senior managers are likely to explain decisions that compromise ethical standards in terms of helping the organization to survive whereas those in more junior positions see themselves as simply following orders. Those in the middle see the necessity of compromises in order to hit targets. Each interprets the situation through their own lens and it seems that more dialogue may help each understand the other's perspective and challenges.

If breaches of values and organizational ethics may both undermine trust, how trusting are employees of the organizations they work for? Lucy et al. (2016) used Gillespie and Dietz's (2009) trust model to measure workers' level of trust in their organization. The model has three components:

- Ability – the ability of the organization to reliably and effectively meet its goals and objectives.
- Benevolence – how effectively the organization demonstrates care and concern for the wellbeing of its staff.
- Integrity – how effective the organization is at consistently adhering to moral principles and a code of conduct acceptable to its employees.

For each dimension, there was a decreasing level of trust by level of management. For example, whilst 84 per cent of board directors felt their organization effectively shows care and concern for employees, only 44 per cent of junior managers felt the same. The data are also partly patterned by sector, with managers in the public sector less positive about their organizations' ability to act according to moral principles and show due care and concern for staff. This may be reflective of current pressures in the sector, where the risk may be that the pressure to do well overrides the purpose of doing good.

This suggests that HR could, and perhaps should, be adopting an active stewardship role, tackling in particular senior management behaviour that is not in line with the values. Only one of the HR leaders saw integrity as the mark of a good HR leader. This HRD described how a senior manager who, as he retired from the company after 30 years' service, paid her what she said was a huge compliment, describing her as a person of consistency and high ethics and one didn't see her constantly changing. Her word was her bond, and what he said was terribly important to her.

The talent agenda

Perhaps not surprisingly, given that the HR leader interviews took place during the worst of the recession, conventional talent processes, such as succession planning, high potential identification and development were less of a priority for HRDs, than was managing people out of the organization.

As Cappelli (2015) reminds us, one of traditional HR's biggest difficulties has been in supporting business strategy, because it is such a moving target these days.

> Companies seldom have long-term plans with straightforward talent requirements. Instead they generate streams of projects and initiatives to address successive needs. But HR is by nature a long-term play. Developing talent, heading off problems with regulations and turnover, building corporate culture, and addressing morale problems all take time. Often, leadership teams and priorities change before such initiatives have paid off. And when companies don't meet their performance goals for the quarter, those programs are among the first to go.

And this neglect of the longer-term view is also reflected in the 2016 Management Agenda. With the ongoing downsizing of the public sector in the UK, succession planning was amongst the top three people challenges HR practitioners identified. This is perhaps a consequence of the focus having been on making redundancies and trimming the salary bill at the expense of ensuring the leadership pipeline is strong. As one person commented:

> We've had a lot of people leave. We've done voluntary exit. What we haven't done is look across the piece and identify those people who are really valuable and really up and coming and who will be our leaders of the future and do something to keep them.

In the production and manufacturing and services sectors, succession planning was also among the top three people challenges since there is growing concern that individuals with mission-critical technical skills may be reaching retirement age or are looking for new challenges whilst there is a dearth of job-ready replacements.

Discourse shapers

The new orthodoxy or 'regime of truth' in HRM is that business counts, first and foremost. While most HR leaders were initially attracted to a career in HR because of their strongly

134 *Managerialism and HRM*

people-centred values, few of the respondents seemed to be looking for their successors to have a similar passion for people. Instead they were looking for high-calibre individuals with good business understanding and relationship skills. As one HRD put it, 'you can learn to "do" people'. Although I surmise that, for those HR leaders who retain a strong 'people' orientation, the essential duality of the HR role must produce some cognitive dissonance, these HR leaders seem mostly to have accommodated to the market discourse and the related rewards of power, prestige and influence that go with this. Indeed, two of those HRDs who appeared to be most strongly employee-centric, and to be conflicted by the business exigencies of their role, had subsequently gone on to become CEOs, roles in which they were freer to think about ways in which people could be managed, developed and supported to achieve business success.

It would appear that most of these HR leaders had been normalized to see the process of HR transformation as inevitable and necessary. As careerists and 'thrivers' they secured their own position of power and influence by executing managerial directives. They promoted the discourse of business by inculcating norms of conduct into their teams which reflected the primacy of business interests over employee interests. These norms were enforced through the fear of HR being seen as irrelevant and a costly overhead. Some appeared to be driving this transformation because they genuinely believed it would make HR more effective, while others believed there was no choice but to be seen to be reducing costs and improving the quality of HR delivery. All were finding the process of transformation difficult. In a sense the old dictum 'damned if you do and damned if you don't' seemed to apply. HR leaders felt obliged to make the transformation but if it proved problematic, more energy went into improving the new arrangements. Consequently, internal stakeholders may see little value from the transformation and key areas of HR contribution, such as ethics and talent, may be lost.

Conclusion

So the extent to which these powerful individuals are agents or subjects is unclear. On the one hand, some HR leaders willingly embrace the neo-liberal managerial agenda (in which employees have to 'fit'). They actively drive through the business agenda, using HR mechanisms and discourses to shape the subjectivities of others. Yet some also recognize their own vulnerability to the perceptions and political manoeuvrings of others and seek to maintain and grow their own power and influence through nurturing senior stakeholder relationships. Their credibility is earned by delivering the exclusively business-driven agenda. Even though HR leaders who are members of the 'charmed circle' appear to be highly influential, membership is fragile, and how much room HR leaders have, for instance to offer genuine challenge to unethical business practice, is not clear.

On the other hand, many HR professionals were originally attracted to a career in HR by the thought of working with people and helping them to have satisfying work lives. In its current state of evolution, the HR function, as an instrument of managerialism, largely loses focus on people unless they are perceived to have talent or power or are becoming a scarce resource. For some HR professionals the conflict of values may create cognitive dissonance.

Given the global shocks to the financial system and the ensuing economic crisis, it is perhaps fair to say that there has arguably never been a clearer need to question the dominant discourse about the shareholder-driven needs of business being the ultimate end in itself. The HR discourse reflected here suggests that, in today's politicized, short-termist and self-interested new work cultures (Sennett, 2006), HR leaders are unlikely to seriously 'rock the boat' and promote an ethical agenda which disturbs vested interests. It also suggests that the importance accorded to the 'employee-champion' role will wax and wane according to the relative power of labour and capital at any given time.

Nevertheless, there appear to be growing calls for HR to take a more muscular and strategic approach to people, culture and business issues. This in turn suggests that HR may need to reshape its own role and contribution. For instance, Charan (2014) argues that a structural overhaul of HR functions is needed that would simplify the focus and ensure that HR capabilities are deployed in the most effective ways. He suggests that many chief HR officers are unaware of how key business decisions are made, and they have great difficulty analysing why people – or whole parts of the organization – are not meeting the business' performance goals, largely because few HR leaders have experience of other business roles than HR. Charan argues that HR functions should be split into HR-A (for administration), which would primarily manage compensation and benefits and report to the chief financial officer, who would have to see compensation as a talent magnet, not just a major cost. The other, HR-LO (for leadership and organization), would focus on improving the people capabilities of the business and would report to the CEO. While yet another phase of HR transformation would not be welcome, such a proposed split at least acknowledges that it is time to question what HR's core role is, and how that can be configured to offer scope for HR to better meet the needs of different stakeholders.

In the next chapter I shall consider further the effects of the new work culture on the changing social and psychological contracts of employees, examining in particular the reported effects of loss of existential meaning in work.

Points to ponder

*   What do you consider should be HR's core focus?
*   What might resolve the 'no-win' situation many HR functions appear to find themselves in?

Section III

The impact of the new work culture on employees

8 The emerging psychological contract

In Chapters 4 and 6 we looked at some of the reported changes taking place in the workplace in the early years of the twenty-first century. We considered how the work culture of new capitalism was emerging, characterized by restructurings, flexibilization, work intensification, performativity and more political work climates.

In this chapter we shall look at how these changes affected individuals, using the lens of psychological contract, a component of social exchange theory (see Chapter 2). In an environment of rapid organizational change, where ideas of employee satisfaction and motivation could be seen as potentially meaningless, psychological contract is useful as an analytical device in social and organizational research to describe, understand and predict the consequences of changes occurring in the employment relationship (Shore and Tetrick, 1994). It also provides an integrative concept to make sense of people's accounts of their working lives and around which to converge the concerns of the contemporary workplace.

Guest (2004) argued that the worth of the psychological contract is in seeing employees as active agents in, rather than passive recipients of, the processes involved in the managing of individuals, and that close attention required to be paid to all possible factors that contributed to the individual psychological contract. Guest (2004) also suggested that greater consideration of content at the level of the individual would facilitate analysis of the employment relationship and greatly enrich research into psychological contracts in general.

In particular, we shall explore:

- What was the impact of the work culture on the (collective) psychological and social contract?
  - The effects of job insecurity.
  - To what extent was the 'employability thesis' working?
  - What support did employees expect/hope for from their employers?
  - How was trust affected?
  - How well did employees appear able to cope with the increasing demands made of them?
- How much were employees able to exercise agency in the new work culture?
  - What evidence exists that employees were, and remained, willing to comply with managerial demands for increasing workloads?
  - To what extent did people adopt what Sennett (2006: 5) calls 'the cultural ideal of new capitalism', i.e. a 'self oriented to the short term, focused on potential ability, willing to abandon past experience'?

140 *Impact of new work culture on employees*

A fair deal?

Employee relations based on individualized HRM approaches have generally resulted in UK employees having relatively less employment protection compared with that enjoyed by their counterparts in many parts of mainland Europe. Nevertheless, HRM approaches to employee relations seek to secure employee commitment and performance by perpetuating the illusion of mutuality of interest between employers and employees. This mutuality is inherent in the 'old' white-collar psychological career contract. As a reminder, this was based on an exchange of responses to mutual needs – job security and the possibility for career progression for employees – in exchange for hard work, performance and loyalty for employers.

Guest (1995) argued that the psychological contract is operationalized in the minds of employees by the extent to which an organization (through its management) has kept its promises/commitments with respect to job security, careers and the demands of the job. Perceived fairness of treatment in general, and more specifically with respect to reward allocation (the effort–reward bargain) is crucial. When such conditions are satisfied, Guest argued, the consequences would be attitudinal, in terms of organizational commitment, life satisfaction, employment relations, feelings of security; and behavioural, in terms of motivation, effort, innovation, organizational citizenship, intention to stay/quit and performance. Thus a relationship of trust would exist between the parties and employees would be likely to feel 'engaged'.

On the other hand, breaches or violations of the old psychological contract would be evident in the 'end of career', loss of job security, the increase in workload and working hours, the ending of collective industrial relations and the currency of individualized employee relations, together with growth of the contract culture. Guest proposed that what explains the variations in psychological contracts most strongly are HRM practices, such as appraisal, interesting and challenging work, care over selection, development and guarantees of no compulsory redundancies. Hartley (1999) argues that, when the organization deliberately or unwittingly breaks psychological contracts, employees may behave in a variety of ways, depending on the size of the gap between expectation and reality. Withdrawal and exit are examples of such responses. In addition, employees can experience anxiety and stress.

Job insecurity

The expectation of job continuity is a major component of the old psychological contract. The damage that workforce reductions cause to 'old' psychological contracts has been examined in a number of studies (Rousseau and Anton, 1991; Rousseau and Aquino, 1993). Job insecurity is defined by Hartley et al. (1991: 10) as 'a discrepancy between the security employees would like their jobs to provide and the level they perceive to exist'. A study carried out for the Joseph Rowntree Foundation (Gordon, 1999) found that professional workers went from being the most secure group in the mid-1980s to the most insecure group in the mid-1990s. The study examined the multidimensional character of job insecurity. If job security was part of what employees hoped for, and expected from their employer, then job insecurity would arise as a consequence of psychological contract breach or violation.

There is debate about the extent of job insecurity at the turn of the century. Herriot and Pemberton (1995b) for instance argue that job security for white-collar workers was reduced from the 1980s onwards but was further undermined by the extent of downsizing from the mid-1990s. They argue that downsizing has fundamentally transformed the employment relationship. Similarly, longitudinal data (Organisation for Economic Co-operation and

Development, 1995) suggests that between 1985 and 1995 British workers registered the sharpest decline of confidence in employment security in Europe. Moreover, an International Survey Research (1995) survey of 400 companies in 17 countries employing over 8 million workers throughout Europe, showed that the employment security of workers had significantly declined in the previous ten years, with the UK figures revealing the sharpest drop in security levels from 70 per cent in 1985 to 48 per cent in 1995. On the other hand, Guest (1998) argues that the extent of job insecurity has been exaggerated and limited to certain groups of more vulnerable employees who may fear being unable to find other jobs.

There is also debate about the impact insecurity has on individual employees and on important organizational outcomes. Many theorists agree that, in terms of individual wellbeing, job insecurity is linked with stress. For many people the threatened disruption of job continuity constitutes a major breach of the psychological contract, causing in some cases a serious personal crisis. Some theorists argue that, with respect to organizational outcomes, job insecurity can be beneficial since it may cause employees to increase their work effort; others suggest that this then becomes a source of employee 'burnout' and leads to a drop in productivity (Maslach and Leiter, 2008).

Victor and Stephens (1994) note how the security of a role anchored in an organization and codified in a job description is being supplanted by stress-ridden, 'hyper-flexible workplaces' where roles are defined by the task of the moment, and where rights become ephemeral as everything is driven by the demand to be adaptive and innovative. These 'high-velocity' workplaces, Victor and Stephens (1994: 481) contend, 'offer no ongoing relationships, no safe haven, no personal space'. Everything is negotiable and disposable.

Hartley (1999: 136) argues that the extent to which changes in the work environment lead to a stressful perception of job insecurity hinges on three major factors:

1. The beliefs about what is happening in the environment, or the appraisal of the threat posed by change.
2. The resources available to the person, as perceived by him or her, to counteract the threat.
3. The perceived seriousness of the consequences if the threat is realized and the employee loses his or her job.

Thus the threat of job loss does not even have to be realized in order to create stress. Hartley argues that, while job loss is often very damaging to individuals, job insecurity is potentially more damaging since it represents a chronic condition. This loss of job security is progressive, occurs within a familiar workplace setting and represents a subjective change to the job and the organization. This reduces the visibility of the events and the social support for those involved. As Hartley (1999: 132) points out, 'Whatever the repercussions of job insecurity, they tend to develop subtly, not necessarily with any observable or formal role changes'. In the Gordon (1999) study, even people who did not fear losing their jobs experienced increased uncertainty in their career due to the changed nature not just of their career, but of their working conditions and the way they were treated in general. Many employees were very concerned about losing valued job features such as their control over the pace of work and their opportunities for promotion. Whilst some employees reported an increase in their responsibilities, more than a quarter of respondents reported that their promotion prospects had decreased over the previous five years. The study also found that employees were unable to maintain a 'sense of security' if they did not trust their employer to look after their best interests.

This was reflected in the Management Agenda between 1999 and 2006. For instance, in 2001, 88 per cent of respondents reported that their organizations were undergoing change

142 Impact of new work culture on employees

programmes involving job losses and that they were experiencing job insecurity. When asked what was driving this sense of insecurity, the majority of respondents referred to having witnessed job losses in the previous decade and the climate of continuous change in which the implications for individuals were not yet clear, or where future changes were anticipated. Poor communication was also a key factor. Respondents stated that they neither knew what was going on, nor what the future might hold for the organization, or their role in it. Moreover, many respondents reported that they did not believe what they were being told, largely because they did not trust management, nor did they feel their needs were heard or considered important. In 2004, only 24 per cent of Agenda respondents trusted their organizational leaders to any extent.

How did insecurity affect people? In 2000, 68 per cent of people reported insecurity as having a negative effect on their loyalty to the organization (Figure 8.1) and 52 per cent on their motivation (Figure 8.2).

Yet despite uncertain employment prospects, unclear expectations and the reportedly heavy demands made of them, most 2000 respondents stated that they remained loyal to their organization. By 2004, regular restructurings and related job losses and job insecurity appeared to be taking their toll on occupational commitment, with 44 per cent of respondents reporting that they were no longer committed. Of these, 19 per cent reported that they were looking to leave at the first opportunity. Since employees base their psychological contract in part on implied contracts, even when an employee is not directly affected, workforce reductions can do serious damage to the psychological contract. Trust and the expectation of a fair deal evaporate and, far from notions of 'a job for life' or even of 'employability', as one 'survivor' commented, 'Security now depends on sponsorship rather than skills and competencies'.

Martin et al. (1998) found that the changing demand conditions, redundancies, different types of jobs, prospects of alternative employment and types of work undertaken by employees influenced employee perceptions and feelings of powerlessness to shape their expectations

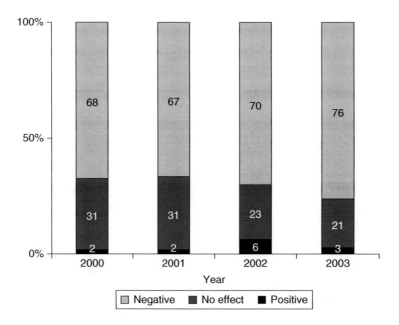

Figure 8.1 The effect of insecurity on loyalty (2000–3)

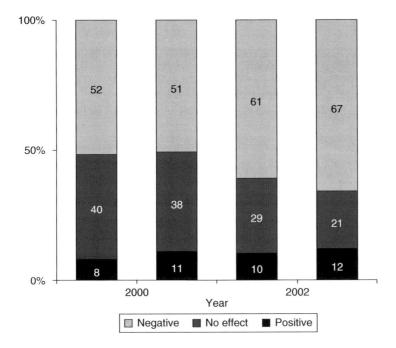

Figure 8.2 The effect of insecurity on motivation (2000–3)

of training and careers. Moreover, Herriot and Pemberton (1996) argue that if, as a result of restructuring, people end up in jobs which are at a lower level than before (i.e. when the new job is a step down/lower quality), individuals will be underemployed, which is as stressful as having too much to do, because it generates feelings of relative deprivation. As one financial services manager whose job had been 'delayered' from a more strategic role and now found himself a front-line 'team leader' put it, 'it's bad enough having to do work you moved on from years ago. The worst thing is explaining to my mother-in-law what being a "team-leader" is all about.'

The nature of perceived contract breach reported in the Agenda (2000–2005) extends beyond 'old' psychological contract expectations about job security and career progression to the quality of working life as a whole. The context of restructurings, flexibilization of organizational forms, significant work pressure, changes to work patterns, increasing levels of management control and reduced worker autonomy was increasingly reported to be problematic for employees. Indeed, it could be said that a new social contract was emerging that put the onus on individuals to rethink their expectations about careers and continuity of employment. Perhaps not surprisingly, concerns about work–life balance started to take precedence over careers for many employees.

Stress

As discussed in Chapter 4, to manage their increased workloads, individuals were putting in longer hours at work, which then led to feelings of stress and loss of control. Stress was a common part of working life for the majority of Management Agenda respondents (there were no significant differences by age, gender or sector). The major sources of stress in 1998 were reported as increased workload and lack of time to cope. The main reasons are summarized in the phrase 'when the demands placed upon me exceed my ability to deliver'.

In 2000, 87 per cent of Agenda respondents reported that they consistently worked longer than their contracted working week, with 46 per cent working between five and ten extra hours, a quarter working an extra 11–15 hours and 20 per cent working on average more than 15 extra hours per week. Half the sample stated that, in addition to coping with longer working hours and heavy workloads, they were now also expected to focus on innovation within their role.

In 2000, as Agenda respondents struggled with organizations' excessive demands, the boundaries between home and work had become blurred for many people. Given the growing importance of the topic, in 2000 I ran a series of focus groups with Agenda respondents who were asked to define what they meant by 'stress'. The main themes were 'anxiety, overload, loss of control and pressure'. The main source of stress was the growing gulf they perceived between the demands organizations made of them and their personal ability to deliver, and reported that this led to sleeplessness, the feeling that nothing is done well, a sense of being overwhelmed by the volume and complexity of work and an inability to balance home and work life. As Figure 8.3 suggests, the number of employees who perceived that their organization made excessive demands of them rose steadily between 2000 and 2003. Unsurprisingly, those who reported their organization makes excessive demands of them were more likely to report that they experienced stress at work.

The effects of stress were clearly undermining employee wellbeing. In the 1999 survey the word 'anxiety' featured over 600 times in open-ended statements. People reported being anxious over deadlines; about work issues 'that keep me awake at night'; 'pressure from family to work shorter hours'; 'affects mood with family and friends' and an inability to relax. Typical comments included, 'Screaming by Tuesday' and 'Never feeling I have done enough despite

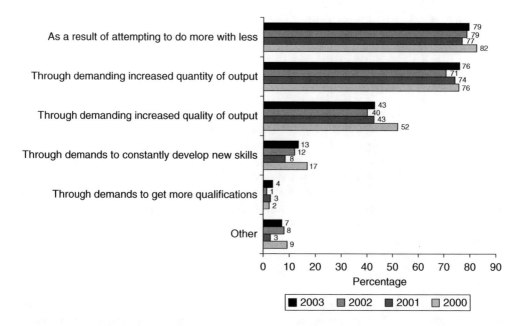

Figure 8.3 How does your organization make excessive demands of you?

The emerging psychological contract 145

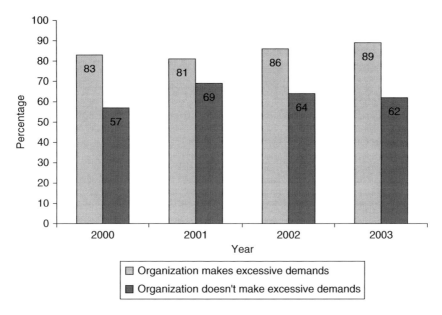

Figure 8.4 Percentage who experience stress as a result of work

an 80 hour week'. 'I am burning out! Can I maintain my position, and is it worth it?' In the 2002 Agenda there were over a hundred mentions of insomnia and poor quality sleep in the open-ended responses to the question of how stress affects people.

Symptoms of the stress reported included feeling out of control; 'I'm exhausted at the end of the day so I need to sleep before I can even eat'; 'upset stomach', 'tightness across the chest/palpitations'; uncharacteristic emotional outbursts; and even bad handwriting! One person reported having taken an overdose due to pressure. The situation appeared to be compounded by command and control management styles, lack of recognition from the manager or any real opportunity for 'empowerment'. One person reflected Sennett's 'specter of uselessness' in the phrase 'If only I was younger!'

In the 1999 survey some of the reported personal costs of heavy workloads included loss of social life, lack of time for family/interests/hobbies, postponed holidays, 'some disturbance to marriage', 'having to relocate family', 'moving home constantly' and a 'smaller circle of friends'. The majority of people making these sacrifices believed they were necessary in order to perform well. The ways in which employees were responding to the uncertainties and pressures of the workplace seemed to polarize into two camps: those who viewed the additional demands made of them as stressful, in some cases causing their health to suffer ('the strugglers' – the majority, of all ages), and those who did not ('the survivor thrivers') (see Figure 8.4).

Only a small number of people appeared to fit Bunting's (2004) 'willing slave' description by describing themselves as having willingly chosen to make these shifts to meet these new requirements. Some of their reasons for doing so included 'Because by then I was a workaholic', 'I push myself hard', 'to meet the quality standards I aspire to' and 'desire to be seen as an effective manager'. Other comments fell into the category of 'I'm not sure why I did this'. Respondents reported having only a small number of coping strategies such as: 'allowing some things to drop off the end'; 'by dropping "would like to do" type work'; 'job-sharing to maintain my energy'; 'fighting back when I think the workload is totally unreasonable'.

146　*Impact of new work culture on employees*

By 2003, stress was reported to be the biggest single health and safety problem facing the UK workforce, according to a TUC report (2004), which estimated 13.5 million working days lost each year to stress-related illness. The Health and Safety Executive (2007) introduced new standards on stress in 2003 which employers were expected to meet. Sources of stress were reported in the Agenda in 2003 included bullying at work, the long-hours culture, having to work at high speed, uncertainty about job roles, lack of control, redundancies, increasing workloads on those left behind, 'glass' and ethnic 'ceilings', and poor management of change.

By 2005, with a tight labour market, there was evidence that the number of full-time hours worked in the UK was beginning to fall, and the overall number of people in the Agenda reporting that they worked more than 48 hours per week declined between 1998 and 2005 by 7.5 per cent. By 2006, the Agenda reported that, while stress levels remained high (67 per cent), there was some improvement over the previous year (78 per cent in 2005), since some people seemed to be developing 'coping' strategies – which included looking for other jobs.

Coping strategies

In 2002 Agenda respondents were asked what coping strategies they used to deal with stress. These could be clustered as follows:

- Defensive/denial – examples include cynicism, block it out.
- Seeking consolation – alcohol, lots of chocolate, music.
- Looking after health/relaxation – gym, prayer, meditation, calm breathing, reflexology.
- Talking with others – talking things through with friends and family, socializing.
- Perspective – take a balanced view, switch off when I leave office, grin and bear it, rationalization, try to prioritize and manage time, moved to four-day week, move laterally to less stressful job.

One comment from a young marketing executive sums up many similar remarks: 'A large scotch and a rant to my understanding fiancée helps with letting off steam at the end of the day. The rest is probably denial.' Only a few comments suggested that some people were coping with pressure by learning to say 'no' and by assertively managing other people's expectations: 'I just ignore some work and prioritize the key issues. Also by making it quite clear that dates won't be met.'

Work–life balance

Throughout the Agenda study, 'work–life balance' became an increasingly prominent theme, although it only became categorized in this way in 2004 having been earlier described variously as an 'equal opportunities', then a 'working families', then a 'diversity' issue to reflect changing policy fashions and initiatives. In 1998, with no real job security, people were expected to work harder and smarter. In 1999, 85 per cent felt it necessary to make sacrifices in other areas of their lives to achieve career success while 63 per cent of respondents reported that their organizational culture expected them to make sacrifices which included missing out on time with children (64 per cent), suffering health problems (32 per cent) and even broken relationships (20 per cent).

Importance of work–life balance

In 2003, 98 per cent of respondents said that balance was personally important to them but only 52 per cent believed they had a satisfactory work–life balance. As managers themselves, 94 per cent of respondents believed they supported their own staff to achieve work–life balance. Slightly fewer respondents in 2005 (51 per cent versus 59 per cent in 2004) believed that they had satisfactory balance (Table 8.1).

By 2005 there was a growing disparity of views about the importance attached to the subject of work–life balance by employees and employers (Table 8.2). For employees, the trend was for work–life balance to increase in importance (70 per cent versus 49 per cent in 2004) while 66 per cent reported that their senior managers did not 'buy in' to the idea of work–life balance and therefore did not take it seriously.

Adaptation

In more recent years, there was a drop in the number of respondents reporting that they consistently worked longer hours (1998: 96 per cent; 2005: 85 per cent; 2007: 76 per cent), perhaps because they were better able to manage workloads. As Warr (2007) points out, processes of adaptation may contribute to an increased ability to handle environmental demands after a period of exposure to those demands. In that respect, everyday experience suggests that many people's capacity to manage a substantial workload becomes 'ratcheted up' after a period of coping with increased pressure; workload that would otherwise cause difficulties and strain can more easily be handled after a person has become adapted to a raised level. The impact of workload itself (an environmental feature) depends in part on judgements about one's situation.

Table 8.1 Work–life balance-related questions

		1998 %	2001 %	2002 %	2003 %	2004 %	2005 %
Do you currently have a satisfactory balance between your work and personal life?	Yes	56	53	61	52	59	51
Are you considering leaving your organization to achieve a better balance?	Yes	/	38	35	38	19	43
Do you as a manager actively support your staff in relation to home/work balance?	Yes	88	86	93	90	94	/
Do you experience any difficulties in trying to enable your team to achieve a balance between their work and personal lives?	Yes	/	37	44	44	51	/
Have you made sacrifices for your career in the past?	Yes	/	83	81	78	73	/

Table 8.2 How important is work–life balance?

	2004 %		2005 %	
	To you	*To your organization*	*To you*	*To your organization*
Increasingly important	49	32	70	21
Important	48	41	28	46
Unimportant	3	28	2	33

148 *Impact of new work culture on employees*

Were people receiving organizational support to help them cope? This seems unlikely. HR professionals, as organizational agents involved in negotiating (or imposing) the 'new deal', were described by Agenda respondents as too fragmented in focus and distribution to really deliver any perceived organizational support and career 'partnership'. Indeed, during this period, many HR teams were aware that delivering the employer side of the deal was not a business priority.

Of the organizational support available, 'truly flexible working' was considered the main enabler of work–life balance, i.e. where career advancement is not sacrificed for taking up flexible working. The take-up rate of flexible working in 2005, the year after the Employment Act came into force that offered parents of children under six the 'right to request' to work flexibly, was low and appeared to be highest in small organizations. By 2006, 67 per cent of respondents said they would refuse a promotion if it affected their work–life balance.

There may be several reasons for this. Over this period, 'work–life balance' gradually ceased to be considered as solely a 'women's issue' and the need for work–life balance was actively championed by a number of high-flying executives, some of whom were men. Furthermore, the Agenda in 2005 suggested that managements were perhaps starting to recognize that there was no financial benefit to be gained for organizations from expecting their managers to work longer hours. In other words, long hours did not equate to better financial performance, so managers in some organizations were perhaps seeking to change the long-hours culture. Moreover, employees were perhaps growing more confident about using more personal 'leverage' to renegotiate their psychological contract with their organization. In some cases, this meant very explicit transactions in which 'valued' employees negotiated for instance a sabbatical, or chance to study full-time for an MBA, in exchange for a commitment to return to the firm afterwards.

The 2006 Agenda highlighted that recruitment and retention were growing challenges for organizations, and employees were certainly in a better negotiating position to achieve what they wanted in 2006 than in 1998. Employees generally appeared to be gaining in confidence with regard to their own employability and, mirroring the lack of loyalty shown to them by organizations, seemed prepared to leave their employer if a better offer arose. As employees asserted their employability, organizations had to reassess the demands they were making of their workforce in order to emerge as an employer of choice. In such circumstances employees were better able to exercise agency.

Also, technology was enabling more flexible ways to manage workloads so that, although the number of hours worked remained the same, employees had more options around when and where they worked, thus enabling them to prioritize home and work issues differently. In other words, employees may no longer have believed they needed to sacrifice their personal life for their career.

The 'new deal'

It is perhaps in the theme of careers that the changes to the 'old' psychological contract are most evident. The downsizings of the 1990s appeared for the first time to significantly affect professional and managerial workers as well as those in blue-collar jobs. The former were people who were more likely than the latter to envisage their working lives as being about 'career'. Pervasive definitions of organizational or managerial careers have long encompassed notions of hierarchical progression. The traditional career-management processes of many large corporations, which often involved a dedicated team of HR professionals organizing ex-patriate and other development assignments for those deemed to be high-flyers, were gradually dismantled during the 1990s. For people on such schemes, the organization was largely responsible for managing individual careers.

For many professionals and managers, the flattening of organizational structures (delayering) resulted in fewer opportunities for vertical career progression in the form of promotion. Traditional definitions of career started to seem no longer appropriate (Arthur and Rousseau, 1996) and some theorists argued that the fundamental changes in the forms of organizations since the mid-1990s have led to the 'death of the career' (Hall, 1996; Cappelli, 1999). While this may be an exaggerated notion, the inherent short-termism of business within Anglo-American forms of capitalism means that the nature of 'careers' and 'employment' have been dynamically redefined. This section examines the extent to which white-collar employees appeared to be adjusting to the 'new deal'.

Was the employability thesis working?

The Agenda reflects the embedding of the new 'psychological career contract' or 'new deal' (see Herriot and Pemberton, 1995a: chapter 2). One of the constants in the Agenda over the period of study is the importance of careers to the people who respond. Almost every year over 80 per cent of respondents reported that careers were important or very important to them; less than 5 per cent reported that they were unimportant. Whilst there were no significant gender differences in how important career issues were to individuals in any year of the survey, age was a relevant factor, with younger people more frequently reporting career issues to be important or very important.

The 'employability thesis' (Rajan, 1997) suggests that 'enlightened' employers have been offering a 'new deal' to employees since they can no longer offer job security. This assumes that, in order to be successful in their career, employees will be willing to be flexible, self-manage their career and actively learn and accumulate new knowledge and skills that can be adapted and applied across different settings and jobs (Inkson and Arthur, 2001). Since the onus is on individuals to acquire relevant skills, this thesis implies that the new deal will drive an increase in demand for training which will be less employer driven and more employee driven.

Did people accept that they were responsible for managing their career?

Certainly there was growing recognition by individuals of the need to manage their own careers (Figure 8.5). In 1998, 53 per cent of Agenda respondents reported that they recognized the need to take responsibility for managing their own career. In 1999, most respondents (especially those aged 35 and over) reported frustration with the lack of opportunities for career progression and 'glass ceilings'. By 2004, 91 per cent of respondents reported that they had to manage their own careers since some respondents, especially senior managers, stated that their organizations no longer offered careers at all. In contrast, the importance of careers ascribed to organizations throughout that time, as perceived by respondents, averaged 12–14 per cent until 2003 when this figure rose to 26 per cent and has continued to rise slightly as organizations returned to career management and 'talent management' in the light of challenges with respect to recruitment, retention, succession planning and skill shortages noted in the 2005–7 surveys.

However, the vast majority of respondents in the early years of the twenty-first century still equated 'career' with 'within the context of being employed by an employer'. Only 9 per cent of Agenda respondents in 2001 (mainly aged 55 and over) were contemplating self-employment. This echoes the research of Pascale (1995) who concluded that only around one

150 *Impact of new work culture on employees*

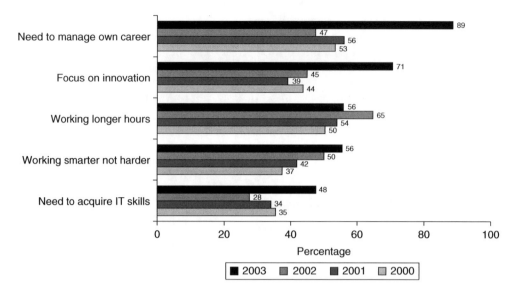

Figure 8.5 What impact has change had on your role?

tenth of the US workforce possessed the entrepreneurial traits and initiative deemed necessary to be able to implement the new free-agent relationships characterized by the new deal psychological contract.

Certainly the development message of employability was getting through. In the 2001 Agenda, 94 per cent of respondents claimed to have actively done something to develop themselves the previous year. For instance, 65 per cent were reflecting on how to develop their own career and 76 per cent were actively developing their skill sets for the future. In 2001 just 50 per cent of respondents reported feeling secure in their job. Nevertheless, with a buoyant job market, 98 per cent of respondents considered that they had the skills needed to be employable and many felt confident about finding other work.

With the advent of the knowledge economy, knowing what to learn and having access to learning opportunities was becoming problematic. Sparrow and Cooper (2003) argue that, since old-style career structures have been replaced by short-term jobs and tasks, flexible competence is key to employability. Moreover, career self-management would require relationship management skills.

Similarly, the cultural ideal of the 'enterprising worker' was becoming widespread. Agenda respondents (2001) recognized the need to be enterprising; they considered that the skills required to be successful in the new work culture were networking, flexibility, political acumen, ability to forge alliances, cultural awareness and 'extreme competitiveness'. Respondents reported that they were expected to be innovative and creative but many pointed out cultural mismatches between the rhetoric of 'enterprising' – such as no specific rewards for creativity – and reward systems which reinforced sticking to procedures and maintaining the status quo. People also reported having no time to be creative and limited processes to 'capture' creativity in a way that benefited both themselves and the organization. They also feared the consequences of making mistakes in the increasingly performative work cultures of the day. Many Agenda respondents argued that the new psychological contract must be accompanied by a change in management style, away from the old 'command and control' approach to one of 'empowerment', involving being given more responsibility, learning new skills and leaders getting better at communicating the direction of the organization.

Employees were increasingly expected to 'work on self' to comply with the new ideal employee specification. Increasingly, HRM assessment processes defined employees' performance and 'potential' in terms of the skills, attributes, behaviours and attitudes required of them, such as 'emotional intelligence' (Goleman, 1996). Emotional intelligence, with its components of self-awareness, awareness of other people's emotions and self-control, was reported in the Agenda to be widely integrated into assessment processes for recruitment and performance-appraisal purposes. It was thus a technology of control since it encouraged 'work on self', in order to self-regulate and comply with the template of 'ideal' employee or manager.

Though people recognized the need to learn new skills, the majority of 2002 Agenda respondents still wanted their organization to act as their 'partner' with respect to careers. They wanted more time to develop themselves, as well as more resources and organizational signposts to the development and career opportunities available, preferring to remain within the firm if possible. The main organizational support employees wanted was secondments and mentors. The 2002 Agenda suggested that the organizational side of the new deal was slow to materialize. In 2003, less than a third of organizations in the Agenda offered lateral career development opportunities (i.e. sideways moves at the same hierarchical level).

Responses to contract breach

While Agenda respondents in general appeared to be adjusting to the new deal in the period 2000–3, for many the violation of their 'old' psychological contract had had a significant effect on their motivation, commitment and sense of wellbeing. For many, the violation of psychological contract appeared to have occurred less over career development and more arising from workload issues, other disenchantment with their employer or a desire for better balance, in line with Herriot et al.'s (1997) findings. As a result, over half the sample group in 2001 were planning to leave their employers in the near future. A few people lamented being 'stuck' with their current employers as they were 'trapped' by pensions. In 2002, Agenda respondents said they were thinking more short-term with respect to their current jobs and career planning and it seemed that loyalty had been firmly replaced by 'me plc'.

Of those who were optimistic about job opportunities within their profession or sector, about half each year were considering moving jobs in the near future. From 2000, people who were considering leaving their organization were asked why they might move. Some people were contemplating 'downshifting', i.e. moving to a less demanding and less well-paid job, because of 'sheer overwork: I want a break'; 'less stress and more time with the family'.

The responses in Figure 8.6 show some interesting similarities and differences across the years. Compared with previous years, respondents in 2003 were more likely to report they would leave due to no opportunities to broaden skills, no challenges and a lack of responsibility, but proportionately fewer reported they would leave due to lack of (vertical) promotion prospects. Thus the 2003 respondents wanted stimulating work but not necessarily promotion. Poor money and incompatible ethical aims were also reported proportionately more in 2003 compared to previous years. As one professional put it, when asked what would attract him to another job, 'Money is not the issue, neither is promotion. Challenge and ethics are important.' Poor management, lack of appreciation and long hours were key reasons reported each year.

People who felt secure in their jobs were less likely to report that they would move jobs than those who did not feel not secure. This was observed each year and corresponds with respondents reporting that insecurity has a negative effect on loyalty and motivation.

152 *Impact of new work culture on employees*

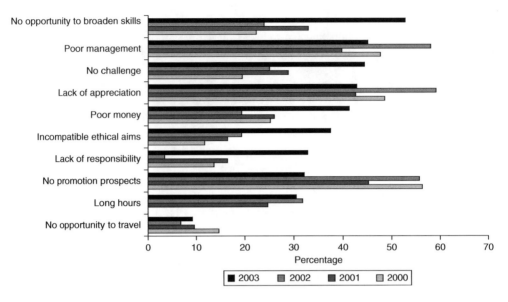

Figure 8.6 Why are you considering leaving your organization?

How people react to changes and perceived violations of their psychological contract may depend on a variety of factors. For instance, various studies report evidence that older workers lose trust in their organizations when their psychological contract is perceived to be violated (Herriot et al., 1997), while younger workers may have different reactions (Turnley and Feldman, 2000; Smithson and Lewis, 2000), reflecting a more 'realistic' understanding of the modern labour market (Brannen and Nilsen, 2002).

Alienation and cynicism

Central to the concept of psychological contract is the notion of trust. The assumption is that both parties will deliver their obligations to the other. When trust is lost, because one party reneges on their obligations, employees suffer contract breach. They are likely then to rebalance the contract perhaps by becoming cynical and less committed, or to rebalance the contract in other ways, perhaps by withdrawing their goodwill, sabotage or even exit, with potentially damaging consequences for employers. Cynicism towards employers is often seen as a symptom of loss of trust and potential breaches of psychological contracts as a result of organizational change efforts.

The 2004 Agenda reported high levels of employee cynicism,[1] accompanied by a lack of trust, particularly in senior managers, with only 24 per cent of respondents trusting their senior managers to a great extent. Typical reasons given for lack of trust at that time included unclear vision; an overload of and poor communication; a lack of consultation; unprofessional behaviour; lack of honesty; broken promises; poor performance management; political behaviour; and overall poor leadership. Some people appeared to cope through accepting a reduction in job satisfaction: 'I was rather blown off course. I have now a survival approach in an area that holds less intrinsic interest for me.'

The mutuality implicit in HRM approaches is especially put to the test through the issue of careers which for most Agenda respondents remains important but is perceived to be less important to employers. This mismatch is reflected in the lack of initiatives and management attention given to career issues and the increasing cynicism of employees towards the notion of 'career partnership' between themselves and their employer.

Similarly, any job, no matter how exciting, that spills over into one's personal life and takes up to 70–80 hours per week can drive out other fulfilling aspects of life such as family, friends or community. The growing need to take control of one's life is reflected in the fact that, for 89 per cent of Management Agenda 2004 respondents, work–life balance was of increasing importance, with only 3 per cent suggesting that balance was unimportant to them. On the other hand, 29 per cent claimed that their organization was dismissive of the issue. Similarly, 73 per cent had made sacrifices for their careers in the past, while 46 per cent would not be willing to do so in the future.

Of course the extent of employee alienation may be exaggerated. Gallie et al. (2001) explored employee-commitment factors in a comparison of employee surveys between 1992 and 1997, finding stable levels of employee commitment over that time. On the other hand, they also commented that 'while there is little evidence that British employees are hostile to their organisations, there is little sign of strong positive commitment'.

Disidentification theory (Kreiner and Ashforth (2004) suggests a negative association with organizational reputation (Dutton et al., 1994) and positive association with negative affectivity, cynicism and psychological contract breach (Rousseau, 1998). Participants in Management Agenda surveys reported that many facets of the new work culture had contributed to their disidentification from their employer. These included the relationships and behaviours characteristic of the new work culture – such as the more politicized and transactional relationships, lack of congruence by leaders, or failure to 'walk the talk' on values, workplace pressure and employee stress, anxiety and loss of wellbeing, loss of control, autonomy and balance. Cavanagh (1999) argues that business people working 50–70 hours a week, separating them from family life and faith, are thus unable to lead an integrated life. As Anderson and Schalk (1998) note, once these changes which cause fluctuation in the overall perception exceed certain boundaries, the psychological contract will either be revised or abandoned.

Moreover, a person's identity is now seen as an emergent, contingent process (Trevor-Roberts, 2006) rather than as a static connection to an organization or job. Identity is created and shaped through action (Rose, 1999). Changing careers, therefore, also involves changing one's identity. Evidence of this is most apparent during periods of unemployment when a rapid 'renegotiation' of identity occurs. Amundson (1994) argued that the more closely a person's identity is linked to work, the greater will be the individual's difficulty in coping with the unemployment period.

In addition, people differ with respect to how much agency or self-efficacy they can exercise in such contexts. Bandura's (2001) theory of self-efficacy refers essentially to what you are actually capable of doing in specific contexts or, more generally, who you may become as a person. This stands in contrast to perceived self-efficacy – that is, what you think you can do or become. For Bandura, your set of beliefs about what you can do and the extent to which you see yourself as having control over your life are by far the most central and persuasive aspects of personality. As a consequence, rather than by design, employees who are able to adapt and who have the behavioural and cognitive competencies associated with flexibility find themselves, rather than their roles, taking on the characteristics of permanent or core employees (Sennett, 2003: 630). These are the 'employable' employees, whereas those without such competency face the prospect of downgraded or outsourced roles.

But structuration theory suggests that individual agency is to a large extent tempered by structures. The extent to which people feel self-efficacy may be related to the specific

154 *Impact of new work culture on employees*

nature of the context, such as the scope it offers for individual discretion, as well as to personal differences, such as ambition and actual employability. For instance, while the numbers of Agenda respondents reporting confidence in their ability to maintain their effectiveness through change had dropped to 79 per cent in 2001 from 93 per cent in 1998, a minority of respondents (mainly between 25 and 35 years of age) in the years 1998–2003 felt the increased demands made of them were a positive thing, giving them a developmental 'stretch', especially if their roles had grown broader (86 per cent of respondents had changed job roles in the previous two years as a result of restructurings).

The main motivator for these younger respondents was a challenging job and most admitted that ambition was their key driver. As one middle manager reflected in 2002, 'I didn't know how else to behave'. Such employees risked becoming the 'willing slaves' described by Bunting. Hall (1996: 22) argued that, if employees are ambitious and driven to succeed, organizations can exploit them by making them work ever harder and longer since 'We too are prime candidates to be exploited to serve someone else's ends if we are talented, have the ability to learn…and are greedy. Ironically, these are precisely the qualities that our schools, professions and employers strive to instil in us.' Agenda respondents were divided about whether their employer expected more of them than they were prepared to offer. The majority of those who had no complaints about what their organization required of them were people who had set up their own businesses and were prepared to do what was necessary to succeed. In these cases, the individuals had a considerable degree of autonomy and were able to exercise agency, even though they were under personal pressure to succeed.

While in 2005, 85 per cent of Agenda respondents still reported working longer than their contracted working week (96 per cent in 1998), less than a quarter said they needed to do so in order to be successful. After workload, the most common reason for working longer hours was 'enjoyment of the job', suggesting that some managers at least had a choice. As Hall points out (1996: 30) many people have deep intrinsic satisfaction from their work which for them has many of the qualities we associate with play. These people choose to be overinvolved.

Over time, respondents generally appeared to be coping better with their heavy workloads. This is supported by findings from the Agenda 1999 survey where 30 per cent of respondents reported having sacrificed their physical health for career success, and 18 per cent had sacrificed their mental health (Figure 8.7). There were, however, significant differences between the sacrifices reported by men and women. Men were particularly likely to report they missed out on time with their children for their career, whereas women were more likely to report their physical health had suffered.

People who had not made sacrifices for their career were asked if they had sacrificed their career for their personal life (Figure 8.8). In previous years, women had always been more likely to respond that they had sacrificed their careers for their personal life but data from 2003 revealed an increase in men reporting they too had sacrificed their careers for their personal life. While until 2002 most employees reported that they were willing to make sacrifices for the sake of their careers by working long hours, by 2003 there was the beginning of a growing cohort of men and women managers who were no longer prepared to sacrifice everything else for their careers, as suggested in Figure 8.8.

There were no significant age or sector differences. As one 40-year-old manager explained, 'Work is less enjoyable and satisfying than home and social activity', while another respondent commented 'there's more to life than being what you do'. Getting older was a key factor for a number of respondents, causing them to change priorities. Others talked of 're-evaluating priorities' and needing to establish balance after 'seeing others burn out'. For many people, this re-evaluation has led them to consciously take charge of their own life, as in this example: 'I am not going to sell my soul to an organisation again. Family life is more important and I need

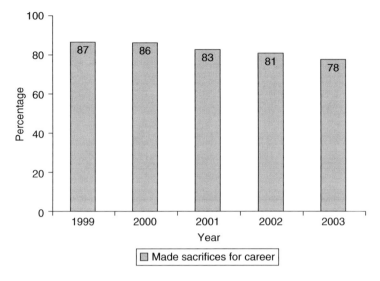

Figure 8.7 I have made sacrifices for my career

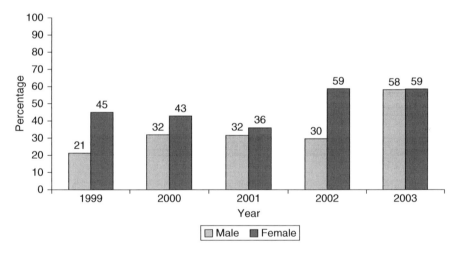

Figure 8.8 Have you sacrificed your career for your personal life?

to have more balance.' Sadly, a number of respondents, some of whom were also facing the prospect of redundancy, were motivated negatively to focus on things other than work, as in this comment from one manufacturing manager: 'I no longer feel secure. One day I will be made redundant and I have no outside interests so I had better develop some!'

Was the 'old' career deal dead?

Guest (1998) argues that the psychological contract concept has shown resilience despite the breaches which have arisen from changes in the business environment such as the disappearance of the concept of lifetime employment; the declining importance of the unions

156 *Impact of new work culture on employees*

which has resulted in a shift from industrial relations to employment relations; reductions in the number employed as subcontracting; the fragmentation of the workforce through flexible working and virtual teaming; and the greater diversity in the workplace both in terms of gender and race.

The new deal appears to represent a less benign and more ruthless alternative to the old deal.

The emerging social contract was one of instability, uncertainty and indeterminacy. 'Obedience for security' was replaced by 'initiative for opportunity' (Herriot and Pemberton, 1995a). This was being normalized within organizations whose work culture was characterized by short-termism, performativity, more aggressive and conflicted work climates, declining job quality, heavy pressures on individuals from work intensification, the continuous exposure to measurement and control, the absence of trust and loss of autonomy. Thus Agenda respondents recognized that they bear the risks in the employment relationship and expect to look after their own interests rather than trust employers to do so.

Who suffers most?

Much of the literature suggests that contract breach has more intense emotional implications than contract fulfilment. Atkinson (2007) finds that trust is generally low in purely transactional contracts and only becomes important in relational ones: transactional components relying on cognitive trust and relational components on affective trust. Breach of a transactional component leads to lower perceived obligations for the employee or higher obligations for the employer. Breach in a relational component, however, is more severe as this has an emotional impact; this may change the nature of the relationship and result in ongoing loss of trust.

Johnson and O'Leary's study (2003) suggests that employees suffer more than their employers from the combined effects of psychological breach and cynicism. They studied the different effects of two types of social-exchange violation: those that generate perceptions of psychological contract breach and of organizational cynicism. They found that only psychological contract breach (not cynicism) predicted employees' behavioural responses (low performance, absenteeism). Further, affective cynicism fully mediated the relationship between psychological contract breach and emotional exhaustion, suggesting that cynical attitudes have negative consequences for the attitude holder.

With respect to careers, most Agenda participants seemed to accept the 'employability thesis' – recognizing that they would need to continue to learn and develop throughout their lives and to be responsible for managing their own careers. Whilst some people appeared to welcome the more transactional nature of the new employment relationship, others felt betrayed by their employer over the one-sided ending of the 'old deal'. Mostly people said they were too busy to think about their career and they wanted to carry on working for their then employer, largely because they were not sure what other employment possibilities they had.

Breach of a relational contract is therefore likely to have the proportionally greater impact on employee emotions, attitudes and behaviours such as job satisfaction, citizenship behaviours, organizational commitment, turnover intentions and actual turnover, perceived job security and motivation and performance. These findings suggest that when work and the workplace lack meaning, people are alienated, morale suffers and people *dis*identify from the organization, start to look for other jobs or consider self-employment. Change also becomes more difficult to manage. Equally, many people appeared to feel obliged to continue to work for their organization and comply with the behavioural norm of the new work culture, even though this may cut across their personal values and cause them discomfort. The consequences

The emerging psychological contract   157

of alienation for their own health and wellbeing are reflected in this comment by Jim Collins (2001: 210): 'It is impossible to have a great life unless it is a meaningful life. And it is very difficult to have a meaningful life, without meaningful work.' This loss of meaning, I argue, is synonymous with violation of psychological contract and worker alienation. We shall return to this topic in the next chapter.

Discussion

This historical review of the changing workplace (1998–2007) suggests that, throughout this period, the changed nature of production and the radically altered work environment in which careers are constructed shifted the balance of power in the employment relationship towards employers and, as a result, psychological and social contracts were significantly revised in their favour.

Herriot and Pemberton (1997) suggest that employee reactions to the 'new deal' may be exaggerated and that organizations may be in danger of underestimating the fundamentally transactional nature of the employment relationship for many of their employees. Indeed, they argue that many employees would be perfectly happy if they were to receive pay above the going rate. In contrast, Sennett (2006) suggests that, in banishing old ills, the new economy model has instead created new social and emotional traumas. The culture of the new capitalism demands an ideal self, oriented to the short term, focused on potential ability rather than accomplishment, willing to discount or abandon past experience. Loyalty between the company and employees is no longer evident because workers know that they are simply a tool that can be replaced with the twist of a wrench.

And for many Agenda respondents, representing a more general white-collar population, who still appeared to aspire to job security and a long-term employment relationship with their employer, the effects of the ending of the old psychological contract appeared largely negative. Sennett argues that as work is reshaped to stress short-term goals, this leads to alienation, or 'corrosion' of character, since character is expressed by loyalty and mutual commitment, and through the pursuit of long-term goals. He describes what we are doing to ourselves as we chop and change professional paths, decentralized structures, incessant risk and teamwork as against the hierarchies of yesteryear: 'Only a certain kind of human being can prosper in unstable, fragmentary institutions', he argues (2006: 3).

Schein (1965) argued that, for the psychological contract to exist, agreement between the parties is necessary, which includes a process of negotiation and renegotiation. Herriot and Pemberton (1997) suggested that, while the content of the psychological contract may vary, the process of contracting is a social process and is likely to be similar wherever contracts are made. The ability to renegotiate career contracts will therefore vary according to the relative power balances in the employment relationship.

With respect to the employability thesis, in these early Management Agenda findings, the gap appeared to be widening between what employees wanted and what they perceived their organization to offer. Because even though most employees accepted that they must manage their own careers, most also wanted organizational support for development. These findings suggest that organizational support was generally not very forthcoming.

Yet, if people are genuinely employable, and are valued by their employer, they will have more power in the employment relationship than employers. If labour market conditions change, the nature of psychological contracting may change again. For many employees in this study, it seemed that the negotiated relationship was becoming a more informed transaction as time went on, rather than a passive exchange. As reflected in the Agenda, work–life balance

158 *Impact of new work culture on employees*

grew to be a significant element of what employees aspired to achieve in their careers, in the light of eroding control over workloads. So important did these issues appear to become, that many employees increasingly reported being unwilling to sacrifice other parts of their lives for the sake of career development.

In a sense, these employees came to exercise agency in response to these structural pressures, even if this meant re-evaluating and modifying their own career aspirations. For many, achieving work–life balance appeared to become more important than achieving conventional career success in the form of promotion up a hierarchy. Some were contemplating or actually 'downshifting' in the way that Bunting (2004) advocated, reducing their working days, taking less demanding jobs, working from home or taking time out from their working life to study, travel or in other ways regain a sense of time sovereignty in their lives. Whether these choices represented employees' pragmatic accommodation to the demanding working conditions they experienced within the new work culture, or reflected individual employees' life stages, it is not possible to tell from this study. In this evolving social contract, definitions of work–life balance were also extending beyond the balance between work and the family unit, to considerations about the wider impact of business on society and community life.

I agree with Herriot and Pemberton (1997), who argue that the damaging effects of change on the white-collar psychological contract call for a more reciprocal employment relationship which recognizes and permits pluralism of interests, a topic we return to in Chapter 12.

Conclusion

In this chapter and Chapter 4 I have argued that, in the employer-led drive to increase profit through labour flexibility, the seemingly mutual employment exchange between employers and employees, as reflected in the 'old' psychological contract, became unbalanced in favour of employers. The Management Agenda data presented in this chapter suggest that employer commitments to a collective social contract akin to the 'old' psychological contract of white-collar work were gradually reduced or abandoned altogether over this period. As a consequence, Sennett (2006: 5) argues, individuals found themselves caught in 'unstable, fragmentary social conditions' that generate 'ontological insecurity'.

The psychological contract is inherently subjective. It is based on perceptions by the employee about mutuality. Yet the cultural ideal of today's organizations, Sennett contends, is short-term and 'damages many of the people who inhabit them' (2006: 6). For instance, Hartley (1999) argues that while job loss is often very damaging to individuals, job insecurity is potentially more damaging since it represents a chronic condition. This loss of job security is progressive, occurs within the familiar workplace setting and represents a subjective change to the job and the organization. This reduces the visibility of the events and social support for those involved. As Hartley (1999: 132) points out, 'Whatever the repercussions of job insecurity, they tend to develop subtly, not necessarily with any observable or formal role changes'. Hartley argues that this chronic job insecurity is much more a 'socially and psychologically constructed phenomenon' (1999: 133). 'Since job insecurity exists within a person as a result of his or her perceptions and cognitions, it is not open to direct observation: rather it is a construct that is inferred from the employees' verbal report or observed behaviour' (1999: 134). Since the effect of job insecurity is subtle and not visible, could this explain why so many Management Agenda respondents reported experiencing various forms of loss or lack, without being able to name what was missing? We shall explore what we subsequently named 'the search for meaning' in the next chapter.

Points to ponder

- To what extent do you consider job insecurity to be an issue these days? Given its 'invisibility', how would you find out about its prevalence?
- How much do you believe that people entering employment these days would expect the kinds of careers their predecessors experienced? What would be the same/different?
- Should employers offer some employees at least a longer-term employment relationship? If so, why? If not, why not?

Note

1 Cynicism represents an attitude composed of negative beliefs and feelings that influences individuals' perceptions of events and behaviour, which in turn affects their trust (Whitener et al., 1998: 513). Cynicism has both cognitive and affective elements (Dean et al., 1998). In the Management Agenda there were many instances of employee cynicism reflected in the increasing numbers of comments relating to gaps between management rhetoric around values, and actual practice, such as 'The restructure has given senior management the chance to do yet more Empire building' and 'Decisions driven by personal agenda of Director and his peers'.

9 The search for meaning

> Ever more people today have the means to live, but no meaning to live for.
> (Viktor Frankl, 2006)

In previous chapters I have argued that, from the 1980s on, as part of the neo-liberal drive for organizations to increase profit through labour flexibility, the seemingly mutual employment exchange between employers and employees, as reflected in the 'old' psychological contract, appeared to become unbalanced in favour of employers. Labour flexibility was being achieved at the expense of employees' job security. I have also argued that the new work culture, with its work-intense and performative managerial practices, together with both the commodification and the commoditization of white-collar work, generally appears to have resulted in reduced employee autonomy and wellbeing.

In this chapter my focus returns again to an exploration of the impact of the new work culture on the psychological contracts of white-collar workers at perhaps a deeper level. Here I examine the findings from a strand of research carried out in 2004 arising from the Management Agenda surveys of 2000–3, namely an exploration of why many employees were reporting a loss of meaning at work.

I begin by explaining my interest in this topic and provide a brief overview of the methods of data collection and analysis used. I then outline some key literature themes and go on to interweave selected themes from the study's findings throughout this chapter. This includes how people define 'meaning', why people feel the need for greater meaning at work, how meaning is destroyed, what people find meaningful in work and how meaning at work is enabled. I also consider the role of corporate purpose in enabling meaning at work. I conclude by evaluating the strengths and limitations of the research, and by outlining an emerging model suggesting possible future research possibilities.

Why did I research this topic?

I initially became interested in the issue of meaning and work in 2001. The choice of topic arose from a subtheme emerging from a rising number of apparently unrelated open-ended responses in the Management Agenda since 1999. These were thematically analysed into clusters which all related to variations on a sense of 'lack' or a 'loss'. These themes included a lack of purpose, trust and commitment; a general loosening of emotional and other ties relating to colleagues and the workplace; a loss of motivation and of personal direction; a feeling that the nature and purpose of the organization and/or respondents' work was not worthwhile.

In 2003–4, when a colleague, Nigel Springett, and I carried out this research, the British economy was enjoying a period of relatively unbroken growth, despite occasional downturns.

The labour market was relatively buoyant, the consumer economy was booming, and to paraphrase Harold Macmillan it might be argued that people 'had never had it so good'. And yet there were increasing numbers of people each year in the Management Agenda (70 per cent in 2002; 76 per cent in 2003) reporting that they lacked meaning at work.

I initially assumed that this subtheme, which I termed 'Quest for meaning at work', was symptomatic of the zeitgeist and temporary economic downturn at the turn of the millennium. Another characteristic of the macro-context backdrop at the time was the widespread socio-economic and political turbulence on a global scale, not least the aftermath of 9/11, the War on Terror and home-grown terrorism, wars in Iraq and Afghanistan, which unsettled and disturbed large sections of the UK population. I was conscious that in such a context, as Overell (2008: 6) comments: 'It seems impossible to imagine that in times of deep hardship, industrial strife, hunger and war, ideas so superficially fey as meaningful work might have some appeal.' However, I was curious to understand whether, given the persistence and volumes of 'lack/loss' comments in the Management Agenda, these reflected a deeper, longer-term phenomenon. I decided to investigate the question of meaning more specifically in 2003.

The aim of the research was to investigate people's understandings of 'meaning', especially with regard to the workplace, and to explore what constitutes 'meaning-full' and 'meaningless' experiences:

- What did employees mean by 'meaningful' work?
- What conditions were present when people experienced a sense of meaning, or a lack of this, in the workplace?
- To what extent were employees experiencing existential loss of meaning in the new work culture?
- How did meaning/loss of meaning manifest itself?
- If people were searching for more meaning at work, why was this?

These issues are not well grounded in empirical data in much of the literature and research and our aim in this enquiry was to 'ground' the definition of 'meaning' at work. In particular, we wanted to discover if there were links between people's experience of the new work culture, changes to their psychological contract and their loss of/search for meaning at work.

In terms of conceptual framework, Giddens' 'structuration theory' (1986) is very useful in synthesizing micro and macro issues, seeing connections between the most 'micro' aspects of society – individuals' internal sense of self and identity – and the big 'macro' picture of the state, multinational capitalist corporations and globalization. In this strand of research I focus on the micro, but also on the interaction between the two. On a micro scale, Giddens argues, an individual's internal sense of self and identity becomes a reflexive project that has to be interpreted and maintained.

Yet this micro-level change cannot be explained only by looking at the individual level, as people do not spontaneously change their minds about how to live; nor can it be assumed that they are directed to do so by social institutions and the state. On a macro scale, globalization offers vast new opportunities for business, but crises such as 9/11 can affect the entire world, spreading far outside the local setting in which they first developed, and directly influencing individuals. A serious explanation of such issues must lie somewhere within the network of macro and micro forces. These levels should not be treated as unconnected; in fact, Giddens argues, they have significant relation to one another.

So while interest in meaning at work is almost certainly not a new phenomenon, our starting point was to argue that the rising interest in meaningful work may be explained as a consequence of organizational changes that derive from a neo-liberal agenda and which have become more pronounced in the recent past. I saw this as Thatcherism working its

162 *Impact of new work culture on employees*

way ever-more profoundly through the system, at an accelerating pace, with consequences for employees and society as a whole. The banking crisis of 2008 represents just one manifestation of the practices and values which derive from the unbridled pursuit of a neo-liberal agenda.

The initial research method involved a literature review and analysis of specific multiple-choice response and open-ended questions included in the Management Agenda surveys in 2003 and 2004. I believed that qualitative methods were most likely to lead to deeper insights into people's perceptions and experiences. As Hall (1996) points out, when we look at career and occupational experiences, we need to see these experiences in the context of that individual's total life, encompassing all the other important current roles and subidentities as well as hopes and dreams for the future:

> We need to look at the individual's overall quest for meaning and purpose as she or he pursues what Shepard (1984) calls the 'path with a heart'. This requires the use of concepts and research methods that will let us probe individuals' sense of direction in the search for work that has personal meaning…relational influences are powerful methods for the task.
>
> (Hall, 1996: 7)

Accordingly, a series of three focus-group meetings, involving a total of 30 people, explored the topic using appreciative inquiry methodology (Cooperrider and Srivastva, 1987). I wrote up the management implications of the study for my work purposes in a Roffey Park report, *In Search of Meaning at Work* (2004).

In the next section I provide an overview of key literature themes relating to meaning, and how these informed our research questions.

Literature on meaning

At the time we carried out this strand of research (2004), much of the literature considering the perennial nature of mankind's existential search for meaning was reflected in several literatures, focusing on leadership, spirituality, psychology and philosophy (e.g. Jung and Victor Frankl).

Meaning – a perennial quest?

Much of the literature relating to the concept of 'meaning' concerned the notion of spirituality. Indeed, the notion of spirituality has been employed to explain and understand a deeper, more defining sense of meaning at work since the new spiritual movements of the 1960s (Lonergan, 1957). 'Spirituality', however, is a problematic word in the literature, meaning different things to different people. The complexity is demonstrated by the many labels given to each that refer to a particular discourse of leadership or management or social practice at work. One of the major differences is about whether spirituality in the workplace is given a religious meaning.

Emotion in general and spirituality more specifically represent core concepts within the organizational transformation literature (Cooper, 1997; Argyris, 1964). Particularly in American management texts, spirituality is generally used to describe numerous organizational phenomena, including organizational change, value systems, identity, managing, leadership, executive development and empowerment (Conger, 1994). The expected benefits of spirituality are supposed to include a better work environment, ethical business practice and a satisfied workforce. And a better balance with the structurally short-termist perspectives of management that are thought to constrain consideration of the larger picture.

Mitroff and Denton (2000), proponents of the 'spiritual paradigm' for management, argue that renewal – both individual and organizational – affects the essence or core and is associated with spirituality. Characteristics of renewal in the workplace are entrepreneurship, courage, passion, creativity and innovation. In particular they associate spirituality at work with self-fulfilment: 'the workplace is one of the most important settings in which people come together daily to accomplish what they cannot do on their own, that is, to realize their full potential as human beings' (2000: 7). There is also an extensive popular literature consisting of self-development texts. The latter mainly consists of works focused on improving self-effectiveness, for instance through mindfulness and variations on meditative practices (Harris, 2008; Hayes, 2004).

Search for meaning: a post-modern phenomenon?

Since 2004 there has been a steady rise in the number of research studies (mostly American) exploring meaning in the workplace. Within the literature, several themes suggest that there is a growing 'search for meaning' arising from:

1. The intensifying search for individual self-fulfilment, which reflects the stage of development of society.
2. Crises of late capitalism and contemporary harsh working conditions.

I shall now explore these themes in more detail.

Stage of development of society

The function of work as a means of self-actualization (in Maslowian terms), and through which people experience a sense of personal identity and purpose, is explored by many writers. Marx argued that work is central to humanity, since: 'In creating an objective world by his practical activity, in working-up inorganic nature, man proves himself a conscious species being, i.e. a being that treats the species as its own essential being' (Marx and Engels, 1988: 76–7). It is from this belief that self-directed work is the essential quality of being human that Marx exalted work itself as a 'liberating activity', 'the first premise of all human co-existence'; at one point, he wrote of 'attractive work, the individual's self-realisation' (1973: 611). Marx further argued that work under capitalism was both alienating and destructive. He considered that the commodification of work under industrial capitalism causes alienation – the loss of humanness experienced when workers lack control over work and are forced to sell an inherent part of themselves. Marx viewed alienation as embedded in work under capitalism.

Tischler (1999) explains the growing interest in meaning and spirituality as a theory of social consciousness and motivation. He also argues that the search for meaning at work is a natural reflection of the evolution of society over the past 200 years, from an agrarian society of little change for the majority of people through an industrial society that, through a machine orientation, created:

- comparatively enormous wealth for most people in developed countries;
- a mass society with attendant changes in social structure and social consciousness; and
- an unimaginably faster and increasing pace of change.

Changing values, he argues, are related to the experience of fragmentation in a highly organized society since we are now in a post-industrial society that focuses on individual achievement

164 *Impact of new work culture on employees*

and self-actualization growth for as many people as possible in a socially, economically and environmentally sustainable and responsible manner.

Sociologist Ronald Inglehart has carried out a World Values survey since 1970 that he claims is now representative of 70 per cent of the world's population. This provides empirical evidence of a shift in people's values and motivations around work, particularly among the most developed nations, away from an emphasis on instrumental rationality, economic growth and physical and material security above all, towards 'post-material values' emphasizing quality of life, self-expression and personal and cultural growth – an echo, perhaps, of the psychological needs theories of Maslow and Herzberg. Maslow's (1987) hierarchy of needs theory suggested that there are five basic levels of need: physical or survival needs, security needs, social needs, achievement needs and self-actualization needs. Inglehart argues that, for a growing proportion of people, once their physical and material security has been achieved, new priorities emerge: 'The disciplined, self-denying and achievement-oriented norms of industrial society are giving way to an increasingly broad latitude for individual choice of lifestyles and individual self-expression' (1997: 44). This has meant 'a growing insistence on interesting and meaningful work'. Thus, as workers decreasingly look to outer situations and their structures to motivate their behaviour and impact their feeling and thinking, they look increasingly inward for direction, esteem and the creation of their own happiness. The increasing focus on individual fulfilment means, inevitably, less deference towards tradition and organizations. 'A major component of the postmodern shift', Inglehart argues, 'is a shift away from both religious and bureaucratic authority, bringing declining emphasis on all kinds of authority, for deference to authority has high costs: the individual's personal goals must be subordinated to those of a broader entity' (1997: 39).

Arising from contemporary harsh working conditions

Under this heading, many authors argue that, with fewer of the certainties of earlier societies, people are increasingly looking for something meaningful to frame their existence. Overell (2008) argues that, rather than an evolutionary development, the search for meaning at work is historically new and arises from unprecedented changes that have occurred recently in advanced Western societies which threaten individual identity. Weick et al. (2005) note that people in organizations invest their settings with meaning and then come to understand them. Work has become an important factor in how people define themselves, as well as a source of personal growth:

> Self-realisation is about identity, of expressing ourselves in our own way and of being recognised by others for that identity; self-realisation is finding a way of life that makes sense as a whole, with work and relationships and all our activities somehow blending into a coherent unity.
>
> (Overell, 2008: 10)

Budd (2010) agrees that today work is increasingly conceptualized as being about self-fulfilment, and seen as a source of psychological wellbeing because it can satisfy human needs for achievement, mastery, self-esteem and self-worth. Meaningful work may depend on the achievement of economic and physical security, on the belief that there is no realistic alternative to contemporary market capitalism, yet while risk is in the air, this is of a more personal, more inward nature than in previous ages. But Budd (2010: 5) also adds that: 'lousy work – work with mindless repetition, abusive co-workers or bosses, excessive

The seeming mismatch between individuals' desires for self-actualization and the realities of work within the new work culture is reminiscent of Braverman's proposition that the tendency under capitalism for work to be degraded inevitably leads to worker alienation (1974: 4). Braverman claimed that the modern trend of work, by its 'mindlessness' and 'bureaucratisation', is 'alienating ever larger sections of the working population' (1974: 36). It could therefore be argued that the reported degeneration of meaning and purpose for many workers is a reflection of worker alienation arising from the degradation of work within the new work culture. Ellsworth (2002) argues that such 'bankrupt' conditions have contributed to a sense for many employees that they are expendable cogs in a corporate wheel. Many people feel they have become means to ends they do not value. The result has been an erosion of loyalty among the corporation's key source of competitive advantage – its people. Consequently, many people at work have turned their focus inward, away from the common good, to their own narrow self-interest.

Dean et al. (1998) point out that rising levels of employee cynicism are symptomatic of the modern workplace, typical components of which include a belief that their organization lacks integrity, negative affective attitudes and emotions towards the organization and a tendency for employees, consistent with their beliefs and emotions, towards disparaging and critical behaviours of their organization. The apparent growth of interest in meaning at work by employees may be prompted by the personal consequences for them of their deteriorating social and psychological contracts within the new work culture.

For his part, Sennett (1998, 2006 and 2008) has been concerned with exploring why people lack the cultural anchor of a more secure and coherent work existence. He argues that the large bureaucratic institutions of the Fordist era (what he calls the period of 'social capitalism') created a sense of time and enabled people to think about their lives as narratives. It became possible, for instance, to define what the stages of a career ought to be like, even though few ever managed to climb to the top of the career 'ladder'. Sennett argues that this sense of time and narrative was important because it allowed workers to construct themselves as having some agency, albeit in a highly constrained, institutionalized form. But the new world of flexible organizations and casualized labour undermines any sense of linear time or narrative.

Moreover, Sennett (2006) argues that new capitalism takes away the worker's sense of being useful. Institutional knowledge is neglected or destroyed, and new communications technology allows for organizational orders to be sent out without workers mediating them or moderating them in accordance with their experience. In the past, Sennett (2008) argues, one of the traditional defences against uselessness was skill, or the cultivation of craftsmanship, 'doing something well for its own sake'. But craftsmanship seems obsolete in the institutions of flexible capitalism. 'Instead, the flexible organization puts a premium on portable human skills, on being able to work on several problems with a shifting cast of characters, cutting loose action from context' (2008: 142). Sennett claims that, 'those judged without inner resources are left in limbo. They can be judged no longer useful or valuable, despite what they have accomplished' (2008: 130). Sennett argues that three abilities are the basis of craftsmanship: the ability to localize, the ability to question, and the ability to open up (2008: 42). In his conclusion, Sennett holds out 'narrative, usefulness, and craftsmanship' as potential 'anchors' for a new, healthier culture of capitalism.

So is the 'lack of life narrative' described by Sennett reflected in research participants' attitudes towards their own careers? Is there evidence that the effects on employees of proletarianization and commodification of white-collar work are reflected in loss of meaning at work? Is there evidence that research participants feared the 'specter of uselessness' in due course?

166 *Impact of new work culture on employees*

Findings – the meaning of 'meaning'

The initial topic of focus-group discussions was what people meant by the words 'meaning' and 'meaningful'. Participants were invited to recall and describe moments in their lives where they had experienced 'elevated meaning'. From the themes which emerged the experience of 'meaning' appears to have an existential and 'mind-full' quality for many people. People's stories were about connection to (special) people and memories, having a sense of personal purpose, a heightened understanding of what is really important, of what it is to be human. Meaningful moments appeared to elevate people's focus and desire to give to others and to fulfil themselves.

Many of these stories suggested that this existential sense of 'meaning' is central to mental and physical health and wellbeing. Some of the story elements were about balance – becoming more 'centred', 'finding out what's important to me', 'making new'. Others were about autonomy – more meaningful choices, gaining a different perspective on life in general, being free to achieve. For almost all the focus-group participants, the experience of heightened meaning took place at defining moments which enabled the individual to glimpse life's journey, looking deeper than the demands of daily life would normally permit.

Participants told stories which held strong emotional depth for them, such as finding one's life partner, helping someone in difficulty, holding one's baby for the first time, about being authentic in testing circumstances, achieving something special against the odds. For several participants, the experience of childbirth had enabled them to touch something transcendental. As one person put it,

> It's a feeling of 'I am'. A feeling of being part of someone or something else that's unreachable by any other conscious effort – uniqueness yet universality (since time immemorial) – basic yet powerful. You see things from a completely different place – it was nothing to do with what I had done – something had shifted. Gosh! – it could have been 2000 years ago – a bigger sense of connection, a shared meaning and sense of community.

For some people meaning arose from 'dark night of the soul' experiences, which heightened their awareness of something fundamental and made them determined to live life to the full. Two focus-group participants described how, having been seriously ill, they now had different priorities and deeper, more important motivations. One participant learned that she had a medical condition for which medical science currently has no known cure. She said of her reaction after being told the news:

> The moment stays with me and has impacted/changed the course of how I've lived since. It is the 'embracing of life' rather than postponing it. I promised myself that I would live every day to the full – to step out of the safety of my then world, explore and live those dreams that had been on hold – waiting for tomorrow.

She had been true to this intention, setting herself up as an independent consultant and starting to write her first book.

One participant remembered her grandmother who had been her primary carer as a child. She recalled her last conversation with her grandmother before the latter's death, in which her grandmother had given her some loving messages to help her through her life. The participant could recall the place where the conversation had taken place in fine detail, right down to the perfume of the flowers in the garden. This experience had given the participant a sense of being part of something of a more universal order. Death was not death *per se*, but provided a sense of continuity. The participant told us that if she ever felt low, just recalling this experience helped her to cope.

Another participant had a son who had lost three years of schooling due to serious illness. This had taught the participant what it is to be a parent, at a deeper level, compared with the person's previous habit of 'breezing along'. Similarly, another person recalled meeting an old friend whom he had not seen for a very long time. He found this experience a sort of recognition/validation that he exists beyond the present moment – being with someone who can testify to his existence and to the journey travelled. This sense of continuity and connection was a common thread in several stories.

Meaning at work

When asked to describe times when people had experienced intense meaning at work, the underlying themes from group conversations were about feelings, identity and a sense of purpose. 'Meaning-full' moments involved feelings of:

- belonging and connection;
- harmony and balance;
- everything being in order;
- having the freedom to be genuine and fully oneself;
- giving selflessly;
- release, and being at ease with oneself.

It is in these states that people appeared to feel most able and eager to give their best – to be in what Csíkszentmihályi (1998) describes as 'flow', or the optimal state of intrinsic motivation, where the person is fully immersed in what he or she is doing. Flow is characterized by a feeling of great absorption, engagement, fulfilment and skill, during which temporal concerns (e.g. time, food, ego-self) are typically ignored. In short, flow is described as a state where attention, motivation and the situation meet, resulting in a kind of productive harmony or feedback.

What participants aspired to was akin to this statement by American author and historian Studs Terkel (1974: xiii): 'Work is about a search for daily meaning as well as daily bread; for recognition as well as cash; for astonishment rather than torpor; in short, for a sort of life, rather than a Monday to Friday sort of dying.' Some participants felt that meaning at work was really about making their mark on the world and finding answers to questions such as: 'What contribution am I making? Why am I doing what I'm doing? What difference do I make?' Achieving something exceptional against the odds, and proving something to themselves, was a common theme, such as setting themselves major challenges at different stages of their lives in order to heighten the intensity of their life experience.

Given the length of time most people spend 'at work', having a role and work context which offer the chance to achieve something significant, to make a difference, appeared vital to the possibility of work being 'meaning-full'. For many participants, 'meaning' appeared strongly linked to their greatest source of motivation, with the possibility of achieving satisfaction and contentment at both work and at home being very important. As one woman personnel manager put it, 'I want to have a happy and fulfilling personal life, nicely balanced with achieving success at work'. For several participants, meaning at work was linked to their faith, and being able to 'live' their spiritual values through their work.

168 *Impact of new work culture on employees*

'Meaning at work' seemed to be closely linked to how people defined themselves, and also to the kinds of organizations they wanted to work for, or had previously enjoyed working for. These included stories of bygone days in their current organizations, typically before aspects of the 'new work culture' produced a shift in practice or in what was valued. One person spoke fondly of a former colleague who represented to her what had been lost with a shift towards a more commercial and competitive culture:

> I used to have a colleague...who used to really irritate me in some ways, but I was fond of him in other ways. He was a consultant too and worked very hard for his clients but he also drove the admin team mad because he was always in the main office, organising things in detail, because they were pretty amateur and sloppy. Whenever you went in to the main office, there he was, making lists and plans – and he was not even in charge of that team. And he was always there so he was always someone you could talk to and knew what was going on. When he was forced to retire at sixty (and he did not want to go), we all soon realised how much we missed him, not just because he'd kept the wheels on the wagon but also because he sort of stood for getting things right for clients. He was the last of the old guard in that respect. Clients loved him too, because although he was a fuss-pot, they knew he had their best interests at heart. Not as commercial as you're supposed to be of course, but actually his figures were pretty good because people always asked for him. He'd not have survived now though, not commercial enough.

'Loss of meaning' as a result of changing context

One macro discussion theme affecting the 'micro' was the fast-changing nature of contemporary UK society.

Market-driven social transformation

People commented disparagingly about the decline in moral values and standards of behaviour reflected in popular culture over recent years, exemplified in the market-driven transformation 'dumbing down' of television output in the UK. Reality TV was then gaining ground, in which participants willingly exposed themselves to a public panopticon in pursuit of 'celebrity', popular TV programmes such as 'The Weakest Link' appeared to celebrate cruelty and bullying, and what would previously have been considered 'underhand' and dishonourable behaviour was now normalized as 'smart' tactics. Participants felt that such graphic demonstrations of dog-eat-dog behaviour were also reflective of competitive workplace practice and micro politics, and the tendency for people not to trust each other.

The reasons for increasing mistrust in Britain are complex. For focus group members, lack of trust in the workplace echoed this phenomenon in wider society, with politicians, the media and other institutions under the spotlight of public suspicion. Participants remarked on their general scepticism towards authority, reflecting the Halpern study's findings (Elliott and Quaintance, 2003) about falling public trust levels. Similarly, ethical standards among business leaders were a cause for dismay. The Enron, Worldcom and other accountancy scandals, the Maxwell pension scandal of years before, and 'fat cat' pay issues made people feel that business leaders were not to be trusted and could be expected to 'feather their own nests', regardless of whether their actions caused problems for their business and its employees.

Individualistic society

The seeming tidal wave of materialism and consumerism that had engulfed daily life in the UK was commented on, with many participants admitting that they were very much part of the credit-based consumer revolution. At the same time some remarked on the lack of satisfaction spending alone provides. Today's more secular Western societies, the discrediting of institutions such as the Catholic Church, scandals affecting even parliamentary democracy itself, the trivializing of contemporary popular culture, appear to offer little substance on which people can rely, or moral compass by which to steer one's life, what one respondent referred to as a 'God-shaped hole'.

The increasing secularization of UK society as a whole, as reflected in the decline of organized religion, was considered to leave people with few outlets for organized faith-based spirituality. Instead, as one participant suggested, religion had not in fact disappeared – it had just translated into 'Who wants to be a millionaire?' or was reflected in people's affiliations to football clubs. In contrast, it was felt that some faith-based communities within multicultural Britain retain some of the cohesiveness which might once have characterized indigenous communities in the past.

Many participants felt that contemporary UK society was becoming reflective of Margaret Thatcher's dictum that 'There is no such thing as society'. People talked of the growth of a 'me-first' attitude embodied in an ethic of individual entitlement without individual responsibility, encouraged by companies providing 'ambulance-chasing' claims pursuit services. The combined effects of an individualistic and uncaring society and people's busier, more fractured lives meant that people were much less likely to live near relatives, or contribute to community activities or to know their neighbours than 20 years before. In 2004, Management Agenda respondents were working long hours, with 83 per cent of respondents consistently working longer than their contracted week. Fifty-seven per cent maintained that their workload had increased over the previous year. Boundaries between work and non-work were blurred. Changing technology allowed a tenth of the working population to telework. Work became the focus around which the rest of life revolved.

People also perceived a loss of community. With small shops, pubs and post offices in villages and town centres closing down because they were unable to compete with out-of-town supermarkets, supermarkets had become community focal points. Increasing fear of crime was reinforced by the construction of 'gated' upmarket housing developments and the prevalence of CCTV. Andrew Solomon (2001) talks of the climbing rates of depression which are a consequence of post-modern fragmentation and the breakdown of systems of belief. It is in this layer that matters relating to the importance of human relations, of personal identity and of the meaning and purpose of life reside. Marquand (2008a: 408) in contrast argues that during the same period as this study:

> Despite marketisation, consumerism, unstable relationships, family breakdown, job insecurity, gross inequality, brutish media and other forces threatening the public realm, there was no significant decline in 'social capital' – in the membership of social networks outside the family such as tenants' or residents' associations, profession groups, sports groups, churches, amenity groups and the like.

More recently, a report for the Mental Health Foundation, *The Lonely Society* (Griffin, 2011) found that while Britain has never been so crowded, we are spending more time alone (12 per cent of households in 2008). As Marquand (2008a: 48) concedes: 'The extraordinary growth of the

170 *Impact of new work culture on employees*

internet, from 16 million users worldwide in December 1995 to 1.2 billion in June 2007... Virtual communities of lone individuals, glued to their computer screens are poor substitutes for real people talking to each other.' There was general consensus that participants were interested in a 'wider experience' linked to a more ethical, responsible, values-based approach to life which would help them answer questions such as:

- Why am I doing what I am doing?
- What difference do I make?

Loss of meaning at work

While focus-group participants considered the search for meaning to be an inherent aspect of the human condition, most believed that the search for meaning at work had been heightened by the vicissitudes of contemporary working life and disenchantment with work. The backdrop of uncertainty and wider economic and political instability was causing people to have concerns about the future. They were conscious of 'overspill' into the workplace of the changing nature of UK society and other macro issues discussed earlier.

Focus-group participants also considered the possibility of a significant relationship between age and the quest for meaning. In the 2004 Management Agenda sample it was the younger people (82 per cent of 20–30-year-old respondents) who were most likely to report that they wanted a greater sense of meaning at work, followed by people aged between 41 and 50 (76 per cent) and those over 60 (70 per cent) and 31–40 year olds (59 per cent). Those aged between 51 and 60 appeared least likely to report a search for meaning at work (33 per cent). Participants speculated about whether the high turnover among young people, who tend to be idealistic and radical in their views, arises if they feel no connection with the organization's higher purpose. Managers in particular, it was felt, did not have a clear understanding of the transitions people experience in life, especially mid-life.

People discussed the ways in which 'loss of meaning' at work manifested itself. Symptoms of loss of meaning at work were grouped initially into the following themes:

- loss of control
    - lack of influence
    - a feeling of not having control over one's life and events that impact on it;
- loss of important things
    - loss of interest in life
    - lack of enjoyment
    - lower self-confidence;
- a feeling of inability to cope
    - anxiety about the future;
    - knock-on effects on motivation, personal life and psychological health
    - panic attacks
    - losing sleep over wrestling with issues;
- feelings of injustice;
- lack of meaningful work that makes a difference
    - unsatisfying work
    - feeling unfulfilled in the work I do
    - inability to achieve meaningfully;

- ethical problems with work/superior/company practices
  - political behaviour
  - mismatch between own values and company values
  - actual management behaviour and espoused company values out of sync;
- feeling pulled out of balance
  - a feeling there is not time for own life
  - becoming less patient at home, tired and reclusive towards family
  - ill-health.

In his book, *Alienation and Freedom*, Robert Blauner (1964) argues that alienation is not solely an objective state and that work has different meanings for different people. His perspective was sociological, or 'social psychological'. He began from the proposition that 'alienation is a general syndrome made up of a number of different objective conditions and subjective feeling states' (p. 15), 'alienation is viewed as a quality of personal experience which results from specific kinds of social arrangements'.

I argue that the search for more meaning and disenchantment with work evident in many of the Management Agenda (2004) findings and the focus-group discussions are expressions of worker alienation as described by Blauner (1964).

Loss of autonomy

In the focus groups, the process of degradation of work through performativity was a common theme. There were frequent mentions of jobs structured to provide the most control for management and the least for those who actually perform the work. The spread of what Budd (2010a) calls 'lousy' work was evident in participants' comments. For instance, one local government worker now found her job effectively dissected by the 'purchaser/provider' splits then commonplace. She resented the loss of autonomy, control and job satisfaction, and the changes in work relationships which this had forced upon her. Blauner (1964: 15) argues that:

> Alienation exists where workers are unable to control their immediate work processes, to develop a sense of purpose and function which connects their jobs to the overall organisation or production…and when they fail to become involved in the activity of work as a mode of personal self-expression.

People discussed the personal consequences of new 'social arrangements' which resulted in debased new roles, with some describing work as drudgery. Some people argued that the more an individual's sense of identity becomes subsumed by their work role, the more they experience loss of meaning when external forces, such as government targets and inspections, interfere with their own view of their role. For example, one person's partner was a very experienced primary school teacher. A variety of child-protection measures which had been put in place – from quality-assurance measures to prohibitions on physical contact, including cuddling a distressed child – had undermined her professional autonomy, sense of what her job was about and confidence in her own judgement, with corresponding loss of meaning and job satisfaction.

Loss of community and trust at work

Waddock (1999) argues that work organizations are replacing other types of communities in many people's lives. Pressure to do more substitutes for real teamwork. Layoffs, downsizings,

172   *Impact of new work culture on employees*

re-engineering and restructurings of all sorts combine in the devaluing of local communities, not to mention community among employees. In addition, there are numerous virtual organizations where people interact less frequently than in traditional organizations. Many people commented that restructurings and redundancies of recent years appeared to have reduced people's trust in others, especially their employer, to protect their interests, as well as a loss of social relations in the workplace which in many cases had become more 'dog eat dog' and political. One focus-group participant described social relations at one of the organizations he had worked for:

> The other organisation that I have worked for, for about six years, was a biomedical company. It was a small company with about thirty or forty people and a lot of the emotional concern seemed to go into putting other people down. It was quite negative, inward looking, that was not trying to look outside, so, it is difficult even to put into words – it is more of a feeling and the politics is a reflection of the culture, but yeah I have had experiences where it is not possible to work well.

Trust is likely to be a casualty of poor leadership, as one respondent noted:

> This used to be a great place to work – nice colleagues, interesting work, a real 'buzz'. Then with the new CEO we lost half our section. The new director is a cold fish and you can never do things right for her. Everyone's on edge and watching their own backs. You find people whispering about who's 'in' or 'out' with the boss, and before you know it, that person's got rid of.

Another manager described his personal strategy of denial for dealing with competitive and political behaviour from others:

> Well, I think there is probably an element of never really wanting to believe that somebody is out to get you, or that somebody could really be that nasty about someone, so it is always trying to turn a negative into a positive, maybe somewhere shutting it out in that if it is that nasty don't go there sort of thing. I can cope with that kind of thing because I do have the ability to turn that sort of thing out. I pretend to be able to block that out, and not really believe that they mean that and it has to be really in front of me to think that is what they are like. So I go on daily as if it is not happening I suppose and deal with it because I am ignoring it. But also being positive in what I want to achieve can help. Does that make sense?

People reported feeling increasingly 'disconnected' from fellow humans by the increasingly impersonal nature of work. In contrast, one participant described how, when he was visiting a relative in hospital, an elderly person in the same ward had died. The curtains were drawn while staff prepared to move the body of the dead person. Despite the curtains, the participant was able to see one nurse gently put her hand on the hand of the dead person, as if to communicate and reassure them. While such behaviour would not form part of any government target, it meant a lot to the participant to see that this nurse clearly considered it important to treat the dead person with respect and dignity, whether or not she was measured on this behaviour.

Lack of chance to reflect

The pressure to be busy, to perform and produce results prevented people from feeling able to reflect and make personal choices. Participants reported sensing a void, wanting some 'space' where they could 'be' rather than 'do' all the time:

The lack of meaning is mainly in 'human terms', such as an appreciation by management that staff are more important than targets, paperwork etc. – that staff should have a 'quiet' staff area, that breaks are important and should be taken, that a 37 hour week means just that – all too often missing!

These comments echo remarks by Alison Webster (2002) who describes how lives are becoming textured by technology. She argues that the increasingly fluid boundary between people and machines – through the use of mobile phones, texting, voicemail and internet chat rooms – creates an illusion of community. Webster points out the paradox that, despite the wider range of contacts made possible by the internet, email and social media, there is a heightened sense of loneliness (when the computer is turned off). Making time to reflect, and (re)discovering the capacity to reflect has to be sanctioned and aided officially – through organized 'Awaydays'. Webster questions what is happening to relationships – whether they are becoming many layered or whether the negatives are coming more into focus.

Loss of identity

Social identity theory (Tajfel and Turner, 1986) focuses on how individuals construct their identities by categorizing themselves into various groups. This might include one's occupation, employer or other work-related group constructs. The interactionist approach suggests that individuals create identities through social interactions with others. From this perspective, the social roles attached to occupations and careers are a major source of our self-presentation and identity during adulthood.

One focus-group participant, a professional coach, argued that lack of self-awareness with respect to one's own values restricts people's sense of who they are, their choice of occupation and freedom to act:

> I do wonder whether people even think about what their values are. They go into a career or a job because that is what they have been good at, or that is what they have studied and it just happens. They are not then able to move out or that or even think about, 'well what are my values? What is it that I value? What is it that I really need from the job and your life? And what are the values that are important to me?'

'Balance' was frequently used to refer to being happy at work and at one with the world. As reported in the Management Agenda 2004 survey, the short-term focus of many organizations appeared to leave little time for reflection and affiliation. Typical comments include: 'Disquiet and the overriding temporal issues and relentless pursuit of (short-term) goals, each at the expense of the "inner person".' The effect of this short termism, according to one respondent, was 'Greater resistance to change than I have experienced/witnessed during 33 years, coupled with a desire to "touch" the present and its meaning to self and organisational unit'.

Sennett (2006) argues that work pursuits require individuals to manage short-term relationships, to do without institutions that give them a long-term frame of reference, and to 'improvise' life narratives without a sense of self sustained by lasting relationships to work, colleagues and social environments. Indeed, many focus-group participants felt that their values and sense of identity were under attack in the new work culture. Many felt that they were being forced to suppress fundamental parts of themselves at work, being asked to give more, without being valued in return. Some participants reported that their personal values were tested regularly by working with other people whose values were very different. One senior partner from a professional services firm described some of the challenges of working with

174 *Impact of new work culture on employees*

his managing partner: 'He is a very powerful character and I suspect that part of his power is due to the fact that he's very self-centred and will step on people to get where he wants to be. I'm afraid I just don't have the stomach for that.' Another participant, a senior manager from a large international organization, described how he frequently stood out against some of the less than ethical practices among his peer group and sometimes had to suffer the penalty of being ostracized: 'I do get frustrated but I've got to live with myself first. And I can't believe that some of the senior managers in my company behave the same way at home, they can't possibly.' However, he also talked about being pragmatic, and having to compromise his values because, 'All of a sudden, you don't (challenge) because the chairman's secretary says "Are you free for lunch?" and that's always a bad sign'.

Grounding – search for meaning at work

While people's definitions of 'meaning' and 'lack of meaning' varied, the common elements were values, connectivity, trust and identity, autonomy, growth and worthwhile achievement.

To ground definitions further, data from the Management Agenda 2003 and 2004 were analysed to identify correlations with a 'loss' or 'search for' meaning at work. For Blauner (1964), the different objective conditions and subjective feeling states relating to alienation emerge from certain relationships between workers and the socio-technical settings of employment. Alienation is multidimensional and can be broken down into four dimensions: powerlessness, meaninglessness, isolation and self-estrangement. Different employees will be affected differently by these dimensions and will therefore have different alienation profiles and experience alienation differently. But Blauner was less concerned with looking at the differences between individuals than the differences that existed between entire occupational groups.

Given that our samples were from a wide range of sectoral and occupational backgrounds, we chose instead to use Ken Wilber's (2001) model – 'Four Dimensions of Phenomena' – to develop a multidimensional perspective on the interplay between structure and agency. Wilber discusses intersubjectivity, which conventionally refers to relationships between human beings, and particularly those that result from our use of language, and argues that intersubjectivity is also manifested in non-linguistic forms, seeing intersubjectivity as a universal principle of which we humans experience just one particular example. Though Wilber, in his desire to make his four-quadrant model as comprehensive and inclusive as possible, is criticized for applying the notion of intersubjectivity in a very sweeping manner, this model lent itself well to organizing correlations without seeking to establish causality.

Search for meaning correlates

Outer collective (organizational characteristics)

In the 2003 Management Agenda, the people wanting more meaning tended to work for large organizations which had flattened their management layers and gone global (Figure 9.1). People ended up having large spans of control, many responsibilities and pressures. Conflict within organizations had increased in recent years (45 per cent) and relationships at work had become more transactional, characterized by mutual suspicion and lack of trust. Respondents were least trusting of senior managers (only 24 per cent trusted to a great extent), while subordinates (59 per cent) and peers (49 per cent) were the most trusted groups. High stress

Inner individual	Outer individual
• Search for meaning • Spiritual aspect to personal values • Tensions between work and spiritual values • Job insecurity and stress	• Work demands too high or too low • Work/life unbalanced • Views not heard • Considering leaving
Inner collective	**Outer collective**
• Low morale • People not encouraged to be creative • Top managers not seen as acting as leaders	• Large organization • Large spans of control • Delayering • Globalizing

Figure 9.1 Correlations of meaning
Source: Holbeche and Springett, 2004

levels were reported (74 per cent). Respondents from the public sector appeared most likely to suffer from stress (77 per cent), while respondents from the charity sector were least likely to report suffering from stress (36 per cent).

Eighty-eight per cent of respondents reported a growing demand for more flexible working patterns and 68 per cent said they would like a more flexible working pattern. Those wanting more meaning were typically looking for a more flexible working pattern (82 per cent). Just 35 per cent suggested that their organization was going beyond the minimum requirements of the Employment Act and extending the right to request flexible working beyond parents of young children.

Inner collective (culture and shared meanings)

Similarly, lack of meaning correlated to competitive and demanding organizational climates in which top managers did not act like leaders. People had neither the time nor the encouragement to be creative and they reported having low morale. They typically wanted:

*   a more ethical organization;
*   a better match between their own values and those of the organization;
*   a self-employed situation.

Outer individual (behaviours)

People who were looking for more meaning in the workplace tended to report low levels of involvement in organizational decision-making and felt their views were not heard (Management Agenda 2004). The search for meaning correlated with work demands being too high or too low, together with a lack of control over workload (33 per cent) or the length of the working day (30 per cent). They also experienced a lack of work–life balance. These people were generally considering leaving their jobs, typically looking for roles with the same or less responsibility (47 per cent) and many (25 per cent) were considering going self-employed. People working in small organizations (up to 50 employees) fared best and reported experiencing the highest levels of commitment and meaning.

Inner individual (search for meaning)

In the 2003 Management Agenda, people looking for more meaning tended to report tensions between the spiritual side of their values and their work (65 per cent). Women (44 per cent) were more likely to report that they experienced these tensions than men (35 per cent). They were also more likely to value the opportunity of discussing spirituality in the workplace with colleagues and were interested in learning meditation and mindfulness practices. Such employees took their own development – in the broadest sense – seriously.

They tended to be worried about the future and to experience more job insecurity than people who were not looking for more meaning (36 per cent versus 25 per cent). They were also more likely to report experiencing stress as a result of work (79 per cent) than those who were not looking for meaning (63 per cent), especially if they felt they had to conform and play politics just to survive.

In practice, disenchantment with the workplace was evident in this research, especially since many people worked long hours and felt under heavy workload pressure. On the whole, in both the 2003 and 2004 Management Agendas, people working in larger organizations appeared to experience less meaning than those in small organizations. I would speculate at this stage that people working in small organizations (50 or fewer employees) are more likely to identify with their organization and its leader, have more control over their work, more rounded jobs, a shared sense of responsibility, closer working relationships with managers and colleagues and a clearer line of sight to organizational purpose than people working for large organizations.

In attempting to synthesize different forms of data, we developed an emergent model of how the search for meaning appears to link with both the changing macro and micro contexts.

This would suggest that a combination of an insecure macro context, a loss of purpose and identification with organization and a longing for, and insight into, something better are characteristic of a 'search for meaning' (Figure 9.2). Many participants developed coping strategies to help them deal with these less than ideal circumstances but still remained dissatisfied. Some people preferred to remain true to their values in order to achieve a more meaningful balance in their lives, even if this cost them in terms of career development.

Figure 9.2 An emerging model of meaning
Source: Holbeche and Springett, 2004

'Meaning' equates for the people in this study with a sense of belonging and connection, a chance to be fully oneself, to be free to be altruistic and to obtain deeper levels of self-fulfilment. Applied to work, 'meaning' appears linked with having an uplifting sense of purpose, a harmonious working environment, worthwhile jobs through which people can grow, control over one's own destiny, ethical practice, trust among colleagues and the opportunity to achieve work–life balance. When people have meaning, they appear to believe that they can fulfil themselves and make a contribution to society.

In the next section we consider whether it is possible that, by aligning to corporate purposes which employees find worthwhile, some employees can develop a meaningful work–life narrative.

Corporate purpose

Having a cause or important purpose is recognized as a source of cohesion and high performance within organizations in much of the literature (Ellsworth, 2002). Sandelands (2003: 170) suggests that: 'Employees perform most energetically, creatively and enthusiastically when they believe they are contributing to a purpose that is bigger than themselves.' In his study of long-lived or 'living' companies, De Geus (1997) argues that cohesion and a strong sense of identity are key to organizational survival amid change. Purpose can excite and mobilize the members of an organization to work in greater alignment to each other. Similarly, Deal and Kennedy (2000: 203) argue that purpose is at the heart of social cohesion and point out: 'People still want to belong. They yearn for something that elevates their work from routine drudgery to a higher purpose. They will listen to what seems thoughtful, authentic, and comes from the heart.' A sense of community is a common thread for scholars. As Sennett comments (1998):

> One of the unintended consequences of modern capitalism is that it has strengthened the value of place, aroused a longing for community. All the emotional conditions we have explored in the workplace animate that desire: the uncertainties of flexibility, the absence of deeply rooted trust and commitment, the superficiality of teamwork, most of all the spectre of failing to make something of oneself in the world, to get a life through one's work. All these conditions impel people to look for some other scene of attachment and depth.

Waddock (1999) argues that people need and want to belong to communities where they can make meaningful contributions that build a better world. Many people discover that, from a certain point, money is not going to make their lives better. Turned off by work that is, at its roots, meaningless and in some cases even unethical, many people opt out of their organizations psychically, turning their productive energy and attention to family, civic matters or self-development. Community, where it can be found or created, can be a countervailing force to stress, isolation and anomie that characterizes organizations that have cut out too much of what was community in their efforts to become competitive.

The importance of purpose is reflected in the Management Agenda 2005, where the quest for (lost) meaning was inversely related to the extent to which individuals considered their organization's purpose uplifting, especially with respect to environmental and social responsibility. But not just any purpose – Anderson (1997: 34) suggests that: 'By itself, shareholder wealth provides an incomplete sense of identity and uniqueness, and does not motivate long-term creativity the same way community does.' Commercial organizations

178 *Impact of new work culture on employees*

with a strong client or customer focus may be tapping into similar motivations (Ellsworth, 2002). Konz and Ryan (1999) also suggest that individuals are searching for meaning in their work that transcends mere economic gain. Even the authors of a book which attempted to puncture the rhetoric about 'de-alienated knowledge work' noted that, among their often resigned and pressurized interviewees, the economic motivation was overlain by many others: 'Wherever possible people at work look for something beyond that, a sense of purpose or redemption, a source of challenge or enjoyment, or the ability of the work to confer or reinforce social identity or identities' (Baldry et al., 2007: 40). In focus groups there was a general consensus that people felt more connected if their work served, and made a positive difference to, an identifiable group of stakeholders. One participant had left his corporate role for self-employment, having become disenchanted with the relentless pursuit of shareholder value. He argued that organizations will have to do more to connect with people if they are to attract and retain them. Another participant who had previously worked for British Rail and now, since privatization, worked for a franchise holder, suggested that his colleagues were not motivated by shareholder value; instead their affiliations tended to be with their colleagues and trade unions.

A senior manager within a subsidiary service to the NHS, described how having a patient-centred purpose united the people working in the service, despite poor working conditions:

> I think there's a common feeling that at the end of all this there's the patient who…we can do things that can make a difference to a patient by improving their lives or saving their lives. So I think there is a common feeling. I think it's different from the feeling of, oh it's just made money. I think that, with the…Service, you've got a common purpose, it isn't just money and you've got a fairly common way of actually achieving that. I think that helps; there are still things that go terribly wrong and people then pick up the pieces.

Other NHS participants described their disenchantment with the contrast between the original noble aims of the NHS and its growing business orientation. They also considered that the greater degree of managerialism, with its targets and weightings, had left people feeling 'I'm not trusted any more'. Similar views were expressed by a participant working for a major charity, who saw conflicts of values between the charitable aims and the commercial side of the work leading to ongoing clashes in the workplace.

One participant, a CEO of a newly formed social enterprise that had previously been an NHS mental health trust, described how she persuaded most NHS staff at the Trust to join the new enterprise by engaging them around the original purpose of the NHS:

> Well, it would be an organisation outside of the NHS. A lot of the [management] discussion we've had was around what is it that makes us what we are? I did a range of workshops last year and that brought us to around 1500 staff – over 800 of them with me personally – and one of the key messages that was coming through was…what they wanted was to remain as part of the NHS. But actually when you questioned that, what they wanted was to maintain the beliefs they had in what the NHS was. My argument to that, or my discussion with them then was, well what makes up the NHS in this part of the world? It's the people who are within it, not some magical thing that makes you an NHS person/employee.
>
> And once we started to debate that, their view was that this was what they went into the NHS for. Those beliefs around putting people first, caring for them; for most clinicians not actually having to consider what it costs at that point in time, so doing it because

of what the needs were. So the argument was, well, if we believed that and we were the people who made that up, we could then move that to any organisation and what we might find is that the stuff we have been unable to do on the edges – and I could give some examples of that – with the freedoms we might have as part of any social enterprise or social enterprises, we could plough back our profit and that would allow us to do those things. So that is some of the discussion with staff.

The CEO also described how re-engaging staff with the core NHS purpose appeared to have a galvanizing effect on people's behaviour and focus:

Once that thinking happened, what we all agreed was, if every single person in each of those groups walked around, we would see waste. It wasn't about getting people to admit to be part of causing that waste, it didn't go that far, but people talked for example about the waste when we were ordering things. So the discussion then went along the lines of, 'well if we all owned a part of this new organisation, if we felt valued within it and we believed in it and we wanted it to be successful, what we could do away with would be waste? Because if we were doing that at home, we would try not to waste money, we'd watch the heating, and we'd watch what we spent in the supermarkets, you know those sorts of things. If we applied that to owning part of this organisation then the feeling was that people would feel more responsible for it and to it. And actually we talked about how what we saved on the waste would be invested to do what we wanted to do. So I know it is quite a simplistic view but there were enough people that bought into that and really felt that there would actually be a way for us to do that.

These discussions suggested that people wanted their work to have a higher (uplifting) purpose and workplace behaviour characterized by congruence, respect, integrity, authenticity and honesty. However idealistic, they wanted the chance to achieve something worthwhile and to be part of a community they could be proud of.

Discussion

Reverting to psychological contract theory, I argue that the search for 'meaning' is a 'weather gauge' of the quality of the exchange relationship between employers and employees at a profound level, and that this has implications for both employees and employers.

According to identification theory, people tend to identify with their organizations when they perceive synergy between their own goals and values and those of the organization. For Edwards (2005: 209), the notion of identification involves a 'significant psychological linkage between the individual and the organisation whereby the individual feels a deep, self-defining affective and cognitive bond with the organisation as a social identity'. From these various data, 'meaning' is associated with a sense of community and having a higher sense of purpose, especially a customer-focused purpose, and above all with autonomy and balance; these are mostly perceived to be missing.

This bond produces organizational commitment, a broad and all-encompassing notion consisting of a feeling of membership and belonging, and a self-categorization into the organization. Organizational commitment also involves more behaviourally oriented aspects as well, or at least intentions to act or behave in a certain way, such as involvement or motivation to do things not just for oneself but for the good of the organization and loyalty or intention to stay in the organization.

180 *Impact of new work culture on employees*

These findings suggest that many people do want to identify with their organization, but in order to do so they must perceive a strong values connection. They appear to aspire to work as a means of self-actualization, and want more control over their own work, but many have experienced reduced job quality, insecurity and work intensification, job insecurity and loss of job satisfaction.

Although some authors differentiate between the emotional side of identification and affective commitment (e.g. Johnson and Morgeson, 2005), it seems sensible to assume a close relationship between them. When people experience greater meaning, they appear to be 'in flow', able to give their best. If they want to belong and feel uncertainty and anxiety about the future, they are more likely to tolerate shifts which reduce meaning for them. The driver of social categorizations is also a very emotional driver, that of reduction of anxiety by making sense of the confusing social world around us (Tajfel and Turner, 1986). Rousseau (1998) argues that both parties gain from such an exchange: a) individuals have a strong drive to believe that they are part of, or belong to the social settings in which they work, and b) member identification enhances the success of firms based upon coordinated corporate action. When one combines both a and b there is an exchange. Employees get to feel a sense of belonging when identifying, and the organization benefits (ultimately financially) from employees' increased effort and motivation. In other words, there is a mutual benefit for both employees and employers.

What motivates the individual to build identification with the organization? Research participants in my study wanted to feel involved, to be treated like adults, and to be able to balance work with other aspects of their lives. They wanted the opportunity to be a 'whole person' at work, able to reflect on deeper matters with colleagues. They wanted challenging jobs through which they could experience personal growth and the chance to achieve something worthwhile. People wanted to work for ethical organizations where leaders 'walk the talk' on values, as reflected in this comment by Collins (2001: 210):

> Perhaps, then, you might gain that rare tranquillity that comes from knowing that you've had a hand in creating something of intrinsic excellence that makes a contribution. Indeed, you might even gain that deepest of all satisfactions: knowing that your short time here on this earth has been well spent and that it mattered.

However, in practice, work is seldom like this utopian dream. Overell (2008) argues that employees who seek to fulfil themselves through work are doomed to disappointment. He suggests that the pursuit of self-actualization through realizing one's potential in work (which is partly the rationale behind ideas of employee engagement) is a self-delusion or heterotopia. According to this ideal, work is part of the 'project of the self', and the organization is a 'blank canvas' onto which worthwhile lives can be drawn in cooperation with sympathetically minded managers and colleagues, the interests of employees and employers reconciled at last. However, the drive for self-fulfilment through work risks producing 'willing slaves' who must progressively face the 'specter of uselessness' if they can no longer keep up with the pace or the working conditions. Karasek (2002) found that ill health is more frequent when employees face high levels of psychological demand whilst enduring low levels of autonomy. In such a context, as Brown et al. (2010b: 141) point out, it is employees who pay the price of a one-sided employment relationship:

> The personal costs of the trap continue to mount as individuals and families are forced to redouble their efforts to secure an advantage. Rather than opportunities extending

individual freedom and fulfilling our dreams, they are making people increasingly self-centred, stressed, and unfulfilled as more and more effort, money and time is spent doing what is necessary, rather than for any intrinsic purpose. These unintended consequences of securing success reflect a lack of freedom for people to express their social worth or contribution to society other than through the job market.

Conclusion

In this chapter we have considered whether the vicissitudes of modern working life – the ending of a job for life, ongoing change, work–life imbalance, work intensification, performative work cultures and a commodity approach to work and workers – may have 'alienated' many employees and given spur to the quest for meaning at work. Meaning appears to correlate with deep motivation, and the search for meaning could represent a retreat from the conditions in which 'work has enslaved us' (Bunting, 2004).

Should organizations (and HR in particular) attempt to develop initiatives to enhance meaning in the workplace? Given the assumed benefits of meaning for employee motivation and organizational performance, it is not surprising that high-commitment models of HRM (Storey, 1992; Guest, 1999) should seek to play an important role in organizational meaning making. With respect to enabling 'meaningful work' (Garrow et al., 2009), HR can help line managers design fulfilling roles. Through such roles, people have a chance to achieve and can actively engage in a discourse that helps them construct their identities, or sense of 'self' in an age where there is increasing orientation for self-expression and self-realization (Overell, 2008; Garrow et al., 2009). And it is important to be aware of what appears meaningful to employees, and seek to avoid eroding meaning unnecessarily through corporate actions.

However, from a critical standpoint, the ethics and practicalities of employers drawing on the language of commitment and engagement (e.g. Keenoy, 1997, 1999; Storey, 1992; Townley, 1998; Legge, 2005), increasing productivity by eliciting employees' discretionary effort can appear less a concern for mutuality between employers and employees and 'more like straight-forward corporate take-over of psychological space' (Overell, 2008: 14). Overell also points out the risks to employees of these approaches: 'Has a fresh page in the nature of work really been turned? Have fundamental antagonisms been dressed up in emollient, perhaps manipula-tive language? The goal of self-realisation seems to lend itself all too easily to being padded out with company logic' (2008: 15). I share Overell's scepticism. Sennett too is convinced that the new economy cannot last and concludes that: 'a regime that provides human beings no deep reasons to care about one another cannot long preserve its legitimacy' (1998: 148). It would seem that their message is not yet being heard.

Points to ponder

- Should employers take the search for meaning seriously? If so, why? If not, why not?
- What might be some of the actions that employers could undertake in order to avoid eroding people's sense of meaning at work?

Section IV

Phoenix out of the ashes?

10 The 'crisis' of capitalism

> A way of life that bases itself on materialism, i.e. on permanent, limitless expansionism in a finite environment, cannot last long.
>
> (Schumacher, 1974: 156)

A central argument of this book is that neo-liberalism, globalization and the availability of technology have provided the political rationale in Anglo-American capitalist economies for organizations to drive through radical changes in business structures and employment practices which have resulted in a largely one-sided employment relationship, with the balance tipped in favour of the organization and investors, at the expense of employee interests. In society at large there are growing inequalities thanks to the huge income disparities between elite workers and those in precarious jobs, as well as those with no job at all. Surveys reveal half the population of the UK are experiencing income insecurity. As a result, Hutton (2010) argues, Britain in 2010 was more polarized than ten years earlier: the economic bubble had created both a new super-rich and a disenfranchised underclass.

How sustainable is this trajectory for capitalism and for society as we have known it? In his many works (published and unpublished), Marx suggested that, at different points and under certain circumstances, capitalism would experience a crisis, or a period during which the normal reproduction of an economic process suffers from a temporary breakdown. A key characteristic of these theoretical factors is that none of them is natural or accidental in origin but instead arises from systemic elements of capitalism as a mode of production and basic social order. Marx (1958) argued that capitalism has the capacity to overcome crises by radically transforming itself periodically, so that economic expansion can continue.

In his book, *The Spectre at the Feast* (2009), political economist Andrew Gamble distinguishes between periods of 'capitalist crisis' and conventional recessions and 'economic downturns'. He argues that, while there were several 'crashes', there were only two real crises for capitalism during the twentieth century – these were during the 1930s and the period of 'stagflation' in the 1970s. Following the economic crisis that began in 2008, which Gamble (2009) describes as the 'third crisis of capitalism', we could be said to be at an inflection point in capitalism. In this chapter we shall explore:

- The broader consequences of the third 'crisis of capitalism'.
- Trust deficits.
- Drivers of future change including information technology, demographics, new ways of working, social legitimacy and the sharing economy.
- What might characterize the next phase of capitalism?

186 *Phoenix out of the ashes?*

Crises as political events

Jürgen Habermas (1977), a sociologist and philosopher in the tradition of critical theory and pragmatism, pioneered ways of thinking about crises as political events which arise because the dominant interpretations of political reality are no longer accepted. Periods of crisis are usually accompanied by fundamental changes of political economy which lead to major changes in the rules of employment and production, and what might be called the 'moral economy' (Klein, 2007; Gamble, 2009; Peston, 2008). According to Habermas' theory of legitimation, these changes do not just happen – they are usually political experiments to reshape the economy. For instance, during the prolonged Great Depression in the 1930s, US President Franklin D. Roosevelt was able to gain political and financial consensus for his 'New Deal' programme which involved committing to vast spending programmes on national infrastructure building, and helped lift thousands of US workers out of unemployment (Garraty, 1973).

Following the Great Depression, the world was plunged into the Second World War. The post-war consensus on economic management embraced the 'efficient government thesis', the belief that government could acquire enough knowledge and capacity to manage capitalism successfully. The 1950s and 1960s were recorded as a period of successful progress. Orthodox Marxists argued against the discourse of the welfare state and the mixed economy which Keynesianism promoted. Some supported Kondratieff's theory that, rather than the conventional ten-year business cycle of the nineteenth century, there were longer economic cycles, lasting 50 to 60 years, and characterized by boom in their first half. In the periods studied by long-wave theorists – the 1850s in Europe, the 1900s and 1950s across the globe – it was arguably thanks to the power of organized labour that corporations were forced to innovate since they could not simply maintain old business models through cutting wages (Mason, 2015).

The Institute for Precarious Consciousness (2014) argues that each phase of capitalism has its own dominant affect, and dominant narrative, that holds it together. In the nineteenth century (until the post-war settlement), the dominant affect was misery (of the working class) and the dominant narrative was that capitalism leads to general enrichment. The first wave of social movements in the nineteenth century were set up to fight misery. Tactics such as strikes, wage struggles, political organization, mutual aid, cooperatives and strike funds were effective ways to defeat the power of misery by ensuring a certain social minimum for all. Some of these strategies still work when fighting misery.

In the mid-twentieth century, the dominant public narrative was that the standard of living – which widened access to consumption, healthcare and education – was rising. Mid-century capitalism gave everything needed for survival; everyone in the rich countries was happy, and the poor countries were on their way to development (Institute for Precarious Consciousness, 2014). Job security and welfare provision reduced anxiety and misery, but jobs were boring, made up of simple, repetitive tasks. This was an effect of the Fordist system which was prevalent until the 1980s – a system based on full-time jobs for life, guaranteed welfare, mass consumerism, mass culture and the cooptation of the labour movement which had been built to fight misery.

The Thatcherite 'project'

Keynesianists predicted that the boom of the post-war period would eventually wind down and lead to another period of crisis which governments would be unable to control. By the 1970s, as Britain's old model of mass industrial production and capital accumulation began to fail and the UK economy was increasingly uncompetitive, the oil crisis and growing pressure from labour for increased wages, and adversarial industrial relations triggered the first major crisis of Anglo-Saxon capitalism since the Great Depression. Gamble argues that the 1970s stagflation was of a lesser scale than the Great Depression of the 1930s though it still resulted in major changes which were politically managed in the structure of the economy, in national and international politics and in dominant ideologies. Out of this arose a new and invigorated global capitalism which originated in Britain and the US.

As we discussed in Chapters 1 and 3, in the 1980s both Britain under Margaret Thatcher and the United States under Ronald Reagan adopted 'neo-liberalism', a political project for facilitating the restructuring and rescaling of social relations in accord with the demands of an unrestrained global capitalism (Bourdieu, 1998). The influential Chicago School of economic theorists, led by Milton Friedman, promoted the efficient markets thesis – the belief that markets, if left alone, would always price assets accordingly. Under Thatcher in particular, there was an orchestrated attempt by the right-wing political elite to redraw the UK political economy to achieve what they considered to be the only remedy to the intractability of those elements involved in the crisis. Milton Friedman's 'shock therapy' was applied to the British economy and to the working class. Neo-liberalism became a 'formidable discourse', especially in the Anglo sphere but also more broadly (Klein, 2007).

The Canadian author and social activist Naomi Klein takes legitimation theory further in her book *Shock Doctrine: The Rise of Disaster Capitalism* (2007) in which she describes how political elites take advantage of the opportunity afforded by economic crisis to override democratic will by bringing in unpopular policies and claiming that these are unavoidable: 'I call these orchestrated raids on the public sphere in the wake of catastrophic events, combined with the treatment of disasters as exciting market opportunities, "disaster capitalism"' (Klein, 2007: 6). Political economist Will Hutton (2010) argues that the free-market hypothesis was the biggest intellectual mistake made by various governments, behind which were vested interests: US Republican politicians and their think tanks identifying 'truths' which became the benchmark for the West. The market rewarded itself handsomely: wholesale money markets paid themselves huge sums of money (salaries and bonuses of partners in UK hedge funds averaged £10–20 million per annum. Regulators and New Labour did not question economic agents who were chasing profits on what seemed a rational model and therefore there was no basis for challenge. Consequently, the few warnings about the impending crisis emanating from academics were not heeded.

The current 'crisis' of capitalism

'Long-wave' theorists predicted that the next real crisis of capitalism was due in the early years of the twenty-first century. Just as the crises of the 1930s and 1970s have been seen in retrospect as major turning points in the way in which the global economy and its governance developed, so, Gamble argues (2009: 69), the economic crisis which began in 2008 may come to be seen as another such turning point for capitalism: 'The global financial crash of 2008 did not just prick the asset bubbles of the financial markets; it also burst the bubble of neo-liberalism which had been inflating for three decades, and cast doubt on the claims of the hyper-globalists.' For Gamble, politics and economics are intertwined and, at the present time, politics drives economics.

As Marquand (2008b) put it in a *Guardian* article:

> The crisis stems, above all, from lax and incompetent public regulation of private economic power. That in turn stems from a profoundly dangerous economic philosophy,

188   *Phoenix out of the ashes?*

which holds that government failure is more prevalent and more damaging than market failure, that markets are always wiser and more rational than governments, and that if private market actors are allowed to pursue their private interests without interference from public authorities, the invisible hand of the market will necessarily deliver the best possible outcome for society as a whole. As we now know, thanks to a variety of corporate scandals, markets can be rigged in favour of those who profit most by them.

Mason (2015) argues that neo-liberalism has morphed into a system programmed to inflict recurrent catastrophic failures. In large part this is due, he argues, to neo-liberalism being the first economic model in 200 years that was based on the premise that economic upswing could be achieved by suppressing wages and smashing the power and resilience of the working class. Similarly, Morgan (2010) argues that the material policies of neo-liberalism have dramatically changed economic conditions: 'Turning the world over to the market has produced an accelerated erosion of the ecosphere and an ever-widening gap of inequality in American and global society, to say nothing of the persistence of destructive and arguably counterproductive American wars.'

Keynesian economists such as John Gray (2008) argue that there is an existential problem at the heart of market economics in the way the financial system relates to the real economy, with the 'crowd effects' of the market happening faster within the financial system than in the real economy. The 2008 crash wiped 13 per cent off global production and 20 per cent off world trade. Gray (2008) and others argue that the implosion of financial institutions is irreversible; that normalcy in the form of debt-based financial capitalism based on a global free market cannot be re-established. Whether this is the case remains to be seen.

In the real economy, the impact of the current 'crisis of capitalism' has not only been profound, but enduring and widely felt. Many Western countries adopted austerity measures ranging from years of spending cuts to driving down wages and living standards. In Europe, various national economies are under severe pressure, with some being bailed out by loans from the International Monetary Fund. There are high levels of youth unemployment and widespread public-sector cuts. Indeed, with the income and prospects of so many people seriously affected, the potential is growing for organized protests, serious civil unrest and increasing fragmentation in some countries. The crisis aftershocks in Europe, together with the continuing mass influx of migrants since 2015, are potentially tearing Europe apart.

Marxist scholars consider all capitalist crises as crises of overproduction and immiseration of the workers. Marx himself envisaged that the working class would rise up during periods of economic collapse and would cause the old order to be overthrown. A century later, Schumacher too foresaw potential revolt against the conditions within which work is carried out under the monopoly capitalist system:

> The modern world has been shaped by technology. It tumbles from crisis to crisis; on all sides there are prophecies of disaster, and indeed, visible signs of breakdown. Human nature revolts against inhuman technological, organisational and political patterns, which it experiences as suffocating and debilitating.
>
> (Schumacher, 1974: 101)

People tend to be either 'work rich', i.e. overstretched and under pressure, or 'work poor', i.e. bored without the stimulus of work. Indeed, for the majority in work, conditions have deteriorated and pay levels remain mostly static. People without employment have been subject to ever more punitive sanctions and restricted benefits. Inequalities are increasing and working lives are becoming more precarious. While the UK employment scene appears rosy, the main growth is in part-time work or self-employment.

For those in precarious forms of work, or with no work at all, the dominant affect is anxiety across the whole of the social field, which is seen as the linchpin of subordination according to the Institute for Precarious Consciousness (2014). Precarity is a type of insecurity which treats people as disposable so as to impose control. This leads to generalized hopelessness; growing proportions of young people are living at home. Substantial portions of the population – over 10 per cent in the UK – are taking antidepressants. The birth rate is declining, as insecurity makes people reluctant to start families.

However, Mason (2015) argues that, after 25 years of capitalism underpinned by neo-liberalism in the UK and USA, the proletariat are unlikely to rise up since the market, individualism and technology have become normalized under neo-liberalism. As a result, he proposes, individuals and the public at large have come to see such crises and related effects as 'business as usual'. Instead, Mason proposes, 'post-capitalism' will arise largely unnoticed from within the midst of capitalism in crisis.

Business ethics and social legitimacy

The financial crisis has highlighted how business practices and ethics are often in tension, yet it appears as yet not to have led to any fundamental reappraisal of the nature of capitalism, nor how to govern it. For instance, how seriously does business take ethics? Arguably not very. Ethics are enacted through decision-making, leadership, culture and permitted or condoned behaviours and practices that either build or undermine trust.

The negative consequences for society of unethical corporate cultures, as well as the benefits of ethical ones, have become apparent during and since the financial crisis. Hutton (2010) highlights how unfair it is that the British have lived through the biggest bank bail-out in history and the deepest recession since the 1930s, yet they are being warned that they face a decade of unparalleled public and private austerity, while: 'Those who created the crisis – the country's CEOs and bankers, still living on Planet Extravagance, not to mention mainstream politicians – all want to get back to "business as usual": the world of 1997 to 2007' (Hutton, 2010: 4). In the UK, the state intervened to attempt to mitigate the effects of financial crisis, not only by bailing out failing banks but also by attempting to respond to international proposals to reregulate the financial-services industry and to curb excessive bonuses for bankers, though these measures have apparently been largely subverted. Despite the demand for better regulation of the financial-services industry, there is a reported return by various financial institutions to some of the now notorious money-market practices which led to the financial crash of 2008. Scandals such as the widespread mis-selling by banks of purchase protection insurances and the manipulation of the LIBOR rate continue to undermine public trust in the banking system. Much of the learning from the latest crisis of capitalism appears to have gone unheeded.

And yet, the topic of business ethics does not go away and there is growing pressure on businesses to at least appear to be operating ethically. With the topic of business ethics regularly in the media spotlight often for all the wrong reasons, there is a growing public backlash against certain firms whose supply-chain practices have been found to be exploitative of workers in the developing world. How seriously firms will amend their practices to respond to consumer pressure remains to be seen. For instance, in the UK there was extensive media coverage in 2015–16 of the ways in which big international businesses appear to wield more power than national governments over matters like tax. Several large international corporations were using

190   *Phoenix out of the ashes?*

apparently legal loopholes to pay little or no corporation tax on their enormous UK earnings. While the coverage provoked some reputational damage to the firms involved, there is little evidence of sustained harm to their business. After all, given the international popularity of their products and services, firms such as Starbucks and Google appear largely able to manage their tax affairs as they wish and do tax-settlement deals with national governments on their terms, without fear of losing too much consumer custom as a result of bad publicity.

Perhaps more impactful are the growing shareholder revolts over executive pay packages that have grown to huge levels, often for unspectacular or even failed performance that have reduced share prices.

Corporate social responsibility

At the same time as business' reputation is deteriorating, its reach and impact is growing. Business today has more power than ever before to enhance or to diminish overall wellbeing in society. With the collapse of socialism and the decline in the authority of other institutions, global corporations could be expected to have a major role to play as global citizens. Yet neo-liberalism does not truly embrace the notion of corporate social responsibility (CSR). Even firms which adopt well-publicized CSR practices are often accused of embracing CSR for PR purposes. Milton Friedman (1962:133), probably the best known of the neo-liberal theorists, stated that

> There is one and only one social responsibility of business – to use its resources and engage in activities designed to increase its profits so long as it stays within the rules of the game, which is to say, engages in open and free competition without deception or fraud.

With respect to workers, are firms providing good jobs? The explosion of consumerism in the early decades of the twentieth century has led to the proliferation in high streets of inexpensive clothing retailers who have sourced their goods from the developing world, coffee shops and fast food outlets. While these provide some employment, by and large these jobs require volume and throughput of trade, and that applies to the workforce too where staff turnover can be over 90 per cent in many cases. As Mason (2015) points out, the business class is rewarded by late neo-liberal culture not for creating high-value, purposeful jobs that contribute to the good of mankind and the planet, but instead low-value, poorly paid and long-hours jobs that are available to a transient workforce.

Corporate schizophrenia

With respect to customers, are firms putting their interests first? Although Ellsworth (2002: x) found that in high-performing organizations, clients always remain the primary focus as the driving force for high-performing businesses, more generally 'corporate schizophrenia' abounds: too many companies pay lip service to the customer being their number one priority and employees as their number one asset. In practice, they pursue a purpose of shareholder wealth maximization that subordinates the interests of customers to those of shareholders and treats employees as expendable means to these financial ends. This results in a purpose focused on the capital market (shareholders), which often conflicts with strategies oriented toward product markets and with employees' values, resulting in widespread mistrust and cynicism about corporate statements of purpose and values.

With respect to society, are firms making a meaningful contribution? Corporate schizophrenia is also reflected in McKinsey's research (Bonini et al., 2010) which found that, while

The 'crisis' of capitalism   191

most executives endorse the idea that their organization should serve the public good, in practice most executives see their engagement with the public good as a risk, not an opportunity. They frankly admit that they are ineffective at managing this wider social and political issue which they tend to delegate to public-relations departments and corporate-affairs teams even though they recognize that they themselves need to lead on these issues.

There are growing debates about the ethics and responsibility of business with respect to the environment and the social good. Since large corporations typically exercise their power in promoting their own interests, they increasingly risk social legitimacy, and heavy financial penalties, if their practices are found morally wanting. Despite talk of the 'triple bottom line', tensions are in evidence at the intersection between profitability, employee satisfaction and societal value.

One of the most blatant examples of alleged frauds in 2015 was the emissions scandal of Volkswagen, which ran commercials of its engineers as angels even when company officials were setting up elaborate software systems to get around pollution control. When Volkswagen revealed in September 2015 that it had installed software on millions of cars in order to trick the US Environmental Protection Agency's emissions testers into thinking that the cars were more environmentally friendly than they were, investors understandably deserted the company. As a result, Volkswagen lost approximately $20 billion in market capitalization, as investors worried about the cost of compensating customers for selling them cars that were not compliant with environmental regulations. Thus unethical conduct harmed the business. However, business ethics should not be seen simply as a means to an end – to protect or advance investor interests. Like it or not, business is looked to for more than that.

With regard to the environment and the wellbeing of the planet, as Binnie (2005) points out, sustainability is not just the job of governments, and global warming has raised the stakes. Business clearly has a key role to play in addressing practices which impact on the health of the planet. Consumer power is being used not only to exert pressure on errant firms but also to exert influence on governments to intervene. After all, the number of environmental disasters that can be laid at the door of large corporations, such as the pollution catastrophe in the Gulf of Mexico caused by the BP Deepwater Horizon explosion in 2010, continues to rise unabated. It is no longer just a question of a 'licence to operate'. If global companies want to be seen as responsible citizens of a world community, they can no longer wait for others to intervene or to regulate. Arguably the threats are too serious and go beyond individual interests, representing a clear shared need.

Unfortunately, current business thinking does not easily grasp systems interdependencies, and therefore often lacks ecological consciousness or a sense of responsibility for other constituencies, or other stakeholders, besides investors. Of course at one level companies are obliged to develop policies showing their intent to deliver their environmental and corporate social responsibilities. Whether the motivation for business embracing an ethical agenda is for the sake of appearances, or because companies truly believe in the substantive benefits that can be gained by facilitating an ethical context, perhaps matters less than the actions they take. For despite the claims of many organizations to adhere to strict ethical rules, policies and guidelines, in practice unethical behaviour across supply chains is still regularly reported. For instance, a study by Amnesty International revealed that a number of technology companies are linked to child labour through their supply chains. Those companies argue that it is impossible to track the source of their raw materials or to verify, at arm's length, if their supply chain is operating irresponsibly or unethically.

Zane et al. (2016) claim that a possible explanation for this contradiction can be found in the concept of 'wilful ignorance', referring to the unwillingness of organizations to actively

192 *Phoenix out of the ashes?*

research their supply chains for fear of what they might find out and possible costly outcomes. Wilful ignorance does not mean that organizations will not take action when reports reach them about unethical behaviour. However, they will choose to appear ignorant of the problem until the problem is revealed and they are under public pressure to appear to act. This suggests that more research is needed that puts a spotlight on the ethical practice within supply chains.

Loss of trust

Not surprisingly perhaps, there are reportedly low levels of public trust in business, public institutions and their leaders, and growing demands for greater transparency. Arguably, organizational culture is a primary driver of employee behaviour and leaders shape this culture and related behaviour. The rash of business scandals of 2001–3 (Enron, Worldcom, etc.) and later, during the economic crisis from 2008 onwards, illustrated just how far out of kilter corporate-values statements and people's behaviour can become. For instance, before the firm ceased trading, Enron's then chairman Ken Lay had circulated staff with Enron's code of ethics on 1 July 2000:

> Enron stands on the foundation of its vision and values. Every employee is educated about the Company's vision and values and is expected to conduct business with other employees, partners, contractors, suppliers, vendors, and customers keeping in mind respect, integrity, communication, and excellence. Everything we do evolves from Enron's vision and values statements.
>
> (www.agsm.edu.au/bobm/teaching/BE/Cases_pdf/enron-code.pdf)

Despite Enron's statement of its core ethical values, senior leadership actions created a culture of greed that encouraged unethical behaviour at all levels that eventually led to the company's collapse.

More recently a seemingly endless series of scandals involving public figures from all walks of life, including political, business and religious leaders, has reduced public trust in leaders to low levels. There is also a good deal of concern about the amoral culture which has supported the capitalism of the past three decades. One example is the FBI's indictment of FIFA officials for racketeering, fraud and other offences in 2015. This was not surprising given that FIFA officials had long been suspected of 'feathering their own nests', but had been able to get away with their misdemeanours.

In the UK, trust in big charities is falling too, undermined by stories ranging from aggressive fundraising practices – blamed for the death of a 92-year-old woman – and allegations of mismanagement, to reports of high salaries for executives, debatable investment practices, huge cash surpluses and sizeable funds spent on administration. In 2016, one major charity was found to have greatly profited from promoting to its beneficiaries the services of a utilities supplier who did not offer the best rates to the charities' intended beneficiaries. Indeed, research published by the Charities Aid Foundation in September 2015 suggested that public trust in charities had fallen significantly in a year. When asked in 2014 whether most charities are trustworthy and act in the public interest, 71 per cent of over 1,100 people agreed, a figure broadly in line with previous years. In 2015, this had fallen to 57 per cent.

Given that leadership and organizational culture are areas in which HR has some deep expertise, it might be expected that HR leaders would take seriously the need to improve businesses behaviours which fall below ethical standards. HR is also directly involved, at least in an advisory capacity, on issues relating to executive pay. However, various reports suggest that HR does not see ensuring ethical practice as its role and one HR director was reported to have commented on the topic by saying, 'I don't do ethics, I'm commercial'.

Disruptive technologies

It is not only corporate behaviours and decision-making that have contributed to the current 'crisis of capitalism'. Arguably technology too is triggering the development of a new era. Indeed, Mason (2015) equates the breakthroughs possible through information technology with technical advances of earlier epochs such as the printing press that led to pivotal changes of system.

Corporations today are faced with a climate of disruption in a competitive landscape marked by turbulence, complexity, ambiguity and relentless speed. In our highly connected, fast-changing world, 'black swan' events (those of low probability and high impact) also seem to be more significant. Social disruption in general and the fast evolution of emerging businesses and markets are causing many business leaders to question the sustainability of their business models and drawing attention to the need for organizational and individual agility.

In particular, it is the sheer pace of change and disruption that is exponential, not incremental, and propelling a new era of globalization, economic value creation, innovation and discovery. Digital technology is now everywhere, disrupting business models and radically changing the workplace and the way work is done. In global banking, for instance, digitization is expected to penetrate a third to nearly a half of all European revenue pools by 2020, according to McKinsey analysis.

The pervasive nature of mobile technology and social networks has increased the size of the network, giving voice and economic opportunity to many previously silenced by a lack of connectivity. It is predicted that by 2020 there will be 80 billion connected devices worldwide and 5 billion internet devices. Indeed, there may soon come a time when everyone across the globe will have just-in-time access to information and learning platforms, potentially corroding capitalism through the free exchange of information. This is increasing the need to be innovative and is causing a rethink about what we do in organizations, for instance how to apply mobile technology – already accepted as the norm in terms of communications, music and healthcare – at work. With multiple digital competitors emerging, traditional firms are under pressure to match disruptive new business models while maintaining valuable customer relationships. Companies that fail to adapt are just likely to fail.

Such big shifts in the world economy combine to make it challenging for companies to sustain competitive advantage, and are resulting in new definitions of how and where companies create value, and for whom. Organizations have to become agile in order to respond and reposition themselves quickly to meet new challenges. For most companies, the business imperative is shifting from creating value through scaled efficiencies to creating value through a portfolio of transient advantages (Gunther-McGrath, 2013). Thus innovative experimentation and rapid prototyping are becoming the new 'business as usual'. Many consumers now rely on one digital channel or another to interact with companies, saying that they prefer shopping through mobile devices or laptops for ease of use, greater choice and control, and timely delivery of products and services, among other benefits. In retail, online operators have lower overheads than their bricks-and-mortar rivals so major physical retailers have been forced to rise to the competitive challenge by developing an online offering alongside running their stores, or face shrinking sales. In retail banking physical bank branches are rapidly disappearing from small towns as banks work on the basis that online banking is now the norm – ignoring the fact that many older customers do not use computers.

194 *Phoenix out of the ashes?*

Technology is already being used to target specific products to specific customers. For companies, mobile and big data offer vast opportunities for product and service development, as well as for how we manage our economies within communities across the globe. Technologies such as mobile devices, 3D printing, sensors, cognitive computing and the Internet of Things are changing the way companies design, manufacture and deliver almost every product and service. How big data about the market is gathered will no longer rely on market surveys but on 'user cases' with respect to customer analytics, according to McKinsey. They argue that leaders need to tune into social media to pick up weak signals and use these to drive product development, stocking and distribution channels. Already, i-beacons (small Bluetooth devices attached to smartphones) aimed at consumers are designed to draw on specific consumer-preference data and use proximity-based messaging to alert people/potential customers about deals they can find as they are passing by their local stores. While such a service can in theory appear customer-centric in intent, it is also a means of invading customers' personal space and enticing them into behaviours they may come to regret.

Accessing real-time information processed by advanced artificial-intelligence tools may create an enhanced reality in everyday lives and interactions, potentially transforming how people live, work and consume. The growth of artificial intelligence and robotization, combined with the continued pressure to improve productivity and output, is driving profound changes for the future. Digitally effective companies such as Amazon and Google are achieving tremendous operating leverage, with process automation driven by algorithms that allow them to manage billions of transactions and to upsell and cross-sell products and services without human intervention. In the UK alone, the Bank of England forecast in 2015 that within ten years 15 million jobs could be automated. So, does the increasing automation of work currently present a crisis, or an opportunity for liberation?

Automation may lead to richer roles as people are liberated from dull, repetitive tasks and are able to focus on the higher value-added job elements. From an employee perspective, the latter option of course would be preferable. In flatter structures, more and more organizations are pushing responsibilities and decision-making to the lowest level possible in an effort to increase commitment, task variety, organizational flexibility and employee ownership of work outcomes. Additionally, work is more and more likely to be designed and performed by teams, either formally or informally assembled. Already a new organizational model is on the rise: a 'network of teams' in which companies build and empower teams to work on specific business projects and challenges (Deloitte, 2016a).

Technology as risk

However, for all its positive potential, the use of technology has a more troubling shadow side since the multifaceted omnipresent web of surveillance is contributing to the social underpinning of anxiety. The Institute for Precarious Consciousness (2014) points to the mass proliferation of surveillance mechanisms such as CCTV and the constant examination and classification of even the youngest schoolchildren as examples of the outer shell of a neo-liberal idea of success inculcated inside the subjectivities and life stories of most of the population.

Within organizations, too, performance-management reviews and the growing use of CCTV in work premises prompt employee suspicion that they, rather than possible intruders, are under surveillance. Workplaces like call centres are increasingly common, where workers are subject to constant monitoring, retesting and potential failure both by quantitative requirements on numbers of calls and a process which denies most workers a stable job (they have to work for six months to even be offered a job, as opposed to a learning place).

Big data in particular arouses major concerns about privacy. On the one hand, governments worldwide want to know how they can protect the public from terrorism risks and consumers from privacy risks; on the other hand, some businesses are embracing the persona of protector of the public from a potentially malevolent and intrusive state. For instance, the 2010 WikiLeaks exposure of confidential memos obtained from 'secure' US government websites appeared to confirm cynical assumptions about the degree to which the state is to be trusted.

Apple fought a federal magistrate's order to help the Obama Administration break into an encrypted iPhone belonging to one of the terrorists who carried out the deadly San Bernardino terror attack in December 2015, the deadliest attack on US soil since the 9/11 catastrophe. Apple's CEO argued that this could lead to wider problems of phone hacking. This brings into question a private company's power to protect its customers, especially when Apple alone apparently has the means to address the issue. Amidst widespread concerns about where a 'snoopers' charter' might lead, there are also considerable ambiguities about who occupies the moral high ground on such issues. Whether such corporate stances are motivated by an inherent distrust of state intervention into private-sector activity, or are about companies acting on principle, championing free speech, remains to be seen. For as Mason (2015) points out, the business models of all the modern digital giants are designed to prevent the abundance of information and to ensure that nobody but the corporation can utilize the results. After all, 'by building business models and share valuations based on capture and privatisation of all socially produced information, such firms are constructing a fragile corporate edifice at odds with the most basic need of humanity, which is to use ideas freely' (Mason, 2015).

The transformation of work

Digital disruption and social networking have changed the way organizations hire, manage and support people. Our growing ability to leverage information through the smart–data movement has the potential to be one of the greatest productivity drivers to date. These analytics should enable managers and HR to move from being reactive to being predictive, requiring entirely new approaches, solutions and perspective.

The advance of digitization is already transforming work itself. While the evolution of modern robotics, or artificial intelligence, has made our lives easier in some ways, it has also raised concerns as to how human workers will be affected. Whether this trend is a positive development for workers remains to be seen. As we have discussed in earlier chapters, the use of technology in the workplace may be revitalizing scientific management practice (digital Taylorism), enabling a high level of managerial control over employee work practices. The coming waves of automation, which will reduce the amount of work carried out by labour, have barely got under way. Machine learning, algorithms and easy-to-teach robotics are becoming available to transform assembly operations that were once relegated to unskilled or semi-skilled human labour. In the first decade of the twenty-first century, many industrial and low-paying jobs disappeared from the UK or moved to other countries. With little collective resistance from the workforce, and technology at the heart of the latest wave of innovation, there is no real pressure on employers to re-employ the old workforce in new jobs. The resulting gap of decent jobs will no doubt test our social structures and economic systems.

Digitization, artificial intelligence and learning machines are likely in due course to extend commoditization of all forms of work, including professional, highly skilled work. Automation is likely to further destabilize jobs since it allows these to be disaggregated into

196 *Phoenix out of the ashes?*

their component tasks and subtasks and the hiving off of those that can be automated. As the nature of work becomes more fluid, jobs are less likely to be defined by a clear description and become more a fixed set of tasks determined by management. These are more likely to be made up of constantly changing activities or by a role in a work process, or responsibility for a specific outcome. Thus employee flexibility becomes mandatory. Employers will increasingly expect employees to shift roles, responsibilities and tasks quickly.

This destabilization of jobs has the potential to be harmful to the interests of workers, since it has the potential to speed up work processes, creating ever greater demands. Additionally, the rapid pace of technological advancement requires employees to understand more than just the current program or system they are working with since this will soon be obsolete, so continuous learning becomes essential for continued employment. Through short-term and project-based employment, businesses can meet their short-term staffing needs, without a long-term employment commitment to the workforce. The rapid increase in the use of temporary employees and contractors presents an increasingly common hiring trend with teams of permanent and non-permanent workers working alongside each other.

The use of big data and other forms of analytics are increasingly being applied to recruitment. Indeed, many employers see the onset of the information economy as heralding new opportunities for an on-demand talent market. Digital disruption and social networking are changing the way organizations hire, manage and support people. One high-tech company receives approximately 85,000 applications for 850 graduate jobs each year. The firm has reduced the cost of filtering these applications by developing personality templates based on the firm's current most highly performing graduate 'ideal workers' against which computers can automatically scan applications. Ninety-seven per cent of applications are screened out without further consideration, thus diversity of approach is not required. Similarly, some firms are using psycho-analytic tools such as sentiment analysis to screen current and potential employees' social media activity both to assess workers' interests and the risks they pose to the company. Since Millennials tend to use social media very widely, there is usually plenty of data available to firms to assist in the screening-out process.

Some firms are presenting workers with fitness trackers as a benefit – which employees are encouraged to use and which tend to be enthusiastically embraced, especially by young people. However, the data these generate are also available to the firms to help them understand the health levels of their employees. Such data could potentially be used during restructurings to weed out those who are least healthy and likely to represent a costly risk to the employer.

So on the one hand, technology's positive potential to help mankind is evident in the use of advanced technology to teach both people and machines. On the other hand, such technology is also being used to replace human labour. Even 'emotionally intelligent' work is susceptible to replacement, as Braverman had predicted. For instance, artificially intelligent 'chat bots' will replace customer-service assistants in the next decade and are already being trialled by Facebook, according to Mark Zuckerberg (Dean, 2016). Meanwhile, robotics is being used for some surgical procedures, remotely controlled by an ever-shrinking number of specialists who may be based on the other side of the globe from the patient.

As Schumacher, Braverman and Sennett have all pointed out, technology is not neutral with respect to domination. Professor Stephen Hawking (Cellan-Jones, 2014) too warns that as artificial intelligence advances yet further, it could take off on its own and redesign itself at an ever-increasing rate. As Professor Hawking argues, 'Humans, who are limited by slow biological evolution, couldn't compete, and would be superseded'.

This suggests that large corporations that are still grounded in a theoretical model that does not acknowledge the complex interdependencies of all the various constituencies are unlikely to reach their fullest potential in the twenty-first century. Ehrenfeld and Hoffman (2013) identify two core facets of our culture that drive the unsustainable, unsatisfying and unfair social and economic machines that dominate our lives. First, our collective model of the way the world works cannot cope with the inherent complexity of today's highly connected, high-speed reality. Second, our understanding of human behaviour is rooted in this outdated model. Arguably the new economy will require new types of leadership. Embracing such trends may require a mindset change for today's leaders – with those who 'get it' recognizing the dramatic transformation needed in the way we work.

The model of the firm is changing

Not only are business models put under pressure in today's environment, but the model of the firm is, too. In the quest for business-model innovation and agility, some organizations are undertaking a significant redesign of the workforce that entails a shift in how, where, by whom and with whom business is done, how leadership is leveraged, and how individuals self-organize to increase productivity while creating new forms of value.

Perhaps the pre-eminent reason why organizations are rethinking how they operate is people power. Why is there such an emphasis on people and their interactions these days? Meeting the complex demands of customers requires not only higher skill levels and greater specialization, but flexibility and a willingness on the part of workers to contribute over and above what is specified in written rules. Traditional command and control-management practices, with employees required simply to carry out instructions, are increasingly at odds with what is needed for people and businesses to succeed today. It leads employees to have little interest in their work and low levels of commitment to their employers – and ultimately to conflict or personal withdrawal.

The emphasis today is on the creation of organizations that are able to keep pace with sudden alterations in consumer preference and technology and that are able to learn and to innovate. Given the competitive pressures facing businesses, contemporary themes in this genre include the pursuit of agility; organizations becoming flatter, leaner, less insular, hierarchical and rule-bound and more flexible, change-focused, enterprising and collaborative; the use of technology and implementation of high-performance work systems including team working. Workplaces are being redesigned, with more and more companies moving to 'virtual offices', in which employees no longer have dedicated office space, but can work from home or visit a satellite office to check in, pick up materials or have face-to-face meetings.

Since the creation and delivery of sophisticated products and services does not lend itself well to monitoring or controlling through rules, the demise of hierarchy is increasingly heralded. Owing to the devolution of decision-making and new forms of team-based work organization, some workers are able to use their initiative and to exercise autonomy in the quest of generating competitive advantage. Thus, in theory at least, we are witnessing the emergence of a new, more liberating 'post-bureaucratic' era.

Heckscher and Donnellon (1994) argue that this type of post-bureaucratic organization is not merely different from bureaucracy but is an evolutionary development beyond it, generating a greater capacity for human accomplishment. That is because, as everyone, at each level of hierarchy, takes responsibility for the success of the whole, the nature of bureaucratic, hierarchical control in work organizations becomes largely redundant and should be replaced by notions of shared leadership and the manager as leader. If that happens, then the basic notion of regulating relations among people by separating them into specific, predefined functions must be abandoned to be replaced by the use of influence rather than of hierarchical power.

198 *Phoenix out of the ashes?*

Similar points apply to the notion of trust. Faced with rapid change, often involving part-nerships, alliances and networks, effective influencing to a large extent depends on trust – on the belief by all members that others are seeking mutual benefit, rather than maximizing personal gain. Thus trust is a more efficient coordinating mechanism than power, hierarchy, money or markets. The challenge is to create a system in which organizational control occurs through the management of relationships; where people can enter into relations that are determined by problems to be solved rather than predetermined by the structure; where people's ability to persuade and the use of influence carry more weight than power or official position.

The major source of this kind of trust is a recognition of interdependence: a shared under-standing of the ways in which different parts of the organization contribute to the accom-plishment of the overall strategy and acknowledgement that the fortunes of all depend on combining the performances of all. In an organization that relies less heavily on job definitions and rules, the mission and purpose plays a crucial integrating role; spelling out what the com-pany actually seeks to achieve rather than universalistic values statements. Employees need to understand the key objectives in depth in order to coordinate their actions intelligently as they go along. Because this model is based on dialogue rather than command or 'tell-and-sell' style communication, Heckscher refers to this type of organization as the 'interactive type' since the influence hierarchy is to a far greater degree than bureaucracy based on the consent of, and the perceptions of, other members of the organization.

In turn, this implies the kind of relationship where work is characterized by the principles of consent and participation rather than command and control – indeed by something deeper than mere consent. Intense competition has meant the commitment, motivation, loyalty and willingness of people to invest their creativity in their work is one of only a few sources of differentiation (Overell et al., 2010).

Symptomatic of the growth of the people-centred firm is the extent to which many of them have come to stress their 'social' as opposed to their 'economic' characteristics. Over recent years, all firms have had to adapt to changing social expectations about the role of employers. Organizations are viewed as sources of friendship, happiness and personal devel-opment. Childcare, eldercare, maternity, paternity, work–life balance, equality, diversity, stress, wellbeing; such issues now need to be 'managed'.

So are we moving in a post-bureaucratic direction?

Sturdy et al. (2015) point out, as is so often the case in claims of fundamental change, that there is good reason to be sceptical about the apparent demise of bureaucracy and the birth of this 'new' twenty-first-century organizational ideal. Based on their extensive analysis of Australian and British corporations, they argue that, while large organizations are indeed changing, with managers becoming less explicitly hierarchical and more market and change oriented, there are also strong resonances with the past and the move away from bureaucracy, departmental silos and hierarchical control is exaggerated.

Rather, they argue, we have entered an age of 'neo-bureaucracy' in which elements of tra-ditional organizational practice are morphing with other more recent trends such as a focus on change, projects, 'client' relationships and boundary spanning. For example, in the organi-zations they studied, previously specialist functions were integrated through cross-functional project teams. Firms sought to generate change and innovation via standardized change pro-grammes and methods. Managers needed to use both authority and influence in managing relationships and organizational politics. Companies delegated some authority but balanced this with quasi-market checks and balances. Moreover, the identity of the manager has also changed with an emphasis on personal branding and network building.

Sturdy et al. (2015) suggest that a hybrid form of neo-bureaucracy is also emerging, founded on the example of management consultancy. Firstly, large organizations are increasingly recruiting former external consultants into management positions, especially those from 'blue-chip' management consulting firms who bring with them a particular approach to managing that favours, for example, analytical and often standardized change and project management tools. Secondly, management groups within organizations such as those in information technology, accounting and HR are increasingly taking on consulting roles and identities. The aim is to enhance the occupational status of specific internal managerial groups by borrowing from the prestige of external consulting. The third way is through the creation of specialist internal consulting units, now being modernized through a focus on 'programme management' and 'culture and change'. As companies seek out new ways to improve their performance, reduce costs and increase efficiency, these internal consulting groups provide another example of how managerial work is increasingly focused on project-based change across the organization for various internal 'clients'.

However, Sturdy et al. (2015) found that the new group of consultant managers in large private and public-sector organizations tended to focus on short-term gains, 'value added' and were using analytical, often mechanistic tools such as those taught on MBA programmes. In this scenario, alternative approaches to management that stressed longer-term goals and capability-building risked becoming marginalized.

Moreover, this new hybrid role of management as consultancy also suffers from the same precarity as other workers, since activities become increasingly framed as discrete change projects, ongoing employment depends on the availability of relevant projects and these are subject to the whim of new CEOs or waves of job cuts.

Taken together, such changes have important implications for the future of management and leadership as both an activity and occupation. Whatever the future holds, as Wright points out (2015),

> contrary to the rosy view of a post-bureaucratic nirvana, contemporary organisational life involves a curious blend of old and new; multifunctional projects, the standardised innovation of change programmes, a need to manage peers and subordinates as 'clients', and delegated autonomy of quasi-market structures across organisational relations. This is the brave new world of management as consultancy!

Conclusion

Today, in the wake of a global financial crisis, it is appropriate to question and challenge the direction of business development and the financial and economic models that drive it. The old paradigm of maximizing profits and shareholder value as the sole purpose of business has created negative unintended consequences. The single-minded pursuit of short-term profit maximization now lies discredited. Business is seen as despoiling the environment and causing harm in the world. Capitalistic business practices and their outcomes – such as the decline of trust in large corporates and growing wage inequality – raise fundamental questions about the role of business in society, the legitimacy of bureaucratic structures and the meaning of organizational justice. And, to extend this argument further, it could be that capitalism as we have known it is not fit for the twenty-first century.

In particular, the ethics of business and its leaders are in the spotlight. A seemingly endless series of corporate and institutional scandals have produced corporate reputation damage, huge financial losses, led to an anti-corporation rhetoric and shareholder revolts against the enormous compensation packages paid to executives of such firms. Loss of key staff and

Phoenix out of the ashes?

disenchanted customers are just some of the symptoms of an organization that has lost its way. Such scandals have led to deeper questions being asked in all sectors – civil society, governments and the business community itself – about the nature of business and indeed about neo-liberal, free-market 'casino' capitalism itself.

However, in *The Enigma of Capitalism*, David Harvey (2010) argues that the essence of capitalism is its amorality and lawlessness and to talk of a regulated, ethical capitalism is to make a fundamental error. Similarly, Mason (2015) points out, capitalism was structured around something purely economic. However, Mason also makes the case for containing crises of the current sort within the constraints of capitalism, and for a social order that would allow us to live within a system that really could be responsible, just and humane. Given that, in today's more connected world, companies can no longer call all the shots because they have become so interdependent upon their wider network of stakeholders, the challenge for organizations is how to really engage, openly and honestly, with their stakeholders.

So will this latest crisis of capitalism trigger major change and innovation as have previous crises? Predicting what the future will hold is difficult since it is full of 'unknown unknowns', as former US President G.W. Bush's economic adviser Donald Rumsfeld put it. Gray (2008) argues that the global economy is in the first stages of a deep shift, a geo-political change involving the meltdown of the neo-liberal model of debt-ridden capitalism – and it is not yet clear what will replace it. Gray suggests that this is unlikely to be a new universal paradigm and more likely to be fragmented, akin to what happened to former Soviet Bloc governments following the collapse of communism.

Gamble (2009) proposes that this latest crisis of capitalism is likely to lead to a new political economic settlement. This will take time, and there will be much resistance from entrenched interests, but we are seeing this process already in the reaction to finance capital – and especially the 'bonus culture'. Hutton argues that at this historic turning point in British capitalism we need to return to our core moral values and find a new way of making a living: 'There is a genius in capitalism, but the paradox is that it flowers best in an environment that capitalists themselves think is hostile. Paradoxically, fairness is capitalism's indispensable value' (Hutton, 2010: x). Mason (2015) suggests that post-capitalism will emerge from within the relics of neo-liberal forms of capitalism. He points out a key contradiction between the possibility of free, abundant goods and information versus a system of monopolies, banks and governments trying to keep things private, scarce and commercial.

Whichever way things turn out, over the next few years we will need answers to the fundamental questions arising from today's changing environment and its related challenges for work and working lives. Are today's business leaders and HR professionals preparing themselves to deal with the challenges these known-unknowns will create for organizations in every sector? How will this changing context drive new definitions of organizational effectiveness? These are questions we shall explore in the next chapter.

Points to ponder

- To what extent do you believe that the financial crisis that began in 2008 was the onset of a crisis of capitalism?
- In your view, will business continue to operate much as before, or will a new paradigm for doing business emerge? What might this look like?

11 New organizational effectiveness

> Efficiency is doing better what is already being done. Effectiveness is deciding what to do better.
>
> (Peter F. Drucker)

After the last few chapters, it might be possible to conclude that neo-liberal capitalism as we have known it has run its course. As we discussed, the world of business today is urgently in need of a new paradigm because 'business as usual' is simply not working well any more. The pursuit of profits without heed to broader consequences, as manifested in the wake of the collapse of Lehman Brothers, has had damaging and long-lasting consequences for many national economies and for generations of workers who have lost or never gained employment. Public distrust of business is at a historic high; many employees, customers and other stakeholders of businesses are disconnected from, and disillusioned with, the companies they interact with. Inequalities and inequities exist around the world and there is increasing social unrest as well as anti-capitalist movements.

Yet capitalism can also be a force for good – so in this book I am not advocating jettisoning capitalism, but rather amending capitalism's potentially harmful aspects. As the power and influence of business grows, corporations must rethink why they exist, become holistic and integral in their aims, with deeper, more comprehensive purposes. Mackey and Sisodia (2014) argue that we can remove most of the hostility toward business and capitalism if businesses work at becoming better citizens. Thus as new definitions of the role and purpose of business emerge, so too will different metrics be needed to evaluate organizational performance and effectiveness.

In this chapter we shall consider if it is time to move on from a shareholder-focused strategy to one focused on creating value for stakeholders. If so, how would business success then be defined?

In this chapter we will cover:

- A changing basis for competitive advantage.
- A new paradigm for doing business.
- Who are today's legitimate stakeholders?
- Corporate purpose.

Changing basis for competitive advantage

Today the global economy and business are in transition, driven by technology, new ideas, population changes and political instability. If the trigger for change in the 1980s and 1990s was globalization, today technology is driving the next era of economics, enterprise and leadership. It is increasing the need to be innovative and is causing a rethink about what we do in organizations, for instance how to apply mobile technology – already accepted as the norm in terms of communications, music, healthcare and at work.

202   *Phoenix out of the ashes?*

Ellsworth (2002: 10) highlights a number of trends that he believes are changing the face of competition and collectively will determine competitive advantage in the twenty-first century. I add my interpretation of these trends below.

The coin of competitive advantage is rapidly evolving to knowledge

Today the creation and management of knowledge is becoming the primary source of competitive advantage. Mason (2015) argues that in the information economy, social knowledge, as Marx envisaged it, could 'blow capitalism sky high' since the whole of society is a network through which we share knowledge and discontent that cannot be silenced. 'By creating millions of networked people, financially exploited but with the whole of human intelligence one thumb-swipe away, info-capitalism has created a new agent of change in history: the educated and connected human being' (Mason, 2015).

On the other hand, the next raft of knowledge work will be automated. Who will be impacted and will new jobs replace those being eliminated? Can today's workers be retrained for this emerging world of work?

Loyalty and commitment of employees are increasingly essential to knowledge-based competitive advantage

In the knowledge-based economy, people are the source of innovation and business success. There is a raft of literature on the topic of employee engagement, much of which argues that in any field, employees must be willing to release their discretionary effort if they are to produce outstanding results. In the case of knowledge work, the difference between the output of a highly engaged individual and that of a person who is less engaged can be marked. Companies prize the workers who produce these outstanding performances and want to retain them. Such skilled employees can enjoy the whip hand in the employment relationship and are often able to enjoy 'i-deals', i.e. idiosyncratic employment deals that meet their personal needs (Rousseau, 2005).

As demand for higher-skill work continues to increase, in certain sectors there are reported to be growing talent shortages which jeopardize business success, thus increasing the influence of talent further. Scase (2006) predicted that there would be a growing systemic 'talent crisis' in the West (referred to as the 'demographic time bomb'). Throughout Western Europe and the US, the workforce is ageing, with declining birth rates generating future shortages of both employees and consumers. In practice, demographic upheavals have made the workforce both culturally more diverse and also younger and older, with Millennials now making up more than half the workforce. By 2020 there will be 2.7 workers to every non-worker, compared with 4:1 in 1990 (Department of Trade and Industry statistics).

It is predicted that people of the 'Baby Boomer' generation will be among the last to be able to enjoy a comfortable retirement from the age of 60. Conversely, the ending of the default retirement age and the closure of most final salary pension schemes, and other pensions concerns, are forcing many older workers to postpone their retirement. Many Baby Boomers are working into their 70s and 80s and are being challenged to adapt to new roles as mentors, coaches and often subordinates to junior colleagues. Consequently, the labour pool for many jobs is becoming ever-more multigenerational.

More generally, the changing composition of the workforce may be altering the dynamic of employer–employee relations. While businesses pursue talent wherever it is to be found, low-skill workers are increasingly replaced as their work is automated. In addition, the anticipated capability gap (i.e. increased demand for, and greater scarcity of, high-level skills) in the workforce raises issues of group differences and an increased emphasis on trainability. The diverse nature of the global workforce highlights a need for inclusion and shared beliefs to tie people together.

As the most 'connected' generations, younger workers bring particular value to organizations. Millennials are reported to bring high expectations for a rewarding, purposeful work experience, constant learning and development opportunities and dynamic career progression. While pay remains a top priority for Millennials, work–life balance, integrity and career development are all important factors too. A Deloitte (2015) survey of Millennials from 29 countries found that one in four would quit their job to join a new organization or do something else during 2016 if the opportunity arose. Only 16 per cent of Millennials saw themselves with their current employer in ten years' time. Consequently, employers will need to provide different kinds of development opportunities for younger generations of workers (often stereotyped as Generations X, Y and the 'Net Generation') who may have different value-sets and expectations of employers from their Baby Boomer forebears.

Technology underpins the growth of social networking and the burgeoning of online communities. Increasing use of chat rooms and services such as My Space, Facebook and YouTube seems to potentially counter-balance the apparent fragmentation of society by enabling people to create their own online identities or avatars and have access to thousands of new 'friends'. Erickson (2010) argues that younger workers in particular have been strongly influenced by their exposure to multimedia stimuli, and in a short-term focus workplace, develop a fractured and externalized sense of self which can only be experienced through their latest achievement. This, she argues, leads to a desperate search for recognition at the individual level, and through Facebook and other social media sites, the construction of an ersatz life. Underneath this, Erickson proposes, young people have a strong desire for community.

The sources of managerial influence are changing

For instance, the term 'conscious capitalism' is gaining currency. This perhaps reflects the fact that people today are more aware of the world around them than ever before and, in the wake of numerous corporate scandals, expect companies to behave ethically. The advent of the World Wide Web has accelerated this trend, simultaneously connecting hundreds of millions of people and placing great demands on companies for transparency. There is growing public consciousness about widening inequalities between social groups and the inherent unfairness of extremes of wealth and opportunity. Similarly, there is greater environmental awareness. Amongst the new management 'fashions', Smart is the new Green.

Firms with different concepts of corporate purpose are competing head to head

On the one hand, as Binnie (2005) points out, new sources of competition are creating an ever-more cut-throat backdrop to organizations and their supply chains:

> There is a feeling that short-term cost advantages take priority over long-term relationships. Whoever in the world can pop up now on the Internet and offer to supply at the lowest cost, will get the business – and the long-term welfare or development of the supplier is of no importance.

At the same time, post-capitalism is social and based on the precondition of abundance. This in turn is challenging traditional business models. For instance, we are witnessing the

204 *Phoenix out of the ashes?*

rise of the so-called 'sharing' or 'collaborative economy' – where goods and services are produced and exchanged by volunteers for free (as with Wikipedia) and no longer respond to the demands of the market. A variety of cooperative car sharing and food-supply arrangements, new forms of ownership and new forms of lending are surfacing. Companies that are pioneering the commercialization of the 'sharing economy', such as Uber and Airbnb, are aiming at system-wide change since their valuations depend on their ability to win highly localized political arguments all over the world, city by city. They have to navigate complex rules and regulations, which were not designed to deal with their business model. Consequently, they are attempting to completely redefine the way cities and platforms coexist.

Emerging models such as Uber's, that rely on technological advances to spearhead social and business-practice changes, appear to shift the competitive paradigm at the expense of existing suppliers. In various European cities Uber is winning over from traditional taxi firms increasing numbers of customers who appreciate the ready availability and relatively lower costs of on-demand taxis. Meanwhile the black-cab drivers who have learned their trade the traditional craftsman way by acquiring the 'the knowledge' of their routes before gaining their license to operate find their business undermined by unlicensed Uber drivers who rely instead on their global navigation system. Not surprisingly, the potential conflicts of interest run at multiple levels and are not easily resolvable.

Need for a new paradigm of business

Consequently, business models are needed that are more in touch with our complex, post-modern, information-rich world. In today's self-adaptive system all of the various constituencies connect together and affect one another. As Mackey (2006) points out,

> we will need to create a new business paradigm that moves beyond simplistic machine/ industrial models to those that embrace the complex interdependencies of multiple constituencies. This is the reality in which corporations exist today and our economic and business theories need to evolve to reflect this truth.

This change is perhaps underway. The shareholder approach, which states that managers are required to manage a firm in the interests of its shareholders, has always been the overriding concept in the Anglo-American corporate governance (Dolenc et al., 2012). However, by the late 1980s, triggered mainly by challenges to US competitiveness and poor growth in productivity, concern was growing over the failure of management and the narrowness of the criteria used to measure organizational effectiveness in practice. In the wake of the financial crisis, these concerns have grown even more. Accounting-determined measures such as return on investment, assets, equity or assets and earnings per share were highly intercorrelated but were subject to distortion, and did not take account of risks to the reported finances (Sparrow and Cooper, 2014). For Hitt (1988), the financialization of organizational effectiveness measures created an over-reliance on financial measures of performance and short-run profits.

By the 1990s, the need for innovation and longer-term criteria that could allow organizations to evolve and adapt to changing circumstances was starting to be recognized. Moreover, shareholder value-based organizational effectiveness measures failed to take account of the changing nature of stakeholders and more collaborative ways of working. For instance, in the sharing economy, information is, or should be, abundant. Wikipedia is one example of a peer-based sharing platform operating initially on the basis of voluntary sharing of information – 'creative commons' in action. Gradually though, e-business models emerged that were based on old-style monopolizing and protecting data that had been generated for free by social interaction. Early contributors of information on some sites soon found that they were unable to access that information without signing up to a 'service' of some sort for which they had to pay a price.

Today, investors are increasingly shifting away from looking at businesses simply from the profit/revenue/customer/cost perspective towards a broader range of success measures that reflect a wider stakeholder perspective, moving from purely financial measures to social. Moreover, thanks to regulatory and other pressures today, shareholders around the world are pressuring companies to link executive compensation packages to the company's sustainability performance, motivated in part by the prevalence of short-term and stock market-linked metrics in many executive compensation schemes (Ethical Funds Company, 2006: 8).Viewing the production of profits for investors as business' sole goal is therefore increasingly exposed as myth.

Increasingly, therefore, with regard to organizational effectiveness, the performance of an organization is evaluated in terms of its responsibility to, and its relationships with, its various stakeholders. Even Michael Porter, a leading proponent of shareholder value in the late twentieth century, now asserts that CSR and core business are not mutually exclusive (Porter and Kramer, 2011). Indeed, businesses 'must seek out opportunities to create shared value', both for the organization and other stakeholders.

Although stakeholder theory was popular until the 1980s in the UK and USA, it was difficult to operationalize in practice and had fallen out of fashion by the end of the twentieth century, replaced by the pursuit of shareholder value, particularly in the UK and US (Donaldson and Preston, 1995). On the other hand, stakeholder theory has long held sway in other countries.Yoshimori (1995) examined the views of managers from a variety of countries and found that, in contrast to the American and English managers who believe the only valid stakeholder is the shareholder, managers in Japan, Germany and France believe that the firm exists for the interests of all its stakeholders.

Stakeholder theory

'Stakeholder theory begins with the assumption that values (ethics) are necessarily and explicitly a part of doing business' (Freeman et al., 2004: 364). Freeman's (1984) stakeholder theory is essentially a normative strategic management theory with instrumental and descriptive dimensions. It tells managers and organizations how to treat the interests of stakeholders in a moral and appropriate way (Phillips et al., 2003). In the stakeholder approach to CSR, the organization is to maximize business-value creation based on relevant stakeholder interests, and fair allocation of business value to stakeholders (Phillips et al., 2003). Organizations which ignore or harm these other constituencies are likely to do lasting damage to their corporate reputations.

Much of the research on stakeholder theory has addressed the subject of which stakeholders deserve or require management attention (Mitchel et al., 1997), referred to as stakeholder salience. Freeman's stakeholder concept refers to 'any group or individual who can affect or is affected by the achievement of an organization's purpose' (Freeman, 1984). The main groups of stakeholders are shareholders, customers, employees, local communities, suppliers and distributors. In a later publication, Freeman referred to stakeholders as 'those groups who are vital to the survival and success of the corporation' (Freeman, 2004). Additional groups were identified by Friedman to include academics, non-governmental organizations, government and the media (Friedman and Miles, 2006). Similarly, Paauwe (2004) argues that the survival

206 *Phoenix out of the ashes?*

of an organization not only depends on financial competitiveness, but also on its ability to legitimize its existence towards society and relevant stakeholders of the organization (e.g. employees, customers, trade unions, local government).

Approaches to the question of stakeholder salience have focused on stakeholder–organization relations based on power dependencies, legitimacy claims and urgency (Donaldson and Preston, 1995; Mitchel et al., 1997). Therefore, within a stakeholder model, the stakes of specific stakeholders need to be recognized by managers and other stakeholders and it is the responsibility of managers, and the management function, to select activities and direct resources to obtain benefits for legitimate stakeholders.

Effective stakeholder mapping should provide a response to the following questions:

- Who are our current and potential stakeholders?
- What are their interests/rights?
- How does each stakeholder affect us?
- How do we affect each stakeholder?
- What assumption does our current strategy make about each important stakeholder?
- What are the 'variables' that affect us and our stakeholder?
- How do we measure each of these variables and their impact?
- How do we keep score with our stakeholders?

(Freeman, 1984)

Central to stakeholder theory is the assertion that 'managers must develop relationships, inspire stakeholders and create communities where people strive to give their best to make good on the firm's promises' and 'manage the relationships with its stakeholders in an action-oriented way' (Freeman et al., 2004: 364). That is because the success of stakeholder relationships largely depends on the degree of commitment of the involved parties from the outset.

Since conflicts in stakeholder interests are inevitable, these must be anticipated and resolved so that stakeholders do not exit the relationship (Freeman et al., 2004). The aim should be to arrive at a win–win situation for all stakeholders, irrespective of the motive. Hence, engagement processes should inform the strategic decision-making of all stakeholders throughout the life cycle of a product, service or activity over the long term. This ensures the continued willingness of stakeholders to engage in the organization to the advantage of all participants.

In principle, a series of stages leading to stakeholder engagement can be applied to the context of a single organization or that of organizations embedded in the life cycle of a product, service or activity (Espinosa-Orias and Sharratt, 2006):

1. Acknowledge the existence of stakeholders around a product, a service or an activity. As a result, it is possible to establish that the organizations are accountable to the stakeholders for the actions, omissions and decisions taken along the life cycle.
2. Methodically identify and categorize both stakes and stakeholders of the life cycle under consideration. Then prioritize them for the allocation of commensurate weighting, attention and resources.
3. Identify, map and establish relations between stakes and stakeholders in a number of ways. Such relations will depend on the context, the nature of the stake and the characteristics of the stakeholders.
4. Manage stakeholder relations by developing engagement strategies to pursue with stakeholders with the purpose of establishing, maintaining or strengthening relationships

which will inform decision-making processes. These might include the exchange of information, expertise and experiences to build transparency, trust and credibility among organizations and stakeholders alike.

5. Monitor and measure and control relationships.

The above-mentioned stages do not necessarily follow a sequential application, though they are mutually dependent.

Who are today's legitimate stakeholders (in addition to shareholders)?

Customers

While investors remain the primary stakeholder of business under neo-liberalism, looking back to the 1970s, customers were seen as the key stakeholders and nominally still are today. For Peter Drucker (1954) the only valid definition of business purpose is to create a customer. Similarly, the pioneer of the total quality movement, W. Edwards Deming (1986), argued that quality followed the simple principles of putting the customer's needs first and placing the product before profits. For Deming, quality comes from people who believe in the corporate ends and are entrusted to work positively for the common good (Ellsworth, 2002: 9).

Suppliers

A healthy and ethical supply chain is fundamental to a corporation's brand positioning and operational effectiveness. Corporations which take advantage of their suppliers, for instance supermarket chains who exploit small farmers and fail to pass on their cost savings to customers, risk putting their suppliers out of business and losing their corporate reputations.

Labour

Whether these are employees or contractors, labour is a key stakeholder of business efforts. Even Jack Welch (in Guerrera, 2009), an arch proponent of shareholder capitalism, called the pursuit of shareholder value the 'dumbest idea in the world' and pointed out that 'shareholder value is a result, not a strategy. Your main constituencies are your employees.' We shall discuss what an employee-centric approach to labour management might look like in the next chapter.

Society

Drucker also observed that a company's purpose must lie outside of the business itself; in fact, it must lie in society since a business enterprise is an organ of society. Of course, corporations have for years been encouraged to be both profitable and ethical with regard to their financial practices and their social and environmental responsibilities. They have been urged to demonstrate their 'stewardship'/trusteeship by embracing the 'triple bottom line' (people, planet, profit), rather than financial accounting measures alone.

However, such arguments have had relatively little traction until recently. As we discussed in the last chapter, conventional business wisdom views CSR issues as a burden – a necessary cost of doing business in a multistakeholder environment. For many companies, the challenge of delivering value to all possible stakeholders – such as people in the community, those who work in organizations, natural systems and the earth itself – remains too abstract a goal. Indeed,

208 *Phoenix out of the ashes?*

increasing shareholder value and serving the needs of society's stakeholders are often seen as mutually exclusive: the *Great OR* of business (Marquard and Graham, 2010).

Moreover, given the examples of unethical behaviour revealed in various corporate scandals, there are risks in shifting from the traditional shareowner orientation to a stakeholder orientation since this could make it more difficult to detect and discipline self-serving behaviour by managers, who may always claim to be serving some broad set of stakeholder interests while they increase their powers and income (Donaldson and Preston, 1995).

The environment

With regard to the planet, after years of debate, claim and counter-claim, today there is a broad consensus among nations that climate change represents a threat and that mankind has a responsibility to avoid accelerating the pace of global warming. In December 2015, 195 nations signed the Paris Agreement – the first legally binding global climate accord. The intention is to work to reduce greenhouse emissions that contribute to global warming. However, Ehrenfeld and Hoffman (2013) argue that, driven by the old guard, sustainability has become little more than a fashionable idea, a reputational 'sticking plaster' to the problem that has largely been created by mass industrialization, toxic waste and emissions. As a result, they argue, both business and government are following the wrong path – at best applying temporary, less unsustainable solutions that will fail to leave future generations in better shape.

Pressure from the investment community may force companies to take sustainability issues seriously. The Economist Intelligence Unit's (EIU) report (2015) on the impact of global warming warns the investment community of the huge financial risks in play with regard to climate change and suggests that this is likely to represent an obstacle for many asset owners and managers to fulfil their fiduciary duties. Fiduciary duty requires managers to act in the best interest of their beneficiaries. In practice this means they need to deliver the best, risk-adjusted returns possible. 'Unfortunately, too many investors currently over-emphasize short-term performance at the expense of longer-term returns' (Economist Intelligence Unit, 2015: 3).

The EIU report proposes that institutional investors can collectively influence the companies in their portfolios to adapt and prepare for a lower carbon future as something that is in their collective self-interest. Some are seeking to reduce long-term climate risks by decarbonizing their portfolios. This need not come at the expense of short-term performance. The Swedish public pension fund AP4, for instance, has identified the 150 worst performers, in terms of carbon intensity, in the S&P 500 index and divested its holdings in them. The remaining 350 stocks track the performance profile of the index closely but have 50 per cent of its carbon footprint.

In various global sustainability indices there is growing evidence that sustainability is now being taken seriously by analysts when assessing the value of a company (http://sustainability-indices.com). For instance, Danone, one of the companies high on the Climate, Performance and Leadership Index outperforms other companies on that index, including with respect to financial performance. It's about corporate reputation and place in society, and involves taking deliberate action to contribute positively on a range of fronts, not simply financial, for instance by paying attention to packaging, thinking of the consequences of your actions. In another example, to improve standards of organic farming among its suppliers, in late 2014, Whole Foods rolled out a new rating system called Responsibly Grown, which measures factors like energy conservation, waste reduction and farmworker welfare.

Increasingly, therefore, an organization's reputation, its valuation and its sources of funding depend on the genuineness of its approach to sustainability issues, even though opinion is

New organizational effectiveness   209

divided about the best way to achieve sustainable outcomes. Indeed, Marquard and Graham (2010) argue that:

> We have come to a point now where this agenda of sustainability and corporate responsibility is not only central to business strategy but will increasingly become a critical driver of business growth…how well and how quickly businesses respond to this agenda will determine which companies succeed and which will fail in the next few decades.

Quadruple bottom line

So if shared value is becoming recognized as the goal of business, operating according to this paradigm requires expanding our aspirations and changing our assumptions. Instead of rules we need principles; transparency and commitment rather than superficial compliance. Shared value from a conscious capitalism perspective involves protecting and enhancing the earth and its people, building a world with healthy employees, communities and natural systems. Sustainability requires us to be better stewards of the world's resources – to consider these as held in trust for future generations and therefore to be left in a better condition than they are now.

Cambridge Leadership Development argues that triple bottom line accounting and related measurement frameworks (competitive productivity for profit, quality of life for people and sustainability of the planet's resources for the survival and flourishing of species and ecosystems) fail to emphasize the foundations of sustainable prosperity in continuous and competitive entrepreneurship and innovation. Hence the notion that corporations should be held accountable according to a quadruple bottom line, though there is debate about the nature of the fourth bottom line. Cambridge Leadership Consultancy advocate that '(Enterprising) Progress' in the lives of individuals and their communities should be the fourth 'P' (or 'bottom line') to be measured. This requires adaptive innovation – successful implementation of new combinations – in all aspects of sustainable prosperity. These interrelated 4Ps of the quadruple bottom line – people, profit, planet and progress – are proposed as the basis for a more comprehensive framework for developing measures of sustainable prosperity, as in Table 11.1.

Measurement is a key starting point on the journey towards sustainability practice. Lawler et al. (2015) argue that, with the new metrics that are being developed as a result of big data and the tremendous computing and analytic power that is now available, it is more and more

Table 11.1 Quadruple bottom line

Sustainable prosperity: 4Ps	Measures
People – quality of life	Quality of life for people, e.g. health, vigour, wellbeing, flourishing.
Profit – competitive productivity	Competitive productivity in producing and distributing goods and services for consumption and profit with scarce resources.
Planet – sustainable ecosystems	Individual, community and ecosystems survival across lifespans and generations.
Progress – adaptive innovation	E.g. adaptive learning and change; trial and error risk taking and discovery – in all aspects of people, profit and planet – and innovations in being innovative.

Source: http://cambridgeleadershipdevelopment.com/quadruple-bottom-line-for-sustainable-prosperity/

210   *Phoenix out of the ashes?*

possible to measure their performance in all four areas. Therefore, executives and HR must devise and implement strategies, clarify priorities and measure performance in ways appropriate to their organization's context. For this to happen effectively:

> When incorporating the new technologies that are being developed into how organizations are designed and operated it is critical that the quadruple bottom line be the criterion against which change is conceived, implemented, and evaluated. Only if this is done are organizations going to perform in ways that warrant support by the societies that create them and allow them to exist.
>
> (Lawler, 2014b)

Means–ends argument

Corporate management has the legal and fiduciary responsibility to maximize long-term shareholder value, but is a focus on stakeholders incompatible with shareholder value? Milton Friedman quoted Bakan (2004) to argue that: 'Executives who choose social or environmental goals over profits are immoral since the company is the property of the shareholders and must act in their interests'. However, he goes on to say: 'There is, however, one instance when social and environmental aspirations can be tolerated – when they are insincere. The executive who treats social and environmental values as means to maximise shareholders' wealth commits no wrong.' Thus for neo-capitalists, if social or environmental goals are a means to the end of increased profitability, all well and good.

Freeman's stakeholder theory disputes the separation thesis (Freeman et al., 2004: 364), which asserts that ethics, and for that matter CSR, and economics are mutually exclusive. Similarly, Marquard and Graham (1995) cite Peter Drucker's statement, 'Every single social and global issue of our day is a business opportunity in disguise'. They argue that leaders must that find the AND and so transform corporate social responsibilities into corporate social opportunities; then they should convert those opportunities into sustainable profits and competitive advantage. This means leaders asking themselves: 'How can we satisfy that business need AND serve a social good?' and 'How can we serve that social need AND increase shareholder value?' These authors propose that the entry point for finding the AND should be tailored to the unique needs and culture of the company. CSR strategy should be focused on a specific mission that the company is best equipped to help resolve and from which it can gain the greatest competitive benefit.

Sustainability texts tend to emphasize the 'three pillars' of sustainability (economic, social and environmental), though in practice the economic pillar tends implicitly to be the dominant concern. Indeed, as John Ehrenfeld (Ehrenfeld and Hoffman, 2013) argues, this corporate conception of sustainability reinforces shareholder value and any positive social and environmental impacts are incidental. Indeed, in the corporate reconceptualization of sustainability, what we are often really talking about is being just a little less 'unsustainable'.

However, sustainability cannot become simply a way to achieve business success. This is about business contributing to solving difficult problems, collaborating in the quest to build a global economic system governed by equity and justice. Achieving change that affects a broader set of outcomes requires major corporations, with their financial clout, to carry out economic roles that protect our planet. Mohrman and Shani (2011) argue that most organizations are barely at the start of the journey towards differentiating themselves on sustainability performance. Some corporate leaders recognize that policies and action are needed on ethics and other corporate responsibility issues, together with greater engagement with stakeholders

New organizational effectiveness   211

and increased transparency about the risks of products and processes. A few major corporate heads, such as Paul Polman of Unilever, are playing a leading role in global forums on how corporations can do this.

The power of corporate purpose

But how to align stakeholder needs in a meaningful way? For the Center for Effective Organizations, the fourth 'P' or bottom line of the quadruple bottom line, is Purpose, often expressed as spirituality or culture. Corporate purpose sits at the confluence of strategy and values. It expresses the company's fundamental value – the raison d'être or overriding reason for existing, the end towards which the strategy is directed (Ellsworth, 2002: 4). Corporate purpose also defines the contribution management seeks to make to its various constituents – the corporation's owners, employees and customers and the communities in which it does business – and specifies a firm's ultimate priority among its responsibilities, be that priority the maximization of shareholder wealth, satisfying customer needs, providing for the employees' welfare or serving the national or community interest (Ellsworth, 2002: 5).

Binnie (2005) argues that a strong sense of 'Why do we exist?' and 'What is the essence of how we do things around here?' was what gave exceptional companies a compass to steer by, and enabled them to adapt and thrive in periods of great economic and social change. Similarly, in their book *Built to Last*, Collins and Porras (1994) argue that enduringly success- ful organizations are marked out, not by charismatic leaders, choice of business area, particu- lar systems, processes or people, but by an enduring sense of purpose and values. However, since their book was published we have seen the rapid advance of globalization and the rise of China, amongst other significant features of the changing context. Many of the compa- nies highlighted as successful in the book have slipped from the top ranks of companies in terms of financial performance. Nevertheless, Ellsworth's research into organizational pur- pose in corporate America suggests that a genuine and sustained focus on corporate purpose directly affects an organization's ability to respond constructively to turbulence (Ellsworth, 2002: x, xi).

The effect of purpose on employees

Ellsworth argues that, in today's corporation, a firm's purpose profoundly influences employees' ideals and sense of personal fulfilment. He proposes that the purpose of maximizing shareholder wealth has failed to energize employees within the firm – those individuals whose knowledge and effort create the competitive advantages of today and the future. Consequently, he argues, as do Sennett and I, many people experience difficulty finding meaning in their work, and for many employees the deep longings of the human spirit – the desire for a life rich in meaning, passion, creativity and a sense of belonging – are being left unsatisfied. The result is a hollowness of work. Similarly, most corporations are failing to realize their potential to make people's lives better – the lives of the people who use their products, work within their boundaries and invest in their future (Ellsworth, 2002: 3).

In contrast, a deeper, more transcendent purpose is highly energizing for all of the vari- ous interdependent stakeholders, including the customers, employees, investors, suppliers and the larger communities in which the business participates. Fred Kofman (2014), author of *Conscious Business*, suggests that in 'conscious capitalism' companies have a purpose that tran- scends profit maximization, and are managed for the benefit of all stakeholders in their eco- system, not just shareholders.

212　*Phoenix out of the ashes?*

John Mackey (Mackey and Sisodia, 2014), CEO of the US organic food retailing firm Whole Foods Market, is a leading proponent of conscious capitalism and an advocate of a new form of business leadership. For Mackey, conscious capitalism is a mode of doing business that attempts to create value for all stakeholders – employees, customers, community, shareholders – rather than sublimating the needs of the first three to those of the last. As with Bill Gates' 'creative capitalism', the fundamental precept is that profits and purpose should go together – and that companies that combine the two authentically will outperform the competition over the long term.

Mackey's firm aspires to express the ideal of 'Service to Others' as its primary purpose. This deeply motivating purpose provides tremendous emotional fulfilment to individuals who truly embrace this ideal. An example of the stakeholder model in action is the company's quarterly 'community giving days', in which 5 per cent of a Whole Foods store's net sales are given to a local non-profit. This creates goodwill with customers, motivates team members and takes care of communities. With more than 400 stores and 87,000 team members in three countries, the company has been named by *Fortune* magazine as a 'Best Company to Work For' for 17 consecutive years.

Mackey categorizes other types of corporate purpose as 'excitement of discovery and the pursuit of truth' and cites Google, Intel, Medtronic, Apple, Berkshire Hathaway and Four Seasons Hotels as examples of companies that have greatly benefited humanity through their successful fulfilment of this great purpose. The 'heroic business' is motivated by the desire to change the world, not necessarily through 'service to others' or through 'discovery and the pursuit of truth', or through 'the quest for perfection' (all three motivations that can have definite 'heroic' impulses), but through the powerful desire to really change things – to truly make the world better, to solve what appear to be insoluble problems, to do the really courageous thing even when it is very risky, and to achieve what others say is impossible. He cites the Ford Motor Company in its early days and Microsoft as examples of companies having this kind of purpose.

Binnie's (2005) research into corporate purpose in a range of organizations selected from the 'Fortune Global Most Admired Companies 2005' and the 'PWC Most Respected Global Companies 2004' found that the most common expressions of purpose focused on balancing the needs of different groups and interests and on serving customers. While most of these organizations had purpose statements that included expressions about ethical behaviour, sustainable development and the development of employees, these 'balanced' purpose statements did not give priority to any one group of stakeholders. For instance, Johnson and Johnson's famous 'Credo' states:

> We believe that our first responsibility is to the doctors, nurses and patients, to mothers and fathers who use our products and services. In meeting their needs everything we do must be of high quality. We must constantly strive to reduce our costs in order to maintain reasonable prices. Customers' orders must be serviced promptly and accurately.

It goes on to describe the obligations to employees and to the community before concluding with:

> Our final responsibility is to our stockholders. Business must make a sound profit. We must experiment with new ideas. Research must be carried on, innovative programs

developed and mistakes paid for. New equipment must be purchased, new facilities provided and new products launched. Reserves must be created to provide for adverse times. When we operate according to these principles, the stockholders should realize a fair return.

(Binnie, 2005)

Some firms do give priority to specific kinds of stakeholder interest or emphasize specific values. For instance, Coca-Cola, Disney, Caterpillar and Vodafone, among others, have made particularly strong statements about ethical behaviour. Other companies emphasize sustainable development and green issues – primary product producers such as BHP Billiton, Gazprom and Alcan, as well as companies in other business areas, such as Walmart, Toyota and Tata.

The paradox of profits

Based on his research, Ellsworth (2002: 2–3) highlights a number of paradoxes with respect to corporate purpose and business results. He argues that:

- Long-term shareholders are not best served when a company puts the interests of shareholders above all others. Instead, they benefit most when customers are made the primary reason for the firm's existence and employees are given priority over shareholders.
- Similarly, employees' interests are not best served when the corporation's purpose places top priority on their interests. Instead, the highest level of individual development and the greatest happiness are derived from serving ends beyond the self – ends that employees value, that enable them to feel they are 'making a difference' and consequently bring increased meaning to their lives through work.
- The value a company creates for society is not synonymous with its shareholder-wealth creation. Most critical for society is the firm's total value-generating ability, not the value created for shareholders alone, but also for customers, employees and communities.

The paradox of profits then is that they are best achieved by not aiming directly for them. John Kay (2010) describes this as the principle of 'obliquity' – by directing all your efforts at a specific group of stakeholders, such as customers, other stakeholder groups including investors will benefit too (indirectly, as a consequence). So if a company's purpose is to provide customer excellence, and if employees believe in serving the customer and do so successfully, existing customers are likely to remain with the firm and new customers are likely to be attracted. Business results then improve, so everyone benefits. Mackey and Sisodia (2014) also argue that long-term profits are the result of having a deeper business purpose, great products, customer satisfaction, employee happiness, excellent suppliers, community and environmental responsibility. Indeed, focusing purely on shareholder value is missing the fundamental point made by Drucker: the creation of value for shareholders is a means, and not an end.

However, corporate purpose can be a double-edged sword. While strategic actions consistent with the purpose can build trust, corporate actions that are inconsistent with corporate purpose will lead stakeholders to view it, and the company, with mistrust and cynicism. As Binnie (2005) points out, the true currency of purpose and values is not so much the official

214   *Phoenix out of the ashes?*

statements as the stories, the gossip that circulates around an organization that capture far more subtly the essence of purpose and values.

Moreover, Overell et al. (2010: 10) argue that corporate purpose may also be used to manipulate employees in ways detrimental to themselves:

> The shortcoming of models of the employment relationship based on common purpose ideologies is that they allow little scope for people to have and fulfil their own desires, aspirations and expectations within the work that they do, rendering them passive recipients of a company's brand messages – mere resources, as opposed to people.

Leaders and purpose

Therefore, a strong onus is placed on leaders to build a responsible and ethical business culture, infusing an organization with a worthy purpose that reaches beyond subservience to shareholders and that is meaningful (and not harmful) to its stakeholders. Binnie (2005) points out that corporate leaders profoundly influence the sense of purpose and values in the organizations they lead, whether they like it or not, since they are highly visible and keenly watched by employees and others to see which way they turn, what they give priority to, who they favour.

For Kofman (2014: 5), this means that leaders should be conscious of their role in creating shared purpose.

> To be conscious means to be awake, mindful. To live consciously means to be open to perceiving the world around and within us, to understand our circumstances, and to decide how to respond to them in ways that honor our needs, values, and goals…A conscious business fosters peace and happiness in the individual, respect and solidarity in the community, and mission accomplishment in the organization.

So to create a truly credible and authentic corporate purpose, leaders need awareness, an understanding of the firm's strengths and weaknesses and what drives or motivates its actions and how these affect key stakeholders as well as the environment. This means that, in developing the purpose, leaders need to scan the environment, taking into account the changing place of the organization in society, involving the people who will be implementing it, embedding purpose in all key business decisions, policies and business practices. If not, the purpose risks being seen as an irrelevant platitude.

Corporate reputation

Corporate reputation, how outsiders are judging the firm, is increasingly seen by investors as a key indicator of organizational health. Building corporate reputation is often seen as an exercise in brand building which requires authentic and consistent corporate purpose intent, with aligned strategy and action. For example, IKEA invests heavily in renewable energies such as wind farms and is committed to becoming totally carbon neutral by 2020 because it believes this is the soundest long-term business decision in alignment with its corporate purpose. Thus corporate reputation becomes a differentiator in the marketplace.

Reputation is also a major risk factor (Davies et al., 2003), so building reputational capital is about mitigating reputational risk. Reputational capital is earned every day, mainly in the way firms treat their people and customers. This requires deliberate and ongoing effort (Jackson, 2004), for instance by the company becoming actively and authentically involved in the community and becoming known to be a good place to work. On the other hand, reputation can be quickly and irremediably lost if businesses are seen to ignore their corporate responsibilities or to tolerate poor practice, including across their supply chain, as companies like Nike know only too well.

Taking stock of how a firm is viewed provides a benchmark for improving reputational capital. The Harris–Fombrun Corporate Reputation Quotient (Fombrun and Van Riel, 2003) was created specifically to capture the perceptions of any corporate stakeholder group such as consumers, investors, employees or key influencers. The instrument enables research on the drivers of a company's reputation and allows reputations to be compared both within and across industries. This business–reputation model assesses six drivers of corporate reputation with subsequent 20 attributes:

Emotional appeal

- good feeling about the company
- admire and respect the company
- trust the company

Workplace environment

- is well managed
- appears to be a good company to work for
- appears to have good employees

Products and services

- company believes in its products and services
- company offers high-quality products and services
- develops innovative products and services
- offers products and services that are good value

Financial performance

- history of profitability
- appears a low-risk investment
- strong prospects for future growth
- tends to outperform its competitors

Vision and leadership

- has excellent leadership
- has a clear vision for the future
- recognizes and takes advantage of market opportunities

Social responsibility

- supports good causes
- environmentally responsible
- treats people well

Making random checks, these criteria taken together result in lists of most reputable and/or most visible companies.

216   *Phoenix out of the ashes?*

How might a stakeholder-management approach work?

As discussed above, there is increasing focus on creating value for a range of stakeholders. Management's role is to optimize the health and value of the entire complex, evolving and self-adaptive system, managing any conflicts of interest as they do so. As Mackey (2006) points out: 'The best way to maximize long-term shareholder value is to simultaneously optimize the value for all other constituencies. The health of the entire system is what really matters.' Without consistent customer satisfaction, employee happiness and commitment and community support, the short-term profits will probably prove to be unsustainable over the long term (assuming its competitors manage their businesses to create value for all of their stakeholders).

But how does a traditional profit-centred business fare when it competes against a stakeholder-centred business? Mackey cites *Firms of Endearment: The Pursuit of Purpose and Profit* by Rajendra Sisodia, Jagdish Sheth and David Wolfe (2007) as proof that a stakeholder-centred purpose works. The authors identify 30 companies that are managed to optimize total stakeholder value instead of focusing strictly on profits and track long-term stock performance of those that are publicly traded compared to the S&P 5001. These companies have had extraordinarily high stock-market returns both over the short term and the long term. Mackey argues that this success is the result of all 30 firms creating a superior business model – the business model that will, he believes, become the dominant business model of the twenty-first century.

Inevitably, there will be tensions and conflicts between stakeholder groups at different times and as circumstances change and management's task is to address and seek to resolve potential conflicts. This is where a set of principles can be helpful in 'doing the right thing' (Seglin, 2006). The Clarkson Principles of Stakeholder Management (1999) originate from four conferences that were hosted between 1993 and 1998 by the Centre for Corporate Social Performance and Ethics in the Faculty of Management (now the Clarkson Centre for Business Ethics and Board Effectiveness). These represent an early-stage general awareness of corporate-governance concerns (Table 11.2). The Clarkson Principles could be regarded as 'meta-principles', encouraging and requiring management to develop more specific stakeholder principles and to implement those in accordance with the Clarkson Principles.

Strategic evolution towards a more responsible and ethical business culture

According to Andrew Hoffman (2011), Professor of Sustainable Enterprise at the University of Michigan, the first wave of sustainability thinking began in 1970 and was primarily around environment and regulatory compliance. The second wave began around 1990 and was about corporate environmentalism as corporate strategy. Hoffman sees the current, 'third wave' of sustainability as adopting systems thinking to bring the full scope of social and environmental into sustainability, challenging us to think systemically, pay attention to life-cycle analysis, understand and influence system dynamics. Chris Laszlo and colleagues (2014) argue that the notion of responsible business has infiltrated our markets, and 'going green' is now a part of our mindset. But, sustainability as we know it is not enough. Flourishing – the aspiration that humans and life in general will thrive on the planet forever – should be a key goal for every business today. This is a bold concept, like sustainability was a decade ago. Just as sustainability has become a matter of course, so too, they argue, will flourishing become a cornerstone of business tomorrow.

Table 11.2 The Clarkson Principles of Stakeholder Management

Principle 1	Managers should acknowledge and actively monitor the concerns of all legitimate stakeholders, and should take their interests appropriately into account in decision making and operations.
Principle 2	Managers should listen to and openly communicate with stakeholders about their respective concerns and contributions, and about the risks that they assume because of their involvement with the corporation.
Principle 3	Managers should adopt processes and modes of behaviour that are sensitive to the concerns and capabilities of each stakeholder constituency.
Principle 4	Managers should recognize the interdependence of efforts and rewards among stakeholders, and should attempt to achieve a fair distribution of the benefits and burdens of corporate activity among them, taking into account their respective risks and vulnerabilities.
Principle 5	Managers should work cooperatively with other entities, both public and private, to ensure that risks and harms arising from corporate activities are minimized, and where they cannot be avoided, properly compensated.
Principle 6	Managers should avoid altogether activities that might jeopardize inalienable human rights (e.g. the right to life) or give rise to risks which, if clearly understood, would be patently unacceptable to relevant stakeholders.
Principle 7	Managers should acknowledge the potential conflicts between (a) their own role as corporate stakeholders and (b) their legal and moral responsibilities for the interests of stakeholders, and should address such conflicts through open communication, appropriate reporting and incentive systems and, where necessary, third-party review.

Source: Clarkson Centre for Business Ethics, 1999: 4

For companies aiming to move from adopting sustainability aims as a bolt-on to current strategies to strategically embedding sustainability there is a strategic evolution. Some organizations may approach this evolution incrementally, while others might adopt radical innovation regarding what they are making and how. Hoffman (Ehrenfeld and Hoffman, 2013) outlines four phases of transition to sustainability effectiveness. The first phase is one of simple compliance, which is about doing the minimum of initiatives to comply with what is required. Moving beyond this, the second phase is one of active engagement, which involves trying out new approaches to achieve expanded outcomes. Mohrman (2011) refers to DIY retailer Kingfisher whose aims have moved on from 'doing less harm' to becoming a net positive contributor to solving the problems of the earth by 2050, for instance by selling goods that can be repaired, rather than thrown away. In a similar vein, instead of serving only the well-off, some luxury clothing retailers are attempting to be more socially inclusive. Several are running pilot schemes involving offering customers their garments on a loan rather than buy basis so that even the less well-off can afford smart clothing and there is less wastage.

While some firms are embracing sustainability aims because they believe this is the right thing to do, for others competitive challenges can provide the spur to engagement. Several major shopping centre firms are suffering a fall-off of trade with the growth of online shopping. They are aiming to add value to the physical shopping experience in a way that attracts customers to visit shopping malls in person. For instance, sports-clothing retailers within these malls are offering free public classes in yoga and keep fit; others offer spaces for book clubs and community groups to meet while out shopping. While the commercial motive is to keep people shopping in person as opposed to online, such activities still have a beneficial effect for

218 *Phoenix out of the ashes?*

the business, the customer and contribute to the social good. Social awareness is now key to many company brands and brand-building activities. For instance, in its 2016 global 'World Recycle Week' fashion retailer H&M offered customers the opportunity for a 30 per cent discount on new clothes in return for recycling used clothes in their stores.

The third, integrated phase is reflected in aligning strategies, operations and design. Companies that perform well with respect to sustainability have a clear strategy guiding their sustainability activities, and the relationship between sustainability and their business strategy is clearly articulated, according to research by the Center for Effective Organizations. In such companies, sustainability is a part of how these companies operate, with sustainability objectives and activities coordinated and integrated into their organizational design and management processes. Finally, the proactive phase is where stewardship is integrated into the larger ecosystem.

The Center for Effective Organizations outlines the transitional process towards sustainability as follows:

- embracing the problem;
- developing a values framework;
- mission, purpose, strategy;
- breaking down organizational boundaries, since connecting with customers requires cross-functional activity;
- inter-organizational collaboration, action networks addressing the full value stream;
- redefining success – integrated reporting (quadruple bottom line), goals, measurement and transparent feedback.

In 2007 under its former CEO Stuart Rose, UK high-street retailer Marks and Spencer launched a social and environmental campaign called 'Plan A', because 'there is no Plan B'. Plan A became an active strategy, involving staff in all stores and incorporating customer suggestions. In the first phase of Plan A, Marks and Spencer made 100 commitments to reduce the social and environmental footprint of their business across hundreds of stores and thousands of supply-chain locations. In 2010, the second phase involved 80 new commitments and a goal to become the world's most sustainable major retailer. Plan A was integrated into management processes enabling them to capture a significant business case.

In the third phase – Plan A 2020 – there are still 100 commitments but there is a heavy emphasis on engagement, of customers, employees and suppliers. Why? According to Mike Barry, director of Plan A, this is because Plan A 2020 is seeing a shift of thinking, from improving today's business model to imagining what a very different, truly sustainable Marks and Spencer might look like in the future.

> We cannot yet define fully what this sustainable model will look like (a number of our commitments focus on understanding and testing new ideas) but one thing we do know is that we cannot shift from today's business model to tomorrow's without the full engagement of the vast majority of our millions of customers, 86,000 employees and 1,000s of suppliers.
>
> (http://corporate.marksandspencer.com/blog/stories/plan-a-2020)

Moving from pilot mode to scaling system change requires agile capability, the ability to continuously change. It will also require new approaches to organization design. Leaders and employees need to see stewardship as a core responsibility. This means that stewardship aims must be built into corporate purposes, strategies, goals and objectives, decision-making models, reporting, structures, employee and management accountabilities and rewards and integrated into core business functions.

Hybrid organizations

While business and environmental concerns are often at odds with one another, Hoffman (2011) argues that hybrid organizations are emerging that straddle the increasingly blurred line between the non-profit and for-profit worlds. These companies are innovators in business design and are experimenting with merging business strategy and sustainability concerns. Unilever is perhaps one such example. Unilever recognizes that the global challenge of a growing population relying on limited resources is very real. Its Sustainable Living Plan includes a number of sustainability goals, such as ethically produced products, gender parity, access to water and energy sources for all. To enable a focus on long-term sustainability effectiveness, not just short-term financial outcomes, Unilever has abandoned short-term financial reporting and refuses to have the quarterly analyst conversations which can drive a narrow, exclusively shareholder-value focus.

One of Unilever's sustainable growth ambitions, as well as its commitment to become resource resilient and tackle climate change, is to achieve zero waste across its value chain. Over 600 Unilever sites in 70 countries around the world including factories, warehouses, distribution centres and offices have now eliminated non-hazardous waste to landfill and have found alternative routes for the waste from these sites. This has been achieved through the 4Rs approach of reducing, reusing, recovering or recycling, proving that waste can be seen as a resource with many alternative uses, from converting factory waste to building materials to composting food waste from staff cafeterias. Unilever hopes that by working with, and learning from, suppliers, partners and other organizations, they can inspire a wide-scale movement.

Another example of a successful 'hybrid' organization is the US food retailer, Whole Foods Market, whose founder and CEO John Mackey has embraced the ideals of conscious capitalism in the way he runs his business. With reference to the transition process outlined by the Center for Effective Organizations, a key element is developing a values framework. John Mackey (2006) here explains how Whole Foods Market pursues its values with regards to sustainability.

> When businesses have a purpose beyond maximizing profits, that purpose is often expressed in the business mission. At the center of the Whole Foods Market business model, illustrating holistic interdependence, are the Core Values and Business Mission. Core values constitute the guiding principles the business uses to realize its purpose. Whole Foods Market's core values very succinctly express what the purposes of the business are – purposes that include making profits but also include creating value for all of the major constituencies. Everything else extends from the purpose of the business reflected in the Core Values. Surrounding these central purposes are the various constituencies: customers, team members, suppliers, investors, and the community and environment.

As Mackey points out,

> Our business talks and walks our values; we share them with our constituency groups, and invite feedback in the form of dialogs. The core values are: selling the highest quality

220   *Phoenix out of the ashes?*

natural and organic products available, satisfying and delighting our customers, supporting team member happiness and excellence, creating wealth, profits, and growth, and caring about our communities and environment.

Breaking down organizational boundaries

In a retail business like Whole Foods, the cross-boundary interdependencies are recognized. Management's role is to hire good people, train them well and do whatever it takes to have those team members flourish and be happy while they are at work. The team member's job is to satisfy and delight the customers. As Mackey says, 'If we have happy customers, we will have a successful business and happy investors'. Management helps the team members experience happiness, team members help the customers achieve happiness, the customers help the investors achieve happiness, and when some of the profits from the investors are reinvested in business, there is a virtuous circle. Market analysis increasingly illustrates that the businesses with a sole purpose of maximizing profits, in other words, those that do not understand that their profits are produced by an interdependent system of constituencies, are less successful over the long term.

Interorganizational collaboration

Mackey's desire to contribute positively to the entire ecosystem is evident:

> Whole Foods Market trades throughout the world and we recognize our responsibilities as global citizens, as well. Poverty remains one of the most serious global challenges, and one of the ways we are trying to be good global citizens is through the creation of Whole Planet Foundation. Our mission with Whole Planet Foundation is to create economic partnerships with the poor and developing world communities that supply our stores with products. Through innovative assistance for entrepreneurship, including direct micro-credit loans, as well as intangible support for other community partnership projects, we seek to support the energy and creativity of every human being we work with in order to help create wealth and prosperity in emerging economies.

John Mackey continues:

> In meeting our responsibilities as citizens, Whole Foods Market donates five percent of our after tax profits to non-profit organizations, with nearly 75 percent given away on a local basis. Whole Foods Market supports various local community events and support health initiatives such as fighting AIDS, and breast and childhood cancers. With 188 stores currently, we give to thousands of local organizations. Many of our customers belong to or volunteer with the organizations we support, and as they trade with Whole Foods Market, we are in turn supporting them in the communities in which we live and do business. Many of our stores also compensate team members for community service work, either on an individual basis, or as a group.
>
> The silent stakeholder that can never speak for itself is the environment. All of our other constituencies can speak up when they are unhappy about something. We consider the environment as linked to our community constituency. As a business, we exist within both a local and global environment. Whole Foods wants to be a responsible citizen in the

environment in which we live. We do this by supporting organic and sustainable agriculture and by selling sustainably-harvested seafood.

From its start in 1978 as Safer Way, Whole Foods Market has promoted organic food and the agricultural systems from which it derives. By helping to develop markets, customers, distribution networks, and even the national standards for labeling for organic foods, Whole Foods has also promoted the environmental benefits that accompany the increasing number of organic farms, dairies, ranches and sustainable agricultural practices. For example, organic farms utilize no synthetic fertilizers and pesticides, resulting in reduced usage of fossil fuels, and less chemical contamination entering food chains and water supplies. While some products are transported long distance to meet consumer demand, Whole Foods Markets also stock as many locally-grown and/or manufactured products that meet our quality standards as are available in our market areas.

This is one example of what is possible when a stakeholder approach to business is genuine. All the constituencies benefit.

Conclusion

Stakeholder engagement is not a new concept, but this requires managements to be able to align the interests of a much more diverse set of stakeholders in a mutually rewarding way and to be held more accountable according to a broader definition of performance – for how organizations perform financially, environmentally, socially, as well as in how they treat their employees. However genuine or otherwise their interest in sustainability, businesses need to embrace sustainability aims in order to gain or restore their 'social licence to operate'. Even if not driven by desire, business engagement with sustainability is thus a form of risk management. Business schools too should consider for whom they are training future leaders, and teach them how to complement the typical mechanical analysis with a focus on why companies exist.

Which of the stakeholder needs to place first remains a source of ongoing debate. Some theorists advocate that even in a stakeholder approach, shareholder value should remain the primary focus of business efforts, since this produces clarity and, as business results improve, other stakeholders can benefit too. Increasingly theorists advocate putting sustainability and business' social responsibilities first. Others argue that the main organizational focus should be earlier in the value chain – on customers – since by meeting their needs, business results improve and all stakeholders, including shareholders, benefit. The intended beneficiaries of a business effort tend to be reflected in its corporate purpose. Whatever the aspiration, this needs to be translated into an overall mission and, ultimately, into guiding principles for frontline behaviour.

In the debate about which stakeholder counts most, an increasing number of executives are placing employee needs ahead of those of other stakeholders. This is not questioning the importance of providing benefit to shareholders: it is more a recognition that focusing more intently on the intermediaries of that shareholder value, i.e. customers and employees, may produce greater benefits to all. Although the way in which organizations treat their employees often gets included in the triple bottom line definition of the social category, Lawler argues that it warrants a separate and distinct set of measures and a high level of accountability since in the knowledge and service economy, people are the vital 'unit of production'. This is an area where the impact of organizations is measurable, significant, and may be quite different from the impact on the communities in which they operate.

222 *Phoenix out of the ashes?*

We shall discuss how a more employee-centric HR approach might work over the next few chapters.

Points to ponder

- What would need to shift in conventional management thinking and practice to fully embrace a stakeholder purpose? What dilemmas might this create and for whom?
- Who do you consider should be the salient stakeholder group?

Section V

HR influencing organizational effectiveness

12 HRM, stewardship and organizational effectiveness

For too long the benchmark for good HR has been so-called 'best practice'. These solutions that worked in the past are now proving unreliable across a range of business, economic, and political contexts that are not just fluid but positively metamorphosing due to the impact of global trends like changing workforce demographics and digitisation.

Ksenia Zheltoukhova, Research Adviser, CIPD

As we discussed in the last chapter, the discourse on the 'new capitalism' is gaining ground, even if the values that should underlie a reinvigorated and more responsible capitalism of the future are under debate. We discussed how, now more than ever, the emerging business paradigm will define what it means to become a high-performing, sustainably effective organization. The notion of measuring performance according to a quadruple bottom line is gaining credence and it is clear that the needs of different stakeholders are often in tension. Achieving a fair distribution of performance benefits will require a shift in contemporary business priorities and practices. Adopting a stakeholder approach implies opting for a multidimensional concept of performance. If the definition of business performance viewed through a stakeholder lens becomes more complex, the means to achieving desired results must also be reconsidered.

In this chapter we shall consider how HR, as the people- and organization-behaviour experts, could influence organizational effectiveness according to the stakeholder paradigm. Sparrow and Cooper (2014) argue that HR practitioners should focus on influencing the intermediate organizational variables that lead to business results. Therefore, improving the working practices, climate and culture of organizations becomes central to HR's agenda. Above all, since many firms now recognize 'talent' and 'human capital' as the foundation of their business models, and the most important source of value, HR must exercise stewardship with respect to one of a firm's key stakeholder groups – its workforce. This may mean revising HR's primary focus and priorities since acting as business partner to deliver HR's contribution to shareholder value often appears to be achieved at people's expense. What would 'sustainable' look like with respect to people?

Taking a stakeholder perspective in today's challenging employment context would require a new approach to HRM that is business focused but more 'human'. In a more 'human' (or 'employee-centric') HR practice, HR would seek to work towards achieving a balance of mutually beneficial outcomes for the business and its workforce. In what will be uncharted waters for many, the risk is that we reach for the latest bright, shiny, new idea or for tried and tested 'best-practice' models of the past. While these no doubt contain useful nuggets, we need to rethink *what* might work *when* and *where*, since context relevance is everything. As Paauwe and Boselie (2005) point out, 'Along with corporate or business strategy, a whole range of other

226 *HR influencing organizational effectiveness*

factors play a role in shaping the relationship between HRM and performance, among which the institutional context is critical'.

Of course, I recognize that in this section of the book I am shifting my stance away from analysing what is and what has been, to advocating what might be (Watson, 2010). In one sense therefore this cannot be a fully evidence-based approach, but there are sufficient indications emerging from various studies to suggest a possible (and desirable) direction of travel. In the remaining chapters of this book we shall consider in more detail how HR might better influence organizational effectiveness to equip their organizations and their stakeholders to thrive in the twenty-first century. I shall include case examples of practice which hint at 'new organization' approaches that overcome some of the limitations of what has gone before, and also produce more social justice and organizational effectiveness.

Here we shall cover:

- What employee-centric HR might look like;
- Towards a new employee relations approach;
- A positive work environment;
- Employee wellbeing;
- Job quality; and
- Careers.

An evolution in priorities

We have discussed in earlier chapters some of the trends that are reshaping work and organizations as we know them. As businesses pursue agility, we can anticipate some of the future changes both for organizations and employees. There are potentially many conflicting outcomes, as Paauwe and Boselie (2005) point out. For instance, as businesses seek to increase productivity, which managers will appreciate, there will be increased levels of stress, which workers will probably dislike. Labour intensification through increased employee participation, decentralization and emphasis on performance management (practices that can be seen as high-performance work practices) might create competitive advantage in terms of financial performance, but the individual worker might experience increased levels of stress and anxiety (Legge, 1995). Being aware of, and making choices regarding conflicting HR outcomes in HR practice is an important step.

By anticipating what lies ahead, HR professionals can help build their organizations' resilience by focusing on the people and cultural enablers of good business outcomes – such as effective leadership and management; governance, transparency and ethics; the ability to attract and retain key talent the business needs; diversity; the ability to operate fluidly across boundaries; and enabling knowledge exchange and collaboration. For many HR teams this broader remit is relatively new territory. HR's skill set needs to expand accordingly to include business acumen, effective role and organization design, analytical capability, awareness of organization-development principles and significant influencing ability.

The HR profession has a major role to play in ensuring that technology-enabled cultural trends shape the future of work in a way which meets stakeholder needs and produces sustainable value for everyone. HR needs to keep asking the fundamental questions about the purpose of work and the kind of future we aspire to, since this provides a platform from which to influence business decision-makers and achieve win–win outcomes. Encouragingly, the CIPD, HR's professional body for the UK and Ireland, is now championing a vision of better work and working lives. This implies an evolution in labour–capital relations, with HR practices helping shape harmonious working relations and workplaces in which there are high levels of staff engagement, voice, training and empowerment.

This means HR must address questions relating to the changing nature of work. We need to make sure that the future of work is human, that we are designing workplaces that help people work well and realize their potential. For instance, automation is already affecting entry-level jobs, and mid- and higher-skill jobs will be soon impacted by artificial intelligence in ways that have not been seen before. The number of people working flexibly, part-time and on contract is set to rise considerably over the next five years. In such a world, according to Peter Cheese, CEO of the CIPD, work might be displaced more to individuals than organizations, to trade and craft skills and a gig economy. As Cheese asks, if many of the jobs we know today could be automated in the future, then what kinds of jobs will we all be doing? And how can people working in HR and learning and development actively design for that future, for example by developing new skills, shifting reward mechanisms or adopting new norms relating to working hours and relationships?

This means tackling questions for which there are no easy answers such as, how can flexibility be made to work for both organizations and workers? How can HR ensure that business achieves its ends and that employees are treated ethically and fairly? Some consider the 'gig economy', where largely self-employed individuals use online platforms to choose parcels of work that suit them, to be mutually advantageous. Employers benefit from a 'human cloud' of talent they can dip into at will, while employees can work the hours that suit them – in theory. However, in situations where the flexibility demand is driven by employers, the consequences for employees can be largely negative.

For example, Wood (in Jeffrey, 2015) studied a large high-street retailer that uses a system of 'labour-matching reviews' to plan how its employees' shifts should be scheduled. This is a common practice in many industries, but has previously been an annual or biannual process aligned to financial results. Technology, says Wood, has transformed it entirely: the retailer was using complex information on footfall, weather and buying patterns to shift its forecasts on an almost weekly basis. This meant staff were told with just a few days' notice when and if they would be required to work, their precise shifts (and weekly pay) changing from one week to the next. All were permanent workers with pensions and employment rights, but their contracts stated only a minimum number of hours and no guarantees over consistent patterns or suitable notice of changes. Mental ill health arising from labour-matching reviews and general insecurity over hours is so great, Wood believes, that it is a health and safety issue, and employees could potentially bring a case for a breach of relevant Health and Safety Executive legislation.

With respect to the 'zero-hours' debate, some of its principal advocates are occasional academics who enjoy being paid for a few lectures on a piecemeal basis while on a permanent contract elsewhere and enjoying a healthy income. On the other hand, care-home workers or the average barista have no such choice and may not benefit from such supposed autonomy, especially if they end up having to juggle two or three such precarious jobs to make ends meet. This new transient category of workers is still aligned to the business but less known to HR, and in some cases disenfranchised from engagement initiatives and development opportunities. The risk is that the shift in the UK to a service-driven economy has facilitated, 'not a race but a weary trudge to the bottom' (in CIPD, 2014).

HR needs to take a view about how the wider workforce should be treated. For instance, the rise of the gig economy raises questions about workplace protection in the future – such as pensions, benefits and healthcare. How, if at all, should employers look after a workforce that could be very transitional in nature? There will always be different styles of work relationships

228   *HR influencing organizational effectiveness*

and contracts that work for the employer': these need to be appropriate for the individual as well. HR's challenge is to find solutions that meet both sets of needs.

If the relationship between the employer and the individual employee is out of balance – for example, in the case of increased performance pressures without fair pay – employees might feel they are being exploited, resulting in low commitment levels towards the organization (Paauwe, 2004). This is where principles can help guide decision-making and practice. In an employee-centric approach to the management of people, the guiding principle is fairness, not simply expediency, with the aim of achieving the best outcomes for both the organization and the people.

Employee–centric HR

'Employee-centric' HR approaches are not simply about being nice to people. Mainstream HRM theory views people as a resource, so when we factor in the importance of 'knowledge workers' to the productive aims of the firm, competitive labour economics theory (Blundell and MaCurdy, 2008) suggests that people are *the* key competitive resource and should be treated as such. This aligns with the mainstream strategic thinking that says that only firms with unique and valuable resources or capabilities will gain and maintain competitive advantage. Capital is a fungible, non-differentiating resource that rarely provides a competitive edge (Barney, 2001). Today it is labour's generation and use of knowledge that is the greatest source of advantage for most firms. Employees with high levels of skill are shown to be those that bring most value to the firm (Wright et al., 1994) and highly skilled people are rare and not easily substituted by other factors. Moreover, it has long been assumed that a motivated, engaged and inspired workforce generates higher long-term productivity, yet UK surveys regularly report widespread disengagement. Indeed, the need for committed, engaged workforces who are able and motivated to contribute to the success of organizations is arguably the most pressing business question of the twenty-first century.

So, employee-centric approaches are increasingly being adopted, more often than not by CEOs who recognize the need to create better value through and for employees. For instance, Vineet Nayyar, CEO of HCL Technologies, the India-based global information-technology services company, and author of *Employees First, Customers Second: Turning Conventional Management Upside Down* (2010) argues that putting employees first is a philosophy, a set of ideas, a way of looking at strategy and competitive advantage that came from observing the company closely. 'We create value in one very specific place: the interface between our HCL employees and our customers. The whole intent of Employees First is to do everything we can to enable those employees to create the most possible value.' This has led to the hierarchy being reconfigured, essentially turning the organizational pyramid upside down so that management is as accountable to the people in the value zone as the people in the value zone are to management. This is an example of benign unitarism, or progressive HRM (Budd, 2004), in which the interests of employees and the business are assumed to be identical and therefore aligned. Here the focus is on designing the organization to facilitate the creation of value through people, rather than on simply saving cost which is a common driver of restructuring from a neo-liberal perspective.

Under HRM the collective employee voice has largely fallen silent, leaving workers potentially at risk of exploitation. There are encouraging signs that some multinational companies are beginning to use their might across jurisdictions to improve conditions for their workers globally. For instance, the US is the only developed country that does not guarantee paid maternity or parental leave to its citizens. Vodafone introduced a policy to provide 16 weeks' paid maternity leave to all applicable staff worldwide, together with full pay for a four-day working week for up to six months on returning to work. This is thought likely to result in an overall saving for the company of billions of dollars. While employees benefit, so does the business since providing this benefit is thought to cost less than the business disruption, recruitment and training costs involved when valued female employees do not return to work following maternity leave. With multinational companies the impact can be global and Vodafone's example will perhaps lead other large companies to look at the 'bigger picture' rather than short-term costs, to the benefit of thousands of employees, including those in developing countries (Lewis Silkin LLP, 2016).

Similarly, Microsoft is raising employment standards across its supply chain by requiring that all of its more sizeable suppliers provide their employees with at least 15 days' paid annual leave (which can include sick leave) or Microsoft will not do business with them. This is in a context where many US employees are entitled to no paid leave at all. They believe that paid time off often results in a happier workforce, which results in a more productive workforce. Additionally, paid sick leave helps improve overall health in the workplace (www.theguardian. com/us-news/2015/mar/26/microsoft-require-suppliers-provide-paid-leave-workers).

Towards a new employee–relations approach?

The changing nature of work, coupled with the changing face of the workforce, creates new employer–employee dynamics and it seems that a new social contract is developing between companies and workers, driving major changes in the employer–employee relationship (Deloitte, 2016b). In an 'employee-centric' HR approach, the employment relationship is recognized as of strategic significance because the core fact of employment is the interdependent nature of the relationship between worker and employer in which cooperation is required in order to secure respective goals.

We have discussed previously how under managerialism and HRM, the employment relationship has become largely one-sided, in favour of employers. Budd (2004) argues that, while the effective use of scarce resources (efficiency) is an important objective of the employment relationship, 'a sole focus on efficiency, however, reduces the employment relationship to a purely economic transaction that workers endure solely to earn money'. Unitarism's promises of mutual benefit and commitment have gradually become untangled by employers and a residual transactional form of employment relationship has emerged in its place, with unitarist discourse vestiges. 'Relationship' no longer applies.

A new settlement is needed but, typically, there has been a lack of strategic thinking about what kind of settlement for the twenty-first century workplace is needed. The nature of the employment relationship always reflects wider societal changes and itself changes society. Historically, the employment relationship has favoured the interests of the employer over the employee because of the former's exclusive ownership of physical capital. In recent years, as capitalist enterprises have restructured, flattened layers and dismantled the foundations of job security, the big risk taker is labour, not capital. Today, contingent, contract and part-time workers make up nearly one third of the workforce and many companies lack the HR practices, culture or leadership support to manage this new workforce. As organizations become more diverse, both in terms of their operating models and in the nature of their workforces, a one-size-fits-all approach to HR and people development no longer applies.

To some authors, the knowledge economy is a key driver of the evolution of the employment relationship because it signals a rebalancing of power. In the knowledge economy, capital is increasingly 'intellectual capital', which – in the heads of individuals – cannot easily be

230 *HR influencing organizational effectiveness*

claimed as the exclusive property of employers or shareholders. Intellectual capital is, in part at least, worker-owned (Robertson and Swan, 2004) – and its owners can walk out the door. Ellsworth (2002: 13) is unequivocal: 'The future belongs to those with the greatest ability and willingness to deploy capital, to create and leverage knowledge, and to realize the latent potential of their employees'.

When we factor in the swings and balances of power in the labour market for 'talent', particularly in times of talent shortage, it is clear that business growth and profit can be constrained by the availability of people with key skills and knowledge. Indeed, Ellsworth argues: 'loyalty and commitment are essential to knowledge-based competitive advantage'.

Yet Deloitte's Millennial survey (Nabaum et al., 2014) suggests that loyalty and commitment are in short supply. Retention of Millennials is likely to be a growing problem with 44 per cent of nearly 7,700 Millennials from 29 countries saying that they would leave to pursue other opportunities within two years and two out of three saying they would be open to doing something else by the end of 2020. Only 16 per cent of Millennials saw themselves with their current employer ten years from now. In sector after sector, there is a reported 'battle for talent' as organizations compete to attract, motivate and retain more of the knowledge workers who are key to their success. The same logic of ethics and competitiveness that once supported shareholder-value maximization now leads to the conclusion that firms should focus on maximizing returns for labour. The change would be greater in the UK and US, where corporate governance typically is concerned primarily with protecting investor interests. In contrast, many leading German and Japanese companies are directed by boards that represent both labour and capital (Yaziji, 2008).

Thus, the balance of the employer–employee relationship is said to have shifted towards the latter, which enables knowledge workers to make greater demands to their employers, such as flexibility, time sovereignty and autonomy (Overell et al., 2010). This raises the question about what kinds of employee relations are likely to be more sustainable between employers and workers – whether these are employees or contractors. In a more balanced employment relationship, HR's role would be to act as a real employee champion, with a strong focus on, and understanding of, employee engagement and wellbeing. So important is the issue of employee voice that Budd (2004) advocates the creation of the field of human resources and industrial relations.

Employers are increasingly attempting to understand what they offer in terms of the employee experience. Why does it matter? As we discussed in the last chapter, studies show that intrinsic factors – the meaningfulness and purpose of work, for example – can motivate employees more effectively than traditional extrinsic rewards such as pay. Furthermore, with the advance of automation, thanks to artificial intelligence, into even high-skill jobs, some employees may be feeling vulnerable. Improving the employee experience can help balance that feeling of vulnerability.

Attracting and retaining Millennials

Each year in the Roffey Park Management Agenda, HR managers are asked what they see as their key people challenges for the future. Each year, managing the needs and expectations of different generations appears high on the list since HR managers are aware of how workplace demographics are shifting, with older employees staying in work for longer. Much is written about the different values of newer generations, though increasingly there is recognition that each generation has more in common with its predecessors than was previously recognized.

Nevertheless, there are some stereotypical differences. HR's conventional 'kitbag' of extrinsic motivator tools such as pay, long thought to be a retention factor ('golden handcuffs') appear to be losing their sway with respect to Millennials. The 2016 Agenda report finds that the main reasons why younger people intend to leave their employer include lack of promotion prospects, poor leadership and lack of opportunity to make a difference. Lack of appreciation, insufficient financial rewards, lack of opportunity to broaden skills and lack of challenge are also high-scoring reasons. Similarly, in the Deloitte Millennial study (Nabaum et al., 2014), even though pay remains a top priority, work–life balance, integrity and career development are also important factors.

Millennials are also reported to be values-driven, with 87 per cent of Deloitte respondents believing that 'the success of a business should be measured in terms of more than just its financial performance'. Only in Germany (22 per cent) and South Korea (30 per cent) do more than a fifth of Millennials say business should be measured in purely financial terms. Millennials are also reported to be likely to refuse a project that does not align with their personal values and morality.

Such data suggest that, in order to attract and retain employees, employers need to work with young people to understand the kinds of motivational practices that work well for them. This means that many employers are having to rethink conventional strategic HR processes, such as benefits and succession planning. Clearly, it is in the interests of employers who wish to attract and retain key employees to do so. In particular, HR will need to work with line managers to create a positive and uplifting work environment, with which Millennials' values align. Ellsworth (2002) argues that, especially in a context of talent scarcity, organizational purpose becomes ever more important for the following two reasons:

> First it helps people transcend the boundary between the self and others…
>
> Second…loyalty is increased. Loyalty brings with it lower turnover, more stable relationships and the subordination of narrow self-interest to the common interest. The firm's knowledge is less likely to walk out the door and knowledge creating networks remain intact. Trust is enhanced.

However, it is crucial that the reality of the aspiration is delivered or trust and employee loyalty are likely to be undermined. So employers should be not only developing their enticing external employment brand in an increasingly transparent job market, but also ensuring that the brand and its values are delivered in reality. HR should therefore be acting as stewards of the employer brand, challenging practice and decision-making that is not in line with the purpose and values.

What form of employment relationship might work best?

So if the balance of power in the employment relationship appears to swing in favour of (elite) workers, temporarily at least, what form of employment relationship might work best? For Edwards (1995), the employment relationship is about organizing human resources in the light of the productive aims of the firm but also the aims of employees. It is necessarily open-ended, uncertain, and a blend of inherently contradictory principles concerning control and consent.

Given that today's workforces are increasingly diverse, there may be no single employment relationship which works for all. Here John Budd's frames of reference on the employment relationship can be helpful (Figure 12.1). According to the Egoist frame of reference, if employers and employees are equals in self-regulating competitive labour markets,

232 *HR influencing organizational effectiveness*

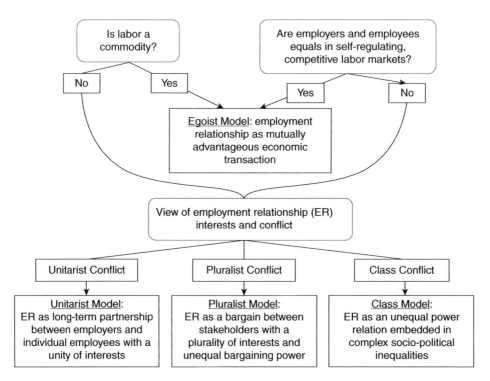

Figure 12.1 Models of national and international regulation: a frames of reference approach

Source: Diagram printed with permission from John Budd from his presentations. www.slideshare. net/NuBizHRMWE/john-budd, 2015; Models of National and International Regulation: A Frames of Reference Approach, ESRC Seminar Series (Seminar 3, International Regulation), University of Minnesota, 15 September 2014, www.ilera-directory.org/15thworldcongress/files/papers/Track_4/Thur_W4_BUDD.pdf

the mutually advantageous economic-transaction nature of the relationship is made explicit, without the broader psychological, relational and social aspects of the conventional employment relationship. Thus pay would be a significant contractual element. However, employers and employees aspiring to a longer-term relationship might seek to create a more unitarist relationship. After all, as Budd (2004) argues, work is a fully human activity: 'in addition to being an economic activity with material rewards undertaken by selfish agents, work is also a social activity with psychological rewards undertaken by human beings/citizens in democratic communities'. In such a case, to build explicitly on social exchange theory, this would imply broadening the meaning of HRM and a move away from the Attitude, Motivation, Opportunity model (Appelbaum et al., 2000).

This would involve building an authentic partnership with employees, characterized by open and genuine dialogue as circumstances change. Therefore, alongside efficiency and economic performance, equity and voice are equally important objectives, as Budd (2004) points out. Equity represents employees' entitlement to fair treatment (such as justice, security and non-discrimination); voice denotes the opportunity to have meaningful input into decisions, autonomy, free speech and industrial democracy. Only through a greater respect for these human concerns can broadly shared prosperity, respect for human dignity and equal appreciation for the competing human rights of property and labour be achieved, Budd (2010b) argues. There would also be a closer match between HR rhetoric and practice reality.

In forging a new employment relationship with employees on behalf of the organization, HR should embrace the principles of employee voice and equity, take a wider stakeholder perspective and work to provide the foundation for sustainable success for all parties. With respect to voice, given that today's workplaces are constantly changing, it makes perfect sense that those contributing the most valuable resource – labour – should contribute to the decisions about matters that affect them and have the rights to residual returns (Yaziji, 2008; Wilkinson and Fay, 2011). Ackers (2014) proposes that neo-pluralist employee relations are needed that move beyond both classical and radical pluralism to bring cooperation back into the centre of the pluralist equation, allowing the scope for good employers and unions to co-construct shared values and interests. He argues that there is more sociological space for cooperation at work than the radical-pluralists would have us believe because conflict and cooperation are 'indeterminate' and shaped by institutional context. People and politics really can shape workplace institutions and relationships.

Others argue that, especially in a context where there is union decline, or in small organizations, and to avoid covert types of discrimination, mutual gain approaches may be more appropriate. Mutuality is about achieving a happy blend of outcomes that both workers and organizations want. HR has the power to bring about change through collaboration, bringing people together. This would mean embracing the principle of give and take, with employers and employees both taking risks and receiving mutual gains, rather than adopting conventional adversarial stances. In such a case, each group of stakeholders could give and take in turn in support of achieving a commonly agreed valued outcome (such as increased market share, improved jobs, efficiency or flexible working), with even greater benefit for all the stakeholders involved in the giving and taking. Such an approach would arguably represent a fair social exchange.

I am not advocating a return to the kinds of old-style paternalism that bred dependency – rather HR practice that works on the basis that employees are adults and is fair to all parties. At Netflix, for example, the aim is to hire only the brightest and best employees. HR processes reflect the principle that people should be treated as fully formed adults who can be trusted to do their jobs. Adult-like behaviour is expected from everyone and this means people talking candidly with the boss, without fear of blame and recrimination. Communication is key to people understanding how they can succeed. Patty McCord (2014), former chief talent officer for Netflix, argues that, instead of reaching for best practice, HR should think of themselves as businesspeople and be innovative in their approach, crafting relevant practice in answer to questions such as: What's good for the company? How do we communicate that to employees? How can we help every worker understand what we mean by high performance? Colleagues whose skills no longer meet job requirements are not passed from pillar to post but are told the truth and offered 'spectacular' severance packages. Managers are charged with recruiting and developing great teams and leaders are held responsible for the company culture.

Development and learning

Working to the fairness principle means that employers should invest in developing their workforce. There is certainly plenty of scope for HR to make a difference here since over half the respondents in the 2016 Management Agenda reported 'rarely' or 'never' receiving any coaching from their line manager. Of those managers who had received coaching of one form or another during their career, the vast majority felt it would have been helpful earlier

234   *HR influencing organizational effectiveness*

in their career. So an employee-centric HR provision would include widening access to development and learning opportunities, ensuring that managers have the skills to coach and develop their staff.

The changing workplace is making greater demands of workers and is driving the need for different skills and behaviours. The demand for 'soft skills' such as communication, collaboration, teamwork, creativity and relationship management reflect the forces driving greater interactivity at work. Despite widespread political fragmentation, collaborative working is becoming a growing feature of communities, between organizations and among groups who share a common purpose. In particular, organizations in the digital economy tend to be more horizontal, collaborative and flexible (have blurred boundaries) than their traditional counterparts and work towards new conceptions of value. These more fluid structures are leading to new forms of management and leadership. In open-software communities such as Linux, leaders arise because others rate their skills and trust them. Gandini (2016) defines this as the 'Reputation economy' – where people's reputation is generated through collaborative relations. The challenge is how to integrate individuals and networks so that they can work sustainably beyond person-to-person collaboration.

If organizations want more from employees – in the form of higher skills, identification with and commitment to the company, as per the conventional unitarist employment relationship – arguably employers will have to offer employees a more substantial commitment in return, for instance in the form of improved working conditions, greater employee voice, improved opportunities for learning, growth and careers and appropriate forms of management support, according to employee needs and context.

Employee hunger for development is reflected in Deloitte's annual survey (2015). A new type of employee learning is emerging that is more 'consumer-like' and that brings together design thinking, content curation and an integrated model offering an end-to-end designed learning experience. However, companies still face tremendous challenges in realizing this vision. There were also signs of increasing recognition among executives and HR leaders that learning must adapt to a world where employees demand continuous learning opportunities through innovative platforms tailored to their individual schedules. The focus on learning seems appropriate, as learning opportunities are among the largest drivers of employee engagement. Companies were reported to be making strides in adopting new technologies and embracing new learning models such as incorporating massive open online courses and advanced video into their learning platforms.

A positive work environment

Key to an enduring new settlement would be the development of a positive and healthy work environment. HR professionals understand better than most the importance of a positive company culture to overall business success. Organizational culture and climate are often pivotal to how people feel about their organization and how 'engaged' they feel.

Employee engagement

In a people business, employee engagement is the key. Many definitions of employee engagement highlight the assumed links between engagement, performance and organizational outcomes. Engagement is 'a positive attitude held by the employee towards the organisation and its values' (Robinson et al., 2004), and 'the connection and commitment employees exhibit toward an organisation, leading to higher levels of productive work behaviours' (Society for

Human Resource Management, 2011). When employees feel uncomfortable contacting their supervisors or have a negative opinion about their jobs, they are far less likely to succeed. According to service-value chain thinking, disengaged workers tend to feel negatively about their jobs, and that translates onto customers as well. Conversely, when workers are engaged they tend to feel committed to the organization, its goals and the task at hand, feel optimistic about their jobs and are more receptive to the idea of strengthening client relationships. As a result, customers spend more and business results improve. Little wonder then that managers in every sector are keen to ensure that employees become and remain engaged.

Employee engagement is thought to reflect the state of the employment relationship between employers and employees, which is most obviously delivered on a daily basis through their relationship with their line managers. High engagement is likely to occur when people are able to satisfy their intellectual, social and affective or emotional needs and drivers at work (Kahn, 1990). How well they are able to do this depends on many factors, not least their own situations and dispositions. Yet two underpinning principles – voice (Am I informed? Am I heard?) and equity (Am I treated fairly?) – appear to be particularly important modifiers of engagement levels if employee needs are otherwise being met (Holbeche and Matthews, 2012).

In the current context, as we have discussed in previous chapters, these key engagement drivers and principles are being widely flouted. With unpredictable markets and public-sector budget cuts, many employers are attempting to increase flexibility, reduce cost and surplus capacity – zero-hours contracts are just one example of this tendency. Though affected by such decisions, staff are typically not involved in them. When the employees' voice and equity are reduced in this way, resulting in loss of trust and job security, the employment relationship between employers and employees can be damaged, often beyond repair.

Improving the quality of work life: the humanization of work

Consequently, some organizations are attempting to offer employees the best possible quality of work life (QWL), measured by employee perceptions of their working environment. Factors that are thought to affect the quality of working life include job security, pay, occupational stress, adequacy of resources and social relationships. Aiming to improve the QWL has come to be seen as part of the process of the 'humanization of work'. The aim is to make work more attractive and provide benefits to workers, though the ultimate aim is to create positive attitudes, job satisfaction and increase productivity.

More broadly QWL has come to mean the degree to which members of a work organization are able to satisfy important personal needs through their experiences in the organization. According to Walton (1973, 1980), QWL's main components can be divided into four categories: work meaningfulness, work social and organizational equilibrium, work challenge and richness. Moreover, employee involvement and participation feature large in Robbins' (1989) definition of QWL as a process by which an organization responds to employee needs by developing mechanisms to allow them to share fully in making the decisions that design their lives at work. Today QWL is a dynamic multidimensional concept that includes such concepts as job security, reward systems, working conditions, promotional opportunities, organizational and interpersonal relations, involvement in decision-making processes and people's idiosyncratic experience of meaning at work.

Well-designed HRM practices should be a key managerial mechanism for improving the quality of working life. Whether initiatives that result are expressed as 'leadership', 'strategic HRM', 'talent', 'high-performance working' or 'engagement', these different HR approaches are a means of aligning the extrinsic and intrinsic interests of employees, employers and other

236 HR influencing organizational effectiveness

stakeholders and place line managers centre stage in delivering better people management (Overell et al., 2010).

Benefits of investing in QWL

There are several key benefits to employers in investing in QWL activities. First, they should provide 'good' employers with opportunities to attract the best employees. Younger workers in particular will work where they like and will look to work for organizations which show high commitment to employees and offer development opportunities to increase their employability. Furthermore, as discussed earlier, there is growing evidence that Millennials (and other generations) want to work for organizations whose purpose is not solely financial. According to a paper published in the *Academy of Management Review*, employee motivation stems from working on highest-order goals with which employee values align, and in roles that offer opportunities for status, autonomy, achievement and interacting with others.

Employee retention is likely to be higher in organizations in which there is a mutual employment relationship and that offer a high-quality working life, since employees tend to be more committed. Transactional psychological contracts are unlikely to have this retention effect. One study (McInnes et al., 2009), for example, examined the link between employee commitment and how employees in two very different groups perceived the psychological contract found clear correlations between levels of commitment (positive and negative) and the ways in which the psychological contract was perceived. In particular, psychological contracts that correlated positively with employee commitment were based on mutual trust rather than formal agreements; the sense of collective wellbeing of employees rather than more narrowly defined individual interests; equality of partnership rather than the assumption that the employer's interest must come first; forging a long-term rather than short-term relationship; and negotiation with the employee rather than imposition by the employer.

Social exchange is a key mechanism mediating potential outcomes around wellbeing, in particular, interactional fairness (Farndale and Kelliher, 2013). So while it is important to be clear what the organization wishes to achieve – such as more innovation and creativity, better customer service, higher skills – it is crucial to consider what arrangements, practices, incentives and structures (and attitudes) will help deliver these and also improve employees' quality of working life. Job satisfaction is an important enabler of both productivity and quality of working life. If the aim is to develop a working environment with a strong work ethos that stimulates the creative ability of employees and generates cooperation, the related aim is to achieve this without leading to employee burnout.

First, it is useful to take stock of how people perceive the quality of working life at a given point in time. The measurement of climate and culture can also serve as a starting point in diagnosing and influencing changes required in the organization to facilitate the achievement of job satisfaction and organizational goals (Sempane et al., 2002). Employee-engagement surveys can be used to identify issues for further inquiry with groups of employees. QWL initiatives, even when based on employee-engagement survey data, should not be initiated 'top down' by HR. After all, it is mainly line managers and employees themselves who are likely to implement the initiatives. Instead they should originate from many levels and departments. Feedback from middle managers and other staff can help refine plans and ensure that all employees feel ownership and are connected with the efforts in progress at a company.

Then it is important to take action on those key variables that significantly and positively aid in creating a high-quality work experience. Signalling theory suggests that employees' attitudes can be influenced by the actions of those around them in the workplace. Line managers play a crucial role in delivering HRM, so if line managers show that they value employees and care about employee wellbeing, job satisfaction and affective commitment may increase and perceptions of work pressure may decrease. HR should therefore work closely with line managers to ensure that there is appropriate supervision, good manager–employee relations and suitable working conditions. According to context, this might require HR action to improve the quality of line-manager interactions and help managers to design rewarding jobs that address employee motivations and cut down staff turnover.

Teams should be designed and developed to be as self-managing as possible. In such teams, employees have the chance to take up new opportunities for learning and growth and to plan, control and manage their own workloads. When people are part of autonomous work groups or integrated project teams they are able to collaborate with others and directly participate in decision-making.

Employee wellbeing

From an employee-centric HR standpoint, workplaces should be designed to promote employee wellbeing. Why the growing focus on wellbeing today? The argument goes that, because in modern societies goods and services are plentiful, and because simple material needs are largely satisfied, in theory people have the luxury of focusing their attention on the 'good life' – a life that is enjoyable, meaningful, engaging and fulfilling (Diener and Seligman, 2004: 2). Though there is debate about causality, as we have discussed in earlier chapters, many popular management texts talk about a happy worker being a productive worker; a happy worker is one who is devoted and committed to the organization (Stenner, 2010; Helliwell et al., 2012).

In particular, employee wellbeing has become central to much 'employee-engagement' thinking in recent years. Wellbeing includes pleasure, engagement and meaning, and the concept of life satisfaction may reflect all of these (Seligman, 2002). Current research on wellbeing has been derived from two general perspectives: the hedonic approach, which focuses on happiness and defines wellbeing in terms of pleasure attainment and pain avoidance; and the eudaimonic approach, which focuses on meaning and self-realization and defines wellbeing in terms of the degree to which a person is fully functioning.

However, as we have also discussed, for many people, working life is anything but enjoyable. With echoes of Braverman's observations about worker alienation and Sennett's 'new work culture', Richard Ellsworth (2002) describes the modern workplace as the site within which: 'the historical battle between work as a source of drudgery and alienation and work as a creative, fulfilling experience continues today. It is within senior management's power to shape the outcome of this conflict.' Wood and Ogbonnaya (2016) argue that if employers and HR fail to 'get to grips' with the changing workforce of the future, it could have a detrimental effect on employees' mental health. Aided by a proliferation of contracts, and a loosening of the psychological bonds between large organizations and their employees, a greater number of people than ever are suffering a level of instability at work that seems less related to temporary economic fluctuations and more a permanent shift. Even high-performance work systems are associated almost entirely with high performance – very rarely with wellbeing since the pursuit of performance often involves work intensification or overengagement, which can actually diminish employee wellbeing.

The benefits of employee wellbeing are thought to be legion, not only for individuals and employers but for society as a whole.

> People high in well-being later earn higher incomes and perform better at work than people who report low well-being. Happy workers are better organizational citizens, meaning that they help other people at work in various ways. Furthermore, people high

238   *HR influencing organizational effectiveness*

in well-being seem to have better social relationships than people low in well-being. For example, they are more likely to get married, stay married, and have rewarding marriages. Finally, well-being is related to health and longevity, although the pathways linking these variables are far from fully understood. Thus, well-being not only is valuable because it feels good, but also is valuable because it has beneficial consequences.

(Diener and Seligman, 2004: 1)

However, Diener and Seligman warn that:

Well-being is not a panacea that will in itself solve all of the world's problems. Even if well-being one day becomes the dominant paradigm, it must be supplemented by other values of societies, and people must be socialized for humane values for the well-being economy to be a desirable concept.

(Diener and Seligman, 2004: 25)

So in a more human HRM, as part of its constructive social exchange with employees, HR would aim to develop a positive employment relationship and to ensure employees can enjoy a high quality of working life, resulting in higher employee wellbeing and satisfaction.

Making the case for improving employee wellbeing

It is therefore important that organizations monitor the wellbeing of workers, and take steps to improve it. Yet a CIPD positioning paper on health and wellbeing found that only 8 per cent of organizations have strategies to improve employee wellbeing. Making the business case for improving employee wellbeing can be difficult since this is often seen as a subjective, individual concern. Yet in a broader evaluation of organizational success and return of investment, wellbeing has been linked to employee satisfaction, organizational commitment, job satisfaction, organizational citizenship behaviour, employee turnover, absenteeism and productivity.

Stress is perceived to be the opposite of wellbeing (Walton, 1985). Stress is also a very subjective concept; people may react differently with happiness or unhappiness to the same environmental features (Warr and Clapperton, 2010). Moreover, occasional stress can sometimes produce a positive outcome (for instance, working to a tight deadline can act as a spur to short-term achievement). However, there is a widely growing awareness of the potentially damaging effects of chronic stress on workers' mental health and emotional wellbeing if not managed efficiently and effectively. Stress has been linked negatively to:

- the mental and physical health and safety of employees – accidents on the job, illness and even death;
- financial impact of healthcare – absenteeism, hospitalization, increased healthcare costs;
- organizational effectiveness – reduced quality and quantity of work, missing deadlines, decreased productivity, lower individual and team performance, loss of passion for work; and
- legal compliance with worker-compensation programmes.

(Based on Yahaya et al., 2012)

In recent times, organizations have become concerned about not only the financial, but also the reputational implications of stress. Ideally workplaces should be designed to promote wellbeing for its own sake, not just because of its instrumental benefits for morale or efficiency.

Stress tends to be measured in terms of employees' perceptions of their physical and psychological wellbeing at work and self-reported evaluations of stress are just as valid as 'objective' data, such as statistics on accidents or absenteeism. There is growing demand for an evidence base about the causes and effects of wellbeing. Available research evidence broadly falls into two categories:

- Outcomes of a positive employment relationship. For instance, the ongoing reviews of the 100 best companies to work for (Fulmer et al., 2003) suggest a link exists between wellbeing and a positive employment relationship. Guest's work suggests an association between a positive psychological contract, higher wellbeing and lower absence (Guest and Conway, 2004).
- Outcomes of positive wellbeing. For example, WERS 2011 suggests an association between job security, supportive management and employee wellbeing. Various studies suggest a direct impact of wellbeing on:
  - trust levels, occupational citizenship behaviour and performance (Whitener et al., 1998);
  - job satisfaction with performance (Judge et al., 2001; Schneider et al., 2003);
  - work engagement (Guest and Conway, 2004), leading to higher performance outcomes.

Building a convincing case may require HR to master business and HR analytics to provide in-house evidence of the issue to be addressed. Gaining executive support for wellbeing activities may depend on the relative balance of power in the employment relationship at a given time. Situations of decreasing competitive advantage could result in senior managers either embracing or rejecting such a case. For instance, the introduction of the national living wage in the UK, that requires employers to increase the pay of the low-paid, has proved an unpopular move in the business community. Some employers are choosing to get rid of people, while others are finding other ways to make cost savings. Several large employers have been accused by their staff of slashing employee benefits in an effort to offset the costs of the national living wage. Some employers have considered reducing pay for overtime and bank holidays or are flattening their structures and reducing the number of better-paid supervisory roles. The same cost pressure could also bring a desire to improve productivity – to improve motivation, invest in and use people better.

Clearly the case to be made must fit the context and the people involved. For instance, the 2016 Management Agenda highlighted that managers in the UK public sector are doubtful of their organization's ability to show care and concern for staff in a context of ongoing cost-cutting and where employers expect more for less. Yet failing to look after the wellbeing of public-sector staff may ultimately impact their ability to care for those they serve.

Implementing wellbeing initiatives

When it comes to implementing improvements, the HR function must take on the role of steward and designer of new people processes that will enable employee wellbeing and deliver the lived reality of the employee-value proposition in a sustainable and cost-effective way. Psychologists are in an ideal position to work with HR to develop and improve relevant measures and design interventions that would be maximally effective in increasing wellbeing.

Various studies offer good evidence that increasing job control and autonomy reduces sickness absence and has positive effects on mental health (Marmot Review Team, 2010).

240 *HR influencing organizational effectiveness*

According to the Demand–Control model, employees who can decide for themselves how to meet their job demands do not experience job strain (e.g. job-related anxiety, health complaints, exhaustion and dissatisfaction). Therefore, people should have manageable workloads, free from excessive demands, roles in which they can exercise some personal control over their job and support from supervisors.

The aim should be to lower stress levels and improve the quality of work life. Deloitte's Global Human Capital Trends 2015 report identified some HR attempts to 'simplify' the work environment as a response to the 'overwhelmed employee' situation. This means HR simplifying its own processes, helping employees manage the flood of information at work, challenging practices which lead to excessive workloads and building a culture of collaboration, empowerment and innovation.

Some HR organizations are attempting to incorporate design thinking into their approach to wellbeing. Instead of building training programmes, they are developing interventions, apps and other tools that help make employees less stressed and more productive. For instance, as discussed in Chapter 10, some companies encourage employees to stay healthy by providing them with fitness trackers which monitor exercise and stress levels, while others encourage employees to stay mentally focused by subsidizing their further education costs. Health information is one of a number of categories of data considered particularly sensitive, so the employer then, of course, is obliged to process any personal information gathered in this way in accordance with data-protection laws.

Wellness, diversity, work–life balance and flexi-time policies are CSR programmes directly within the HR manager's purview. Wellness programmes can become a platform for engaging employees in discussions about 'personal sustainability' and provide support for employees in the areas of stress management, spirituality at work, health and fitness, healthy lifestyles, etc. A related policy could be the development of an unpaid leave programme for employees to pursue personal projects aligned with company values. New policies around working time and annual leave may help but they must be backed up by genuine support from the top. For example, Virgin and Netflix have replaced their conventional annual leave policies by allowing employees to take as much holiday as they wish. While no doubt well intended, having such a policy does not mean employees will use it – that will depend on the corporate culture and the messages they get from the top. If employees believe that they are expected to be up to date with every project before taking leave, they risk taking less rather than more leave. (In the UK, workers are legally entitled to take at least 5.6 weeks of paid annual leave.)

Career development

Since the concept of 'talent management' entered the HR lexicon about the year 2000, the aim has been to ensure that organizations have the future leaders and other talent they need for success over the medium term. Just some of the new approaches to standard HR practices that some HR teams are adopting include embracing digital technology as a means of locating and sourcing scarce talent, developing valid and reliable selection measures to hire and promote employees, providing training and development opportunities and ensuring appropriate methods of supervision.

As Cappelli (2008) argues, although the central talent-management concerns – anticipating human-capital needs and setting out plans to meet them – may not be new, traditional solutions are no longer appropriate because the certainty that was required for them no longer holds. Some of the organizational design and structural factors that are influencing the changing nature of careers include the advent of technology, flattening of organizations, increased reliance on teams, the changing nature of the employment contract and the drive to be lean.

Sennett (1998) observes that flexibility in the working environment has made it difficult for the individual to make long-term commitments and to shape a 'life narrative'. Effective career-development programmes are informed by sound HR planning through which organizations can identify the skills that will be needed in the future, the areas of job growth anticipated, and existing competencies that will no longer be required. A career-development programme informed by this type of information can serve employees better by directing them toward areas that the company will need and value, and can serve the organization better by developing internal talent to meet future needs. With today's more fluid workforces it could be argued that, in their talent planning, HR should take into account the changing nature of employee expectations with respect to their careers. However, PwC (2016) research with around 10,000 employees, and 500 HR professionals from China, India, Germany, the UK and the US, suggests the majority of HR teams are not doing this. Results outlined in the Future of Work report showed that just 31 per cent of businesses across the world are building their future talent strategy around the rise of the portfolio career and are hiring a diverse mix of people on an ad hoc basis.

Increasingly, careers-a long-neglected facet of talent management – is becoming once again a key focus for many HR teams as they attempt to address the needs of an increasingly multigenerational, diverse and more fluid workforce. In the past, careers and career planning within large corporations involved internal advancement supported by early training and regular movements within the firm to provide development opportunities. Despite the major shifts in the way organizations have managed their workforces over the last three decades of change and restructurings, much of the existing literature on talent management even today continues to focus on practices associated with lifetime careers in corporations. This is despite 46 per cent of HR professionals in PwC's Future of Work survey predicting that at least 20 per cent of their workforce will be made up of contractors or temporary workers by 2020.

Employers have long since abandoned offering job security except to the favoured few and conventional career paths in any single organization are mostly gone. Traditional hierarchies are becoming weaker, with feedback from peers becoming more valued than that from traditional leaders. As organizations have become flatter, there are fewer jobs in middle and upper management, and the opportunity for traditional career advancement up a career ladder has decreased. How work is performed is in a state of reinvention. In organizations in which there is an increased reliance on teams, teams in some cases are expected to take the place of middle managers, as the team members develop the ability to self-manage. In addition, jobs may be less clearly defined within a team environment, making career planning more difficult for employees used to seeing a linear career path.

These changing employment factors have reduced the stability of a traditional career, as well as affecting employee morale, loyalty, commitment and expectations. As the line between one's personal and professional life becomes ever more blurred in the modern world of work, the overall responsibility for developing and enhancing careers has shifted more heavily to the employee.

With that evolution, and given that employees must manage their own careers, the area of career development has become more important, and more challenging, than ever. For many young people today, the notion of a 'career' is one spanning multiple employers and periods of self-employment. This leads to expectations for rapid career growth, a flexible workplace

242   *HR influencing organizational effectiveness*

with a compelling proposition, an enriching experience at every stage and a sense of mission and purpose at work. The Deloitte Millennial survey (2016b) found that salary and financial benefits are the top retention factor for Millennials, but once this is stripped out, work–life balance and opportunities to progress and take leadership roles stand out. According to the PwC 'Future of Work' report, 44 per cent of global respondents said the most important aspect they looked for in a job is security, while 29 per cent of employees wanted a chance to take control of their career.

How would an employee-centric approach to talent management shift the dial? While retaining the focus on business needs for talent, a more balanced approach would take into account employees' career aspirations.

Career-development programmes

Employee-centric HR practitioners will remember the 'new deal' described by Herriot and Pemberton (1997). This suggests that if employers no longer offer people job security, they ought at least to support them in their efforts to become and remain competitively 'employable', even if job security is not on offer.

Career-development activities are ways to show employees that they are valued. This means employers being open to dialogue with employees about their career aspirations, offering career coaching, for instance, that can help people understand how the nature of the career is changing:

- competition for good jobs is global, not local;
- the search for more meaning and satisfaction from work;
- increased use of technology – workers need to be both 'hi-tech' and 'hi-touch';
- acting like an entrepreneur, even when employed';
- more shared leadership at all levels;
- increased need for networking and self-marketing;
- lifelong learning and taking on of various roles, jobs and industries; and
- increased representation of women and minorities in the workforce.

Given the increasingly fluid nature of organizations, people are less likely to remain in one job or area of specialization for long; career plans are more likely to be made up of lateral and diagonal moves. Effective performance in many jobs requires continuous learning and acquisition of new skills. Employees must re-evaluate their capabilities and career plans regularly and flexibly, continuously assessing the 'fit' of the work with their own career stage and needs. Workers will need portable skills. The tech-savvy recruit is likely to be at an advantage over those who are not. Having the opportunity to develop their skills may help employees develop both their competence and self-esteem.

Workers need to be adaptable and open to new ideas, willing to explore and experiment and make the most of new opportunities. Getting involved in professional associations, attending seminars and continuous networking are useful ways to meet like-minded professionals. They will need to be proactive; look for, and make their own opportunities, keep their skills up to date, working towards the kind of work–life balance that is right for them. Given that career 'paths' rarely run smoothly, employees also need to develop career resilience, the ability to bounce back from setbacks, sudden changes and twists and turns along the career path.

Stewardship and organizational effectiveness   243

Box 12.1 Growth and development at IKEA

A dynamic career planning and development would aim to meet both organizational needs and employee needs and would be an example of mutuality in action. One organization which actively works in partnership with its employees to help them develop their careers is IKEA.

Selection

Selection criteria include a strong emphasis on value fit. New recruits are assigned a co-worker as a mentor for some time.

Job enrichment

Co-workers at IKEA who have mastered their current job are encouraged to seek new challenges through job enlargement and enrichment, often involving changing the job scope/location. Annual development talks take place to discuss and outline career paths. A wide range of on-the-job training is complemented by traditional classroom courses. In addition, there is a wide range of web-based training activities available for all aspects of IKEA operations.

Compensation and incentive system

Line management takes a direct role in the design and determination of reward policy in IKEA. IKEA has developed global, mandatory guidelines for compensation and benefits. Thus each country must offer the same benefit structure for all co-workers in the country. The benefits are to be based on core IKEA values as well as local laws and market conditions. With regard to incentives, the emphasis is on designing reward systems that best fit the local context.

Encouraging diversity in the workplace

About 40 per cent of the co-workers are women with a great mix of nationalities. IKEA's purchasing and retail operations in 41 different countries are led by country managers of 14 different nationalities.

Career development

Internal promotion is one of the motivation-enhancing HRM practices. Any co-worker with potential can apply for a one-year development adventure programme at the beginning of their career with IKEA. Participants travel to two different countries for six months each to work in different fields from what they are used to. These co-workers are then encouraged to take on leadership responsibility, forming a pool of highly skilled IKEA managers of the future.

Today's career-development practice is likely to include creative approaches to skill building, more sophisticated assessment and development tools and links to other HR systems. For instance, future job analysis and work analysis can be used to identify logical connections among jobs that can form meaningful career paths. By identifying the skill requirements of

244 *HR influencing organizational effectiveness*

multiple job families within a company, we may be able to identify jobs for which a similar requirement profile exists, even if the titles and organizational locations are very different. When it comes to job matching and opportunities for skill building there is a need for creative dialogue between employees and employers about how to put employees' talents to good use. Structured and tailored development plans could include on-the-job opportunities and assignments in combination with formal learning opportunities.

Mentoring programmes can help people develop relationships that can assist their career success and growth. The Deloitte Millennial report (2016b) found that having a mentor was 'incredibly powerful' in achieving this. Traditional mentoring programmes may assign people with more organizational experience and a higher job level as mentors to newer, lower-level employees; given the speed with which organizational structures and needs are changing, new forms of mentoring programmes may be needed to assign mentors who can help employees navigate their careers in fast-paced, ever-changing organizations (Kram, 1996).

As with any organizational intervention, evaluation of career-development programmes is important since these take up significant amounts of employee and managerial time, as well as a substantial financial investment in some cases.

Conclusion

In this chapter we have considered how an employee-centric approach might reshape the employment relationship. We have talked about how HR can help increase employee wellbeing, improve the quality of the working environment and reintegrate career development within HR offerings. CIPD's research on the causes and consequences of high-quality work suggests that positive HRM, investing in employees, employee voice, manageable work hours, trust and fairness are all aspects of social exchange which benefit not only employees but employers too since they are seen as antecedents to high performance.

In the next chapter we shall consider what a fair deal – in terms of pay and opportunities – might look like from a mutual gains perspective. We shall look at how HR can influence the development of a high-performance climate that may be critical to stimulating both employee engagement and performance. Creating a high-quality workplace that engages people, developing a new model of leadership and building a more meaningful culture may require HR to redesign almost everything it does – from recruiting to performance management to onboarding to rewards systems. In particular, we shall consider how approaches to performance management might evolve to produce more mutual benefits for all concerned.

Points to ponder

- Is a new form of pluralism needed, in which employee needs are represented collectively alongside those of other stakeholders of the firm? How could this work?
- What would a 'mutual gain' approach involve?

13 A high-performance workplace

> Without continual growth and progress, such words as improvement, achievement and success have no meaning.
>
> (Benjamin Franklin)

In the last chapter we considered how a more employee-centric HR approach might transform HR's priorities. In this chapter we consider how, at the dawn of the truly digital age, organizations must respond to the great corporate challenge of the age – harnessing the creativity and the productive power of people against a background of incessant organizational change. With respect to performance and productivity, people issues come to the fore. Since many UK organizations are knowledge or service based, people are their principal source of value production. Business success increasingly depends on an employer's ability to attract, motivate (engage) and retain the 'right' employees. Little wonder that many leaders are wondering how to create an adaptable, high-performance culture that attracts the people they need, and keeps them engaged with the organization and the work they are doing. The challenge is often expressed through approaches that seek to foster commitment and effort – release discretionary effort, more for less, the 'extra mile', engagement.

We discussed how high-performance work systems (HPWS) have generally failed to catch on and, if applied in a largely instrumental way, can do more harm than good (Combs et al., 2006). After all, employees are not passive pawns to be manipulated into high performance. Unless there is fair exchange, some people can and do exercise their agency through resisting or undermining the work effort. From an economic-exchange perspective, research has shown that perceptions of equity relate to some key HPWS outcomes including pay satisfaction and commitment (Tekleab et al., 2005) and increased workload (Brockner et al., 1994). When employees perceive the exchange is fair, they will be more satisfied and committed to the organization (Ambrose and Schminke, 2003).

So is there a way in which HR practices can more obviously achieve a balance between employer needs for performance and productivity and employee needs for a high-quality work experience and a fair deal? In this chapter we shall consider employees' need for 'good work' and go on to focus on two of the most contested areas of HPWS from an organizational justice perspective – performance management and reward. We shall also consider how HR can directly influence organizational effectiveness with respect to one of the other quadruple bottom line elements – the customer.

In particular, we shall cover:

- Job quality and 'good work'.
- Customer-centric HR.
- The design of high-performance workplaces that offer a high-quality working life.

246   *HR influencing organizational effectiveness*

- How performance-management systems might evolve in tandem with this.
- How reward systems might reflect the mutual gains approach.

The quality of work

Work quality is a profoundly important issue in the twenty-first century. Today people are the most important source of value. The skill requirements of jobs have been increasing in recent times and are likely to continue to do so. Modern technologies require more educated and intellectually capable workers to get the best out of them. With better educational opportunities, modern workers tend to look for work which interests them. In general, work has become progressively more complex and engaging – and potentially more meaningful and fulfilling as a result. Indeed, many people invest great hopes of individual fulfilment and self-expression in their work and employment relationship and more skilled and complex jobs afford the opportunity for workers to fulfil themselves more through their work.

However, too many people endure what Budd (2010a) calls 'lousy work'. In the 2016 Management Agenda survey (Lucy et al., 2016), 61 per cent of respondents self-reported that their skills are higher, or much higher, than the skills they need to do their present job. In effect, they could be considered to be 'underemployed'. Those in more junior roles are marginally more likely to feel their skills are underused. The potential relevance of this is twofold. Firstly, the UK has a productivity problem and part of that involves managers not making the most effective use of the skills that are available. More needs to be done to ensure that skills are more effectively utilized in the workplace (Overell et al., 2010). Secondly, if people believe they do not have the opportunity to use their skills and develop, they risk becoming demotivated and may leave their organization for pastures new.

The risks to job quality

Looking ahead, there are potential storm clouds gathering as job quality is at risk of declining. As organizations pursue agility, many low-skill jobs are being outsourced and automation is increasingly applied to a wide range of jobs. The process involves breaking down jobs into their component tasks/parts, some or most of which can be done more efficiently by computers. Computers cannot substitute for all types of labour, and jobs that involve non-routine tasks that require flexible judgements and personal attention (caring occupations, for example) cannot be fully replaced in the same way as routine jobs. Nevertheless, automation is already being applied to some professional tasks previously carried out by lawyers or doctors. For high-skilled workers, work risks becoming both more intensive and less interesting as roles are 'hollowed out'.

Moreover, in today's increasingly networked organizations, to gain the most from new technology, organizational structures are being radically altered as new operations are created, networks formed and functions and jobs reorganized. Job design is now conceived as being less about fixed job descriptions composed of set tasks and more about encapsulating the processes and outcomes of how work is structured, organized, experienced and enacted (Morgeson and Humphrey, 2008). This broader definition reflects the emergence of dynamic roles and changes in work from project to project (Parker et al., 2001).

This puts organizational and employee needs on a potential collision course. In traditional bureaucracies, people knew where they stood and where responsibility lay. In flexible networks, it can be hard to discern who is boss, where responsibility lies or how problems should be resolved. The resulting lack of clarity may lead to low morale, confusion, duplication and job strain.

On the other hand, agility is not just about speed and disruption; it also requires 'dynamic stability' (Abrahamson, 2004; Holbeche, 2015) or the ability to stabilize and standardize while also keeping pace with fast-moving disruptive innovators (Christensen et al., 2015). Jobs represent a key form of stability. McKinsey's Agility research found that workers' roles and the processes that support them are the first and fourth most important factors that differentiate truly agile companies from the rest.

Whichever ways automation is applied to jobs and work processes, core foundations of organization such as structures, autonomy, influence and control will need to be looked at anew. And if people are an essential engine of growth, job quality logically becomes more strategically significant as a result. As Overell et al. (2010: 17) point out: 'There is little merit in seeking engagement or adopting "high performance" models of work organisation without a concomitant willingness to pay attention to the quality of the experience of work: they are two sides of the same coin.'

Good work

HR should work to create sustainable value for everyone. This means leading thinking within the organization about how roles can be reconfigured to reconcile organizational needs for efficiency with people's need for what the International Labour Organisation term 'decent work' and what Budd, the Work Foundation and others term 'good work'. For instance, (how) can automation be used to give people opportunities for roles in which they can become 'craftsmen' (Sennett, 2008), acquire new skills and responsibilities and gain great job satisfaction from their work? If creativity is required, how will this affect the ways people should be managed? As Paul Edwards (1995) has argued, imposing control and releasing creativity involve very different approaches.

At one level, the duality and tension between competing moral and the economic drivers for good work are illustrated in the International Labour Organisation concept 'Decent Work for All'. This was formulated by the its constituents – European governments, employers and workers – and reflects priorities on the social, economic and political agenda of countries and the international system. It assumes that productive employment and decent work are key elements to achieving a fair globalization, reducing poverty and achieving equitable, inclusive and sustainable development.

The Decent Work agenda is based on the understanding that work is central to people's wellbeing. It is a source of personal dignity, family stability, peace in the community, democracies that deliver for people and economic growth that expands opportunities for productive jobs and enterprise development. In addition to providing income, work can pave the way for broader social and economic advancement, strengthening individuals, their families and communities. Such progress, however, hinges on work that is decent. Decent work is characterized by opportunity and income; rights, voice and recognition; family stability and personal development; fairness and gender equality.

Similarly, 'good work' (Bevan, 2012; Overell et al., 2010) conjures up a vision for the future of the employment relationship that seeks to balance the interests of individuals, employers and society in order to deliver performance, engagement and fairness. It identifies the principles which should guide choices around how work is organized across different sectors, firms and workplaces. Good work is work that is rewarding for employees, employers and society. For employees, good work provides: secure and interesting jobs; choice, flexibility and control over working hours; autonomy and control over the pace and timing of work and the working environment; a say in the critical decisions that affect their future; and a fair and appropriate balance between effort and reward. From a business perspective, good work is: productive and efficient; aims to involve and engage employees and to encourage their contribution to

248   *HR influencing organizational effectiveness*

organizational success. And from a society perspective, good work is socially aware, ethical and sustainable.

Good work is defined as 'whatever advances development by supporting the fulfilment of individual potentialities while simultaneously contributing to the harmonious growth of other individuals and groups' (Csíkszentmihályi et al., 2001: 244). Under this rubric, employees should have 'voice', i.e. not only be kept informed of developments by management but also have the chance to participate actively in issues relating to business and the workplace. Consequently, employees are assumed to want to exercise agency, and to be motivated to achieve mutual benefits for themselves and their employers.

Finally, the concept of 'Feel Good Management' (Frenking, 2016) has been gaining traction in Germany, where it originated, in recent times. In the 'knowledge economy', given the increasing competition for talent, the key to holding onto skilled employees is to understand their needs and expectations, and match it with the organizational culture, creating a win–win situation for people and the organization. This is not about large bonuses, but delivering a workplace that reflects individuals' core values. For workforce groups such as Millennials, this may be meaningful work and a fair work–life balance. This is essentially an employee-centric approach that recognizes that 'factors other than mere numbers measure success', and no matter how much the company grows, not to lose the human touch.

Developing a good work context involves primarily HR-related responsibilities, conveying the unique culture to potential new talent, involvement throughout the employee lifecycle, from the recruitment process to onboarding events, manager training, and developing work–life balance options. The focus is on achieving immediate and sustained wellbeing for each employee. Meaningful work is central to this. Serey (2006) observed that meaningful and satisfying work is generally viewed as a career-growth vehicle since it offers individuals:

- an opportunity to realize one's potential and utilize one's talents, to excel in challenging situations that require decision-making, initiative and self-direction;
- a meaningful activity perceived as worthwhile by the people involved;
- an activity in which one has clarity of role necessary for the achievement of overall goals; and
- a feeling of belonging and pride associated with what one is doing, and doing this well.

This is where the role of the manager comes in, with the aim of developing and fostering a value-oriented corporate culture. To be successful, such an approach must engage each manager and team member to shape the overall culture, and be fully supported by senior leaders.

Crafting jobs

Since it is mostly managers who make decisions about how to design jobs for employees, HR can help managers to design roles to avoid job strain and improve job quality. Many new jobs require a raft of higher-level cognitive and interactive skills so it is vital that people's skills are matched with the complexity of their jobs and that people retain a degree of autonomy in how they do their work. HR can help ensure that there are appropriate communications and employee voice – do people have the information they need to do the job? Do they have opportunities for participation and involvement in decision-making? Are their views sought and heard?

With respect to the quality of work, one of the best known models is the Job Demands-Resources (JD-R) Model (Bakker and Demerouti, 2006; Demerouti et al., 2001). This is helpful for understanding both employee burnout and engagement, and consequently organizational performance. According to the JD-R, job characteristics can have a profound impact on employee wellbeing (e.g. job strain, burnout, work engagement). The combination of excessive demands and low resources represents a risk to health and wellbeing.

However, the JD-R model also highlights the importance of job resources – their lack is primarily related to disengagement. When job resources are present, such as social support, performance feedback and autonomy, they may instigate a motivational process leading to low burnout levels, job-related learning, work engagement and organizational commitment (e.g. Bakker et al., 2014; Demerouti et al., 2001; Salanova et al., 2005; Taris and Feij, 2004). Resources may be located at the level of the organization at large (e.g. pay, career opportunities, job security); at the level of interpersonal and social relations (e.g. supervisor and co-worker support, team climate) and the organization of work (e.g. role clarity); and at the task level (autonomy, feedback and task significance). So arguably people can remain engaged in their work even when job demands are high if job resources are also high.

Hackman and Oldham's (1980) work on job characteristics suggests that when task significance, task identity and skill variety are present, employees will perceive their work as more worthwhile and valuable. They also predicted that autonomy would lead employees to take greater personal responsibility or ownership over their work, and that job feedback would lead employees to experience greater knowledge of results, or awareness of effectiveness. Overell et al. (2010: 17) argue that 'the greater accountability and sense of responsibility among employees that many organisations are keen to foster depend for their legitimacy on a view of the control people have over their work and the basis of the stake they have in an organisation'.

Good job design is central to a decent job quality, the most important aspects of which are pay, skill, effort, autonomy and security. Pay is not only essential to workers' financial wellbeing, it also provides recognition and, if not too low, a sense of fairness. Roles should have the right blend of demands and resources; be worthwhile, offer scope for growth and development and have manageable workloads. This means ensuring that people have the right balance of job demands (implications for autonomy) and resources (i.e. organizational support). To gauge the qualities of 'good jobs', Green (2009a) suggests five 'core' indicators: pay, skills and skill utilization, security, autonomy and task discretion, working time and work intensification.

Job enrichment

From a motivation perspective, the ideal is for jobs to be designed to match the skills and interests of the workers. The concept of job enrichment was devised by Herzberg in the 1950s. This essentially involves giving employees opportunities for personal growth, increased responsibility, opportunities for decision-making and task discretion through which people have the chance for achievement, recognition and self-actualization. Some of the on-the-job approaches to skill building that seem to work well within today's organizations include cross-training and job rotation to provide people with the opportunity to develop new skills or enhance existing skills. Other ways through which jobs can be enriched include:

- Implementing participative management – encourage team members to participate in decision-making and get involved in strategic planning.
- Combining tasks – combine work activities to provide a more challenging and stimulating work project.

250　*HR influencing organizational effectiveness*

- Identifying project-focused work units – break up traditional functional units to form projects-focused units.
- Creating autonomous work teams – who can make their own decisions at group level.
- Increasing employee-related feedback – make sure that people know how well, or otherwise, they are doing their jobs. Be open to feedback.

Job enrichment thus becomes a vehicle for mutual gains as employees achieve personal growth and the organization retains key staff.

Customer–centric HR

Most HR professionals maintain strong relationships with employees to help them to succeed, though it is less common for HR teams to actively engage with another key stakeholder group – (external) customers. Indeed, even the notion of internal consultancy and working on projects for internal 'clients' is still alien in many quarters. Customer-centric HR is the next level of HRM that will revolutionize the way companies operate, according to prominent HR guru Dave Ulrich. In their book, *HR from the Outside In*, Ulrich and colleagues (2012) argue that external customers are also HR's clients, albeit indirectly, since the quality of customer–employee interactions and customer service often depends on HR's systems that help train, retain and reward employees. Indeed, these authors argue that almost every HR practice can be filtered through the eyes of the customer.

This means shifting HR's stance from strategic to 'outside-in'; from acting as a 'mirror' (i.e. reflecting business strategies in HR practices) to informing HR practices by looking through a 'window' into the external world of customers or investors. Therefore, in order to better understand the company's offering through the eyes of its customers, an HR department should shift focus to include external influences, particularly the customer experience. This means reflecting on questions such as:

- What is a company's appetite for change in the near term?
- What is the gap between the needs and wants of customers and what they actually experience?
- How can the company gain a customer-experience advantage against competitors?
- At which point in the experience should the company concentrate to have a real impact?

Ulrich argues that, instead of aiming to become an employer of choice, organizations should strive to become an employer of employees whom customers would choose – and, in some cases, do choose. This in turn should raise awareness of the extent to which the overall capabilities of the staff support the customer experience the company wants to provide, and what needs to be done to strengthen these.

Developing a customer-centric HR policy could involve (Ulrich et al., 2012; Fox, 2013):

- Learn more about clients in order to understand what the customer really wants and values

This is about more than letting customers give you feedback about what's good and bad about your company, what they expect from your company, and how your service teams are doing. Surveys alone tend to produce a biased or limited view. HR should attend sales meetings and participate in online customer forums in which customers share their opinions on products and services.

- Involve top customers in selecting your key staff members

Clients know what is required of the job, especially in a personal field such as long-term care. One UK NHS mental health trust involves long-term service users as panel members to help select key care staff and to give feedback on the quality of care they receive.

- Implement training programmes

If a company wants to improve its client relationships, training is usually the first place to start. With sales- or customer service-based companies, HR professionals can enlist the talents of top salespeople or employees who best exemplify the customer-centric traits a company is striving for. It's important for managers and supervisors to train employees how to develop and maintain positive client partnerships. HR can develop training packages and programmes that show new recruits the best ways to forge these relationships, as well as effective techniques to dealing with difficult clients. Let customers be part of training – invite them to share a story about a bad experience with the company, which was rectified by someone in customer service. This lets new hires know it's okay to make mistakes, as long as these are remedied and learned from. Such training sessions remind employees of the importance of clients in their business and can improve sales and communication skills across an organization.

- Invite customers to reward employees

While it is common for companies to set up plans that financially reward strong sales numbers, it is far rarer for companies to set up systems that recognize the hard work it takes to improve client retention and satisfaction. For instance, Richer Sounds encourages customers to write to the firm about very good service they receive from staff. This leads on to a variety of rewards for the staff who have provided exceptional service.

Example: luxury hotel chain

Of course, every industry has its own particular challenges, so context counts above 'best practice'. What might work for Google might not work in a care home. For example, in an industry notorious for high staff turnover, one luxury hotel chain's HR is directly integrated into the sales function, not just to provide training but also to improve working practices and to seal the 'leaky bucket' of turnover. This means that HR has to deeply understand the commercial dynamics. For example, recurring problems in customer service were the result of staff not applying standard operating procedures. HR recognized that this was because recruits were not being properly inducted so this was soon put right and customer service improved significantly.

With respect to recruitment, HR takes a proactive approach and incentivizes all staff to be the same. Staff can undertake 'proactive hours', for instance giving careers talks in schools as part of the recruitment drive. The firm has developed an online presence and sophisticated databases enabling targeted recruitment and a speedy process since in a highly competitive labour market 'the fast eat the slow'. The firm targets customers with tailored special offers, using detailed information about customer preferences from their databases. The firm is now applying these marketing techniques to staff, to be able to better understand, support, develop and retain their own workforce.

252 *HR influencing organizational effectiveness*

Example: Unipart – HR's key role in solving the productivity puzzle

With UK productivity still not recovered from pre-recession levels, nearly every employer would like to know how to increase the output of their staff. According to John Greatrex, group HR director of automotive parts manufacturer and consulting company Unipart, this is an area where HR can really make a difference: 'Of all the different influences HR faces, technology will be important, but as I see it, it's the productivity puzzle, how we produce more with less, that is the critical challenge facing private- and public-sector employers, and UK plc,' he says.

In Unipart, managers use lean tools and techniques to empower people to take ownership of their own work. The more people are empowered to take ownership, the more engaged and effective they are. In lean processes, responsibility and accountability for solving problems is devolved to teams and good practices spread across the organization. Greatrex estimates that techniques such as allowing workers to solve problems at the very lowest level, rather than pushing them on to managers, can improve productivity by as much as 40 per cent in just 12 months.

Although 'lean' techniques are long established in manufacturing (having been popularized by car companies such as Toyota), they are arguably highly relevant to employers in other sectors, too. Unipart's approach has been so successful internally that the company now helps other organizations embed it for themselves, with consulting clients including major financial services companies and NHS trusts. Greatrex adds: 'Take an A&E department as an example. If you empower nurses and porters who are frontline staff to understand processes and how to make improvements, they become a lot more efficient. People understand their own jobs better than anyone else.'

Take ownership and improve

Crucially, too, HR does not lose sight of engagement. Lean processes often get a bad press, according to Greatrex, because they are 'anything but engaging', with all the focus on efficiency improvements at the expense of staff happiness. At Unipart, employees at all levels learn problem-solving skills and other approaches such as process stream mapping so they can review how they work and improve if necessary. By learning how to codify what they do and teach it to new people, in order to 'take ownership and improve', employees in turn feel engaged with their work.

Employee engagement

When it comes to measuring that engagement, Unipart uses traditional employee-engagement surveys, but measures both at the beginning and end of processes so managers can see how behaviours have changed, rather than simply capturing an attitude at a certain point in time. Staff are encouraged to address any gripes that arise through the survey head on; only those they cannot control are dealt with centrally.

At Unipart Rugby, for instance, acting on feedback from the employee-engagement survey, a number of initiatives were put in place at the firm's Rugby site with the aim of engaging employees. They include:

- A 'Swampy Forum' was set up to improve environmental management on site including layout and flow of waste areas, local initiatives to reduce power and reduce waste to landfill.

- A sports and social committee was set up which organized a number of events including 'Gunge the Manager', which was very popular and raised £670 for charity.
- The employee forum set up a question-and-answer process where answers to questions raised are displayed on TV screens in the problem-solving area.
- The look and feel of the rest area was improved with redecoration and new furniture.
- A recognition scheme was introduced where cash rewards were recognition 'cheques' presented to colleagues by anybody across the business to say 'thank you' or 'well done' for behaviour or performance that deserves recognition. The cheques themselves don't have a monetary value, but every quarter they are collated and a small award payable in shopping vouchers is presented to an employee at each site.

The lean HR function

Since Unipart has a diverse range of businesses, an annual turnover of more than £1 billion and employs more than 10,000 staff worldwide, the company's HR model borrows 'a bit of everything'. In order for the lean approach to be effective, HR acts as a role-model function, applying lean HR models aligned to the business to increase engagement and productivity. Greatrex and his team have revolutionized their output and engagement through drawing on 'lean' manufacturing approaches to constantly review and improve its processes and empower staff to solve problems. As John Greatrex says,

> I believe in HR that you have to make sure that the key capabilities in your organisation are also the key capabilities of the function. One of our key principles at Unipart is that no problem is a problem. Instead, when we make mistakes, we say, let's look at this as a source of improvement.
>
> So HR needs to start by looking at the efficiency of its own processes. This involves asking questions such as, how good are we at measuring what's important in what we do? How well do we understand processes and working out ways of improving them? How good are we at cascading strategy right from the top of the organisation?
>
> Thus HR has been transformed into an enabler of engagement and continuous improvement.
>
> (John Greatrex; Jo Faragher on 29 October 2015 and
> Frank Nigriello, Director of Corporate Affairs at Unipart)

Performance management for mutual outcomes

Performance-management systems and processes have been a mainstay of HR systems for decades and the impact of performance-management practices stands out as highly significant in most research studies on high-performance working (Combs et al., 2006). Yet, as we discussed in Chapter 6, in practice, performance management is often seen as a performative and ineffective process that wastes time and can actually reduce employee engagement and performance in the long term if the performance-appraisal discussion seriously deflates people's sense of self-worth. Far from feeling like 'assets', many employees are left feeling like disposable commodities.

Indeed, Keith Grint (1995) stated that 'rarely in the history of business can a system have promised so much and delivered so little'. More recently a raft of articles and reports suggests that performance management is in crisis. A large study conducted by WorldatWork

254   *HR influencing organizational effectiveness*

and Sibson Consulting (2010) found that 58 per cent of organizations considered their performance-management system as disappointing.

So, according to different viewpoints, appraisal systems are either a key driver of high performance or alternatively they are, at best, a waste of time and effort or, at worst, a destructive force with regard to employee engagement and performance. And in today's fast-moving and highly pressurized climate it's easy to understand why something better is needed. HR should be leading on this issue, considering the true impact of the performance-management system, going back to first principles, providing evidence, suggesting options, helping spark new thinking and decision-making with regard to what might work better for all concerned.

Revising performance management

Today many major companies are amending or abandoning their performance-management schemes altogether. A Deloitte Consulting report (Nabaum et al., 2014) found that 70 per cent of respondents were either currently reviewing or had recently reviewed their performance-management systems, mostly to address the problems caused by forced rankings. Microsoft is reported as having abandoned rankings since employees believed these were 'capricious' and resulted in 'power struggles among managers, and unhealthy competition among colleagues' (Ovide and Feintzeig, 2013). Other companies following suit by removing ratings include Juniper Networks, Accenture, Kelly Services and Motorola (Kirton, 2015; Nabaum et al., 2014). Even GE, whose well-known 'Rank and Yank' practice became feared, is stepping away from it.

Rock et al. (2014) challenge readers with the question: What would happen if you simply abandoned performance-management ratings? They argue that the consequences might be much more positive than you think.

Similarly, PwC's 2015 report *Transforming Performance Management* revealed that many employers were having to re-evaluate their performance-management processes in response to technological advances, combined with economic recovery, and requests for more immediate feedback from younger generations. In the 2016 Management Agenda, only a quarter of respondents felt that their manager was effective at giving praise and recognition for work done. The more junior the manager, the more likely they were to feel that their line manager was ineffective at giving praise and recognition. With one third of junior managers feeling that their motivation is low and regarding recognition as a key motivator, saying 'thank you' for work well done would seem to be a 'quick win' for boosting employee morale.

The general direction of travel today is towards creating a continuous feedback culture, rather than relying on once-a-year reviews. These are typically replaced with informal and regular in-depth conversations about performance between the individual and someone senior in their team, drawing on multiple data points and with the individual typically having gathered feedback from other stakeholders first. This is in part to enable more agile responses to changing business conditions and also to change the dynamic of the conversation from the often stressful, low-return models to a more engaging and productive conversation in line with business values and the spirit of fairness. For instance, in the hotel-industry example above, given employee expectations of rapid career progression, appraisals have been replaced by quarterly conversations about development. The firm has set up its own Chef's Academy training school to fill its own talent pipeline.

A CIPD report (Kirton, 2015) identified that many high-technology companies, such as Microsoft, Adobe, Expedia and Google, are leading the shift away from annual appraisals to more frequent, less formal catch-ups. Other examples of firms who have abandoned traditional performance appraisals and moved toward a model of ongoing conversation designed to improve skills and results include Accenture, Gap, PwC and Juniper Networks. Netflix, an American provider of on-demand internet-streaming media, has replaced formal performance reviews by getting managers and employees engaged in conversations about performance as an 'organic part of their work' (McCord, 2014). When Netflix stopped doing formal performance reviews, they instituted instead informal, fairly simple 360-degree reviews. People were asked to identify things that colleagues should stop, start or continue. In the beginning they used an anonymous software system, but over time they shifted to signed feedback, and many teams held their 360s face to face.

Another detectable shift is away from evaluating individual performance to focusing on team performance. In most contexts today, especially firms whose output is creative, business success is not based on individual brilliance alone since people are generally working collaboratively. High-performing teams are characterized more by the communication and knowledge sharing that goes on between them than by individual excellence so the old individualistic performance-management models made famous by Jack Welch and others are not so useful when it comes to encouraging teamwork. In 2013, Microsoft changed its forced ranking from one that rated its top people as individuals to one that assessed teams.

Making the change

In most cases, the answer is not to jettison the performance-management system outright but rather to take a step back and consider what you most importantly want it to do; and then make sure every bit of it helps deliver that. Let's be clear – this is not about HR designing yet another sophisticated competency framework to add to an existing process. It's about going back to fundamentals, taking a broader look at what's needed to stimulate and sustain high performance.

To achieve managerial objectives, a performance-management system should be company-wide, flow from the business plan and be designed to enhance overall performance. To be considered of value, performance management needs to be owned and championed by line management, with senior managers modelling the process. To improve employee job satisfaction and engagement, it should also be about the recognition of good performance and the development of potential, not just control. Promoting and facilitating a 'growth mindset' is essential. This is particularly important when giving feedback, and the language used can have a significant influence.

The underpinning principles for effective performance management could include:

- Effective performance results from a partnership between the job holder and the organization.
- The employee has adequate skills for the job.
- The employee knows his/her role in the process.
- The employee's responsibilities match her/his accountabilities.
- The employee has access to the information needed, at the right time.

So it's worth paying attention to the following areas:

1. A simple performance-management and grading system should provide people with clarity about how to succeed. A conventional PMS tends to be process-driven whereas

256 HR influencing organizational effectiveness

effective performance management is primarily relationship-based. So it's important to get line managers (and employees) involved in redesigning the appraisal process to make it more stimulating, relevant and useful.

2. Strengthen the link between organizational purpose, strategy and people's work. Wherever employees work, they need to know what 'good' looks like and what their part is in delivering the company's vision. Start with the strategic drivers and what you are trying to achieve overall in your business, short-term and longer-term. A broad scorecard of performance can be far more useful than a disparate set of KPIs since it is possible to define clear performance measures that really add value and link specific jobs or tasks to business outcomes.

   At Carphone Warehouse, a leading telecoms retailer and provider, the company has used its Compass scorecard of five sets of criteria to drive a major culture change and higher financial performance. In its retail stores this represents a shift from the short-termist view of achieving quick sales towards driving profit through giving brilliant service. The performance-management process – and bonuses – drives the strategy down into everyone's performance-management goals and rewards. Leading indicators are as important as short-term financial metrics and there is a wide range of tools and guidance available to managers and staff. The strategy has also compelled a rethink of the company's reward strategy as a result of which basic wages in store have been increased and the variable pay element is more team-based and geared to rewarding excellent customer service.

3. Design the PMS to encourage and recognize continuous improvement rather than just to prevent performance failure. Instead of the system encouraging people to work ever-harder, use it to help them work smarter; the emphasis should be on the quality of output rather than input or hours worked.

4. As HR has long known, supervisors need the training, the time and the incentives to have serious conversations with subordinates about performance and growth. Concentrate on improving the quality of the conversation. Encourage managers to stop relying on email and memos and make time to have personal conversations with the people in their group and learn to listen. A strengths-based approach to performance conversations and reviews can bring many benefits since it builds on employee's strengths and energy levels, rather than diminishing and demotivating them.

   Therefore, developing quality leadership and management becomes a priority. KPMG extensively trained more than 300 performance-management leaders across their business to act as the vanguard of a movement to build continuous, ongoing performance feedback and review throughout the organization. As a result, the proportion of staff who feel they have clear goals related to the organization's strategy and who feel their reward is linked to their performance has improved significantly.

5. How well people perform can be as much a function of how they've been treated as what they are capable of. The challenge for managers is to produce the conditions in which people are doing, and believe they are doing 'good work', for which they willingly release their discretionary effort and achieve satisfaction from a job well done. So work with line managers to identify and remove bottlenecks that prevent smooth workflow or create unmanageable workloads. Help managers create a high-performance climate in which people are trusted and expected to do what's needed and have the resources – including information – and the authority they need to be truly empowered. Patty McCord (2014), former chief talent officer at Netflix, argues that if you are careful to hire people who will put the company's interests first, 97 per cent of employees will do the right thing. Trust is the basis of Netflix's willingness to treat people as adults.

6. Employees usually thrive in roles which give them scope to use their initiative and chance to develop, so HR should work with line managers to design jobs that will make best use of the talents of employees and deliver business value and also provide employees with real stretch, growth and job satisfaction.

Revamping performance management at Deloitte

In 2015, professional services firm Deloitte revealed that it would be revamping its own traditional appraisal system in favour of a more continuous coaching and development model of performance management, decoupled from compensation (Buckingham and Goodall, 2015).

In researching its own needs, Deloitte calculated that roughly 2 million work hours were being spent on producing appraisals for their 65,000 staff. They drew on other research, such as that conducted by Mount et al. (1998), that found that assessing someone's skills tends to produce inconsistent data, since variance in ratings can often be accounted for by the peculiarities of perception of individual raters. Actual performance accounted for only 21 per cent of the variance. They also recognized that the defining characteristic of the very best teams at Deloitte is that they are strengths-oriented.

As a consultancy offering service or knowledge work, performance in Deloitte requires an emphasis on customer empathy and the ability to innovate and drive changes through teams. Such capabilities need to be developed in a more fluid and chaotic work environment than in the past, where goals shift, strategies evolve and employees move between multiple projects and managers over short periods of time. Conversations about year-end ratings are therefore generally less valuable than conversations conducted in the moment about actual performance. Deloitte concluded that the conventional performance-management system with its annual appraisals did not meet emerging needs.

A radical redesign

The firm has therefore radically redesigned its performance-management system to be simpler than its predecessor and to be fast, tailored, agile and to encourage constant learning.

They began by articulating three objectives for the new system:

- to recognize performance, particularly through variable compensation;
- to recognize each person's performance clearly (to avoid the idiosyncratic rater effect); and
- to streamline their traditional process of evaluation, project rating, consensus meeting and final rating.

The new system is underpinned by a new way of collecting reliable performance data. Rather than asking more people for their opinion of a team member (in a 360-degree or an upward-feedback survey, for example), they will ask only the immediate team leader about their own future actions with respect to that person at the end of every project (or once every quarter for long-term projects), for instance 'I would always want him or her on my team'. The aggregated data over a year, weighted according to the duration of a given project, provides a rich stream of information for leaders' discussions of what they, in turn, will do – for instance, succession planning, development paths or performance-pattern analysis. Once a quarter the organization's leaders can use the new data to review a targeted subset of employees (those eligible for promotion, for example, or those with critical skills) and can debate what actions Deloitte might take to better develop that particular group.

258   *HR influencing organizational effectiveness*

When it comes to compensation, Deloitte want to factor in some uncountable things, such as the difficulty of project assignments in a given year and contributions to the organization other than formal projects. So the data are intended as the starting point for compensation, not the end point. The final determination, which will be called a 'performance snapshot', will be reached either by a leader who knows each individual personally or by a group of leaders looking at an entire segment of Deloitte's practice and at many data points in parallel.

The third objective is to fuel performance. Team leaders conduct regular weekly check-ins with each team member about near-term work which allow leaders to set expectations for the upcoming week, review priorities, comment on recent work and provide course correction, coaching or important new information. The conversations provide clarity about what is expected of each team member and why, what great work looks like, and how each person can do his or her best work in the upcoming days – in other words, reflecting the combination of purpose, expectations and strengths that characterizes the firm's best teams. Deloitte have so far found a direct and measurable correlation between the frequency of these conversations and the engagement of team members. They have learned that the best way to ensure frequency is to have check-ins initiated by the team member – who more often than not is eager for the guidance and attention they provide – rather than by the team leader. A strengths-based self-assessment tool will help team members to explore and present those strengths to their teammates, their team leader and the rest of the organization.

These three interlocking rituals to support them – the annual compensation decision, the quarterly or per-project performance snapshot and the weekly check-in – are in line with the three objectives at the root of their performance management – to recognize, see and fuel performance.

Case example: performance management at Buckinghamshire County Council

From a very different sector, another organization that has transformed its performance, reward and talent-management system is Buckinghamshire County Council (CC). Local government in the UK has been undergoing considerable change as central-government funding is progressively reduced. In common with all local authorities throughout the UK in recent years, Buckinghamshire CC was facing increasing demand for its services in a context of massively shrinking budgets.

Unlike many other councils, which have sought to achieve savings by shedding large numbers of staff, Buckinghamshire CC sought instead to improve productivity in partnership with its employees, and to effect a culture change which would produce more sustainable benefits to all stakeholders. Increasing productivity from a shrinking workforce and achieving cost savings and efficiencies would be no mean feat. In general terms productivity can be calculated by dividing the cost of output by the cost of input (i.e. total headcount). In Buckinghamshire CC, if a 1 per cent productivity improvement could be achieved, this would equate to 3 million pounds of savings.

The HR department took two main routes to achieve this. The first involved redesigning the HR service itself, achieving savings of £4.2 million by increasing self-service options, providing access to more services online, automating some services and outsourcing others to less expensive providers.

The second main initiative was to create a strong performance culture across the reduced workforce through the introduction of an automated performance and talent-management framework known as 'Delivering Successful Performance'. Essentially this is a more commercial approach to performance management, reward and talent management that links an individual employee's contribution to their pay.

The approach taken was devised and led by Gillian Quinton, Director of Resources and Business Transformation. The project had multiple aims – for instance to give managers the ability to drive performance improvement and to manage poor performance more effectively. The intention was also to give employees clarity about performance expectations, recognition for their contribution and the possibility of additional reward once at the top of the pay range. As a result, it was hoped that the organization would benefit from productivity improvements and some flexibility around the management of the pay bill and employees would feel fairly treated.

The first step of redesign was to carry out research into the nature of productivity and how this could be improved. This highlighted some elements common to many research studies into the links between employee engagement and performance such as:

- Knowing how what I do links to the overall goals of the organization.
- Having clear objectives.
- Strong values and behaviours that colleagues are expected to demonstrate.
- High levels of employee engagement.
- Good leadership and management.
- Strong performance management.
- Recognizing and rewarding high performance.

The new automated performance-management framework, closely linked to the council's business strategy, was introduced in April 2012. This system replaced cumbersome paper-based appraisals and an inflexible approach to reward, with a more commercial and integrated approach to performance management, reward and talent management that now links an individual employee's contribution to their pay. The framework clarifies the links between personal performance, organizational objectives and pay progression. Metrics allow high performers to be identified, retained and offered access to mentoring and cross-organization projects.

Objective setting has been considerably improved under the new system and there is a stronger emphasis than before on measurable objectives deriving directly from key business-strategy objectives. Every employee has objectives in each of the balanced scorecard quadrants shown in Figure 13.1. Alongside this, a new Values Framework, with positive and negative

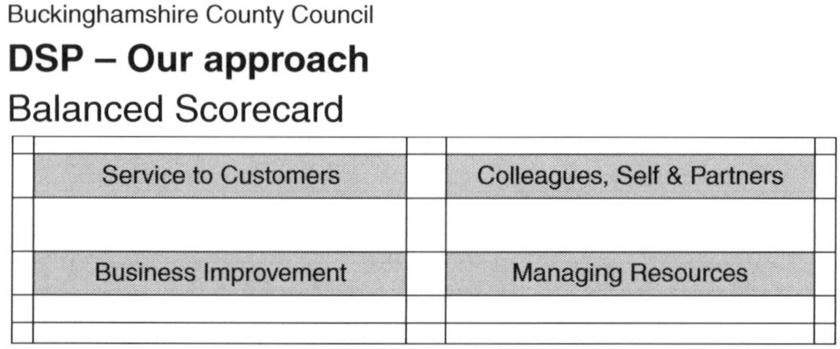

Buckinghamshire County Council

DSP – Our approach

Balanced Scorecard

Service to Customers		Colleagues, Self & Partners	
Business Improvement		Managing Resources	

Figure 13.1 Values and behaviours framework

260 HR influencing organizational effectiveness

indicators, segmented to reflect different hierarchical levels, highlights the behaviours expected of all employees:

- Committed to making a difference:
  - We will do our best for people even when we are making difficult decisions.
  - We will deliver what we promise.
  - We will take pride in working with our communities.
  - We will make public money go as far as possible.
- Working together to find solutions:
  - We will support each other to do our jobs well.
  - We will work as one council and with our partners.
  - We will celebrate our success and good news.
  - We will learn from our and others' experiences.
- Change starts with me:
  - We will take responsibility for our work.
  - We will be open to change and other people's ideas.
  - We will look for ways to improve how we do things.
  - We will act with honesty and treat others with respect.

Performance is reviewed every six months not only on *what* has been achieved but also, equally important, *how* (behaviours). Performance (results and behaviours) are assessed as follows:

- inspirational;
- exceeding;
- successful;
- needs development;
- unsatisfactory.

Objectives are weighted so that only by succeeding at both task and behaviours can employees' performance be rated as 'exceeding' or 'inspirational'.

Initially the new system received a somewhat sceptical response from many employees: some did not believe that performance in the public sector could be measured; others had concerns about consistency and fairness. Consequently, a thorough, tiered quality-check process was implemented, starting with a 'grandparent' check, i.e. managers of line managers assessing their assessments; the top team assess mid-year and end-of-year ratings for consistency, right up to elected cabinet members assessing top team assessments for consistency. And while many staff welcomed the new approach, seeing it as a big improvement on what had gone before, criticisms remained, such as why there was no direct link with pay.

Gillian Quinton wanted first to be sure that the new performance-management process had started to work before linking performance with pay – an even more contentious issue, especially in the public sector. The old reward system was one of incremental progression (pay date in April) up a five-point pay scale until people reached the top of the scale. Incremental progression was equivalent to 2 per cent, plus an annual additional uplift on top.

The new system is linked to people's performance assessments and is based on contribution. It has an entry point, a central reference point and an advanced reference point, together with the opportunity for a non-consolidated bonus on top. Overall the pay bands are 1 per cent higher than the old pay bands. The pay date has moved to July from April. The pay for the job is based on market rates and progression involves moving to the competence reference point at which you are likely to stay, unless you consistently achieve exceeding or outstanding ratings.

The online nature of the system provides real-time evidence of when employees are not performing. Those who fail to improve either 'flat-line' in terms of pay progression or leave.

The offer to employees

The new scheme was made voluntary due to trade-union resistance. However, after extensive consultation involving focus groups and face-to-face workshops led by the directors, 92 per cent of staff signed up to the new reward system. Each person doing so received a one-off payment of £750 (in recognition of moving the pay date and transferring to the variable scheme). The new scheme initially received a mixed reaction, with some people arguing that consistency would not be possible to achieve and that it must be unfair since it is difficult to differentiate between 'Exceeding' and 'Inspirational' performance. However, the quality-check process has to a large extent allayed such concerns.

Costs and benefits

Costs to the employer, including software and one-off payments to employees, amounted to 2 per cent of the total pay bill. In addition, 580 managers were trained in setting objectives and giving effective feedback on performance. However, these costs are likely to be significantly outweighed by the various benefits.

Thanks to the new system, the whole organizational culture is becoming more performance-focused. People are very focused on their objectives and the behavioural changes are tangible. There is much greater emphasis than before on innovative thinking – with people becoming risk aware rather than risk averse. After 18 months of operation, 98 per cent of employees have performance objectives and 100 per cent of these are linked to corporate objectives. Flexibility is built in: objectives are changeable as the organization evolves and corporate objectives can be set for specific groups of staff. Rather than being 'judged' solely by managers, employees themselves are now responsible for providing portfolios of evidence for their twice-yearly appraisals. For their part, many managers have developed greater competency with respect to people management and it has become much easier to identify high – and low – performance.

Talent data on the whole workforce can be broken down in any way to provide greater insight – such as the location of high-performing employees, etc. There are now clearer career pathways across the organization through the job-family approach, together with integrated succession planning and talent programmes. Talent-development programmes are now linked to job levels.

Above all, the original objectives – to achieve cost savings and improve efficiency – are on course to be delivered thanks to low turnover and sickness-absence levels, and the introduction of this completely paperless performance and talent-management system. Furthermore, the two performance meetings per annum have resulted in efficiency savings of £1.4 million in the first year of operation. Since the new system is online, it is not only cheaper to administer than before, but it also allows for greater transparency. The rationalization of more than 1,000 job descriptions across the county's 3,800 non-school workforce into ten job families and generic role profiles brought £50,000 of savings in job-evaluation costs. Thanks to the new system and the culture it has engendered, Buckinghamshire CC is on target to achieve a 1 per cent increase in productivity per annum, saving £3 million in the process.

Of course implementing such a scheme can be challenging and requires considerable persistence. Gillian Quinton's advice to fellow practitioners is as follows:

- Make sure that you have a robust performance system in place before linking pay to contribution. We implemented the online performance system a year in advance of the

262 *HR influencing organizational effectiveness*

link to pay to ensure that managers were applying the scheme consistently and that we could train people to have those difficult conversations that can sometimes be needed to give realistic ratings.

- Set an expectation across the whole organisation about where the performance benchmark sits. We said that we expected around 80 per cent of our workforce to be rated as 'successful'. We were clear that 'successful' was a reflection of an employee meeting their targets and doing a good job. Anything above this would have to be supported by evidence and would need to be outstanding or exceptional. The tendency, we found, was that managers wanted to mark people up so we have had to be clear from the outset where the standard benchmark sat.
- Take good legal advice along the way. You need to test out the employee relations implications and be certain that you don't offer what can be seen as an incentive to encourage people to move away from collective bargaining processes if the trade unions don't support your direction of travel. We were clear that financial payments made were in compensation for making changes that could affect employees and not a financial inducement
- Make sure that this is visibly led from the top. One of the interventions that worked really well for us were the numerous face to face presentations the Directors' Team made to all staff across the organisation.

Questions for you

- How would you manage information coming out of the system so that it could link to talent processes?
- What other ways can you think of for ensuring fairness and consistency? How could you make the quality-check process more robust? How could you ensure employee voice was heard?

Reward

Reward systems symbolically and literally tell employees what the firm values and are an important element in ensuring that workforce efforts are aligned with the needs of the organization. Intel, for example, has incorporated its corporate responsibility goals into its compensation system (Barrett and Niekerk, 2013).

Ensuring fair pay is also an important element of quality of work life and puts the principle of equity to the test. As Lawler (2003) points out, perceived fairness of the distribution of 'rewards' such as opportunities to learn, develop and contribute, and of outcomes such as pay and promotions within the firm, including benefits such as flexible working options that enable employee wellbeing, are manifestations of the company's orientation to social justice. These are indicators to employees of the integrity of the firm's claims to care about fairness and how people are treated; how can reward and recognition systems become fair and reinforce varied contributions? How can benefits foster personal growth, security and work–life balance?

In recent years there has been a good deal of experimentation around pay systems, with many variations of apparently employee-centric 'total-rewards' systems having been adopted. Flexible working in particular is thought to be a key enabler of work–life balance. Sadly, increasingly total-rewards systems are being perceived as a means for the organization to save on its benefits bill rather than providing a meaningful and flexible offer to employees.

Shared capitalism

A growing number of firms are now offering share ownership to their employees, often referred to as 'shared capitalism', as part of their overall reward package. In today's firms, most of the added value comes from innovations, specialized products and services. Such activities often demand investments in human capital, which make workers involved in the risk of a firm. Proponents of the stakeholder approach argue that it is therefore not only shareholders who should be entitled to a firm's residual (Freeman, 1984; Blair, 1995; Turnbull, 1997; Blair and Roe, 1999; Tirole, 2006; Vinten, 2001). According to these authors, offering shares, or stock, to employees is important (and only fair) in a situation when workers engage in firm-specific investments in human capital, for example, in technology-intensive production.

There is a common belief that employee-ownership schemes strengthen employees' motivation and commitment and ultimately boost productivity. The John Lewis partnership in the UK and Netflix in the US are well-known examples of such schemes. Thus a common research topic has been the effect of shared capitalism on employee outcomes, such as standard employee attitudes in organizational psychology (e.g. job satisfaction, organizational commitment, turnover intention, motivation and company loyalty). Such schemes tend to create a sense of ownership among employees if they provide significant stock contributions and continually reinforce employee-ownership status through managerial recognition and greater employee participation in firm decision making (Rosen and Rodgers, 2007).

However, employee-share ownership (ESO) schemes are not without their difficulties or detractors. One criticism is that it promotes free-riding in the workplace and that it creates too much financial risk for employees. Instead, a set of studies by Freeman, Blasi and Kruse (2010) found that workers who received shared capitalism are more likely to engage in co-monitoring of employees, which potentially mitigates against free-riding. They also found that most employees in companies with shared capitalism have not taken on undue financial risk by excessively investing in company stock, and that shared capitalism can provide a financial asset that is part of a diversification strategy of the type advised by portfolio theory in economics, as long as the level of stock funded by worker savings is kept within reasonable parameters.

In addition, the literature also suggests that, for shared capitalism to produce its positive effects, it needs to be offered as an additional reward on top of existing wages and other benefits rather than as a replacement. An alternative example is that of Netflix.

Box 13.1 A balanced approach

A few years ago, in addition to market-based pay rates, Netflix used equity compensation differently from the way most companies do. They let employees choose how much (if any) of their compensation would be in the form of equity. If employees wanted stock options, Netflix reduced their salaries accordingly. Management believed in treating people like adults who were sophisticated enough to understand the trade-offs, judge their personal tolerance for risk and decide what was best for them and their families. Options were distributed every month, at a slight discount from the market price, and unlike most tech companies that have a four-year vesting schedule and try to use options as 'golden handcuffs' to aid retention, Netflix options could be cashed in immediately as management did not want to hold workers hostage who may want to leave to work elsewhere (McCord, 2014).

264   HR influencing organizational effectiveness

Effects on performance

Another common research theme has been the effects of shared capitalism on corporate performance. While a number of studies have found evidence of a positive effect of ESO schemes on performance, there is still a lack of evidence about the mechanisms driving performance gains, and most of this attention has focused on ESO plans.

Rather than being introduced to improve labour productivity through participation, many ESO schemes are introduced with the aim of restructuring employee wages or to facilitate the privatization of state-owned enterprises (Blasi et al., 2003; Lowitzsch et al., 2008). For instance, financial participation of employees in the form of share ownership and profit sharing has been particularly prominent in Ireland in the transformation of the public sector over the past 20 years. Such ESO schemes involve little change in firm governance or management, nor do they offer substantial financial returns, and therefore fail to establish a greater sense of ownership among employees (McCarthy and Palcic, 2012).

McCarthy and Palcic (2012) describe an example of substantial employee ownership at Eircom, Ireland's former national communications company. They outline the complex history of Eircom from its rapid commercialization in the 1980s; part then full privatization from 1996 to 1999; the rise, fall and subsequent rise in its debt; reflotation and further highly leveraged buyouts; and the headcount reduction in the workforce. Alongside this, the authors track the rise of the ESO programme (ESOP), which started in 1998 with 14.9 per cent of shareholding and rose to 35 per cent by influencing and benefiting from the various buyouts. For individuals with a full share allocation, the ESOP paid out over €80,000 between 2002 and 2010.

Yet despite the substantial payouts, the ESOP's impact on employee productivity was mixed. In their analysis, the authors first consider the rise in Eircom's productivity from eight years before to eight years after the ESOP was introduced. They conclude that there are too many potentially intervening factors to attribute the rise in productivity directly to the ESOP. Moreover, they were unable to establish that the ESOP achieved its official aim: 'to incentivise and motivate employees through giving them a shareholding in their company, leading to improved productivity'.

Similarly, if ESOs are forced on to individuals, their potential motivating effect may backfire. The UK Conservative government attempted in 2012 to introduce a major deregulation of the labour market through the back door by proposing to fast-track legislation that would enable companies to force many workers to accept shares in their employer's company worth between £2,000 and £50,000, with the incentive that any gains in those shares would be exempt from capital gains tax, in return for giving up a host of employment rights – over redundancy, requests for flexible working, access to unfair dismissal tribunals and time off for training. The main driver for this is to get rid of employee rights that are suspected to be stifling economic growth. While the proposed 'employee-owner' status would be optional for existing employees, existing companies and new startups would offer only this type of contract for new hires, making it a compulsory condition of employment for new recruits.

In contrast, Carberry (2011) points out that employee ownership works best when combined with increased decision-making opportunities for employees and other HR practices associated with the high-performance work systems model (Appelbaum et al., 2000). Similarly, Freeman et al. (2010: 23) observe that 'shared capitalism works best when it combines monetary incentives with employee decision-making and personnel and labor policies that empower and encourage employees'. The idea is to create cultures of ownership by combining participation by employees in decision-making, extensive information sharing about the business and in-depth training and education about ownership and financial literacy (Rosen et al., 2005). In short, shared capitalism appears to work well only when it is used as a way to promote workplaces that distribute power and authority more broadly.

Some critics argue that ESO may create unrealistic expectations among employees in terms of their influence over firm decision-making and their legal rights. Failure to meet such expectations can result in reduced employee sense of ownership and thus lead to reduced work effort and motivation. Therefore, to facilitate improved employee understanding, ESO should be accompanied by training on how firms work and extensive sharing of financial information sharing with employees and effective employee participation in firm decision-making (Ben-Ner and Jones, 1995; Pendleton et al., 1998).

Nevertheless, systems of participative-management and ownership cultures seem to unlock the potential of shared capitalism, when implemented under certain conditions, to have positive effects on psychological and economic outcomes of employees at all occupational and organizational levels, as well as positive effects on firm performance, growth and long-term stability. However, these gains are much more likely to occur when shared capitalism is implemented as a way to fundamentally enhance an existing culture, or as a way to transform more traditional top-down cultures and authority structures along the lines of shared commitment, sacrifice, information and rewards. What is not clear from research is whether the performance gains emerge from the ways in which decentralized decision-making structures capitalize on the knowledge and experience of all employees. Could ESO be a vital tool in the creation of a cohesive collectivist culture united by a shared purpose? HR needs to have a view and be prepared to articulate it.

Conclusion

So as HR professionals adapt their HR practices, including performance-management and reward systems, to today's context and their organizations' needs, it is right to focus effort on improving the things that matter in the short term. However, it's important to avoid the temptation of simply going for the quick win by tightening up the performance-management system to get 'more for less' out of the workforce, metaphorically squeezing the lemon until the pips squeak.

Really successful performance management is about achieving a better balance of employer and employee needs over time – and is more about building trust, performance and capacity to drive the organization forward in the years to come. By understanding and responding to the business drivers, recognizing the vital motivational effects of these processes and developing innovative and tailored solutions, HR can make a valuable contribution to their organization's effectiveness. There are now enough examples emerging of firms making the high-engagement/high-performance connection to demonstrate that the real task for HR is to ensure people are treated fairly and to equip line managers with the tools and ambition to develop talent and build sustainable high performance through employee engagement. A positive goal that's really worth going for!

14 Building a healthy, ethical and changeable organization

> It is a commonplace executive observation that businesses exist to make money, and the observation is usually allowed to go unchallenged. It is, however, a very limited statement about the purposes of business.
>
> Daniel Katz and Robert L. Kahn in *The Social Psychology of Organizations* (1966)

In this chapter we shall consider how to build an organization's capability for ongoing change. After all, the business world is in a state of constant flux (with some sectors moving at a faster rate than others), in what is still described as a VUCA environment (volatile, uncertain, complex, ambiguous). Writing in the *Harvard Business Review*, Kotter (2012) states that 'perhaps the greatest challenge business leaders face today is how to stay competitive amid constant turbulence and disruption'. As national economies slowly get back into growth mode, business leaders in every sector are facing common challenges, not least improving performance and productivity, and also bringing about change. Not surprisingly, when asked to use one word to describe their organizations' climate, Management Agenda 2016 respondents use words such as 'changing', 'uncertain' and 'challenging'. They see navigating change in this environment as their most salient challenge

Yet, as many as 70 per cent of change efforts are deemed failures. More often than not, change programmes driven top-down fail to engage properly with the front-line staff who are essential for the delivery of high-quality products and/or high levels of customer service. Mergers and acquisitions, in particular, are notorious for their high failure rates – largely because of the way the people aspects of merger integration are handled. Moreover, conventional top-down 'more-for-less' approaches to change management, with their linear change models offering 'ten steps', 'eight lessons' and Gantt charts, prove too slow and cumbersome to be effective in a VUCA environment.

Some businesses choose to do nothing and hope for the change to dissipate and for former market conditions to re-emerge. In a context where speed and agility are crucial, this 'crisis of adaptation' reaction often results in failure to recognize and capitalize on opportunities, such as Kodak's denial of digital trends and Blackberry's market-share erosion to smartphones, to name but a few. Today many firms are failing to exploit the potential of digital in their operations (Management Agenda 2016). This then results in business casualties in terms of bankruptcy, market-share erosion, wasted investments and shareholder dissatisfaction. As is often said, the greatest danger in times of turbulence is not the turbulence. It is acting with yesterday's logic.

So if doing nothing is not an option, and if sustainable success is the aim, we should instead be looking to build an adaptable, healthy, ethical and resilient organizational culture in which change is the norm. With organizational agility in mind, advantage goes to firms that can adapt better and faster than others on a continuous basis and sustain their performance. Building their organization's changeability is fundamentally a leadership and management challenge that requires a different view of change. In conventional, episodic change, the aim is to return to stability as soon as possible. In continuous change, change itself is seen as effective; stability is useful only up to a point.

We shall cover:

- The challenges of culture change.
- Developing a healthy and ethical, changeable culture.
- New organizational development.
- The nature of leadership required for continuous change.
- HR and the ethical agenda.
- Diversity and CSR.
- A learning culture as key to changeability.

The challenges of culture change

A 2016 survey, co-sponsored by Crawford International, pointed to the impact of an adaptive culture on financial growth. They found that investing in strengthening leadership and culture to improve adaptability can have a significant impact on long-term financial performance of a company (www.crawfordinternational.com/research). Various surveys suggest that leaders generally recognize the need for a culture change to improve practices, boost employee engagement and therefore productivity, yet very few feel equipped to drive culture change. Indeed, leaders recognize managing change as their central leadership challenge (Management Agenda 2016).

Culture change is not easy, yet it can be essential and mean the difference between business success and failure. Corporate crises such as the debacle of the Jimmy Saville scandal for the BBC highlight some of the risks of getting leadership, culture and behaviours wrong. Similarly, the financial crisis has highlighted the way in which company norms and practices became a negative force in several financial-services institutions. In an article entitled 'What price principles?' in the CIPD's *Work* magazine, the Volkswagen scandal is described as one of the most systemic and damaging examples of a business focusing on financial return while deceiving its other stakeholders. Once more business ethics come to the fore, demonstrating that people and their behaviours are the biggest drivers of both value and risk in organizations.

Some of the main reasons why change is so difficult are reported in the 2016 Management Agenda. Central to navigating the complexity of change is the ability to learn, to ask questions and sense-make. Culture change often begins as the result of a shared and open inquiry into how best to understand and respond to changing conditions. HR managers commonly report their organization failing to review and learn as change progresses. They view their leadership population as lacking the ability to foster a learning culture, or to create an environment in which there is an openness to different views and a spirit of enquiry.

Similarly, for successful culture change to occur, HR managers highlight the importance of leaders being able to steer through uncertainty and manage change, adapt effectively to new organizational structures (i.e. matrix working) and lead rather than manage. However, over half of HR managers believe their leaders fail to establish a clear purpose and direction to engage and motivate the workforce. What emerges, then, is a picture of change that is driven top-down, rather than collaborative.

Above all, when the success of the business depends on the motivation of the workforce, involving employees in the process of change is paramount. When employees are engaged in change, they can observe the influence of their contributions, so everyone is invested in its success. Conversely, when change is imposed and employees feel unable to influence change within the organization, this may lead to a lessening of both engagement and accountability within the workforce. Most managers recognize that their own staff are best suited to solving the issues facing the business, yet leaders are clearly struggling to harness the skills and

268 *HR influencing organizational effectiveness*

know-how of their workforce. The picture presented in Roffey Park's 2016 Management Agenda (Lucy et al., 2016) is one of hard-pressed leaders doing their best to manage constant change. There is clearly a need to better manage complex change and to engage with employees in a way that helps them achieve their full potential.

Developing a healthy, ethical and changeable culture

So if managing change can be difficult enough, perhaps the greater challenge is thinking through how to manage change as 'business as usual' – to create a more sustainably flexible, innovative and resilient way of operating that can help organizations thrive in a constantly changing environment. This again puts organizational culture centre-stage. Growing and adapting to the changing marketplace requires firms to pursue significant behavioural shifts from time to time. HR practitioners (including learning and development and OD practitioners) are key players when it comes to corporate culture, team building and change management processes. In any deliberate attempt to create significant behavioural change, an appropriate strategy is needed that must be owned and driven from the top, or it is unlikely to be taken seriously.

The 'what' – changeability

But what kind of culture might provide this more changeable foundation? I would argue that a changeable culture is one which develops and grows its capabilities to serve all its stakeholders, rather than simply shareholders. This means that successful cultures will be those in which diversity flourishes, where people focus on their external constituencies and work effectively beyond their organizational or disciplinary boundaries, where there is participation, collaboration, innovation and shared learning, and where people believe they are treated fairly In such cultures there is a determined focus on building dynamic organizational capabilities.

Dynamic capabilities

Dynamic capabilities have been described as the firm's capabilities to change (e.g. Zahra et al., 2006) and as 'the firm's ability to integrate, build and reconfigure internal and external competencies to address rapidly changing environments' (Teece et al., 1997). Teece adds that dynamic capabilities are deployed by 'entrepreneurial management' to enable organizations to 'sense' and 'seize' opportunities/threats and to 'transform' accordingly (Teece, 2007).

Dynamic-capabilities theory was originally proposed as an extension to the resource-based view, where each organization develops 'firm-specific capabilities' (Teece and Pisano, 1994). Yet dynamic-capabilities theory addresses two aspects beyond the traditional scope of resource-based view theory:

1. The 'shifting environment' faced by the firm; collecting available information, filtering it, building a paradigm of industry/market evolution.
2. The 'key role of strategic management in appropriately adapting, integrating and reconfiguring internal and external organizational skills, resources and functional competences toward a changing environment' (Teece and Pisano, 1994). This involves a proactive (not simply adaptive) role for management and *internally* seizing opportunities by achieving new combinations, reorganizing if necessary.

By building on these ideas, dynamic-capabilities theory responds to one of the main critiques of the resource-based view – namely that it is static and does not explain the organizational capabilities of flexibility, innovation and responsiveness which are so critical to dynamic marketplaces. In the absence of dynamic capabilities, the resource-based view's 'path-dependent strategic logic of leverage…lacks a logic of change that is crucial in dynamic markets' (Eisenhardt and Martin, 2000: 1118).

This logic of change is vital for firms in sectors which face 'rapidly changing environments' (Teece et al., 1997) such as technology, e-commerce, etc. In these and other 'high-velocity' industries, market boundaries are blurred, successful business models are unclear and market players (i.e. buyers, suppliers, competitors, complementers) are ambiguous and shifting (Eisenhardt and Martin, 2000).

Teece develops the concept of the 'ecosystem' to describe 'the community of organizations, institutions, and individuals that impact the enterprise and the enterprise's customers and suppliers' (Teece, 2007). Helfat et al. (2007) perceive the issue of external relations so critical that they refine their definition of dynamic capabilities to embrace 'alliance partners' (Helfat et al., 2007: 66). They assert that organizations must be open to the wider investigation and coordination of possibilities in their extended networks 'outside the boundaries of the firm' (Helfat et al., 2007). The role of leadership in this more complex landscape lies not so much in management, but in the effective 'orchestration' of assets inside and beyond traditional firm boundaries (Helfat et al., 2007). Managers must leverage both 'internal and external competencies' (Teece et al., 1997) in a strategy which transcends 'the question of optimal firm boundaries' (Helfat et al., 2007). This chimes with the logic of 'open innovation' proposed by Chesbrough (e.g. 2006).

Teece's notion of the ecosystem encourages us to explore the significance of collaborative relationships with stakeholders situated beyond the traditional boundaries of the firm. One example of such collaboration is in the development of 'co-specialised assets' (e.g. Teece, 2007). For instance, credit cards are not much use to cardholders without merchants that will accept them, and vice versa. Thus dynamic capabilities can be used to '*create market change*' (Eisenhardt and Martin, 2000) and 'help shape [the firms'] environments' (Augier and Teece, 2009).

A broader form of collaboration is depicted by Astley (2015). He coins the phrase 'orchestrated stakeholder dialogue', through which firms exploit the expertise of internal and external stakeholders, including their customers, in order to build innovative solutions or business models. Examples include an IT firm which adopts a 'consortium' model comprising representatives from many different clients, who collaborate, thereby enabling it to invest more on building one higher-quality core solution, with clients paying less and further benefits and cost savings in terms of upgrades and ongoing support. Another example of orchestrated stakeholder dialogue is the integration of a customer chat lounge (called an 'experience tab') at the heart of an online fashion retailer. Dialogue amongst users of the tab flags to management those products and styles which are in vogue. It informs decisions about stock requirements and signals future trends. The dialogue is also a vital sales tool because, in the words of the person involved 'when other people talked about it… that's where we score our sales from. We don't do [sales]. Others do it for us' (Astley, 2015). Developing and deploying dynamic capabilities may require a collective shift in thinking, behaviour and business practice.

The 'how'

How can organizational effectiveness play into this?

According to Richard et al. (2009), organizational effectiveness captures organizational performance plus the myriad internal performance outcomes normally associated with more efficient or effective operations and other external measures that relate to considerations that are broader than those simply associated with economic valuation (either by shareholders, managers or customers), such as corporate social responsibility. These authors argue that organizational effectiveness practitioners can influence organizational effectiveness by focusing on the following:

- Decision-making – how real people make decisions; enabling them to make good decisions real time; helping them improve the quality of their decisions by exposing them to adjacent disciplines; replicating relevant experiments, creating new ones and implementing their results to make organizations effective.
- Change and learning – how real people learn, change, adapt and align, get 'affected' by dynamics in the environment and leveraging this knowledge to create effective organizations that are pioneers of change and learning.
- Group effectiveness – how real people work well together, especially in bringing new ideas and innovation; the impact of digitization and virtualization on people-to-people protocols.
- Self-organizing and adaptive systems – how self-organizing systems and highly networked systems work; learning from them and the tangible ways by which they can be put together to help make organizations more effective.

This is where an organization development approach can help. Organizations are essentially the sum of their parts – people, the way they work, how they are organized, how they behave. OD focuses on human dynamics, on how people and organizations function, and on how to help them function better within a clear value framework. It is 'a process (and its associated technology) directed at organisational improvement' (Margulies, 1978). Organization design and change management are OD subdisciplines.

OD is concerned with stimulating organizational renewal by building organizational capabilities required for current and future success. Foremost among these is the ability to learn, in order to become 'changeable', i.e. agile and capable of ongoing change while also improving performance (Holbeche, 2005, 2015). Building these capabilities requires forward-looking management teams, swift and competent decision-making processes, a happy blend of innovation and risk management and, above all, flexible, resilient and engaged employees. It is about getting the organization's total system to work coherently, to improve organizational effectiveness, health and performance.

Just how best to develop organizations is a rich source of debate within OD practice, which is derived from many fields (and stereotypically divided between humanists and systems thinkers). Some of these differences are also evident in the development of 'new' OD approaches and in the language of change (Cheung-Judge and Holbeche, 2015).

'New' OD

More recent approaches to OD embrace complexity and social-construction theories and more organic metaphors for change. Complexity theory suggests that organizations are complex adaptive systems that are changing all the time anyway. Similarly, social-construction theory argues that all knowledge, including the most basic everyday common sense, is derived from, and maintained by, social interaction (Berger and Luckmann, 1966). The well-known OD dictum, 'I own what I help create' highlights the importance of involving and engaging employees in decisions that affect them.

Thus, 'new' OD sees change as continuous and potentially self-organizing. Meaningful change involves creating new mindsets or social agreements, sometimes through explicit or implicit negotiations (Marshak and Grant, 2008: S9).

Stakeholder dialogue

So while change occurs naturally through conversation, such conversations can be provoked. Astley's (2015) concept of orchestrated stakeholder dialogue describes how organizational strategy is delivered through the meticulous orchestration of dialogue between 'stakeholders' that may occur inside or outside the organization's traditional boundaries. Managers are not always directly involved in the dialogue, but they orchestrate it to achieve strategic goals. Dialogue is sometimes face to face (for example in the form of conversations between change agents and those employees who are change targets) and sometimes virtual (for example where product insight is gathered via feedback from the customer-services function or from the industry press). There can also be a symbolic dimension, for example in the choice of a certain member of staff to 'champion' a change initiative or in the espousal of a particular organizational culture embodying fairness or trust, which influences the behaviours of certain stakeholders.

Indeed, the development and assurance of trust between stakeholders operating within such interorganizational networks is absolutely central to the development of organizational agility through dynamic competencies. The benefits of trust for organizations include:

- People feel able to rely upon each other and there is a culture of cooperation.
- People feel able to be open and honest with other employees at all levels.
- The top team operates more effectively by relying on their staff to deliver.
- People experience greater belief in communications from managers and leaders.
- Increased likelihood that people will buy into the organization's mission and values.
- Things get achieved more quickly – and more effectively.

Astley (2015) found that the 'clear framework' of a culture of fairness, reciprocity or trust facilitates the kind of dialogue, i.e. stimulation of insight, nuanced dialogue and stakeholder integration, that is necessary to achieve agility. These correspond to the three classes of dynamic capability defined by Teece (2007), namely 'sensing', 'seizing' and 'reconfiguration', and therefore constitute an underlying component of all dynamic capabilities.

Collective sense-making

Another challenge is collective sense-making. Of course today's work world is awash with data, much of it superfluous, which overwhelms many people, causing confusion, making it hard to see the 'wood' for the 'trees'. Bringing clarity through meaningful metrics – dashboards and analytics, applying statistical models and using predictive intelligence-based decision support can help transform background 'noise' into useful information through which people can gain insight and ultimately knowledge and wisdom.

Formal communication programmes used to convey the corporate direction, objectives, innovation and performance can also convey what the organization stands for and values. To bring messages to life, it can be useful to frame business events in story-telling to illustrate, for instance, a reversal, turning point or 'Aha!' moment to help people deduce root causes and simple rules that they and others can adopt. Of course the reputation and perceived

272   *HR influencing organizational effectiveness*

trustworthiness of the messenger – as someone who knows what they are talking about and can be trusted – plays a big part in getting lessons accepted. To aid diffusion further, make videos, train people in story-telling.

To bring the values message to the workforce – in ways that are attuned to the communication channels of the employee, which are changing rapidly in this age of web 2.0 – intranets, websites, blogs, wikis, social networking sites, podcasting, videos, forums, town hall meetings, regular team briefings, webcasts, voicemails, print and electronic newsletters and other forms of social media need to be deployed. Through social media people can create serendipitous connections and have informal conversations rather than wait for the systematic communication cascade to reach them.

The nature of leadership required for continuous change

How to apply adaptive system thinking in practice? Marshak (2002) calls for new words such as 'morphing' to better express continuous whole-system change. The key principles of 'morphing' include:

- creating limited organizational structures and principles, such that there is both enough form and fluidity for rapid, organized action;
- creating resource flexibility in terms of both availability and application;
- ensuring organizational learning to quickly develop and deploy new competencies;
- bridging from the present to the future, with clear transition processes, while avoiding focusing on the future to the detriment of the present; and
- having top management mindsets that fully embrace the concepts of continuous change and flexible organizational forms, i.e. managers with 'morphing mindsets' (Marshak, 2002: 283).

This has implications for the nature of leadership required. Over time it is possible that traditional top-down leadership approaches will fade away as the need for agility increases. Effective organization development is not about aligning people to organizations by rendering them passive subjects of organizational requirements, but instead, about enabling greater employee agency. It is a fundamentally different way of thinking about how power and control are exercised, and forms of leadership variously described as 'distributed', 'dispersed' and 'shared' reflect the socially constructed nature of change in which people can make sense of what's happening and are empowered to make necessary changes at the right level. As groups of employees see trends ('sense'), they need to be willing and able to chase opportunities ('seize') without constant checking from higher up. Therefore, when employees become more active 'producers' not merely 'consumers' of HR policies and practices, the results are likely to include greater innovation and employee wellbeing.

However, if the Management Agenda findings reflect what is happening more widely, we are not there yet. As organizations grow, there is a natural tendency to adopt more bureaucratic structures. To make the collective behavioural and power shift required to create and sustain an empowered organization, it is essential that leaders and managers instil the right values and just enough structure to enable the entire organization to flourish. This requires strong conviction from senior leaders, a willingness to make fundamental changes within their organizations and constant attention to how things are working. Such a shift can be threatening for employees, too, who may see such a move as disruptive. So senior managers must deliberately introduce new structures and ways of working that enhance the effective sharing of power, knowledge and control at the workplace. The challenge is getting the balance right between empowerment and top-down direction.

To shift to a distributed leadership model will require revisiting the embedded values that have been reinforced within the organization, and the values of the current leaders. What is rewarded within the organization? How are leaders selected? What are the consequences for leaders who don't live up to the desired values?

Rebuilding trust

Lack of trust in leaders, especially in times of change, is a major obstacle to successful change. People often judge whether someone is to be trusted across three key dimensions:

- ability (the ability of their organization to reliably and effectively meet its goals);
- benevolence (how effectively their organization demonstrates care and concern for the wellbeing of its staff); and
- integrity (how effective their organization is at consistently adhering to moral principles and a code of conduct acceptable to its employees).

In the 2016 Management Agenda, a third of respondents reported a disconnect between espoused values and those demonstrated in practice, especially by leaders. Values imposed top-down tend to generate employee cynicism and distrust. People in operational roles commonly refer to change fatigue as a barrier to change and feeling pressured to compromise their organization's ethical standards. This again erodes trust, particularly in the middle and lower levels of management where breaches are most likely to occur as a result of overly aggressive targets or the perceived need to follow orders. It is easy to see why people do not often surface their concerns about possible fraud or other malpractice in a context where they do not trust senior management or HR. More often the whistle-blower falls victim to the organization's protective governance carapace.

Given the generally low levels of trust, leaders may need to rebuild it. Without the commitment of the board, CEO and senior management to the values, employees will become cynical and unmotivated.

Principles that drive trust can be taught to leaders and line managers such as:

- being transparent in decision-making;
- being consistent in messaging;
- delivering on promises;
- being consistent with the organization's values;
- modelling reciprocity with direct reports;
- being more visible locally; and
- creating more dialogue with the rest of the business.

So, role modelling by executives and the HR department is essential for communicating and bringing ethical values to life. Leaders must not only model the organization's values – they must create alignment to the values throughout the organization. The ultimate goal should be to engage employees in the ethical mission of the firm, thus building the firm's ethical DNA.

HR and the ethical agenda

Ensuring that the organization operates ethically is perhaps where HR contributes most to organizational effectiveness from a stakeholder perspective. By implication, the organization's practices should benefit individuals, businesses, the economy, communities and society as a whole. The needs of these different stakeholder groups are often in tension yet organizations tend to focus on only one stakeholder group – shareholders or funders. HR often finds itself in the middle of dilemmas arising from such tensions.

Given that, for many HR practitioners, tackling the ethical culture agenda is relatively new territory, and there are no easy answers to some of the dilemmas that practitioners may face, the CIPD advocates HR becoming principle led rather than policy/best-practice led. This means looking behind the policy to work out what principle it is based on, e.g. fairness? Protecting employees? This also means knowing what you stand for; where you draw a line in the sand. As Laura Harrison (2016: 3), CIPD's People and Strategy Director puts it:

> We believe that good HR should be defined by broad principles, not just by best practice. These high-level fundamental priorities of the profession could provide a framework for situational judgement that goes beyond policy development and implementation. Based on a sound professional knowledge base and ethical competence, principled practice is the kind of HR that business leaders and people would trust with critical issues of long-term organisational survival.

Harrison argues that, in order to advance their social and ethical responsibilities, HR not only needs a globally defined body of professional knowledge and skills but also 'situational judgement'. This allows people to make decisions within an ethical framework even if they do not have all the answers to 'wicked' problems. The underpinnings of situational judgement include the ability to understand the requirements of local contexts; the ability to evidence decision-making through measurement; balancing business needs with fairness and other values.

Principles also relate to the corporate governance world. For instance, is the employee voice being heard? After all, in so many of the corporate scandals, it is possible that no one 'blew the whistle', or if they did, that no one was listening. So whatever channels for employee voice are used – such as social media, intranets and so on, these must not be one way but community spaces, with employee-initiated innovation streams. HR should be promoting these channels and stimulating dialogue; then paying attention, keeping their ear to the ground to find out what is happening in different places, sensing when things are becoming chaotic and where there are opportunities to learn from what works. In social media, employee voice is often fragmented and atomized, dominated by more active individual communicators. Where there are trade unions, collective employee voice can play into the overall picture so that employees' voices are actively heard and responded to.

HR's societal contribution is likely to include managing new and diverse employment 'deals' for different workforce populations; managing the organization's brand and building organizational trust; creating shared value for the business, for employees and the customer. Employee wellbeing, shareholder value and customer delight should not be mutually exclusive. This is about HR 'finding the AND'. This is also where examples of what works, and what to avoid, can be helpful.

And it is possible to produce a significant shift in practice to create a more ethical culture, as the following example of HR-led recovery at RBS illustrates.

HR-led revival

HR has been central to cultural shift at the troubled bank RBS. RBS returned unexpectedly positive financial results in 2015 and believes it can face the future with confidence after its near implosion at the height of the financial crisis. Much of this positive revival is HR led.

HR had collectively taken a decision to roll up its sleeves, get involved and do the right thing to support the business in its recovery – especially when it came to redundancies. HR made sure people were treated people well, and even brought in competitors like Barclays to see if there was exiting talent in RBS that they could employ. HR had to define what was needed, and HR had to measure it, too, because if they didn't, someone else would.

Emerging from its part in the financial crisis, for which the bank is still paying fines, RBS wants to become 'one bank' again. Future pay principles have been agreed which have removed sales incentives from front-line staff and reduced bonuses to 10 per cent of the salary bill.

New cultural pillars were key to changing behaviours: 15,000 people have been trained in the new common plan for leading teams, 'Determined to lead'. This captures what RBS is and what it stands for in a way that has meaning internally. Proof that the new leadership principles are working is provided by the fact that leadership scores are now at 'global high-performing' level.

HR itself has transformed, with a strong focus on culture. A so-called 'Yes Check' runs right through the business – where people say 'Does X idea pass the "Yes Check?"

As the chief HR officer Elaine Arden puts it,

> HR has to be bold. If you've got a CEO who doesn't want to listen to you, you've got the wrong CEO. HR needs a point of view, and needs to front up to that point of view without waiting for leaders to do it for them.

> (Crush, 2016)

Cappelli (2015) urges HR to set the agenda – show executives what they should care about and why, highlighting financial risks and benefits if necessary. So if HR wishes to be influential and authoritative on people issues, HR needs to be business credible. This means understanding business dynamics; looking out, exploring the trends which are changing the world of work; prompting the need for internal change that will increase the business' social licence to operate and having the courage of one's convictions.

Diversity and inclusion

In her article 'You Can't Fix Culture' (Reid, 2016), the author argues that 'culture isn't something you "fix"': rather, cultural change is what you get after you've put in place new processes or structures to tackle tough business challenges like reworking an outdated strategy or business model.

Diversity and inclusion are a case in point. Diversity is an inherent aspect of corporate agility since it allows firms to access talent, wherever talent is to be found. Without inclusion, talent soon goes elsewhere. Today, with an open social network, people's voices are being heard regardless of diverse backgrounds. Teams are often virtual, and often deal with diversity in process ways, for instance overcoming language differences through technology aids. However, is diversity providing new ways of thinking about change? For instance, one communications company operates extensively through virtual teams. The standard practice is that two people

276   *HR influencing organizational effectiveness*

who have similar expertise are put onto each global team, enabling flexibility and continuity so that teams can meet at different times.

Changing cultures isn't something that can be done overnight. It has to start with sustained, deep commitment from directors who need to lead from the top. Mindsets and behavioural change come about through role modelling, building awareness and generating desire (what is in it for me?) and conviction, then developing knowledge and ability. Diversity must be built into the way change happens, as a normal, strategic, embedded way of getting things done, rather than being something that is nice to have. The values need to be reflected in all processes starting with how you attract and recruit employees, to decision-making and rewards and incentive programmes. A starting point for many is awareness raising, as the following example illustrates.

High-technology company – Company X

As a huge and successful company built and led by a member of Generation Y (Gen Y), and whose workforce too is primarily Gen Y, Company X could truly be said to be a Gen Y company. Its mission is 'to make the world more open and connected'.

As a fast-growing global company with vigorous expansion plans, and with a current workforce of 12,000, Company X is constantly recruiting to meet its growth needs. Its talent pool is global and diverse with the workforce comprising people of 54 nationalities who between them speak 74 languages. That said, in some other respects, Company X's workforce reflects conventional stereotypes: 94 per cent of the software engineers are men; the salesforce is equally split between men and women; the workforce is mostly White. All employees tend to be in the top 5 per cent of their peer groups.

Culture and values

As a Gen Y company it is perhaps not surprising that values and mission lie at the heart of the company culture. And while the word 'culture' is rarely used in Company X, it is clear to insiders such as the learning and development manager EMEA, that the corporate values define the culture and are fuelling growth.

Practising the values is what makes the mission real to employees. On the company website's careers page, people are encouraged to 'Do the most meaningful work of your career. People are at the heart of every connection we build. We design products and deliver services that create a more human world – one connection at a time.'

The values are reflected in everything, including the design of physical office space. Executives have the same size desks as everyone else; offices have glass walls so people can see who is meeting whom. What drives the executives is not money (since they are all multi-millionaires who are there by choice) but the company mission.

Authenticity and openness is a key value. With a large skilled talent pool to recruit from, Company X employees are hired not just because they are talented but because they are able to demonstrate that they share the company values in their own life experience. People are encouraged to be themselves at work – to dress as they do when they feel at their best, for instance at the weekend. If they wish to, people can put flags at their desks which declare their nationality or their gender orientation. Being accepted and included for who you are is what this is about.

HR policies

Freedom is another key value. Company X has few formal HR policies and these too reflect the values. For instance, with regard to parental leave the assumption is that fathers and mothers alike deserve the same level of support when they are starting and growing a family, regardless of how they define 'family'. The CEO extended the 'baby leave' policy from the US to the rest of the world in 2016. This offers the company's expectant fathers four months' paid paternity leave. The policy is open to same-sex couples and adopters, too.

With regard to flexible working there is no formal working from home policy. Instead people are trusted to do what they say they will do. When the learning and development (L&D) manager inquired about this when he first joined Company X, the response he received was, 'why would we care where you work?'

Similarly, there is little in the way of formal leadership development or talent management. Succession planning is limited to a tiny number of key executive roles and there is no high-potential programme. After three months in the firm, the L&D manager attempted to introduce the possibility of using a conventional nine-box grid (potential versus performance) to assess for high potential, a typical 'best practice'. He was told, 'the only time you should be in a box is when you're dead. Come up with something new.' So the L&D manager now recognizes that, when coming up with new possibilities to solve a problem, what's needed is 70 per cent creativity and just 30 per cent of your current knowledge and experience. Recruits to Company X tend to be very able and, as the L&D manager points out, if you change the context, you can change people's potential. What's considered more important is that each person can succeed, rather than having successors for roles. So one of the L&D manager's two key areas of focus (the other is new people) is developing managers who can more broadly create a context where people thrive.

The only formal HR process is performance management. Again there is no 'one-size-fits-all' approach. Directors of different functions and business units, such as sales and engineering, devise the leadership capabilities for their areas so that they are relevant. People are accountable for their own performance. For those who have performance issues there are performance-improvement plans, complaints and grievance procedures. The job of managers is to coach rather than direct. People are encouraged to talk with their managers – to have a conversation to agree objectives and measure these carefully. The assumption is that as long as people understand what their goals are, they will take responsibility for sorting out their own problems and mistakes.

Developing an even more inclusive, values-based culture as the company grows

So this unusual values-led culture is clearly giving Company X a distinctive edge in its market. The challenge is how to keep the best of the values and become even more diverse as the company grows. Since its mission is to connect the world, Company X wants its workforce to reflect the diversity of its customers. The L&D manager believes that, the more diverse a company becomes, the more diversity it will attract. There is also a shared belief that creating an open and inclusive culture is simply the right thing to do. The L&D manager argues that this becomes a more difficult task once companies become large global players such as banks, who tend to have rigid procedures, low staff turnover and only a small percentage of ethnic minority staff. The L&D manager's advice to other companies aspiring to become more diverse is to persevere and to take the long-term view: 'It's going to be difficult. You have to actively sponsor this work and put money in. Don't look for any results until at least 3 years out' – a challenge for large companies that are typically working to very short-term agendas.

So for Company X, getting the right mix now is vital before it grows to the size of its competitors over the next couple of years. While recruitment is a vital tool in creating a truly diverse organization, by changing the current mix of the workforce, there is also an urgent need to operationalize Company X's open culture to ensure this vital differentiator is not lost. Because while recruiting the right people is crucial, helping them to embrace and thrive in the culture is another challenge. The L&D manager argues that if new recruits are not connected with the corporate values they will fail. Even if they share the values, some new recruits may struggle to adjust to working amongst such very bright colleagues since in their previous companies they may have been among the highest performers in their peer groups. At Company X they typically find that the bar has gone up. Some indeed may suffer from 'imposter syndrome' for a while.

So one of the L&D manager's key priorities is to ensure that new people are helped to be the best that they can be and to thrive in the culture. There is a thorough three-day onboarding programme and the HR team check in with new recruits every 30 days during their first 90 days to make sure that all is well.

The L&D manager's other key focus is on training managers to manage in such a way that people of diverse backgrounds feel welcome and accepted. In much HRM literature, the importance of having the right values at the top is emphasized but there is general consensus that what most affects an employee's work experience is the relationship they have with their immediate boss.

The L&D manager has put together a powerful training programme which is being rolled out globally to help people to explore their own unconscious biases and understand the effect of these on their own actions and on other people. It also helps people understand the impact of other people's attitudes and what it feels like to be viewed through a biased lens, which is a revelation for many. The training is owned and championed by the CEO and chief operating officer who co-devised and helps present the programme, which at the time of writing has reached 70 per cent (9,000) of Company X's 12,000 people globally. While it is too early to say what the impact of the programme will be, there is some evidence that people are now more aware of biased dynamics. For instance, there are now more complaints when things go wrong rather than people feeling obliged to passively accept another person's prejudiced behaviour.

Other interventions to stimulate and embed values

While raising people's awareness of their biases is a good start, the L&D manager recognizes that developing and embedding an inclusive culture will take time and will require ongoing attention and effort, especially from top leadership. The CEO holds an open Q&A session every Friday and often has challenging questions to respond to. The L&D manager believes that leaders will have to do even more active communication around the values since with so many new people joining they may find it harder to make the personal connection. The L&D manager believes that people who are counter-cultural should be managed out. 'Our culture is our biggest asset. We need to be close to our values and help people see what that looks like.'

Corporate social responsibility

CSR is another key plank of sustainable business practice. Keeping true to CSR values is a critical guidepost to change management and team alignment; similarly, incorporating a CSR ethic throughout the firm necessitates a change-management approach. This of course needs genuine sponsorship from the top; even then, resistance can be anticipated. The Canadian government advisory booklet on CSR offers change agents the following advice: do not attempt to use the same approach to win support from all stakeholders since these are likely to fall into different camps according to their view of CSR:

A. Those that have the value and the behaviour.
B. Those that have the value but not the behaviour.
C. Those that do not have the value or the behaviour.

To advance CSR it is important to tailor your change strategy appropriately:

A. Recognize Group A for their behaviour to encourage them to continue it.
B. Promote, incentivize and reward Group B for behaviour changes. Ensure that these 'tools' are specifically designed so that the benefits are meaningful and the barriers to change are removed for this group.
C. Leave Group C alone. Do not cut them out, just don't tailor your promotions, incentives, etc. to their needs. A large percentage of the Cs will change their behaviour once the Bs have changed their behaviour so that they do not stand out as the minority. The remainder of the Cs will not change and they truly will be the minority (and perhaps a group you no longer find a fit with in your organization).

To educate employees and achieve awareness about CSR, many HR teams become actively engaged in awareness-raising events and initiatives, such as contests and the like. Some firms actively sponsor the establishment of 'CSR champions teams' in which employees throughout the organization are encouraged to join a group that meets on company time to conceive and launch CSR initiatives that both green the company's operations and achieve social value in the community. Other firms have initiatives underway to support employees and their families to learn about, and take action on, their social and environmental concerns at work, at home and in their communities. This is employee CSR engagement at its most engaged level.

HR is also in a position to drive policy development and programme implementation in HR areas that directly support CSR values. In organizations committed to reducing their carbon footprint, HR practitioners can develop programmes enabling employees to use alternative transport to get to work (e.g. providing showers, secure bike lock-ups, parking spots for co-op or hybrid cars, shared car journeys, bus passes, etc.) and work remotely, including other forms of headquartering and 'hoteling', teleworking, etc. Employee volunteering programmes are also within the HR mandate, and can help build the employee-value proposition and employer brand while concurrently delivering on the firm's CSR goals for community engagement and investment. Successful wellbeing, carbon reduction and employee-volunteer programmes require management support, role modelling and ongoing communications – which, if in place, become further vehicles to fostering employee awareness of, and engagement in, the firm's CSR approach.

Similarly, some HR departments have responsibility for procurement. Those that do could incorporate their CSR commitments into their purchasing programme. By adopting a sustainable purchasing policy, and integrating their social and environmental objectives into supply-chain management, HR practitioners can influence the sustainability performance of their suppliers. Benefits providers, recruiters and other suppliers to the HR department can be asked to demonstrate how their practices align with the buyer's CSR values. Requests for proposals can incorporate questions and requirements for a certain level of sustainability or CSR performance on the part of vendors, thereby cascading CSR into the supply chain as further demonstration of how the organization is walking its talk.

280   *HR influencing organizational effectiveness*

By embedding CSR into everyday practice, HR can help normalize ethical practice as 'the way we do things around here'.

Building a changeable, learning culture

The challenge of continuous change is how to manage ongoing transitions. This is where shared learning is vital to building a changeable culture. HR, OD and organizational effectiveness consultants can bring specific forms of expertise to help organizations to make transitions. Such transformations require not broad, shallow knowledge but deep, broad expertise. The task of OD/organizational effectiveness is to be a 'dot connector', bringing together different people to think about what the organization needs and introducing relevant interventions to unblock or enable key aspects of organization. Through continuous engagement with people who are linked together in a learning capacity, being nimble, agile and dealing with capability requirements, learning occurs across the organization as an important part of building change capability.

Almost certainly, developing changeability will be challenging to people whose mindsets are based on previous recipes of success. Therefore, the organizational-effectiveness task is to stimulate different behaviours and practices through a focus on adaptive learning. Key to it all is selecting and simplifying change processes and involving people to clarify what must change now. Then it's about proactively making tweaks to the organization's design to solve the problems the organization needs to solve now – constant tailoring, ensuring timeliness and speed on the right things. Ongoing monitoring is crucial – did you get it right?

The starting point is building awareness of the external environment. By anticipating what's happening, the firm can proactively make continuous changes to get ahead of the curve. What's needed is a multidirectional approach to data gathering, with an unbiased information flow that makes sense within the business context. This is about helping people understand the complexity without overwhelming them. Then it's about working with people to analyse what needs to change, helping them figure out how to make the emerging design work so that changes can be made in an agile way.

One organizational-effectiveness consultant (an HR director) worked in a company that wanted to introduce a new IT platform which would represent a radically new way of working across the organization. She set about creating a partly 'top-down' and partly 'bottom-up' change process, first establishing a cross-boundary steering committee, which had C-level support. She was clear that their task was to lead by example. She then set up a non-hierarchical project team, inviting people 'where the energy is' to work with her. This self-filtered team of change agents developed an adaptive plan, on the principle of sense and respond. They brought together 600 clients to give feedback to staff about the service challenges they were currently experiencing and to share ideas for what might work better.

In communicating the rationale for the change, the organizational-effectiveness consultant focused both on how the new work process would aid the customer and also employees. Thus the inspiring and people-centric reason for change, developed with staff, was 'to upgrade our employees' working day and improve our performance and well-being; in other words, to make us happy at work, share happy moments'. Her advice is as follows:

1. Start with current realities in workflow:
   - Look at external business trends.
   - Observe operational realities.

An ethical, changeable organization 281

- Client platform and event – bring together clients and staff; working group to address issues. Link tools to broader intent so people get it.
- So what might 'better' look like?
- Crowdsource ideas in company.
- So what do I do differently now?

2. Evolve a framework:
   - Work with what already exists as triggers for learning and change, e.g. demographics, other initiatives – piggyback on these.
   - Minimize technical boundaries – signpost channels, ensure easy access and interconnectivity.
   - Preparation
   - Make it real and test user experience.
   - Review launch readiness.
   - Engage WIFM – Will I be safe enough? Do I have the necessary resources – psychological, physical, emotional? (Kahn, 1990; May et al., 2004)

3. Stay connected to the top, sow seeds that can lead to innovation:
   - Convince senior managers/inspire reticent users.
   - Use real-world examples.

4. Build momentum but do not force:
   - Scale and accelerate the change virally.
   - Share stories – 'happy moments' – 'work out loud' as people experience the new platform – make stories visible.
   - Get ready to onboard staff – to start experiencing new ways of working (user journey is non-linear).

5. Working across ecosystems:
   - Need to tailor messages to needs of different audiences.
   - Be open and transparent – communicate in nuanced way with different groups.

6. Rolling out change – go viral:
   - Build 'the muscle' – by getting influencers from across the organization trialling new approach.
   - Start with the enthusiasts and develop a group of ambassadors and advocates (go where the energy is). Create a group who use all the process tools rather than dispersed – creates desire within the system for more people to use them.
   - Sense and respond to feedback – modify system.

7. Evolve a framework to stimulate and bound the degree of learning:
   - Use case examples that convince people, e.g. people who 'get it' who are now working in a different way.
   - Encourage engagement at all levels.
   - Remember training may be needed.

8. Maintain top-down alignment:
   - Review emerging patterns in light of company strategy – do they contribute positively or negatively?
   - Management and leadership practices that encourage engagement – nudge the ecosystem – 'strengthen the elbows' of champions.
   - Leadership-development programme – one conversation at a time – taken to social platform to reflect.

9. Reinforce over time by personal experience (NOT by force from senior management):
   - See the benefit in this – share with colleagues – build new reflexes every moment.

282 *HR influencing organizational effectiveness*

- Create attractive user space for sharing stories/learning.
- Build into induction, operating-procedure guidance, etc.
- 'Every wave of transformation begins with a small ripple.'

Developing change–agent capability

To build changeability, it helps to develop change agents who have relevant skills and expertise. In the following case study, from an English NHS institution, the change agent in question is Catherine Heaney, OD manager at Frimley Health NHS Foundation Trust. This case example looks at how Cath developed her own change-agent/OD expertise and how she is helping others do the same, thus building the organization's 'muscle' for thriving in ongoing change.

There are many routes into OD. For Catherine Heaney, it was via a project-management background and a mission to develop service-improvement capacity at the trust during a period of major organizational change.

As with many NHS institutions, Frimley Health has been subject to considerable cost pressures in recent years. In 2010, a transformation director was brought in both to find significant cost savings and also to improve the service. One of the first casualties of spending cuts was a two-day offsite programme, *Essential Skills in Service Improvement*, which had been run for the trust by an external provider for several years. Initial internal attempts to fill the gap left by the service-improvement programme lacked impact and soon fell by the wayside.

About this time the L&D function carried out a detailed training needs analysis of the top three tiers of management asking people to rate themselves on a wide range of skills on a scale from beginner to expert/possible trainer of others. The idea was to make better use of internal training capacity. The analysis revealed clear gaps in in-house skills relating to organization development and service improvement.

For Cath, this proved a spur to her own development as an OD practitioner. Having been trained in lean thinking in a previous role at a primary care trust, Cath recognized that, if she was to become skilled in OD, she would need to extend her skillset. As Cath puts it, 'OD found me'.

So Cath embarked upon an accelerated development journey towards becoming an effective OD practitioner. She built on learning gained at the trust's development centre in 2009; was trained in a variety of personal effectiveness skills including influencing and political awareness; became licensed to use psychometrics such as the Myers-Briggs Type Indicator and tools such as 360-degree feedback. Cath also took part in the NHS Institute for Improvement's online Vanguard Programme, gaining access to learning from world-class experts and virtual-action learning sets.

Cath now had the opportunity to start shaping a new type of development offering aimed at service improvement. Cath's aim was to build capacity to bring about real change – she was keen to ensure that people taking part in the programme could acquire transferable skills and apply these to real improvement challenges in the workplace and so make a real difference.

The two-day Tools for Change Projects programme is designed and delivered by Cath with an independent 'lean' consultant with a background originally in automotive manufacturing, followed by ten years working in healthcare. Participants must nominate a real work project that relates to service improvement, preferably one that is business critical. Participants come from all parts of the organization and they are invited to attend the programme with a partner whose work is co-dependent on theirs. Partners are not exclusively front-line staff; they may be managers and subordinates, or cross-disciplinary or cross-departmental teams. For instance, a data analyst responsible for stroke-care data partnered with a stroke-specialist nurse on an improvement project. Amongst the advantages of having partners take part is that it is easier to measure real progress towards improvement – a usually challenging task that is often not the same as audit. Working together helps both parties identify the key aspects of service improvement required and find meaningful ways of measuring progress. Moreover, many people find lack of time is the greatest obstacle to implementing service improvements, so attending with their colleagues means that people can support and challenge each other back in the workplace and keep progress toward improvement on track.

The training days are held offsite and are content rich, with practical workbooks and space for participants to discuss and reflect on what is feasible. There is a month gap between the two study days, so that participants can test out initial learning and participate in action learning with their cohort. In this way they build collaborative learning and benefit further from the multidisciplinary environment the open programme affords. Then participants apply their learning to their real work projects, coming together again six months later to give a short presentation in which they review what has been achieved, as well as what they have learned. Of course during the six-month period much may have changed and some initiatives may have stalled or been blocked. The review day allows people to reflect on what is feasible and continue to develop the skills and confidence to make change happen even when things are difficult.

There are also many successes to report. For instance, one project resulted in improved turnaround times for urgent sample results from blood sciences (pathology). Each project group creates a poster to illustrate what has been improved and their managers are invited to hear, recognize and celebrate with participants what has been achieved. Cath is keen to develop institutional knowledge so has evaluated and catalogued as 'Tools for Change' over 80 project improvements since the programme began. These are easily accessible by staff and managers. For Cath, the aim of work such as this is to develop the capacity of the organization to sustainably improve its service and patient outcomes and also to make working lives better: aspirations entirely in line with OD's values and purpose. Many roads lead to Rome!

In the following case study, we look at how one recently merged organization managed to develop a high-engagement, high-performance, learning-based culture in record time, using training as a key enabler of cultural integration, capability building, talent spotting and employee engagement. Training can play a key part in developing such a culture, yet its value is often overlooked by senior leaders. The case study that follows the management of Ashfield Meetings and Events, an international event-management company, recognized and championed the use of training to equip people to succeed and to help build a high-performing organizational culture. The company was the worthy gold award winner of the 2014 *Training Journal* Award in the Organizational Development category.

Training as the spur to developing a changeable, creative culture

Ashfield Meetings and Events is the product of a merger between Universal Procon and WorldEvents. From the outset, senior leaders were ambitious for the new company to become a high-performing learning organization. Yet, based on their previous experience of acquisitions, they were aware that merging two companies with different cultures can cause disruption. Therefore, they commissioned the Denison Culture Survey (this assesses an organization's progress toward a high-performance culture) in order to better understand the thoughts and feelings of staff across the newly merged company. Results suggested some

284 *HR influencing organizational effectiveness*

weaknesses, especially in the company mission, consistency and empowerment categories of the Denison model. The capability development and learning segments also showed scope for improvement.

The initial challenge was to ensure that the combined company's business operations were legally compliant and of a high standard, so it was crucial that staff were familiar with Ashfield's internal standard operating procedures and best practice, and also with changes to the latest legislation that govern how they do their day-to-day jobs, with advances in technology and changes to preferred suppliers.

The Bitesize programme

The 'Bitesize' training programme was devised to ensure that employees can learn relevant skills, network and share best practice across a broad range of subjects – including company initiatives, best practice and legislation – in a way that is accessible and relevant to each individual. Since the events industry is fast-paced and time-demanding, Bitesize sessions, as the name implies, are short – usually just an hour – interactive, informative and available in a range of formats, including face to face.

The nature of the programme is fluid, ever evolving and implemented in agile fashion to ensure that courses remain aligned to changing business requirements, company culture and employee development needs. In 2013/14, Ashfield delivered 74 Bitesize courses covering 33 different subjects in six different countries. On average, each employee attends six courses in a calendar year.

Bitesize training is proving useful for rolling out new operational processes and procedures. Some sessions are compulsory, since, as the company grows and as legislation changes, it is crucial to ensure that everyone keeps abreast of legal requirement changes and continues to meet Ashfield's high standards. By delivering process change in this format, Ashfield has seen efficient transformation and fostered a more collaborative employee resource.

However, Bitesize is not a purely top-down initiative. Self-organizing principles underpin much of what is on offer. Employees themselves can suggest the subjects they would like to see scheduled for the future. While some sessions are run by external partners, Bitesize also harnesses a plethora of internal talent for the benefit of the company. Anyone, from senior project executives to business directors can run Bitesize sessions across a broad range of subjects. Management believes that exposing employees' knowledge and sharing best practice incentivizes individuals and also raises their profile within the company. Thus, Bitesize provides a structure for staff to exercise shared leadership and to have a voice.

The Bitesize programme provides a career path, tailored to each individual, delivering a framework of transferable skills, and learnings including 'soft skills' to help employees develop their personal skills and attributes. Employees have autonomy – they can take control of their own development and are even empowered to sign themselves up for training sessions, which are scheduled in advance so that employees can plan ahead. The intention is win–win.

Bitesize training is now an ongoing programme and a fully integrated component of the company's people-management practices. It forms a key element of induction programmes, equipping new recruits with the tools they need to fit quickly into their new roles. It also forms a key part of each employee's staff-development plan, which is monitored regularly through appraisals and one to ones. The training has improved staff morale and contributed to attracting a top-quality workforce within the business.

Among its many benefits, the training has proved an effective way of communicating with employees, keeping them up to date with the latest company information and changes to legislation that can affect their industry. Thus, employees are participants in the strategic conversation. This has strengthened consistency and led to process improvement. At the same time, it has provided opportunities for employee voice and self-development and plays into the human desires for excitement, innovation and the urge to act autonomously. The Bitesize courses are helping to motivate employees and enhance relationships across the business. The programme also acts as a vehicle for talent spotting and succession planning. Indeed, there is a strong correlation between attendance at Bitesize courses and internal promotions. In 2013/14, 70 per cent of promotions went to people who had run Bitesize courses for their colleagues.

What's next?

A year after the introduction of the Bitesize programme, Ashfield Meetings and Events undertook the Denison Culture Survey again, and the company leapt from the forty-first to the ninetieth percentile. The Bitesize courses are clearly having the desired effect, especially with respect to the company mission and consistency. All employees now have a much clearer understanding of the overall purpose and direction for the company moving forward. In the same timeframe, during a challenging period for the events industry, Ashfield has registered double-digit EBIT growth.

Since winning the *Training Journal* Award, Ashfield continues to resource and develop Bitesize further, to reflect ever-changing customer needs, regulations, technology developments and employee-engagement trends. The focus now is on innovation and, in true 'morphing' manner, management have again introduced simple structures that can help staff and management to act as partners in the development of new approaches. In 2014, the company introduced Spark Thinking, an approach to harnessing different capabilities in order to generate fresh ideas and new solutions for their clients who face shared problems in fast, and sometimes unforeseen, change. Office space at the new UK headquarters has been designed to be more engaging. The ingenuity room, for instance, is a completely white space with resources to assist staff with creative thinking. This is proving a great success with some very exciting sessions taking place in this space.

'Spark Shorts' have been added to the training programme to get staff thinking about disruptive trends in an engaging way, and to strengthen individual and collective creative confidence. Each session lasts just 30 minutes and takes the informal style of TED Talks. Ashfield has also recently relaunched the employee forum, to give staff a platform to discuss collective initiatives and issues, ensuring that the staff feel that their voices are heard and that they are involved in shaping the future of the company. By using training in an imaginative, holistic way to upskill employees and to stimulate genuine involvement, participation and empowerment, Ashfield is finding that change approaches can gain more traction. Above all, the training programme has aided cultural integration in a way that meets both business and employee needs. Thus, training is making a key contribution to the development of a high-performance, innovative culture and proving a strategic enabler of business success.

Conclusion

In this chapter we have looked at how, in today's fast-changing environment, organizations need to be equipped not just for episodic change but to thrive in continuous change. Dynamic capabilities are essential and key to these is trust. A changeable organization has an ethical,

286   *HR influencing organizational effectiveness*

values-based, learning culture where people are open to change and where stakeholder needs are pursued. Developing changeability requires new contributions from all concerned: employees need to be willing to step up to the plate, to be 'empowered' and take responsibility for advancing their organization's success; leaders need to be willing to share power and develop the kind of iterative direction setting that makes sense in fast-changing times; managers need to embrace change as the norm and adopt agile working methods that fit the context. HR needs to be willing to champion the ethical agenda, highlighting dilemmas, taking risks and implementing change in order to improve practice and ensure that stakeholders are well served by the organization's actions.

To enable all this requires much more active dialogue, support and challenge to ensure that people are operating consistently with the values and are able to embrace change as the norm, rather than as a threat. A shared learning approach is vital – both in intent and in practice – to enabling the organization and its people to proactively sense and seize opportunities to the benefit of all concerned.

Points to ponder

- The question for your organization might be, what attitudinal, behavioural, structural or process update is needed to create an environment that would promote learning and development?
- What sorts of principles should underpin decision-making with respect to ethical dilemmas?

15 Conclusion

> Being good is good business
> Anita Roddick 1942–2007, British founder of The Body Shop

In this book I have examined evidence for the existence of Sennett's 'work culture of new capitalism' in UK organizations at the turn of the twenty-first century and considered what that means for white-collar workers' satisfaction. I have set out to provide an historical analysis of the nature and impact of the neo-liberal 'new work culture' on white-collar workers in the UK during the period 1997–2016, focusing more particularly on the period 2000–6. I have drawn on a variety of literature and research data to examine evidence for the claims made by Harry Braverman in his book *Labor and Monopoly Capital* (1974), which was in a sense a cry of protest against the degradation of work in late Modernity.

I have considered the contribution of HRM to the installation of a work culture of 'new' capitalism. I have also examined evidence for the disorienting effects and personal consequences for white-collar workers of working conditions within the 'new work culture', as described by Sennett (2006), using the lens of the psychological contract through which to view these effects. Against this backdrop I have also considered changing definitions of organizational effectiveness and HR's actual and potential contribution to this.

In this final chapter I consider the extent to which I have been able to evidence Braverman's and Sennett's propositions. The questions I have examined are:

1. What were the macro-political, economic and technological changes which have led to the emergence of a 'new work culture'?
2. How do HRM practices contribute to the development and perpetuation of the new work culture?
3. What were the characteristics of the new work culture, as perceived by employees?
4. How did employees experience the 'new work culture'?
5. To what extent were employees able to exercise agency?
6. How did HRM professionals view their role with respect to the new work culture?
7. What is meant by organizational effectiveness?
8. How might HR influence organizational effectiveness in future?

In the rest of this chapter I will summarize what I am concluding on each of these questions, though not in this order. Given the historical nature of my analysis, I shall permit myself some speculation about possible future trends, looking at a couple of scenarios based on inferences I draw from my research. In concluding I shall highlight possible areas for future research.

288   *HR influencing organizational effectiveness*

A timely analysis?

Throughout the period in question (late 1990s to the present day) work has been in flux. I have attempted to chart elements of the rapid advance of the work culture of 'new' capitalism and set this alongside social and political shifts. This period represents one of interesting transitions in its own right; between the late phase of neo-liberal capitalism and an emerging form of capitalism; it also reflects the increasing confluence of capital and knowledge as the basis of economic growth; and it represents the emergence of post-modernity from the late stages of modernity. Moreover, this period is relatively clearly bounded; first because it marks a period of relative growth leading to a period of economic crisis and downturn; then because it largely shadows the period of New Labour in office.

Before the recession, this was on the whole a period of economic growth in the UK in which capitalists reaped high rewards. Gamble (2009) terms this period 'the feast'. Since then there has been a significant global economic trauma in the form of the banking crisis which began in 2007–8 and subsequent recession in many developed economies, including the UK's. Gamble (2009: 4) argues that since the last 'crisis of capitalism' in the 1970s, we now face the 'spectre at the feast' of a significant crisis of capitalism which would: 'Signal a much more far-reaching political and economic impasse, manifested in unpredictable and sometimes uncontrollable events, and which at the extreme threatens slump, depression, polarization, political unrest, even war, affecting all parts of the global economy and the international state system'. I believe that Gamble's observations are entirely pertinent to current conditions. In such circumstances, the working practices of the new work culture, of which I have charted elements in this book, will themselves need to be revised again in the light of the failings of the current system, in particular with respect to their impact on white-collar workers.

Summarizing evidence for Braverman's predictions

Braverman's argument was closely linked to that of Marx, if a century apart. In *Capital*, Marx argued that under capitalism, the goals of workers and capital are fundamentally different. Management itself only existed because capitalism was a system of property relations, in which a large majority worked, while a tiny minority owned or administered capital. Workers, according to Marx, ought to live to work, but under capitalism they work to live, and this is because the exclusive goal of the capitalist is to maximize profit.

Marx argued that, under capitalism, workers would inevitably be alienated. In his early writings, like Hegel, he sees alienation as a necessary feature of human life prior to the final realization of true human nature, so that there has been alienation under all modes of production; however, he does see this as being brought to an extreme under capitalism. In *Grundrisse*, he describes the capitalist mode of production as so inhuman as to make the worker 'a mere appurtenance' of the machine whose work would be 'such a torment that its essential meaning is destroyed' (1973: 376). Secondly, alienation involves a loss of self as the worker is subsumed in the process of productive activity. Moreover, the worker's labour does not belong to him or herself. Marx argued that alienation has profound consequences for humanity since it is through work that people express creativity, produce the means of their own existence and become themselves. Under capitalism, work becomes not a form of creative freedom but a form of compulsion. For Marx, therefore, employee alienation was structural since it is the structures of capitalism that determine the objective state of alienation.

Braverman too described capitalism as a system 'dominated and shaped' by the needs of capital. He saw managerialism as a technology of domination; because of the pressure of competition, management has continually been forced to renew and extend its control over the employed workforce. In this way, capital has constantly renegotiated its dominance over labour through managerial control over the labour process. While Braverman agreed with Marx that it was primarily the relations of production which distinguish capitalism and that work in a capitalist society is alienating, he regarded work in the twentieth century under monopoly capitalism as particularly alienating. Braverman's contribution was to re-examine the productive process in a precise and detailed way, updating Marx's theory, showing that alienation (or, in his phrase, the 'degradation of labour') was a process which was constantly being created and recreated by capitalist management.

Braverman advanced the argument that, in the twentieth century, this dominance was achieved through scientific management or 'Taylorism', which prescribes the separation of conception from execution, with only managers allowed to control the labour process, while workers become the 'doers', forced to comply to the will of management. In a context where production is based upon the purchase and sale of labour, it is in the interest of managers, acting on behalf of capital, to break down the labour process into smaller and smaller parts making the individual parts cheaper to obtain. Since Taylorism prescribes conditions of work, the length of the working day and the process of work, these are not only beyond the control of workers, they are in the control of forces hostile to workers because capitalists and their managers are driven to make them work harder, faster and for longer stints.

Braverman recognized the potential of technology, in particular automation, to commoditize and commodify work and deskill the workforce. The resulting rigidly repetitive process buries the individual talents or skills of the worker. Braverman (in Davies, 1986: 37) claimed that under modern capitalism 'labour power has become a commodity', which was one of the distinctive features of capitalism for Marx. With reduced labour power, workers are rendered subject to meaningless work and become ultimately expendable. However, Braverman was fiercely critical of the idea that the uses and consequences of technology are neutral; that if machinery cuts jobs, or reduces skills, this is an inevitable price of progress. In his view capitalism drives technology, and it was not the machinery of production but management that was to blame – and the class divisions which shaped how the machinery was used.

Braverman argued that while science and technology skills have increased, this has only increased the gap or 'polarization' between the lower and higher ends of the labour scale. However, Brown et al. (2010b) argue that while digital Taylorism continues the degradation of the labour process today, the polarization in earning potential between the low-skilled and people described in current political jargon as the 'squeezed middle' seems to be levelling out, as the earning power of high-skilled workers declines in the face of global competition for knowledge work. In contrast, there are increasing gulfs opening up between the new capitalist class divisions – the super-rich elite employees who are 'winners' in the 'global auction' and everyone else. For those not in the super-league, the degradation of work is reflected in reduced quality of jobs and of working life.

According to the data I have drawn on in this book, Braverman's predictions have largely been realized. Thus, with respect to the first core research question, the macro-political, economic and technological changes which have led to the emergence of a 'new work culture' include the ascendancy of neo-liberalism within a globalized economy. A few years after Braverman published his book in 1974, neo-liberalism became the dominant hegemonic economic ideology of the US and UK. Neo-liberalism gives capital an advantage in its struggle with labour as it pursues greater capital accumulation through competitive strategies on a global scale enhanced by labour flexibilization.

290 HR influencing organizational effectiveness

Moreover, Braverman predicted that the commodification of white-collar work would be progressively and systematically applied beyond clerical to high-skilled work. Since his day, as a consequence of Thatcherism and neo-liberal economic policies, white-collar work, especially professional work, has been progressively proletarianized as UK governments have sought to reduce the labour power of professional workers in public institutions such as education, the BBC and the civil service. The technologies used to achieve these ends include wide-scale restructurings and the installation of new work cultures characterized by performativity.

With respect to research questions 3 and 4, i.e. what are the characteristics of the new work culture, as perceived by employees, and how did employees experience the 'new work culture', the data I have presented suggest that the new work culture of neo-liberalism has consolidated into a harsh and uncompromising regime. The increase in performativity in many organizations over the period of study would suggest that the individual had less scope and freedom to respond to change (Dearlove, 1998; Salauroo and Burnes, 1998). Within organizations the neo-liberal new work culture is short term in focus, highly utilitarian and controlling with respect to employees. With the ending of employment practices based on assumptions of job security, many white-collar workers have had to accept the imposition of short-termist and performative new work cultures, in which they are subject to work intensification and at risk of casualization, outsourcing or redundancy.

Among the effects on them reported by respondents in Management Agenda surveys were long working hours, lack of work–life balance, pressure, anxiety and ever increasing demands. Developments such as the internet and advanced communications technology have enabled work intensification by accelerating the flow and increasing the volume of work still further. As reported in their accounts, for many workers, the boundaries between work and other aspects of life became blurred and work came to dominate life. Many workers appeared to accept their subjectivity to this regime as inevitable, due to their apparent lack of viable alternatives. And while they used 'coping' strategies, the resignation and anomie felt by many people was reflected in my study of 'meaning' which found that, on the whole, people were experiencing work as meaningless.

HRM practices: management by consent or coercion?

Braverman argued that management rules by coercion but prefers to appear to manage by consent, using tactics of encouragement and consensus. He regarded HRM (or HR) as an element of scientific management which was used as a means of habituating workers to oppressive conditions. In practice, workers would be treated as machines, with the aim of transforming the subjective element of labour into objective, measurable, controlled processes. Sennett (1998) argues that emphasis on these performative concepts, as reflected in HRM's performance-management systems, is affecting character as expressed by loyalty and commitment and ultimately leads to the decline of values that are desirable in society.

With respect to research question 2 – how do HRM practices contribute to the development and perpetuation of the new work culture – I have charted the shifting role of the HR management and noted that, during the period addressed in this book, HRM has become embedded as the dominant form of HR practice in organizations, largely replacing 'Personnel'. According to HRM theory, HR practice must be closely aligned to the needs of the business. Moreover, with the decline of trade unions and the lack of a collective approach to employee relations, individualized HRM approaches to employee relations have left employees on their own in dealing with any grievance against their employer.

HR practitioners are influential in the psychological-contracting process since they are usually involved in recruitment and selection activities; they devise reward and other policies, as well as induction and performance-management processes; they play a crucial role in shaping employees' expectations about the employment relationship. I have argued that HRM high-commitment theory represents a strong, persuasive ideology that can manufacture consent, just as neo-liberalism in the political and economic sphere can have the same effect. I have reported the scepticism expressed by many Management Agenda respondents about human-resource practices, and in particular drawn attention to the ethics of 'management of meaning' through the use of HRM discourse of high performance and high commitment, such as contemporary concerns about 'employee engagement'. This is in the context of highly utilitarian, performative approaches to people management, where the underlying drivers of HRM are to manage and reduce the costs of people as a resource.

How did HRM professionals view their role with respect to the new work culture? On the whole, for the HR leaders I interviewed, business concerns took priority over employee concerns. Indeed, even apparently employee-focused initiatives, such as those concerned with employee engagement or talent management, appear to reflect a more instrumental 'hard' approach to managing humans as resources, rather than as people. Such initiatives derive from what they perceive as their organizations' needs for higher performance output and/or to meet current and future skills shortages. Moreover, many of these HR practitioners do not appear to question their own roles in large scale layoffs which they have organized and indeed have derived power from these activities. As discourse shapers and HR careerists these practitioners are keen to be seen to be shaping the future of the HR profession. They are concerned to ensure that such business-centric approaches to HRM are embedded in their own teams and beyond.

By and large, I have reported that the positive rhetoric of HRM appears to be very much at odds with employee accounts of their experience of HRM practices. If anything, I would agree with a Management Agenda respondent who considered that performance management is actually damaging to individuals. Ironically, then, HRM practices which purport to lead to increased productivity may actually reduce it because of employees' cynicism and loss of autonomy in their own jobs. Moreover, the extent to which HR practice can in any case really be mutual is questionable given that, according to mainstream theory, HRM is unambiguously an intrinsic part of the management structure and in practice represents the employer in cases of dispute. It is therefore not really surprising that, in Management Agenda surveys since 1998, the HR function was generally reported by employees to be reactive, counter-productive and not to be trusted.

Can employees exercise agency?

For Marx and Braverman, workers were seemingly powerless to resist the structural forces – the social machinery, bureaucracies and states – which reduced their autonomy and quality of their working lives. Marx had argued that human beings are social beings who have the ability to act collectively to further their interests. However, under capitalism that ability is reversed by the anarchic drive for profits, submerged under private ownership and the class divisions it produces. Marx believed, of course, that as capitalism experiences ever more severe crises of overproduction, if the working class act collectively in economic and political terms, then capitalism can be overthrown.

Some Marxists disagree with Braverman that scientific management is the predominant method of control in the latter part of the twentieth century, or that management control is necessarily complete. Edwards (1978) for instance sees the workplace as a contested domain,

292 HR influencing organizational effectiveness

where worker resistance and other situational factors can influence the outcome. Burawoy (1979) argues that consensual negotiation tactics often succeed. Friedman (1977) proposes that, at all stages of capitalism, direct control, where every aspect of the worker's labour is rigidly controlled, co-exists with responsible autonomy, where workers are invited to identify with the objectives of the business as a whole. Friedman also comments on the distinction between central and peripheral workers, with central workers being essential to the long-term prospects of the company and therefore more powerful.

However, both Burawoy and Friedman appear to accept the argument that capitalism is a process through which workers have increasingly been denied real control over their work. Furthermore, Paul Sweezy saw the structures of monopoly capitalism wreaking havoc on people's working lives and he described the consequences for employees in his Foreword to *Labor and Monopoly Capital*:

> The sad, horrible, heartbreaking way the vast majority of my fellow countrymen and women, as well as their counterparts in most of the rest of the world, are obliged to spend their working lives is seared into my consciousness in an excruciating and unforgettable way. And when I think of the talent and energy which daily go into devising ways and means of making their torment worse, all in the name of efficiency and productivity but really for the greater glory of the great god Capital, my wonder at humanity's ability to create such a monstrous system is surpassed only by amazement at its willingness to tolerate the continuance of an arrangement so obviously destructive of the well-being and happiness of human beings.
>
> (Sweezy, 1974: ii)

Similarly, Sennett (1998, 2006) proposes that, within the new work culture, 'character' is 'corroded', that is to say that employees, with high levels of job insecurity, adjust to thinking short term, lack the opportunity for real achievement and struggle to sustain a life narrative that comes out of one's work.

I have reported the impact on employees of the new work culture of neo-liberal capitalism in Chapters 4, 6, 8 and 9. This suggests widespread work intensification and performativity and employer-driven dismantling of the 'old' psychological contract. I have reported characteristic aspects of the new work culture such as the constant change, short termism, growth of internal competitiveness and loss of collegiality, conflict, micro politics, lack of leadership and insecurity experienced by people working in the new work culture. I have argued that these growing demands and the reduction of the quality of working life represented a breach or violation of the psychological contract of many employees. Indeed, it could be argued that these effects on individuals were symptomatic of a more widespread shift in the social contract with respect to white-collar work.

This raises the question of how far consensus at work can go, and how far workers may be participating in their own subordination at work. Where I might take issue with Braverman is over the extent to which he assumes that workers will be powerless to resist capitalist managements. In this book I have considered the question of how much agency workers can exercise in the face of significant structural change. Between 2000 and 2003, the majority of respondents increasingly questioned and resented the long working hours, ever increasing demands and loss of work–life balance. Nevertheless, people seemed by and large to accept that they had no option but to work hard and for long hours. Moreover, for many people, technology brought some freedom in that, with laptops, the internet and mobile phones, work could be carried out anywhere, thus in theory aiding better work–life balance; in practice this meant that work *was* carried out everywhere, thus undermining work–life balance.

Gradually though Management Agenda surveys showed a small but perceptible trend for increasing numbers of employees to take control of their own situation in order to improve it. Indeed, a tiny minority of respondents seemed to thrive in the new environment, choosing to embrace ever more demanding work. Mostly these were employees aged between 25 and 35 years of age, for whom career ambition was a strong motive.

More generally though, it seemed that most employees were learning to adjust to the demands of the new work culture, in many cases finding ways to work round the system, or becoming more assertive and no longer being prepared to sacrifice their health or personal lives for the sake of job security or career advancement. Throughout this period many people lamented a perceived loss of meaning at work. From about 2004 onwards, some employees at least appeared to more assertively be exercising their choice not to put up with work conditions which they found to be personally unsustainable, perhaps by 'opting out', 'downshifting' or moving to less stressful jobs. Some people chose to set up their own businesses rather than endure employment in the new work culture. Indeed, this trend has continued, with 'micro businesses' of the self-employed as the fastest-growing sector of the UK economy.

While I recognize the need to be mindful of the potentially manipulative/harmful effects of HRM noted above, I take the view of Keenoy (2009) and others, that employees are not simply passive receptacles for management ideas or corporate 'mono-cultures' (Francis, 2007; Grant and Shields, 2002) and that more needs to be understood about the exercise of agency and ways in which people exercise choices, even within a 'constrained employment context' (Bolton and Houlihan, 2009: 6).

Psychological and social contracts

This book has examined the impact on employees of work degradation in the new work culture, through the lens of the psychological and social contract. Unlike many traditional theories of management and behaviour, the psychological contract and its surrounding ideas are still quite fluid; they are yet to be fully defined and understood, and are far from widely recognized and used in organizations. In examining the extent to which the employment relationship between employers and employees appears mutual or one sided I have referred to two forms of exchange relationship. Social contracts represent a commonly held view of the obligations that define appropriate employment relationships, while the psychological contract describes the specific expectations an employee has of their employer that defines their actual employment relationship.

I have argued that a major reason for the increasing significance of, and challenges posed by, the psychological contract was the rapid acceleration and deepening severity of change in business and organized work which began in the 1980s. The employer/employee relationship – reflected in the psychological contract – has progressively grown in complexity, especially since globalization and technology in the late twentieth century shifted organized work onto a different level – in terms of rate of change, connectivity and the mobility of people and activities. In particular, I have considered how the macro thrusts of neo-liberalism, technological advances, labour flexibility and resulting regimes of significant workplace restructuring and performativity, have impacted on the stereotypical 'old' psychological contract of white-collar workers.

I have argued that the pursuit of labour flexibility since the 1990s has led to the deliberate undermining by employers of the 'old' psychological contract, or 'deal'. Like Guest (2004),

294   HR influencing organizational effectiveness

I argue that the breakdown of the traditional 'deal' of a career in return for loyalty, a fair day's work for a fair day's pay, and the individualization of the employment relationship, together with considerable amounts of organizational change, have represented widespread violation of the 'old' white-collar psychological contract, manifest for instance in the loss of professional autonomy, job security and the possibility of career progression. The significant trust deficits in many organizations are perhaps reflective of this violation.

At the heart of the psychological contract is a philosophy of mutuality which reflects its deeply significant, changing and dynamic nature. Based on the evidence I have drawn on, I have argued that the employment relationship has become one-sided in favour of employers as a result. While the 'old' psychological contract might only have become widespread in white-collar work since the 1960s, and never really applied to blue-collar or contract workers, nevertheless the career and employment expectations of many respondents at the start of my study were forged within this stereotype. I have therefore been interested to consider new ways of managing employment relations to meet the interests and concerns of both white-collar employees and their employers. Latterly, the balance in the employment relationship may be swinging towards knowledge workers. This is likely to trigger new demands of employers who wish to attract and retain scarce talent.

Work as self-fulfilment

The experience of work is increasingly impacted by factors outside of work, as well as those that arise inside work. During the period in question, as a result of globalization, technology and knowledge capitalism, the 'knowledge content' of much of white-collar work has increased. Social change has also facilitated the rise of identity as a preoccupation for many employees, especially people with creative and professional jobs. People are aware of more, they have more, and want more from life – and this outlook naturally expands their view of how work can help them achieve greater fulfilment. That may be perhaps because, as Sennett (2006) argues, in large modern businesses, the majority of workers face uncertainty and find it difficult to conceive of a life narrative. In a 2006 survey for the Work Foundation, 69 per cent of respondents said work was a 'source of personal fulfilment'. A 2008 Roffey Park survey (Sinclair et al., 2008) found that 90 per cent of employees were looking for happiness and fulfilment at work.

While there is a danger in extrapolating trends based on this variety of samples of white-collar populations, nevertheless there appears to be a general trend for employees to want to pursue self-actualization through work. In the Management Agenda the main motivators in 1999 were personal drive and achievement, challenge and enjoyment of the job. These remained exactly the same in 2007 and also in 2016, along with the 'desire to make a difference'. Financial rewards remained well down the list.

Yet I argue that over this period the social contract within which people struggle to negotiate individual psychological contracts has become skewed to one in which individuals must watch out for their own interests. Since trust between the two parties is crucial to building a relational psychological contract, the lack of job security inherent in the new work culture would make it difficult to build this trust. In today's harsher work environments, individuals' ability to renegotiate their individual psychological contracts will be determined by their perceived market value.

Thus, as De Meuse et al. (2001) suggest, the loss of job security has made the employee focus on developing transferable skills and contacts, resulting in a transactional contract being formed. In my study, respondents appear well aware of the need to develop their skills and to have been actively developing their employability, in line with the 'employability thesis' (Rajan, 1997). For many people in my study, rather than providing a means of self-fulfilment, work appears to have become increasingly bound up by questions of 'survival' in the workplace. Indeed, recent newspaper reports have suggested that some UK employees will not even take their annual holidays for fear of losing ground in their absence.

I argue that people who pursue self-fulfilment or seek to advance their careers within the new work culture are likely, in a context of performativity and ever growing workloads, to suffer significant frustration and/or may try even harder, thus risking becoming 'willing slaves' and ultimately 'burnt out'. Due to automation and technical advances and the need for upskilling, employees are likely to experience different fortunes akin to a Darwinian 'survival of the fittest'. While perhaps some younger and ambitious employees may be able to absorb the increasing pace for a long time, other employees, less able to sustain the pace, face the possibility of obsolescence, and the 'spectre of uselessness' that Sennett (2006) described.

The reported loss of 'meaning' at work over this period perhaps reflects the degree of potential mismatch between what employees aspired to and what they actually experienced. The career implications of the ending of the 'old deal' remained important to many employees, though most people appeared to be more concerned about their loss of autonomy, as reflected in the increasing concerns about lack of work–life balance, and loss of job quality in these pressurized and challenging work contexts. And people also appeared increasingly as anxious and uncertain about what was happening in society at large as they were about what was happening to them personally in the work context. Thus it could be argued that the macro-context changes, including the market-driven, individualistic and secular values of contemporary society and the turbulent political and economic scene, together with performative and insecure work contexts, were resulting in a challenging new social contract emerging within which individuals were attempting to maintain or improve their own psychological contract at work.

This suggests that the situation facing many workers in the first few years of the twenty-first century was worsening, with workers increasingly feeling trapped in harsh working conditions. There were signs that large amounts of organizational change, and related sense of loss of direction, were having a negative effect on employee attitudes, weakening employees' belief that their managements knew what they were doing. HRM practices in particular appeared to result in a significant reduction in employee trust, reflecting the tensions and dualities of HRM, i.e. the rhetoric of mutuality implicit in high-commitment HRM concealing a machine metaphor view of labour. While many organizations were reported to have high-commitment HRM practices, such as organizational values, there was a degree of cynicism expressed about the gaps between 'rhetoric' and 'reality'. HRM practices which appeared to reduce employee trust included more draconian policies relating to job tenure, performance management, training, communication and redundancy programmes in particular.

Thus many participants in this study appear to have experienced a deteriorating employment relationship. Employers generally did not fulfil their part of the 'new deal'. Over time, some people at least were no longer prepared to passively tolerate excessive employer demands or to make the sacrifices required, including potential loss of authenticity, in order to make career progress. In one way then, this could be viewed as employees getting back in control of their own destinies and looking for more work–life balance. Moreover, there is an argument that, if breaches of relational psychological contract are so damaging to individuals, ironically they might perhaps be less vulnerable to exploitation by employers, and be better able to secure a 'good deal', including meaningful work, if they were to embrace a more transactional approach to renegotiating their psychological contract: 'Because if I can't have meaning, I'm goddamn-well going to have money' (Barber, 2008). For employers, the cost of negotiating transactional psychological contracts is likely to be considerably higher than enticing employees with an implied promise of a mutual exchange relationship.

Nevertheless, despite the vicissitudes of work in the new work culture, many people in this study appeared to prefer to remain in 'permanent' employment with their employer, and by implication, perhaps continued to aspire to a relational contract with their employer. The freewheeling protean career was not what many people aspired to. In that sense, the 'employability thesis' (Rajan, 1997) did not seem to be working in full.

The 'Meaning at Work' study perhaps suggests what many people aspired to with respect to their employment relationship. People's definitions of 'meaning' were complex. These reflected emotions as well as cognition; they related to individual and social identity; they combined existential elements with longings for connection and purpose. By and large these definitions did not reflect materialistic values and no one defined 'success' in financial terms. These definitions might be said to reflect both people's desire for self-actualization and fulfilment, and also their desire to belong. People wanted the chance to achieve and to feel part of a community doing worthwhile work that makes a difference. An uplifting purpose appears to provide meaning for some people and to act as a 'bonding' mechanism with their organization, thus becoming an inherently relational psychological contract which provides individuals with a means for self-actualization and fulfils the desire to belong.

As a concept, the psychological contract will continue to evolve and change, in both its effects and its definitions, especially given the increasing casualization of work. It has been argued that the psychological contract needs extending to give greater weight to context and to what is described as the state of the psychological contract, incorporating issues of fairness and trust that lie at the heart of employment relations (Guest, 2004). For instance, in terms of context, there are significant changes under way specifically involving attitudes to traditional corporations, markets and governance. Examples of extremely potent 'community'-driven enterprises are emerging. Social connectivity and technological empowerment pose a real threat to old-style corporate models of organization. Moreover, each new generation of workforce will have its own social-contract expectations. Younger generations have seen the free-market model and traditional capitalism fail, and fail young people particularly.

The significance and complexity of the psychological contract has grown in response to all of these effects, and given that the world of work will continue to change, so the significance and complexity of the contract will grow even more. Like Sparrow and Cooper (2003), I recognize its dynamic quality, and the social and emotional factors. Clarity of mutual expectations will be vital for a healthy employment relationship. The basic principle – that people seek fair treatment at work – is simple. Complexities and dynamics come to life as soon as the principle is seen in a practical context. Essentially the psychological contract is driven by people's feelings which cannot be measured or defined in fixed terms. I propose that 'meaning' is a barometer of the health of the psychological contract which reflects core issues in the employment relationship of trust, exchange and control. More research would be needed to explore the links between meaning, purpose and organizational outcomes such as commitment and performance.

In the following sections I consider the implications of the current macro context for the emerging psychological and social contract.

The developing crisis of capitalism

So while Braverman began the debate, many of the issues he raised remain unanswered or with incomplete responses. Are these modes of control – the separation of craft and professional work and the deskilling of professionals – happening now? Arguably yes.

Unlike in the first period addressed in this book (1998–2006), the UK economy since 2007 has experienced recession and ongoing downturn as well as a change of government. On the world scene, political and economic turbulence continues unabated. Gamble (2009) argues that, as the creaking mechanisms of neo-liberal monopoly capitalism become more destabilized, we will experience another crisis of capitalism. This will typically be triggered when super-exploitation proves counter-productive, when workers do not have the wealth to purchase goods, consumption declines and hence investment slows down. Prior to this happening, he argues, there is no role for workers in the short term other than as victims. Arguably, we have seen the effects of this in the collapse of the financial system (including the 'credit crunch') following the banking crisis of 2007–8.

Zuboff (2010: 5) argues that we are currently experiencing a historic transition of capitalism: 'The pattern of change is one of overlapping and interwoven fields of transition rather than clean, unidirectional breaks. For those of us living through these transitions they can be confusing and frustrating.' The nature of the new form of capitalism which may emerge is unclear. Marx had argued that, under capitalism, workers are alienated from fellow human beings, especially from those who exploit their labour and control the things they produce, and are unlikely to come together spontaneously in collective action. Ollman (1996: 143) argued that human beings are social beings who have the ability to act collectively to further their interests, given political organization. Under capitalism though, that ability is submerged under private ownership and the class divisions it produces:

> We have the ability to consciously plan our production, to match what we produce with the developing needs of society, but under capitalism, that ability is reversed by the anarchic drive for profits. Thus, rather than consciously shaping nature, we cannot control, or even foresee, the consequences of our actions.

Reflecting on the banking crisis, Sennett (interviewed by Ember, *Financial Times*, 5 November 2008) argues that the inherent short termism of neo-liberalism has driven highly individualistic behaviours, particularly from those who 'control' capital:

> One of the striking things about this is that the people who are involved in trading these financial instruments had almost no sense that they could do an injury to large numbers of other people. I do not think that is just greed. I think it is the way that the search for very short-term profit and the organisation of work in a very short-term time frame gradually begins to eclipse other people. You do not think socially under those conditions.

Perhaps Sennett is being charitable. At the time of writing, the UK economy, though buoyant relative to those of its European neighbours, is struggling to maintain consistent growth. There are significant ongoing public-sector 'cuts' under way, including changes to public-sector pensions, and record levels of youth unemployment. Instability applies to workplaces right across the economy. It is not surprising that employees are reported to be anxious and uncertain about the future, even though their own jobs may not be at risk of redundancy (McCartney and Willmott, 2010). As my study has found, work can be undignified and damaging to worker wellbeing, owing to pressure, the demand to do more with less, the seemingly never-ending flow of work and less individual autonomy. This level of uncertainty could encourage some employers to make ever greater demands and also induce employees to comply even more. In such a situation, will employees continue to seek identity and self-actualization through work (in Maslowian terms) or will more basic concerns such as safety

298   *HR influencing organizational effectiveness*

and security take precedence? If the latter, the notion of 'meaningful work' would simply be a 'fey' issue (Overell, 2008: 6), a luxury residue of the times of growth.

However, Pink (2009) suggests that, despite successive economic downturns in the past 60 years, the broad trend in Western societies has been towards 'less materialist values'. Zuboff argues that potential clashes inherent in this transition include those between the interests of worker and organization; between the shared duties of professional ethics and the personal values of individuals; and between down-to-earth industrial relations issues and a more psychological emphasis on self-realization. If Zuboff and Pink are correct, this does mean that the employment relationship must, by definition, have multiple objectives, since, as Budd (2004) points out, organizations cannot be run with efficiency as the only goal, and it is incumbent upon individuals to look further than their own direct personal interests? Will a new form of capitalism need to embrace a new form of collectivism, one that takes into account the needs of different stakeholders and has a longer-term perspective?

Moreover, the apparent widespread public revulsion at the causes and ongoing consequences of the banking crisis, and at the disparity between the 'rewards for failure', by which bankers continue to award themselves huge bonuses, and the ways in which the rest of society are left to pay the price for their actions, suggests that continuing with the neo-liberal status quo is likely to lead to growing protest. At the very least, there are likely to be growing demands for genuine accountability and a new form of social justice, as outlined by Brown et al. (2010b: 160).

> Social justice is also about giving people a sense of dignity and recognition for their contribution to society regardless of whether they are an all-out winner in the global auction. This part of a new bargain challenges the winner-takes-all society based on neo-liberal assumptions about talent, contribution, and rewards. It challenges an economic world of empty suits that knows nothing other than bottom-line numbers and return on investment. It also questions the perverse social priorities that lead talented professionals to dedicate themselves to finding novel ways of making bigger profits or personal bonuses even if it threatens the viability of the financial system if not the whole economy.

If social justice is not seen to be done, it could be envisaged that, at least over the medium term, social protest will grow, as we have already seen in England with student protests over the rise in university tuition fees and proposed changes to public-sector pensions. As Braverman (1974: 151) points out, underlying hegemonic struggles mean that worker acceptance of the new modus operandi should not be taken for granted:

> The apparent acclimatization of the worker to the new modes of production grows out of the destruction of all other ways of living, the striking of wage bargains that permit a certain enlargement of the customary bounds of subsistence for the working class, the weaving of the net of modern capitalist life that finally makes all other modes of living impossible. But beneath this apparent habituation, the hostility of workers to the degenerated forms of work which are forced upon them continues as a subterranean stream that makes its way to the surface when employment conditions permit, or when the capitalist drive for a greater intensity of labor oversteps the bounds of physical and mental capacity. It renews itself in new generations, expresses itself in the unbounded cynicism and revulsion which large numbers of workers feel about their work, and comes to the fore repeatedly as a social issue demanding solution.

Conclusion   299

I believe there are signs of such action by individuals, acting as collectives, to change structures today, not least in the 'Arab Spring' uprisings of 2011, and the growing use of social media as a means of spurring individuals to take part in collective action, as was seen in the London student protests against proposed rises in university tuition fees. Arguably, the publication by WikiLeaks of US classified information and the dogged journalism which resulted in the revelations about the Westminster MPs' expenses scandal, are examples of how the power of monopolies to control can be challenged by individuals acting in concert.

Future scenarios?

Gamble (2009: 166–7) argues that the economic crisis perhaps provides some temporary breathing space before 'enormous and unsustainable pressure' builds up: 'We face the daunting task of learning from this present crisis, and trying in the future to attempt something more different than we have ever attempted before'. Given that, without a crystal ball, it is not possible to predict with accuracy what might happen to work, workers and workplaces in the future, in this final section I would like to present a couple of speculative future scenarios, one perhaps utopian, the other pessimistic.

Scenario A: Pessimistic

Of course, things may go on much as before. If so, we are likely to see increasing polarization between the few, super-rich elite workers and the majority of white-collar and other workers whose earning power, job quality and wellbeing are reduced. Braverman, in the absence of any extended discussion of resistance by workers against management control, gives the impression that managers have all the initiative; that workers are passive and resistance cannot succeed. This is my main criticism of Braverman's book. For while I broadly agree with his thesis, nevertheless I think that he underestimated the potential for individuals to exercise agency in the face of seemingly inevitable workplace change. And, as other Marxists (e.g. Friedman, Edwards and Burawoy) have argued, structures are the products of people, and people have the power to change the structures.

Ironically, as we perhaps start to emerge from the 'Age of Individualism' (Scase, 2006) to a more connected (if fragmented) age, people are finding new means of gaining collective support in ways trade unions have not been able to muster for decades.

I suspect that, unless there is genuine movement towards a more inclusive form of stakeholder capitalism, perhaps along the lines of the 'good-work' thesis, the interests of workers and those of capital are likely ultimately to be on a collision course once again. Marx considered that, since alienation is rooted in capitalist society, only the collective struggle against that society carries the potential to eradicate alienation, to bring our vast, developing powers under our conscious control and reinstitute work as the central aspect of life. I agree with Cox (2006) that capital can be endured, or it can be resisted, but the greatest hope comes when people fight back.

In this scenario, HR's contribution to organizational effectiveness will go on much as before, with the holy grail being to align HR spending and strategies geared to supporting an ever more short-termist agenda. Industrial-relations problems may sporadically break out, temporarily forcing employers onto the back foot. Some HR teams may perhaps attempt a bridging position between the shareholder-value drive and the needs of an ever more diverse workforce, though this will be viewed with suspicion by all concerned. Cost considerations will be an ever-increasing driver of the way people are treated, so as 'business partner' HR is

300 *HR influencing organizational effectiveness*

likely to become ever more instrumental in delivering a flexibilized, transient workforce, with only a small minority of elite workers singled out to be richly rewarded. These people are unlikely to see a problem with the current situation and will expect HR to provide i-deals tailored to their needs. In this scenario, the ethical agenda will be seen as a luxury PR 'nice to have' and there will be little embedding of better practice. HR's role will remain largely administrative and operational.

Scenario B: Utopia

The more optimistic scenario assumes that a confluence of thinking and aspiration may converge to creating a 'tipping point' towards 'Good work'. In the nineteenth century, in the lecture *Useless Work versus Useless Toil*, William Morris (1884) distinguished 'good' from 'bad' work as follows:

> Here you see are two kinds of work – one good, the other bad; one not far removed from a blessing, a lightening of life; the other a mere curse, a burden to life. What is the difference between them then? This one has hope in it, the other not…hope of rest, hope of product, hope of pleasure in the work itself…pleasure enough for all of us to be conscious of it while we are at work; not a mere habit, the loss of which we shall feel as a fidgety man feels the loss of the bit of string he fidgets with.

It could be argued that there are detectable signs of a growing trend towards demands for a new form of industrial democracy, not least in the increasing flow of writing and conferences on the theme of 'good work'. Good work is defined as being about 'employment with a human face' (Budd, 2004), while for Schumacher (1974) 'good work' is about:

*   providing useful goods and services;
*   cooperation with others; and
*   exercising stewardship.

Schumacher's philosophy was one of 'enoughness', appreciating both human needs, limitations and the appropriate use of technology.

For Gardner (2007: 3) 'good work' is work that is of excellent technical quality, ethically pursued and socially responsible. Gardner argues that most people aspire to something more in return for their work than the pay cheque. In particular, most people want to do 'good work' – to accomplish something significant in their work, and to take pride in doing their jobs well. People who achieve financial success without satisfying these other aspirations, he argues, may end up feeling barren and dispirited, especially when they feel obliged to compromise their own professional standards. The 'Meaning at Work' study suggests that many employees are experiencing these dispiriting feelings, and are seeking a more meaningful work life. Some are exercising choices which reduce their financial success but provide more satisfaction of what matters more to them, such as work–life balance. By so doing, employees are no longer rendered subject to conditions which might previously have 'enslaved' them.

How might 'good work' become more widespread? Braverman (1974: 445–6) argued that the antidote to the capitalist labour process is granting workers democratic control over their workplace and society. This involves taking labour-process control away from experts and committees, demystifying pseudo-science claims and privileged ideologies (e.g. managers are the experts), and returning technical and system knowledge back to the workers. It is skilling up instead of skilling down. It is broadening the unitary goal of maximizing profit to include worker control of work, social accountability and environmentally sustainable designs. It means an education system that educates wage earners in self-governance, science, technology, ecology and democracy. Sennett (2008) too points to the dynamic of craftsmanship and longer-term skill development as an antidote to the commoditization of work and to the utilitarian short termism of the new work culture.

My study of what people found meaningful at work points strongly in this direction. People wanted to do work that was fundamentally worthwhile, that felt authentic and served a higher purpose, and therefore gave them the chance to achieve something that mattered. They wanted to be part of, and identify with, something they could be proud of, rather than serving shareholder interests alone. To enjoy good work, Gardner argues, employees must experience engagement. This is underpinned by employment security and has the following features:

- autonomy;
- workplace relations;
- sense of fairness; and
- balance – what you put in you might expect to get out in some form.

Again the study of meaning suggests that autonomy was crucial to employees' experiencing meaning. Most also appeared to have strong affiliation drives and wanted to be part of a community embarked on achieving a common purpose. Trust was a vital ingredient to a meaningful work experience – not naive, blind trust by which one is easily manipulated, but a relationship based on mutual respect and authenticity, where words were matched by deeds.

A context for meaningful work?

Like Coats, Esland, Gardner, Gordon, Hutton, Isles, Mill, Overell, Schumacher and Sennett, I consider the creation of a 'good-work' context to be not only an economic but also a moral issue. Gardner argues that there needs to be a thriving industrial democracy in place for good work to flourish. Gordon (1996) concluded *Fat and Mean*, published shortly after his untimely death, with a chapter devoted to policy recommendations designed to ensure fairer business practices and promote more democratic and cooperative 'high-road' approaches to labour management. Schumacher (1974) established the vision 'small is beautiful' in which he advocated the restoration of community and control, seeking low-tech solutions and implicitly a rejection of modern industrial society. He emphasized a restoration of our relationship with nature and was a prime mover in the development of the new environmentalism which supports the idea that nature is equal to, or more important than humanity.

For Sennett (2006), meaningful work has concrete characteristics. First, people must feel there is procedural justice in work; that is, when they do something right that they are rewarded and if they are maltreated that there is some way in which they can find redress. The second has to do with autonomy. What gives workers a sense of meaningful work is when they are recognized for doing something distinctive and are not treated just as a commodity. The third has to do with craftsmanship; when people feel they can build a skill in the course of a working life they take real satisfaction out of their work. However, Sennett argues, with short-term work in unstable institutions, it is hard for people to get better at something. If people feel their skills get stalled, that their jobs don't build up their capacity to work well, they become very unhappy. Sennett (in an interview by Barber, 2008) points out that, in the past two decades, management has not paid enough attention to these three requisites of meaningful work: 'They have

302   HR influencing organizational effectiveness

assumed that all workers are kind of entrepreneurial – they are just there for the money. That the content of work is not something employers really have to focus on. The idea is to get a task done.' Isles (2010) suggests that employers will have to rethink their mode of operation to ensure that workers have ownership of what they do – both financial and intellectual – in the craft tradition. In practice this is about ensuring that workers enjoy the interdependent and inter-related sovereignties of task, time and place. By so doing, Isles argues, people will feel they own their own destiny and will want to give of their best. Then employers should identify what reduces employee motivation within the organization system and design; simplify, reduce or remove processes such as performance-management systems which appear geared to reducing poor performance rather than recognizing and celebrating good performance:

> Then we need to work towards an adult–adult employment relationship, one that is re-lational but underpinned by lifelong learning so that employees have the means to move on when no longer needed and where the relationship needs to be actively worked at on both sides.

> (Isles, 2010: 48)

Trust will be the enabling factor of such relationships. Behaviour and standards will be values-driven and rhetoric must match practice. Equity will be more widely interpreted within such a context, allowing for personalized contracts within an ethical base, where people are united in pursuit of a shared purpose.

Above all, good work is an attempt to advance a point of view on how to arrive at a new settlement for work in the twenty-first century that breaks out of the straightjacket of interest-group gains and losses and instead aims at work that is able to deliver performance, engage-ment and fairness.

Is this scenario realistic? That is debatable but it seems likely that the pressure on businesses to behave ethically and to be more humane institutions will grow, just as the pressure on various authoritarian heads of state has grown in recent times. Corporate reputation can no longer be just about public relations; it has to be grounded in people's lived experience. I believe that this study highlights the desire by employees for an employment relationship which is more mutual and authentic than what they have experienced in recent years. As the workforce becomes increasingly diverse and multigenerational, as long as employers require particular sorts of skills and 'talent', labour power may force improvements in the employment relationship.

The extent to which labour can exercise power in these contexts will reflect the relative strength of the market for employees' skills at any given time. It is possible that in the after-math of recession, the market for high-level skills has become saturated and that the demand for it has peaked. This seems unlikely, especially given underlying demographic and longer-term economic trends, but the current economic downturn presents possibilities for further degradation of work and commodification of workers. For instance, some employers may seek to exploit their advantage in the labour market while labour power is relatively low.

Alternatively, labour may seek to remobilize its collective power by connecting with wider social protests about the consequences of unbridled market freedoms and the protracted reces-sion for people's livelihoods and lives.

How would HR influence organizational effectiveness within this scenario?

HR would be proactive in leading the way to the development of new organizational practice that is fit for the world we live in today. Working within an ethical, stakeholder-oriented

Conclusion 303

framework, HR could contribute significantly to organizational effectiveness. We have discussed just a few ways this might happen, for instance:

- Raising stakeholders' awareness of external drivers for change.
- Developing more employee-centric HR practice.
- Simplifying HR policies.
- Becoming principle rather than policy based.
- Challenging the status quo of priorities that limits the business focus to creating shareholder value at the expense of other constituencies.
- Challenging unethical practice and championing ethical practice.
- Revising performance management and other procedures so that they ensure fair treatment and help, rather than hinder performance.
- Ensuring a fair deal for all.
- Co-designing organizational roles and structures that can enable good work.
- Supporting managers and leaders to make the transition to new ways of leading.
- Acting as organizational 'pulse taker' and 'alternative therapist' – helping people to help themselves.

And that is not even taking into account the continuing quest to attract and retain talent, grow leadership across the organization and ensure that people have healthy and safe working conditions. In this scenario, HR would be operationally effective, embracing technology and providing tailored solutions. It would also become more strategic, leader-like and increasingly valued for its well-judged contributions to organizational effectiveness.

Such a scenario would of course be welcome. The challenge would be knowing what is appropriate in any given context.

Conclusion

So on balance I believe that I have found evidence for Sennett's 'work culture of new capitalism' and for Braverman's predictions being realized with respect to the proletarianization of white-collar work in UK workplaces (1998–2016). On the whole my study suggests that the work culture of new capitalism, spawned by neo-liberalism, has largely proved damaging to the working lives of employees and has been corrosive of character in the ways Sennett has described. Its practices have led to the degradation and commoditization of much white-collar work and workers. Performativity, technology and HRM practices have been used by managements to dismantle the 'old' psychological contract, in ways that F.W. Taylor might have dreamed of, in order to secure control over, and produce greater output from, insecure, proletarianized, overworked, overmanaged and alienated employees. HRM and performativity in particular appear to have been used for their panoptic effects to secure worker compliance under the rhetoric of consensus and mutuality.

Given that many white-collar workers appear to want to achieve greater fulfilment from work, since it now occupies so much space in their lives, employer and employee interests may be on a collision course. To date, it seems that it has mainly been employees who have borne the brunt of market fundamentalism. How long this situation will continue in the face of talent shortages, and growing disparities of wealth and opportunity between the elite workers of capitalism and everyone else, remains to be seen.

In carrying out this study I have used a multimethod approach within an emergent research design. In addition to re-examining longitudinal survey data, and carrying out a thematic

304   *HR influencing organizational effectiveness*

analysis to investigate employees' experience of the new work culture, I have also used qualitative methods to explore emerging issues. I have considered HRM within historical and theoretical contexts and used critical discourse analysis to dissect the power dimensions implicit in HRM/performativity. I have reflected on practitioner accounts and critiqued these from a critical theorist standpoint. I have made connections between the lived reality of the new work culture and broader society to provide a more unified analysis.

Of course I recognize that there is the danger of overgeneralizing from what were various sources of data and samples gathered over a number of years. It is possible that many of these issues may have been specific to the period in which I was researching the changing workplace. It is possible that my interest in the 'good-work' agenda may have caused me to overlook factors which were important but which did not fit within this agenda's paradigm. Moreover, I am aware that, in my desire for breadth, I may have sacrificed depth by not considering the changes by specific sector, firm size, age or gender grouping. My focus has been on UK-based employees, on 'permanent' rather than on contingent workers.

However, I believe that this generality is also one of the strengths of this book. By analysing and, in some cases, reanalysing data over this period I have been able to detect potential connections between the micro and the shifting macro context which I was not aware of at the time. I have attempted to ask the right questions to connect organizational phenomena such as careers, work–life balance and meaning to the psychological contract. My aim has been to find logical connections between these and other organizational outcomes such as learning, performance and profits.

Moreover, drawing on these strands of research has given me a chance to reflect on my own career journey over this period and on the 'plural selves' (Harré and Van Langenhove, 1999) which I have brought to this study. My interests are those of a practitioner – as employee, manager, management developer and adviser to HR professionals – and also as researcher and writer about people management. On the whole I have embraced a mainstream interest in high performance from an employee perspective but I have always considered that, for this to be sustainable, it would be essential that the employment relationship was genuinely mutual.

I have progressively taken a more critical stance, though I hope not a pessimistic one, about the possibilities of mutuality being achievable in neo-liberal work contexts. I have empathized with HR practitioners who may be experiencing cognitive dissonance between what they are required to do at work and their personal values and aspirations because I too have felt increasingly less comfortable focusing on helping people to comply with the demands of the system, for instance by running performance-management training courses for managers. I applaud the new trend towards discarding such clunky processes in favour of new practice better suited to delivering positive intent in today's fast-changing context.

In recent times the rapprochement between critical and mainstream HRM theory offers me some hope of being able to reconcile these tensions and dualities. Watson (2010) argues that a coherent critical HRM theorization requires a clear acknowledgement of the sociological, socio-psychological, economic, political and ethical aspects of working, managing and organizing. As Watson suggests, pragmatism is not about pursing absolute or final truths about reality. It is about attempting to make theoretical generalizations which might inform human practices and help us better appreciate the relationships between individuals' predicaments and institutional and historical patterns better than others. I agree with Spicer et al. (2010), that the task of scholars should be to encourage progressive forms of management.

Of course there is considerable scope for further research to investigate, for instance, whether white-collar employees will continue to seek self-fulfilment and meaning through work, given the current economic challenges and as labour markets become less buoyant. Other research could explore the nature of 'mutuality' in the employment relationship from the perspectives of different stakeholders. It could also seek examples of where mutuality within the employment relationship has been achieved and what difference this makes in terms of different stakeholder outcomes. Future research could also examine the nature of leadership required for a more mutual employment relationship to exist.

This book represents an attempt to bridge the stereotypical 'knowing–doing' gap described by Pfeffer and Sutton (1999). I believe that this historical picture of what it is like to be an employee working in the new work culture has highlighted a number of important issues and complexities. I have attempted to reveal the reality of the daily experience of the new work culture as reported by employees, in particular of HRM policy and practice, within which the state of the psychological contract acts as the weather gauge of the employment relationship. I have attempted to both acknowledge these aspects and also 'strengthen the elbow' of those seeking to develop more ethical approaches towards work, the treatment of workers and organizational practice. I believe that HR has potentially a pivotal role to play in delivering these, and that the time is now right for HR to take a lead on these issues. In short, I agree with Hutton (2010: 395) when he says: 'We are starting to understand the link between fairness, prosperity and the good life. Now we just have to deliver it. After all, we deserve better.'

References

Abrahamson, E. (2004): *Change without Pain*. Cambridge, MA: Harvard Business School Press

Ackers, P. (2014): Rethinking the employment relationship: a neo-pluralist critique of British industrial relations orthodoxy. *International Journal of Human Resource Management*, 25 (18): 2608–25

Ackers P., Smith, C. and Smith, P. (eds) (1996): *The New Workplace and Trade Unionism*. London: Routledge

Alvarez, K.M. (1997): The business of human resources. *Human Resource Management*, 36 (1): 9–15

Alvesson, M. (2003): Beyond neopositivists, romantics, and localists: A reflexive approach to interviews in organizational research. *Academy of Management Review*, 28: 13–33

Alvesson, M. and Deetz, S. (2005): Critical theory and post-modernism: Approaches to organisation studies. In Willmott, H. and Grey, C. (eds), *Critical Management Studies*. Oxford: Oxford University Press, pp. 60–106

Alvesson, M. and Sköldberg, K. (2000): *Reflexive Methodology: New Vistas for Qualitative Research*. London: Sage Publications

Alvesson, M. and Willmott, H. (eds) (1986): *Work, Self and Society: After Industrialism*. London: Routledge

Alvesson, M. and Willmott, H. (1996). *Making Sense of Management: A Critical Introduction*. London: Sage Publications

Alvesson, M. and Willmott (2002): Identity regulation as organisational control: Producing the appropriate individual. *Journal of Management Studies*, 39 (5): 619–44

Alvesson, M. and Willmott, H. (eds) (2003): *Studying Management Critically*. London: Sage

Ambrose, M.L. and Schminke, M. (2003): Organization structure as a moderator of the relationship between procedural justice, interactional justice, POS and supervisory trust. *Journal of Applied Psychology*, 88: 295–305

Amin, A. (1997): Placing globalisation. *Theory, Culture and Society*, 14 (2): 123–37

Amundson, N. (1994): Negotiating identity during unemployment. *Journal of Employment Counselling*, 31: 98–105

Anderson, C. (1997): Values-based management. *Academy of Management Executive* (11) 4: 25–46

Anderson, N. and Schalk, R. (1998): The psychological contract in retrospect and in prospect. *Journal of Organizational Behavior*, 19: 637–47

Antonacopoulou, E.P. (2009): *HRM in Context: A Case Study Approach*. Basingstoke: Palgrave

Appelbaum, E., Bailey, T., Berg, P. and Kalleberg, A. (2000): *Manufacturing Advantage: Why High-Performance Work Systems Pay Off*. Ithaca, NY: Cornell University Press

Archer, M. (1995): *Realist Social Theory: The Morphogenetic Approach*. Cambridge: Cambridge University Press

Argyris, C. (1960): *Understanding Organizational Behavior*. Homewood, IL: Dorsey Press

Argyris, C. (1964): *Integrating the Individual and the Organization*. New York: John Wiley and Sons

Armstrong, M. and Baron, A. (1998): *Performance Management: The New Realities*. London: CIPD

Aronowitz, S. and Difazio, W. (1999): The new knowledge work. In J. Ahier and G. Esland (eds), *Education, Training and the Future of Work* (Vol. 1). Buckingham: Open University Press

Aronson, J. (1994): A pragmatic view of thematic analysis. *Qualitative Report*, 2 (1): 1–3

Arthur, M. and Rousseau, D. (1996): *The Boundaryless Career: A New Employment Principle for a New Organizational Era*. New York: Oxford University Press

Astley, M.R. (2015): Orchestrated stakeholder dialogue: Its place in dynamic capability theory and its practical value for business. PhD, London Metropolitan University

Atkinson, C. (2007): Trust and the psychological contract. *Employee Relations*, 29 (3): 227–46

Atkinson, J. and Meager, N. (1986): Is flexibility just a flash in the pan? *Personnel Management*, 18: 26–9

Augier, M. and Teece, D.J. (2009): Dynamic capabilities and the role of managers in business strategy and economic performance. *Organization Science*, 20 (2): 410–21

Bach S. (2000): Performance management. In Bach S. and Sisson K. (eds), *Personnel Management: A Comprehensive Guide to Theory and Practice*. Oxford: Blackwell

Bain, P., Watson, A., Mulvey, G., Taylor, P. and Gall, G. (2002): Taylorism, targets and the pursuit of quantity and quality by call centre management. *New Technology, Work and Employment*, 17 (3): 170–85

Bakan, J. (2004): *The Corporation: The Pathological Pursuit of Profit and Power*. London: Constable.

Bakker, A.B. and Demerouti, E. (2006): The job demands–resources model: State of the art. *Journal of Managerial Psychology*, 22 (3): 309–28

Bakker, A.B., Demerouti, E. and Sanz-Vergel, A.I. (2014): Burnout and work engagement: The JD–R approach. *Annual Review of Organizational Psychology and Organizational Behavior*, 1 (March): 389–411

Baldamus, G. (1961): *Efficiency and Effort*. London: Tavistock

Baldry, C., Bain, P. and Watson, A. (2007): *The Meaning of Work in the New Economy*. Basingstoke: Palgrave Macmillan

Ball, S.J. (1990): *Foucault and Education*. London: Routledge

Ball, S.J. (1994): *Education Reform: A Critical and Post-Structural Approach*. Buckingham: Open University Press

Ball, S.J. (1999): Performativity and fragmentation in postmodern schooling. In Carter, J. (ed.), *Postmodernity and the Fragmentation of Welfare*. London: Routledge

Ball, S.J. (2003): The teacher's soul and the terrors of performativity. *Education Policy*, 18 (2): 215–28

Bandura, A. (2001): Social cognitive theory: An agentic perspective. *Annual Review of Psychology*, 52: 1–26

Baran, P.A. and Sweezy, P.M. (1996): *Monopoly Capital: An essay on the American Economic and Social Order*. New York: Monthly Review Press

Barber, P. (2008): Beyond the pay cheque. *Financial Times*, 5 November, www.ft.com/cms/s/0/10e64e7e-ab34-11dd-b9e1-000077b07658.html#ixzz1GskFVa9e

Bardwick, J. (2007): *One Foot out the Door: How to Combat the Psychological Recession that's Alienating Employees and Hurting American Business*. New York: Amacom

Barney, J.B. (2001): Is the resource-based theory a useful perspective for strategic management research? Yes. *Academy of Management Review*, 26 (1): 41–56

Barrett, C.R. and Niekerk, G. (2013): Sustainable business: A Fortune 500 company perspective. In Huffman, A.H. and Klein, S.R. (eds), *Green Organizations: Driving Change with I-O Psychology*. New York: Routledge

Barrick, M.R. and Mount, M.K. (1993): Autonomy as a moderator of the relationship between the Big Five personality dimensions and job performance. *Journal of Applied Psychology*, 78: 111–18

Bauman, Z. (1992): *Mortality, Immortality and Other Life Strategies*. Stanford, CA: Stanford University Press

Bauman, Z. (2002): *Society under Siege*. Cambridge: Polity Press

Bazely, P. (2009): Analysing qualitative data: More than 'identifying themes'. *Malaysian Journal of Qualitative Research*, 2: 6–22

Beard, K.M. and Edwards, J.R. (1995): Employees at risk: Contingent work and the psychological experience. In Cooper, C.L. and Rousseau, D.M. (eds), *Trends in Organizational Behavior* (Vol. 2). New York: Wiley, pp. 109–26

Beardwell, I. and Holden, L. (2001): *Human Resource Management: A Contemporary Approach* (3rd edn). London: Financial Times Management

Beardwell, I., Holden L. and Claydon, T. (2004): *HRM: A Contemporary Approach* (4th edn). London: Financial Times Management

Becker, B.E. and Gerhart, B. (1996): The impact of human resource management on organizational performance: Progress and prospects. *Academy of Management Journal*, 39: 779–801

Beer, M. (1997): The transformation of human resource function: Resolving tension between a traditional administrative and a new strategic role. *Human Resource Management*, 97 (36): 49–56

308   *References*

Beer, M., Spector, B., Lawrence, P.R., Quinn Mills, D. and Walton, R.E. (1984): *Managing Human Assets*. New York: Free Press

Beer, M., Spector, B., Lawrence, P., Quinn Mills, D.Q. and Walton, R. (1985): *Human Resource Management: A General Manager's Perspective*. New York: Free Press

Befort, S.F. and Budd, J.W. (2009): *Invisible Hands, Invisible Objectives: Bringing Workplace Law and Public Policy into Focus*. Stanford, CA: Stanford University Press

Ben-Ner, A. and Jones, D.C. (1995): Employee participation, ownership and productivity: A theoretical framework. *Industrial Relations*, 34 (4): 532–54

Berger, P.L. (1974): *Pyramids of Sacrifice: Political Ethics and Social Change*. New York: Basic Books

Berger, P.L. and Luckmann, T. (1966): *The Social Construction of Reality*. New York: Anchor Books

Bernstein, L. (1981): *The Unanswered Question: Six Talks at Harvard*. Cambridge, MA: Harvard University Press

Best, S. (1995): *Politics of Historical Vision*. New York: Guilford Press

Bevan, S. (2012): High performance, good work and productivity. *Work Foundation*, www.theworkfoundation.com/Reports/316/High-performance-good-work-and-productivity

Binnie, G. (2005): *Tomorrow's Global Company – The Challenges and Choices: Corporate Purpose and Values – Time for a Re-think?* London: Tomorrow's Company

Blair, M.M. (1995): *Ownership and Control: Rethinking Corporate Governance for the Twenty-First Century*. Washington, DC: Brookings Institution Press

Blair, M.M. and Roe, M.J. (eds) (1999): *Employees and Corporate Governance*. Washington, DC: Brookings Institution Press

Blasi, J., Kruse, D. and Bernstein, A. (2003): *In the Company of Owners: The Truth About Stock Options (and Why Every Employee Should Have Them)*. New York: Basic Books

Blau, P.M. (1964): *Exchange and Power in Social Life*. New York: Wiley

Blauner, R. (1964): *Alienation and Freedom*. Chicago, IL: University of Chicago Press

Blinder, A. (2007): How many jobs might be offshorable? *CEPS working paper 142*, Princeton, NJ: Princeton University

Blundell, R. and MaCurdy, T. (2008): Labour supply. *The New Palgrave Dictionary of Economics* (2nd edn). Basingstoke: Palgrave Macmillan

Blyton, P. and Morris, J. (1992): HRM and the limits of flexibility. In Blyton and Turnbull (2004)

Blyton, P. and Turnbull, P. (2004): *The Dynamics of Employee Relations* (3rd edn). Basingstoke: Macmillan

Boje, D.M. (2010): Labor process theory and other grand narratives, business.nmsu.edu/~dboje/grand.html

Boltanski, L. and Chiapello, E. (2006): *The New Spirit of Capitalism*. London: Verso

Bolton, S.C. and Houlihan, M. (2009): Beyond the control-resistance debate: A fresh look at experiences of work in the new economy. *Qualitative Research in Accounting and Management*, 6 (1–2): 5–13

Bonini, S., Gorner, S. and Jones, A. (2010): How companies manage sustainability. McKinsey Global Results, www.mckinsey.com/insights/sustainability/how_companies_manage_sustainability_mckinsey_global_survey_results

Boselie, P., Dietz, G. and Boon, C. (2005): Commonalities and contradictions in research on human resource management and performance. *Human Resource Management Journal*, 13 (3): 67–94

Boselie, P., Brewster, C. and Paauwe, J. (2009): In search of balance: Managing the dualities of HRM: An overview of the issues. *Personnel Review*, 38 (5): 461–71

Boudreau, J.W. and Ramstad, P.M. (2007): *Beyond HR: The New Science of Human Capital*. Cambridge, MA: Harvard Business Review Press

Bourdieu, P. (1998): A reasoned utopia and economic fatalism. *New Left Review*, 227: 25–30

Boxall, P. and Macky, K. (2009): Research and theory on high-performance work systems: Progressing the high-involvement stream. *Human Resource Management Journal*, 19 (1): 3–23

Boxall, P. and Macky, K. (2014): High-involvement work processes, work intensification and employee well-being. *Work, Employment and Society*, 28 (6): 963–84

Boxall, P. and Purcell, J. (2008): *Strategy and Human Resource Management*. Basingstoke: Palgrave Macmillan

Boxall, P., Purcell, J. and Wright, P. (2007): *Oxford Handbook of Human Resource Management*. Oxford: Oxford University Press

References 309

Boxley, S. (2003): Performativity and capital in schools. *Journal for Critical Education Policy Studies*, 1 (1), www.jceps.com/?pageID=article&articleID=3

Brannen, J. and Nilsen A. (2002): *Lone Parents and the Labour Market: Literature Review and Secondary Review of the Labour Force Survey*. Sheffield: Employment Office

Brannan, M.J., Parson E. and Priola, V. (2011): *Branded Lives: The production and consumption of meaning at work*. Edward Elgar Publishing

Braverman, H. (1974): *Labor and Monopoly Capital: The Degradation of Work in the Twentieth Century*. New York: Monthly Review Press

Brayfield, A.H. and Crockett, W.H. (1955): Employee attitudes and employee performance. *Psychological Bulletin*, 52: 396–424

Briner, R. (2007): Is HRM evidence-based and does it matter? Opinion paper OP6, Institute for Employment Studies, March

Brockner, J., Konovsky, M., Cooper-Schneider, R., Folger, R., Martin, C. and Bies, R.J. (1994): Interactive effects of procedural justice and outcome negativity on victims and survivors of job loss. *Academy of Management Journal*, 37 (2): 397–409

Brooks, I. (2009): *Organisational Behaviour: Individuals, Groups and Organisation*, (4th edn). Harlow: Pearson Education

Brown, A., Forde, C., Spencer, D. and Charlwood, A. (2008): Changes in HRM and job satisfaction, 1998–2004: Evidence from the Workplace Employment Relations Survey. *Human Resource Management Journal*, 18 (3): 237–56

Brown, D., Caldwell, R., White, K., Atkinson, K., Goodge, P. and Emmott, M. (2004): *Business Partnering: A New Direction for HR*. London: CIPD

Brown, P., Ashton, D. and Lauder, H. (2010a): Skills are not enough: The globalisation of knowledge and the future UK economy. *Praxis*, 4 (March)

Brown, P., Lauder, H. and Ashton, D. (2010b): *The Global Auction: The Broken Promises of Education, Jobs and Rewards*. New York: Oxford University Press

Buckingham, M. and Goodall, A. (2015): Reinventing performance management: A Deloitte case study. *Harvard Business Review*, April, https://hbr.org/2015/04/reinventing-performance-management

Budd, J.W. (2004): *Employment with a Human Face: Balancing Efficiency, Equity, and Voice*. Ithaca, NY: Cornell University Press

Budd, J.W. (2010a): Theorizing work: The importance of conceptualisations of work for research and practice. Presentation given at the 25th Cardiff Employment Research Unit Annual Conference, Cardiff Business School, 13–14 September

Budd, J.W. and Bhave, D. (2010b): "The Employment Relationship," in A. Wilkinson, T. Redman, S. Snell, and N. Bacon, eds., Sage Handbook of Human Resource Management (London: Sage), pp. 51–70

Budd, J.W. and Bhave, D. (2008): Values, ideologies, and frames of reference in industrial relations. In Blyton, P., Heery, H., Bacon, N. and Fiorito, J. (eds), *Sage Handbook of Industrial Relations*. London: Sage, pp. 92–112

Budd, J.W., Gomez, R. and Meltz, N.M. (2004): Why a balance is best: The pluralist. Industrial relations paradigm of balancing competing interests. In Kauffman, B.E. (ed.), *Theoretical Perspectives on Work and the Employment Relationship*. Champaign, IL: Industrial Relations Research Association, pp. 195–228

Bunting, M. (2004): *Willing Slaves: How the Overwork Culture Is Ruling Our Lives*. New York: HarperCollins

Burawoy, M. (1979): *Manufacturing Consent: Changes in the Labor Process under Monopoly Capitalism*. Chicago, IL: University of Chicago Press

Burnes, B. (2009): *Managing Change* (5th edn). Harlow: Pearson Education

Burrell, G. and Morgan, G. (1979): *Sociological Paradigms and Organisational Analysis*. Aldershot: Ashgate Publishing

Byrne, R. (2001): Employees: Capital or commodity? *Learning Organization*, 8 (1): 44–50

Cafferkey, K. and Dundon, T. (2015): Explaining the black box: HPWS and organisational climate. *Personnel Review*, 44 (5): 666–88

Caldwell, R. (2003): The changing roles of personnel managers: Old ambiguities, new uncertainties. *Journal of Management Studies*, 40 (4): 983–1004

Cannon, D. (1997): *Generation X and the New Work Ethic*. London: DEMOS

Cappelli, P. (1999): *The New Deal at Work*. Boston, MA: Harvard University Press

310 *References*

Cappelli, P. (2008): Talent management for the twenty-first century. *Harvard Business Review*, 86 (3): 74–81

Cappelli, P. (2015): Why we love to hate HR…and what HR can do about it. *Harvard Business Review* (July–August), https://hbr.org/2015/07/why-we-love-to-hate-hr-and-what-hr-can-do-about-it

Carberry, E.J. (ed.) (2011): *Employee Ownership and Shared Capitalism: New Directions in Research*. Ithaca, NY: Cornell University

Cascio, W.F. (2007): Evidence-based management and the marketplace for ideas. *Academy of Management Journal*, 50 (5): 1009–12

Cavanagh, G.F. (1999): Spirituality for managers: Context and critique. *Journal of Organizational Change*, 12: 186–99

Caye, J-M., Dyer, A., Leicht, M., Minto, A. and Strack, R. (2008): *Creating People Advantage: How to Address HR Challenges Worldwide through 2015*. Boston, MA: BCG and Dusseldorf: EAPM

Cellan-Jones, R. (2014): Stephen Hawking warns artificial intelligence could end mankind. *BBC*, 2 December, www.bbc.com/news/technology-30290540

Charan, R. (2014): It's time to split HR. *Harvard Business Review*, July–August

Chesbrough, H.W. (2006): *Open Innovation: The New Imperative for Creating and Profiting from Technology*. Cambridge, MA: Harvard University Press

Cheung-Judge, M.-Y. and Holbeche, L.S. (2015): *Organization Development: A Practitioner's Guide for OD and HR* (2nd edn). London: Kogan Page

Christensen, C.M., Raynor, M.E. and McDonald, R. (2015): What is disruptive innovation? *Harvard Business Review*, December, https://hbr.org/2015/12/what-is-disruptive-innovation

Christensen, T., Laegreid, P. and Wise, L.R. (2002): Transforming administrative policy. *Public Administration*, 80 (1): 153–78

Chomsky, N. (1975): *Reflections on Language*. New York: Pantheon

CIPD (2007): *Employee Attitudes and Engagement Survey*. London: Chartered Institute of Personnel and Development

CIPD (2014): *HR: Getting Smart about Agile Working*. London: CIPD

CIPD (2016): *From Best to Good Practice HR: Developing Principles for the Profession*. London: CIPD

Clark, A. (1997): *Being There: Putting Brain, Body and World Together Again*. Cambridge, MA: MIT Press

Clark, M.S. and Waddell, B. (1985): Perceptions of exploitation in communal and exchange relationships. *Journal of Social and Personal Relationships*, 2: 403–18

Clarke, J. and Newman, J. (1997): *The Managerial State: Power, Politics and Ideology in the Remaking of the Welfare State*. London: Sage

Clarkson Centre for Business Ethics (1999): Principles of stakeholder management. Joseph L. Rotman School of Management, University of Toronto

Coats, D. and Lehki, R. (2008): *Good Work, Job Quality in a Changing Economy*. London: Work Foundation

Collins, J.C. (2001): *Good to Great: Why Some Companies Make the Leap…and Others Don't*. London: Random House Business

Collins, J.C. and Porras, J.I. (1994): *Built to Last: Successful Habits of Visionary Companies*. London: HarperCollins

Colquitt, J.A., Wesson, M., Porter, C., Conlon, D. and Ng, K.Y. (2001): Justice at the millennium: A meta-analytic review of 25 years of organizational justice research. *Journal of Applied Psychology*, 86 (3): 425–45

Combs, J., Longmei, L., Hall, A. and Kecthan, D. (2006): How much do high performance work practices matter? A meta-analysis of their effects on organisational performance. *Personnel Psychology*, Autumn

Conger, J.A. (1994): *Spirit at Work: Discovering the Spirituality in Leadership*. San Francisco: Jossey-Bass Management

Constas, M.A. (1992): Qualitative analysis as a public event: The documentation of category development procedures. *American Educational Research Journal*, 29 (2): 253–66

Conway, E., Fu, N., Monks, K., Alfes, K. and Bailey, C. (2015): Demands or resources? The relationship between HR practices, employee engagement, and emotional exhaustion within a hybrid model of employment relations. *Human Resource Management*, 9 March

Cooper, R. (1997): Applying emotional intelligence in the workplace. *Training and Development*, 51 (12): 31–8

Cooperrider, D.L. and Srivastva, S. (1987): Appreciative inquiry in organizational life. In Woodman, R.W. and Pasmore, W.A. (eds), *Research in Organizational Change and Development*, 1: 129–69

Costea, B., Crump, N. and Holm J. (2007): The spectre of Dionysus: Play, work, and managerialism. *Society and Business Review*, 2 (2): 153–65

Costea, B., Crump, N. and Amiridis, K. (2008): Managerialism, the Therapeutic Habitus and the Self in Contemporary Organizing. *Human Relations*, 61 (5): 661–85

Coyle-Shapiro, J. and Kessler, I. (1998): The psychological contract in the UK public sector: Employer and employee obligations and contract fulfilment. In Havlovic, S.J. (ed.), *Academy of Management Best Paper Proceedings*, pp. 1–7

Coyle-Shapiro, J. and Kessler, I. (2000): Consequences of the psychological contract for the employment relationship: A large scale survey. *Journal of Management Studies*, 37 (7): 903–30

Coyle-Shapiro, J. and Shaw, L. (2007): The employee–organization relationship: Where do we go from here? *Human Resource Management Review*, 17 (2): 166–79

Cox, J. (2006): An Introduction to Marx's Theory of Alienation, http://pubs. socialistreviewindex.org.uk/isj79/cox.htm

Crouch, C. (1998): *Corporatism: International Encyclopaedia of Business and Management*. London: Thomson

Cruikshank, B. (1996): Revolutions within: Self-government and self-esteem. In Barry, A., Osborne, T. and Rose, N. (eds), *Foucault and Political Reason: Liberalism, Neo-Liberalism, and Rationalities of Government*. Chicago, IL: University of Chicago Press

Crush, P. (2016): 'We lost our way' admits RBS HR chief. *CIPD Scotland*, 7 March

Csíkszentmihályi, M. (1998): *Finding Flow: The Psychology of Engagement with Everyday Life*. New York: Basic Books

Csíkszentmihályi, M., Damon, W. and Gardner, H. (2001): *Good Work: When Excellence and Ethics Meet*. New York: Basic Books

Cullinane, J. (1996): Theorising human resource management. In Harbridge, R., Gadd, R. and Crawford, A. (eds), *Current Research in Industrial Relations*. Melbourne: Victoria University Press

Cullinane, N. and Dundon, T. (2006): The psychological contract: A critical review. *International Journal of Management Reviews*, 8 (2): 113–29

Cunningham, B. (1997): The failing teacher in further education. *Journal of Further and Higher Education*, 21 (3): 365–71

Cutler, T. and Waine, B. (1994): *Managing the Welfare State*. Oxford: Berg

D'Art, D. and Turner, T. (2008): Workers and the demand for trade unions in Europe: Still a relevant social force? *Economic and Industrial Democracy*, 29 (2): 165–91

Davies, A. (1986): *Industrial Relations and New Technology*. Dover: Croom Helm

Davies, G., Chun, R., daSilva, R. and Roper, S. (2003): *Corporate Reputation and Competitiveness*. London: Routledge

Davies, P. (2009): The Griffiths Report: 25 years on. *Health Service Journal*, 5 June

Davis, G. (1997): Implications, consequences and futures. In Davis, G., Sullivan, B. and Yeatman, A. (eds), *The New Contractualism?* Melbourne: Macmillan, pp. 224–38

De Geus, A. (1997): *The Living Company*. Boston, MA: Harvard Business School Press

De Jonge, J. and Schaufeli, W.B. (1998): Job characteristics and employee well-being: A test of Warr's Vitamin Model in health care workers using structural equation modelling. *Journal of Organizational Behavior*, 19: 387–407

De Meuse, K.P., Bergmann, T.J. and Lester, S.W. (2001): An investigation of the relational component of the psychological contract across time, generation, and employment status. *Journal of Managerial Issues*, 13 (1): 102–18

Deal, T.E. and Kennedy, A. (2000): *Corporate Cultures: The Rites and Rituals of Corporate Life*. New York: Basic Books

Dean, J. (2016): Intelligent 'chat bots' to replace humans on customer service helplines. *The Times*, 13 April, www.thetimes.co.uk/tto/technology/article4731931.ece

Dean, J.W., Brandes, P. and Dharwadkar, R. (1998): Organizational cynicism. *Academy of Management Review*, 23: 341–52

Dearlove, J. (1998): Fundamental changes in institutional governance structures: The United Kingdom. *Higher Education Policy*, 11: 111–20

312 *References*

Deem, R. (1998): New managerialism and higher education: The management of performances and cultures in universities in the United Kingdom. *International Studies in the Sociology of Higher Education*, 8 (1): 47–70

Deem, R. (2004): The knowledge worker, the manager-academic and the contemporary UK university: New and old forms of public management? *Financial Accountability and Management*, 20 (2): 107–28

Deery, S. and Kinnie, N. (eds) (2004): *Call Centres and Human Resource Management: A Cross-National Perspective*. Houndsmill: Palgrave Macmillan

Deetz, S. (1992): *Democracy in an Age of Corporate Colonization: Developments in Communication and the Politics of Everyday Life*. Albany, NY: University of New York

Deetz, S. (2003): Disciplinary power, conflict suppression and human resources management. In Alvesson, M. and Willmott, H. (eds), *Studying Management Critically*. London: Sage

Delbridge, R. (1998): *Life on the Line in Contemporary Manufacturing: The Workplace Experience of Lean Production and the 'Japanese' Model*. Oxford: Oxford University Press

Delbridge, R. and Keenoy, T. (2010): Beyond managerialism? *International Journal of Human Resource Management*, 21 (6): 801–19

Deloitte (2015): Mind the gaps: The 2015 Deloitte Millennial survey. www2.deloitte.com/global/en/pages/about-deloitte/articles/millennialsurvey.html

Deloitte (2016a): Deloitte HC trends 2016. The new organization: Different by design. Westlake, TX: Deloitte University Press, www.workdayrising.com/pdf/Deloitte_GlobalHumanCapitalTrends_2016_3.pdf

Deloitte (2016b): The 2016 Deloitte Millennial Survey: Winning Over the Next Generation of Leaders. Westlake, TX: Deloitte University Press

Demerouti, E., Bakker, A.B., Nachreiner, F. and Schaufeli, W.B. (2001): The job demands-resources model of burnout. *Journal of Applied Psychology*, 86: 499–512

Deming, W.E. (1986): *Out of the Crisis*. Cambridge, MA: Massachusetts Institute of Technology

Den Hartog, D., Boon, C., Verburg, R.M. and Croon, M.A. (2013): HRM, communication, satisfaction, and perceived performance: A cross-level test. *Journal of Management*, 39 (6): 1637–65

Dent, M. (ed.) (2004): *Managing Professional Identities*. London: Routledge

Department of Trade and Industry (2008): *Workplace Employee Relations Survey*. Colchester: DTI

Dessler, G. (1994): *Human Resource Management*. Englewood Cliffs, NJ: Prentice-Hall

Devanna, M. and Tichy, N. (1990): Creating the competitive organization of the 21st century: The boundaryless corporation. *Human Resource Management*, 29 (4): 455–71

Diener, E. and Seligman, M.E.P. (2004): Beyond money: Toward an economy of well-being. *Psychological Science in the Public Interest*, 5, 1–31, http://dx.doi.org/10.1111/j.0963-7214.2004.00501001.x

Dietz, G., Wilkinson, A. and Redman, T. (2010): Involvement and participation. In Wilkinson, A., Bacon, N., Redman, T. and Snell, S. (eds), *The Sage Handbook of Human Resource Management*. London: Sage Publications

Doherty, N. (1996): Surviving in an era of insecurity. *European Journal of Work and Organizational Psychology*, 5 (4): 471–8

Doherty, N., Viney, C. and Adamson, S. (1997): Rhetoric or reality: Shifts in graduate career management? *Career Development International*, 2: 173–9

Doi, Y. (2005): An epidemiologic review on occupational sleep research among Japanese workers. *Industrial Health*, 43: 3–10

Dolenc, P., Stubelj, I. and Laporsek, S. (2012): What is the objective of a firm? Overview of theoretical perspectives. In Bojnec, Š., Brada, J.C. and Kuboniwa, M. (eds), *Overcoming the Crisis: Economic and Financial Developments in Asia and Europe*. Koper: University of Primorska Press, pp. 51–64

Donaldson, T. and Preston, L.E. (1995): The stakeholder theory of the corporation: Concepts, evidence and implications. *Academy of Management Review*, 20 (1): 65–91

Drucker, P.F. (1954): *The Practice of Management*. New York: Harper Business

Drucker, P.F. (1993): *Post-Capitalist Society*. London: Harper Paperbacks

Du Gay, P. (1996): Organizing identity: Entrepreneurial governance and public. In *Consumption and Identity at Work*. London: Sage

Du Gay, P. and Salaman, G. (1992): The cult(ure) of the customer. *Journal of Management Studies*, 29 (5): 615–33

Dundon, T. and Ryan, P. (2010): Interviewing reluctant respondents: Strikes, henchmen, and Gaelic games. *Organizational Research Methods*, 13 (3): 562–81

Dutton, J.E., Dukerich, J.M. and Harquail, C.V. (1994): Organizational images and member identification. *Administrative Science Quarterly*, 39: 239–63

Dyer, S. (2007): Crafting critical HRM in the management classroom. CMS Conference proceedings, www.mngt.waikato.ac.nz/ejrot/cmsconference/2007/proceedings/whereiscriticalhrm/dyer.pdf

Economist Intelligence Unit (2015): The cost of inaction: Recognising the value at risk from climate change, www.economistinsights.com/sites/default/files/The%20cost%20of%20inaction.pdf

Edwards, J.C. and Karau, S.J. (2007): Psychological contract or social contract? Development of the employment contracts scale. *Journal of Leadership and Organizational Studies*, Spring

Edwards, M.R. (2005): Organizational identification: A conceptual and operational review. *International Journal of Management Reviews*, 7 (4): 207–30

Edwards, P. (1986): *Conflict at Work*. Oxford: Blackwell

Edwards, P. (1995): The employment relationship. In Edwards, P. (ed.), *Industrial Relations*. Oxford: Blackwell

Edwards, P. (ed.) (2003): *Industrial Relations: Theory and Practice* (2nd edn). Oxford: Blackwell

Edwards, R. (1978): Social relations of production at the point of production. *Insurgent Sociologist*, 8: 109–25

Ehrenfeld, J.R. and Hoffman, A.J. (2013): *Flourishing: A Frank Conversation about Sustainability*. Stanford, CA: Stanford University Press, www.theatlantic.com/national/archive/2011/12/a-conversation-with-andrew-j-hoffman-professor-of-sustainable-enterprise/249891/

Eisenhardt, K.M. and Martin, J.A. (2000): Dynamic capabilities: What are they? *Strategic Management Journal*, 21 (11): 1105–21

Ellig, B.R. (1998): Employment and employability: Foundation of the new social contract. *Human Resource Management*, 37: 173–5

Elliot, J. and Quaintance, L. (2003): Britain is getting more suspicious. *Sunday Times*, 18 May

Ellsworth, R.E. (2002): *Leading with Purpose*. Stanford, CA: Stanford Business Books

Erickson, T. (2010): *What's Next, Gen X? Keeping Up, Moving Ahead and Getting the Career You Want*. Cambridge, MA: Harvard Business School Press

Esland, G., Esland, K., Murphy, M. and Yarrow, K. (1999): Managerializing organizational culture. In Ahier, J. and Esland, G. (eds), *Education, Training and the Future of Work* (Vol. 1). London: Open University/Routledge, pp. 160–85

Espinosa-Orias, N. and Sharratt, P.N. (2006): A hierarchical approach to stakeholder engagement. Proceedings of 13th CIRP International Conference on Life Cycle Engineering, pp. 525–9, www.mech.kuleuven.be/lce2006/145.pdf

Ethical Funds Company (2006): Shareholder action program 2006 status report. BC, Canada and personal communication, Robert Walker, Vice-President, 2 November, www.ethicalfunds.com/do_the_right_thing/sri/ethical_principles_criteria

Fairclough, N. (2001): *Language and Power* (2nd edn). London: Longman

Fairclough, N. (2003): *Analysing Discourse: Textual Analysis for Social Research*. London: Routledge

Farndale, E. and Kelliher, C. (2013): Implementing performance appraisal: Exploring the employee experience. *Human Resource Management*, 52 (6): 879–97

Farnham, D. (ed.) (2002): *Managing Academic Staff in Changing University Systems: International Trends and Comparisons*. London: Society for Research into Higher Education

Felstead, A., Gallie, D., Green, F. and Zhou, Y. (2007): *Skills at Work (1986–2006)*. Oxford: Oxford University Press

Fineman, S. (2000): Emotional arenas revisited. In Fineman, S. (ed.), *Emotions in Organizations*. London: Sage, pp. 1–24

Fisk, C.L. (2002): Reflections on the new psychological contract and the ownership of human capital. *Connecticut Law Review*, 34: 765–85

Fiss, P.C. and Zajac, E.J. (2004): The diffusion of ideas over contested terrain: The (non) adoption of a shareholder value orientation among German firms. *Administrative Science Quarterly*, 49 (4): 501–34

Fleetwood, S. and Hesketh, A. (2006): High performance work systems, organisational performance and (lack of) predictive power. *Journal of Critical Realism*, 5 (2): 228–50

Fleetwood, S. and Hesketh, A. (2010): *Explaining the Performance of Human Resource Management*. Cambridge: Cambridge University Press

314   *References*

Flood, P.C., Turner, T., Ramamoorthy, N. and Pearson J. (2001): The causes and consequences of psychological contract among knowledge workers in the high technology and financial services industries. *International Journal of Human Resource Management*, 67: 845–55

Foley, M., Maxwell, G. and McGillivray, D. (1999): The UK context of workplace empowerment: Debating HRM and post-modernity. *Participation and Empowerment: An International Journal*, 7 (6): 163–77

Fombrun, C.J. and Van Riel, C.B.M. (2003): *Fame and Fortune: How Successful Companies Build Winning Reputations*. London: FT Press

Fombrun, C.J, Tichy, N.M. and Devanna, M.A. (1984): *Strategic Human Resource Management*. New York: Wiley

Foucault, M. (1977): *Discipline and Punish*. New York: Pantheon

Foucault, M. (1980): *Power/Knowledge*. New York: Pantheon Books

Foucault, M. (1997 [1978]): What is critique? In Lotringer, S. and Hochroth, L. (eds), *The Politics of Truth*. New York: Semiotext(e)

Foucault, M. (2004): *Society Must Be Defended*. London: Penguin

Fournier, V. and Grey, C. (2000): At the critical moment: Conditions and prospects for critical management studies. *Human Relations*, 53 (1): 7–32

Fowler, A. (1987): When chief executives discover HRM. *Personnel Management*, January

Fox, A. (2013): Customer-centric HR. *HR Magazine*, 58 (6), www.shrm.org/publications/hrmagazine/editorialcontent/2013/0613/pages/0613-customer-centric-hr.aspx#sthash.0EE6LtdG.dpuf

Francis, D. (2001): Managing people in agile organisations. In *Agile Manufacturing: The 21st Century Competitive Strategy*. Amsterdam: Elsevier Science BV, pp. 193–202

Francis, H. (2003): HRM and the beginnings of organizational change. *Journal of Organizational Change Management*, 16 (3): 309–28

Francis, H. (2006): A critical discourse perspective on managers' experiences of HRM. *Qualitative Research in Organizations and Management: An International Journal*, 1 (2): 65–82

Francis, H. (2007): Discursive struggle and the ambiguous world of HRD. *Advances in Developing Human Resources*, 9 (1): 83–96

Francis, H. and D'Annunzio-Green, N. (2007): The impact of emotion management training on the 'shifting sands' of the psychological contract. In Hill, R. and Stewart, J. (eds), *Management Development: Perspectives from Research and Practice*. London: Routledge, pp. 177–96

Francis, H. and Keegan, A. (2006): The changing face of HRM: In search of balance. *Human Resource Management Journal*, 16 (3): 231–49

Francis, H and Sinclair, J. (2003): A processual analysis of HRM-based change. *Organization*, 10 (4): 685–706

Frankl, V. (2006): *Man's Search for Meaning*. Boston: Beacon Press

Freeman, R.E. (1984): *Strategic Management: A Stakeholder Approach*. Boston, MA: Pitman Publishing

Freeman, R.E. (2004): A stakeholder theory of modern corporations. In Donaldson, T. and Werhane, P. (eds), *Ethical Issues in Business: A Philosophical Approach* (7th edn). Englewood Cliffs, NJ: Prentice Hall, pp. 38–48

Freeman, R.E., Wicks, A.C. and Parmar, B. (2004): Stakeholder theory and 'the corporate objective revisited'. *Organization Science*, 15 (3): 364–9

Freeman, R.B., Blasi, J.R. and Kruse, D.L. (2010): The extent and operation of shared capitalism. In Kruse, D.L., Freeman, R.B. and Blasi, J.R. (eds), *Shared Capitalism at Work*. Cambridge, MA: National Bureau of Economic Research, www.nber.org/chapters/c8085.pdf

Frenkel, S.J., Lloyd, L., Restubog, D. and Bednall, T. (2012): How employee perceptions of HR policy and practice influence discretionary work effort and co-worker assistance: Evidence from two organizations. *International Journal of Human Resource Management*, 23 (20): 4193–210

Frenking, S. (2016): Feel good management as valuable tool to shape workplace culture and drive employee happiness. *Strategic HR Review*, 15 (1): 14–19

Friedman, A. (1977): Responsible autonomy versus direct control over the labour process. *Capital and Class*, 1

Friedman, A.L. and Miles, S. (2006): *Stakeholders: Theory and Practice*. Oxford: Oxford University Press

Friedman, M. (1962): *Capitalism and Freedom*. Chicago, IL: University of Chicago Press

References   315

Friedman, M. and Schwartz, A.J. (1963): *A Monetary History of the United States*. Princeton, NJ: Princeton University Press

Fulmer, I., Gerhart, B. and Scott, K. (2003): Are the 100 best better? An empirical investigation of the relationship between being 'a great place to work' and firm performance. *Personnel Psychology*, 56: 965–93

Gallie, D., Felstead, A. and Green, F. (2001): Employer policies and organizational commitment in Britain 1992–7. *Journal of Management Studies*, 38 (8): 1081–101

Gamble, A. (2009): *The Spectre at the Feast: Capitalist Crisis and the Politics of Recession*. London: Palgrave Macmillan

Gandini, A. (2016): *The Reputation Economy: Understanding Knowledge Work in Digital Society*. Basingstoke: Palgrave Macmillan

Gardner, H. (2007): *Responsibility at Work: How Leading Professionals Act (or Don't Act) Responsibly*. San Francisco, CA: Jossey-Bass

Garraty, J.A. (1973): The new deal, national socialism, and the great depression. *American Historical Review*, 78 (4): 907–44

Garrow, V., Varney, S. and Lloyd, C. (2009): Fish or bird? Perspectives on Organisational Development (OD). *Research report 463, Institute for Employment Studies*, May, www.employment-studies.co.uk/resource/fish-or-bird-perspectives-organisational-development-od

Geary, J.F. and Dobbins, A. (2001): Teamworking: A new dynamic in the pursuit of management control. *Human Resource Management Journal*, 11 (1): 3–21

Giddens, A. (1982): *Sociology: A Brief but Critical Introduction*. London: Macmillan

Giddens, A. (1986): *Constitution of Society: Outline of the Theory of Structuration*. Berkeley: University of California Press

Giddens, A. (1999): *Runaway World: How Globalization Is Reshaping Our Lives*. London: Profile

Gillespie, N. and Dietz, G. (2009): 'Trust Repair After an Organizational-level Failure', *Academy of Management Review*, 34 (1), 127–145.

Goleman, D. (1996): *Emotional Intelligence*. London: Bloomsbury Publishing

Goleman, D. (2011): *Leadership: The Power of Emotional Intelligence*. Florence, MA: More Than Sound

Goodman, J. (2010): Cosmopolitan women educators, 1920–1939: Inside/outside activism and abjection. *Paedagogica Historica*, 46 (1–2): 69–83

Gordon, D. (1996): *Fat and Mean: The Corporate Squeeze of Working Americans and the Myth of Managerial 'Downsizing'*. New York: Free Press

Gordon, D. (1999): Poverty and social exclusion in Britain, *Joseph Rowntree Foundation report*

Gowler, D. and Legge, K. (1983): The meaning of management and the management of meaning: A view from social anthropology. In Earl, M.J. (ed.), *Perspectives on Management*. Oxford: Oxford University Press

Graeber, D. (2015): *The Utopia of Rules*. New York: Melville House

Gramsci, A. (1971): *Selections from the Prison Notebooks*. London: Lawrence and Wishart

Grant, D. and Shields, J. (2002): In search of the subject: Researching employee reactions to human resource management. *Journal of Industrial Relations*, 44 (3): 313–34

Gray, J. (1999): *False Dawn: The Delusions of Global Capitalism*. London: Granta

Gray, J. (2008): A shattering moment in America's fall from power. *Observer*, 28 September

Green, F. (2004): Work intensification, discretion, and the decline in well-being at work. *Eastern Economic Journal*, 30 (4): 615–25

Green, F. (2009a): Employee involvement, technology and job tasks. National Institute of Economic and Social Research, Department of Economics, discussion paper no. 326

Green, F. (2009b): Job quality in Britain. Praxis No 1, November, UK Commission for Employment and Skills

Grey, C. (1996): Towards a critique of managerialism: The contribution of Simone Weil. *Journal of Management Studies*, 33: 591–612

Grey, C. and Mitev, N. (1995): Management education: A polemic. *Management Learning*, 26 (1): 103–7

Grey, C., Knights, D. and Willmott, H.C. (1996): Is a critical pedagogy of management possible? In French, R. and Grey, C. (eds), *Rethinking Management Education*. London: Sage, pp. 94–110

316   *References*

Grice, S. and Humphries, M.T. (1997): Critical management studies: Oxymorons in outer space. *Journal of Organisation Change Management*, 10 (5): 412–25

Griffin, J. (2011): The Lonely Society, The Mental Health Foundation.

Grint, K. (1995): *Management: A Sociological Introduction*. Cambridge: Polity Press

Griffiths, B. (1988): *Community Care: Agenda for Action: A Report to the Secretary of State for Social Services*. London: HMSO

Guerrera, F. (2009): Welch condemns share price focus. *Financial Times*, 12 March, https://next.ft.com/content/294ff1f2-0f27-11de-ba10-0000779fd2ac

Guest, D.E. (1987): Human resource management and industrial relations. *Journal of Management Studies*, 24 (5): 503–21

Guest, D.E. (1995): Human resource management, trade unions, and industrial relations. In Storey, J. (ed.), *HRM: A Critical Text*. London: Thomson

Guest, D.E. (1997a): Human resource management and performance: A review and research agenda. *International Journal of Human Resource Management*, 8: 263–76

Guest, D.E. (1998): Is the psychological contract worth taking seriously? *Journal of Organizational Behavior*, 19: 649–64

Guest, D.E. (1999): Human resource management: The workers' verdict. *Human Resource Management Journal*, 9 (3): 5–25

Guest, D.E. (2000): Management and the insecure workforce: The search for a new psychological contract. In Heery, E. and Salmon, J. (eds), *The Insecure Workforce*. London: Routledge

Guest, D.E. (2001): Human resource management: When research confronts theory. *International Journal of Human Resource Management*, 12 (7): 1092–106

Guest, D.E. (2002): Human resource management, corporate performance and employee well-being: Building the worker into HRM. *Journal of Industrial Relations*, 44 (3): 335–58

Guest, D.E. (2004): The psychology of the employment relationship: An analysis based on the psychological contract. *Applied Psychology*, 53 (4): 541–55

Guest, D.E. (2011): Human resource management and performance: Still searching for some answers. *Human Resource Management Journal*, 21 (1): 3–13

Guest, D.E. and Bryson, A. (2008): From industrial relations to human resource management: The changing role of the personnel function. *National Institute of Economic and Social Research working paper*

Guest, D.E. and Conway, N. (1997): *Employee Motivation and the Psychological Contract*. London: Institute for Personnel and Development

Guest, D.E. and Conway, N. (2001): *Employer Perceptions of the Psychological Contract*. London: Chartered Institute of Personnel and Development

Guest, D.E. and Conway, N. (2004): *Employee Well-Being and the Psychological Contract: A Report for the CIPD*. London: Chartered Institute of Personnel and Development

Guest, D.E. and King, Z. (2004): Power, innovation and problem-solving: The personnel managers' three steps to heaven? *Journal of Management Studies*, 41 (3): 401–23

Guest, D.E., Michie, J., Conway, N. and Sheehan, M. (2003): Human resource management and corporate performance in the UK. *British Journal of Industrial Relations*, 41 (2): 291–314

Guest, D.E., Conway, N. and Dewe, P. (2004): Using sequential tree analysis to search for 'bundles' of HR practices. *Human Resource Management Journal*, 14 (1): 79–96

Guetal, H.G. and Stone, D.L. (2005): *The Brave New World of E-HR: Human Resources Management in the Digital Age*. San Francisco, CA: Jossey-Bass

Gunther-McGrath, R. (2013): Transient advantage. *Harvard Business Review*, June, https://hbr.org/2013/06/transient-advantage

Habermas, J. (1977): Hannah Arendt's communications concept of power. *Social Research*, 44 (1): 3–24

Hackman, J.R. and Oldham, G.R. (1980): *Work Redesign*. Reading, MA: Addison-Wesley

Hakim, C. (1994): *We Are All Self-Employed: The New Social Contract for Working in a Changed World*. San Francisco, CA: Berrett-Koehler Publishers

Halbesleben, J.R.B. and Buckley, M.R. (2004): Burnout in organizational life. *Journal of Management*, 30: 859–79

Hall, E.T. (1977): *Beyond Culture*. New York: Doubleday

Hall, D.T. (1996): *The Career Is Dead: Long Live the Career.* San Francisco, CA: Jossey-Bass

Hall, D.T. and Moss, J.E. (1998): The new protean career contract: Helping organizations and employees adjust. *Organizational Dynamics,* 26: 27–37

Hammer, M. and Champy, J. (1993): *Reengineering the Corporation: A Manifesto for Business Revolution.* New York: Harper Business

Handy, C. (1987): *The Making of Managers: A Report on Management Education, Training and Development.* London: National Economic Development Office

Handy, C. (1994): *The Empty Raincoat.* London: Hutchinson

Hansmann, H. and Kraakman, R. (2000): End of history for corporate law. Harvard Law School Discussion Paper 280

Harley, B. and Hardy, C. (2004): Firing blanks? An analysis of discursive struggle in HRM. *Journal of Management Studies,* 41 (3): 377–400

Harley, B., Allen, B.C. and Sargent, L.D. (2007): High performance work systems and employee experience of work in the service sector: The case of aged care. *British Journal of Industrial Relations,* 45: 607–33

Harré, R. and Van Langenhove, L. (1999): *Positioning Theory.* Oxford: Blackwell

Harris, R. (2008): *The Happiness Trap.* London: Trumpeter Books

Harrison, L. (2016): *From Best to Good Practice HR: Developing Principles for the Profession.* London: Chartered Institute for Personnel and Development

Hartley, J. (1999): Models of job insecurity and coping strategies. In *Labour Market Changes and Job Insecurity.* Copenhagen: World Health Organization, pp. 127–50

Hartley, J., Jacobson, D., Klandermans, P.G. and Vuuren, C.V. (1991): *Job Insecurity: Coping with Jobs at Risk.* London: Sage

Harvey, D. (2010): *The Enigma of Capital and the Crisis of Capitalism.* London: Profile Books

Hasegawa, H. and Hook, G.D. (eds) (1998): *Japanese Business Management.* London: Routledge

Hassard, J. and Rowlinson, M. (2001): Marxist political economy, revolutionary politics and labour process theory. *International Studies of Management and Organisation,* 4: 85–111

Hatcher, R. (2001): Getting down to business: Schooling in the globalised economy. *Education and Social Justice,* 3 (2): 45–59

Hay McBer (2000): *Research into Teacher Effectiveness: A Model of Teacher Effectiveness.* London: DfEE

Hayes, S.C. (2004): *Get out of Your Mind and into Your Life.* Oakland, CA: New Harbinger Press

Health and Safety Executive (2007): *Managing the Causes of Work-Related Stress.* London: Office of Public Information

Heckscher, C. and Donnellon, A.M. (eds) (1994): *The Post-Bureaucratic Organization.* London: Sage Publications

Heffernan, M. and Dundon, T. (2016): Cross-level effects of high-performance worksystems (HPWS) and employee well-being: The mediating effect of organisational justice. *Human Resource Management Journal,* 26 (2): 211–31

Helfat, C.E., Finkelstein, S., Mitchell, W., Peteraf, M., Singh, H., Teece, D. and Winter, S. (2007): *Dynamic Capabilities: Understanding Strategic Change in Organizations.* London: Blackwell

Helliwell, J., Layard, R. and Sachs, J. (eds) (2012): *World Happiness Report.* New York: Earth Institute, Columbia University

Hendry, C. and Jenkins, R. (1997): Psychological contracts and new deals. *Human Resource Management Journal,* 7 (1): 38–45

Herman, J.B. (1973): Are situational contingencies limiting job attitude–job performance relationships? *Organizational Behavior and Human Performance,* 10: 208–24

Herriot, P. and Pemberton, C. (1995a): *New Deals: The Revolution in Managerial Careers.* Chichester: Wiley

Herriot, P. and Pemberton, C. (1995b): *The Career Management Challenge.* London: Sage

Herriot, P. and Pemberton, C. (1996): Contracting careers. *Human Relations,* 49 (6): 757–90

Herriot, P. and Pemberton, C. (1997): Facilitating New Deals. *Human Resource Management Journal,* 7 (1): 45–56

Herriot, P., Manning, W.E.G. and Kidd, J.M. (1997): The content of the psychological contract. *British Journal of Management,* 8: 151–62

318   *References*

Hesketh, A. (2014): *Valuing Your Talent: Managing the Value of Your Talent – a New Framework for Human Capital Measurement*. London: CIPD

Hesketh, A. and Hird, M. (2009): *The Golden Triangle*. Lancaster: Lancaster University

Hiltrop J-M. (1996): Managing the psychological contract. *Employee Relations*, 18 (1): 36–49

Hirsch, P.M. (1975): Organizational effectiveness and the institutional environment. *Administrative Science Quarterly*, 20 (3): 327–44

Hirsh, W., Holbeche, L., Garrow, V. and Devine, M. (1999): *Mergers and Acquisitions: Getting the 'People Bit' Right*. Horsham: Roffey Park

Hitt, M.A. (1988): The measuring of organizational effectiveness: Multiple domains and constituencies. *Management International Review*, 28 (2): 28–40

Ho, V.T., Weingart, L.R. and Rousseau, D.M. (2004): Responses to broken promises: Does personality matter? *Journal of Vocational Behavior*, 65 (2): 276–93

Hodgkinson, G.P. and Rousseau, D.M. (2009): Bridging the rigor-relevance gap in management research: It's already happening! *Journal of Management Studies*, 46 (3): 534–46

Hoffman, A. (2011): Talking past each other? Cultural framing of skeptical and convinced logics in the climate change debate. *Organization and Environment*, 24 (1): 3–33

Holbeche, L.S. (1996): *Career Development in Flatter Structures*. Horsham: Roffey Park

Holbeche, L.S. (1997): *Motivating People in Lean Organizations*. Oxford: Butterworth-Heinemann

Holbeche, L.S. (1999, 2005 and 2009): Aligning HR and Business Strategy, Oxford, Butterworth-Heinemann

Holbeche, L.S. (2005): *Understanding Change: Theory, Implementation and Success*. Oxford: Butterworth-Heinemann

Holbeche, L. (2012): The strategic context of new OE. In Francis, H., Holbeche, L. and Reddington, M. (eds), *People and Organisational Development: A New Agenda for Organisational Effectiveness*. London: CIPD

Holbeche, L.S. (2015): *Organizational Agility*. London: Kogan Page

Holbeche, L.S. and Springett, N. (2004): In Search of Meaning at Work, Horsham, Roffey Park

Holbeche, L.S. and Matthews, G. (2012): *Engaged: Unleashing the Potential of Your Organization through Employee Engagement*. Chichester: John Wiley/Jossey Bass

Holbeche, L. and Springett, N. (2004): *In Search of Meaning in the Workplace*. Horsham: Roffey Park Institute

Hope-Hailey, V., Farndale, E. and Truss, C. (2005): The HR department's role in organizational performance. *Human Resource Management Journal*, 15 (3): 49–66

Höpner, M. (2001): *Corporate Governance in Transition: Ten Empirical Findings on Shareholder Value and Industrial Relations in Germany*. Köln: Max-Planck-Institut Für Gesellschaftsforschung

Hoskisson, R.E., Hitt, M.A., Wan, W.P. and Yiu, D. (1999): Theory and research in strategic management: Swings of a pendulum. *Journal of Management*, 25: 417–56

Hudson, R. (1989): Labour market changes and new forms of work in old industrial regions. *Environment and Planning Society and Space*, 7: 5–30

Humphries, M. (1998): For the common good? New Zealanders comply with quality standards. *Organisation Science*, 9 (6): 738–49

Huselid, M. (1995): The impact of human resource management practices on turnover, productivity, and corporate performance. *Academy of Management Journal*, 38 (3): 635–72

Hutton, W. (2010): *Them and Us: Politics, Greed and Inequality – Why We Need a Fair Society*. New York: Little, Brown and Company

Hutton, W. and Giddens, A. (eds) (2001): *On the Edge. Living with Global Capitalism*. London: Vintage

Hyman, R. (2003): Stakeholder capitalism. *European Journal of Industrial Relations*, 9: 249–50

Iles, P. and Salaman, G. (1995): Recruitment, selection and assessment. In Storey, J. (ed.), *Human Resource Management: A Critical Text*. London: Routledge

Inglehart, R. (1997): *Modernization and Postmodernization: Cultural, Economic and Political Change in 43 Societies*. Princeton, NJ: Princeton University Press

Inkson, K. (2008): Are humans resources? *Career Development International*, 13 (3): 270–9

Inkson K. and Arthur M.B. (2001): How to be a successful career capitalist. *Organizational Dynamics*, 31 (3): 48–61

Institute for Precarious Consciousness (2014): Anxiety, affective struggle, and precarity consciousness-raising. *Interface*, 6 (2): 271–300

International Survey Research (1995): *Employee satisfaction: Tracking European trends*. London: ISR

Isles, N. (2010): *The Good Work Guide: How to Make Organizations Fairer and More Effective*. London: Earthscan

Jackson, T.K (2004): *Building Reputational Capital: Strategies for Integrity and Fair Play that Improve the Bottom Line*. Oxford: Oxford University Press

Jacques, R. (1999): Developing a tactical approach to engaging with 'strategic' HRM. *Organization*, 6 (2): 199–222

Janssens, M. and Steyaert, C. (2009): HRM and performance: A plea for reflexivity in HRM studies. *Journal of Management Studies*, 46 (1): 143–55

Jeffrey, R. (2015): The new workforce: Meet the employees of tomorrow. *People Management*, 27 October

Jensen, M.C. (2001): Value maximization, stakeholder theory and the corporate objective function. *European Financial Management*, 7 (3): 297–317

Johns, G. (2001): In praise of context. *Journal of Organizational Behavior*, 22: 31–42

Johnson, J.L. and O'Leary, A.M. (2003): The effects of psychological contract breach and organizational cynicism: Not all social exchange violations are created equal. *Journal of Organizational Behavior*, 24 (5): 627–47

Johnson, M.D. and Morgeson, F.P. (2005): Cognitive and affective identification in organizational settings. Paper presented at the 64th Annual Meeting of the Academy of Management, Honolulu

Joyce, W., Nohria, N. and Robertson, B. (2003): *What (Really) Works: The 4+2 Formula for Sustained Business Success*. New York: HarperBusiness

Judge, T.A., Thoresen, C.J., Bono, J.E. and Patton, G.K. (2001): The job satisfaction–job performance relationship: A qualitative and quantitative review. *Psychological Bulletin*, 127 (3): 376–407

Kahn, W.A. (1990) Psychological conditions of personal engagement and disengagement at work. *Academy of Management Journal*, 33: 692–724

Kahneman, D. (2013): *Thinking: Fast and Slow*. New York: Farrar, Straus and Giroux

Kallinikos, J. (1996): Mapping the intellectual terrain of management education. In French, R. and Grey, C. (eds), *Rethinking Management Education*. London: Sage

Karasek, R.A., Jr. (1979): Job demands, job decision latitude, and mental strain: Implications for job redesign. *Administrative Science Quarterly*, 24 (2): 285–308

Karasek, R.A., Jr. (1998): Demand/control model: A social, emotional, and physiological approach to stress risk and active behaviour development. In Stellman, J.M. (ed.), *Encyclopaedia of Occupational Health and Safety*. Geneva: ILO, pp. 34.06–34.14

Karasek, R.A., Jr. (2002): Toward job stress social policy analysis: Could the JCQ be used? 3rd International Conference Work and CVD, Dusseldorf, March

Katz, D. and Kahn, R.L. (1966): *The Social Psychology of Organizations*. New York: Wiley and Sons

Katzenbach, J.R. (2000): *Peak Performance: Aligning the Hearts and Minds of Your Employees*. Cambridge, MA: Harvard Business School Press

Kay, J. (2010): *Obliquity*. London: Profile Books

Keegan, A. and Boselie, P. (2006): The lack of impact of dissensus-inspired analysis on developments in the field of human resource management. *Journal of Management Studies*, 43 (7): 1492–511

Keegan, A. and Francis, H. (2008): HRM, technology and strategic roles: Considering the social implications. In Martin, G., Reddington, M. and Alexander, H. (eds), *Technology, Outsourcing and Transforming HR*. Oxford: Butterworth-Heinemann

Keenoy, T. (1990): HRM: A case of the wolf in sheep's clothing? *Personnel Review*, 19 (2): 3–9

Keenoy, T. (1997): Review article: HRMism and the languages of representation. *Journal of Management Studies*, 34 (5): 825–41

Keenoy, T. (1999): HRM as hologram: A polemic. *Journal of Management Studies*, 1 (36): 1–23

Keenoy, T. (2009): Human resource management. In Alvesson, M., Bridgman, T. and Willmott, H. (eds), *The Oxford Handbook of Critical Management Studies*. Oxford: Oxford University Press, pp. 454–72

Keenoy, T. and Anthony, P. (1992): HRM: Metaphor, meaning and morality. In Blyton, P. and Turnbull, P. (eds), *Reassessing HRM*. London: Sage

320 *References*

Keenoy, T. and Reed, M.I. (2007): Managing modernisation: Introducing performance management in British universities. In Mazza, C., Quattrone, P. and Riccaboni, A. (eds), *European Universities in Transition: Issues, Models, and Cases*. Cheltenham: Edward Elgar Publishing, pp. 298–329

Kelly, J.E. and Kelly, C. (1991): Them and us: Social psychology and the 'new industrial relations'. *British Journal of Industrial Relations*, 29 (1): 25–48

Kelly, G., Kelly, D. and Gamble, A. (eds) (1997): *Stakeholder Capitalism*. Basingstoke: Palgrave Macmillan

Kenny, D.T. and McIntyre, D. (2005): Constructions of occupational stress: Nuance or novelty? In Antoniou, A.S. and Cooper, C.L. (eds), *Research Companion to Organizational Health Psychology*. Cheltenham: Edward Elgar Publishing

Kenton, B. and Yarnell, J. (2005): *HR: The Business Partner: Shaping a New Direction*. Oxford. Butterworth-Heinemann

Kersley, B., Alpin, C., Forth, J., Bryson, A., Bewley, H., Dix, G. and Oxenbridge, S. (2005): *First Findings from the 2004 Workplace Employment Relations Survey*. London: Department of Trade and Industry

Kickul, J. (2001): When organisations break their promises: Employee reactions to unfair processes and treatment. *Journal of Business Ethics*, 29 (4): 289–307

Kickul, J.R., Neuman, G., Parker, C., and Finkl, J. (2001): Settling the score: The role of organizational justice in the relationship between psychological contract breach and anti-citizenship behavior. *Employee Responsibilities and Rights Journal*, 13: 77–93

Kirton, H. (2015): Appraisals, but not as you know them. *People Management*, 4 September

Klein, N. (2007): *The Shock Doctrine: The Rise of Disaster Capitalism*. Toronto: Alfred A Knopf, Random House

Knights, D. (1990): Subjectivity, power and the labour process. In Knights, D. and Willmott, H. (eds), *Labour Process Theory*. London: Macmillan

Knights, D. (1997): Organisation theory in the age of deconstruction. *Organization Studies*, 18 (1): 1–19

Knights, D. and Willmott, H. (1989): Power and subjectivity at work. *Sociology*, 23 (4): 535–58

Kochan, T.A., Katz, H.C. and McKersie, R.B. (1986): *The Transformation of American Industrial Relations*. New York: Basic Books

Kochan, T. (2007): Social legitimacy of the HRM profession: A US perspective. In Boxall, P., Purcell, J. and Wright, P. (eds), *Oxford Handbook of Human Resource Management*. Oxford: Oxford University Press, pp. 599–620

Kofman, F. (2014): *Conscious Business: How to Build Value through Value*. Louisville, CO: Sounds True

Konz, G.N. and Ryan, F.X. (1999): Maintaining an organizational spirituality: No easy task. *Organizational Change Management*, 12 (3): 200–10

Korten, D. (1999): *The Post-Corporate World: Life after Capitalism*. San Francisco, CA: Berrett-Koehler

Kotter, J.P. (2012): Accelerate! *Harvard Business Review*, November: 44–58

Kotter, J.P. and Heskett, J.L. (1992): *Corporate Culture and Performance*. New York: Free Press

Kram, K. (1996): A relational approach to career development. In Hall, D. (ed.), *The Career Is Dead – Long Live the Career: A Relational Approach to Careers*. San Francisco, CA: Jossey-Bass, pp. 32–157

Kreiner, G.E. and Ashforth, B.E. (2004): Evidence toward an expanded model of identification. *Journal of Organizational Behavior*, 25 (1): 1–27

Krzywdzinski, M. (2014): Do investors avoid strong trade unions and labour regulation? Social dumping in the European automotive and chemical industries. *Work, Employment and Society*, 28 (6): 926–45

Kuhn, T.S. (1970): *The Structure of Scientific Revolutions* (2nd edn). Chicago, IL: University of Chicago Press

Lankhuijzen, E.S.K., Stavenga de Jong, J.A. and Thijssen, J.G.L. (2006): Psychological career contract, HRD and self-management of managers. In Streumer, J.E. (ed.), *Work-Related Learning*. Dordrecht: Springer, pp. 309–31

Lansbury, R.D., Kitay, J. and Wailes, N. (2003): The impact of globalisation on employment relations: Some research propositions. *Asia Pacific Journal of Human Resources*, 41 (1): 62–74

Lash, S. and Urry, J. (1994): *Economies of Signs and Space*. London: Sage

Laszlo, C. and Brown, J.S. with Ehrenfeld, J.R., Gorham, M., Pose, I.B., Robson, L., Saillant, R., Sherman, D. and Werder, P. (2014): *Flourishing Enterprise: The New Spirit of Business*. Stanford, CA: Stanford University Press

Lawler, E.E. III (1986): *High Involvement Management*. San Francisco, CA: Jossey-Bass

Lawler, E.E. III (2003): *Treat People Right*. San Francisco, CA: Jossey-Bass

Lawler, E.E. III (2014a): HR should own organizational effectiveness. *Forbes Leadership*, 11 February, www.forbes.com/sites/edwardlawler/2014/02/11/hr-should-own-organizational-effectiveness/#7ad75e707074

Lawler, E.E. III (2014b): The quadruple bottom line: Its time has come. *Forbes Leadership*, 7 May, www.forbes.com/sites/edwardlawler/2014/05/07/the-quadruple-bottom-line-its-time-has-come/#9acf8476630d

Lawler, E.E. III, Mohrman, S.A. and O'Toole, J. (2015): *Corporate Stewardship: Achieving Sustainable Effectiveness*. Saltaire: Greenleaf

Leary-Joyce, J. (2004): *Becoming an Employer of Choice: Make Your Organization a Place Where People Want to Do Great Work*. London: CIPD

Legge, K. (1978): *Power, Innovation and Problem-Solving in Personnel Management*. London: McGraw-Hill

Legge, K. (1995): *Human Resource Management: Rhetorics and Realities*. London: Macmillan

Legge, K. (2001): Silver bullet or spent round? Assessing the meaning of the 'high commitment management'/performance relationship. In Storey, J. (ed.), *Human Resource Management: A Critical Text*. London: Thomson Learning, pp. 21–36

Legge, K. (2005): *Human Resource Management: Rhetorics and Realities*. New York: Palgrave Macmillan

Legge, K., Clegg, C. and Walsh, S. (eds) (1999): *The Experience of Managing: A Skills Guide*. Basingstoke: Palgrave Macmillan

Lemke, T. (2001): The birth of bio-politics: Michael Foucault's lectures at the College de France on neo-liberal governmentality. *Economy and Society*, 30 (2): 190–207

Lemke, T. (2002): Foucault, governmentality, and critique. *Rethinking Marxism*, 14 (3): 49–64

Lepak, D.P., Bartol, K.M. and Erhardt, N. (2005): A contingency framework of the delivery of HR practices. *Human Resource Management Review*, 15: 139–59

Lepak, D.P., Youndt, M.A., Snell, S. and Dean, J.W., Jr. (2007): The status of theory and research in human resource management: Where have we been and where should we go from here? *Human Resource Management Review*, 17: 93–5

Lewis Silkin LLP (2016): Back to the future of paternalistic capitalism? 31 March, www.futureofworkhub.info/allcontent/2016/3/31/back-to-the-future-of-paternalistic-capitalism

Lievens, F., Van Hoye, G. and Anseel, F. (2007): Organizational identity and employer image: Towards a unifying framework. *British Journal of Management*, 18 (1): 45–59

Ling, T.M. (1954): *Mental Health and Human Relations in Industry*. London: H.K. Lewis

Linstead, S. (1996): Understanding management: Culture, critique and change. In Linstead, S., Grafton-Small, R. and Jeffcutt, P. (eds), *Understanding Management*. London: Sage, pp. 11–13

Littler, C.R. and Salaman, G. (1982): Bravermania and beyond: Recent theories of the labour process. *Sociology*, 16: 251–69

Locke, E.A. (1970): Job satisfaction and job performance: A theoretical analysis. *Organizational Behavior and Human Performance*, 5: 484–500

Lonergan, B.F. (1957): *Insight: A Study of Human Understanding*. London: Longman

Lowitzsch, J., Bormann, A., Hanisch, S., Menke, J.D., Roggemann, H. and Spitsa, N. (2008): *Financial Participation for a New Social Europe: A Building Block Approach*. Rome/Berlin: Inter-University Centre/Institute for East European Studies

Lucero, M.A. and Allen, R.E. (1994): Employee benefits: A growing source of psychological contract violations. *Human Resource Management*, 33 (3): 425–46

Lucy, D., Poorkavoos, M. and Thompson, A. (2014): *Building Resilience: Five Key Capabilities*. Horsham: Roffey Park Institute

Lucy, D., Poorkavoos, M., Sinclair, A. and Hatcher, C. (2016): *The Management Agenda 2016*. Horsham: Roffey Park

Lukacs, G. (1974): *Soul and Form*. Cambridge, MA: MIT Press

Maas, E. Van der. (2004): British Labour and the European Union: The Europeanisation of trade unions? Conference paper for UACES/ESRC Seminar on Europeanisation, Sheffield, 16 January. *Archive of European Integration*, pp. 1–29

322 *References*

MacDuffie, J.P. (1995): Human resource bundles and manufacturing performance. *Industrial and Labor Relations Review*, 48: 197–221

Mackey, J. (2006): Conscious capitalism: Creating a new paradigm for business. Blog, 9 November, www.wholefoodsmarket.com/blog/john-mackeys-blog/conscious-capitalism-creating-new-paradigm-for%C2%A0business

Mackey, J. and Sisodia, R. (2014): *Conscious Capitalism: Liberating the Heroic Spirit of Business*. Cambridge, MA: Harvard Business Review Press

Macky, K. and Boxall, P. (2007): The relationship between high-performance work practices and employee attitudes: An investigation of additive and interaction effects. *International Journal of Human Resource Management*, 18 (4): 537–67

Maguire, H. (2002): Psychological contracts: Are they still relevant? *Career Development International*, 7 (3):167–80

Mandel, E. (1968): Workers under neo-capitalism. *International Socialist Review*, 29 (6): 1–35

Mandel, E. (1973): The debate on workers' control. In Hunnius, G., Garson, G.D. and Case, J. (eds), *Workers' Control: A Reader on Labour and Social Change*. New York: Vintage

Manning, K. (2010): Strategic human resource management and the Australian public sector. *Transylvanian Review of Administrative Sciences*, 30E: 150–61

Maravelias, C. (2009): Make your presence known! Post-bureaucracy, HRM and the fear of being unseen. *Personnel Review*, 38 (4): 349–65

March, J.G. and Simon, H.A. (1958): *Organizations*. New York: John Wiley and Sons

Marchington, M.P. and Wilkinson A. (2005): *Human Resource Management at Work: People, Management and Development*. London: CIPD

Marchington, M.P., Grimshaw, D., Rubery, J. and Willmott, H. (2005): *Fragmenting Work: Blurring Organizational Boundaries and Disordering Hierarchies*. Oxford: Oxford University Press

Marcuse, H. (1964): *One-Dimensional Man: Studies in the Ideology of Advanced Industrial Society*. Boston, MA: Beacon

Margulies, N. (1978): Perspectives on the marginality of the consultant's role. In Burke, W.W. (ed.), *The Cutting Edge: Current Theory and Practice in Organization Development*. La Jolla, CA: University Associates

Marks, A (2000): 'Caught in the cross-fire': The complexity of psychological contracts in teamworking. *Management Research News*, 23 (9–11): 106–8

Marks, A. and Lockyer, C (2004): Self-interest and knowledge work: The bugs in the programme for teamwork? *Economic and Industrial Democracy*, 25 (2): 213–38

Marks, A. and Scholarios, D. (2004): Work life boundary, reciprocity, and attitudes to the organization: The special case of software workers. *Human Resource Management Journal*, 14 (2): 54–74

Marmot Review Team (2010): *Fair Society, Healthy Lives: Strategic Review of Health Inequalities in England Post 2010*. London: Marmot Review

Marquand, D. (2004): *Decline of the Public: The Hollowing Out of Citizenship*. Cambridge: Polity Press

Marquand, D. (2008a): *Britain since 1918: The Strange Career of British Democracy*. London: Orion Books

Marquand, D. (2008b): Never mind the role of the state. *Guardian*, 11 December

Marquard, W.H. and Graham, A.B. (2010): Shareholder value OR social responsibility? How corporations find the AND. Unpublished manuscript

Marshak, R.J. (2002): Changing the language of change: How new contexts and concepts are challenging the ways we think and talk about organizational change. *Strategic Change*, 11 (5): 279–86

Marshak, R.J. and Grant, D. (2008): Organisational discourse and new organisation development practices. *British Journal of Management*, 19: S7–S19

Martin, G. (2008): Employer branding and reputation management. In Cooper, C. and Burke, R. (eds), *High Performing Organizations*. London: Routledge

Martin, G. and Dyke, S. (2010): Employer branding and corporate reputation management: A signalling model and case illustration. In Collings, D. and Scullion, H. (eds), *Global Talent Management*. London: Routledge

Martin, G., Staines, H. and Pate, J. (1998): Linking job security and career development in a new psychological contract. *Human Resource Management Journal*, 8 (3): 20–40

Martin, G., Reddington, M. and Alexander, H. (eds) (2008): *Technology, Outsourcing and Transforming HR*. Oxford: Butterworth-Heinemann

Martin, G., Reddington, M. and Kneafsey, M.B. (2009): *Web 2.0 and Human Resource Management: Groundswell or Hype?* London: CIPD

Marx, K. (1958): *Capital* (Vol. 1). Translated by Moore, S. and Aveling, E. Moscow: Foreign Languages Publishing House

Marx, K. (1973): *Grundrisse*. Harmondsworth: Penguin

Marx, K. and Engels, F. (1988): *The Economic and Philosophic Manuscripts of 1844 and the Communist Manifesto*. Translated by Milligan, M. Amherst, NY: Prometheus Books

Maslach, C. and Leiter, M.P. (2008): Early predictors of job burnout and engagement. *Journal of Applied Psychology*, 93: 498–512

Maslow, A. (1987): *Motivation and Personality* (3rd edn). Hong Kong: Longman Asia

Mason, P. (2015): *Post-Capitalism*. London: Allen Lane

Maxwell, J., Briscoe, F. and Temin, P. (2000): Corporate health care purchasing and the revised social contract with workers. *Business and Society*, 30: 281–303

May, D.R., Gilson, R.L. and Harter, L.M. (2004): The psychological conditions of meaningfulness, safety and availability and the engagement of the human spirit at work. *Journal of Occupational and Organisational Psychology*, 77: 11–37

McCarthy, D. and Palcic, D. (2012): The impact of large-scale employee share ownership plans on labour productivity: The case of Eircom. *International Journal of Human Resource Management*, 23 (17): 3710–24

McCartney, C. and Willmott, B. (2010): *The Employee Outlook*. London: CIPD

McCord, P. (2014): How Netflix reinvented HR. *Harvard Business Review*, January–February, https://hbr.org/2014/01/how-netflix-reinvented-hr&cm_sp=Article-_-Links-_-End%20of%20Page%20Recirculation

McHugh, M. (1997): The stress factor: Another item for the change management agenda. *Organisational Change Management*, 1 (4): 345–62

McInnes, K.G., Meyer, J.P. and Feldman, S. (2009): Psychological contracts and their implications for commitment: A feature-based approach. *Journal of Vocational Behaviour*, 74: 165–80

McKinsey and Co. (2001): *The War for Talent: Organization and Leadership Practice*. New York: McKinsey and Company

Michie, J. (2003): *The Handbook of Globalisation*. Cheltenham: Edward Elgar Publishing

Miller, P. (1996): Strategy and the ethical management of human resources. *Human Resource Management Journal*, 6 (1): 5–18

Millward, N., Stevens, M., Smart, D. and Hawes, W.R. (1992): *Workplace Industrial Relations in Transition: The ED/ESRC/PSI/ACAS Surveys*. Aldershot: Dartmouth Publishing

Millward, N., Bryson, A. and Forth, J.A. (2000): *All Change at Work? British Employment Relations 1980–1998*. London: Routledge

Mintzberg, H. (1988): *Mintzberg on Management: Inside Our Strange World of Organizations*. New York: Free Press

Mintzberg, H. (1994): *The Rise and Fall of Strategic Planning*. New York: Prentice Hall

Mitchel, R.K., Wood, J.D. and Agle, B.R. (1997): Towards a theory of stakeholders identification and salience: Defining the principle of who and what really counts. *Academy of Management Review*, 22 (4): 853–87

Mitroff, I.I. and Denton, E.A. (2000): *A Spiritual Audit of Corporate America*. San Francisco: Jossey Bass

Mohrman, S.A. (2011): Organizing for sustainable effectiveness. In Mohrman, S.A and Shani, A.B. (eds), *Organizing for Sustainability*. Bradford: Emerald Group Publishing

Mohrman, S.A. and Shani, A.B. (eds) (2011): *Organizing for Sustainability* (Vol. 1). Bradford: Emerald Group Publishing

Mohrman, S.A., Lawler, E.E., and Mohrman, A.M. (1992): Applying employee involvement in schools. *Educational Evaluation and Policy Analysis*, 14 (4): 347–60

Monbiot, G. (2000): *Captive State: The Corporate Takeover of Britain*. London: Pan

Morgan, E.P. (2010): *What Really Happened to the 1960s: How Mass Media Culture Failed American Democracy*. Lawrence: University of Kansas Press

Morgeson, F.P. and Humphrey, S.E. (2008). Job and team design: Toward a more integrative conceptualization of work design. In Martocchio, J. (ed.), *Research in Personnel and Human Resource Management* (Vol. 27). Bradford: Emerald Group Publishing, pp. 39–91

324   *References*

Morris, W. (1884): Useful work versus useless toil. Originally a lecture, reproduced in full, www.marxists.org/archive/morris/works/1884/useful.htm

Morrison, E.W. (2014): Employee voice and silence. *Annual Review of Organizational Psychology and Organizational Behavior*, 1 (1): 173–97

Morrison, E.W. and Robinson, S.L. (1997): When employees feel betrayed: A model of how psychological contract violation develops. *Academy of Management Review*, 22 (1): 226–56

Mount, M.K., Barrick, M.R. and Stewart, G.L. (1998): Five-factor model of personality and performance in jobs involving interpersonal interactions. *Human Performance*, 11 (2/3): 145–65

Nabaum, A., Barry, L., Garr, S. and Liakopoulos, A. (2014): Performance management is broken. Westlake, TX: Deloitte University Press, http://dupress.com/articles/hc-trends-2014-performance-management/

Nayyar, V. (2010): *Employees First, Customers Second: Turning Conventional Management Upside Down.* Cambridge, MA: Harvard Business Press

Nichols, T. and Benyon, H. (1977): *Living with Capitalism.* London: Routledge and Kegan Paul

Nonaka, I. and Takeuchi, H. (1995): *The Knowledge Creating Company: How Japanese Companies Create the Dynamics of Innovation.* New York: Oxford University Press

O'Doherty, D. (1993): Strategic conceptions, consent and contradictions: Banking on part-time labour. Paper given to the 11th International Labour Process Conference, Blackpool

O'Doherty, D. and Willmott, H. (2001): Debating labour process theory: The issue of subjectivity and the relevance of poststructuralism. *Sociology*, 35: 457–76

Ollman, B. (1996): *Alienation.* Cambridge: Cambridge University Press

O'Reilly, C.A. and Tushman, M.L. (2004): The ambidextrous organization. *Harvard Business Review*, 82 (4): 74–81

Organisation for Economic Co-operation and Development (1995): *Governance in Transition: Public Management Reforms in OECD Countries.* Paris: OECD

Overell, S. (2005): Nonsense on jobs. *Personnel Today*, January

Overell, S. (2008): *Inwardness: The Rise of Meaningful Work.* London: Work Foundation

Overell, S., Mills, T., Roberts, S., Lekhi, R. and Blaug, R. (2010): *The Employment Relationship and the Quality of Work.* London: Work Foundation

Ovide, S. and Feintzeig, R. (2013): Microsoft abandons 'stack ranking' of employees. *Wall Street Journal*, www.wsj.com/news/articles/SB10001424052702303460004579193951987616572

Paauwe, J. (2004): *HRM and Performance: Achieving Long-Term Viability.* Oxford: Oxford University Press

Paauwe, J. (2007): HRM and performance: In search of balance. Inaugural address of Professor of Human Resource Management at the Department of HR Studies at Tilburg University

Paauwe, J. (2009): HRM and performance: Achievements, methodological issues and prospects. *Journal of Management Studies*, 46: 129–42

Paauwe, J. and Boselie, J.P. (2005): HRM and performance: What's next? Visiting fellow working papers, Cornell University ILR School, http://digitalcommons.ilr.cornell.edu/cgi/viewcontent.cgi?article=1012&context=intlvf

Palley, T.I. (2004): From Keynesianism to neoliberalism: Shifting paradigms in economics: Public understandings of the economy also matter. *Foreign Policy in Focus*, 5 May, http://fpif.org/from_keynesianism_to_neoliberalism_shifting_paradigms_in_economics/

Parker, M. (2002): *Against Management: Organization in the Age of Managerialism.* Cambridge: Polity Press

Parker, S.K., Wall, T.D. and Cordery, J.L. (2001): Future work design research and practice: Towards an elaborated model of work design. *Journal of Occupational and Organizational Psychology*, 74: 413–40

Pascale, R. (1995): In search of the new employment contract. *Human Resources*, 12 (6): 21–6

Patton, M.Q. (1994): Evaluation Practice, Elsevier

Peccei, R. (2004): *Human Resource Management and the Search for the Happy Workplace.* Rotterdam: Erasmus Research Institute of Management

Pendleton, A., Wilson, N. and Wright, M. (1998): The perception and effects of share ownership: Empirical evidence from employee buy-outs. *British Journal of Industrial Relations*, 36 (1): 99–123

Peston, R. (2008): *Who Runs Britain?* London: Hodder and Stoughton

Peters T. and Waterman, R. (1982): *In Search of Excellence*. New York: Harper Row

Pettigrew, A.M. and Whipp, R. (1991): *Managing Change for Competitive Success*. Oxford: Basil Blackwell

Pfeffer, J. (1998): *The Human Equation: Building Profits by Putting People First*. Cambridge, MA: Harvard Business School Press

Pfeffer, J. and Sutton, R. (1999): *The Knowing-Doing Gap: How Smart Companies Turn Knowledge into Action*. Cambridge, MA: Harvard Business School Press

Phillips, R.A., Freeman, R.E. and Wicks, A.C. (2003): What stakeholder theory is not. *Business Ethics Quarterly*, 13 (4): 479–502

Piketty, T. (2014): *Capital in the Twenty-First Century*. Cambridge, MA: Harvard University Press

Pink, D. (2009): *Drive: The Surprising Truth about What Motivates Us*. New York: Riverhead

Pollitt, C. (1990): *Managerialism and the Public Services: The Anglo-American Experience*. Cambridge: Basil Blackwell

Pollitt, C. (1993): *Managerialism and the Public Services: Cuts or Cultural Change in the 1990s?* Oxford: Blackwell Business

Porter, M.E. (1985): *Competitive Advantage*. New York: Free Press

Porter, M.E. and Kramer, M.R. (2011): Creating shared value. *Harvard Business Review*, 89 (1/2): 62–77

Power, M. (2001): *The Audit Society: The Rituals of Verification*. Oxford: Oxford University Press

Price, A. (2003): *Human Resource Management in a Business Context*. Boston, MA: Thomson Learning

Pullen, A. and Linstead, S. (eds) (2005): *Organization and Identity*. London: Routledge

Purcell, J. and Hutchinson, S. (2007): Front line managers as agents in the HRM-performance causal chain: Theory, analysis and evidence. *Human Resource Management Journal*, 17 (1): 3–20

Purcell, J. and Kinnie, N. (2006): HRM and business performance. In Boxall, P., Purcell, J. and Wright, P. (eds), *The Oxford Handbook of Human Resource Management*. Oxford: Oxford University Press

Purcell, J., Hutchinson, S., Kinnie, N., Rayton, B. and Swart, J. (2003): *Understanding the Pay and Performance Link: Unlocking the Black Box*. London: CIPD

Purcell, J., Kinnie, N., Swart, J., Rayton, B. and Hutchinson, S. (2009): *People Management and Performance*. London: Routledge

PwC (2015): *Transforming Performance Management*. PwC Research

PwC (2016): The future of work: A journey to 2022. PWC Research, www.pwc.com/gx/en/managing-tomorrows-people/future-of-work/assets/pdf/future-of-rork-report-v16-web.pdf

Quinn, J.B. (1980): *Strategies for Change: Logical Incrementalism*. Homewood, IL: Richard D. Irwin

Raja, U., Johns, G. and Ntalianis, F. (2004): The impact of personality on psychological contracts. *Academy of Management Journal*, 47: 350–67

Rajan, A. (1997): Employability in the finance sector: Rhetoric vs. reality. *Human Resource Management Journal*, 7 (1): 67–78

Ramsay, H., Scholarios, D. and Harley, B. (2000): Employees and high-performance work systems: Testing inside the black box. *British Journal of Industrial Relations*, 38 (4): 501–31

Reed, H. (2010): *Flexible with the Truth? Exploring the Relationship between Labour Market Flexibility and Labour Market Performance*. London: TUC

Reich, R. (1991): *The Work of Nations: Preparing Ourselves for 21st Century Capitalism*. New York: Alfred A. Knopf

Reid, E. (2016): You can't fix culture. *Harvard Business Review*, April, https://hbr.org/2016/04/culture-is-not-the-culprit

Reilly, P. (2009): Pulling in different directions. *Public Servant*, September

Reilly, P. and Williams, A. (2003): *How to Get Best Value from HR: The Shared Services Option*. Farnham: Gower

Reilly, P. and Williams, A. (2006): *Strategic HR: Building the Capability to Deliver*. Farnham: Gower

Reilly, P., Tamkin, P. and Broughton, A. (2007): *The Changing HR Function: Transforming HR?* London: CIPD

Richard, P.J., Devinney, T.M., Yip, G.S. and Johnson, G. (2009): Measuring organizational performance: Towards methodological best practice. *Journal of Management*, 35: 718

Robbins, S.P. (1989): *Organizational Behavior: Concepts, Controversies, and Applications*. Englewood Cliffs, NJ: Prentice-Hall

326 *References*

Robertson, M. and Swan, J. (2004): Going public: The emergence and effects of soft bureaucracy within a knowledge-intensive firm. *Organization*, 11 (1): 123–48

Robinson, D., Perryman, S. and Hayday, S. (2004): *The Drivers of Employee Engagement*. Brighton: Institute for Employment Studies

Robinson, S.L. and Morrison, E.W. (1995): Psychological contracts and OCB: The effect of unfulfilled obligations on civic virtue. *Journal of Organizational Behavior*, 16: 289–98

Robinson, S.L., Kraatz, M.S. and Rousseau, D.M. (1994): Changing obligations and the psychological contract: A longitudinal study. *Academy of Management Journal*, 37: 137–52

Rock, D., Davis, J. and Jones, B. (2014): Kill your performance ratings. *Strategy+Business*, 76, 8 August, www.strategy-business.com/article/00275?gko=c442b

Romero, D. and Molina, A. (2011): Collaborative networked organisations and customer communities: Value co-creation and co-innovation in the networking era. *Production Planning and Control*, July: 1–26

Rose, M. (2011): *A Guide to Non-Cash Reward*. London: Kogan Page

Rose, N. (1999): *Governing the Soul: The Shaping of the Private Self* (2nd edn). London: Free Association Books

Rosen, C. and Rodgers, L. (2007): *The Ownership Edge*. Oakland, CA: National Center for Employee Ownership

Rosen, C., Case, J. and Staubus, M. (2005): *Equity: Why Employee Ownership is Good for Business*. Cambridge, MA: Harvard Business School Press

Rousseau, D.M. (1989): Psychological and implied contracts in organizations. *Employee Responsibilities and Rights Journal*, 2: 121–39

Rousseau, D.M. (1990): New hire perceptions of their own and their employer's obligations: A study of psychological contracts. *Journal of Organizational Behavior*, 11: 389–400

Rousseau, D.M. (1995): *Psychological Contracts in Organizations*. Thousand Oaks, CA: Sage

Rousseau, D.M. (1998): The 'problem' of the psychological contract considered. *Journal of Organizational Behavior*, 19: 665–71

Rousseau, D.M. (2001): The idiosyncratic deal: Flexibility versus fairness? *Organizational Dynamics*, 29 (4): 260–73

Rousseau, D.M. (2005): *I-deals: Idiosyncratic Deals Employees Bargain for Themselves*. Armonk, NY: M.E. Sharpe

Rousseau, D.M. (2006): Is there such a thing as evidence-based management? *Academy of Management Review*, 31: 256–69

Rousseau, D.M. and Anton, R.J. (1991): Fairness and implied contract obligations in job terminations: The role of contributions, promises and performance. *Journal of Organizational Behavior*, 12: 287–99

Rousseau, D.M. and Aquino, K. (1993): Fairness and implied contract obligations in job terminations: The role of remedies, social accounts and procedural justice. *Human Performance*, 6: 135–49

Rousseau, D.M. and Fried, Y. (2001): Location, location, location: Contextualizing organizational research. *Journal of Organizational Behavior*, 22: 1–14

Rousseau, D.M., Hornung, S., and Kim, T.G. (2009): Idiosyncratic deals: Testing propositions on timing, content, and the employment relationship. *Journal of Vocational Behavior*, 94 (2): 547–56

Rowan, J. and Cooper, M. (1999): *The Plural Self*. London: Sage

Rushkoff, D. (2005): Commodified vs commoditized, http://zomobo.net/Douglas-Rushkoff

Rutherford, J. (2008): The culture of capitalism. RINF.com, 13 May

Saad-Filho, A. and Johnston, D. (2005): *Neo-Liberalism: A Critical Reader*. London: Pluto Press

Saks, A. (2006): Antecedents and consequences of employee engagement. *Journal of Managerial Psychology*, 21 (7): 600–18

Salanova, M., Agut, S. and Peiró, J.M. (2005): Linking organizational resources and work engagement to employee performance and customer loyalty: The mediation of service climate. *Journal of Applied Psychology* 90: 1217–27

Salauroo, M. and Burnes, B. (1998): The impact of a market system on the public sector: A study of organizational change in the NHS. *International Journal of Public Sector Management*, 11 (6): 451–67

Sandelands, L. (2003): Spirituality in organizations. *Journal of Organizational Change*, 23 (1): 71–86

References   327

Scase, R. (2006): *Global Re-Mix: The Fight for Competitive Advantage*. London: Kogan Page

Scheck, C.L. and Kinicki, A.J. (2000): Identifying the antecedents of coping with an organizational acquisition: A structural assessment. *Journal of Organizational Behavior*, 21 (6): 627–48

Schein, E. (1965): *Organizational Psychology*. Englewood Cliffs, NJ: Prentice Hall

Schein, E. (1978): *Career Dynamics: Matching Individual and Organizational Needs*. Reading, MA: Addison-Wesley

Schneider, B., Hanges, P.J., Smith, D.B. and Salvaggio, A.M. (2003): Which comes first: Employee attitudes or organizational financial and market performance? *Journal of Applied Psychology*, 88 (5): 836–51

Schramm, C.J. (2006): Entrepreneurial capitalism and the end of bureaucracy: Reforming the mutual dialog of risk aversion. American Economic Association Meeting, Boston, MA, January

Schuler, R.S. (1992): Strategic human resource management: Linking the people with the strategic needs of the business. *Organizational Dynamics*, Summer: 18–32

Schumacher, E.F. (1974): *Small Is Beautiful: A Study of Economics as if People Mattered*. London: Vintage

Schwab, D.P. and Cummings, L.L. (1970): Theories of performance and satisfaction: A review. *Industrial Relations*, 9: 408–30

Scott, A. (1994): *Willing Slaves: British Workers under Human Resource Management*. Cambridge: Cambridge University Press

Scott, J.C. (1990): *Domination and the Arts of Resistance: Hidden Transcripts*. New Haven, CT: Yale University Press

Scott, J.C. (1992): *Domination and the Arts of Resistance: Hidden Transcripts*. New Haven, CT: Yale University Press

Seglin, J.L. (2006): *The Right Thing: Conscience, Profit and Personal Responsibility in Today's Business*. Kittery, ME: Smith/Kerr Associates

Seligman, M.E.P. (2002): *Authentic Happiness: Using the New Positive Psychology to Realize Your Potential for Lasting Fulfillment*. New York: Free Press

Sempane, M.E., Rieger, H.S. and Roodt, G. (2002): Job satisfaction in relation to organizational culture. *SA Journal of Industrial Psychology*, 28 (2): 23–30

Senge, P., Kleiner, A., Ross, R., Roth, G. and Smith, B. (1999): *The Dance of Change*. New York: Currency Doubleday

Sennett, R. (1998): *The Corrosion of Character: Personal Consequences of Work in the New Capitalism*. New York: W.W. Norton

Sennett, R. (2003): *Respect, in an Age of Inequality*. New York: W.W. Norton

Sennett, R. (2006): *The Culture of the New Capitalism*. New Haven, CT: Yale University Press

Sennett, R. (2008): *The Craftsman*. New Haven, CT: Yale University Press

Serey, T.T. (2006): Choosing a robust quality of work life. *Business Forum*, 27 (2): 7–10

Sewell, G. and Wilkinson, B. (1992): Someone to watch over me: Surveillance, discipline and the just-in-time labour process. *Sociology*, 26 (2): 271–89

Shephard, H.A. (1984): On the realization of human potential: A path with a heart. In Arthur, M.B., Bailyn, L., Levinson, D.J. and Shepard, H.A. (eds), *Working with Careers*. New York: Columbia University, pp. 25–46

Shierholz, H. and Lawrence Mishel, L. (2013): A decade of flat wages: The key barrier to shared prosperity and a rising middle class. *Briefing Paper 365*, 21 August, Economic Policy Institute

Shore, C. and Wright, S. (1999): Audit culture and anthropology: Neo-liberalism in British higher education. *Journal of the Royal Anthropological Institute*, 5 (4): 557–75

Shore, L.M. and Tetrick, L.E. (1994): The psychological contract as an explanatory framework for the employment relationship. In Cooper, C.L. and Rousseau, D.M. (eds), *Trends in Organizational Behaviour* (Vol. 1). Chichester: Wiley, pp. 91–109

Shore, L., Tetrick, L., Taylor, M, Coyle-Shapiro, J., Liden, R., McLean Parks, J., Wolfe Morrison, E., Porter, L., Robinson, S., Roehling, M., Rousseau, D., Schalk, R., Tsui, A. and Van Dyne, L (2004): The employee-organisation relationship: A timely concept in a period of transition. *Research in Personnel and Human Resources Management*, 23: 291–370

Siegrist, J. (1996): Adverse health effects of high effort–low reward conditions. *Journal of Occupational Health Psychology*, 1: 27–41

328   *References*

Sinclair, A., Robertson-Smith, G. and Hennessy, J. (2008): *The Management Agenda*. Horsham: Roffey Park

Sisodia, R., Sheth, J. and Wolfe, D. (2007): *Firms of Endearment: The Pursuit of Purpose and Profit.* Philadelphia, PA: Wharton School Publishing

Smith, C. (2011): The short overview of the labour process perspective and history. Background to the International Labour Process Conference, 5–7 April, www.ilpc.org.uk/Portals/56/ilpc-docs/ILPC-Background.pdf

Smithson, J. and Lewis, S. (2000): Is job insecurity changing the psychological contract? *Personnel Review*, 29 (6): 680–702

Society for Human Resource Management (2011): *Developing and Sustaining Employee Engagement.* Alexandria, VA: SHRM

Solomon, A. (2001): *The Noonday Demon: An Atlas of Depression*. New York: Scribner

Sparrow, P.R. (1996): Transitions in the psychological contract in UK banking. *Human Resource Management Journal*, 6 (4): 75–92

Sparrow, P.R. and Cooper, C.L. (2003): *The Employment Relationship: Key Challenges for HR.* Oxford: Butterworth-Heinemann

Sparrow, P. and Cooper, C. (2014): Organizational effectiveness, people and performance: New challenges, new research agendas. *Journal of Organizational Effectiveness: People and Performance*, 1 (1): 2–13

Sparrow, P.R. and Marchington, M. (eds) (1998): *Human Resource Management: The New Agenda.* London: Financial Times, Pitman Publishing

Spicer, A., Alvesson, M. and Karreman, D. (2010): Critical performativity: The unfinished business of critical management studies. *Human Relations*, 62 (4): 537–60

Starkey, K., Hatchuel, A. and Tempest, S. (2009): Management research and the new logics of discovery and engagement. *Journal of Management Studies*, 46 (3): 547–58

Steers, R.M. (1975): Problems in the measurement of organizational effectiveness. *Administrative Science Quarterly*, 20 (4): 546–58

Stenner, P. in Newman, M. (2010): Get happy and get on with it. *Times Higher Education Supplement*, 21 January

Stevens, J.M., Beyer, J.M. and Trice, H.M. (1978): Assessing personal, role and organizational predictors of managerial commitment. *Academy of Management Journal*, 21 (3): 380–96

Storey, J. (1985): The means of management control: Levels and circuits. *Sociology*, 19 (2): 193–211

Storey, J (1992): *Developments in the Management of Human Resources: An Analytical Review*. Oxford: Blackwell Publishing

Storey, J. (ed.) (2001): *Human Resources Management: A Critical Text* (3rd edn). Boston, MA: Thomson Learning

Sturdy, A., Wright, C. and Wylie, N. (2015): *Management as Consultancy: Neo-bureaucracy and the Consultant Manager*. Cambridge: Cambridge University Press

Sutton, R.I. (1990): Organizational decline processes: A social psychology perspective. *Research in Organizational Behaviour*, 12: 205–53

Sweezy, P. (1974): Foreword. In Braverman, H., *Labor and Monopoly Capital: The Degradation of Work in the Twentieth Century*. New York: Monthly Review Press

Sweezy, P.M. (2004): Monopoly capitalism. *Monthly Review*, 56 (5)

Tajfel, H. and Turner, J.C. (1986): The social identity theory of intergroup behaviour. In Worchel, S. and Austin, W.G. (eds), *Psychology of Intergroup Relations*. Chicago, IL: Nelson-Hall, pp. 7–24

Tamkin, P. (2016): *Performance Management, a Tale of Two Practices? IES Perspectives on HR*. Brighton: Institute for Employment Studies

Taris, T.W. and Feij, J.A. (2004): Learning and strain among newcomers: A three-wave study on the effects of job demands and job control. *Journal of Psychology*, 138: 543–63

Teece, D.J. (2007): Explicating dynamic capabilities: The nature and microfoundations of (sustainable) enterprise performance. *Strategic Management Journal*, 28 (13): 1319–50

Teece, D.J. and Pisano, G. (1994): The dynamic capabilities of firms: An introduction. *Industrial and Corporate Change*, 3 (3): 537–56

Teece, D.J., Shuen, A. and Pisano, G. (1997): Dynamic capabilities and strategic management. *Strategic Management Journal*, 18 (7): 509–33

References   329

Tekleab, A.G., Bartol, K.M. and Liu, W. (2005): Is it pay levels or pay raises that matter to fairness and turnover? *Journal of Organizational Behavior*, 26 (8): 899–921

Terkel, S. (1974): *Working*. London: Random House

Terry, L.D. (1998): Administrative leadership, neo-managerialism, and the public management movement. *Public Administration Review*, 58 (3): 194–200

Thompson, P. (2009): Labour process theory and critical management studies. In Alvesson, M., Bridgman, T. and Willmott, H. (eds), *The Oxford Handbook of Critical Management Studies*. Oxford: Oxford University Press

Thompson, P. and Hartley, B. (2007): HRM and the worker: Labor process perspectives. In Boxall, P., Purcell, J. and Wright, P. (eds), *Oxford International Handbook of Human Resource Management*. Oxford: Oxford University Press, pp. 147–65

Thorsen, D.E. and Lie, A. (2006): *What Is Neoliberalism?* Oslo: University of Oslo

Tinker, T. (2002): Spectres of Marx and Braverman in the twilight of postmodernist labour process research. *Work, Employment and Society*, 16 (2): 251–81

Tinker, T. and Feknous, B. (2003): The politics of the new courseware: Resisting the real subsumption of asynchronous educational technology. *International Journal of Accounting Information Systems*, 4 (2): 141–64

Tirole, J. (2006): *The Theory of Corporate Finance*. Cambridge, MA: MIT Press

Tischler, L. (1999): The growing interest in spirituality. *Journal of Organizational Change Management*, 12 (4): 272–9

Towers Watson (2008): *Closing the Engagement Gap: A Roadmap for Driving Superior Business Performance*. London: Towers Watson

Townley, B. (1993): Foucault, power/knowledge and its relevance for human resource management. *Academy of Management Review*, 18 (3): 518–45

Townley, B. (1994): *Reframing Human Resource Management: Power, Ethics and the Subject at Work*. London: Sage

Townley, B. (1998): Beyond good and evil: Depth and division in the management of human resources. In McKinlay, A. and Starkey, K. (eds), *Foucault, Management and Organization Theory*. London: Sage

Townley, B. (2004): Managerial technologies, ethics and management. *Journal of Management Studies*, 41 (3): 425–45

Trevor-Roberts, E. (2006): Are you sure? The role of uncertainty in career. *Journal of Employment Counselling*, 1 September

Tsui, A.S., Pearce, J.L., Porter, L.W. and Tripoli, A.M. (1997): Alternative approaches to the employee–organisation relationship: Does investment in employees pay off? *Academy of Management Journal*, 40 (5): 1089–121

TUC (2004): Focus on health and safety. Trade Union Trends Survey 04/03

Turnbull, S. (1997): Stakeholder co-operation. *Journal of Co-operative Studies*, 29 (3): 18–52

Turnley, W.H. and Feldman, D.C. (2000): Re-examining the effects of psychological contract violations: Unmet expectations and job satisfaction as mediators. *Journal of Organizational Behavior*, 21: 24–42

Tyson, S. and Fell, A. (1986): *Evaluating the Personnel Function*. London: Hutchinson

Ulrich, D. (1997): *Human Resource Champions: The Next Agenda for Adding Value and Delivering Results*. Boston, MA: Harvard Business School Press

Ulrich, D. and Brockbank, W. (2005): *The HR Value Proposition*. Boston, MA: Harvard Business School Press

Ulrich, D. and Ulrich, W. (2010): *The Why of Work: How Great Leaders Build Abundant Organizations that Win*. New York: McGraw-Hill Education

Ulrich, D., Younder, J., Brockbank, W. and Ulrich, M. (2012): *HR from the Outside In*. New York: McGraw-Hill

Van der Ven, A.H. (2007): *Engaged Scholarship: A Guide for Organizational and Social Research*. Oxford: Oxford University Press

Victor, B. and Stephens, C. (1994). The dark side of the new organizational forms. *Organization Science*, 5, 479–482

Vinten, G. (2001): Shareholder versus stakeholder: Is there a governance dilemma? *Corporate Governance: An International Review*, 9 (1): 36–47

330   *References*

Visser, J. (1998): Learning to play: The Europeanisation of Trade Unions. In Pasture, P. and Verberckmeos, J. (eds), *Working Class Internationalism and the Appeal of National Identity: Historical Debates and Current Perspectives*. Oxford: Berg

Waddock, S.A. (1999): Linking community and spirit: A commentary and some propositions. *Organisational Change Management*, 12 (4): 332–44

Walker, J. (1978): Linking human resource planning and strategic planning. *Human Resource Planning*, 1: 1–18

Walton, R.E. (1973): Quality of work life. *Sloan Management Review*, 15 (1): 11–12

Walton, R.E. (1980): Improving the QWL. *Harvard Business Review*, 19 (12): 11–24

Walton, R.E. (1985): Toward a strategy of eliciting employee commitment based on policies of mutuality. In Walton, R.E. and Lawrence, P.R. (eds), *Human Resource Management: Trends and Challenges*. Boston, MA: Harvard Business School Press

Warr, P.B. (1990): Decision latitude, job demands and employee well-being. *Work and Stress*, 4: 285–94

Warr, P.B. (2007): *Work, Happiness, and Unhappiness*. Mahwah, NJ: Erlbaum

Warr, P.B. and Clapperton, G. (2010): *The Joy of Work? Jobs, Happiness, and You*. New York: Routledge

Watkins, C. (2010): Learning, performance and improvement. *INSI Research Matters*, 34, Summer

Watson, T.J. (1996): *Management, Organisation and Employment Strategy*. London: Routledge

Watson, T.J. (2002): Professions and professionalism: Should we jump off the bandwagon, better to study where it is going? *International Studies of Management and Organization*, 32 (2): 94–106

Watson, T.J. (2004): HRM and critical social science analysis. *Journal of Management Studies*, 41 (3): 447–67

Watson, T.J. (2007a): HRM, critique, pragmatism and the sociological imagination. Research paper, University of Nottingham

Watson, T.J. (2007b): HRM, ethical irrationality, and the limits of ethical action. In Pinnington, A., Macklin R. and Campbell, T. (eds), *Human Resource Management: Ethics and Employment*. Oxford: Oxford University Press

Watson, T.J. (2010): Critical social science, pragmatism and the realities of HRM. *International Journal of Human Resource Management*, 26 (6): 915–31

Weber, M. (1978 [1922]): *Economy and Society: An Outline of Interpretive Sociology*. Berkley: University of California Press

Webster, A. (2002): *Wellbeing*. London: SCM Press

Weick, K.E., Sutcliffe, K.M. and Obstfield, D. (2005): Organising and the process of sense-making. *Organization Science*, 16: 409–21

Wheen, F. (2004): *How Mumbo-Jumbo Conquered the World: A Short History of Modern Delusions*. London: HarperCollins

Whitener, E.M., Brodt, S.E., Korsgaard, M.A. and Werner, J.M. (1998): Managers as initiators of trust: An exchange relationship framework for understanding managerial trustworthy behaviour. *Academy of Management Review*, 23: 513–30

Whittington, R. and Mayer, M. (2002): *Organising for Success in the Twenty-First Century: A Starting Point for Change*. London: CIPD

Wilber, K. (2001): *A Theory of Everything: An Integral Vision for Business, Politics, Science and Spirituality*. Boston, MA: Shambhala Publications

Wilkinson, A. and Fay, C. (2011): New times for employee voice? *Human Resource Management*, 50 (1): 65–74

Willmott, H. (1993): Strength is ignorance; slavery is freedom: Managing culture in modern organizations. *Journal of Management Studies*, 30 (4): 515–52

Willmott, H. (1994): Bringing agency (back) into organizational analysis: Responding to the crisis of (post) modernity. In Hassard, J. and Parker, M. (eds), *Towards a New Theory of Organizations*. London: Routledge

Willmott, H. (1995): From Bravermania to schizophrenia: The d(is/ec)eased condition of subjectivity in labour process theory. Paper presented at the 13th Labour Process Conference, Blackpool

Willmott, Hugh (1997): Rethinking Management and Managerial Work: Capitalism, Control and Subjectivity. Human Relations. Vol. 50 No. 11, pp. 1329-1359

Willmott, H. (2003): Organization theory as critical science. In Tsoukas, H. and Knudsen, C. (eds), *The Oxford Handbook of Organization Theory: Metatheoretical Perspectives*. Oxford: Oxford University Press

Winstanley, D. and Woodall, J. (eds) (2000): *Ethical Issues in Contemporary Human Resource Management.* Basingstoke: Palgrave

Wong, W., Sullivan, J., Albert, A., Huggett, M. and Parkin, J. (2009a): *Quality People Management for Quality Outcomes.* London: Work Foundation

Wong, W., Sullivan, J., Blazey, L., Albert, A. Tamkin, P., and Pearson, G. (2009b): *The Deal in 2020.* London: Work Foundation

Wood, S. (1999): Human resource management and performance. *International Journal of Management Reviews,* 1 (4): 367–413

Wood, S.J. and de Menezes, L.M. (2011): High involvement management, high-performance work systems and well-being. *International Journal of Human Resource Management,* 22 (7): 1586–610

Wood, S.J. and Ogbonnaya, C. (2016): High-involvement management, economic recession, well-being, and organizational performance. *Journal of Management,* July

WorldatWork and Sibson Consulting (2010): 2010 study on the state of performance management. WorldatWork, www.worldatwork.org/waw/adimLink?id=44473

Wright, C. (2015): The age of neo-bureaucracy. *Climate, People and Organizations,* 14 April, https://climatepeopleorg.wordpress.com/2015/04/14/the-age-of-neo-bureaucracy/

Wright, P.M. and Snell, S.A. (2005): Partner or guardian? *Human Resource Management,* 44: 177–82

Wright, P.M., McMahan, G.C. and McWilliams, A. (1994): Human resources and sustained competitive advantage: A resource-based perspective. *International Journal of Human Resource Management,* 5 (2): 301

Yahaya, A., Chui Ing, T., Yahaya, N., Boon, Y., Hashin, S., and Taat, S. (2012): The impact of workplace bullying towards work performance. *Archives Des Sciences,* 65 (4): 11–28

Yaziji, M. (2008): Time to rethink capitalism? *Harvard Business Review,* November, https://hbr.org/2008/11/time-to-rethink-capitalism

Yoshimori, M. (1995): Whose company is it? The concept of the corporation in Japan and the West. *Long Range Planning,* 28 (4): 33–44

Zahra, S.A., Sapienza, H.J. and Davidsson, P. (2006): Entrepreneurship and dynamic capabilities: A review, model and research agenda. *Journal of Management Studies,* 43 (4): 917–55

Zane, D., Irwin, J. and Reczek, R.W. (2016): Why companies are blind to child labor. *Harvard Business Review,* https://hbr.org/2016/01/why-companies-are-blind-to-child-labor

Zuboff, S. (2010): Creating value in the age of distributed capitalism. *McKinsey Quarterly,* www.mckinseyquarterly.com/Creating_value_in_the_age_of_distributed_capitalism_2666

Index

accountability 44, 110
Ackers, P. 42, 92, 233
agency 19, 103–4, 153, 291
agility 197, 226, 246, 266
alienation 23–24, 67, 116, 152–3, 157, 163, 165, 171, 174, 288
Alvesson, M. and Willmott, H. 10, 38, 80, 88, 101
Amin, A. 40, 46
analytics 195
appreciative inquiry 162
Archer, M. 55–56
Argyris, C. 15, 25
Aronowitz, S. and DiFazio, W. 65
artificial intelligence 195–196
Ashfield Meetings and Events 283–285
Astley, M.R. 269, 271
Attitude, Motivation, Opportunity 82–83
automation 4, 49, 50, 194, 195, 202, 227, 289
autonomy 61, 72, 83, 85, 101, 109, 113, 154, 171

Bain, P. 49–50, 112–13
Ball, S. 23, 44, 89, 103, 107, 110–11, 116
Bandura, A. 19–20, 61, 153
Bardwick, J. xi
Barney, J.B. 79, 228
Beer, M. 79, 82, 85
Berger, P.L. xiv, 270
Best, S. 101
Big Data 81, 114, 194–95
Binnie, G. 48, 191, 203, 211–14
'Black box' 82
Blauner, R. 171, 174
Boje, D.M. 101
Boselie, P. 87, 91
Boudreau, J.W. and Ramstad, P.M. 88
Boxall, P. xiv, 79, 80, 85–86, 106
Boxley, S. 111, 112
Braverman, H. xii, xvii, 12–13, 23–24, 33, 36–37, 42, 49, 59, 72, 90, 102, 104, 165, 288, 298
Brayfield, A.H. and Crockett, W.H. 6
Brexit xviii
Briner, R. 10

Brown, P. 21, 48, 50–51, 64, 106, 180, 289, 298
Buckinghamshire County Council 259–262
Budd, J.W. 22, 92–96, 164, 171, 228–229, 246–247
Bunting, M. 64, 85, 99, 102, 105, 145, 154
bureaucracy 58, 63, 78, 94, 197; neo-bureaucracy 198–9; post-bureaucracy 198
business models 204, 269
business partnering 13, 17, 22, 42, 80, 82, 90, 120–125, 299
business schools xiv, 40, 43

Caldwell, R. 81, 121
call centres 49, 60, 113
Cannon, D. 117, 201
capitalism: anti-capitalism 37; crises of xiv, 4, 37, 52, 65, 92, 134, 162, 185–200; conscious capitalism 203, 214; knowledge capitalism 50, 294; monopoly capitalism 11, 36–37, 289; new capitalism xvii; shared capitalism 263–265; stakeholder capitalism xviii, 41, 209, 217, 266–86, 299
Cappelli, P. 29–31, 120, 133, 149, 240, 275
careers 14, 24, 28–30, 148, 240
Cascio, W. F. 10
casualization 50, 56 see also flexibility and flexible working
Center for Effective Organizations 218
change (organizational): effects on employees 54–70, 139–159, 160–181
changeability 55, 58, 266–286
Charan, R. 135
CIPD 130, 228, 238, 254, 274; Employee Outlook survey 89
Clarkson Principles of Stakeholder Management 216
Coats, D. xiii
collaboration 204, 211, 269
Collins, J.C. 157, 180
Combs, J. 245, 253
commitment 179, 236, 263
commodification xii, 12, 19, 22, 36, 41, 44, 51, 54, 60, 72, 80, 289–90, 302

Index 333

commoditisation 50, 90, 93, 96, 100, 111, 116, 181, 195, 289, 301
communication 5, 50, 60, 94, 96, 193, 198, 233, 271–2, 279
complexity theory 270
conflict 93, 232
Cooperrider, D.L. and Srivastva, S. 162
corporate reputation 214–216, 278–280
corporate social responsibility 190, 205
critical HRM theory xiv, 78, 88–90, 96–114
critical management theory 9–10, 33, 88–90, 97
critical pragmatism xv, 10–11
Cullinane, J. 36, 105, 107
culture (corporate, organizational) 89, 233–4, 236, 240, 245, 248, 254, 261, 269; see also 'New' Work Culture
culture change 256–286
customer 3, 39, 44, 54, 80, 100–101, 178-9, 190-192, 194–195, 251

Deal, T.E. and Kennedy, A. 177
Deem, R. 43
De Geus, A. 177
degradation of work xvii, 12, 16, 19, 21–24, 72, 162, 171, 287
Delbridge, R. 16, 87, 92, 97
Deloitte 257
Demerouti, E. 248–250
demographics 3, 49, 185, 202, 302
deskilling 11–12, 19, 21, 24, 44, 77, 77, 90, 107
Diener, E. and Seligman, M. E. P. 237–238
Digital Taylorism 50, 60, 195, 289
digitization see technology
discourse analysis 88, 100
diversity 202, 275–278
Drucker, P.F. 48, 205, 207, 210, 213
Dyer, S. 87, 101
dynamic capabilities 120, 268–9, 271

Edwards, P. 26, 92, 179, 247
Ehrenfeld, J.R. and Hoffman, A.J. 197, 208, 210, 217
Eisenhardt, K.M. and Martin, J.A. 269
Ellsworth, R. E. 165, 190, 202, 211, 230, 237
employability 15, 27, 29–30, 65, 69–71, 142, 149–159, 236, 295–6; see also 'New Deal'
employee: centricity 95, 225, 228–244; development and learning 233, 243–244; engagement 57, 70, 79, 167, 228, 234–238; share ownership (see shared capitalism); subjectivities 88, 101–117, 290; voice 39, 93–94, 228; well-being 61, 236–240
employee relations 40–1, 72, 78, 81, 94, 127–8, 130, 140, 202, 228–30, 290
employment governance 79, 100, 103, 107–8, 301
employment relationship 11, 45, 78–79, 92–94, 295, 301

emotional intelligence 151
equity theory 61
Erickson, T. 203
ERI model 62
Esland, G. 47, 80, 89–90, 99, 111
Espinosa-Orias, N. and Sharratt, P.N. 205
ethics 9, 11, 189–190, 203, 210
European Union (EU) xviii

Fairclough, N. 97
fairness 231, 233, 236, 245
'false consciousness' 92, 105
Felstead, A. 102, 114
financialization 47
flatter structures 46, 149
flexibility 45, 97, 196
flexibilization 56
flexible firm theory 31, 45
flexible working 148, 262
Flood, P.C. 59
Foley, M. 101
Fombrun, C.J. 79
Foucault , M. 32, 99, 104, 111–112
Francis, H. 85, 97
Freeman , R.E. 205, 210
Friedman, M. 37, 153, 187, 190, 210

Gallie, D. 94, 114
Gamble, A. 38, 40, 185, 187, 200, 288, 297, 299
Gardner, H. 301
Generation X 117; see also demographics
Generation Y see Millennials
Giddens, A. 19, 52, 59, 103
global warming 208
globalization 3, 39, 46
Goleman, D. 151
Goodman, J. xiv
Good Work xiii, 246–248, 301
Gordon, D. 66
governance (corporate) 47, 81, 187, 204, 216, 226, 230, 264, 273–4, 296
Graeber, D. 59, 104
Gramsci, A. 11, 200
Gray, J. 188
Greatrex, J. 252–254
Grey, C. xiv, 9, 97, 100
Grint, K. 253
Guest, D. E. 27, 61, 63, 80, 85, 87, 121, 139, 155, 239
Gunther-McGrath, R. 193

Habermas, J. 186
Hall, D.T. 6, 9–10, 30, 149, 154, 162
Harris-Fombrun Corporate Reputation Quotient 215
Harrison, L. 131, 274
Hartley, J. 141, 158

334 *Index*

Harvard model 79, 85
Heaney, C. 282–283
Heckscher, C. and Donnellon, A.M 197
Herriot, P. and Pemberton, 25, 29, 31–32, 71, 91,
140, 143, 149, 156–7, 242
Hesketh, A. 6, 128–129
High Performance Work Systems (HPWS)
83–84, 91, 105, 245; *see also* HRM mainstream
theory
higher education 44, 104
Hirsch, P.M. 5
Hodgkinson, G.P. xi
Hoffman, A. 216
Holbeche, L.S. 46, 121, 235, 270
HR function 133–135; customer-centricity
250–251; leaders 119–135; policies xiv,
230–231; power 130–133; practice 101–117,
140; stewardship 225; transformation 80,
125–126, 134–135
human capital 7, 48, 84
HRM 77–88; analytical 15; discourse 9, 11,
42, 77–80, 82–3, 86–7, 91, 97, 99–110;
emergence 41–42; ethics 11, 91, 96, 110, 130,
131–134, 274–275; evidence-based 10; high
commitment 85–87; mainstream theory 10, 22,
42, 78–80, 82–89, 94–97; performance link
see HPWS, HRM mainstream theory
Human Relations School 6
Hutton, W. 51, 53, 185, 187, 189, 200, 305

inclusion *see* diversity
individualization 11, 22, 25, 35, 41–2, 44, 96, 140,
169, 290, 294, 299
industrial relations 57, 78, 80, 91, 93–4, 96–7, 140,
156, 187, 230
inequality 4, 33, 39, 48–9, 52–53, 92, 102, 169,
185, 188–9, 199, 201, 203
information and communication technologies
49–50, 60
Inglehart, R. 164
Inkson, K. 100, 110, 149
Isles, N. 302

'Japanese' management practices 46, 87
Jensen, M.C. 39
job: characteristics 249; demands-resources
(JD- R) model 248–250; design 246, 249;
enrichment 249–250; quality 61, 245–246;
security 46, 140–142, 158, 241; strain 61, 63
Judge, T.A. 83
justice 56–57, 87–88, 94, 101, 226, 232, 245, 262,
298, 301

Kallinikos, J. 112
Karasek, R. A. Jr 61, 180
Katz, D. and Kahn, R. L. 6
Kay, J. 51, 213

Keenoy, T. 11, 16, 79, 88–89, 91, 96–97,
100, 111
Keynes, J.M. 59
Keynesian economics 36–37, 186
Klein, N. 186–187
Knowledge economy 48, 229
kofman, F. 211, 214
Kuhn, T. S. 20

labour process theory 11, 20–21, 33, 36, 113
Lawler, E. E. III 85, 88, 120, 208, 210, 262
Lazlo, C. 216
leadership 69, 214, 272–273
Legge, K. xiv, 89–90, 97–98, 111, 119, 120
line managers 69, 80, 82, 108–9, 117, 119–21,
126, 231, 233, 235–7, 254, 256
Ling, T. M. 54
local government 57
long-hours culture 62–63
long wave theory 186
Lucy, D. 71, 132, 246

Mackey, J. 39, 201, 211–212, 216, 219
Mackey, J. and Sisodia, R. 201, 213–221
mainstream management theory xiv, 9–10,
15–16, 22
Management Agenda xii, 16, 54, 60, 86, 112–
113, 120, 122, 131–132, 141–159, 161, 174,
177, 233, 239, 246, 254, 267–268, 290,
292–293
managerialism 9, 42–43, 78, 105–107
Mandel, E. 24, 92
Manning, K. 87
Marcuse, H. 11, 23
Marks, A. 87
Marks and Spencer 218
Marquand, D. 33, 37, 41, 43, 47, 169, 187
Marquard, W.H. and Graham, A.B. 208–209
Marshak, R.J. and Grant, D. 270
Marx, K. 36, 56, 92, 163, 185, 188, 288
Mason, P. 186, 188–190, 193, 195, 200, 202
Matthews, G. 235
McCord, P. 256
meaning xiii, xv, 88, 102, 160–171, 173–181, 295,
300–301
measurement 112, 209, 271
mental health 238; *see also*
Michigan model 79
Millennials 31, 197, 202–203, 230–231
Miners' strike 41
Mitev, N. 9
Mohrman, S. A. 85, 215
monitoring 21–22, 50, 56, 84, 102, 110, 112–5,
194, 197, 263, 280
Morgan, E. P. 188
Moore's Law 3
mutuality 89–90, 112, 140, 233

National Health Service (NHS) 43, 178–9, 251, 282–3
Nayyar, V. 228
neo-liberalism xi-xii, 33, 35–52, 187, 289
Networks 197
'New Deal' 29–32
'New Labour' 23, 44, 57
new public management 43–44, 49
'new' work culture xi-xii, 10–11, 54–70, 137
normalization 104

Ollman, B. 297
organization design 269
organization development 269
organizational effectiveness; and shareholder value 5, 39, 82; and stakeholder value 200–220, 225–228
organizational structures 46–47, 197; matrix 56
outsourcing 56
Overell, S. 91, 110, 164, 180–181, 198, 214, 230, 236, 246

Paauwe, J. 16, 87, 91, 97, 205, 225, 228
Palley, T.I. 37, 39, 52
pensions 31, 57, 96, 151, 202, 227, 297–8
performance management 84, 107–9, 253–265
performance related pay 84, 86, 115
performativity 11, 22, 44, 110–111, 290
Peters, T. and Waterman, R. 101, 105
Pfeffer, J. 84, 305
Piketty, T. 48
Pink, D. 298
PIRK model 85
pluralism 16, 78, 81, 88, 92–3, 95–6, 158, 232-233
political behaviour 65
Pollitt, C. 43–45
power 95–96
price 78
productivity 245–246
psychological contract 14–15, 23–32, 57, 72, 82, 139–159, 179, 293–295
Purcell, J. 82–3
purpose (corporate, organizational) 22, 39, 91, 160–1, 176–80, 190, 198–9, 201, 203, 207, 211–214, 216, 219, 231, 236, 256, 265

quadruple bottom line 5, 209–11, 225, 245
quality of working life 235–236
Quinton, G. 259–262

Rajan, A. 29, 71, 149
redundancies 27–28, 31, 56–58, 70, 107, 130–133
reflexivity 56
Reich, R. 48–49, 65, 72
Reilly, P. 82
resilience 71

resource-based theory 79
reward 262, 269–270
Richard, P.J. 5, 84
Robinson, D. 235
Rock, D. 109, 254
Roffey Park xx, 71, 89
Rousseau, D. M. xi, 25–27, 30, 72, 140, 153, 202
Rowan, J. and Cooper, M. 103

Saad-Filho, A. 48
SCARF framework 109
Scase, R. 202
Schein, E. 157
Schumacher, E.F. 59, 72, 185, 188
scientific management 20–21, 50–51, 77, 101, 104, 112
Scott, A. 22, 80, 93–96, 100, 113
Scott, J.C. 56, 92, 94, 105, 107
self-efficacy theory 61, 105, 153
self-esteem 112
Senge, P. 20, 177
Sennett, R. xii, xvii, 11, 13–14, 24, 50, 52, 54, 65, 69, 94, 102, 106, 116, 157, 165, 173, 181, 241, 247, 290, 297, 301
Serey, T.T. 248
shared service centres 82, 125
Shore, L.M. and Tetrick, L.E. 14, 25, 139
short-termism 48
skills 68–69
Smith 33
social contract 11, 26, 65, 156, 294–295
social exchange theory 24–25
social identity theory 173
Sparrow, P. R. and Cooper, C. L. 5, 6, 25, 29, 95, 115, 150, 204, 213, 225, 296
Spicer, A. 10, 16, 304
spirituality 162–164
Springett, N. xiii, 160
stakeholder: capitalism 41, 205; dialogue 271; engagement 214–221
Steers, R.M. 5, 6
stress 62, 71, 143–147, 238
structuration theory 19–20, 153
structure 19–20
Sturdy, A. 198–199
surveillance 194
sustainability 191, 208, 216
Sweezy, P. 292
systems models 5, 103–4

Tajfel, H. and Turner, J.C. 173, 180
talent management 133, 240–242
Tamkin, P. 108
Taylor, F.W. 45
Taylorism see scientific management
teams 102, 106
technology 4, 20, 49–50, 59–61, 113, 188, 289

336   *Index*

Teece, D.J. 268, 271
Thatcher, M. 40, 43, 187
Tischler, L. 163
Townley, B. 103
trade unions 40–42, 92, 129, 290
trust 15, 26, 52, 61, 65, 110, 132, 140, 152, 192, 197, 271, 273, 302

Ulrich, D. 22, 53, 57, 79, 82, 121, 250
Unilever 219
unitarism 9, 41, 78, 93–94, 103, 121

values 105, 116, 173, 180, 192, 219
van der Ven, A.H. xv
Victor, B. and Stephens, C. 141
virtual 46
vitamin model 62

Waddock, S.A. 171, 177
Walton, R.E. 89–90, 96, 235, 238

War for Talent 67–8
Warr, P.B. 62
Watkins, C. 115
Watson, T. J. xiv–xv, 10, 16, 41, 78, 88, 122, 225, 304
Weber, M. 13, 78, 88, 119
Webster, A. 173
WERS 106, 114
Wilber, K. 174–175
Willmott, H 10, 22, 33, 38, 80, 94, 96, 101, 103, 114
Winstanley, D. and Woodall, J. 103, 119
Wong, W. 34, 117
Wood, S. J. 103
work 163, 227; intensification 58, 60, 64–64, 113; -life balance 65, 67, 71, 146–8, 153, 157–8, 175, 177, 198, 203, 231, 240, 242

Zheltoukhova, K. 225
Zuboff, S. 297–298